The Salt Companion to Harold Bloom

Edited by

GRAHAM ALLEN is Senior Lecturer in Modern English, University College Cork. He is the author of *Harold Bloom: A Poetics of Conflict* (Harvester, 1994), *Intertextuality* (Routledge, 2000), *Roland Barthes* (Routledge, 2003), *The pupils of the University*. Ed. parallax 40 (2003) and is currently working on a monograph on Mary Shelley (to be published by Palgrave in 2007) and a first collection of poetry, provisionally entitled *Some Things I Never Did*.

ROY SELLARS is Senior Lecturer in English literature at the University of Southern Denmark, Kolding; in 2005–06 he is in residence at the Kierkegaard Library, St. Olaf College, Minnesota. A graduate of St. Edmund Hall, Oxford, where he discovered Bloom thanks to his tutor Ann Wordsworth, he has also worked at Marburg University, the University of Geneva, Cornell University and the National University of Singapore. He has published on topics in literature and theory, and is completing a book on Milton; he is also co-editor, with Per Krogh Hansen, of *Glossing* Glas (Nebraska, forthcoming). He welcomes notice of any relevant writings for a complete bibliography of Bloom in progress.

The Salt Companion to Harold Bloom

Edited by
GRAHAM ALLEN
ROY SELLARS

CAMBRIDGE

PUBLISHED BY SALT PUBLISHING
PO Box 937, Great Wilbraham. Cambridge PDO CB1 5JX United Kingdom

All rights reserved

Selection © Graham Allen and Roy Sellars, 2007
Copyright of the contributions rests with the authors
as cited in the acknowledgements.

The right of Graham Allen and Roy Sellars to be identified as the
author of this work has been asserted by them in accordance
with Section 77 of the Copyright, Designs and Patents Act 1988.

This book is in copyright. Subject to statutory exception
and to provisions of relevant collective licensing agreements,
no reproduction of any part may take place without the written
permission of Salt Publishing.

First published 2007

Printed and bound in the United Kingdom by Lightning Source

Typeset in Swift 10/12

*This book is sold subject to the conditions that it shall not,
by way of trade or otherwise, be lent, re-sold, hired out,
or otherwise circulated without the publisher's prior consent
in any form of binding or cover other than that in which
it is published and without a similar condition including this
condition being imposed on the subsequent purchaser.*

ISBN-13 978 1 876857 20 2 paperback

Salt Publishing Ltd gratefully acknowledges
the financial assistance of Arts Council England

1 3 5 7 9 8 6 4 2

For Harold, at 75

Contents

Cover art: original work by Gregory Botts
Key to Abbreviations — ix
Preface: Graham Allen and Roy Sellars, — xiii
 "Harold Bloom and Critical Responsibility"

1

Graham Allen, "Passage"	1
Norman Finkelstein, "Aliyah"	4
John Hollander, "A Merrie Melody for Harold"	6
Geoffrey Hartman, "The Song of Solomon's Daughter in the Paradise of Poets, Exulting that She Exists"	8
Peter Abbs, "Voyaging Out"	11
Paolo Valesio, Three Poems	13
Kevin Hart, "The Trader's Wife"	23
John Kinsella, "Field Notes from Mount Bakewell"	25
Nicholas Royle, "The Slide"	33

2

Roger Gilbert, "Acts of Reading, Acts of Loving: Harold Bloom and the Art of Appreciation"	35
Graham Allen, "The Anxiety of Choice, the Western Canon and the Future of Literature"	52
R. Clifton Spargo, "Toward an Ethics of Literary Revisionism"	65
Heidi Sylvester, "Sublime Theorist: Harold Bloom's Catastrophic Theory of Literature"	120
Barnard Turner, "Bloom and the School of Resentment: An Interrogation of the 'Prelude' and 'Preface' to *The Western Canon*"	133
Christopher Rollason, "On the Stone Raft: Harold Bloom in Catalonia and Portugal"	149
T. J. Cribb, "Anxieties of Influence in the Theatre of Memory: Harold Bloom, Marlowe and *Henry V*"	170

Gregory Machacek, "Conceptions of Origins and Their Consequences: Bloom and Milton"	183
Milton L. Welch, "The Poet as Poet: Misreading Harold Bloom's Theory of Influence"	199
John W. P. Phillips, "To Execute a Clinamen"	213
Martin McQuillan, "Is Deconstruction Really a Jewish Science? Bloom, Freud and Derrida"	235
Roy Sellars, "Harold Bloom, (Comic) Critic"	255
Anders H. Klitgaard, "Bloom, Kierkegaard, and the Problem of Misreading"	290
Nicholas Birns, "Placing the Jar Properly: The Religious and the Secular in the Criticism of Harold Bloom"	303
Gwee Li Sui, "I, J, K"	319
Leslie Brisman, "Bloom upon Her Mountain: Unclouding the Heights of Modern Biblical Criticism"	332
Moshe Idel, "Enoch and Elijah: Some Remarks on Apotheosis, Theophany and Jewish Mysticism"	347
Sinéad Murphy, "'From Blank to Blank:' Harold Bloom and Woman Writers"	378
Stephen Da Silva, "A Queer Touch and the Bloomian Model of Authorial Influence"	393
Peter Morris, "Harold Bloom, Parody, and the 'Other Tradition'"	425
María Rosa Menocal, "How I Learned to Write Without Footnotes"	479
Afterword: Harold Bloom	487
Notes on Contributors	490
Index: Milton L. Welch	00

Key to Abbreviations
(Printed Texts by Harold Bloom)

References to texts by Bloom are made in parentheses in each essay according to the following abbreviations. We have not distinguished between American and British editions of the same book. In the case of *Anxiety* and *Map*, pagination of the text is identical between the first and second editions; the new prefaces to the latter are listed below separately.

Agon	*Agon: Towards a Theory of Revisionism.* New York: Oxford UP, 1982.
Alone	"Preface." *Alone With the Alone: Creative Imagination in the Sūfism of Ibn 'Arabī.* By Henry Corbin. Trans. Ralph Manheim. 1969. Bollingen Series 91. Princeton: Princeton UP, 1998. ix–xx.
American	*The American Religion: The Emergence of the Post-Christian Nation.* New York: Simon and Schuster, 1992.
Anxiety	*The Anxiety of Influence: A Theory of Poetry.* New York: Oxford UP, 1973.
Apocalypse	*Blake's Apocalypse: A Study in Poetic Argument.* Ithaca: Cornell UP, 1963.
Ashbery	Introduction. *John Ashbery.* Ed. Bloom. Modern Critical Views. New York: Chelsea House, 1985. 1–16.
"Beard"	"The One with the Beard Is God, the Other Is the Devil." *Portuguese Literary and Cultural Studies* [Dartmouth, MA] 6 (2001): 155–66.
Best American	*The Best of the Best American Poetry.* Ed. Bloom. New York: Scribner Poetry, 1998.
Best English	*The Best Poems of the English Language: From Chaucer through Frost.* Ed. Bloom. New York: HarperCollins, 2004.

"Breaking"	"The Breaking of Form." *Deconstruction and Criticism*. By Bloom, et al. New York: Seabury, 1979. 1–37.
Canon	*The Western Canon: The Books and School of the Ages.* New York: Harcourt, 1994.
"Daemonic"	"The Daemonic Allegorist." Rev. of *The Prophetic Moment: An Essay on Spenser*, by Angus Fletcher. *Virginia Quarterly Review* 47 (1971): 477–80.
Deconstruction	*Deconstruction and Criticism*. By Bloom, et al. New York: Seabury, 1979.
Exodus	*Exodus*. Ed. Bloom. Modern Critical Interpretations. New York: Chelsea House, 1987.
Figures	*Figures of Capable Imagination*. New York: Seabury, 1976.
"Foreword"	"Foreword." *Absorbing Perfections: Kabbalah and Interpretation*. By Moshe Idel. New Haven: Yale UP, 2002. ix–xvii.
Futur	*El futur de la imaginació*. Barcelona: Anagrama / Empúries, 2002.
Genesis	*Genesis*. Ed. Bloom. Modern Critical Interpretations. New York: Chelsea House, 1986.
Genius	*Genius: A Mosaic of One Hundred Exemplary Creative Minds*. New York: Warner, 2002.
Hamlet	*Hamlet: Poem Unlimited*. New York: Riverhead, 2003.
How	*How to Read and Why*. New York: Scribner, 2000.
"How"	"Preface: How to Read Milton's Lycidas." *A Map of Misreading*. 2nd ed. New York: Oxford UP, 2003. xiii–xxiii.
"Introduction" *JM*	Introduction. *John Milton*. Ed. Bloom. Modern Critical Views. New York: Chelsea House, 1986. 1–7.
"Introduction" *JMPL*	Introduction. *John Milton's* Paradise Lost. Ed. Bloom. Modern Critical Interpretations. New York: Chelsea House, 1987. 1–11.

"Introduction" PL, PR, SA	Introduction. *Paradise Lost, Paradise Regained, Samson Agonistes*. By John Milton. Ed. Bloom. New York: Collier, 1962. 5–11.
J	*The Book of J*. Trans. David Rosenberg. Interpreted by Bloom. New York: Grove Weidenfeld, 1990.
"J to K"	"From J to K, or The Uncanniness of the Yahwist." *The Bible and the Narrative Tradition*. Ed. Frank McConnell. New York: Oxford UP, 1986. 19–35.
Kabbalah	*Kabbalah and Criticism*. New York: Seabury, 1975.
Kierkegaard	Introduction. *Søren Kierkegaard*. Ed. Bloom. Modern Critical Views. New York: Chelsea House, 1989. 1–4.
King Lear	Introduction. *William Shakespeare's* King Lear. Ed. Bloom. Modern Critical Interpretations. New York: Chelsea House, 1987. 1–8.
Map	*A Map of Misreading*. New York: Oxford UP, 1975.
Merrill	Introduction. *James Merrill*. Ed. Bloom. Modern Critical Views. New York: Chelsea House, 1985. 1–7.
"New Poetics"	"A New Poetics." Rev. of *Anatomy of Criticism: Four Essays*, by Northrop Frye. *Yale Review* 47 (1957): 130–33.
Omens	*Omens of Millennium: The Gnosis of Angels, Dreams, and Resurrection*. New York: Riverhead, 1996.
Peripheral	Introduction. *Peripheral Light: Selected and New Poems*. By John Kinsella. New York: Norton, 2003. xiii–xxviii.
Poetics	*Poetics of Influence: New and Selected Criticism*. Ed. John Hollander. New Haven: Henry R. Schwab, 1988.
Poetry	*Poetry and Repression: Revisionism from Blake to Stevens*. New Haven: Yale UP, 1976.
Pope	*Alexander Pope*. Ed. Bloom. Modern Critical Views. New York: Chelsea House, 1986.

"Preface"	Preface. *The Anxiety of Influence: A Theory of Poetry.* 2nd ed. New York: Oxford UP, 1997. xi–xlvii.
Ringers	*The Ringers in the Tower: Studies in Romantic Tradition.* Chicago: U of Chicago P, 1971.
Ruin	*Ruin the Sacred Truths: Poetry and Belief from the Bible to the Present.* Charles Eliot Norton Lectures, 1987–88. Cambridge, MA: Harvard UP, 1989.
Shakespeare	*Shakespeare: The Invention of the Human.* New York: Riverhead, 1998.
Shelley	*Shelley's Mythmaking.* Yale Studies in English 141. Ithaca: Cornell UP, 1959.
Stevens	*Wallace Stevens: The Poems of Our Climate.* Ithaca: Cornell UP, 1977.
Vessels	*The Breaking of the Vessels.* Wellek Library Lectures at the University of California, Irvine. Chicago: U of Chicago P, 1982.
Visionary	*The Visionary Company: A Reading of English Romantic Poetry.* 1961. Rev. ed. Ithaca: Cornell UP, 1971.
Wisdom	*Where Shall Wisdom Be Found?* New York: Riverhead-Penguin, 2004.
Yeats	*Yeats.* New York: Oxford UP, 1970.

Preface
Harold Bloom and Critical Responsibility

GRAHAM ALLEN
AND
ROY SELLARS

It is difficult to read. The page is dark.
Yet he knows what it is that he expects.
—STEVENS, "Phosphor Reading by His Own Light"

Opposition is true Friendship.
—BLAKE, *The Marriage of Heaven and Hell*, plate 20

Harold Bloom is the most famous living literary critic in the English-speaking world.[1] Such a statement is easy enough to make in terms of its truth-value; however, it also brings with it a host of paradoxes and complications. For a long time now, Bloom has been presenting himself as a solitary voice, ignored by an academic audience who should—but never will—listen. The role sounds like a painful one; but is it anything more than a role, played with a mask? Bloom's customary self-presentation does not sit neatly with our opening statement. Writing in 1988, Peter de Bolla began his study of Bloom with a confirmation of Bloom's self-figuring: "while Bloom's notion of 'influence' is probably one of the most widely disseminated concepts at work in literary critical practice today, the books in which this idea is conceptually formulated are little read or commented upon" (8). De Bolla goes on to suggest that there is within Bloom's work itself a resistance to critical imitation and extension, to generating disciples and schools. Indeed, Bloom has forcefully confirmed this resistance to emulation. To take one example, from his

---

[1] Roger Gilbert, in this volume, calls him "the most famous, and in some quarters infamous, literary critic of our time."

essay "Agon: Revisionism and Critical Personality:" "I want first to suggest that on a pragmatic view there is no language *of criticism* but only of an individual critic, because . . . a theory of strong misreading denies that there is or should be any common vocabulary in terms of which critics can argue with one another" (*Agon* 21). While it may be true that Bloom's work is difficult to adopt as a methodology, and that it presents itself as a kind of literature, its unrepeatability does not, on its own, explain the lack of academic dialogue to which De Bolla refers. Kristeva, Barthes, Derrida and De Man are equally unrepeatable, for example, and yet their works, unlike those of Bloom, have been subject to a widespread and intensive (if not always successful) incorporation into academic discourse.[2]

Academic and other worlds have changed significantly since the mid-1980s, and now is a good time to reassess the reception of Bloom's ever-increasing corpus. The first and most remarkable change has been in Bloom's own critical focus. De Bolla refers inevitably to Bloom's famous theory of the anxiety of influence and the idea of literary and indeed critical writing as miswriting. However, if we had to characterise Bloom's work since the mid-1980s, it would be in terms of freedom from influence, originality, authors who are influencers rather than influenced, movers rather than moved. As a number of contributors to this volume explain, Bloom has dramatically altered his orientation in the last twenty years, ceasing to describe and in some ways embody those who are belated and, instead, focusing on that small circle of authors who, as he now likes to put it, have made us all possible, whoever 'we' may be.[3] That reorientation may seem unremarkable; but to many readers who have closely followed Bloom's career, richly and diversely assembled in the current volume, the change of perspective is immense and does not come without a certain sense of loss. Graham Allen, for example, pivots his essay on this commonly expressed regret, foregrounding the ironic fact that, in moving away from the anxiety of influence and the struggle against the poetic burden of the past, Bloom may have temporarily lost sight of the future-orientation of the most vital forms of literature.

---

[2] For a discussion of this issue, see the conclusion of R. Clifton Spargo's essay in this volume.

[3] For a rigorous reading of originality in the context of Bloom's work, readers should turn to Gregory Machacek's "Conceptions of Origins and Their Consequences: Bloom and Milton," in this volume.

We need to avoid premature assumptions about the overall character of Bloom's work. Contributors to this volume often remind us that there exists what we might call an *alternative Bloom*, or *alternative Blooms*. Like any culturally central controversialist, he is not quite the figure that public opinion imagines. There is a Bloom who fiercely defends the art of reading and a dynamic but central canon of strong literary texts. There is also a Bloom who is a highly respected contributor to Biblical studies and religious studies more generally. Nicholas Birns, in this volume, comments that "*The Book of J* seems one of the most 'primary' of Harold Bloom's works." In his "Foreword" to Moshe Idel's *Absorbing Perfections: Kabbalah and Interpretation*, Bloom styles himself a "literary critic and not a Kabbalistic scholar" (x). But his evident ability, in a few pages, magisterially to evaluate the relationship between Idel, the great scholar of Kabbalah in our generation, and the great precursor in that field, Gershom Scholem—added to the very fact that it is he, Bloom, who is prefacing what he calls Idel's "most important volume so far" (x)—runs against his own self-humbling characterisation. The enormous influence that Bloom has had in Biblical studies and related disciplines of reading cannot be ignored if we hope to take full measure of his lifelong achievement. The fact that so many of the contributors to this volume, including Geoffrey Hartman and Moshe Idel himself, focus on this aspect demonstrates its importance for Bloom's thought. Many of these contributions attempt to link Bloom's work on Kabbalah and the Bible with his theories of literary influence and poetic (or critical) agonism. This move is on one level an obvious one, and it is clear that Bloom sees in the realms of religious writing a 'poetics of conflict' similar to the one he has so memorably marked out in the realms of poetry and imaginative literature (see Allen, *Harold Bloom*, esp. ch. 2). Whether Bloom's interventions in different fields can ultimately be reconciled is not for us to judge; the purpose of this heterogeneous collection was never to create a synthetically unified Bloom. Of the many precursors to whom Bloom refers in his moving "Afterword" to this volume, the overriding presence is that of Walt Whitman. Bloom here states that "[t]he politics of pre-civil war America scarcely illuminate *Leaves of Grass* (1855)," and much the same could be said of the eras of Kennedy, Johnson, Nixon, Ford, Carter, Reagan, Bush *père*, Clinton, or Bush *fils* ("Benito Bush," as Bloom calls him) in relation to Bloom's own major writings on literature. However, since the Reagan years another Bloom has emerged who, like Whitman and Emerson before him, is quite prepared to leave the realms of poetic *agon* in order to address the political follies of the day. This Bloom—perhaps more ephemeral, but hardly minor—is still little known to academic readers, for it is a Bloom one will mainly find in the mass media. In the American university system to which he remains attached, he has often been castigated as an elitist or reactionary, but the American university system is not the world, and it is the world, increasingly, that is Bloom's audience. Scourge of Newt Gingrich and other right-wing ideologues, defender of abortion rights, analyst of religious fundamentalisms, Bloom has become one of those American critics who can most help readers outside the US to read the text that the American empire has been writing on minds and bodies around the world. The diversity of his interventions makes Stanley Fish's claim, in 1995, that Bloom is not a "public intellectual" look out of date (*Professional* 118). Much as Bloom likes to mock academic pretensions and pseudo-politics, one cannot survey his work without registering its own political dimension or, if a trope is required, face.

Harold Bloom has many faces, and like his favourite literary character, Sir John Falstaff, or like Whitman, these faces do not amount to a totality. There is a passage in Whitman which is so obvious in this context that many sophisticated critics, fearful of repetition, would no doubt avoid it. The passage comes to us in such a familiar guise that it already reads like a quotation or even cliché. But some clichés are quotations whose apparent staleness can be refreshed, being thus transformed back into moments of literature; and for demonstrating this quickening power, we owe gratitude to Bloom, a critic never anxious about repeating (from memory, naturally) the texts which have, as he puts it, helped him to live his life. Here it is:

> Do I contradict myself?
> Very well then I contradict myself,
> (I am large, I contain multitudes.) (*Song of Myself* 51)

The planet Bloom contains multitudes; we say it here because we know enough about him to know that he might say it himself, smiling at the ironies that such a statement would contain. This reminds us of another Bloom, another face often missed by the multitude of critics and journalists who have pronounced on, or denounced, his work. This Bloom is nowhere better represented than in his own "Afterword" here, a text written on the morning of his seventy-fifth birthday in 2005. This is a Bloom who, as Roy Sellars, alongside a number of others collected here, reminds us, is a comic genius—a man for whom literary life allows for constant irony and pastiche; a man for whom Oscar Wilde is a giant precursor. Bloom deals in tropes and roles, not identities; and he writes aphoristically, at his best, rather than magisterially. One of the principles for "the restoration of reading" that he outlines in the provocative Prologue to *How to Read and Why* is "the *recovery of the ironic*" (25). The Wildean role is hard to sustain, though, in any context, and sometimes it seems as if Bloom is verging on self-parody. It's hard to tell. Bloom's humour is certainly lost on academics trained to be bureaucrats rather than readers, professionalised to the point where vast ironies can go unseen and unmarked. If opposition is true friendship, then the hostile non-reception of Bloom suggests that one can have too much of a good thing.[4] We return, then, to Bloom's readers, whom we hope this collection will create as well as reach.

The shift from the anxiety of influence to the celebration of Shakespearean originality might seem to have confirmed Bloom's academic marginalisation. But then we ask: whose margins? Our contributors are geographically diverse, our publisher is not based in the US, and we question the tendency of the US academy to take for granted its own frames of reference. Furthermore, and again appropriately in our view, our publisher is not a university press–for academics are not the only readers. In the past fifteen years or so, Bloom has gained a worldwide audience who purchase books such as *How to Read and Why* (2000), *Genius* (2002), *The Art of Reading Poetry* (2004), *Where Shall Wisdom Be Found?* (2004) or *Jesus and Yahweh* (2005). This has happened not just in English but also in translation (another aspect of his work that has been little studied). Bloom has become good copy, and each of his new publications is heralded by a degree of media coverage unrivalled by any other living critic. The current foundation stone of this presence in popular culture is his Bardolatry, his uncompromising (and professionally thankless) defence of Shakespeare as the central author in Western and indeed world literature.[5] Herbert Weil, in *Harold Bloom's Shakespeare*, states that Bloom "has managed to capture the curiosity and attention of readers whom professional specialists have failed to reach" (Weil 126). Linda Charnes, in the same book, states that Bloom's *Shakespeare: The Invention of the Human* (1999) has made him "the literary critic of the educated, nonacademic middle class" (Charnes 262). Richard Levin adds: "I think that [the] striking difference between the

---

[4] Readers are referred to Barnard Turner's essay in this volume, a sustained examination of Bloom's contemporary agon with what he calls the School of Resentment.

[5] A significant account of Bloom's approach to Shakespeare is found in T. J. Cribb's contribution to this volume.

book's reception inside and outside the academy should concern us, since it marks the extent to which our vanguard critics have separated themselves from, and alienated, a significant part of the public that used to be included in our audience and our constituency" (Levin 77). In a period in which literary critics increasingly diversify and apply their techniques to analysis of the productions of popular culture, it is Bloom, staunch defender of more traditional ideals of canonicity and close reading, who has himself become both a subject and an object of that culture. The cultural capital of Bloom has probably never been higher. The irony is not lost on him—is irony ever lost on Bloom?—and is part of what allows for his confident and joyfully vengeful prophetic stance, as adopted here at the opening of *The Western Canon*:

> Not a moment passes these days without fresh rushes of academic lemmings[6] off the cliffs they proclaim the political responsibilities of the critic, but eventually all this moralizing will subside. Every teaching institution will have its department of cultural studies, an ox not to be gored, and an aesthetic underground will flourish, restoring something of the romance of reading. (*Canon* 15)

Beyond any other contemporary critic, Bloom stands for a fierce love of literature. Nowhere is this fact better attested to than in María Rosa Menocal's amusing and moving "How I Learned to Write Without Footnotes," below. If this love of literature can only be kept burning outside the techno-bureaucratic university—and that remains a large if—then so be it. Bloom's critical desire to honour literature, and the passion with which he pursues it, has won him a readership on a scale unimaginable to other critics, and those who have followed and cared about his work can only rejoice at such a situation in all its irony. Martin McQuillan expresses this response memorably at the beginning of his contribution: "Thank goodness for Harold Bloom. There is no literary critic writing today who is more encyclopaedic, more prolific, more outrageous, or more camp than Harold Bloom." John Phillips's wonderfully provocative Bloomian treatment of the word 'bloom,' in this volume, is also indicative of the intellectual affection and critical regard Bloom still inspires in many, even in the academy.

Bloom is the most remarkable literary critic today. In an age of apparently irresistible professionalisation, with its concomitant stress on specialisation, his range over world literature appears sublime, beyond

---

[6] On the trope of the lemmings, see the essay by Roy Sellars below.

reason. This fact is frequently celebrated in the pages which follow. In the various discussions of the sublime in this volume (Heidi Sylvester's being the most sustained), we find a resounding testament to the fact that in our age, the sublime cannot be thought about critically without reference to Bloom. He is, as many in this volume argue, an example of the sublime. In his huge body of critical monographs, and in his prefaces for the innumerable Chelsea House volumes of criticism (addressed not only to an undergraduate but also a high-school audience), Bloom has introduced more texts than any other critic now or in the recent past. It would be an interesting exercise to attempt to name a handful of authors, of any note whatsoever, about whom he has not written at all. Many of the essays below may surprise readers who solely associate him with the canonical works of British and American literature. Christopher Rollason, for example, gives us a Bloom who is a champion of literatures from the Iberian, Ibero-American and Luso-Hispanic worlds, while Stephen Da Silva and Peter Morris, in their quite different ways, give us a Bloom relevant to the complex discussion of homoerotic literatures in English. More important than Bloom's sheer range is the astonishing amount of seminal interpretations that he has gifted us. Intertextually complex and original, these readings will remain a vast testament to the importance of literary interpretation and what Bloom calls "the romance of reading."

If we are to understand the phenomenon that is Bloom—at the beginning of his appreciation, Roger Gilbert asks "What is Harold Bloom?"—we need to pay attention to the continuities as well as the twists and turns of his half-century of critical work. A pair of quotations from two of his most characteristic works will suffice:

> If the imagination's gift comes necessarily from the perversity of the spirit, then the living labyrinth of literature is built upon the ruin of every impulse most generous in us. So apparently it is and must be—we are wrong to have founded a humanism directly upon literature itself, and the phrase 'humane letters' is an oxymoron. A humanism might still be founded upon a completer *study of literature* than we have yet achieved, but never upon literature itself, or any idealized mirroring of its implicit categories. The strong imagination comes to its painful birth through savagery and misrepresentation. The only humane virtue we can hope to teach through a more advanced study of literature than we have now is the social virtue of detachment from one's own imagination, recognizing always that such detachment made absolute destroys any individual imagination. (*Anxiety* 85–86)

> If we were literally immortal, or even if our span were doubled to seven score of years, say, we could give up all argument about canons. But we

have an interval only, and then our place knows us no more, and stuffing that interval with bad writing, in the name of whatever social justice, does not seem to me to be the responsibility of the literary critic. (*Canon* 32)

Two things link these passages from *The Anxiety of Influence* and *The Western Canon*. The obvious connection concerns the persistence of Bloom's dark, anti-liberal vision of the literary imagination, one that allies him with Leo Bersani (*The Culture of Redemption*) rather than Allan Bloom (*The Closing of the American Mind*)—with whom, absurdly, he is sometimes conflated. One of the most challenging aspects of *The Western Canon* lies in Harold Bloom's exasperation: despite three decades of demystification, he laments at length, the academic approach to literature has merely intensified its idealisations of its object. The argument presented in *The Anxiety of Influence* about literature's unavailability for social reform—which, as Bloom frequently reminds us, finds one of its greatest statements in the work of the radical Romantic writer William Hazlitt–is presented again in *The Western Canon*. The difference in the presentation is worth remarking upon, however, since in the former text it is a message delivered mainly to academic literary critics, whilst in the latter it is a message delivered in spite of them.

The persistence of the Bloomian vision of the agonistic literary imagination should move us to the second link between these passages. As various contributors to this collection show, Bloom is a critic committed to what he calls above "the responsibility of the literary critic." Aligning literature with implicit or explicit programmes for social reform does not, he consistently states, meet the challenge of critical responsibility. So, we might ask in return, what does?

A significant number of the essays collected here concern themselves with Bloom's engagement with the Judaic tradition of Biblical interpretation (see especially the contributions by Nicholas Birns, Leslie Brisman, Gwee Li Sui, and Moshe Idel). The philosophical and critical work of Jacques Derrida is a recurrent point of reference in such discussions of Bloom's relation to Judaic interpretation and culture.[7] His old sparring partner, Derrida, reminds us in *The Gift of Death* of the Biblical roots of the Western notion of responsibility. The purpose of such a move in Derrida's work is, in particular, to return us to the impossibility of responsibility's call. Working back through Levinas (see R. Clifton

---

[7] See Martin McQuillan's "Is Deconstruction Really a Jewish Science? Bloom, Freud, Derrida," in this volume.

Spargo in this collection) and Kierkegaard (see Anders Klitgaard in this collection), Derrida's text confronts us once again with the terrible logic of responsibility, captured in the Abrahamic paradox which places us between the Other as Totality (God) and the Other as particular (Isaac). This is a paradox which defeats us every time.[8] Reading Bloom, wherever we may start in his prolific corpus, reminds us that for the literary critic this paradox presents itself as an impossible shuttle between Literature and the text: the need for a theory of literature always threatens the critic's desire and duty to do full justice to the individual text. It also reminds us that evaluation, an inherent aspect of Bloom's work that is frequently noted in this volume, is not something which we can simply choose to embrace or reject.

The presence of evaluative criticism within Bloom's work is a feature which has, as Gilbert suggests, received the most inaccurate and skewed forms of response, both in his supporters and detractors. The tendency has been to assert, against Bloom's rhetoric of 'strong' and 'weak' texts, that such evaluation is unnecessary, and even politically conservative. It hardly needs to be said that the majority of Bloom's critics on this issue have been practitioners of various forms of post-colonial or feminist literary criticism (a sophisticated and sensitive version of this latter form of critique can be found in Sinéad Murphy's contribution). The mistake upon which many of these responses have been built is to suppose that Bloom's evaluative statements issue from a stable map of the literary canon, and that such evaluations are essentially comparative in relation to given identities.[9] For Bloom, strength (power, pathos, more life) does not originate from comparison within a totalising (inclusive) map—who actually possesses such a map?—but from a passionate commitment to the text. The ultimate paradox of evaluation, at least in Bloom's committed hands, is that it is not comparative but, rather, competitive. His evaluative method does not give us a hierarchy of literary greats and also-rans but rather, time after time, the experience of a critic gaining power and more life from texts which possess an uncanny excess of vitality (or what he calls 'strength').

---

[8] For a careful reading of Bloom's response to this Biblical scene—a response which demonstrates his "distaste for the trial of Abraham"—readers should turn to Leslie Brisman's essay.

[9] Milton Welch, in this volume, for example, returns us to the complex question of whether Bloom supports or undermines the traditional figure of the author.

Bloom has presented us with a number of literary maps in his time; but he knows that, for the literary critic, responsibility is always first and foremost to the text. What he also knows, with regard to the Abrahamic paradox (which can look like a straight translation of the hermeneutic circle) is that it is not really Totality (the literary universe) which overwhelms us but the particular, singular text as Other. The crucial question facing all literary critics is what such responsibility to the text as Other involves. When we critically confront a text, is it power or knowledge that we seek? Bloom's decades-long *agon* with Derrida and De Man makes it clear that, faced with a choice between an epistemological and a tropological model, Bloom unhesitatingly chooses the latter—or argues that the latter has already chosen what we like to call 'us.' As he writes in "Ratios: The Language of Poetry and the Language of Criticism:"

> We want to be kind, we think, and we say that to be alone with a book is to confront neither ourselves nor another. We lie. When you read, you confront either yourself, or another, and in either confrontation you seek power. Power over yourself, or another, but power. And what is power? *Potentia*, the pathos of more life, or to speak reductively, the language of possession. The idealization of power, in the reading process, or processes, is finally a last brutal self-idealization, a noble lie against our own origins. This lie is against mortality . . . . (*Breaking* 13)

The choice between understanding and power may ultimately be unimportant on the level of critical responsibility, however. What critic, after all, even if armed with an epistemological account of the reading process, will argue that she has read enough because she has spent a lifetime reading X, even if X turns out to be *The Iliad*, *The Divine Comedy*, *Paradise Lost*, *Ulysses*, or even Shakespeare? On the level of responsibility such a statement would be meaningless, since not only does X remain beyond critical closure, but there remain so many other texts with magnificent claims for critical attention which must be sacrificed during the study of X in order for that study to be possible. The truly responsible critic wishes to meet fully and completely not only with X but with every text worthy of attention, since how can she claim to be fully responsible if she has not given critical attention to all texts worthy of such attention? We read Bloom, we have always read Bloom, and we continue to read Bloom, because he is the greatest example in the past fifty years (at least) of this form of critical responsibility.

Critical responsibility is impossible, but for someone of Bloom's unique capabilities only just. His failure "to complete the work," as he often expresses it (*How* 277), comes under the sign of the *only just*. Bloom's lifelong dedication to the duty of the critic (that duty being *to literature, but also in terms of each of its particular manifestations*) throws a gigantic shadow over everyone else who would take up that task. Few could plausibly claim to rival Bloom in terms of critical range. And yet to experience the Bloom of *The Western Canon* unflinchingly facing up to the impossibility of the task of the contemporary critic not only confronts us with our own deracinated critical visions but also compounds our sense of limitation by presenting us with the master's *only just* sense of incompleteness:

> What shall the individual who still desires to read attempt to read, this late in history? The Biblical three-score years and ten no longer suffice to read more than a selection of the great writers in what can be called the Western tradition, let alone in the world's traditions. Who reads must choose, since there is literally not enough time to read everything, even if one does nothing but read. Mallarmé's grand line—"the flesh is sad, alas, and I have read all the books"—has become a hyperbole. Overpopulation, Malthusian repletion, is the authentic context for canonical anxieties. (*Canon* 15)

A fierce dedication to the responsibilities of the critic has, as the following essays demonstrate, placed Bloom himself within the Western canon while giving us an unavoidable and yet unrepeatable example of critical responsibility. That responsibility rests in what Bloom calls strangeness, another word for what we have been calling the unrepeatable. As a critic, his lifelong responsibility has been to "a strangeness" in literary texts "that we either never altogether assimilate, or that becomes such a given that we are blinded to its idiosyncrasies" (*Canon* 4). This collection is dedicated, then, in a spirit of friendly opposition, to preventing Harold Bloom from ever becoming a given.

Last but not least, no collection such as this one (and this one, despite its lengthy gestation, is the first) could possibly do without the attempt, by poets and prose writers, at some original literary contribution (with all the irony that the word 'original' can stand). This book therefore brings together a number of professional creative writers and a number of academics venturing into creative writing. The section, Creative Work, which begins this volume is at least as important as the Critical Work which it prefaces. We can easily imagine whole anthologies of poems dedicated to, or written in agonistic contention with, the work of Harold Bloom. He has already had (as many of the critical essays here recognize) an immense impact on poetry and fiction written in the past thirty years. No other post-war literary critic can come near Bloom's ignition and motivation of radically new literary responses. Our opening creative section is a chance to acknowledge the productive influence of the greatest literary critic of recent years. The fact that the pieces are almost all new to print is an acknowledgement of the continued vitality for literature that Bloom embodies—and a taster, for readers of this collection, of what is already out there, to be discovered in the future.

Acknowledgements

The call for papers with which this collection began, originally as a special issue of the creative journal *Salt*, produced an overwhelming response. No single book can ever hope to be comprehensive or definitive as far as Bloom is concerned, and it is no exaggeration to say that an entire book series could have been constructed as well as this particular volume. We would like to thank all those who submitted proposals and drafts as well as those whose work is actually included in this collection. The contributors have been very patient in enduring delay and accommodating requests for revision. The book has been a long time in the making, and we would like to acknowledge the immense act of faith that its initiator, John Kinsella, and everyone at Salt Publishing, placed in it over the years. We are grateful to Chris Hamilton-Emery for advice and for seeing the volume through the press so efficiently. Above all, we thank Harold Bloom himself for being so generous and supportive with regard to the entire project. Graham Allen, as always, is indebted most profoundly and personally to Bernie, Dani and Chrissie. The debts of Roy Sellars are too huge to list, but he is grateful to all those who have sustained him in different ways during the making of this book, including the librarians at Cornell University, the University of Southern Denmark, and St. Olaf College.

We would also like to take this opportunity to register our appreciation of the many critics who have responded significantly to Harold Bloom's work. We hope and expect that in the near future there will be an adequate bibliography allowing readers to assess these responses for themselves; in the meantime we have especially benefited from responses to Bloom by M. H. Abrams, Jonathan Arac, Elizabeth Bruss, Peter de Bolla, David Fite, Wlad Godzich, Susan Handelman, Jean-Pierre

Mileur, Donald Pease, Louis Renza, Lars Ole Sauerberg, and Ann Wordsworth, among others. John Hollander has not only written the best book to show what Bloomian approaches can actually do for literary criticism (*The Figure of Echo*) but has also edited the best anthology of Bloom's work, *Poetics of Influence*, which we recommend to readers who are new to him or who have come to him in the past fifteen years. It is hard to imagine Bloom's own best work, agonistically, without critics such as Paul de Man, Geoffrey Hartman, Barbara Johnson, J. Hillis Miller—and of course Jacques Derrida.

Thanks are due to the Faculty of Arts, University College Cork, for funding the index of this book, and to the Institute for Literature, Culture and Media, University of Southern Denmark.

Lastly, Graham Allen and Roy Sellars thank Harold for being the medium by which they found each other, thus initiating a true friendship now twenty years long.

Works Cited

Allen, Graham. *Harold Bloom: A Poetics of Conflict*. Modern Cultural Theorists. Hemel Hempstead: Harvester, 1994.

Bersani, Leo. *The Culture of Redemption*. Cambridge, MA: Harvard UP, 1990.

Blake, William. *The Complete Poetry and Prose*. Ed. David V. Erdman. Commentary by Harold Bloom. Rev. ed. Berkeley: U of California P, 1982.

Bloom, Allan. *The Closing of the American Mind*. New York: Simon and Schuster, 1987.

Charnes, Linda. "The 2% Solution: What Harold Bloom Forgot." Desmet and Sawyer 213-68.

De Bolla, Peter. *Harold Bloom: Towards Historical Rhetorics*. London: Routledge, 1988.

Derrida, Jacques. *The Gift of Death*. Trans. David Wills. Chicago: U of Chicago P, 1996.

Desmet, Christy and Robert Sawyer, eds. *Harold Bloom's Shakespeare*. London: Palgrave, 2002.

Fish, Stanley. *Professional Correctness: Literary Studies and Political Change*. Oxford: Clarendon, 1995.

Hollander, John. *The Figure of Echo: A Mode of Allusion in Milton and After*. Berkeley: U of California P, 1981.

Levin, Richard. "Bloom, Bardolatry, and Characterology." Desmet and Sawyer 71-80.

Stevens, Wallace. *The Collected Poems*. New York: Knopf, 1954.

Weil, Herbert. "On Harold Bloom's Nontheatrical Praise for Shakespeare's Lovers: *Much Ado About Nothing* and *Antony and Cleopatra*." Desmet and Sawyer 125-41.

Whitman, Walt. *Song of Myself*. *Selected Poems*. Ed. Harold Bloom. American Poets Project. New York: Library of America, 2003. 11-92.

Passage

—Graham Allen
For Harold Bloom

I

And soon, there being no end,
He forgot how he had begun,
And could not tell
Whether he was falling still
Or rising.

II

Why must there be this untutored clash,
This ever trumpeted division and discord?
Light and dark, east and west,
Full Moon and crescent, frost and fire,
You and I. I deny them all.
In the name of the light that separates itself
Through imperfectly closed wooden blinds
Only to blend together to form one ray,
One undeniable beam, I deny them all.
In the name of You and I, I deny them all.

III

If I injure myself, is it for you?
If I neglect my body,
Tighten my lip,
No longer point my face
Towards what makes me happy;
If I burn myself by the water
Or freeze my bones outside
Of hearth and home,
Do you think it is for you?

I have cut myself so badly
That I begin to feel.

IV

In the garden
He rose above himself
And paused.

He denied the intuition of the sun,
The elective demonstration of hills,
The simple pride of oak and lily.

He presumed there would be other days,
Interrogative, challenged, somewhat straightened.
But he rose above himself on this day.

He paused.
In the garden, he said:
"This is enough. This is home."

V

If I were to have my days again
I would repeat the same mistakes:
The same enemies, the same misguided kisses,
The same unnoticed tragedies and triumphs.

If I were to have my days again,
Knowing what acts were wise, and what unholy,
My hand would still reach out to you
And you would still crumble at its touch.

VI

And soon, there being no end,
He forgot how it had begun,
And could not tell
Whether he was falling still
Or rising.

Aliyah

—NORMAN FINKELSTEIN
For Harold Bloom

From an infinite distance, the corrosive Word
calls to the soul, which had lost itself
      in the mirror of its activities.
The simulacrum dissolves: Go up to the Book
which contains the emptiness. Go up to the Book
      as if everything were forgotten.
Go up to the Book, because the thrice-commanded
have endured the anger, the scorn and the pity,
all the expectations, the normative illusions,
          and cannot be repossessed.

This is the world of the strong fragments,
where all the voices double back on themselves.
It is the world of the going up, where every image
          projects itself upon another
until the soul denies that it was ever privileged,
that it was the element of risk lost in translation,
      that its integrity was jeopardized
          because it had no integrity,
      that love could curl around the tongue
          until it gave birth to truth.

Here among the pages there are no mysteries.
Bird calls to bird as the seasons shift,
      speaking in that ancient language
            that somehow is always new.
They sit on the branches like words in a sentence.
Sweet world! when will you give yourself to the soul,
which has waited so long among its contradictions?
The wind that blows through the wreckage of history
          stirs among the idle leaves.
    Even here in the place that was promised,
    where the sheer light sears every wound,
    the figures are fruitful and multiply
        as if it had been ordained.

The soul falls back into the world of the mirror,
as across an infinite distance the Word withdraws,
    leaving only the faintest trace of itself
    exiled from the delight of continuity.
  They are shaking hands all around;
they are shaking hands and kissing each other,
kissing each other as they kiss the Book.
It is the birth of irony, born again and again
from the dissatisfactions, meager compensation,
  strong fragments, broken speech.

A Merrie Melody for Harold

—JOHN HOLLANDER

Fiddle-de-dee, fiddle-de-dee,
The fly has married the bumble-bee
Then down to fiddle-de-gee
Then up again to fiddle-de-ay
And way up there to fiddle-de-eeeeeeeeeeeeee—
Which is the way to play.
Is this some kind of boring riddle
Or
Is it that I am the cat and the fiddle?
Both—and more:
Hey diddle bloody diddle
Indeed!—And no, I'm not Stephane Grappelli,
Nor Joseph Szigeti, the fiddler of Dooney,
Nor the accomplished busker outside the local deli,
But I'm monumentally looney
If only because the improbable astronomical event
A certain cow was said to jump over,
Instead of munching her clover,
Has become so central to my discontent.
Io sono amalato
And hearing my own most unmellow
Buzzing yet stingless *ponticello*
And watching the dizzying bounce of my *spiccato*
Turns my poor head nightly . . . .

But the centrality I mentioned, of that moon:
The little dog (he was a brown Norfolk terrier, if I remember rightly)
Didn't exactly laugh at it, mind you, but rather lightly
Barked: at it, at the cow, at the cat horsehairing away at the catgut, at
    the song
They were in, and all so perplexed by, for so long:
Were they jailed in it or created by and out of it?
But enough of that. I return to the moon,

Reminded in so doing that (and I have no doubt of it)
Once in a green moon,
Which comes about some time in early—*that's right!*—June,
This sort of thing has been known to occur:
As in a bad joke,
The dish broke—
Not into pieces but, as it were,
Keeping its physical, if not its moral, integrity—
Into the place where silverware
In its soft brown bed of treated cloth lay there
In its trustful tranquility,
And rummaging through a pile
Of mismatched pieces (whispering all the while
The sort of promises that empty bowls
Are full of) persuaded the silly spoon
(They were poles
Apart in knowledge of the world, the sky, the sun, the moon
The cow had overjumped) to run away
With him and children sing about it to this very day
Unseeing of the darker side of what they sing and say,
And all that I have always known about the games they play.

The Song of Solomon's Daughter

in the Paradise of Poets
Exulting that She Exists
The Composer of Yahweh
Editor: Geoffrey Hartman

A prophecy discovered in the crypt of Yale's famous Babylonian Collection after extensive searches inspired by the thesis of Professor Harold Bloom in **The Book of J.**[1]

O yet once more the ancient letters dower
a mortal hand. What confident shadow
strides before my sight? I am reborn!
This critic—surely a renegade priest
or lovesick rabbi—has guessed I was a girl,
a clever daughter of Solomon. (I wonder
who really begat me. Things were pretty wild
at court, in those over-enlightened days.
They're wilder now, of course, in literature.)
I am found, found out. But what game is he playing
anyway? He's smarter than Baalam's ass,
my favorite invention, unless it's the bit
(truly Lady's gothic) about that awful
adult circumcision. It's all the fault
of those poetic tales around my father's knee,
and bubemaizes sucked from jeweled tongues
of strangely-named women who ran in and out
of his chambers,—he couldn't sleep anyway,—
dripping myrrh and chanting about foxes,
vines, kisses, a garden of nuts, she-gods
and dragons of the flood, their dismembered
heroes, the, what was the Greek word?
yes, sparagmos. The ground I stood on,
they said, was alive, and danced and stamped,

---

[1] A first version of this poem appeared in *Kerem: A Journal of Creative Explorations in Judaism* (winter 1992-93); permission to republish is hereby gratefully acknowledged.

merging the roles of hunter and hunted,
while shouting at each final selah-kick:
"The earth is the Lord's, all who live therein!"

That maddening refrain, like a priest's blessing,
covered every Davidic wildness.
A canny gift sprang from uncanny sounds
his tortured love provoked. I was the harp
that observed all this, child, legacy,
who played before him on the moody strings
and acclaimed Shaddai. Sheba herself
smiled on me, as though she knew (o image
of perfumed wisdom, sister-maze and guide)
what I was and was not.

Here the manuscript ends, but scraps survive from another scroll. It is possible that the following fragments, which the editor has revised into a semblance of coherence, may have been composed by someone other than J. They should be treated as a separate document provisionally called MS JJ.

My brother, my spouse, I was locked in the deep
a fountain closed up of living speech
only my eyes declared you in silence:
I was even lonelier than Joseph
abandoned in the pit,
who had a thousand working for me once,
Lilith and Leilah, the redeemed night-spirits.
Then came the withering priests of the chamzin,
terrorists of the unutterable.
Then came a raggedness, rabbis and scribes,
depressing the tongue of the text. I curse
the degrees, o David, though not your psalms,
I bless the dragon exuberance, the roar
of her against envious eye and pierced ear.
I bless my beloved, the spicy crow's* message

---

* Obscure. The Hebrew *kvk*, seems to be a defective reduplicative *kvkv*, with an onomatopoeic meaning (caw-caw).

rousing the Torah's ear in the cool evening.
You appeared, remade me in your image,
in the image of love and strife you exalted me:
I had faded away, shadow of delight,
you arrived and opened, lord of my mouth,
the firstborn speech I dedicate to you.
You are before I was, who was not there,
gone always gone—you found me in the laughter
and bloom** of your spirit

      caetera desunt

** The Hebrew text has *gevurah*.

Voyaging Out

—Peter Abbs
(After Dante's *Inferno*, Canto 26)
For Harold Bloom

Master, I said, *If within these flames this man can speak*
Let me draw close and hear his words. And Virgil replied:
Listen then and Ulysses will tell you how and where he died.

The oval flame before me began to flicker and rise higher
As if the inferno's wind was slowly rising. Then from the fire
I heard a spectral voice. *When I escaped from Circe*

Nothing held me. Neither my son, nor my decrepit father,
Least of all my doting wife. Some inner devil drove me on
To unravel the riddle of the sphinx, to take seductive nature

To the rack and screw. I wanted to map the sordid runnels
Of the mind, break open the hieroglyphs of dreams,
Crack the recalcitrant code of matter, good or evil—

What the hell? So I set out with a motley crew
And crossed the bare sea tracks to Spain, Morocco,
Sardinia—and other slack backwaters where no man spoke

A word we knew. Then we veered out to the sheer edge,
Where maps end, where the coolest trailblazers screw up,
Where great ships stagger back. My gang looked mutinous.

Men, I said, we have come a long way to reach
This black rock which marks the beginning of uncharted seas
And we are aging now. There's not a young man on this deck.

So, in whatever time remains, let us become as gods.
We were not born to live like pigs drooling in the muck
But to follow the flare of knowledge. To live dangerously!

My words drugged my fractious crew. They wolf-whistled
And clapped as if it was some streetwise spiel,
Not a gamble against the odds. So each bent to lift

His oars and lunged with a drunk elation. For five days
We advanced until no-one could decode the programme of the stars;
Then at dawn I saw this mountain drifting through the haze,

Its bulk was large, larger than anything I'd ever seen.
I do not know why, some loudmouth cackled hysterically.
It was the anti-climax of our trip: this towering hunk of rock

Blockading us. But then from nowhere a storm blew in.
It smacked our boat. Three times we spun around, the tall mast
Cracked and snapped, the prow reared up and then went down

And over our reeling heads the water swirled and closed.

Three Poems

PAOLO VALESIO

Translations by Graziella Sidoli

To Harold Bloom,
who understands poetry like a poet

Da Il cuore del girasole (di prossima pubblicazione)

Sal Poeticum

    Il poeta è come il sale
ma non come il pane:
non il sale della terra
ma il sale sulla terra—
quello che, sparso e sperso
sopra i solchi terreni, li fa sterili.
Eppure anche i seni smagriti
possono scintillare seduzione.
Il poeta rivela
il deserto al deserto,
lo rivergina e prepara.

Teatro di Fiuggi
3 gennaio 2002

From *The Heart of the Sunflower* (forthcoming)

Sal Poeticum

    The poet is like salt
but not like bread:
not the salt of the earth,
but the salt upon the earth—
that, dispersed and dissipated
on the furrowed terrain, makes it sterile.
And yet, even barren breasts
can be a sparkling seduction.
The poet reveals
the desert to the desert,
revirginizing it and making it ready.

The Theater at Fiuggi
3 January 2002

Da *Il cuore del girasole* (di prossima pubblicazione)

Sakura Park

    Il più profondo velo della Vergine
era quello che le copriva il cuore.
Adesso solamente l'ho compreso,
adesso che il mio cuore velato per sempre è lo scrigno
custode delle parole
che più non posso dire è la piccola
lanterna cieca
come quel cuore esterno
che è la grande lanterna di pietra
dolcemente vuota alta sulla colonna
nell'aiuola del parco giapponese.

Upper West Side, Manhattan
20 aprile 2005

From *The Heart of the Sunflower* (forthcoming)

Sakura Park

    The most arcane veil of the Virgin
was the one covering her heart.
Only now I know it,
now that my own veiled heart
is forever more the coffer
that guards the words I cannot say
it is the small blind lantern
resembling the uncovered heart
that is the large stone lantern
gently empty and high above the pillar
at the center of the flower-bed
in the Japanese garden.

Upper West Side, Manhattan
20 April 2005

Da *Figlio dell'uomo a Corcovado: Poema drammatico in nove scene*

Scene II:
Il colle di Corcovado

STATUA:
    I libri-guida nordamericani
che non voglion turbare la pace
mentale dei loro lettori
mi chiamano soltanto: il Monumento.
In verità io sono
la statua del Cristo Redentore.
Quasi quaranta metri sono alta,
ogni mio braccio è trenta tonnellate.
In alto sopra il colle germinante
del Corcovado,
da una piazzetta al termine
di una fila di scale di pietra,
guardo la gente della mia città
guardo i visitatori, gli stranieri
e il paese, e più che il paese.
Guarda, Solange, che ti guardo
(*Mira que Jesús te mira*).
Ti vedo in basso che mi stai negando
di fronte alla minuscola cappella
incavata nel mio piedestallo.
Laggiù in basso tu mi stai negando
con il sogghigno dietro il quale resti
sopra la soglia mentre i professori
visitanti, di cui
tu sei la guida a Rio, sbirciano dentro.
Mi stai negando in ogni movimento,
in ogni scatto della testa eretta,
in ogni scintillìo
dei tuoi occhiali rotondi,
in ogni tua carezza

alla tua minigonna di blue-jeans.
Non mi hanno scavato le pupille
dentro le grandi orbite di pietra
ma ciò non m'impedisce di vedere;
e il mio sguardo ha conquistato—
sguardo che più non sa
se è rivolto all'interno o al di fuori—
la precisione di ogni distacco.

   Tu, la non credente,
tu sei libera di dimenticare
o anche addirittura cancellare
intere parti del mondo;
così che tu ti senti più leggera,
più infuocata all'assalto
di quelle che sono per te
le vere realtà della vita.
Io qui in alto sopra il Corcovado
con queste braccia
così enormemente distese—
    tanto che ho dimenticato
    quale dovrebbe essere il mio gesto:
    riflesso di crocefissione?
    movimento di benedizione?
    accoglimento paziente
    di ciò che si estende ai miei piedi?—
non ho questo potere: debbo vedere tutto,
compresi anche i più frivoli dettagli.

Il mio vedere
è di là del piacere.
Ma è anche al di là del dovere;
è l'aura sopra l'aria,
l'aura vertiginosa che mi avvolge.
Ma ho errato (col mio impeto
che rapido sovente mi trascina):
Come puoi tu negarmi, se mi ignori?

2001

From *Son of Man at Corcovado: A Dramatic Poem in Nine Scenes*

Scene II:

The hill of Corcovado

STATUE:
    The North-American guide-books
which do not want to disturb the peace
of mind of their readers
simply call me: the Monument.
I am really the statue of Christ the Redeemer.
I stand almost one hundred twenty feet tall
and each of my arms weighs thirty tons.
High up above the germinating hill of Corcovado
I look down from a small piazza
where the stone steps end,
and I watch my townspeople,
the visitors, the foreigners;
I see my country, and also beyond it.
Look up Solange, I see you
(*Mira que Jesús te mira*).
Down below you are denying me
as you stand facing the small chapel
scooped out of my pedestal.
You are denying me down below
sneering while waiting outside
as the visiting professors peek inside
(you are their guide in Rio).
With each movement you deny me,
with each start of your proud head
each flash of light
darting from your round glasses
and each time you gently fondle
your blue-jeans miniskirt.
They did not carve out my pupils

inside these large eye-sockets of stone
but that does not prevent me from seeing;
and my glance—
a glance that no longer knows
if it is inner or outer—
has reached the precision
of every distancing.
    You, the unbeliever,
you are free to forget
even to erase
entire parts of the world;
which makes you feel lighter
and readier for the fiery attacks
upon those things which to you
are life's true realities.
High above Corcovado, I
with these arms
stretched out so widely
that I have forgotten
what they signify—
    is it a mirroring of the cross?
    a gesture of blessing?
    a patient embracing of all
    that lies at my feet?—
I do not have your power: I must see it all,
even the most frivolous details.
My seeing is beyond pleasure,
but it is also beyond duty;
it is the aura above the air,
the whirling aura that envelops me.
But I err (with the impetuousness
that so often overwhelms me):
How can you deny me, if you ignore me?

2001

The Trader's Wife

—Kevin Hart
(after Li Bo)[1]

When hair was hardly covering my brow
I was out plucking blossom in the sun.
You rode up smartly on your bamboo horse
And chased me round the garden, throwing plums:

Two kids, without a second thought to share,
Both growing up in a small river town.
At fourteen, now your wife, I was so shy
I lived in corners, head forever bowed,

And never once, not once, came round to you.
By fifteen I had learned to smile with you,
And longed to be with you, like ash and dust
Impossible to part! When you were far

You were still here, as steady as my heart,
And so I never thought to scan the road.
At sixteen, trading took you way out west,
Out past those boiling rapids with that rock

Where gibbons thump their chests and screech all night.
Here, by our gate, you held my hand an hour,
The moss grew green and thick in your slow steps:
I sweep the fallen leaves, but it sticks hard.

---

[1] This poem, which is dedicated to Harold Bloom, will appear as a coda to an essay on translation forthcoming in *Meanjin* [Melbourne].

The Autumn winds came quick and cold this year;
September's here, and yellow butterflies
Flit by the garden bed, always in pairs.
I cannot look at them: a lonely face

Will sometimes find a way into my own.
One day you will return, and when you know
Please write and say. I'll leave at once, upstream,
And come as close as sailors think it safe.

Field Notes from Mount Bakewell

—John Kinsella
For Harold Bloom

I.

Bark-stripped upper branches
of York gums—olive dugites
stretched taut, the dry blue
like stark black bitumen,
a torn limb from last night's
high winds, the snake struck
by a vehicle, maybe taking aim:
is it revenge when a snake,
tossed into the chassis, drops
and strikes the driver
searching for an oil leak?

II.

The stubble a bed of nails,
or hypodermics mounted
on mixed-media, piercing
boot-soles, stapling socks—
soaked with blood that rubs.
Up there, through the burn-off
and parrot bush sown like mythology,
the harsh green of heat trees
mocks foliage—an idea
without history here,
on the hillside.   The launch places
of paragliders—best thermals
for four hundred or a thousand
kilometres, depending on whom

you believe: where euros sweat
in small numbers and the minutiae
of reserves are transgressed
by stand of sheoaks: aerial mimics,
clarifiers of vegetable harmonics,
telecommunication dishes
microwaving panoramically,
ingesting and feeding
the collective soul.

III.

Quartz outcrops packed in soil,
crumbling with sheep trails and frantic climbs,
sheoak, York gum, jam tree,
xanthorrhoea lean back to correct
the incline, against the vertical:
air comes out of the mountain
and fumes across the denuded spaces—
where drifts of pesticide settle,
brought by outside draughts.

IV.

"There is all day, all
day to go."
                    Denise Riley

Locusts are starting to move
in small gusts, like plumes
or insistent waves
lapping at dry oats,
stubble. They rise up
like seed dispersal.

V.

In corridors and channels,
flurries, waves, and bands,
fed on first heat, undoing
in simultaneous languid
and accelerated sweeps,
NOT chaos, trite similes
don't work for them,
even biblical comparisons
pall; like water spilt
over a hot surface?
Spitting dispersal?
Plague centre,
splitting to pass the mountain—
failing to reach the crown,
the trigonometrical station,
place of surveys
where altitude makes
for slight variations
in plantlife . . .
"Up top," tracks are cut
and bush is bashed,
yet locusts—so far—
are scarce. They happen
down there, like . . .

VI.

The last plague,
evoking red paint—delisting
gardens, chlorophyll
as blood and threatening
mad cow disease,
or its equivalent,
in locusts. Comparison
is often laconic.

VII.

Non-return valves
are standard in gardens
post the drawback,
the payback from hoses
left in poison tanks,
sucked back, drawn back,
getting into the system.

VIII.

Roos and bronzewing pigeons
can eat 1080 without suffering
ill-effects? That they gut them
rapidly, to keep the eating
safe and sweet? The less said
the better.

IX.

Moving out towards Beverley:
a side journey past Mount Matilda.
Wagyl tracks: no growth,
shining like scales in the sun.
Below, the Avon snaking
its way towards the ocean,
siphoning or drawing
the flood. Swamp sheoaks,
flooded gums, the few deep
water holes remaining.
The rainbow begins or ends
on the Wagyl tracks, and there's
nothing romantic about it.
This is something else,
but the speaking won't fit

these lines: it has,
as do these lines,
its own precise science.
And the tides of the moon
rip through the undergrowth,
fire breaking the crusts of seeds,
the night shadows thrive
and growth is inflammatory.
On the day of a funeral
no stories are told
after dark . . . or six oclock,
depending on
the sun . . .

    x.

Proximity unsettles chat,
the invitation: this body
wormed with holes,
locusts swarms
choking the labyrinth,
the owl bright on night's edge,
struck on rodents
electric, silently
and smokelessly firing
the vanishing grass.

    xi.

The Amish sell corn
as Halloween approaches: a long way
from here, and a short time back.
American corn. Original,
or semi-original seed.
We make good
an exchange. Here,

at the base of the mountain,
a shearer grows corn.
He can plant and watch the growth,
despite injury. The pain
in his arm, in his head,
won't stop the silks forming.
Genetically engineered crops
are sweeping the district.
This corn grows steadily, daily.
The locusts have come. Let
them eat corn, he says, let them strip
the green before the seeds
have even come. They have
no choice, and I have no choice.
The insurance company
twists and turns, lies, hedges
its bets. Medical certificates
shoot the breeze. The locusts
tune in and out, changing frequencies.
No, they don't tell
the same story.

XII.

The road undoes the desire
to step generically: the locusts
so thick on their journeys
that snowfall or sandstorm
dictate coordinates. Like
diving and seeing sediment
flow past in the current,
as the day goes on
the flow increasing.
Like floaters in the eye
first distracting and
then forgotten.
Disaster brings

its minor reconciliations.
Judged monocultures,
comparatively speaking.

XIII.

Ground dyed blue by fallen
Paterson's curse: in the cold,
brilliantly purple. Heat sheds and takes
their colour. Unlike the yellow
everlastings on the mount,
a different yellow,
as dry as paper,
but speaking out
against hungover skies:
clouds looming
in unsettled atmospheres,
the compass showing
its different faces.
Yellow flowers,
desiccating, to turn
suddenly transparent,
feeding back into the sun,
fuelling its reactions
and evocations.

XIV.

Bandwidth locusts mono rain
bending frequency interlock wandoo
rock sheoak the botanist
Ludwig Preiss, priority one taxon,
and, of course, Thomasia montana,
which I don't see: oedipal, unreceptive,
adjusting the bandwidth.

XV.

The guy from the chemical company
drinks a half-glass of Herbicide.
"There you go, harmless to humans."
The farmer, impressed, sprays
and gets his sheep straight back in there.

XVI.

"... like fire and powder,
Which as they kiss, consume."

Place of weeping, sleeping woman,
eloping against tradition
and cursed from bloodshed,
across the town,
across the region,
not hearing the warning,
the passion, the bleeding:
the mountains
breaking up and meeting,
reconciled as erosion
defeats them.

The Slide

—Nicholas Royle

There is this slide, just as you might find in a park for children. The only difference is that it is bigger and not in a park. You do not trouble to reflect upon such matters as you start clambering up. You are not alone. There is an 'almost festival atmosphere,' the sun is shining and people are enjoying themselves enormously. You join in, laughing and making witty remarks as you go. But the climbing is tricky. The rungs of the ladder are wooden and, trodden by so many feet, prove at moments treacherously smooth. Every so often someone slips and falls. This happens, however, without any great commotion. Indeed there is, almost straightaway, no indication that the incident even occurred. You begin to sense that the laughter of those around is not altogether genuine, but rather conceals a pervasive edginess concerning the demands of the ascent. The distance between rungs has increased. You feel you have to launch yourself up and forwards, as if very slowly and clumsily pole-vaulting, from one rung to the next. Each rung is wide and deep enough to give standing room for three or four people. For what feels like the first time, you stop. You pause to take in the view and see with a start how high you have climbed. You feel dwarfed. You gaze out over a tremendous vista of river, fringed with thick jungle. You are so preoccupied with the climb that you scarcely think about how long you have been at it. You find you have to rest more frequently. The river over which you are perched is so wide now that you can no longer make out any of the jungle observed earlier, not even at the farthest horizons. You know that the end is approaching. You are so near the top that you can see where the steel railings curve inwards and the rungs narrow, restricting the passage of climbers to just one person per step. The atmosphere becomes sombre. For the first time it dawns on you that you have not actually seen the chute itself, and that the amazing, endlessly sparkling silver slipway rushing downwards is a thing that exists only in your imagination. You cast your mind back and realise that all your impressions of the slide are based on what you have heard from others and pictured to yourself. You do not look down any more, you are so filled with trepidation. You haul your exhausted body, by now practically useless, quivering, on to the brink. You are at the top now and, immeasurably elevated, on the very verge, can finally see that there is no slide, glittering and swaying, stretching away down before you. There is only a sheer drop. "At last," you tell yourself, as you inch into your final position, "I can start living."

Acts of Reading, Acts of Loving: Harold Bloom and the Art of Appreciation

ROGER GILBERT

What is Harold Bloom? Many answers are possible, depending on whom you consult. He is, among other things, a sensitive yet bold interpreter of poetry, a dazzlingly original literary theorist, a charismatically eccentric teacher and lecturer, an ardent Gnostic theologian, a remarkably prolific editor of critical volumes, and a gloomy if not downright apocalyptic cultural prognosticator. All of these roles have contributed to Bloom's standing as the most famous, and in some quarters infamous, literary critic of our time. Yet at the heart of Bloom's enterprise, I would contend, lies an imperative that has all but disappeared from current critical practice. Harold Bloom is the last appreciative critic. That is to say, he is the last important critic who takes as his primary responsibility the task of persuading readers that a text or author has aesthetic value, and tries to illuminate the nature of that value as fully as possible. For all the brilliance of his work as an interpreter and as a theorist of literature, it is the passion and acuity of Bloom's evaluative discourse that will, I believe, ensure his place among the major critics of the last three hundred years.

This claim is a difficult one to advance in part because we no longer recognize value judgment as an intellectual activity on a par with interpretation and theoretical speculation. The shift away from evaluation as a central function of literary criticism is in fact a relatively recent development. In the first half of this century critics as diverse as Pound, Eliot, Leavis, Winters, Blackmur, and Jarrell all took the assessment of literary value as a primary aim, and even more theoretically minded critics like Richards, Empson, and Burke kept evaluative criteria strongly in view. The American New Critics are generally credited with making close reading the dominant mode of literary analysis, and in the process elevating questions of meaning over questions of aesthetic value. Yet when one looks at the key writings of Ransom, Tate, and Cleanth Brooks, one sees that their strongest claims almost always have an evaluative component. Indeed it is worth remembering that one of the central tenets of New Criticism, the so-called Intentional Fallacy, was originally formulated by W. K. Wimsatt and Monroe Beardsley as a principle not of interpretation but of value judgment: one should never judge the aesthetic success of a work, it stated, by how closely it fulfills the intentions of its author.

Northrop Frye was the figure who most forthrightly challenged the idea that evaluation should be the final aim of all criticism (ironically, Frye was one of Bloom's most significant early influences). Throughout *The Anatomy of Criticism* and particularly in his "Polemical Introduction," Frye argues for a scientific and systematic model of literary study that deliberately excludes value judgment, relegating it to the realm of mere "taste." Firmly rejecting the notion that sound aesthetic judgment requires specific intellectual faculties and modes of expertise, Frye dismissed evaluation as an activity best left to amateurs, journalists, and literati, one hardly suited to serious scholars and critics. For all the shifts in critical fashion that have occurred since Frye's book appeared in 1957, it can be argued that we still inhabit its wake, inasmuch as value judgment has never regained its place as a respectable and necessary function of literary criticism. In this regard as in so many others, Harold Bloom has for the last forty-five years been swimming against the prevailing currents.

Bloom himself has grown increasingly aware of his anomalous position as an evaluative critic in an age that distrusts aesthetic judgment. He reflected wistfully on this status in a 1991 interview with Antonio Weiss:

> I must be the only literary critic of any eminence who is writing today (I cannot think of another, I'm sad to say, however arrogant or difficult this sounds) who always asks about what he reads and likes, whether it is ancient, modern, or brand new, or has always been lying around, who always asks "How good is it? What is it better than? What is it less good than? What does it mean?" and "Is there some relation between what it means and how good or bad it is, and not only how is it good or bad, but why is it good or bad?" Mr. Frye, who was very much my precursor, tried to banish all of that from criticism.... (Weiss 213)

Readers of Bloom are familiar with the elegiac note he has sounded with growing frequency over the years. Here he both mourns and congratulates himself for single-handedly prolonging the tradition of evaluative criticism that runs from Samuel Johnson through Hazlitt, Ruskin, Pater, and Eliot. Yet throughout his career Bloom has aspired to a degree of intellectual breadth and rigor not usually associated with evaluation *per se*. Indeed in an early essay he took R. P. Blackmur to task for attempting "so little *description* and so much value judgment" (*Ringers* 197; Bloom's italics). The later Bloom would almost certainly substitute "interpretation" for "description;" indeed, what separates him from an older school of critical impressionists blithely pronouncing on the relative merits of canonical works is his recognition that evaluation and interpretation go hand in hand. As his critical catechism in the Weiss interview suggests, questions of meaning are for Bloom inseparable from questions of value, and the special power of his work has everything to do with his insistence on treating them together.

To speak of Bloom simply as an appreciative critic is misleading in another way as well. In Bloom's work appreciation is invariably accompanied by deprecation. He has never been content to toss bouquets to those writers he admires while tactfully ignoring those he does not. The literary sphere is, Bloom holds, a deeply competitive or, in one of his favored terms, "agonistic" arena in which a victory for one artist means a defeat for another, and this bitter truth must necessarily inform the attitude of the evaluative critic as well. In the Weiss interview, Bloom rather surprisingly invokes sports to illuminate the nature of aesthetic judgment:

> In the end, the spirit that makes one a fan of a particular athlete or a particular team is different only in degree, not in kind, from the spirit that teaches one to prefer one poet to another, or one novelist to another. That is to say there is some element of competition at every point in one's experience as a reader. (205)

As a poetry critic who has professed in print my devotion to the (old) Chicago Bulls, I am both intrigued and troubled by Bloom's analogy. Can one only admire a particular poet at the expense of another? If the Bulls win, another team has to lose; if Wallace Stevens wins, must T. S. Eliot lose? In fact the precise nature of the competition varies a great deal in Bloom's work. At times the contest may pit contemporaries against one another, though more often the battle is between father and son, precursor and ephebe; at other times the real struggle seems to take place in the critical arena, between competing interpretations, judgments, or methodologies. What does not vary from the outset of

Bloom's career to its most recent phase is the agonistic spirit, the conviction that poet and critic alike can only define their individual worth through combat or competition.

One consequence of this agonistic ethos is that Bloom's strongest positive judgments often share the stage with equally strong negative ones. Bloom is as notorious for his pithy put-downs as for his rhapsodic *hommages*. He is especially fond of invidious comparisons between illustrious moderns and faded minor poets; thus he has more than once predicted that Pound and Eliot will prove to be the Cowley and Waller of our time, while he has disdainfully crowned Sylvia Plath as our Felicia Hemans. To many readers such sweeping dismissals can seem gratuitous and excessive, and Bloom himself over time has softened some of his more severe judgments (he now grants Eliot grudging admiration). But it is worth asking whether a certain amount of sheer bile might not in fact be a necessity of good evaluative criticism. Bloom's great colleague and rival Paul de Man suggested that genuine critical insight is inevitably accompanied by some form of blindness, and the same may be true in the realm of evaluation. The best appreciative critics always seem to have blind spots, not only for specific artists but often for whole aesthetics.

Certainly Bloom's critical sensibility is distinguished as much by its biases as its predilections. Certain moralizing strains of Christian poetry, especially those that preach humility and self-abasement, have always rubbed him the wrong way; hence his dislike of Eliot, Auden and their kin. He has also shown little tolerance for avant-gardists of various stripes, from Pound to Ginsberg (his devotion to Ashbery being a significant exception). More recently Bloom's harshest barbs have been reserved for those writers he suspects of that dreaded disease called 'political correctness.' He has been particularly dismissive of women poets who openly address gender politics, singling out Sylvia Plath and Adrienne Rich for special scorn. I must confess that I find Bloom's animosity toward Plath and Rich disappointing, fueled as it seems to be by ideological intolerance rather than aesthetic discrimination. A remark by Bloom's favorite critic, Hazlitt, on another great critic, Coleridge, may be apropos: "In short, he was profound and discriminating with respect to those authors whom he liked, and where he gave his judgment fair play; capricious, perverse, and prejudiced in his antipathies and distastes" (228). To be sure, the same might be said of Hazlitt himself, or of any number of other major critics, but Bloom has put his antipathies and distastes on display to an extraordinary degree.

From the very beginning of his career in the 1950s, Bloom's work has been driven in equal measure by admiration and disdain. His first book, *Shelley's Mythmaking*, based on his doctoral thesis, was a passionate defense of Shelley from both his New Critical detractors and his Platonizing admirers, in the course of which Bloom mounted a bold polemic against the school of Donne, at that time generally placed above the Romantics for its cultivation of formal integrity and metaphorical unity. He extended this polemic in his landmark study of Romanticism *The Visionary Company*, distinguishing two main lines of English poetry—one High Church and conservative, linking the Metaphysicals to Eliot and his followers, the other Protestant and radical, running from Spenser and Milton through the Romantics and their heirs—and unsurprisingly declaring his allegiance to the latter camp. Even in these early works Bloom was magisterially judgmental, showing not the slightest hesitation in assessing and proclaiming the comparative strength and weakness of the poems he discussed. The word "mythmaking" in the title of his first book is crucial in delineating Bloom's emerging aesthetic. The term 'myth' links him to Frye, but where Frye is interested in continuities, archetypes, shared themes and plots, Bloom is drawn to precisely those aspects of a writer's work that mark its originality and inventiveness, its swerve from existing myths. For Bloom, originality is always a matter of mythmaking or individual vision; he has shown next to no interest in the kinds of formal and stylistic innovations that win praise from critics like Hugh Kenner and Marjorie Perloff.

By the time of his 1970 study of Yeats, Bloom's work had already begun its turn to the theoretical, yet this book too was primarily evaluative in tenor. *Yeats* represented something of an anomaly in Bloom's oeuvre, however, in offering a strongly mixed judgment; indeed its polemical thrust was to question both the degree to which and the terms in which Yeats had been praised up to that point. All Bloom's other single-author studies—on Shelley, Blake, Stevens, even Shakespeare—purport to give their subjects a fuller, more adequate appreciation than they have yet received. Perhaps because Yeats had already been hugely praised under the rubrics of Symbolist, Modernist and neo-Metaphysical poetics, Bloom felt compelled on the one hand to show that Yeats's greatness is inseparable from his roots in Romantic tradition, and on the other to show that many of the qualities for which Yeats had been praised were in fact not so admirable. Hence the book gives us the unusual spectacle of Bloom expressing moral outrage at the later Yeats's glorification of violence. Since Bloom himself would just a few years later put forward the Nietzschean view that all great poems are patricidal, this moralizing judgment of Yeats may strike one as slightly disingenuous, and perhaps had more to do with Bloom's ongoing war against the New Critics than with Yeats himself. Nonetheless the book abounds in powerful readings and subtle discriminations, and served as a valuable corrective to the reverential treatment Yeats had been receiving at the time.

In 1973 Bloom published his critical manifesto *The Anxiety of Influence: A Theory of Poetry*, which fully expounded his now famous claim that literary influence occurs not as a benign process of transmission but as a fierce struggle for supremacy and originality between older and younger poets, or as he terms them "precursors" and "ephebes." At the time of its appearance it was possible to miss the book's fundamental difference from the main tendencies of literary theory, coming as it did amid the first great wave of structuralist and post-structuralist works by Barthes, Derrida, de Man, and others. That difference once again had to do with the essentially evaluative cast of Bloom's project. Though ostensibly descriptive, Bloom's account of intrapoetic relations is informed at every point by value judgment, from his initial assertion that "[w]eaker talents idealize; figures of capable imagination appropriate for themselves" (5) to his late remarks on the embarrassment of reading Matthew Arnold's poetry and "finding the odes of Keats crowding out poor Arnold" (154). Indeed it would be fair to say that *The Anxiety of Influence* presents a theory of poetic value rather than poetic meaning, though Bloom halfheartedly tried to frame it as the latter in a strange "Interchapter" entitled "A Manifesto for Antithetical Criticism." There he proposed that a greater awareness of the way later poems revise earlier ones can allow us to "correct" for the misreadings that build up over time. Bloom quickly backed away from any suggestion that his theory might serve the old-fashioned purpose of generating more accurate interpretations of poems, however, and this claim remains the least persuasive aspect of the book.

One clear sign of the book's preoccupation with the nature of poetic value is its obsessive use of the word "strength," which might indeed be called its central term, more so even than "influence." By abandoning or subordinating older evaluative vocabularies of 'greatness,' 'beauty,' 'truth,' 'wisdom' and the like, and replacing them with a terminology that stresses willful action and competitive struggle, Bloom dramatically redefined the criteria by which he wanted poems to be judged.

Thanks in large part to his enthralled reading of Emerson and Nietzsche in the 1960s, Bloom now exchanged the Romantic humanism of his early work for a radically individualistic ethos in which the poet's only responsibility is to himself and his legacy. In this view what matters most is not the poem's morality, its formal perfection, or its expression of truth or feeling, but its ability to carve out a previously unoccupied imaginative space for itself. Bloom's understanding of poetic originality differs crucially from the familiar avant-gardist imperative to 'make it new' in its insistence on the need for direct engagement with the past rather than blithe dismissal of it. This is where "strength" comes in. Simply to forget the past may not require much strength, but to confront it in the person of a single potent representative, then find a way to appropriate and extend it without being destroyed, calls for great courage, skill and cunning. We must ask, not, is this poem well-made? expressive? truthful? but rather, does it successfully break the grip of the past? mark a new place? find a new stance?[1]

But how precisely *are* we to judge the outcome of a particular contest or encounter between precursor and ephebe? Despite the systematic appearance given by his elaboration of six "revisionary ratios," or specific strategies that poets take up in revising their forebears, Bloom never claimed to ground literary judgment in theoretical principle (a quixotic project that nonetheless has been attempted fairly often in the past). Ultimately it is up to the individual reader to decide whether a given poet has successfully wrestled his precursor. Bloom himself, of course, remained as magisterial and self-assured as ever in offering his own judgments, and these became most explicit in the final chapter of

---

[1] Bloom's most recent attempt to formulate criteria for the evaluation of poetry has come in the Introduction to his 2004 anthology *The Best Poems of the English Language*. Interestingly, his key value word there is no longer "strength" or "originality" but "inevitability," a term he applies to proof texts from Whitman, Tennyson, and Crane, while taking his frequent *bête noire* Poe as an exemplar of mere predictability and derivativeness. The essay is also noteworthy for Bloom's admission that his literary tastes have matured, to the point where he no longer gives exclusive allegiance to "the sequence that goes from Spenser through Milton on to the High Romantics . . . and then to the continuators . . . . With Chaucer and Shakespeare, these remain the poets I love best, but maturation has brought an almost equal regard for the tradition of Wit: Donne, Ben Jonson, Marvell, Dryden, Pope, Byron, and such modern descendants as Auden and Eliot (a secret Romantic, however)" (13–14). We may take that last parenthesis as a sign that Bloom has not completely renounced his youthful *agon* with the New Critics, despite his avowals of a more "mature" and eclectic sensibility.

the book, which expounds the ratio Bloom calls "apophrades." Here he presented not so much an abstract principle as a pragmatic test of poetic strength: can a poet create the illusion that he has influenced his own precursor? Can the later poet insinuate or project his voice backward into the work of an earlier poet, so that in reading the earlier we find ourselves thinking of the later? For Bloom this is the ultimate measure of a poet's ability to win a kind of fictive priority, which in his scheme amounts to literary immortality.

Again, however, it is a test that can only be made subjectively. Bloom singles out Theodore Roethke as an example of a poet who fails to establish his own voice, who lets himself be drowned out by other voices— Yeats, Eliot, Whitman, Stevens. "Of *apophrades* in its positive, revisionary sense," he writes, "[Roethke] gives us no instance; there are no passages in Yeats or Eliot, in Stevens or Whitman, that can strike us as having been written by Roethke" (142). This is of course pure assertion, that sweepingly inclusive "us" notwithstanding, and may well be contradicted by the experience of individual readers. The passages in Roethke that Bloom cites come from his final phase, when he did indeed seem to be haunted by the ghosts of his ancestors, but in works of his middle years like "The Lost Son" he developed a strikingly original voice that at least some readers might hear resonating in, for example, certain passages of Whitman. Bloom's positive instances of *apophrades* include passages from Shelley and Emerson that sound like Yeats and Dickinson respectively, and here his claims are more persuasive, since, once alerted to them, most readers will also hear the retroactive echoes Bloom detects. But a theory of poetry that depends on such impressionistic distinctions can hardly be called rigorous; the book's originality lies precisely in its opening a perspective on literary history that rests as much on individual acts of evaluative judgment as on general narratives and paradigms.

Perhaps because he feared that *The Anxiety of Influence* was vulnerable to charges of impressionism, Bloom's next book, *A Map of Misreading*, moved to bring more theoretical weight to his project by formalizing the system of revisionary ratios and aligning them with rhetorical and psychoanalytic concepts. This and the theoretical books that immediately follow it clearly reflect the general climate of structuralist and post-structuralist thought then prevalent, and more particularly the influence of Bloom's Yale colleague Paul de Man, to whom *A Map* is dedicated and who in a review of *The Anxiety of Influence* first proposed that the ratios be translated into rhetorical tropes. One major effect of this influence was to displace evaluation as a central element of Bloom's discourse. As if conceding that interpretation has now gained the upper hand, he writes in his introduction: "Criticism may not always be an act of judging, but it is always an act of deciding, and what it decides is meaning" (3). And in fact the book is dominated by a hermeneutic vocabulary, whose key terms include "reading," "misreading," and "misprision." The language of "strength" persists, but now only as a modifier: there are "strong misreadings" and "weak misreadings," but Bloom spends little time distinguishing between the two.

In keeping with his new emphasis on meaning, Bloom now converted the literary-historical vision of *The Anxiety of Influence* into an interpretive paradigm by codifying the sequence of six revisionary ratios as a "map" or diagram to be applied to individual poems. This move was problematic for a number of reasons. For one, Bloom had insisted in the earlier book that the number and sequence of ratios was arbitrary, not essential. More significantly, Bloom's shift of focus from broad intrapoetic relations to rhetorical patterns within poems led him to abandon or at least downplay his concern with poetic originality and uniqueness. Now rather than emphasizing the way poets and poems "swerve" from their antecedents, Bloom's main object was to show how all good poems manifest exactly the same deep structure of tropes and psychic defenses. For the rest of the 1970s and well into the 1980s, Bloom's work was marred by his reliance on his Procrustean map, which acted as a kind of critical sausage machine: feed poems (and occasionally prose works like *Beyond the Pleasure Principle* and *Miss Lonelyhearts*) in one end and get identical six-fold "crisis-texts" out the other. Throughout Bloom's map phase there was little room for the kind of subtle evaluative distinctions at which he usually excels; his basic assumption seemed to be that if a poem is good it will fit the map, with the implicit corollary that if a poem does not fit, it must not be good.

Although his book-length studies and theoretical treatises have understandably received more attention, I would suggest that Bloom's most lasting and impressive work may be the series of appreciative essays he has produced over the years, many of them gathered in *The Ringers in the Tower* (1971) and *Figures of Capable Imagination* (1976). In these shorter pieces Bloom was freed equally from the obligation to produce complete readings and to advance broad theoretical arguments, and could thus indulge what seems to me his greatest gift, critical portraiture.[2] Far from being neutral descriptions, Bloom's best

---

[2] Bloom returned to this mode in his recent *Genius: A Mosaic of One Hundred Creative Minds*, which gathers brief appreciations of writers from Homer to Ralph Ellison.

portraits are fueled by an impulse toward praise that verges on the devotional. Reading Bloom on Shelley, on Emerson, on Stevens, Ashbery or Ammons can be a heady experience; one may at times feel swept away by the powerful tide of his enthusiasm. Yet Bloom does more than gush. His aim always is to isolate the unique identifying mark of each writer he considers, what he likes to call the poet's "stance."

It is in this connection that Bloom's theory of poetic influence has proved to have enormous practical value, providing the terms in which to formulate a given writer's originality with subtlety and precision. Thus Shelley's individuality might best be apprehended by seeing exactly how he "swerves" from his primary precursor, Wordsworth; Whitman's, from Emerson; Milton's, from Spenser, and so on. The results are often dazzingly simply at the level of formulation; over the years Bloom has produced a gallery of bold, aphoristic sketches that seem to capture the pith of a poet in a sentence or two. Discussing John Ashbery's relation to Wallace Stevens, for instance, Bloom cites a maxim of Stevens's, "It is not every day that the world arranges itself in a poem," and suggests that Ashbery's swerve from his precursor consists precisely in his faith that the world *will* arrange itself in a poem each day (*Figures* 170). Such a formula tells us nothing about Ashbery's style, his syntactical habits, his figurative techniques, his treatment of verse form, yet it offers a broad insight into the poet's temperament that may help readers organize their own experience of Ashbery.

Bloom's portraits are of course idiosyncratic in the extreme, more Cubist than photorealist. Thus certain features may be pulled forward into high relief, while others recede into the shadows. For all their exaggerations, distortions, and foreshortenings, however, and perhaps because of them, his portraits of many major poets have by now become inescapable 'versions' to be revised, dismissed, reviled, but never ignored. No serious scholar can study Shakespeare, Milton, Blake, Shelley, Browning, Yeats, Stevens, Freud, Ashbery, Ammons, or a handful of other writers without confronting Bloom's portrayals of them. In large part this is because Bloom's reading—or perhaps more accurately troping—of a canonical writer almost always marks a radical departure from received accounts. In this sense his portraits tend to be agonistic 'corrections' of previous portraits, as subject in their own way to the laws of influence and misreading as the work of the poets themselves. Yet as Bloom keeps reminding us, it is precisely through the process of anxious revision that originality is born; and Bloom's portraits are nothing if not original.

My personal favorite of all Bloom's books is *Figures of Capable Imagination*, a collection of essay-portraits on writers ranging from Coleridge, Emerson and Pater to Ashbery, Ammons and Geoffrey Hill. Written concurrently with *The Anxiety of Influence* but before Bloom had developed his one-size-fits-all map, the essays in this book strike a fine balance between passionate admiration of individual achievements and brooding reflection on the vicissitudes of literary history. As a work of eloquent appreciative criticism the book deserves a place beside such twentieth-century classics as Randall Jarrell's *Poetry and the Age* and R. P. Blackmur's *Language as Gesture*. Among the most rhapsodic pieces in the book is a fine essay called "Wallace Stevens: The Poems of Our Climate." Just a few years later Bloom published a full-length study of the poet by the same title, yet beyond their names the two works have almost nothing in common. Written under the aegis of the map, the book on Stevens, though full of invaluable readings, suffers both from a general excess of arcane terminology, and from Bloom's insistence on finding the same sequence of tropes in every poem. The essay, on the other hand, is unabashedly appreciative in tone and makes very little attempt at rhetorical analysis. Here is its opening paragraph:

> Poets influence us because we fall in love with their poems. All love unfortunately changes, if indeed it does not end, and since nothing is got for nothing, we also get hurt when we abandon, or are abandoned by, poems. Criticism is as much a series of metaphors for the acts of loving what we have read as for the acts of reading themselves. Walter Pater liked to use the word "appreciations" for his critical essays, and I present this particular series of metaphors as an appreciation of Wallace Stevens. Precisely, I mean to appreciate his success in writing the poems of our climate more definitively than any American since Whitman and Dickinson. What justifies an estimate that sets him higher than Frost, Pound, Eliot and Williams? If he is, as so many readers now believe, a great poet, at least the equal of such contemporaries as Hardy, Yeats, Rilke and Valéry, what are the qualities that make for greatness in him? How and why does he move us, enlighten us, enlarge our existences, and help us to live our lives? (103)

It is hard to think of another critic with the temerity to write so directly about questions of value at the highest level of the canon, and to do so with this sense of passionate engagement. To define criticism as "a series of metaphors for the acts of loving what we have read" is quite different from calling it "an act of deciding ... meaning," as Bloom does in *A Map of Misreading*. While his own work often seems torn between its evaluative and hermeneutic registers, in an essay like this the appreciative impulse clearly comes to the fore, and the result is a moving and deeply personal exploration of the way Stevens's poetry "help[s] us to live our lives."[3]

Bloom's insistence on measuring his beloved figures against their near contemporaries and producing thumbnail hierarchies has understandably proved to be one of his more controversial procedures. Here we are told that Stevens is greater than Frost, Pound, Eliot and Williams and at least equal to Hardy, Yeats, Rilke and Valéry; in a slightly later essay on Stevens in *Poetry and Repression*, Bloom tentatively elevates him above even Yeats, Rilke and Valéry. (Given the inevitable entropic drift implied by Bloom's picture of literary history, it is no surprise that he rarely claims a later poet to be greater than an earlier one.) There is something deliberately provocative in these gestures; one often hears a muttered "take that, Kenner" (or some other critical foe) beneath such sweeping pronouncements. Yet these canonical comparisons serve another purpose: they raise the bar, forcing Bloom to find terms of praise that can justify the highest possible ranking of his chosen figure. In the Stevens essay those terms are explicitly Emersonian. Stevens, Bloom asserts, "is uniquely the twentieth century poet of that solitary and inward glory we none of us can share with others. His value is that he describes and even celebrates (occasionally) our selfhood-communings as no one else can or does" (109). Bloom acknowledges that this judgment cuts against the grain of much Stevens criticism, citing in particular the "decreative" Stevens of J. Hillis Miller and Helen Vendler, a poet more concerned with the denuding of reality than with the celebration of self. But Bloom's addiction to Romantic affirmation, to what he calls in the Stevens essay "a passion for Yes," however qualified or hedged around by irony, leads him to posit a Stevens much closer to Whitman and Emerson than any previous critic had conceived. His praise of Stevens, or as he puts it his "act of loving," thus becomes an interpretation of him as well, an act of reading that helps us see an aspect of the poet others had missed.

Bloom's appreciations of contemporary writers occupy a special place in his critical oeuvre. Here the need to swerve from prior accounts and judgments is not a primary factor, and so he can give freer rein to his penchant for praise. His essays on John Ashbery and A. R. Ammons were instrumental in establishing those poets' reputations in the 1970s (iron-

---

[3] The use of the first person plural here is characteristic of Bloom's evaluative grammar, locating itself somewhere between the royal and the universal *we*.

ically, as Bloom's own stock has fallen of late the poets may have suffered a little from their association with him). Even in these canonizing pieces Bloom's praise is not unqualified, however. His blind spots or antipathies with regard to certain literary modes can usually be traced within his appreciations of individual writers as well, and this is particularly clear in the cases of Ashbery and Ammons. Bloom's impatience with the radical opacity of Ashbery's early book *The Tennis Court Oath* reflects his general intolerance of formal experimentation as an end in itself. Where many critics see a continuum between such aleatory play in Ashbery and the more traditional lyricism of his later work, Bloom simply expresses exasperation: "a great mass of egregious disjunctiveness is accumulated to very little effect," he grumbles (*Figures* 174). For Bloom, Ashbery's value clearly lies in his ability to take up and extend Romantic themes of solitude, nostalgia, and possibility, and owes nothing to the overtly avant-gardist aspect of his work.

In the case of Ammons, Bloom's blind spot goes rather deeper, and recalls the claim of *The Visionary Company* that "the Romantics were not poets of nature" (vii). For Bloom, Ammons is essentially a transcendental visionary in the line of Emerson. His most authentic epiphanies thus involve a Gnostic sense of the self's autonomy, its separateness from material creation. Clearly this transcendental strain is a crucial aspect of Ammons's vision, yet just as clearly Ammons is a poet deeply preoccupied with the workings of the physical universe. Trained as a scientist, Ammons dwells lovingly on natural processes ranging from the life of cells to the death of stars. Bloom acknowledges this side of Ammons's poetics, but disparages it as a distraction from the real business of transcendence: "The Ammonsian literalness, allied to a similar destructive impulse in Wordsworth and Thoreau, attempts to summon outward continuities to shield the poet from his mind's own force" (*Ringers* 270). For "outward continuities" we can read 'nature,' 'reality,' 'the world,' all of which for Bloom represent mere buffers against the power of the mind. This illustrates a characteristic and rather drastic myopia throughout Bloom's work; for him any investment in the concrete particulars of the physical world can only be understood as a defensive ploy in the drama of the self, not as a genuine attachment to otherness.

Given Bloom's obvious impatience with what he calls "outward continuities," with the mimetic representation of external reality, the direction of his work in the late 1980s and 1990s came as something of a surprise. Moving outside the Romantic tradition that had dominated his work since its inception, Bloom has for the past decade and a half been steadily developing a panoptic vision of literature from antiquity to the present that takes in a much broader range of texts and genres, including narrative and dramatic works. Initially triggered by his agreement to edit a series of volumes for a small publisher called Chelsea House, this expansion of Bloom's critical domain has led him to writers and texts that might previously have seemed alien to his sensibility. The Chelsea House volumes, which now number in the many hundreds, have forced Bloom to offer his views on a host of major figures who cannot be readily assimilated to Romantic paradigms, in particular novelists and playwrights who deal in mimesis rather than mythopoeia. While the brief prefaces Bloom provided for these volumes are usually quite perfunctory, they show him working hard to expand his evaluative vocabulary. This effort eventually issued in *The Western Canon*, his magisterial overview of literary tradition from Homer, the Bible, and Dante to Woolf, Joyce and Beckett.

The greater eclecticism of Bloom's more recent work has not come without its costs. Part of the fascination of Bloom's early work was the picture it gave of a sharply defined, idiosyncratic sensibility as quick to denounce as to praise. The agonistic energies Bloom had once expended against literary and critical modes that threatened his beloved Romantic tradition have lately been redirected into repetitious polemics against political correctness in the academy. At the same time the sharpness and specificity of Bloom's appreciative language have been somewhat blunted by the need to bestow equal value on Jane Austen, George Eliot, Tolstoy and a bevy of figures he had never shown much interest in before. Yet the opening up of Bloom's evaluative criteria in *The Western Canon* and other recent works is more apparent than real. Beneath the overt deference to mimetic values can be detected a continuing commitment to the visionary in its most basic sense. Literary greatness for Bloom has always been and continues to be a matter of radical originality, of imaginative usurpation, of a single mind aggressively imposing itself on reality rather than passively reflecting it. The fact that Bloom can identify Jane Austen as a descendant of the Jahwist and Chaucer and can posit a direct link between Cervantes and Kafka shows just how far he remains from traditional mimetic approaches; he is not the least interested, for example, in how the social and historical milieu of writers enters their work.

Ultimately Bloom's genius as a critic lies in his ability to estrange familiar works by showing how much in them flows from an utterly personal, idiosyncratic, perverse imagination remaking the world in its own image. He is the only critic I can think of for whom "solipsistic" consistently serves as a term of praise. In that sense Blake is his true template or starting point, the figure in whom the visionary or mythopoeic quality appears most clearly and pervasively. With other writers Bloom has had to work harder to foreground the visionary element, and often this self-appointed task leads him to minimize or disparage those strains in a writer's work that pull against the visionary. Thus he has devoted much polemical energy to clearing away Milton's Christianity, Shelley's neo-Platonism, Wordsworth's naturalism, Yeats's occultism, Stevens's decreationism, and so on, so as to permit their essential visionariness to shine forth. The greatest challenge for Bloom in this regard has been Shakespeare, about whom he has written extensively in recent years, culminating in his massive tome *Shakespeare: The Invention of the Human*. Universally received as the most mimetic of literary artists, the one who most fully and truthfully represents the whole of humanity, Shakespeare might seem to resist any imputation of visionary power. Bloom's solution has been almost literally to make him God, to claim that our very sense of humanity has largely been Shakespeare's creation, that all of us are in fact inventions of Shakespeare. Thus Shakespeare becomes in Bloom's account the visionary poet *par excellence*, the poet whose words not only envision but inaugurate a new world. One can hardly go farther in the rhetoric of appreciation.

Harold Bloom has been stirring up controversy since the beginning of his career, but over the last twenty years his persona has shifted from a gadfly puncturing the idealizations of a creaky critical establishment to a gloomy custodian of waning canonical values. In the process he has made himself an easy target for critics and writers invested in opening the canon and enlarging the category of the literary. One recent round of Bloom-bashing came in response to his rather intemperate introduction to the 1998 anthology *The Best of the Best American Poetry*, a selection of poems from the first ten years of the annual *Best American Poetry* volumes. Bloom was particularly harsh in his assessment of Adrienne Rich's selections as editor of the 1996 volume: calling the book "a monumental representation of the enemies of the aesthetic who are in the act of overwhelming us," he declared it to be "of a badness not to be believed, because it follows the criteria now operative: what matters most are the race, gender, sexual orientation, ethnic origin, and political purpose of the would-be poet" (16). A series of responses published in *The Boston Review* accused Bloom of everything from aesthetic conservatism to thinly veiled racism, and even the more sympathetic pieces conceded that his rhetoric had grown too strident and dyspeptic for its own good. The most persistent note in these responses, however, was a fundamental resistance to Bloom's evaluative criteria, with their emphasis on transcendence, isolation and inwardness. For many readers of contemporary poetry, such values have come to seem quaint at best, elitist at worst. For them Bloom has aged into the very image of what he once so vigorously opposed, that figure he himself calls "the Moldy Fig:" the stuffy old scholar struggling to hold back the tides of change.

One may indeed grow impatient with Bloom's endless valorizing of the isolated self and its "inward glory," his refusal to grant poetry a social or communal dimension, his apparent indifference to formal and stylistic effects, his inexhaustible appetite for Romantic solipsism; but reading his best appreciative writing one cannot doubt the passionate intensity of his response to poetry. In the end I would like to suggest that it hardly matters whether Bloom's tastes remain in step with those of his culture or even those of his readers. The final value of his work, as of all appreciation, is not the accuracy of the judgments presented, which in any case can never be verified, but the force, clarity and intelligence with which those judgments are expressed and defended. His magisterial, Johnsonian tone, with its all-engulfing "we," belies a deeply personal investment in poems, reminding us of Kant's insight that aesthetic judgment is always subjective response offering itself as universal truth. Bloom is fond of quoting Oscar Wilde's epigram that criticism is the most civilized form of autobiography, and certainly Bloom's own criticism leaves us with as vivid an image of its author's mind and sensibility as of its subjects. What sets his work apart from that of most other critics is above all its unique balance of head and heart. Few critics are as ostentatiously brainy as Bloom, with his daunting theoretical intellect and encyclopedic knowledge of literary and speculative traditions. Yet few critics have worn their hearts so prominently on their sleeves, have written so unabashedly of literature in the language of love. Bloom's work reminds us that critical intelligence need not preclude aesthetic appreciation, and indeed that depriving either faculty of the other is like looking at the world with one eye closed. Harold Bloom shows us how to read with both eyes open, brain churning, heart pounding.

Works Cited

Frye, Northrop. *The Anatomy of Criticism*. Princeton: Princeton UP, 1957.
Hazlitt, William. *Selected Writings*. Ed. Jon Cook. Oxford: Oxford UP, 1991.
Weiss, Antonio. "Authority and Originality: An Interview [with Harold Bloom]." In *Wild Orchids and Trotsky: Messages from American Universities*. Ed. Mark Edmundson. Harmondsworth: Penguin, 1993.
Wimsatt, W. K., Jr. and Monroe Beardsley. "The Intentional Fallacy." *The Verbal Icon: Studies in the Meaning of Poetry*. By W. K. Wimsatt, Jr. Lexington: U of Kentucky P, 1954.

The Anxiety of Choice, the Western Canon and the Future of Literature

GRAHAM ALLEN

1) The Western Canon

The Western Canon brings to the foreground an issue which has always lurked in the background of Bloom's critical texts; an issue which is repressed in his previous work and which, I suggested in my study of Bloom, poses serious problems for his theories of influence and particularly for his monumental or Romantic brand of literary historicism. There is in Bloom's work since the late 1960s a repressed anxiety which problematizes his explicit theory of poetic and critical anxiety: I call this *the anxiety of choice*.

Right at the beginning of his influence-phase, in an essay entitled "First and Last Romantics," Bloom describes influence (that thing all "strong" writers apparently have anxiety about) as a "liberating burden" (*Ringers* 9-10). In describing his theory of the "poetic scene of instruction," Bloom writes: "It is only by repressing 'creative freedom,' through the initial fixation of influence, that a person can be reborn as a poet. And only by revising that repression can a poet become and remain strong" (*Repression* 27). Influence, "poetic influence" as defined by Bloom, it seems, saves the poet and critic from a "creative freedom." But what is "creative freedom"? What does influence, the anxiety of influence, "the liberating burden of influence," liberate us from?

In scattered moments throughout his work from the late 1960s onwards we can locate the answer in the expression of a mode of influence-anxiety which, strangely, Bloom does not distinguish from his theory of the anxiety of influence—a mode of anxiety captured directly in his interview with Imre Salusinszky:

> What are we to do? Why, after all, do we have one friend rather than another? You must choose. It isn't chosen for you. Why do we read one book rather than another? Why, for that matter, do we read one critic rather than another? Time is very limited. You can read all your life, for twenty-four hours a day, and you can read only a portion of what is worth reading. You can know only so many people. You can look at only so many sunsets. A fresh poem written now, a fresh critical essay written now, a fresh story or novel, competes against a vast overpopulation. That, I think, is what criticism must address itself to.
> But that is not the class-struggle: it is a question of how we individuate. (Salusinszky 69)

Bloom clearly feels that the theory of literature and criticism that he has developed since the late 1960s provides an answer to this experience of temporal and intellectual limits. And yet, in moments like those I have just cited, there is a glimpse of the fact that the entropic interpersonal or monumental history which Bloom constructs from his master theory of influence cannot really explain this form of anxiety. This *anxiety of influence*, it seems, is an anxiety concerned with something other than being captured and belittled by the precursor, or even the 'composite-precursor' which is, finally, for Bloom, the canon. The anxiety described here concerns, rather, a fear of being defeated, erased, overwhelmed by an unmanageable excess, a realm of books representing a kind of apocalyptic version of the Alexandrian Library. The theory of the anxiety of influence, which Bloom would present as the authentic origin of what he calls 'strong' poetry or even 'strong' criticism, is in fact not an origin but a response to a more primal anxiety which Bloom refuses to theorize, because to do so would undermine that theory's authority and explanatory power.

Bloom's position is that time makes the canon; the canon, therefore, can only be furthered by the human will lying (struggling, fighting, defending) against time. Such a thesis denies the relevance of choice (another candidate for the human will) and as a not inconsiderable consequence denies the political, historical and institutional choices which have constructed the canon. It is not surprising to note, then, that what I am calling the anxiety of choice re-emerges in *The Western Canon* with an insistence and visibility unprecedented in Bloom's previous work. Here is the opening paragraph of the book, which is obviously an echo of the previously cited passage from the Salusinszky interview:

> Originally the Canon meant the choice of books in our teaching institutions, and despite the recent politics of multiculturalism, the Canon's true question remains: What shall the individual who still desires to read attempt to read, this late in history? The Biblical three-score years and ten no longer suffice to read more than a selection of the great writers in what can be called the Western tradition, let alone in all the world's traditions. Who reads must choose, since there is literally not enough time to read everything, even if one does nothing but read. Mallarmé's grand line—"the flesh is sad, alas, and I have read all the books"—has become a hyperbole. Overpopulation, Malthusian repletion, is the authentic context for canonical anxieties. Not a moment passes these days without fresh rushes of academic lemmings off the cliffs they proclaim the political responsibilities of the critic, but eventually all this moralizing will subside. Every teaching institution will have its department of cultural studies, an ox to be gored, and an aesthetic underground will flourish, restoring something of the romance of reading. (*Canon* 15)

The opening chapter of *The Western Canon*, in fact, is dominated by this recognition of the burden of temporality for the serious, critical reader. Bloom writes: "we must choose: As there is only so much time" (31). And he goes on:

> If we were literally immortal, or even if our span were doubled to seven score of years, say, we could give up all argument about canons. But we have an interval only, and then our place knows us no more, and stuffing that interval with bad writing, in the name of whatever social justice, does not seem to me to be the responsibility of the literary critic. (32)

Everyone, Bloom argues, to employ his earlier phrase, has the "creative freedom" to read whatever she or he wishes; but the canon is there to limit that freedom, placing upon us the "liberating burden" of its own aesthetic inescapability. Bloom recognizes, however, that even the canon itself has now grown so large that it cannot save us from "creative freedom" or what I am calling the anxiety of choice. He writes:

> Although canons, like all lists and catalogs, have a tendency to be inclusive rather than exclusive, we have now reached the point at which a lifetime's reading and rereading can scarcely take one through the Western Canon. Indeed, it is now virtually impossible to master the Western Canon. Not only would it mean absorbing well over three thousand books, many, if not most, marked by authentic cognitive and imaginative difficulties, but the relations between these books grow more rather than

less vexed as our perspectives lengthen. There are also the vast complexities and contradictions that constitute the essence of the Western Canon, which is anything but a unity or stable structure. No one has the authority to tell us what the Western Canon is, certainly not from about 1800 to the present day. It is not, cannot be, precisely the list I give, or that anyone else might give. If it were, that would make such a list a mere fetish, just another commodity. (37)

So it would seem that the Western Canon itself cannot save us from the anxiety of choice, that this anxiety can be produced by and within it. The canon itself presents us with an unmasterable, unassimilable series of texts. And yet, having noted this aspect of Bloom's argument, we might feel somewhat confused by comments made in the same opening "Elegy for the Canon." I am thinking here of comments such as the following: "The Western Canon, despite the limitless idealism of those who would open it up, exists precisely in order to impose limits, to set a standard of measurement that is anything but political or moral" (35). The confusion is created of course by the apparent contradiction between the idea of the Western Canon as unmasterable, too vast to be assimilated by mortals of three-score years and ten, and the canon as a limit, a "standard of measurement." How can something be a limit and an aesthetic standard if it is no longer assimilable? Bloom's argument that "the only pragmatic test for the canonical" is whether a text is "rereadable" (518) does not help resolve this problem, since knowing what is "rereadable" logically depends on knowing what is not "rereadable," and knowing what is not rereadable means having read both what is rereadable (the canonical works) and what is not rereadable (all the works which lie or ultimately will lie outside the canon). To be able to depend, as a pragmatic guide, on what is rereadable, it would seem, requires that one reads *everything*.

In his "Elegiac Conclusion" to his book, Bloom returns to the problem I am foregrounding here. He writes: "The overpopulation of books (and authors) brought about by the length and complexity of the world's recorded history is at the center of canonical dilemmas, now more than ever. 'What shall I read?' is no longer the question, since so few now read, in the era of television and cinema. The pragmatic question has become: 'What shall I not bother to read?'" (526). A few pages earlier, however, Bloom has attempted to answer his question by reaffirming the major argument of his study as a whole: "The Western Canon *is* Shakespeare and Dante. Beyond them, it is what they absorbed and what absorbs them. Redefining 'literature' is a vain pursuit because you cannot usurp sufficient cognitive strength to encompass Shakespeare and Dante, and they are literature" (521).

Bloom is one of the last great totalizing critics, and as with all such critical totalizers we come to expect from him a certain circularity of argument. So, here, the answer to the questions "what is the Western canon?" and "how can I engage with/assimilate it?" becomes a reaffirmation of Bloom's master thesis of the anxiety of influence. There are, Bloom once again asserts, original authors in the Western tradition (the J-writer, Shakespeare, Dante) and all those who come after them must wrestle agonistically with these factitious originals if they are to gain sufficient revisionary strength to carve a niche for themselves within the tradition/canon which those originals have made possible and still dominate. The Western Canon, in other words, is a grand confirmation of Bloom's own theories about literature developed since the late 1960s and dominated by the theory of the anxiety of influence. Bloom's own theory—that authentic literature is produced within the confines of an agonistic, monumental history of 'inter-personal' relations (or what he calls influence)—is rhetorically presented as marking the limits of the canonical. Or, to put that another way, Bloom's final move is to contain the unassimilable quantity of texts within the unassimilable genius of Shakespeare and Dante: the anxiety of influence absorbs, one perhaps should say represses, the anxiety of choice.

And yet, as I have been attempting to suggest, such an end-position is itself a defence against a logic, of limits and choices, which it cannot itself resolve; since, in order to position this vision of canonicity against the "school of resentment" and their attempts to 'open the canon,' Bloom must be in a position to arbitrate between the merely 'readable' and the authentically 'rereadable;' and to be in such a position presupposes a knowledge of the limits of the 'readable' which Bloom himself describes as beyond our mortal powers. This is another way of saying that, despite his attempt to resolve what I am calling the anxiety of choice through his theory of facticity and consequent revisionism, Bloom can only offer that resolution by embodying in himself an authority, a knowledge, which has sufficient scope and breadth to arbitrate between the choices. Bloom can authoritatively argue that we need liberating from 'choice' ("creative freedom") only by himself encompassing the choices. Bloom in himself comes to contain, embody, the limits. In terms of Bloom himself it might be possible to suggest that he merits occupying this apparently untenable position. Bloom, with his famously preternatural gifts for reading, assimilating and rereading (in the sense of repeating, reciting) texts, is our sublime critic, which means he is a figure who disturbs our sense of the possible and the impossible. The problem of the anxiety of choice emerges so profoundly in Bloom's work on the Western Canon precisely because he himself, as a reader of texts, embodies an impossible, uncanny position with regard to Western literature and so makes visible limits and borders which for all other readers simply do not come to view.

We cannot, however, for ourselves, leave the problem here. Bloom's sublimity is a glorious phenomenon, but it cannot in itself help us in our unelevated states as readers. The anxiety of choice is experienced by anyone who would arbitrate the choices; that is to say, anyone who would speak for the canonical and against the counter-canonical. To speak for the canonical is to represent oneself as a Professor of Literature; to *profess* literature. Indeed, what Bloom's own public struggle with his own anxiety of choice reminds us is that to be a Professor of Literature in this sense depends upon a rhetoric of embodiment. To 'profess' literature one must embody it; one must have negotiated previously the choices, which boils down to having assimilated the merely readable and the re-readable.

I am hardly saying anything new here, but it is worth remembering the idea to which Bloom is addressing his defence of the canon. Bloom's *The Western Canon* is a work written by and to the embodier of culture; that is to say, by and to an idea closely tied to the emergence of the modern university, and particularly here to the rise of literary studies as an academic discipline (see Readings, chs. 5-6). It is addressed to Arnold's cultural arbitrator who knows "the best that has been thought and known," to F. R. Leavis's cultural elite described, in "Mass Civilization, Minority Culture," as "a very small minority who are capable of fending for themselves amid the smother of new books," and to the remainder of that tradition in the present. Whoever would speak for or defend the canon must take up this position and so present himself as beyond what I am calling the anxiety of choice. The professor of literature, as I am styling him (and this figure is, of course, culturally male), must embody/contain the limits; must, that is to say, suppress the anxiety of choice.

I am not the historian of the anxiety of choice, nor was I meant to be. Yet, if historians of this concept did emerge from amongst us, they would surely find themselves describing a rhetorics; a rhetorics centred in the opposition between order and excess, culture and anarchy, organic culture (in whatever form it is being presented) and waste material, or what Roy Sellars has analyzed as *dreck*. *Dreck* is unassimilable Otherness (waste material, effluvia, spiritless by-products); it is what is not cultural (organically produced by the spirit of the nation or, thinking of Bloom's contribution, civilization). *Dreck*, "unassimilable otherness," is what throws us into choice; it is what requires to be concealed if we are to convince ourselves that we can escape from the condition of the impossibility of choice.

Dragging the issue of choice, its rhetorics and its unavoidably destabilizing effects, out of Bloom's celebration of the canon has implications, of course, not merely for our reading of Bloom, but also for our understanding of our own critical positions. Where are we? Are we free of our own anxiety of choice? Are we 'professors of literature' and, if not, what are we? We should certainly resist, I would suggest, exorcising our own anxiety of choice by comfortably projecting it onto those who choose to be defenders of some idealized canon.

John Guillory, discussing the US canon debate of the 1980s, puts a more sociological slant on Bloom's assertion that "No one has the authority to tell us what the Western Canon is." Guillory, working on a logic which might be supported by my comments in this paper so far, reminds us that the canon is an idea, whilst what actually exists in practice are institutional syllabi:

> the canon is never other than an imaginary list; it never appears as a complete and uncontested list in any particular time and place, not even in the form of the omnibus anthology, which remains a selection from a larger list which does not itself appear anywhere in the anthology's table of contents. (Guillory 30)

The meta-list, or canon proper, cannot appear, of course, because it is purely imaginary. Guillory states: "the canon is an imaginary totality of works. No one has access to the canon as totality. This fact is true in the trivial sense that no one ever reads every canonical work" (30). We might wonder here whether Guillory has ever heard of Harold Bloom. Guillory's assertions, however, remind us that it is not in fact the canon that determines the list of texts to be taught and studied, the syllabus; it is in fact the syllabus which posits an imaginary canon from which it derives and from which it takes its institutional and intellectual authority. Guillory writes:

> So far from being the case that the canon determines the syllabus in the simplest sense that the syllabus is constrained to select only from canonical

works, it is much more historically accurate to say that the syllabus posits the existence of the canon as its imaginary totality.... Changing the syllabus cannot mean in any historical context overthrowing the canon, because every construction of a syllabus *institutes* once again the process of canon formation. (31)

I imagine Bloom reading Guillory's analysis of the canon debate and being equally cheered and dismayed. Bloom, of course, much as he recognizes that there can be no one definitive canon, wishes to assert that there are particular texts and authors that we should and must choose over others. In this sense, Bloom could not endorse the notion of the canon as a pedagogical imaginary. However, I imagine Bloom might be cheered by Guillory's arguments against the 'representation' school of syllabus formation: the politically correct, institutionalized forms of radicalism which falsely conflate political representation with representation on a university's syllabus. I also imagine that Bloom would be cheered by Guillory's assertion that what matters is what is done with texts. That is to say that what matters is not representation per se but power. Harold Bloom may be some readers' figure of sublimity, the sublime reader. He certainly fulfils that role for me and has done so since I began to be a conscious reader, a state which has always involved a terrible recognition that I had little more than three-score years and ten within which to read. The still vital relevance of Bloom's example, as a reader, critic and theorist, comes, it must be said, from his assertion of the performative nature of writing and reading, his unfashionable, yet because of that still timely, reiteration of literary and critical pathos (power).

2) How to Read and Why

How to Read and Why, like *The Western Canon*, the book on Shakespeare, and the recent book on *Genius*, is aimed at a general public interested in literature. These books are written against the grain of academic criticism. That, at least, is their rhetorical stance. These recent works position themselves, sometimes with delight, usually with a prophetic melancholy, entirely outside of the modern academic environment. Bloom's current assessment of academic criticism and theory is well known. His sense of the decline in truly *literary* criticism within the academy is total. Once again, in *How to Read and Why*, we come across statements of contempt for an institution which has turned literary study into a one-dimensional field of political correctness and incorrectness. Sadly, in a book which seeks to teach the how and why of critical reading, Bloom sees little chance of anyone, student or teacher, listening from within the confines of politically correct departments of English or Cultural Studies. Those who exist within such confines seem irredeemable, and Bloom directs his book at the only point of orientation which makes sense to his understanding of the literary and critical process:

> Reading falls apart, and much of the self scatters with it. All this is past lamenting, and will not be remedied by any vows or programs. What is to be done can only be performed by some version of elitism, and that is now unacceptable, for reasons both good and bad. There are still solitary readers, young and old, everywhere, even in the universities. If there is a function of criticism at the present time, it must be to address itself to the solitary reader, who reads for herself, and not for the interests that supposedly transcend the self. (*How* 23)

Despite Bloom's own binary rhetoric, it is possible to agree with him about the essentially solitary nature of reading, whilst at the same moment disagreeing with his frequent assertions that authentic literature has no relation to political and ideological issues and interests. The crux of this issue concerns the significant place Bloom attributes to the word 'transcendence' in his book on how to read. "Poetry," he writes, "can be a mode of transcendence, secular or spiritual, depending upon how you receive it" (138). Reading after reading, in this book, ends with a statement regarding a text's "transcendence" of political and ideological agendas and cultures. Ellison's *Invisible Man* is a novel which apparently "transcends politics and ideology" (267); the voice that speaks the ballad "Tom O'Bedlam" is "as little trapped in a particular era as was Shakespeare" (108); Emily Dickinson's poetry allows us, her readers, "to break with the conventions of response that have been deeply instilled in us" (142); and generally literature's importance and truth is rooted in its ability to help us commune with our authentic rather than our ideological selves:

> Only rarely can poetry aid us in communing with others; that is a beautiful idealism, except at certain strange moments, like the instant of falling in love. Solitude is the more frequent mark of our condition; how shall we people that solitude? Poems can help us speak to ourselves more clearly and more fully, and to *overhear* that speaking.... We speak to an otherness in ourselves, or to what may be best and oldest in ourselves. We read to find ourselves, more fully and more strange than otherwise we could hope to find. (79)

The point of tension in Bloom's account of literature's "transcendent" qualities concerns the notion of Otherness and its relation to temporality. Bloom finds it difficult to evade an ambiguity in these and other statements, an ambiguity concerning literature's and the self's relation to the past and the future. Bloom's sense of the transcendence involved in literature can involve the future; he writes, for example, that "Poetry is the crown of imaginative literature . . . because it is a prophetic mode" (69). However, one cannot help but ask what it is that we could possibly find in that future that has not already been established in the great originals of the past. Turgenev, like Shakespeare, for example, "shows us something that perhaps is always there, but that we could not see without him" (34). Is the Otherness we find when reading alone something that we once were but have forgotten, or is it rather something that we could be and must strive towards? Bloom's opening articulation of this problem is significant: "Let me fuse Bacon, Johnson, and Emerson into a formula of how to read: find what comes near to you that can be put to the use of weighing and considering, and that addresses you as though you share the one nature, free of time's tyranny. Pragmatically, that means, first find Shakespeare, and then let him find you" (22). If ideology is conceived as that which limits the self to a specific time and place, then the Otherness Bloom believes the reader can find within literature concerns, as he states, a transcendent human nature "free of time's tyranny." Yet it matters greatly whether that liberation from ideological contexts involves a backwards or forwards temporal movement. I read the passage above and can respond to it until the concluding sentence concerning Shakespeare. The definitive assertion that our authentic self is always already behind us reads to me like a gigantically sad revision of Shelley's grand statement about poetry in his *Defence*. Shelley writes in his famous concluding section:

> Poets are the hierophants of an unapprehended inspiration, the mirrors of the gigantic shadows which futurity casts upon the present, the words which express what they understand not; the trumpets which sing to battle, and feel not what they inspire: the influence which is moved not, but moves. Poets are the unacknowledged legislators of the world. (Shelley 508)

Bloom's fear, that what we are becoming is less and less reliant on literature, is an understandable one. I join him in hoping that our futurity will still depend, in significant ways, upon the visions of our greatest literary texts. However, to state that where we are going is already contained by the imaginative work of Shakespeare is to argue for a vision of literature as a mirror in which the gigantic shadows of the past perpetually diminish and constrain us. Such a vision of literature can only generate a melancholy sense of dependency within its unproductive, uncreative, already read and written readers.

I prefer to remain with Shelley's sense of the dialectical relationship between literature's past glory and its concomitant future orientation. Great literature may come to the reader from the past, but what it shows to that reader is a vision of the possible, a futurity which is worth a lifetime's struggle. Harold Bloom, of course, knows this. The tension, between past and future orientations, runs through Bloom's book on reading literature. I take it that the tension is self-conscious on Bloom's part, and it certainly is foregrounded in the book's moving "Epilogue." There Bloom meditates on two responses to the life-work of writing and reading. The first response is taken from Rabbi Tarphon and has been a recurrent motive in Bloom's texts and, as he tells us, his life. It reads: "It is not necessary for you to complete the work, but neither are you free to desist from it" (277). Balanced against this, Bloom gives us the example of Shakespeare, greatest of all writers, who did indeed "abandon" his work before his life had ended.

Bloom ends his book, then, considering the question concerning "whether one is required to complete the work or whether one is free to desist from the work" (282). This, however, is a rhetorical question, since it is clear that, for Bloom, Tarphon's statement is superior, even to the example of Shakespeare at his end. The work is never completed, but that does not mean we can desist from the work of completion. Tarphon's aphorism seems to me to partner Shelley's conclusion to the *Defence*, in that both tie us to a futurity which makes sense of the present and the past.

Articulating the tension I have pointed to here in the fashion I have allows me also to express my anxiety over Bloom's assessment of the "transcendence" available in and from literature. Literature cannot simply take us outside of the realm of the political and the ideological. That realm is equivalent to our presence within historical time and place. The great works of the past themselves offer a "transcendence" but only with regard to a futurity to which they act as mirrors. Bloom's notion of "transcendence" does not always integrate the future orientation of those authors and texts he wants to teach us to read. Bloom's readers, those readers who love him, need in their reading to return him to that future.

What is particularly interesting about *How to Read and Why*, as I have already suggested, is the fact that within it the need for a future orientation in literary texts and our reading of them constantly, if unintentionally, suggests itself. I find evidence of the pull of this desire for a future orientation in what is for me the most original and vivid section of the book, Bloom's fifth section on the novel in the United States. Starting with Melville's *Moby-Dick*, this section finds its climax in an analysis of the fiercely negative visions of Faulkner (*As I Lay Dying*), Nathaniel West (*Miss Lonelyhearts*), Thomas Pynchon (*The Crying of Lot 49*), Cormac McCarthy (*Blood Meridian*), Ralph Waldo Ellison (*Invisible Man*) and Toni Morrison (*Song of Solomon*). There is something about the negativity of these post-Melvillean novels that Bloom cannot quite capture and which forces him into the critical sublime. Bloom's assertion that "Negativity cleanses, though at the high price of nihilism" (273) is certainly insufficient summation of what he has just shown his readers. A more accurate assessment of Faulkner, and indeed of his whole sample of US novels, follows a little further on in his "Summary Observations:" "I do not think that there is a higher aesthetic achievement by a twentieth-century American writer than *As I Lay Dying*, a work of shattering originality, but 'shattering' is the most precise adjective for the effect of this novel upon me" (273). Bloom tries in his final comments to move back to the cardinal idea that great works of literature heal their readers by reminding them of who they really are. However, this image of the "shattering" of the reader's self remains the strongest response and is the one we take away from our reading of this section as a whole.

The "shattering" Bloom refers to here—and then attempts to back away from—is a shattering of ideology and as a consequence of the self: a "shattering" that, as he convincingly shows, occurs through a literature of stunning negativity. Bloom here becomes, once again, a critic with whom I *must* creatively misread. My 'misreading' would consist in returning Bloom to a Romanticism he has never fully left and yet which he has never fully embraced either. I would refer here to Godwin's decision, upon publishing the gloriously idealist *Political Justice*, immediately to write a novel of a quite astonishing degree of negativity, *Caleb Williams*. Reference could then be made to a similar trajectory between Wollstonecraft's *Vindication of the Rights of Woman* and her unfinished novel *Maria: Or, The Wrongs of Woman*. We might also think of Mary Shelley's reliance on a global negativity in *The Last Man* or a just as equally pervasive negative vision in her most famous work, *Frankenstein*.

Many other examples would be forthcoming, but above them all would be P. B. Shelley's reliance on a method in which ideological assumptions and habits—Shelley frequently refers to them as "masks"—are shattered and thus, at least potentially, at least imaginatively, transcended.

Romantic literature, before Bloom's series of post-Melvillean US novels, knew that literature's war against ideology involved a future-orientation which was frequently only available as a mode of negative vision. Negativity, in realist or romance forms, allows a cut within the present, a wound in the apparently 'real;' it offers us again, usually in 'bad times,' at least the possibility of a transcendence of ideology in the future. I am not trying to import Adorno, Benjamin and the Frankfurt School into our reading of Romanticism and Bloom. What I am trying to suggest is a potential *agon* unleashed by the productive conjunction of a particular reading of Romantic literature with the latest critical work of Harold Bloom. I am after, in other words, the critic who once, whilst engaged in one of the most sustained of all readings of Romanticism and its influence, gave us such notions as transumption, poetic misprision, diachronic rhetoric, and a host of other to my mind still indispensable critical concepts. Bloom's account of reading, as I have endeavoured to show, requires what Tilottama Rajan calls "the supplement of reading" (Rajan, 1990). This "supplement" involves an exchange which takes us beyond "solipsism" into the human mind's capacity to speak to and for the future, whilst also recognizing that that future remains, in the present, unimaginable. The idea that Bloom, who once analyzed this cardinal feature of literature so eloquently and so rigorously, might learn to do so again by reading the modern US novel is a compelling thought. Yet we would also expect such a vision to be not too far away from the Romanticism from which Bloom first learnt to read the *agon* that literature wages with future time. However we might tilt this hypothesis, we do still desperately need Bloom's accounts of how literature struggles for a future. Telling us that Shakespeare encompasses human nature and thus human time—past, present and future— is a sad task, Harold. Come back to us and speak to us where we find ourselves, here in this dark time, and explain to us again how writers have lied, denied, warred against and made pacts with the future. These are beautiful stories; they are the reason we continue to read. We need you, Harold, in our glorious if doomed quest to complete the work.

Works Cited

Arnold, Matthew. *Selected Prose*. Harmondsworth: Penguin, 1970.
Guillory, John. *Cultural Capital: The Problem of Literary Canon Formation*. Chicago: U of Chicago P, 1993.
Leavis, F. R. "Mass Civilization, Minority Culture." *Education and the University: A Sketch for an "English School"*. London: Chatto, 1948.
Rajan, Tilottama. *The Supplement of Reading: Figures of Understanding in Romantic Theory and Practice*. Ithaca: Cornell UP, 1990.
Readings, Bill. *The University in Ruins*. Cambridge, MA: Harvard UP, 1996.
Salusinszky, Imre. *Criticism and Society*. New York: Methuen, 1987.
Sellars, Roy. "Theory on the Toilet: A Manifesto for Dreckology." *Angelaki* 2.1 (1995): 179-96.
Shelley, P. B. *Shelley's Poetry and Prose*. Ed. Donald H. Reiman and Sharon B. Powers. New York: Norton, 1977.

Toward an Ethics of Literary Revisionism

R. CLIFTON SPARGO

During the later portion of his career, in which Harold Bloom came to appear with regularity on the *New York Times* bestseller list, reaching a wide public audience even as he argued for the irrevocably elitist nature of the production and reception of great literature, he firmly entrenched himself against contemporary modes of de-idealizing reading that might seek blandly to democratize literature. Yet even in his later writings, as in *The Western Canon* (1993) where Bloom appears only too happy to embrace not just an elitist but amoralistic, indeed deeply apolitical trajectory for literary aesthetics, limiting the value of literature to the doubly solipsistic enterprise of overhearing ourselves while we talk to ourselves, his hypothesis of literature's withdrawal from the referential, immediately social, or measurably historical pole of language is betrayed by the premise of redoubled overhearing. As the conceit of overhearing bespeaks the impossibility of containment, it inscribes a historical aspect of literary rhetoric upon the author's or reader's ostensibly private intentions.[1] It is as though the Bloomian reader who talks to himself were like Mr. Ramsay

---

[1] Emphasizing literature's amoral, apolitical, and anti-didactic *raison d'être*, Bloom proclaims in perhaps his most widely read work that Shakespeare, as a metonymy for literature itself, "will not make us better, and he will not make us worse, but he may teach us how to overhear ourselves when we talk to ourselves" (*Canon* 31). And yet Bloomian theory has made a significant contribution to our rethinking of the relation between poetry and history. In a chapter dedicated to Bloom in his critical account of the fate of American literary criticism in the 1960s and 1970s, Frank Lentricchia offers a self-professedly "unsympathetic account" of Bloomian theory but nevertheless declares, "No theorist writing in the United States today has succeeded, as Bloom has, in returning poetry to history" (341, 342). Similarly, albeit with more sympathetic attention paid to Bloom's diachronic rhetoric (an emphasis the present essay shares), Peter de Bolla has distilled for us the historical dimension of Bloom's theory of intertextuality.

of *To the Lighthouse*, each of his soliloquizing recitations doomed ahead of time to be intruded upon by an audience. In figuring the necessarily interruptive force of literature and suggesting that even highly literary, hermetic texts are implicitly social speech acts, the conceit suggests the tension in Bloom's project of literary revisionism which simultaneously apologizes for and overthrows the construct of a poet's individuality. For as Bloom advocates a dialectical literary tradition whose only genuinely modern and therefore belated expression must be antithetical, he is in far greater dialogue than might at first appear with exterior or extra-literary influences on poetry, as also with a historical, socio-political view of literary language he seemingly rejects.

The apparent contradiction in Bloom's project might be accounted for as the function of a rift that developed over time—say, between the theoretically innovative segment of his career (especially 1973 to the late 1980s, including the theoretical tetralogy he published between 1973 and 1980) and the period of popularization when Bloom became, like other public intellectuals such as Camille Paglia and Cornel West, part of everyday cultural knowledge.[2] Long before Bloom had embarked on his genuinely public career, Frank Lentricchia pointed in *After the New Criticism* (1980) to an anterior conflict within Bloom's extant canon, between writings from an initial phase, roughly 1959–1972, which included such works as *Shelley's Mythmaking* (1959), *The Visionary Company* (1961), and *Blake's Apocalypse* (1963), and works from a second phase that began with the publication of *The Anxiety of Influence* (1973). In the earlier phase, Bloom had been committed to a largely redemptive, even unitary mytho-poetics, whereas the works of the latter phase skeptically elucidated the poetic imagination as forever caught in the throes of an irreconcilable dualism. Or, to put this in Freudian terms, as of 1973 Bloom's critical poetics suddenly took account of the reality principle, giving emphasis to that aspect of the world or experience that poetry could not enfold into its imaginative overreaching. Ingeniously and provocatively, and with a talent for overstatement that led readers to align him with his imported European colleagues at Yale who had revolutionized literary critical study by declaring that there was nothing outside the text,

---

[2] I am dating the third, largely public phase of his career from the publication of the transitional work *Ruin the Sacred Truths: Poetry and Belief from the Bible to the Present*, even as I suppose that there is considerable continuity in Bloom's overall project and that Bloom's later works, although directed toward a wider audience and less steeped in theoretical argument, remain greatly dependent upon the premises argued in the theoretical tetralogy.

Bloom imagined that the only reality with which a poet significantly contended was an antecedent textual reality. The formidability of the precursor text was to be demonstrated by the obstacle it posed to a belated poet's imaginative capability. Significantly, in this second, high theoretical phase of his career (circa 1973–1989), Bloom's criticism also became more radically demystifying in emphasis, his ongoing critique of New Critical reverences for the autonomous poetic artifact reformed into pronouncements against all stances involving moral praise, aesthetic appreciation, or canonization (whether adopted by poets, critics or readers) for being symptomatic of imaginative lack or weakness, or worse yet mere derivativeness. Shifting the emphasis of influence theory away from the tracing of sources and from honorific notions of intertextuality, Bloom argued that every significant contributor to literary tradition fights fiercely against those poetic voices that are for him or her most compelling. The result was a hermeneutics of literary history tossing off not only the greater share of contextualizing criticism but most of an author's own notions of what creativity entails.[3]

In his writings of that middle period, Bloom notably accused T. S. Eliot of having advocated a mystificatory conservatism with regard to literary tradition, and thereafter, as so often happens with those who ponder the persistent return of the past, Bloom too was interpreted as leaning backward in his orientation. Maligned for being overly invested in the very paradigms with which he contended (Lentricchia speculated that at heart Bloom might really believe in the autonomous text of New Criticism) or for investing all poetic consciousness with his own obsessions about literary ancestry, Bloom seemed, even as he described the terms of cultural and literary apocalypse, to be, much like Eliot himself, incurably nostalgic for that sublimity achieved only by the dead.[4] Still,

---

[3] In Geoffrey Hartman's view, Bloom's bent for heterodoxy springs from his revisionary relation to notions of canonicity based upon Jewish sacred texts, as is evident in his fondness for heresy and iconoclasm in so far as each stance leans away from canonical stability toward originality (Hartman 53).

[4] See Lentricchia 325–31. Lentricchia argues conversely that the Bloomian tetralogy reveals a "desperate humanist effort to establish, in the face of Derrida's massive critique, the priority of voice over discourse" (333)—an effort that fails because the "Freudianism in his theory dissolves the conscious human subject and so robs Bloom of any genuine claim to humanism" (336). Similarly, Daniel O'Hara argues that despite Bloom's uses of Nietzsche he cannot embrace the Nietzschean turn from negative humanism to a pure humanism unweighted by a heavy cultural past. See O'Hara, "The Genius of Irony."

against critics in the Eliotic vein or advocates of humanism, which is to say against anyone who might suppose that we ought to revere the past because we learn so valuably from it, Bloom perceived the burdensomeness of the past to be its greatest legacy. Bloom's own sympathies with American pragmatism, styled after Emerson and running parallel at times to the work of the philosopher Richard Rorty, informed his basic ambivalence about the value of the past—a value which the past might or might not have possessed inherently but which in any case could certainly not be estimated as a *value* such as the ones moral philosophers would have us adopt. True, in the later segment of his career Bloom has sometimes mystified literary canonization, seeming to mask its socio-economically based motives, as though he sought chiefly a stay against the ongoing decadence of a Western cultural heritage. Yet for those who read him closely, even Bloom's canonical apologetics are overwritten by an elegiac theme of futility about the failing luster of the past and a skepticism about most cultural attempts to preserve the past through idealization.[5]

My reading of Bloom herein concentrates especially on the forcefulness of a prevalent metonymy of much 1970s and 1980s literary theory, specifically, the hypothesis that the text substitutes for reality. In Bloom this means that a precursor text stands in for the exteriority threatening poetic voice, and that intertextual agonistics approximate the function of a Freudianly connoted interpersonal *agon*. What I wish to emphasize, however, is that the metonymic force of Bloom's characteristic overstatements concerning the intertextual dynamic necessarily works in the other direction, and not altogether under the sign of self-contradiction. Bloom openly concedes that there are other social influences

---

[5] As an apostate Nietzschean (and a self-professed Viconian critic), Bloom believes that moral and literary values are not stable but rather perceived or interpretively improvised in the present moment, so that any critical elucidation of the play of intertextuality is always also an act of genealogical critique, according to which the present text is found to be insufficient except by its ambitious, revisionary design on a more-than-sufficient—and in a basic sense, more than real—intertext or precursor. Then too the value attached to a precursor text is always determined by an act of overestimation. For a discussion of Bloom's relation to Nietzsche, see O'Hara's "The Genius of Irony," which contrasts the agonistic elitisms of Nietzsche and Bloom to Northrop Frye's typology of literary tradition as a kind of romance idealizing of the principles of belonging in a group or class, but also accuses Bloom of failing to make the Nietzschean leap to embracing an attack on the past that would launch the full freedom of the future; see also Hubert Zapf, 337–55.

informing a literary text, even while supposing that such influences have nothing to do with the difficulties encountered by the poet as poet, which can pertain only to the overwhelming influx of those antecedent poetic texts that might curtail the contemporary poet's voice—in short, only to the living importance of a poem sustained by way of the fiercely interpersonal logic of intertextual *agon*. The myth of poetry, of what Bloom calls "the poet in a poet"—and I suspect Bloom himself would willingly concede at least this much of my point—produces the illusion that the poet's hubristic metonymic substitution succeeds: a poet renames reality as poetry or recasts exterior influence as originally achieved poetic consciousness.[6] Yet the function of criticism, as of the critical consciousness that repeatedly begets the quest for original poetic voice, is to announce the failure of poetry's own visionary terms. With ironic deftness, Bloom intimates that only the dead, or only those who are powerfully dead poets, can be truly ominous to consciousness; and this is so for the simple reason that they seem retrospectively to have obtained the status of incontestable singularity and thereby elicit our need for a critical remembrance akin to the work of mourning in Freud. The resonances of strong poetry bequeath themselves forward in literary history by being vitally adversarial, by impugning the contemporary poet's or reader's consciousness, measured finally by the extent to which we still find a poet worthily bothersome in what he or she tells us about ourselves. Yet according to the twofold premise of this implicit hermeneutic circle, in which present contestation proves past value and in which the peculiar value of the text in lieu of its social context or its overt habit of referentiality is demonstrated by the very sociality premising such value, the Bloomian metonymy always also reverses its trajectory: not only do poetic texts substitute themselves for reality, but reality re-substitutes itself, as a version of interpersonal *agon*, for the hypothetically autonomous text. Much as Bloom's complaint with the critical orthodoxy of a prior generation put autonomous, iconic poetic texts back within reach of the vital, adversarial contestations through which they come into being, so also his de-idealizing focus translates the value of the literary as a sign of psychological and ethical strife.

My critical intervention in intertextual theory, then, is to suppose that Bloom affords us terms of revisionism that, although not explicitly

---

[6] In other words, the cross-fertilization of the terms is not merely metaphoric or associative—intertextuality figured as its own unique mode of interpersonality—but rather always presumptuously and yet inadequately metonymic. See *Anxiety* 11.

formulated in the language of ethics, nonetheless lend themselves to an interpretation of texts via a historically inspired construct of ethics. What the literary text becomes, when viewed through the lens of a dialectical, antithetical, or revisionary theory, is a site of relational struggle, or a mode of contestation that is also implicitly in Bloom a figure for society itself. By this logic, our acts of reading are powerfully and most significantly interpersonal struggles wherein we confront the formidably constituted personalities of precursor texts interpreting us even as we misinterpret them.[7] The conceit of the interpersonal text is, then, not merely illustrative; it characterizes the deeply relational proportion or disproportion presiding over the meaning of any text, and as such bespeaks a preeminently ethical focus.

In speaking of ethics I invoke especially a modern connotation of the term, corresponding roughly to Emmanuel Levinas' formulation. This does not mean I wish to impose a Levinasian reading on Bloom. If my essay draws Bloom toward ethical emphases upon which Levinas' work has cast important light, Bloom himself never bothers in any explicit fashion with the propositions of the Levinasian project. In fact what I wish to argue here is the rather un-Levinasian supposition that dialectics itself is fundamentally ethical, especially in so far as a dialectic might proceed contrary to Hegel's most famous of all dialectical methodologies, recoiling from the properties of liberal, progressivist myth within which alterity is constructed, along the line of a necessary trajectory, as a problem to be encountered and overcome. Against any willful, idealistic assimilation of alterity to predominant political systems or projected cultural models, the ethical meaning I attribute to Bloomian *agon* depends in part on Levinas' rehabilitation of the signifying force of alterity in its unaccommodated state. Yet even so I remain circumspect about Levinas' rejection of Nietzschean, Freudian, or Foucauldian conceptions of the presiding play of power within relationship if only because it might promote an un-realism exempting ethics from its real-life immersion in the politics of power. Bloom, or at

---

[7] Despite Bloom's deliberate swerve from Freud, many of his readers treat Bloomian revisionism as a literary historical application of Freudian 'family romance.' In Bloom, however, the literary text assumes the characteristics of a personality no longer governed by an author's biographical relation to her own text or to a precursor text, so, as de Bolla puts it: "The concept of influence, as articulated by Bloom, describes the relations that pertain between poems; it is that which articulates one poem with another even when the poet may be unaware of the precursor poem" (18).

least the ethical Bloom I put forward in this essay, would remain firmly on the side of those critics of culture who believe that a social poetics of power must first be conceded before it can be demystified. Indeed, according to Bloom's theoretical amalgamation of Nietzsche and Freud, any affirmation of ethics always works, by reinforcing the mechanism of repression, in the name of culture, which is to say, also on the side of power.

Of course ethics just as readily pushes back at Bloomian theory, and we would be justified in concentrating, for example, on the ways in which the presumption of contentiousness as the basis for sociality persists in mimetic proportion to the praxis of social violence, to oppressive ideologies of power, or to an ideological justification of competitiveness as the basis for capitalistically determined political inequities. There are limits, then, to the rapprochement I am suggesting between the Bloomian model of intertextuality and an ethically based theory of sociality, and one might well have to undertake a revisionary misreading of enormous proportions to make Bloom overtly compatible with, say, the Marxist critique of class. As I conceive my task in this essay, it is not only to situate Bloom inside a set of concerns proper to the discourse of ethics, but also to return his work to the context of 1970s theoretical conversations he was having in his own oblique, polemical, and often wry way. I focus especially on *A Map of Misreading* (1975) as the work from his high theoretical phase that most neatly distills, after the highly speculative formulations of *The Anxiety of Influence*, his unique blending of theoretical and practical literary criticism. As it admirably balances theory and literary-critical praxis, offering extended readings of poetry in its second half, *A Map of Misreading* anticipates the structure of my own argument here. Only at the end of the essay do I put forward a practical reading of Toni Morrison's revisionary relation to Virginia Woolf, which is meant to be illustrative of my theoretical musings about an ethical afterlife for Bloomian theory. Ultimately, I argue for a nexus between the ethical and historical elements in revisionistic modes of intertextuality and for the potential of literary voice, in its diachronic aspect, to recover its hypothetical textual debts as sources of political meaning. In so doing, I construe Bloom's theory of revisionism, supremely dialectical in its significatory patterns, to have surprising relevance to questions of social injustice and our capacity to interpret politically determined sufferings by way of literarily mediated modes of cultural consciousness.

1) The Critical Construct and Historical Significance of Poetic Voice

It is far too easy to underestimate the construct of history operative in Bloom's project throughout the 1970s into the early 1980s. If, for Lentricchia and others, Bloom's polemics against a past generation of critics appeared to date his own critical priorities, on his own view he was as adamantly engaged in fighting the hegemonic, literarily stultifying privilege granted to synchronic linguistic theory and to Derrida's innovative account of *écriture* as the absolutely determinative ground of all meaning and expression. In crudest form, the Bloomian credo rejects the premise that language or the written text anticipates the subject by delimiting ahead of time the range of every utterance, instead locating the bar to a subject's entry into language in another's voice, which by having already said what we wish to say has stolen the better part of our communicative valor. This attempt to set literature apart from the hobgoblin of *écriture* could be productively compared to a concurrent struggle waged by common language theorists, from John Searle to Stanley Cavell, against the influence of synchronic linguistics on philosophy and language theory, and in this light Bloom's persistently pragmatic focus on the oracular dimension of poetics, on that sense in which the poem illustrates an inseparability of speech and action implied by the Hebrew word *davhar*, strategically conflicts with the universalizing properties of *langue*. Recognizing Bloom's affinity with other contemporary protests against *écriture* (I will return to Bloom's emphasis on orality shortly) might force us at the very least to distinguish between the diachronic dimension of the Bloomian project and largely mistaken clichés about his conservative defense of canon or his belief in the atemporality of all great literature.

A closer ground of comparison is a work such as *Metahistory: The Historical Imagination in Nineteenth-Century Europe* (1973), in which Hayden White executes a typological analysis, in the spirit of Northrop Frye, that charts the properties of historical writings according to their modes of emplotment, modes of argument, ideological orientation, *Weltanschauung*, and preferred or characterizing tropes.[8] By means of

---

[8] Of course the most exhaustive contemporary theorization of tropes in literary theory was performed by Bloom's colleague at Yale, Paul de Man. For a link between de Man and Bloom, especially focused on where Bloomian rhetoric intersects with de Man's descriptions of the temporal properties of tropes, see de Bolla, esp. 87–101.

what Fredric Jameson in the essay "Figural Relativism" (1976) perceives as a "deep-figural" analysis of historical narrative, White explicates the intersection of formal and ideological types in nineteenth-century histories, which are shown to obtain active cognitive sense by way less of their purported factuality than of a narrativity that formally, argumentatively, and tropologically determines the ordering of facts (Jameson 153–65, esp. 157). Jameson credits White's method with the potential to focus literary scholars' attention on the history of forms as well as on the co-determinative interplay of aesthetic and ideological judgments, even as he also finds, based in his commitment to the Marxian dialectic of historical materialism, that White's structuralism requires a complementary "structural conception of the historical rock bottom" (160). There must be reasons, Jameson maintains, that narratives assume the generic forms they do and so privilege certain ideological positions at certain historical moments, reasons based in the contextual conditions for the emergence of specific forms and their corresponding ideological import. Near the essay's end, Jameson recalls White's criticism of Foucault for treating history as a succession of narrativistic, social-scientific forms strung together as distinct, discontinuous synchronic systems, and reminds us of White's solution: a logic governing the succession of synchronic forms does reveal itself, even if Foucault failed to recognize it, and it is derived from the transformative, deep structural properties of tropes themselves. Even as White assimilates Foucault to a Viconian 'linguistic historicism,' his tropological system fails in Jameson's estimation to account for its own Viconian echoes. While failing to introduce Vico directly, White too confidently substitutes tropes for contextual origins, and by reverting to a structural typology treats historical narratives and their explicit referential or implicit ideological content as merely cyclical, if not altogether arbitrary in a Viconian sense.

The terms of Jameson's critique might just as well have been aimed at Bloom, who in *A Map of Misreading* declares Vico, more so than Nietzsche, to be the prophet of his own critical methodology (*Map* 55). Embracing Vico's turn against Descartes on the ground that God could not be intuited, Bloom celebrates Vico's perception of a dualism characterizing all human experience. Although there is genuine authority in our historical origins, which are for Vico necessarily metaphysical origins, that authority forever eludes us, leaving us to define it anagogically by way of our own interpretive imagination. Vico surrendered what we might call the historicist myth of recovering origins as a discernible principle of causation (since ultimate causation could be located only in God) to focus instead on the place where determinative meanings would have to be discerned, namely, in the receptive, necessarily interpretive reader. In short, Vico modeled for generations of critics thereafter the necessary arbitrariness presiding over every moment of understanding, which is *de facto* also an interpretive act. Much twentieth-century literary criticism came to focus during the time of Bloom's own high theoretical phase on the phenomenological hermeneutics of the reader's meaning-determining responses, and Bloom evades, say, reader-response theory by turning more originally to a Viconian-inspired hermeneutics treating all hypotheses of origin as effectual tropes. By such a logic, not only does Vico's tropological system become synonymous with the act of interpretation itself, not only do tropes (as Jameson perceives) become the covert mechanics of systemic transformation in White's unwittingly Viconian typology, but tropes (literally, 'turns' in phrasing) seem the motivating force of interpretation: they are what we *turn* to, by, or from every time we attempt to return to origins.

In White's view, even dialectics might reduce to a play of tropes: "... dialectic is nothing but a formalization of an insight into the tropological nature of all forms of discourse which are not formally committed to the articulation of a world view within the confines of a single modality of linguistic usage" (428). In other words, in so far as meaning depends on more than the hegemonic suasion of presently extant ideological systems, and in so far as there must be even within a rigorously synchronic view of power some operative principle by which a change in the perception of form, ideology, or system might take place apart from the ascendant normative expression of historiographical and ideological knowledge, the explanation cannot reside in either a dialectic of historical materialism or a Hegelian dialectical idealism for the simple reason that, if conceived along these lines, dialectic allows for nothing arbitrary within the development of history writing. To insist that history might have been written otherwise or that even what we call facts might have come to mean differently, White attributes to tropes a function within discourse that permits of various expression and of arbitrary change, even to the point where a trope might enable an unusual configuration of form and ideology working regressively against the grain of historical context.

On the relation between dialectic and tropes, Bloom probably proves to be a greater believer than White in the necessary forward movement of the dialectic and even in a historicist inevitability attached to what he calls poetic voice. Ever emphasizing how hard it is to overcome the counterpoint of ancestral or precursor voices within the dialectic, Bloom argues against a structuralist view of tropes, such as that described by Paul de Man or White, in which tropes function as rhetorical procedures within a fixed system of *langue* timelessly tracing, by their purely structural determination, arbitrary patterns of differentiation within linguistic structures. According to what is forward-leaning in Bloom's own dialectic, which proceeds roughly along the lines of a liberal historiography viewed askance through the demystifying Nietzschean-Freudian lens of social criticism, he delineates a historicism more psychological than linguistic, more cultural than materialist, and more literary than anything else. It is important to insist upon the peculiar status of the literary in Bloom's hermeneutics, that his version of aesthetics is decidedly not of the exempted, idealized, autonomous realm posited by the New Critics or even of the asocial decadence advocated by such proto-Bloomian critics as Walter Pater or Oscar Wilde. Modernity is post-Romanticism for Bloom; and the Romantics as both skeptics and visionaries—as representatives of the last historical moment, according to Bloom's literary-historical premises, in which it was possible to recreate belief as though it might be true—predict the advent of a truly literary culture. They pronounce a point in Western cultural history when dialectics is no longer mythical (say, the Hellenic era), religious (say, the Judeo-Christian era), philosophical (say, from humanism until the mid-nineteenth century), or historical (say, from the Enlightenment until the onset of fully demythologized twentieth-century modernity). A truly literary era such as ours is characterized by the sensibility of belatedness, marked by the exhaustion of dialectical belief or ideology, as the moorings of dialectic become so loosened that the dialectical memory of culture advances apart from all the mythic or ideological mechanisms by which it was once rationalized.[9]

---

[9] Bloom's sense of the literary, as I have thus described it, resembles the opposition Frank Kermode draws between fiction and myth as he emphasizes the extent to which literature in our modern sense of the word necessarily opposes itself to a mythic worldview. As Kermode deploys the fictional sensibility to elucidate with astute skepticism the apocalyptic structures of belief in Western culture, so Bloom demonstrates a similar suspicion of our cultural and psychological historicisms pertaining to origins. See Kermode, *The Sense of an Ending*.

In Bloom the historical dialectic of poetic voice functions simultaneously with and independently of the tropes, which are always momentary stays, evasions, or lies told against the historicist logic of dialectic—all the tropes of poetic language proving analogous to and possibly even pre-determinative of the basic psychic defenses. Freud recognized that there is nothing more predetermined than a defense, and Bloom would simply remind us that this is true whether we speak of psychic or poetic defenses. There is no turning back history except perhaps in a poet's mind, which seizes upon tropes so as to turn fantastically, if necessarily, against the laws of time, against the inevitability of precedent, and against the complex of familial and social determination. According to its peculiar distinctiveness, then, Bloomian dialectics remains historical-minded precisely in so far as he rejects the exceptional possibilities of mere contingency in determining the achievement of poetic voice as a specifiable event. There is really no way, so Bloom's own version of historicism insists, for a poet to step outside of the overdetermining influence of an always already inherited past. Thus confronted by an overwhelming influx, under which any poet might awaken only to be drowned, poets improvise their visionary autonomy and formulate myths of self-origination, which as improvisations remain necessarily provisional formulations against history, or the law of the fathers, or the importance of poetic precedent. Bloom's further restriction on the idealizing trajectory of Hegelian dialectic is to insist that the projected *telos* of his own dialectic can never be realized, even temporarily: no matter how hard a poet tries to convince herself of a self-sustaining visionary poetics, she can find no durable present or future in which poetic voice would be tantamount to autonomy.

Such a view of dialectic tends obliquely toward what we might call ethical priorities, again in the wider contemporary philosophical sense of ethics as a system of significations emerging on the basis of interpersonal or broadly relational concerns. It also translates historical determination into the interplay between definable persons or voices within a historical moment. Still, since any concession he makes to a non-poetic determination seems to be strictly psychological, I want to insist upon the following point and hereafter demonstrate its relevance: as was the case for Adorno, Benjamin, Marcuse, and Eduard Bernstein (the latter two cited in *A Map of Misreading*), for Bloom the psychological is by definition historical. In focusing this nexus between psychology and history through the discourse of ethics, and thereafter showing how such an ethics is at least in its theoretical potential also political, my method may stretch Bloomian theory, but certainly not to a breaking point. Indeed, even as I here suspend questions about the special social relevance or contextual determinations of poetic language within Bloom's theoretical model, a necessarily historical dimension of poetics emerges in my account via the simple fact that Bloom portrays the achievements of poetic voice as reliant upon a critical activity he takes to be distinctively diachronic.

A first point, made often enough by Bloom himself that I feel confident in proclaiming its centrality in his project, is simply that an element of critical consciousness preoccupies the possibility of poetic composition. Bloom distinguishes this critical consciousness from the devolutions into endless self-consciousness associated with modernism or the playful repetitions of postmodernism (since among other shortcomings such aesthetic strategies are far too manifestly manipulative to bespeak poetic originality), and he argues further that the critical procedure of poetic voice runs against the grain of any criticism finding in poetry vestiges of unacculturated voice or pure linguistic utterance, as it also belies any tendency to ally literature with a mythic, pre-social space. Even though the visionary supposition of poetic voice so fondly described by Bloom may proceed upon a delusive belief in the possibilities of self-creation, the poet's self-genetic hypothesis is always merely convenient and always also delusive. Indeed, even if poets adamantly resist critical awareness of the principles through which they struggle for poetic voice, their poetry is nothing if not illustrative of such critical strife. Much as Freud gives credence to a version of therapeutic remembrance actively bringing to light the drives by which one has been motivated without knowing it, Bloom interprets the critical reckoning of the strife by which poetry is created to be coextensive with the value and possibility of poetry itself. Not only would there be no poetry without such strife, poetry is itself the meaningfulness of that strife—not a byproduct, but rather a codetermined sign of the difficulty by which it comes into existence. The analogy between the critical procedure and Freudian remembrance as a therapeutic praxis is helpful, I think, if only because as Freud finds there to be so many other unconscious modes of remembrance relevant to the position of a subject (which are, by extension, also the cultural and ideological structurings of consciousness), Bloom similarly makes the poet symptomatic of a cultural complex. The greater part of this cultural complex is perceived, if perhaps defensively according to Bloom, through the poetic tradition itself. Lest poetic texts start to seem merely interchangeable with psychological pathologies, or poets with neurotic subjects failing to recognize the motives for their actions or the actions themselves, or perhaps that they have committed them, Bloomian theory suggests that every poet's disavowal of influence depends on a dialectical transumption of ancestral voice simultaneously littered with the self-betraying signs of remembrance. Unlike neurotics, poets are never merely symptoms of that which they cannot remember; they are much more subtly, albeit at times self-deceptively, engaged in an interpretive struggle by which they might be self-realized. Produced by dialectic, they are nevertheless those who extend dialectic as history—or in cultural terms, their texts constitute a site upon which dialectic gets extended as an active mode of historical consciousness. Or, put another way, every significant poem is a site, according to the dialectical principle of poetic tradition, that has to take account of the past as a significant, intrusive alterity.

2) The Otherness of Literary Memory

Nothing in the theoretical sketch I have thus far offered would require us to invoke the philosophical writings of Levinas. Bloom thoroughly avoids Levinas and there is nothing surprising in this, in so far as it corresponds neatly with the basic cultural narrative of Levinas' delayed importation into the United States. Still, there are obvious links. For instance, Levinas' and Bloom's respective indebtedness to Buber may actually contribute to prominent misperceptions that, for either author, culture might be distilled to and explicated by way of the sociality of personal relationship. The point is worth emphasizing, if only so as to prevent a reduction of my argument about the ethics of revisionism to a version of the slogan, often adopted by feminist criticism, that the personal is political. When Bloom routes a poet's access to her own voice through the elective relation to a precursor, the apparent equation of intertextuality to an interpersonal relationality might incline us to emphasize just such a narrowing focus, as though a poet's private struggle with another poet provided a breakthrough insight into her poetics. Indeed, the potential to read the revisionary struggle as focused largely upon a precursor of singular proportions (and Bloom often inclines toward just such a selective reading of intertextuality) might lead us to construe voice as personally conceived meaning, as though poetry, even in its dialectical dimension, were always intent on realigning itself with liberalism's basic mythologies.

By this same cultural logic in which the personal might seem self-sufficiently meaningful, we are cast back upon the long-standing opposition in Western cultural thinking, reified by Hegel's *Phenomenology*, between ethics and politics. This basic antinomy informs Jameson's representatively Marxist rejection of ethics, and by it we would attribute to ethics even in its late theoretical, largely revisionist phase a focus upon the cultural unease of the bourgeois subject—ethics as a mild alternative or antidote to the Freudian couch. Alain Badiou has raised just such objections against ethics and, specifically, against the Levinasian project, suggesting that the respect for otherness encouraged by contemporary ethics coincides with the trajectory of a liberal culture focused on rights, which are themselves nothing more than privileges of identity evolved on behalf of the power-brokers of Western liberal culture. By this line of critique, to invoke a respect for the other as a corrective to the apparent solipsism of poetic voice would do little to alter the prominent perception that the ethical field in Bloom's theoretical paradigm is personal to the exclusion of politics.[10] Intriguingly on this point, Lentricchia's famous critique of Bloom, although constitutively Marxist in method, faults Bloom, as the supremely self-stylized Romanticist, for his failure to meet the terms of a normatively defined Shelleyan ethics. Lentricchia reminds us that Shelley, representing the public-mindedness of the Romantic poets, argued in the *Defence* for poetry as a "great instrument of moral good," imparting empathy and encouraging a mode of consciousness, general in its sympathies, which was notably "un-unique and un-particular" (330). By which standard, Bloom is "so far from touching on the principles of the ethical life that one might suppose that he had deliberately emptied Romantic poetics of all ethical implication;" for in refusing a sense of ethics premised on "awareness of, and respect for, the other's

---

[10] Bloom's highly antithetical posture with regard to any association of literature and morality makes him especially resistant to a mode of so-called Levinasian interpretation that would yield a reverence for others. Badiou has accused ethics conceived in this vein as offering nothing more than pietistic commonplaces, which lack any real opposition to status-quo Western imperialistic and late capitalistic politics. But Levinas' own exposition of ethics as the neglected first philosophical ground of Western phenomenological and ontological traditions reduces neither to a gesture of respect for others nor to a voluntary suspension of the subjective will in its encounter with a resistant, oppressed other. See Badiou, *Ethics*, esp. 18–29; and see my response to Badiou's critique of Levinas in *Vigilant Memory*.

sanctity," he imagines for us poets who move in "the ethically barbarous world of the child" (330).[11]

Ethics as the praxis of empathy and as a corrective for solipsism is not a sufficient reading, I want to insist, of the ways in which ethical responsibility works. What gives ethics priority for Levinas, as I have argued in *Vigilant Memory* (2006), is the significatory value of the other that conditions the field of culture and politics, anterior to without being preemptive of the analyses of existence we render through phenomenology, ontology, epistemology, psychology or sociology. What is most ethical within Bloom's model of intertextuality retains this emphasis on a structural relation to alterity, since all the poet's efforts to make it seem otherwise can be reduced neither to the immediately describable dimensions of an interpersonal relationship nor to the egoistically connoted significances of poetic voice. If we took a slogan such as 'the personal is political' to mean (as some users of the phrase have doubtless intended) that the personal has always to be read vis-à-vis the political—either as a site of cultural meanings never bereft of political significance, or as a sphere of relationship determined by superstructural and infrastructural aspects of society and thus likewise determinative of a person's mode of relating to political systems—then there is perhaps nothing remiss in describing ethics as a field that privileges an always uncancellable unit of particularity, namely, the dyadic relation to that other who preoccupies every personal situation and invests it with an already political importance.

The most obvious common ground between Levinasian ethics and Bloomian intertextuality is Derrida, who proves for each to be a source of some ambivalence. In so far as Derrida stands for the theoretical progress of the rule of *langue* and for a poststructuralist emphasis on

---

[11] Without arguing explicitly for a rapprochement between ethics and politics, Lentricchia adopts a strategy informing the use of ethics, as Geoffrey Galt Harpham has demonstrated, such that the language of ethics gets deployed within late twentieth-century theory as complement and rhetorical force for a wide-ranging trajectory of methods, surfacing in flourishes and sometimes bombastically moralistic flashes that characterize the ideological bias of a critic or theorist's own method. The ground upon which Lentricchia locates a backsliding tendency in Bloom's theory is its reification of private voice. For Lentricchia, Bloom's ultimate failing is to have willingly enfolded himself back within the individualistic mythology of literary genius as the last of the literary metaphysicians of great poetry, and his willingness to embrace the solipsistic ego of the poet and interpretive critic alike cannot take us beyond a view of literature as the product of "egocentric privacy" (345).

synchronic systems that seem complete unto themselves, his contribution for both Bloom and Levinas is a dubious one. From a political standpoint, what any totalizing synchronic system might suggest, as Levinas worries in "The Ego and the Totality" (1954), prior to his philosophical encounter with Derrida, is that an ego's necessary participation in society can be interpreted as though particularity were inherently a position in a totality: "Generalization is death; it inserts the ego into, and dissolves it in, the generality of its work."[12] This also is the central problem of language as a function of knowledge: the conceptual structure governing knowledge absorbs, consumes, or sublimates the ego into the social positions of a universal order, exhausting the alterity of the interlocutor as of the third party. The solution, however, is not to recoil upon the particular, personal point of reference as a self-sufficient corrective to impersonal politics. Defining particularity via the alterity of the other, which cannot simply be overlooked for a truth embedded in philosophical concepts or for political utilitarianisms deciphering moral value as though persons were numbers, Levinas espouses a tension which is in fact (although he is loath to use the term) *dialectical*, in the sense that the challenge of the other in any apparently narrowed interpersonal moment demarcates the resistant significance of alterity within the universal order of language and society.

By foregrounding Levinas' explicit response to Derridean *écriture*, what I hope partly to suggest are the ways in which Bloom's critique of Derrida focuses on concerns about language that run parallel to key aspects of contemporary ethical discourse such as we find it in Levinas. The analysis of language as a system is, of course, central to the legacy of Saussure. And in one sense Derrida inherits Saussurean linguistics in a manner diametrically opposed to Levinas' own response to structuralist linguistics and phenomenology, since where Derrida chooses to extend the differential, arbitrary attributes of the system *langue* by foregrounding the privilege of *écriture* within all language use, Levinas instead focuses on the extra-linguistic source of signification, on the other who cannot be fully assimilated into language. From the Levinasian standpoint, our constant temptation is to discern the other's meaning as perfectly consistent with an act of representation always written for us in advance by the order of *langue*, and this hypothesis of what Levinas calls *adequation* is only strengthened by a fact Levinas fully concedes,

---

[12] Levinas, "The Ego and the Totality" 36 See also Fabio Ciaramelli 83–105.

that the other's signification must take place within the realm of the *Said* (Levinas' term, at least partly indebted to *parole*, for synchronic language). Even as Levinas takes exception to the order of representation for necessarily betraying the transcendent significance of the other by which the very act of signification is inspired, he does not advocate a hypothetical exemption from universalizing language or from the preeminence of reason, as though particularity or historical situatedness might be liberated by virtue of pure contingency from its structural determinations.[13]

Levinas elevates the construct of *Saying*, as a point of priority and resistance to the representational terrain of language, at least partly in response to Derrida's provocation, and in *Otherwise Than Being* (1974), specifically, Levinas argues for the necessary interdependence of two aspects of language, the one (Saying) proceeding from the side of diachrony, the other (the Said) from synchrony. The priority Levinas gives to Saying depends crucially on the prestige of diachrony. Whereas synchrony is assembled time, and the realm of representation (the Said) its site of assembly, Levinas insists that diachrony is primordial time, time in its tendency to lapse from the moment, the immemorial tendency of time intimating what has already escaped our grasp. Levinas' logic becomes a bit hermetic in so far as he uses three terms—the other (*autrui*), Saying, and diachrony—as proofs of one another. Saying takes its inspiration from the face-to-face dimension of signification, which always occurs in relation to the other. As a testament to the signifying force of alterity,

---

[13] Levinas' commitment to a phenomenology evolved in light of structuralist insights into language brings him within the orb of Derrida's critical linguistics, and at least partly to this end Simon Critchley, in *The Ethics of Deconstruction*, has traced the interdependence of the Levinasian and Derridean projects by way of their explicit and implicit responses to one another. In Derrida's "Violence and Metaphysics," the essay largely responsible for introducing Levinas to the English–speaking world, Derrida deconstructed Levinas' break with Husserlian phenomenology and Heideggerian ontology by exposing Levinas' violent distortions of his precursors' arguments while showing how his philosophical terms were yet beholden to the very metaphysical models of ontology with which he was purportedly breaking. A few years later, in the essay "Wholly Otherwise," Levinas was to return the favor by performing, as Critchley demonstrates, a clotural reading *à la* Derrida that redounded the very charge Derrida brought against Levinas back upon the Derridean project and further suggested the harmony between Levinasian ethics and a critical assessment of the workings of language.

speech "proceeds from absolute difference."[14] So too Saying corresponds to diachrony as the anterior order of time, and what concretizes the priority of diachrony for us, as Simon Critchley emphasizes, is precisely the "everyday event of my responsibility for the Other" (166). In this way, language has a priority that is specifically not written or representational, or even expressive of meaning in the Husserlian sense, and the problem here, as also with skepticism's functional relation to philosophy, is how this non-representational priority of language is to take place in a coherent synchronic system corresponding to the contemporary order of cultural knowledge. By way of an interruption, is Levinas' answer.[15] A fissure referred to an anterior time nonetheless real for its impossible-to-realize significance preoccupies the possibility of language; and this devolves the ethical situatedness of speech. Thus Levinas concentrates on the structural core of the communicative transaction, the significance of the face-to-face that bears the meaning of an excess and promise inscribed on every act of signification.

The antinomy of *Saying/Said* does not boil down to an opposition between the orality of language and the representational function of writing, yet there is nevertheless in Levinas a connotative force of orality overflowing language by way of the transcendent force of alterity, as the other's commanding status inclines the subject toward a vocative mode of address and inserts her within an interlocutive priority that situationally characterizes all language. Indeed, according to Critchley, the interruptive force of Saying is performative, in the sense that it elicits its own significance and describes the parameters of the ethical relation. A turn to orality, or return to oral tradition, is the very move Bloom makes on Derrida's *écriture*. What Levinas attributes to language under the name of *Saying*, that aspect of language conditioned by the other before whom every *I* becomes significant and for whom every language act is dedicated in advance, Bloom perceives in the

---

[14] As Levinas says, "The Other remains infinitely transcendent, infinitely foreign; his face in which his epiphany is produced and which appeals to me breaks with the world that can be common to us, whose virtualities are inscribed in our *nature* and developed by our existence. Speech proceeds from absolute difference" (*Totality and Infinity* 194, hereafter *TI*). For Levinas' theorization of Saying as the ethical condition of signification anterior to the written or representational Said of language, see Emmanuel Levinas, *Otherwise Than Being*, 5–9 and 31–51.

[15] As Critchley aptly puts it, "The Saying shows itself within the said by interrupting it" (164).

interpersonal *agon* determining poetic voice, so that for Bloom, as for Levinas, a provocation of otherness begets the vocation of voice. Bloom's agonistic scenario also depends on the fraughtness of a scene of instruction, bringing every user of language, poets most resistantly of all, into culture. In one sense, Derrida serves to reinforce Bloom's impulse to make the determinative element in the struggle for expression always textual, to fill as it were the bereftness of the present via a fullness residing elsewhere. In Bloom such fullness is strictly antecedent, whereas for Derrida it is the result of a deferral in time such that the hypothesis of present meaning depends largely on a text's supplemental rhetorical gestures, by which paradox the written aspect of writing or text stands to fill in its own gaps. Bloom then proceeds to his contrastive reading: for what "Jacques Derrida calls the Scene of Writing," Bloom says, "depends itself upon a Scene of Teaching, and poetry is crucially pedagogical in its origins and function" (*Map* 32). Whereas Derrida privileges the written word over orality and deconstructs all metaphysical gestures as indebted to the irrevocably ambiguous play of signification and written representation, Bloom argues for the primacy of literature as a scene of instruction and transmission, thus attributing to the word a more active, practical sense. For Bloom, our greatest literary texts hold the memory of orality and are themselves acts in the world, not merely the passive recipients or reflections of language, culture, or ideology.[16]

Performing a deft exegesis of Derrida in *A Map of Misreading*, Bloom perceives how writing would become in Derrida the site of its own primal scene of instruction. At the center of Bloom's brilliant involution of *écriture* is Derrida's own "dazzling essay" on "Freud and the Scene of Writing," in which Derrida supersedes the defensive function of repression as a reaction to the hypothetical primal scene by means of an extraordinary hyperbole. Bloom has just insisted, in a strong reading of Freud, upon a point "Freud may not have cared to understand," that primal scenes, as fantasy traumas determining the psyche, finally

[16] The importance Bloom attributes to the scene of teaching, for example, relies explicitly on a Jewish notion of oral tradition, by means of which Bloom oddly recasts much of the English and American literary tradition, but his most significant, agonistic interlocutor on this point is Derrida. Despite Bloom's claim that literature will not teach us anything and his dismissal in *The Western Canon* of any attempt to align literature with normative values (24–35), he repeatedly employs the verb "to teach" to describe what literature does do, most significantly in his articulation of a "Scene of Teaching" (*Map* 41–62).

require an imagination that "has no referential aspect" (*Map* 48); and in Derrida he perceives a partly parallel scenario in so far as Derrida reads Freud as returning us to models borrowed not from oral tradition or referentiality, but from an absent script, or as Bloom says, "a performance of writing that is at play in all verbal representation" (48). By this ingenious reading of Freud's rhetoric, Derrida has gone Jacques Lacan one step further in revising the governing principle of repression—from the logic of the unconscious (Freud) to a linguistically determined structure (Lacan) to writing itself (Derrida). Writing becomes nothing less than the grandest of tropes, and the Derridean system, with its astute revisionary hermeneutics, starts to sound vaguely Bloomian. Or, as Bloom summarizes Derrida, "[p]sychical life thus is no longer to be represented as a transparency of meaning nor as an opacity of force but as an intra-textual difference in the conflict of meanings and the exertion of forces" (48). It is writing that perfectly requires the mechanism of repression, and thus, as memory recedes to such an extent that the referential capacity of language becomes nearly nil, writing in Derrida's estimation structures the forward movement of culture.

Bloom does not believe, however, either that the tradition of writing can ever fully free itself from its oral premises or that writing possesses sufficient cause within itself to elicit the defensive response against origins that every primal scene of instruction must be about. Contesting Derrida by way of a divergent reading of Freud, but also by virtue of the implicit claims of Jewish oral tradition and the Western poetic tradition, Bloom supposes that only speech retains enough primal force to preside over scenes of instruction, which as acts of transmission are "at least quasi-religious [in their] associations" (50).[17]

---

[17] There is more at work here than dubious metaphysics. In crediting Derrida with ingeniously substituting *écriture* for an interpersonal, if unconsciously structured *agon*, Bloom already supposes (as though Derrida's writing were serving the transformative cause of the trope in Hayden White's typology) that this perception is revisionary, dependent on writing as a specific kind of trope (namely hyperbole) that stands in for Derrida's own Nietzschean willfulness. For Derrida writing is a kind of belatedness, behind which there is no longer any anterior presence, whereas for Bloom orality retains the prestige of originality or self-present signification. Thus, in an era after the prestige of oral tradition, which retained for poetry the memory of its origins and the practical if not necessary means of its authority, poets must recreate visionary possibility for themselves through parallel, improvised fictions of origin. For Bloom the oral tradition, by supposing a continuity about which it is supremely unanxious, pronounces itself as finally not our own, even while offering to teach us a lesson about the inevitable prestige of origins upon which every

In *Of Grammatology* (1967), Derrida imagines that a rupture occurs with the advent of writing, such that the place of memory gets usurped by the ever-erasable, self-constituted presence of writing as a hypothetically synchronic whole. In effect, Derrida incorporates temporality into the act of writing, perceiving the claim of presence to be built not only upon the differential play of language within a system but also on the temporality that inheres, in deferral or via the trace, in every representative claim. There is a challenge to synchrony in all of this, far greater than any Saussure was able to imagine. Yet Bloom, and here he comes close to Levinas, insists upon an aspect of diachrony exterior to the act of writing. The poet is in time and given to time no matter how hard she might resist an awareness of this, and we might even go so far as to say that Bloom's primal scene of instruction, which is always about a myth of origin and the psychic/poetic subject's defensive response to it, purports to be that which temporalizes the creative impulse.

If critical consciousness, experienced in poets as belatedness, suggests that every visionary claim is, from what we know of the psyche, only an elaborate defense mechanism against priority, so too every psychic defense is nothing more than a trope against time. A poem is a proposition of mythic synchrony, and yet in our knowledge of poetic tradition we always recognize it also for something else, perhaps even chiefly for its diversionary reading of its own basic inter-relationality. Always as much a scene of instruction as of repression, the Bloomian construed primal scene traces a basic longing for the original act (rendered in fantasy as the site of one's own origin), even as it also charts the competitive, instinctual, or imaginative urge for displacement of the father figure. All of this centers on the plight of diachrony. Poets may magnificently condense and reconstitute a vaster diachronic

---

tradition is constructed and the subsequent progress through repetition by which it is necessarily diminished. Nevertheless, as Lentricchia emphasizes, Bloom draws freely on metaphysics, especially in so far as his clever transpositions of problems pertaining to Jewish oral tradition onto scenes of poetic priority might trace a Hebraic ambivalence about the revelatory authority of a God who is already primogenitively a masked presence. From an early point, however, a revisionary tradition (sometimes apocryphal, sometimes Kabbalistic) ran parallel to the Talmudic tradition of teaching, and Bloom supposes that the revisionary tradition, never satisfied with the anonymity of inherited authority and already experiencing the lapse in relevance, structures all modern consciousness. For a discussion of Bloom's relation to sacred writing, see Hartman 42–62; and for a skeptical view of Bloom's tendency toward an esoteric Gnosticism which is productively contrasted to Hartman's own reading of the gnostic tendency within Romanticism, see Lentricchia 336-41.

anxiety as though it were focused on a seemingly atemporalized precursor poem, and they may even reconceive intertextuality as though it were an invented proposition of intra-textuality, as Bloom follows them part way in their delusions; yet the improvised suppositions of dyadic singularity (an aspiring ephebe who pairs himself with a monumental father-poet) that interpret poetic tradition are also demarcated as defenses against temporal invasion. This is also to say that they reveal a profound anxiety about alterity.

An ethics of literary revisionism, I am proposing, must turn finally on the analogy between the belated writer's anxious apprehension of a precursor text and the *real-life* ethical scenario in which the speaking subject is already signified by, but also becoming conscious of, the relation to the other. In this respect a hypothesis of interpersonality, which in language is fundamentally dependent upon an inter-relational structure, could properly take its cues from Bloom's diachronically conflicted model of intertextuality. I am not suggesting that there is in Bloom anything like an honorific notion of the other as an ethical force who must be reckoned with. The relation to the other is signally unpleasurable in Bloom, and poetry does all it can to swerve from the source of its provocation. Yet as I have argued elsewhere, this unpleasurable function of signification—derived as the signifying force of the shock of injustice—is one of Levinas' most persistent motifs for figuring relation to the other.[18] At least part of the forcefulness of unpleasure as an ethical phenomenon would derive from the quality of diachrony embedded in it, which is a temporal dissonance preventing any self from becoming reconciled to itself or its world. All of which is the consequence of the static generated by the other, who is always in the way of the present in so far as the present is tantamount to a self-justifying state of existence.

In Bloom, the hermeneutical force of unpleasure is overtly Freudian. He imagines the tropes of literary revisionism as analogous to the defenses of the psyche precisely because the sway of a precursor (or threatening other) impinges on the freedom of the belated writer or reader: "This anxiety is impossible to distinguish from defense, for such anxiety is itself a shield against every provocation from otherness. Indeed, such anxiety itself has priority; it does not exist under the reign

---

[18] For a discussion of the relation between ethics, unpleasure, and psychic or cultural economy, and for subsequent discussion of Levinas' emphasis on ethics as inequivalence in ways that resemble Freud's notion of unpleasure as a violation of psychic economy, see Spargo, *The Ethics of Mourning* 120–27 and 168–72.

of the pleasure principle" (*Map* 90). An anxiety about otherness, Bloom declares, apparently tracing in reverse Freud's peculiar formulation of unpleasure as an inundation of new experiences, is operative at every moment in our existence within speech, especially in the inception of poetry as speech's most original, which is to say tropologically inventive, mode. By this model, the reception of otherness is always potentially overwhelming.[19] At the same time, it suggests the urgency of a history that must be coped with in proportion to its renewable function in the present. If we were not so historical in our consciousness, if culture were not the aggregate of histories we live even as we fail to remember them, the threat of the past would not seem so devastating to poets. The insight here is Emersonian, and Bloom repeatedly cites Emerson's attempted swervings from the indomitable past. Poets might attain visionary language without such historical consciousness, Bloom intimates, but their cultural unrealism would in all probability marginalize their relevance. As a compromise formation, then, his model of wrestling with influence—not just hermeneutically but by revisionistically trying to carve out space for the sake of original truths—posits a severe otherness operative within literary history. Inasmuch as historical consciousness is not merely the function of a subject's projective present-tense desire or of her complicity with the status quo of knowledge in a contemporary cultural system, history remains significant as a dissonance or an alterity. In short, history signifies ethically under the aspect of relationship.

To theorize poetry as contestation, as though the scene of instruction founding poetic tradition were also that against which poets must vehemently defend themselves, hardly seems an obvious ground for ethics. But by describing such a model of apparent struggle as ethical, we accomplish at least two things: 1) we separate ethics from idealizing valuations that by distorting or pleasantly underestimating the difference of the other from the subject's desire might limit the possibility of a genuinely political response to the other; and 2) we require ourselves to concede that ethics as a discourse demands from us the capacity to yield our presumptions about, and hypothetical transumptions of, other people. In perceiving an ethics even in *agon*, I am suggesting then that revisionary responses to the past entail a crucial ethical possibility—specifically, that of admitting the importance of an anterior voice, poetic representation, or cultural paradigm without simply acceding to

---

[19] See Freud, *Beyond the Pleasure Principle* 12–17.

a cultural or literary vision as to a different way of understanding the world. This emphasis on the conflictual nature of truth, which is fundamental to both the Hegelian and Marxist dialectics, has a place in all dialectical thought. What becomes most signally ethical about it is the relative failure of the transumptive or appropriative trajectory of dialectic. In deconstructive postcolonialism, for instance, this has meant valuing precisely those people who prove recalcitrant in their subalternity, in their resistantly unmodern ways, or in their hypothetical regressiveness from if not always overt opposition to the progressive dialectic of Western culture. Bloom, much like Levinas, deploys Judaic modes of consciousness for their slant or resistant relation to the incessantly redemptive ideology of the Christianized West; and by attributing to the great poets not so much the capacity to make us better or shape our future as to trouble us, even while we attempt to overhear ourselves, Bloom values the past for its fundamentally diachronic relation to any present-tense design we make on language.

The anti-idealizing nature of Bloom's project gives place to otherness not as that which might be perfectly subsumed by the successful work of art, but as that which persists as an authentic provocation of the poet's voice and, despite avoidance or swerving, repression or regression, returns as a forcible perception in the belated text. This is Bloom's most significant revision of all previous formulations of literary influence, which are based, as he sees it, in a falsely pious paradigm of generosity. By taking the precursor as a metonymy for tradition, Bloom suggests that the relation to tradition is not a romance of sameness in which writers seek to find a meaningful home, but rather an interpersonally troped wrestling with otherness—all tradition becoming, in Bloom's words, "indistinguishable from making mistakes about anteriority" (*Kabbalah* 103). Diachrony, as the authentic sign of language, persists especially in these mistakes. Every modern poet enters into poetry, Bloom supposes, under the sign of a belatedness, with an anxiety about belatedness that is not a nostalgic longing for tradition so much as a description, much like Levinas' account of the ethical structure determining all language, of the inevitable relationality presiding over signification itself.

3) " The Sufferings of History:" Is There Any Substitute for Reality?

No matter how much ethical credit we give to the provocation of alterity within the Bloomian model of sociality, it is nevertheless apparent that the supreme model for otherness in Bloom, as in Freud, is intergenerational and paternalistic. Although Bloom's hyper-literary theory of influence might be returned to historical meanings, it seems overly committed not only to the narrow, bourgeois conception of Freud's individualized subject but also to Freud's own overinvestment in patriarchy. Even so, Bloom's commitment to a quasi-Freudian anthropology must be recognized (much as Lacan had argued on Freud's behalf) for its keenly critical description of the patriarchal moorings of society. The law of the father gets written in Bloom as in Freud largely as a mode of cultural realism, from which any demystificatory account of origins and repressive complexes within society must begin. For this reason, while Bloom's project was still slanted heavily toward demystifying the mechanisms of literary culture (circa 1973–1988), it seemed compatible with thoroughgoing critiques of Western cultural traditions and even methodologically adoptable by feminists, such as Sandra M. Gilbert and Susan Gubar in *The Madwoman in the Attic* (1979), who were struggling to liberate women's voices from the necessarily agonistic determinations of patriarchy. What Bloom shares with several generations of mid-twentieth scholars also under the sway of Freud, including figures from the Frankfurt School such as Adorno and Marcuse, is a belief in the fundamental conflict between ordinary existence and superstructural sociality, or between what we believe we want for ourselves and those ideological workings of desire that really determine us. Civilization, in its inherently repressive function, generates discontentedness not as the accidental byproduct of thwarted desire but according to the processes by which society is advanced.[20] In Bloom this means that the precursor

---

[20] Those tempted to assign Bloom the role of social conservative might do well to recall the basic tension in his mythopoetics: though there is a liberatory idiom at work in Bloom and his Nietzschean emphases yield the impression that by providing a quasi-genealogical description of poetic voice Bloom might deliver literature altogether from piety as from its freighted past, he assumes that the cultural workings of repression can no more be bypassed than the repressed contents of our civilization can be allowed to have freeplay. As Daniel O'Hara has suggested, Bloom's refusal to believe that cultural ancestors and literary forefathers can be so readily refused promotes a political regressiveness in his work. Much as the Freudian superego can be described according to its historic alignment with the peculiarly limited conscience of the bourgeois subject and shown further to be inscribed within the larger imperialistic project of Western culture as well as other reified aspects of the status quo functionings of power, Bloom's esteem for the greatness of the dead poet, who is archetypically and literary-historically male in Bloomian theory, must cooperate with such an ideological order to the extent that

poet is by extension a figure for the ambivalence presiding over every subject's entrance into language and culture, which demands a begrudging acknowledgment that the poet as subject cannot readily do as he wants or cannot simply say what she wishes if only because her own words are always necessarily derivative, at least until she provisionally makes them her own.

As I have already emphasized, Bloomian revisionism elicits a critical consciousness about poetry's diachronic debts. In simplest terms, the task of the modern critic is to expose the conflicts that determine the plot of poetic creation and thus to make the writing of poetry, as the poet partakes of such critical consciousness, a more difficult act. And yet even as poetry abides by Bloom's culturally realistic terms (subjected against a poet's own desire to the laws of poetic fathers), there is no inherent reason that the critical consciousness contained within each poem, signified especially by poetic tropes functioning as defensive strategies, should translate into a mode of cultural criticism. The relation between the praxis of literary criticism and the function of cultural critique is consistently obfuscated by Bloom. And yet the literary sensibility is conceived as representative of a cultural phenomenon: coming after belief and the visionary potential of myth, we have become for better or worse literary beings, conscious of the extent to which our enterprises in meaning are the consequence of interpretive will, symptomatic of a pragmatic, post-moral decadence pertaining to Western culture at large. For Bloom literary language is a privileged locus, if only by degree, for the cultural work performed by rhetoric, especially revealing the active or transformative rhetorical function of tropes. And even

> Bloom also fails to identify an imaginative space outside of such patrilinear contestation. Then again, the same might be said in slightly different terms for the theories of Adorno, Marcuse, Lacan, or Foucault, to name but these few, in so far as any of these thinkers insist upon the political continuity of power even while formulating theories of resistance to it, or in so far as any theoretical description of the political and cultural subject must be evolved, as Judith Butler has suggested, through the philosophically articulated function of subjection. And it is worth noting that, especially during his high theoretical phase, Bloom admires the young or belated poet's struggles to be released from the repressive mechanisms of culture. This is what Bloom finds to be so admirably naive and Romantic about the American poetic tradition: American poets, who as the product of a belated Western nation are the most belated of all poets, yet believe preposterously in their own originality. Slaying the notion of influence, which Emerson made an implausible doctrine of American poetry, they proceed in a trajectory that can never altogether succeed. See Butler, *The Psychic Life of Power* 83–105.

as any trope swerves from the codified, dead-metaphorical dimension of language, or in Hayden White's scheme from the co-determinative expectations of genre and ideology—functioning, in other words, as a site upon which conventional meaning is averted and an original or transformative ground of meaning sought—literary language is that specialized cultural domain granting license to the full significatory possibility of tropes. By extension, literary criticism—as the demystified praxis of reading the relationality, conflict, and tropological deviations that perpetuate language—must also serve as a kind of cultural criticism.

The question I would ask, then, is whether the principle of alterity at work in Bloomian poetics, traced via the function of diachronic resistances in literary tradition, can be regarded as more than merely analogous to the structure of ethics with which I have associated them. In short, does an ethics of revisionism pertaining to the intertextual dynamics of the literary text also produce itself as an act of cultural criticism? In order to answer this question in the affirmative, my first supposition (argued in the previous section) has been that diachrony is generative of a mode of historical consciousness produced under the provocation of the other. History occurs, in this case as a mode of the literary text, in the response to an interlocutor who is less than or more than synchronous with the present order and whose meaning, for a variety of reasons, including all the basic structural limitations on transparency that inhere in language systems, cannot be simply translated, appropriated, or transumed by the subject. A second supposition, which I assert now, is that the peculiar priority precipitated by the diachronic provocation of the other within the present-tense referentiality of a social system, or as a function of the representational project of language, is the relation to injustice.

It matters a great deal, I thus suppose, whether our notions about the functionings of culture within the political system begin as an elaboration of some purportedly extant justice, requiring liberal or reformative modifications to be brought to its already working potential, or instead refer to the facticity of injustice upon which the extant social order is constructed, so that justice is imbricated with and indeed deeply compromised by its coextensive relation to the data of injustice. At the purely conceptual level, we could say of the Western liberal society (drawing, for example, upon the political theory of John Rawls) that it is the accustomed habit of any liberally defined social system to treat the extant ordering of social and political relations as though they were premised on justice. Regardless of the wide array of structural injustices we might name (which include, to cite only a few of the most obviously persistent themes of politicized cultural criticism, the persistent structures of racism within liberal society; the severe economic oppression produced as a historical consequence and the present political praxis of Western imperialistic, capitalistic, and late capitalistic political orders; or the severe gender inequities built upon the history of woman's oppression under patriarchal political systems), justice would be conceived as though it were fundamentally synchronic, inhering conceptually in the order of law already evolved within a given society while proceeding in cooperation with the power structure of the nation-state whence and from within which any citizen speaks. The facticity of injustice, uttered as a term evolved by the liberal paradigm of justice, might at its most extreme force us to confront a dialectical contradiction of the Hegelian sort, in which the forward momentum of the political system and its always implicit systemic trajectory already predicts an overcoming of resistant data (those obtrusive facts of injustice). In such a view, injustice is often stubborn, but hardly recalcitrant. It does not force those who adhere to an extant political system to a process of self-questioning that might eventually threaten the foundational premise of the cultural-political system itself.

Yet the fact of injustice might also be framed differently in our analysis of the workings of culture and political systems, so that not only would we acknowledge injustice as a structurally integral part of the system from within which we name it, but we would prove susceptible to its contradictory influence upon our lives and the political systems upon which we thrive. The fact that injustice seems to occur as an event from outside of justice might imply our relation to what the present social order has specifically eliminated from consideration, and demand moreover that we question how justice characteristically casts the province of its own neglect, and the specific consequences of its structurally determined oppressions, to the outside, as though the poor, the victims of violence, the victims of racism and gendered persecution had always to present themselves at the door of culture as strangers, needing to be newly considered as potential claimants upon an extant system and its purported integrity. This is the emphasis I give here to injustice, supposing the memory of injustice to be fundamental to any revaluation of justice, or in this case the justness of the literary text. Only by means of a radical adjustment in the construct of justice itself, such that injustice is the reciprocally determining meaning of the very construct of justice, can we come to be ethically centered upon that which is inherently less than just in the present social order. I have argued along these lines with regard to Levinas' philosophical writings elsewhere (specifically, in *Vigilant Memory*), and I wish here only to assert the close link between the diachronic determinations of ethics and a vigilance about injustice, proceeding upon the basis of that assertion to illustrate my case for the relevance of the figure of injustice in Bloom, specifically with regard to Bloom's diachronically driven model of intertextuality.

In the Levinasian view, even an individual's particular suffering functions under the sign of the fundamental non-meaning of another person's suffering, and as such it simultaneously designates the responsibility that befalls us through another person's experience of oppression or misfortune. The quality of excess in all responsibility is what gives to Levinasian ethics its peculiarly unpleasurable slant and also generates the aspect of critique that I have argued is endemic to ethics. To the extent that we work with the facts as they are thus far assembled, culture as the expression of an extant political system would determine what we call our cultural realism, but our conventional discourse for reality is always also a substitute for reality in its excesses, those data we cannot imaginatively entail and those responsibilities we perhaps do not wish to answer for in our immediate experience of obligation. Ethics, then, is the sphere of relationality within culture demanding that we look beyond the present ordering of social relations so as to be obligated also by what has been excluded. And even as the raw data of injustice inspires a critique by means of which a normative construct of justice is indicted or deemed not good enough, these occurrences seemingly from outside justice's conventional parameters must still be accounted for as consequences of extant political, so-called just systems, which is to say, by way of an ethics that generates acts of cultural criticism.

To return to Bloom, then, in my theoretical formulation of injustice, I obviously suppose there to be a crucial interdependence between injustice and the theoretical elucidation of otherness, and I have further suggested that the diachronic dissonances within Bloom's theory are the peculiar locus for a sense of alterity that delineates, via Bloom's psychological and seemingly interpersonal model, a historicized, ethical sense of relationship. But does it really make sense for me to propose the facticity of injustice as integral to those resonances of Bloomian intertextuality I have here deemed to be surprisingly, persistently ethical?

Obviously I want to answer yes, and in doing so I might point for starters to Bloom's description of poetic tradition as paradoxically dependent upon the tyrannical injustice of the father figure. In the agonistic revisionism of Bloom, influence itself is a kind of injustice. It is a persecuting sway of consciousness forcing a relationship to the past or to a peculiar precedent that serves as an imaginative fount of both inspiration and malevolence.[21] Admittedly, since the tyranny of the father figure signifies more psychologically than politically, more literarily than culturally, there is a danger in Bloom (as in Freud) of so psychologizing the origins of suffering that we make little distinction between the ordinary plights of subjectivity (which is always in Freudian theory predicated upon a traumatic entry into language and culture) and the desperate political marginality and suffering of those who within any extant social order are radically alienated from it or cast altogether outside its privileges. Nevertheless, in so far as Bloom's description of the father occupies the symbolic, structural place of an injustice, it preserves within poetics (perhaps not through Bloom's explicit intentions) a space for the memory of injustice in a more radical sense, as a mode of suffering pertaining to the experiences of the politically tyrannized or oppressed.

A second kind of emphasis on injustice within Bloomian theory occurs near the beginning of *A Map of Misreading*, where Bloom is surprisingly explicit about the way in which his poetics points, if obliquely, toward larger socio-historical consequences:

> The strong reader, whose readings will matter to others as well as to himself, is thus placed in the dilemmas of the revisionist, who wishes to find his own original relation to truth, whether in texts or in reality (which he treats as texts anyway), but also wishes to open received texts to his own sufferings, or what he wants to call the sufferings of history. (3-4)

---

[21] By the rule of diachrony, Bloomian poetics interprets an implicit yet necessary violence in our relationship to the past, rather than mystifyingly enfolding the past (*à la* Eliot) into the present order. The necessary defensiveness inscribed upon the poet/misreader's reception of literary tradition presumes the basically unpleasurable challenge of the past, which to be overcome must first be characterized as an injustice. Again, this contradiction always operative within literary tradition would be Hegelian if Bloom did not suppose the contradiction also to be largely irreconcilable. Poets do not win in seeking to overcome literary history with their only purportedly self-invented visionariness. As they labor to be free of their own conflicted inspiration, history, like literature, remains significant under this aspect of otherness, as a burden which must still be received.

The ambiguity of the concluding clause depends not only on the good faith of the subject's reading of history, but also on whether we suppose, according to this metonymic substitution of text for reality, that one projects one's own sufferings onto history or reads history into one's sufferings. Yet the psychological reading of personally connoted sufferings does not outreach the historical density of the phrase, which stubbornly clings, if only figuratively, to the historical scene of political injustice.[22] The corollary to the fact that sufferings belong to history (and not, for instance, to our personal or poetic memory) is that history itself becomes significant under the aspect of suffering. Although Bloom finds it impossible to imagine a collective idea of the "sufferings of history" not predicated upon the memory of our individual sufferings, the poet or strong reader reads in her own sufferings a meaning of history *qua* suffering that is not speculatively supposed about history so much as imposed by it. The initial admission of the tyrannical dimensions of the poetic tradition facilitates in this sense a cultural critique of what we might call the social poetics of injustice. Much as poetic tradition functions as a continuity with the past that we must read demystifyingly for what it carries over both of the past's injustice, so too the facticity of injustice must be read for the way it is framed by dialectical contradictions between social systems and their intended and purportedly unintended consequences. Within literary hermeneutics, in so far as they are not only informed by but also generative of cultural hermeneutics, it may be the explicitly dialectical space of intertextuality, especially in its resistant, revisionist emphasis, that yields insights into the ways literature is embedded in oppressive systems and how it comments on them.

---

[22] As an objective genitive, the "sufferings of history" oddly implies that our suffering is an extension of our desire to be historical. If the immediate is the realm of pleasure and satisfaction, our existence untroubled by time or fully within time (according to the synchrony of the extant system), it is nevertheless precisely because we exist in time and under the notice of our death and the death of others that we suffer. Read the other way, as a subjective genitive (i.e., as *history's sufferings*), the phrase means that personal experience gets interpreted via the objective data of others' historical sufferings, those sufferings belonging specifically to history or to that which is simply greater than any individual's recollective capacity. Bloom's equation of suffering with history shares with Levinas' paradoxically unpleasurable definition of responsibility the worry that imagining either history or language through impersonal, structuralist, or systemic terms might surrender the real—interpersonal or ethical—vocation of language.

4) Recollective Tropes; or How Morrison Turns the Figure of Trauma (via Woolf) Toward History

I turn in the last part of this essay to a practical reading of the ethics of revisionism operative in Toni Morrison's intertextual engagement with Virginia Woolf, an example which proves illustrative of the theoretical principles I have raised thus far. Immediately in *Beloved* (1987) we are in a fictional world offering itself as belated history, such that Morrison's insertion of voice into the absences of African-American history seems premised specifically on the untold sufferings of history as though history might be reconceived as the carry-over effect of injustice. Morrison's magical-realist technique constructs her fiction upon a diachronic rift in conventions of representation, which are themselves reflective of a political status quo. What the hegemonic political system in America supposes is the perspective of those citizens (say, enfranchised whites) for whom the law has evolved a good-enough construct of justice, in John Rawls's sense of the term, requiring that the historical facticity of injustices perpetrated against African-Americans be in some way disassociated from the political system by which they were produced until the bare facts of atrocity seem historically irrelevant, banished to the outside of social discourse. In *Beloved* Morrison imagines that the facts of atrocity have been so effectively banished that they can only be recovered from a mythically constituted realm, akin to the landscape of the afterlife in African folklore which is always positioned proximate to the terrain of the everyday social world. If the presumptions of extant justice are to be challenged, the question is from what perspective or by what social means or what fantastic mechanism of belated memory such history can be made to recur in this novel.

My emphasis is on tropological means rather than on any experiential perspective with which the means might be associated. In keeping with my previous essay on Morrison, "Trauma and Specters of Enslavement in Morrison's *Beloved*" (2002), I take the conceit of trauma to be central to the novel's purported recovery of history, even as I concede that trauma in the clinical, psychological sense can bring with it no inherent return of history and that, furthermore, as a provocation of history it ultimately and contradictorily maintains no place in the novel's final vision of community. It is possible, as Cathy Caruth has argued, that the recurrence of an event through psychic symptomology may suggest the extent to which persons are historical without necessarily knowing it, much in the same way that Bloom has suggested that poets are historical without wishing to be. More attention needs to be paid, however, to the irrevocable literariness of such a view of trauma, what I have elsewhere referred to as the rhetoric of trauma. Perhaps trauma, as a sign of diachrony bringing with its historically construed expectations, should also be considered, at least within the literary hermeneutics of trauma theory and according to the usage Morrison makes of trauma, as a revisionary trope in the Bloomian sense, one that in the bargain revisionarily supplements Bloom's own ahistorical, apolitical high-literary tendencies. To understand trauma in this way requires that we interpret some of its basic symptomology as a temporal disruption of an especially textual, indeed intertextual nature.

According to the empirical, psychological hermeneutics encouraged by Gothic or magical-realist fiction, the ghost of Beloved would be an emanation of Sethe's psyche, construing a larger historical meaning from her sufferings and the sufferings of her family than the protagonist herself is capable of developing. In a psychoanalytic formulation, her mind functions as a text overwritten with submerged or recurring meanings; and by adding a Bloomian twist to that formulation, we might say her mind proves to be inadequately defensive against the incursion of history, and so opens itself as text not only to its own sufferings but to the allegorical delusion that its sufferings might be termed the sufferings of history.[23] In keeping with the novel's fantastic means of bringing back Beloved, Morrison eventually underscores the fact that neither Sethe nor her community, most certainly not the superstructurally determinant white society, has a way of enfolding the experience of injustice into contemporary social relations. When the black community reconstitutes itself at novel's end by exorcising this daemon of history, Sethe's futile attempts to love her child again hardly seem adequate to Beloved's spectral historical meaning, which corresponds rather neatly to her novelistic function as a trope for history. Beloved is an occurrence of responsibility within the novel at least in so far as Sethe intuits an obligation for her; and yet as she ultimately suggests the diachronic divide between the present-tense priorities of the black community and the memory of historical atrocities under which they have suffered, she is set apart from anyone's practical ability in the novel to answer for her. Her abiding meaning is textual in a

[23] Recall that it is Sethe who intuits the identity of the stranger—woman to be that of her returned child. In her traumatic state of mind, she formulates this hypothesis so crucial to the novel's larger historical implications, and very little in the novel breaks faith with her interpretive will; even the exorcism itself is premised on rescuing Sethe from a ghostly persecution the community accepts as actual.

manner that corresponds to Derrida's notion of the *supplement*, but Morrison will not quite cede her significatory connotations to the realm of *écriture* if only because she believes fundamentally that the responsibility for injustice is not an already written or overwritten imperative but rather an intuition of not yet written-about suffering. Instead she constructs a myth of orality in which the rhetorical imperatives of revisionism are writ large, with orality serving as a trope of access to history, which is to say, as a trope recalling those politically caused sufferings which are seemingly unrepresentable within the norms of written American history.

According to a dialectical irresolution I have deemed ethical, and according also to an intertextual dynamics similar to Bloom's privileging of orality as a space prior to the synchrony of representation by which poetic voice might obtain an illusory independence from what determines it, Morrison's conceit of orality is highly revisionary, treating those contents for so long forced outside the mainstream of American history as though they were well-preserved in some magical-realist fictional terrain or, even more relevantly, within a mode of orality that is itself not explicitly part of any oral tradition. In other words, the characters' agonistic tensions with normative history signify the inarticulate orality of their latent testimonial voices, hearing the things they have not yet said, never mind written down. The characters in this fictional black community have not effectively preserved the memory of injustice of which the novel itself speaks. If anything, as users of memory in an ostensibly oral tradition the members of the black community indulge a set of defensive strategies tending toward evasiveness, even as the novel *Beloved* conjures a vision of history, not unlike the persecuting burdens of poetic tradition in Bloom, that simply cannot be refused.

To the extent, then, that orality receives a vexed priority over what is written (*à la* Bloom) and even appears to emerge literally from within the written (*à la* Derrida) as a suffering abandoned or severely limited by representation, it designates a quasi-unconscious terrain of personal memory or an alterity within speech itself that elicits history despite a character's most concrete intentions. In its conflicted textual genealogy, Morrison's revisionism seems, however, significantly more Bloomian than deconstructive. In either case, an emphasis on the novel's intertextuality is in opposition to a critical orthodoxy that interprets the recovery of voice in *Beloved* through a strictly experiential lens, as though the absent voices of history could simply speak for themselves, as though Morrison's use of trauma, by providing *entrée* into the psychological devastations of personal history, could also be made to stand for memory in lieu of history.[24] Since the possibilities of Sethe's voice must be identified with Morrison's own authorial voice—which is to say, in so far as Sethe becomes a figure for the creative process and, quite possibly, the agonistic struggle for voice Bloom describes—it would appear that Sethe's relative success involves at best an anxious struggle with representation itself.

Morrison makes all of this rather overt within the novel's largely allegorical tendencies. She figures her own struggle with the agency of representation through the novel's revisionary representation of its Ur-text, an article Morrison culled from her editorial work on an anthology of slavery memorabilia called *The Black Book* (1974), in which we find a historical newspaper article about a slave mother's infanticide. In that article, the real-life reporter muses over an "unfortunate woman" (Margaret Garner) who committed a desperate act of infanticide so that her children would not be returned to slavery, observing with apparent sympathy and yet remarkably unctuous prejudice, that "she [Garner] evidently possesses all the passionate tenderness of a mother's love" (see Harris). Morrison partly displaces the prejudicial force of this Ur-text into her characterization of Schoolteacher, who analyzes the slaves

---

[24] This way of reading the novel has legitimated a line of critique put forward, for one, by Walter Benn Michaels, who takes aim at *Beloved* and more generally the mystified function of memory in contemporary American culture by arguing that the celebration of memory as implausibly extended experience (since memory is already, except in the first generation of oppression, a substitute for the authentic experience of undergoing oppression) substitutes the hypothesis of experience for a thoroughgoing analysis of enduring conditions of political inequity; see Michaels 181–97. Much critical opinion on the novel holds that Sethe's experiments in representation are ethically if not finally successful, supposing that through Sethe, as Morrison's metonymy for the suffering and occluded perspectives of slave women in history, *Beloved* restores the possibility of voice to the oppressed. Most relevant here is Marilyn Sanders Mobley's argument that Morrison's revisionism of the genre of slave narrative acts as a reinscription of female memory, a memory only partly anticipated by Jacobs's *Incidents in the Life of a Slave Girl*. According to Mobley, the "signifying differences" of *Beloved* as compared to the slave narrative are largely formal: "While the classic slave narrative draws on memory as though it is a monologic, mechanical conduit for facts and incidents, Morrison's text foregrounds the dialogic characteristics of memory along with its imaginative capacity to construct and reconstruct the significance of the past . . . . Through the trope of memory, Morrison moves into the psychic consequences of slavery for women, who, by their very existence, were both the means and the source of production" (Mobley 192).

under his watch with quasi-anthropological condescension and, when the white farmhands sexually assault a pregnant Sethe, disapproves of such treatment on the ground that one would not thusly treat animals in one's keep (Morrison 149–50). Schoolteacher's racist dismissiveness serves a double purpose for Morrison—indicating the limits of racially coded cultural norms (which infect even the purported objectivity of scientifically based ideologies such as eugenics), and highlighting the limits of any inherited mode of representation that would overreachingly prescribe a subject's contemporary apprehension of truth. In Bloomian theory, the poetic tradition's overextensive reach inspires the poet's use of revisionary ratios, of which the function pertaining most particularly to the universalizing claims of representation is specifically that of *limitation*. Whereas representation admits a lack and then "refinds what could fill the lack," thereby strengthening the claims of language, tropes of limitation, even as they also represent, "tend to limit the demands placed upon language by pointing to lack both in language and the self," serving to weaken the viability of any given representation (*Map* 104). Morrison's trope of limitation is directed at the written orthodoxy of language itself.[25]

When Morrison also displaces the force of the Ur-text into the black characters' response to an article written about Sethe's unspeakable act (which is extra-textually modeled on the journalistic account of Margaret Garner's infanticide), she depicts Sethe's struggle for words, her faltering orality, as a consequence of written representation's overreaching. Even as Morrison assumes that any social system of language and its semi-official forms of discourse (with the newspaper seeming by convention only the most obvious vehicle of contemporary public opinion) must participate in the society's prevailing ideological biases, she figures the chasm in Sethe's historically metonymic experience as a problem pertaining to the limits of representation, the words of the article lacking "any more power than she had to explain" her own act:

---

[25] Cp. Valerie Smith, who argues that the novel is specifically about the limits of hegemonic cultural discourses (342–55). As Smith argues that the novel reflects a dialectical tension between the inaccessibility of experience to representation and the central place of "black bodies in the construction of narratives of slavery" (346), she associates the limit of representation with the "limits of hegemonic, authoritarian systems of knowledge" (354). By representing the inexpressibility of its subject matter, the novel also signifies the significatory depth of the slaves' subjectivity and suffering, a horizon Smith reads through the referential reality of the black body that suffers.

> Otherwise she would have said what the newspaper said she said and no more. Sethe could recognize only seventy-five printed words (half of which appeared in the newspaper clipping), but she knew that the words she did not understand hadn't any more power than she had to explain. (161)

This is not a simple irony at the expense of the racist newspapers, paraphrased as such: *of course they hadn't any more power to explain Sethe's experience, they had far less.* Instead, the hypothesis of a power the written text might possess but lacks in proportion to Sethe's communicative lack serves to overestimate the significance of Morrison's Ur-text by the very kind of inflationary valuation that often begets (in Bloom's theory) imaginative acts of revision. As Sethe's illiteracy emphasizes her exclusion for the written texts of white society and as the unrepresentative aspect of the conventional written word's representation of suffering seems to authorize a turn to orality, Morrison refuses to imagine that Sethe's experience might be conceived as independent from the historical context and perspective of a mainstream society that typically precludes black perspectives. Nor does she elaborate an oral tradition by which Sethe has or might have been sustained. Rather, by examining the truly dialectical struggle between the standard social act of representation and the realm of unrepresentative experience, Morrison premises orality itself, even in its hypothetical priority, upon a revisionary turn, or a trope of limitation, performed against an inherited, normative representation.

It is hardly obvious that the historically revisionary hermeneutics I have thus far attributed to Morrison should find even an agonistically conceived source in Woolf, but that is nevertheless precisely the claim I would like to make. What connects Morrison to Woolf is especially the lyrical mode of memory she inherits through Woolf's innovative novels. Ralph Freedman in *The Lyrical Novel* (1963), taking Woolf as one of his exemplary cases, has argued that among the most significant generic pressures exerted upon the novel under the experimentalist imperatives of modernism was the introduction of lyrical style and modality into the modern novel. As with the stylistic experimentation of stream-of-consciousness narrative, lyrical prose explores the phenomenological ground of subjectivity, not so much privatizing the entire social world as exploring the crisis of individual consciousness within that world. It is perhaps not surprising, then, to find that with the introduction of a high degree of lyricism into prose fiction, in writers such as Proust, Hesse, Gide, Faulkner, and Woolf, novelistic prose turns frequently upon the epistemological dynamics of memory, concentrating upon those forces in the mind and its social context that challenge identity or suggest an unreliability in selfhood.

The importance of the psychoanalytic revolution for literary modernism cannot be overestimated. Though Woolf in her private correspondence strongly resisted and sometimes ridiculed psychoanalytic theory, she and her husband Leonard Woolf in their capacity as publishers of the Hogarth Press oversaw the introduction of Freud into the English-speaking world, clearly appreciating his revolutionizing influence on the study of the psychic construction of the person within modern bourgeois society. Moreover, Woolf's novelistic experiments with consciousness often focus on those gaps in memory—whether we think of Septimus's war-wounded consciousness in *Mrs. Dalloway* (1925) or the novelistically structured chasm at the center of *To the Lighthouse* (1927)—that exert a pressure on consciousness as if from inside, examining much the same terrain that Freudian theory attempted to account for. Here is a passage from the posthumously published memoir "A Sketch of the Past" in which Woolf attempts to formulate, in specifically autobiographical terms, what Bloom would call a myth of memory:

> I can reach a state where I seem to be watching things happen as if I were there. That is, I suppose, that my memory supplies what I had forgotten, so that *it seems as if it were happening independently*, though I am really making it happen. In certain favourable moods, memories—what one has forgotten—come to the top. Now if this is so, is it not possible—I often wonder—that things we have felt with great intensity *have an existence independent of our minds; are in fact still in existence?* . . . . I feel that strong emotion must leave its trace; and it is only a question of discovering how we can get ourselves again attached to it, so that we shall be able to live our lives through from the start. (Woolf 67; emphasis added)

Woolf opts for something short of a full myth of memory, as should be clear from the qualifying force of her speculative, conditional, and interrogative moods. In opposing the return of forgotten memories to the intentional act of remembering ("making it happen"), she does not rely on, say, a Freudian theory of the unconscious, but instead describes, as if at the behest of memory itself, a phenomenological alterity fundamental to the deep structure of memory. If memories are constituted in "strong emotion" or feelings of "great intensity," Woolf concludes that "strong emotion must leave its trace," supposing that there is a psychic economy determining memory that is as much biological as social. Her emphasis on memory's alienation, although not explicitly psychoanalytic in origin, indicates an immersion in the currents of modernist culture (including the thought of Freud) even as it also intimates an aesthetics newly troubled by scientifically discerned intricacies of the modern mind. The most unusual assertion here is the one pertaining to memory's ostensible independence from the subject, as though memory could be detailed in mythic proportions as an autonomous force, one not merely following internally cued and externally formulated dictates of an unconscious, but resulting from a recurrent crisis in the life-narrative of every person. According to the experience of crisis, any self is thrust into a mysterious dependence on that which, perhaps once belonging to itself, thereafter functions as an external, independently co-existing aspect of self to be recovered, perhaps only hypothetically, from another realm of being. As Woolf's myth of memory takes an ontological turn, she speculates as to the "question of discovering how we can get ourselves again attached" to that quasi-exterior realm, in which memory has being and independence, without ever quite believing in the hypothesis of continuity by which she might resolve the apparent rift in selfhood.

I wish to emphasize two points here: first, that the ontological rift Woolf imagines is dramatically diachronic in emphasis; and second, that in so far as such a rift characterizes memory originally, memory is by such an account inherently traumatic. There are at least three dimensions to Freud's characterization of the trauma, what I would call the ontological aspect of trauma (associated in Freud with the biological trauma of birth and the pre-linguistic oedipal rupture), the phenomenological event of trauma (which is typically a misremembered, psychically wounding event in a patient's life), and the hermeneutical resolution to a traumatic gap in memory that occurs through the act of remembrance. Indeed, since our capacity to remember depends fundamentally on a premise that experience must first be hypothetically lost or unreliably present in order to be recovered, all memory depends upon the definitional resistance posed by the trauma, if only so as to refute the hypothesis of continuous remembrance so central to the notion of a perfectly extant identity. In this sense, we might even argue that trauma is the characterizing trope of memory. In its fully phenomenological or psychologically pathological—as opposed to, say, merely tropological—emphasis, trauma refers us to a realm of consciousness that can never be properly possessed. In its tropological dimension, however, the trauma refers us always to a question of temporal crisis, to the diachronic tensions within the construct of individual or collective identity. Reversing the order of the literary and psychological as he so characteristically does, Bloom goes so far in his book on Wallace Stevens as to describe the trope as though its function were inherently traumatic: "The trope is a *cut* or *gap* made in or onto the anteriority of language, itself an anteriority in which 'language' acts as a figurative substitution for time" (*Stevens* 393; emphasis added).[26] Trauma, in this scheme, interposes itself as both an event of provisional wounding and a defensive psychic complex substituting for therapeutic remembrance. In other words, the trope as a trauma works both phenomenologically and hermeneutically for Bloom, and is supremely rhetorical in so far as it is at least experimemtally enacted by the subject. By making all language rely on the function of a figure, Bloom points toward an understanding of rhetoric in its temporal dimension if only because, in the words of Peter de Bolla, "time is consistently figured away" (89).

In keeping with the convergence of lyric, memory, and trauma that I am here exploring, Bloom's discussion of the traumatic trope occurs in the context of a larger discussion of lyric, which is for Bloom always a hypothesis undertaken in time as though against it. In more basic literary historical terms lyric would offer a hypothesis of continuity or self-possession, always threatened without being undone by time, social exteriority, or the relentless impinging of history. Of all literary modes,

---

[26] Invoking the diachronic plot of literary history through an image of wounding (we note the elision of "cut" and "gap," or wound and time), Bloom figures all relation to the past (or the poetic past) as traumatic—that is, as part of a referential scheme in which the poetic voice enters the world wounded by its past and made to bear an unconscious history in its struggle for autonomy. Trauma seems quasi-mythically associated with the (un)fortunate fall from what Julia Kristeva would call the semiotic wholeness of oedipal meaning into the anxiety-laden order of temporality, the gain of which is the poet's entry into and production of language. Immediately prior to this comment, Bloom considers the two possibilities of tropological defensiveness, which may involve a will that translates itself into a verbal ethos or one that in failing to translate itself successfully abides "as a verbal desire or figure of *pathos*." For Bloom the two possibilities both prove the willful dimension of poetic figuration as a plot against the necessarily diachronic nature of poetic language, and Bloom's description of these alternatives seems quite similar to Adorno's summation of the lyric as a "sphere of expression whose essence lies in either not acknowledging the power of socialization or overcoming it through the pathos of detachment" (37). For both Bloom and Adorno, the relative success of the poet's turn against language and time is less important than the fact that the autonomy expressed is also merely a fiction against time or history.

lyric is preeminently the one in which the past is written into or onto the self apart from the rule of objective history, operating under the persuasion of singularity as a site in which the relation to reality is described by emotion and concentrated in the detail of the image, and as such it has often been opposed to collective voice as to history. In "On Lyric Poetry and Society," Theodor Adorno nevertheless attributes two negatively mimetic functions to the lyric: it is the illusory embodiment of perfected voice, and simultaneously the receptacle of much of the fragmentation or isolation proper to the bourgeois society.[27] Even when it appears to deny the weight of collective thought, the lyric, Adorno argues, is necessarily, if only negatively, a deeper reflection of social reality and collective meanings. The Hegelian overtones of Adorno's antagonistic dialectics anticipate Bloom's antithetical reading of lyric, since both Adorno and Bloom perceive an inevitable social dimension in the poetry, an attachment to society or to the society of poets, that dialectically reveals itself in the moment in which one swerves to avoid such influence. What Adorno helps us see is a point Bloom would readily concede—that even in its most triumphant vision of autonomy, the lyric is always a signifier, if only as anxiety, of a collectivity masked as tradition, troubling the premise of self-reliant subjectivity by what precedes or contextualizes it. For Adorno the contextualization of lyric is primarily synchronic, such that a historical reading of lyrical voice must account for its achievements also as a function of what it excludes socially and politically. For Bloom such contextualization is diachronic, historical in the sense that it exists specifically in relation to what precedes it, as though the order of language were always a synchronic totality until interrupted by the cut or wound, always temporal in emphasis, of the voice that stands within and against time.

[27] This paradox derives largely from the historical contradiction between poetic and communicative language, so that—to borrow Adorno's phrasing—"in striving for an absolute objectivity unrestricted by any considerations of communication, language both distances itself from the objectivity of spirit, of living language, and substitutes a poetic event for a language that is no longer present" (44). The inherent antagonisms of the objective world that produce the lyric also guarantee that its achievement embodies a universal dimension and reflects a collective undercurrent. Adorno recuperates the social or ethical significance of works of art which—based in the sophistication he associates with modernism but Bloom would trace to Romanticism and its strongest precursors, Shakespeare and Milton—fail to offer a straightforward mimetic relation to the world. See Adorno, "On Lyric Poetry and Society" 37–54.

What I am trying to discern in Woolf, as a triggering inspiration for Morrison, is a special affinity for lyric conceived on such a scale—which is to say, as a function of a diachronic rift as well as both the derivative and responsive effects of memory to such a rift. This is the special quality of Woolf's traumatically infused lyricism, in which memory seems more a symptom of than salve to the rift introduced in consciousness, and in which lyrical voice is always predicated on both possibilities. For Woolf as for Morrison after her, lyricism is a hypothesis of subjective self-possession nevertheless dependent on the persistence of traumatic unpleasure, those phenomena that endure beyond our present understanding of them; and memory is generated by the tension between conscious recollections and submerged, temporally irretrievable experiences. In her revision of Woolf's myth of memory, Morrison avails herself of this diachronic emphasis so as to revise lyrical suffering toward historical or collective meanings, speculating even more mythically than her precursor about a past that obtains as a quasi-physical reality exterior to self:

> Some things go. Pass on. Some things just stay. I used to think it was my rememory. You know. Some things you forget. Other things you never do. But it's not. Places, places are still there. If a house burns down, it's gone, but the place—the picture of it—stays, and not just in my rememory, but out there, in the world . . . . Someday you be walking down the road and you hear something or see something going on. So clear. And you think it's you thinking it up. A thought picture. But no. It's when you bump into a rememory that belongs to somebody else. Where I was before I came here, that place is real. It's never going away. Even if the whole farm—every tree and grass blade of it dies. That picture is still there and what's more, if you go there—you who never was there—if you go there and stand in the place where it was, it will happen again; it will be there for you, waiting for you. (35–36)

Morrison's neologism "rememory" alludes to Woolf's "moments of being," or those moments of the past separated from the self's willful remembering or forgetting that endure independently so as to be hypothetically re-encountered. Part of Morrison's revisionary turn on Woolf, as she figures a past that is also independent from the control of consciousness, is to interpret both singular and collective formulations of identity by way of their potential to evade the force of psychic suffering. Sethe is an advocate of such evasion, attempting to pass it on to her children, teaching them to avoid the repetition of suffering. Yet as she does so, she lapses into a present tense description of an encounter with the past ("It's when you bump into a rememory...") suggesting both the contingency and interpersonal determinations presiding over memory's recurrence.

Such a final absence of control within memory, which in Freud is definitive of unpleasure, is given an ethical inflection by Morrison. Even as the subject's own experiences resist the use she might make of them in the present so as to fashion a consistent identity, the facticity of alienation, or of what we might call self-possession in remission, means that one can encounter—indeed, one cannot avoid sometimes encountering—the mythically hypothesized sufferings of others. By this somewhat Woolfian ontology, suffering precedes us; and according to Morrison's revisionary twist, suffering simultaneously inclines us toward an interpersonal interpretation of selfhood. Bumping into someone else's memory signals the possibility of an alterity already inscribed upon one's own memory, as though even in the act of reaching back to understand ourselves by way of our own individual pasts Morrison would read the horizon of an alienation or unpleasure referring us to another person's suffering.[28] Though memory in its lyrical emphasis incorporates externality into the meaning of selfhood and trauma might further conceal ethical relationship in the symptomology of a subjectively constituted reality, memory's dependence on what disrupts or resists it also means that it necessarily preserves the significance of otherness within any cultural definition of identity. In short, Morrison revises memory toward its occasion until memory itself functions as an exteriority to mind, involving the self in a metaphysically or magically real relation to injustice.

It is worth remarking that, according to its psychoanalytically explained phenomenology, the trauma bears no necessary relation to injustice. Indeed the peculiar scandal of the trauma, as of the theory

[28] Indeed, the phenomenology of alienation in Woolf attracted Morrison to her. In her M. A. thesis, Morrison argues, "Mrs. Woolf's emphasis is on the 'moment' and even in her style she tries to give the moment the effect of eternity. She suggests that by isolating oneself into the fragmentary experiences and sensations as they come, the dread of time eating at the edges of life can be avoided. One can live outside time, as it were. Septimus is outside time in a tragic way, and Clarissa struggles, in her rational way, for the same condition. In death only the alienated find freedom and refuge from time—a solution Virginia Woolf may well have believed in to end her life as she did in 1941" (23). This interpretation of alienation as a perverse refusal of attachment and as a configurative tension between the temporality of the moment and death bears itself out in Morrison's own fiction.

that interprets its historical significances, is that it cannot say whether an unjust history will be more traumatic for victims or perpetrators. Trauma is not proportional to justice, allotted only to those who suffer history's egregious injustices. Nevertheless, perhaps only as a matter of cultural convention, the literature that invokes trauma and so much of our theoretical language about trauma continues to deploy trauma as a state of mind both indicative of a perpetrated injustice and especially pertinent to the fate of the victim. I do not propose resolving this aporia within trauma theory (I have addressed it as an ethical problem elsewhere). I wish only to stress that if by cultural convention trauma often functions as a figure for injustice, even when it is not specifically designated, by the rhetorical calculations of a poet or author, as such, this association of trauma and injustice is advanced, as I have already intimated, by the diachronic resistance characterizing the trauma. That which will not be reconciled to the synchrony and sufficiently ordered view of the status quo is interpreted, perhaps more by inference than by an analysis of causal relations, as a result of injustice.

Literary revisionism, which Bloom would haply imagine as traumatic or as a function of unjust, unequal relations, is for Bloom similarly positioned by way of simultaneously diachronic and agonistic emphases. Without any necessary thematic focus upon a question of injustice, revisionism positions itself along a fault-line of historical transitions that mar any straightforwardly positive inheritance of the past. Although a theory of revisionism resembles much of what Hayden White has to say about the tropological determinations that shift connotations or open other possibilities within historical epistemes, its diachrony is dependent on a peculiar quality of literariness, in which the work performed by a trope is always also hypothetical even within the contextually ascribed meanings that apparently determine it. In Bloom's theory, since the revisionary ratio between the precursor and belated text is always determined by the function of a principal trope, intertextuality is not only the consequence of tropes but can serve itself as a kind of trope for inheritance of the historical past. So with reference to Morrison and Woolf, the later writer wrestles with the otherness of her precursor much as one might wrestle with the ethical meaning of the other in the former's writing, even by reclaiming the ethical meaning of Woolf's own transgressive tropes.

Consider the following passage about traumatic memory from Woolf's memoir, in which Woolf conveys a trauma by arresting the transgressive dimension of the trope of catachresis:

> We were waiting at dinner one night, when somehow I overheard my father or my mother say that Mr Valpy had killed himself. The next thing I remember is being in the garden at night and walking on the path by the apple tree. It seemed to me that the apple tree was connected with the horror of Mr Valpy's suicide. I could not pass it. (71)

The displacement of human history onto the natural world stands, as is often the case in scenes of pastoral consolation, for an emotion in excess of the subject's psychic capability. And yet more importantly, what seems only a random association brought about by the child's imagination here configures the apple tree and the dead man, so that the interruption of the crossing signification of catachresis renders the two terms as though they were starkly complicitous in their signification. To pass the apple tree is to pass by or move beyond memory of Mr. Valpy's suicide, and as the child seems suddenly aware of what temporality in its progressive flow would require of her, she cannot pass because she has been arrested by memory of that which is most awful to her child's mind. In composing this passage years later, when she was already an accomplished novelist, Woolf may have implicitly recalled the dilemma of her own character Clarissa Dalloway, who resents the intrusive news of Septimus's suicide at her party and effectively attempts to pass it by. To look beyond such news is in the novel's allegorical terms—which are conspicuously dependent on the figurative reach of trauma—to put memory of World War I and its traumatized soldiers out of mind, so that British society, as it were, might get on with the future. The child's crossing a puddle does not partake of Clarissa's grandiose callousness, but in so far as the act of passing serves as a trope for an ironic, even unconscious retrieval of the past, Woolf intimates how the self-conscious turnings of language might stand within and yet up against history (see de Bolla 134-43).

What seems especially literary about the "moment of being" I have cited from Woolf's memoir is what is not necessary about the association that here codifies memory. The psyche is represented as working by a trope of catachresis inseparable from its interpretive function in the moment of recollection, and in this sense all memoir in its contrived elicitation of the past becomes literary. The diachronic split between the occasion of remembrance and the original occasion deserving of memory is figured itself as a rupture and impossible repair in the sequence of the child's memory. When the young Virginia stops before an apple tree, she is already—to invoke a mixed gardening metaphor—grafting the image of the tree into the psychic space of an awful event she does not wish to remember and yet cannot not remember. By this associative grafting, the trope of trauma functions hermeneutically as filled-in explanation: because she stops and does not pass the apple tree, Mr. Valpy's death remains significant. In this diachronic imposition of the passing of the apple tree upon the event of a suicide, there is glimpsed a literary or textual—or we might say, inter-textual or revisionary—dimension to memory.

Interpreting the prevalent diachrony of Woolf's texts, Morrison realizes this revisionary tension internal to memory through an intertextual conflict between a precursor and her own belated text. Indeed, as the textuality of the traumatic mind in *Beloved* is conceived as an intertextual phenomenon, initially dependent on a journalistic Ur-text and then more significantly relying on Woolf's myth of memory, much of the necessarily literary work trauma does within the novel involves Morrison's efforts to open the received texts of Virginia Woolf to sufferings that stand, in their diachronic import, for history. I cite Woolf and Morrison together:

> There was the moment of the puddle in the path; when for no reason I could discover, everything suddenly became unreal; I was suspended; I could not step across the puddle; I tried to touch something . . . the whole world became unreal. ("A Sketch of the Past" 78)

> As for the rest, she worked hard to remember as close to nothing as was safe. Unfortunately her brain was devious. She might be hurrying across a field, running practically, to get to the pump quickly and rinse the chamomile sap from her legs. Nothing else would be in her mind . . . . Then something. The plash of water, the sight of her shoes and stockings awry on the path where she had flung them; or Here Boy lapping in the puddle near her feet, and suddenly there was Sweet Home rolling, rolling, rolling out before her eyes, and although there was not a leaf on that farm that did not make her want to scream, it rolled itself out before her in shameless beauty. It never looked as terrible as it was and it made her wonder if hell was a pretty place too. Fire and brimstone all right, but hidden in lacy groves. Boys hanging from the most beautiful sycamores in the world. It shamed her—remembering the wonderful soughing trees rather than the boys. (*Beloved* 6)

As Woolf leaves her reader without any causal context or any interpretive grounding for the event's developmental value to the memoir's self (since the rupture occurs "for no reason [she] could discover"), the child's incapability before the puddle in the path figures the writer's vexed effort to cross or recover the irrevocable gap of time. According to the radical discontinuity of this experience, which even inverts the terms of the real, memory is akin to a trauma or the remembering subject's inability to step across. Turned thus toward diachrony or what it cannot accomplish autonomously, the self is subjected to the impasse. Consider, for example, how the empty moment returns during the young Virginia's bath that night—a "dumb horror" overcomes her and she is "exposed to a whole avalanche of meaning" that, as she tells us, "heaped itself up and discharged itself upon me, unprotected, with nothing to ward it off, so that I huddled up at my end of the bath, motionless" (78). In Woolf's memoir, the absence of context—what precisely is the referent of "meaning" here?—brings us so far inside the subjective symptomology of trauma that we cannot discern an exterior source of causation. It is as if both the moments before the puddle and in the bath connoted something prior only so as to signify diachrony itself, or perhaps a concealed past that cannot be drawn forth.

If temporal dichotomy is the overt problem of Woolf's memoir—the task she sets herself of reconciling the "I now" with the "I then"—the significant gaps of Woolf's imagination open unto further significance in Morrison. Indeed, they stand for the possibility of history itself. Throughout *Beloved* the difficulty of personal memory refers unwittingly to an obstinate historical reality, as suffering traces a relation to the other that stands for history itself. This is *strong* reading in the Bloomian sense, and we might protest that Morrison has distorted Woolf's psychic phenomenology (and doubtless we would be right on some level), but in doing so she has also rightly discerned the ethical problem at the heart of a hermeneutical one. When Sethe halts abruptly at the sight of "her shoes and stockings awry on the path" or at her dog Here Boy "lapping in the puddle near her feet," she is taking on the burden of an interpretive or perceptual problem that explicitly recalls young Virginia's delayed crossing of the puddle, returning to the hesitation at the puddle not so much to emphasize a temporal dichotomy within memory that divides us from ourselves as to insist that such an impasse within temporality proceeds from the ineffective or unincorporated memory of injustice.[29]

---

[29] Woolf's suspended moment before the puddle is itself a revision of Wordsworth's first "spot of time" in *The Prelude*, where the sight of a "naked Pool" followed by a girl bearing a pitcher on her head translates into a "visionary dreariness" that invests the naked pool (see 12.248–58). Woolf's reduction of a naked pool to the status of a puddle is parodic or at least privatizing in force. She diminishes the larger associative dimension of Wordsworth's "lone eminence," which casts the Romantic soul into conflict with its natural clime and thus into productive crisis, to a lonely minimalism of the moment. Furthermore, she focuses the horror of the moment not in the association with another story or memory or image, but as she doubts the restorative capabilities of memory in the impossibility of meaning's recovery.

Not only are the dynamics of Morrison's revisionary ethics intertextual, what she elicits from the scene of beauty depends upon a complex demystification of the pastoral scene in which the image is supposed to be somehow proportional to the suffering it connotes. Morrison converts the play of memory into a fatal complicity between the natural world, upon which we project cultural norms such as beauty and self-satisfaction and justice, and the social world. Maybe beauty is just underestimation, Morrison conjectures. Emphasizing through what Bloom would call a revisionary *limitation* the discrepancy between Woolf's minimalistically narrated moment of being and the "avalanche of meaning" in the bath, Morrison's Sethe says of her own trauma and implicitly of Woolf's as well: "It never looked as terrible as it was." Such underestimation of suffering or misrecognition of the scene of suffering is strategic: as it alludes to any psyche's coping mechanism, it also highlights—at a broader, literary level that cannot correspond to Sethe's own limited perceptions—the aesthetic limit of lyricism. There is a nearsightedness that determines our perception of the beautiful. Still, Sethe does not expose beauty as fraudulent—it evidently remains, imbricated with the ugliness of injustice. As the beautiful scenery misrepresents history, making Sethe "wonder if hell was a pretty place too," Morrison locates history not directly within the heroine's traumatized consciousness but rather by way of an inversion of the conventional procedures of lyric memory. Lyric gets turned inside out—what was once a process of incorporation is here depicted, revisedly, as a tension between what the subjective mind can harmoniously perceive and discordant facts that precede and exceed it. In this way we come upon the fact of injustice inscribed upon the lyrical image as though it were a function of diachronic shock—"Boys hanging from the most beautiful sycamores in the world."

I am reading the hanging boys as lynching victims, although it is almost possible to read the passage, especially in light of its lyrically reminiscent tone, as though they were merely children at play in trees. The very possibility of such a mistake is crucial to the imagistic association of the pastoral world of Sweet Home and the horrific past of slavery for which it stands. The trees host both horrible and innocent meanings, and the scene is always hypothetically beautiful. As though the unidentifiable, possibly lynched bodies in the trees were historically inscribed upon aesthetics so as to generate the misrecognitions at the heart of lyrical memory, Morrison revises the myth of memory and makes history independent from memory and yet dependent upon the facticity of suffering that would seem to demand our revisionary remembrance. It is a scene that literalizes the revisionary trope Bloom calls *apophrades* (literally, the "return of the dead") by way of Woolf's own catachrestic association of a suicide victim and an apple tree. Bloom describes the peculiar achievement of this trope as "having so stationed the precursor in one's own work, that particular passages in *his* work seem to be not presages of one's own advent, but rather to be indebted to one's own achievement" (*Anxiety* 141). But in Morrison's rendering there is an additional revisionary effect. For by laying claim to a historical realm of experience that functions as if it were the proper reference to imagistic associations of dead people and nature, and by reclaiming Woolf's vexed crossing scene, Morrison renders the memory of injustice as though it were produced by an imagistic association involving not only a temporal but a radically intertextual catachresis.

Clearly, my selection of *Beloved* as illustrative text, with Woolf interpreted as Morrison's implicit precursor, has been offered as a deliberately loaded example of Bloomian *agon*, not least of all because perceiving the revisionary relation between two women authors, one black and one white, pushes us beyond the heavily patriarchal and racially normative slant of Bloom's own terms and implicitly challenges Bloom's decision to leave *Beloved* off his provisional list of contemporary classics at the end of *The Western Canon*. Nevertheless, by delineating her artful invocation and interpretive misreading of her precursor Woolf, I have juxtaposed Morrison's own literarily constructed ethics to Bloom's so as to extend Bloomian theory. Indeed, the ethics of revisionism as here demonstrated brings to the fore those cultural-critical imperatives inscribed upon literariness within Bloomian theory, showing us that the critical turn to politics may be posited as a more than supplemental, perhaps even complementary, function to the literary itself. Though the rhetorical stipulations of Bloom's own texts will not, and perhaps should not have to, do all the work in the direction I take them, his literary-critical project must necessarily have a trajectory—at least to the extent that Bloom should be fashioned a theorist—beyond his overt propositions or declarations. Any persuasive humanistic theory remains applicable far beyond what can be established as content proper to an author's immediate intentions or from those meanings belonging strictly to its original context.[30] By the link I have forged between the diachronic dimensions of Bloomian rhetoric and a concern with ethics, I hope to have demonstrated how literary revisionism, apart from the explicit ethical or moral premises it espouses, can be made to pertain not merely to historicist concerns but to the very possibility of historical meanings that, in so far as they are always at least in part tropologically inspired, also turn upon the unaddressed facts of injustice in history.

---

[30] Such is the nature, as Thomas Kuhn has helped us to discern, of any humanistic rather than scientific theory: as humanists we continue to reread, say, Marx or Freud, by posing challenges to their work in light of contemporary insights but also by finding ourselves challenged by what they have to say, apart from a standard of empirical verifiability.

Works Cited

Adorno, Theodor W. "On Lyric Poetry and Society." *Notes to Literature.* Trans. Shierry Weber Nicholsen. Ed. Rolf Tiedemann. Vol. 1. New York: Columbia UP, 1991. 37–54.

Badiou, Alain. *Ethics: An Essay on the Understanding of Evil.* 1993. Trans. Peter Hallward. New York: Verso, 2001.

Butler, Judith. *The Psychic Life of Power: Theories in Subjection.* Stanford: Stanford UP, 1997.

Caruth, Cathy. *Unclaimed Experience: Trauma, Narrative, and History.* Baltimore: Johns Hopkins UP, 1996.

Ciaramelli, Fabio. "Levinas's Ethical Discourse between Individuation and Universality." *Re-Reading Levinas.* Ed. Robert Bernasconi and Simon Critchley. Bloomington: Indiana UP, 1991. 83–105.

Critchley, Simon. *The Ethics of Deconstruction: Derrida and Levinas.* Cambridge, MA: Blackwell, 1992.

De Bolla, Peter. *Harold Bloom: Towards Historical Rhetorics.* New York: Routledge, 1988.

Freedman, Ralph. *The Lyrical Novel: Studies in Hermann Hesse, André Gide, and Virginia Woolf.* Princeton: Princeton UP, 1963.

Freud, Sigmund. *Beyond the Pleasure Principle. The Standard Edition of the Complete Psychological Works of Sigmund Freud.* Trans. and ed. James Strachey, et al. Vol. 18. London: Hogarth, 1955. 1–64.

Gilbert, Sandra M. and Susan Gubar. *The Madwoman in the Attic: The Woman Writer and the Nineteenth-century Literary Imagination.* New Haven: Yale UP, 1979.

Harpham, Geoffrey Galt. *Getting It Right: Language, Literature, and Ethics.* Chicago: U of Chicago P, 1992.

Harris, Middleton A., comp. *The Black Book.* New York: Random House, 1974.

Hartman, Geoffrey H. *Criticism in the Wilderness: The Study of Literature Today*. New Haven: Yale UP, 1980.
Jameson, Fredric. "Figural Relativism; Or, The Poetics of Historiography." *The Ideologies of Theory: Essays, 1971–1986*. Vol. 1: *Situations of Theory*. Theory and History of Literature 48. Minneapolis: U of Minnesota P, 1988. 153–65.
Kermode, Frank. *The Sense of an Ending: Studies in the Theory of Fiction*. New York: Oxford UP, 1967.
Kuhn, Thomas. *The Structure of Scientific Revolutions*. Chicago: U of Chicago P, 1962.
Lentricchia, Frank. *After the New Criticism*. Chicago: U of Chicago P, 1980.
Levinas, Emmanuel. *Totality and Infinity: An Essay on Exteriority*. 1961. Trans. Alphonso Lingis. Pittsburgh: Duquesne UP, 1969.
———. *Otherwise Than Being, or Beyond Essence*. 1974. Trans. Alphonso Lingis. Pittsburgh: Duquesne UP, 1981.
———. "The Ego and the Totality." *Collected Philosophical Papers*. Trans. Alphonso Lingis. Phaenomenologica 100. Dordrecht: Nijhoff, 1987. 25–45.
Michaels, Walter Benn. "'You Who Never Was There:' Slavery and the New Historicism—Deconstruction and the Holocaust." *The Americanization of the Holocaust*. Ed. Hilene Flanzbaum. Baltimore: Johns Hopkins UP, 1999. 181–97.
Mobley, Marilyn Sanders. "A Different Remembering: Memory, History and Meaning in *Beloved*." *Toni Morrison*. Ed. Harold Bloom. Modern Critical Views. New York: Chelsea House, 1990.
Morrison, Toni. *Beloved*. New York: Knopf, 1987.
——— [Chloe Ardellia Wofford]. "Virginia Woolf's and William Faulkner's Treatment of the Alienated." M. A. thesis. Cornell U, 1955.
O'Hara, Daniel. "The Genius of Irony: Nietzsche in Bloom." *The Yale Critics: Deconstruction in America*. Ed. Jonathan Arac, Wlad Godzich and Wallace Martin. Minneapolis: U of Minnesota P, 1983. 109–32.
Rawls, John. *A Theory of Justice*. Cambridge, MA: Harvard UP, 1971.
Smith, Valerie. "'Circling the Subject:' History and Narrative in *Beloved*." *Toni Morrison: Critical Perspectives Past and Present*. Ed. Henry Louis Gates, Jr. and K. A. Appiah. New York: Amistad, 1993. 342–55.

Spargo, R. Clifton. "Trauma and the Specters of Enslavement in Morrison's *Beloved*." *Mosaic: A Journal for the Interdisciplinary Study of Literature* 35.1 (2002): 113–31.

———. *The Ethics of Mourning: Grief and Responsibility in Elegiac Literature.* Baltimore: Johns Hopkins UP, 2004.

———. *Vigilant Memory: Emmanuel Levinas, the Holocaust, and the Unjust Death.* Baltimore: Johns Hopkins UP, forthcoming (2006).

White, Hayden. *Metahistory: The Historical Imagination in Nineteenth-Century Europe.* Baltimore: Johns Hopkins UP, 1973.

Woolf, Virginia. *Moments of Being.* Ed. Jeanne Schulkind. New York: Harcourt, 1985.

Wordsworth, William. *The Fourteen-Book* Prelude. Ed. W. J. B. Owen. Ithaca: Cornell UP, 1985.

Zapf, Hubert. "Elective Affinities and American Differences: Nietzsche and Harold Bloom." *Nietzsche in American Literature and Thought.* Ed. Manfred Putz. Columbia, SC: Camden House, 1995. 337–55.

Sublime Theorist: Harold Bloom's Catastrophic Theory of Literature

HEIDI SYLVESTER

Literary criticism can take its origin from two different traditions: one is the Aristotelian, the other Longinian. The Aristotelian tradition, which is currently in mode again, was inaugurated with Aristotle's *Poetics* and has been remarkably influential throughout literary history. This tradition allows and strongly encourages dialogue between literature and philosophy, although for some this tradition subsumes literature into philosophy. The genesis of the other tradition, which is less receptive to theoretical or philosophical rumination, can be located in the Greek treatise *Peri hypsous*, usually translated as *On the Sublime*, ascribed to Longinus or, as German scholars teach us to say, Pseudo-Longinus. No matter which tradition we take, literary criticism stumbles sooner or later upon the idea of sublimity. Now, in both traditions, the idea of the sublime is always tainted with a negativity, although we must keep in mind that there are distinct theories of negativity. Here our concern will be with the negativity of Kant's sublime, rather than that of Hegel's sublime. Literary criticism, from its inception, can be considered under the category of the negative. Whether this endangers literature itself, designating literature as a negative mode, will be left open for the moment. What is of concern here is the way in which modern literary criticism maintains this negative tradition; if modern literary theories are not theories of the sublime, then they are theories heavily dependent upon the sublime, one could say, obsessed by the sublime. One way in which we can trace the sublime as a determining factor in contemporary literary criticism is by turning to the American literary critic Harold Bloom.

Bloom's theory of literature can be construed as catastrophic, taking catastrophe as its fundamental metaphor. What we need to establish from the start is whether Bloom's whole theory is catastrophic or just its founding moment. We can approach this by considering what *catastrophe* means; etymologically, catastrophe denotes a 'sudden turn,' an 'overturning.' Catastrophe considered in this manner throws light on what a Bloomian account of literature as catastrophe signifies. Because the initial moment of the literary process is a *clinamen* or a severe turning from prior poets, it is catastrophic. In Bloom's account of literature this initial moment of severe turning is repeated to a lesser extent in each revisionary ratio, or more precisely, in each of the three dialectics located within the schema of the poetic process.

Although the primary catastrophe or swerve within the literary process is the most severe, this does not rule out the possibility of catastrophe occurring throughout the literary process. So, we can argue that the initial catastrophe, or clinamen, imbues or motivates literature. The literary process at large is catastrophic because literature from its inception is catastrophic. It is important to note that catastrophe is employed as a trope, which should not be considered simply as a figure of speech but recognized as a 'turn' also. The word 'trope,' like 'catastrophe,' is itself etymologically linked to the idea of a turn or turning. Each step within Bloom's account of literature is a turning, a catastrophic swerve against the literary past.

What I want to examine here is not only Bloom's catastrophic theory of literature, and its relation to negativity (on which see Hart), but also how this theory of literature can be read as a continuation of the sublime tradition. Is Bloom's theory of poetry, one which is considered highly idiosyncratic, merely a modern version of the sublime which takes into account post-enlightenment literature? If so, what does this entail for his theory of poetry, and more importantly, what possibilities does it leave contemporary literary theory?

We can follow the sublime through two traditions which describe a number of trajectories. The path we follow will depend upon our concerns, or, saying the same thing from another perspective, the chosen trajectory will place us within a tradition which will then mark out concerns for us. We might discover that despite the different trajectories that are possible, the end point remains the same, a terminus which may be considered sometimes as a dead end or an impasse. However, a path must be taken, and Bloom follows the tradition marked 'Pseudo-Longinus' rather than the one marked 'Aristotle'—although it would be nonsensical to argue that the two traditions are wholly disparate, neither one affecting the other. Whether Bloom is influenced by the more philosophical path is not an issue here. At stake is Bloom's theory of literature turning upon the sublime; the sublime is the point around which his account of misreading turns.

Although Bloom writes overtly about the sublime in a number of places, he gives his first sustained definition of the sublime, or rather the literary sublime, in *Agon: Towards a Theory of Revisionism* (1982). That this considered definition of the sublime appears in an essay devoted to Freud is worthy of note. Since Bloom elects desire, will, and power, rather than being or knowledge, as his guides to the sublime, Freud is a necessary and experienced guide with whom to explore the outreaches of this terrain. How does Bloom define the sublime? Not surprisingly, Pseudo-Longinus' treatise is taken as the starting point for the definition. The sublime is a style of loftiness, "that is of verbal power, of greatness or strength conceived agonistically" (*Agon* 101). From the outset then we can discern at least one reason why Bloom follows Pseudo-Longinus rather than Aristotle. For Bloom, there is no literary culture independent of the *agon*, no aspect to literature which does not concern a struggle for poetic superiority. Bloom's account of the sublime moves from Pseudo-Longinus to the European Enlightenment, marking the major turns and twists to aesthetic theory which occurred at this time. The sublime becomes aligned with terror, and a certain pleasure which accompanies terror; those feelings of terror and pleasure are bound in a relation with freedom. "But in the European Enlightenment, this literary idea was strangely transformed into a vision of the terror . . . a terror uneasily allied with pleasurable sensations of augmented power, and even of narcissistic freedom . . ." (*Agon* 101). "Power" and "freedom" will be two words which frequently arise when speaking of the literary process as set out in Bloom's theory. These, aligned with *agon*, form the dominant tropes of the theory of literature which Bloom proposes.

There is nothing odd in a discussion of the sublime starting with Pseudo-Longinus and then moving towards the Enlightenment. A history of the sublime will begin with *On the Sublime*, normally tracing the waning and then the revival of this treatise once it is translated into French by Boileau in 1674. Later developments in the idea of the sublime will focus on the psychological, as in Edmund Burke, or on metaphysical concerns, as in Kant. Burke's *A Philosophical Enquiry into the Origin of our Ideas of the Sublime and Beautiful* (1759) sets out a new way of configuring the sublime. Unlike the treatise of Pseudo-Longinus, Burke's treatise heavily marks a distinction between the beautiful and the sublime. The sublime is featured as that which produces "delightful horror;" this feature becomes a benchmark for stipulating what the sublime (experience) is: delightful horror but also terror. Terror enters the domain of the sublime because it is considered the strongest emotional response. Strength, once again, is highlighted as a dominant feature of the sublime. After Burke, Kant is the next major figure in a history of the sublime. In short, we can say that Pseudo-Longinus is concerned with a stylistic account of the sublime, Edmund Burke offers a psychological account of the sublime, and Immanuel Kant is concerned with a philosophical account of the sublime.

Kant's third Critique, the *Critique of Judgement* (1790), drastically changes the traditional conception of the sublime. In the *Critique of Judgement*, Kant virtually inaugurates aesthetics; after this the philosophy of art is reset as aesthetics. The third Critique aims to bridge the gulf formed between his two earlier Critiques, which delineate the sphere of necessity and freedom. With Kant, the problem of presentation becomes paramount. It is necessary to circumscribe what we mean by presentation, which necessitates looking at the distinction Kant firmly makes between *Darstellung* and *Vorstellung*. Martha Helfar clearly articulates this difference when she notes: "Whereas *Vorstellung* represents a priori perceptions (intuitions, concepts, and ideas) already present *in* the mind, *Darstellung* renders a concept sensibly present or actual *to* the mind: it provides the mind with the objective reality necessary for cognition" (Helfar 25). *Darstellung* is sensible presentation or representation, whereas *Vorstellung* is representation. The importance of this distinction becomes apparent when discussing the sublime when we realize that the sublime involves a negative *Darstellung*; moreover the sublime's negative *Darstellung* "marks—and transcends—the limits of presentation" (Helfar 42). Ironically, then, the sublime is everything which is supremely great and colossal but is also that which cannot be presented. Kant renders the sublime as that which verges on being presentable, and in doing so inaugurates a problematic which haunts contemporary critical discussions of modern literature. Kant's sublime is a limit experience. We shall come back to the legacy that Kant leaves for contemporary thought, but for the moment it is necessary to return to the trajectory of the sublime that Bloom follows.

We can safely say that Bloom follows a traditional trajectory of the sublime; however, at a certain point he departs from it, altering the usual path by adding a new figure to the history. Freud, not surprisingly, is a key figure in Bloom's reading of the sublime. In fact, Bloom goes as far as to say that Freud's essay "The Uncanny" (1919) "is the only major contribution that the twentieth century has made to the aesthetics of the Sublime" (*Agon* 101). In part, Freud is included in this history because Bloom follows a sublime tradition which privileges the will, human desire and power. For Bloom one cannot fully understand how these tropes function in modernity without turning to Freud. Bloom's interest in the sublime is literary, and for Bloom the literary crucially involves the psychological. Literature is considered an *agon*, a struggle; and so literature is psychical warfare. Bloom extends the importance of the psychological aspects of the sublime by turning to Freud. With the help of Freud, Bloom perpetuates the idea of the sublime as that which produces psychic affects, a theory of the sublime which does not forget the importance of Burke's insights, his insistence on the terror and horror which the sublime produces. However, Bloom takes Burke one step further: the sublime not only causes psychic disturbances, but disturbances so great as to necessitate repression.

Bloom incorporates Freud into the tradition of the sublime. But for what reason, and in what way does Bloom read Freud as being an inheritor of the sublime? In short, Bloom views poetry's driving force to be desire, which can be articulated, with the help of Nietzsche, as the will to power. In Bloom's understanding, desire has always been a dominant aspect of the sublime. Like T. S. Dorsch, Bloom translates Pseudo-Longinus' sublime as signifying "a certain distinction and excellence of expression, that distinction and excellence by which *authors have been enabled to win immortal fame*" (Dorsch 24-25). Bloom is primarily interested in this desire, this compulsion for greatness which underpins the poetic process. Bloom's foremost concern is to reveal over and over again that *agon* is the dynamic at work within poetry. By turning to Freud, Bloom has a vocabulary in which to articulate the poet's will to power, the desire and the compulsion which molds poets into great, enduring poets.

1) The Sublime Moment: Negativity and Catastrophe

I have suggested that Bloom develops a theory of literature which hinges upon the trope of catastrophe. What I will show now is how Bloom's theory of literature is catastrophic; I will then examine its relation with the sublime by sketching out the ways negativity functions with a theory of literature underpinned by the sublime. As we proceed, it will become clear that Bloom's theory of literature is not only catastrophic—

in part his *oeuvre* is a testament to that—but more importantly reading the negative in literature, reading literature as catastrophe creation, is symptomatic of a reading of literature under the gaze of the sublime.

Although the basic tenets of Bloom's account of literary production are by now well known, I will recapitulate them for the sake of clarity. Bloom proposes a literary history in which poets and poems are determined by their anxiety of influence: a history in which poets struggle with one another for poetic greatness, employing any ruse they are able to. The motivating force behind literature, therefore, is anxiety. But what kind of anxiety is this which underpins literature? For Bloom, it is an anxiety which has been well articulated by Freud but also significantly by Kierkegaard. Viewed from a Bloomian standpoint, this is an anxiety which is caused from a sense of belatedness. It is an anxiety that makes strong poets feel that they have come too late, that everything has been written before them, that there is no need for them or their poetry: an unbearable feeling and one which would paralyze the poet if not repressed. In an attempt to overcome the sense of belatedness, or to hide the feelings of anxiety, ephebe poets distort their precursors. In Bloom's account they must do so in order to be able to write. The distortion of precursor poets, and their influence, manifests itself in six defensive techniques. Alongside this portrayal of poetic relations lies another—creation as catastrophe.

Bloom proposes that literature is, in its founding moment, a catastrophe. The catastrophic nature of literary creation is modeled on two stories of creation as catastrophe: the Freudian family romance and the creation of the world in Lurianic Kabbalah. Bloom receives from Lurianic Kabbalah a dialectical structure which he duplicates in developing his dialectic of revisionism. In Kabbalah, the first moment of the dialectic is negative: *tzimtzum* is a moment in which the Godhead limits himself in order for creation to begin. He absents Himself to make room for creation, creating space for something other than Himself to exist. Now the inspiration which Bloom receives from Lurianic Kabbalah is multifaceted; this need to create space in order for creation to occur is only one of the many ideas which Bloom appropriates from the Kabbalistic tradition. Creation as a catastrophe is further set in motion when the vessels holding the Godhead's emanations collapse, shattering into fragments, a moment in the dialectic called *Shevirath ha-kelim* in Kabbalah. The final movement is *tikkun*, restoration of the broken vessels. Bloom sees within this three-part movement of creation a pattern for all literary creation. For Bloom, the dynamic for creation is the same whether it be the creation of the world or of literature. Either way, it is a creation dependent upon catastrophe, and furthermore it is a catastrophic creation which has negativity as its founding dynamic.

Along with Kabbalah, Bloom employs what he calls the "Freudian family romance" as an exemplum for creation as catastrophe. What does Bloom mean by Freudian family romance, and what relation does it have to literary creation as catastrophe? When Bloom talks about poets forming and following a "family romance," he is, of course, alluding to the phenomenon that Freud perceived within family relations. Taking up this idea, Bloom argues that poets, like children in the Freudian account, construct fantasies about their poetic family relations in order to distort ambivalent feelings they have towards their poetic parents. Bloom employs it to show that lying at the heart of the poetic process is ambivalence towards precursor poets by ephebe poets. A poet, in the act of defending himself against precursors, has to lie to himself about his poetic origins. The poet in denying the primacy, dependency, and influence of his true precursors, is forced to delude himself; he lies about his poetic origins by imaging them as other than what they truly are. The catastrophe of creation stems from a problem with origins. As Bloom argues, "poetry is always at work *imaging its own origin*, or telling a persuasive lie about itself, to itself" (*Repression* 7). From this we can see that the poetic genealogy is one based on denial and ambivalence, and this produces a situation whereby poets will deny outright the influence of precursor poets.

It needs to be pointed out that Bloom, like most contemporary critics, is critical of many Freudian concepts while at the same time being heavily indebted to Freud. Bloom's relation to Freud has never been one of simple appropriation; similarly, Bloom is damning in his critique of psychoanalytic theories of creation. With regard to creativity, Bloom often finds psychoanalytic explanations of creativity problematic. In particular he finds that they "discount or repress two particular aspects of the genealogy of aesthetics" (*Agon* 98). The first aspect involves the refusal to accede that the creative moment, what Bloom calls the sublime moment, is a negative moment. The second aspect repressed is that the creative or negative moment encountered by every ephebe mirrors the precursor's own stance as an ephebe. That is, the negative or creative moment is one that is caught up with repetition. Bloom's sense of repetition here mirrors Kierkegaard's sense of repetition being a revision, a re-creation. For Bloom, the genealogy of aesthetics is founded upon negativity; aesthetics is driven by negativity.

We can say that Bloom's theory of literature is based upon the assumption that creation and catastrophe go hand in hand. But where does the sublime feature in Bloom's theory of literature? In Bloom's map of misreading there are three pairs of dialectical ratios and in each dialectical ratio a negative moment can be found which can be considered a crossing, a crisis-point, or an aporia. The crossing or crisis-point occurs "where a figuration of *ethos* or Limitation yields to a figuration of *pathos* of Representation" (*Stevens* 401). Limitation and representation are the two fundamental tropes in Bloom's theory of the poetic process; they correspond to action and desire. For Bloom, it is meaning itself which collects at these crisis-points, these negative moments between limitation and representation. Now Bloom argues that the breaking of the middle, or second crossing, the crossing of Solipsism, is where the sublime moment features in a poem. This crossing takes place between the ratios *kenosis* and *daemonization*; that is to say the crossing of the sublime is a "gap of negation or disjunctive generation of meaning" (*Agon* 238).

Daemonization, or the counter-sublime, corresponds analogically in the map of misreading with the psychic defense repression, the rhetorical tropes hyperbole or litotes, and to images of high and low in poetry. *Daemonization*, the fourth revisionary ratio, represents the stage in the poetic process whereby the ephebe poet renders his precursor as being weaker than himself. *Daemonization* is the moment in which the sublimity of the precursor poet is contested. Never in reality was it a true sublimity but always a counter-sublimity, which is indeed what all figurations of sublimity finally are in Bloom's map. It is important to recognize the difference between the movement Bloom traces in the sublime moment from the movement traditionally articulated as the encounter with the sublime. Bloom writes: "The Counter-Sublime does not show forth as limitation to the imagination proving its capabilities. In *this* transport, the only visible object eclipsed or dissolved is the vast image of the precursor, and the mind is wholly happy to be thrown back upon itself" (*Anxiety* 100–01).

Daemonization corresponds to the psychic defense repression; according to Bloom, within the traditions of the sublime there is a constant association between sublimity and negativity, and within his own writings this relation between sublimity and negativity hinges on the concept of repression. As Freud formulated it, repression bears a relation to negation. Indeed, one could go as far as to say that repression depends upon negation in so far as the only possibility of a repressed image coming into consciousness is conditioned by negation. That is, the repressed image can enter consciousness only once it has been negated, although, of course, for the person involved, the repressed image is still not acceptable.

In Bloom's account, the sublime moment of creativity always involves major repression. He argues that "the Sublime depends upon repression" (*Repression* 74). But what needs to be repressed in the poetic process? It is precisely the sublimity of the prior poet. It is here that we can gauge once again Bloom's need to turn to Freud. Repression, for Bloom, was always a factor in the workings of the sublime, but one that was never fully articulated until Freud—or more precisely, never articulated fully until Bloom himself perceives this relation and begins to articulate it. Bloom turns to Freud in order to elucidate the psychical workings within the creative moment, to articulate with a ready formulated vocabulary what precisely is being repressed in the poetic process.

The sublime, in Bloom's argument, shares a relation to repetition and quotation. Bloom argues that the sublime in poetry is "produced through quotation . . . repressed quotation" (*Agon* 229). It is the revisionary ratio *kenosis*, the ratio before *daemonization* which helps save the poet from simply being a repetition of the precursor. It must be remembered that together *daemonization* and *kenosis* form a dialectic, and it is the crossing within the dialectic which reveals the sublime moment in a poem. The sublime or negative moment occurs in a poem when an ephebe poet represses an earlier poet's writings, in the moment when the ephebe refuses to quote the prior poet. But in the very act of repressing these writings, traces of the earlier poet can be felt. These repressed quotations leave traces in every poet's writings. As Bloom suggests, to become memorable a poem must supersede or overcome the memory left over by previous writings; it must make the reader forget that he or she has heard this speech before. It must lull the reader into believing that the words of the poem have a sublime strength and priority of their own, while in reality they merely over-write a language already written, a poem already composed.

In a similar manner, the sublime is associated with the power of naming and un-naming. The sublime is the un-naming of a precursor, and is accomplished by a purposeful forgetting. What are forgotten are a precursor's anterior texts. The idea of naming and un-naming is central to creation according to Bloom; it is one of the major paradigms of poetry. "I would venture one definition of the literary Sublime (which to me seems always a negative Sublime)," says Bloom, "as being that mode in which the poet, while expressing previously repressed thought, desire, or emotion, is able to continue to defend himself against his own created image by disowning it, a defense of *un-naming* it rather than *naming* it" (*Agon* 108-09). The sublime moment occurs, then, in the presentation of repressed desires, in the presentation of repressed quotations: that is, with every poet's ability to repress and in the act of repressing to render their precursors as being without sublimity in order to gain sublimity for their own poetry.

Let us think for a moment of the legacy that Kant left aesthetics, namely the difficulty of presentation. Although Bloom would not consider himself indebted to Kant, he is. This becomes clear when we consider the problems involved in the presentation of the sublime moment. The sublime is precisely that which cannot be successfully presented. Certainly, Bloom does not tackle this problem in the same manner as other contemporary theorists concerned with aesthetics: Jean-Luc Nancy or Philippe Lacoue-Labarthe, for example. The sublime moment in a poem for Bloom, as I demonstrated earlier, is a moment when one represses a precursor poet. What is repressed is the sublimity of the prior poet's writing. But for *daemonization* to take place, the poet must cite a repressed quotation. The poet must write something which, in the very act of writing, both presents and does not present the precursor poet's writing. The earlier poet is simultaneously there and not there. What is repressed, but also presented in an oblique fashion, is nothing other than the poet's desire: it becomes itself a presentation of repressed desire. In this manner, *daemonization*, or the sublime and negative moment, takes place precisely in the same way as does repression in Freud's account. The content of the repressed material is presented, but presented in an inverse or negated manner. It is the degree to which the ephebe poet negates, or represses, the precursor which determines the ephebe's strength or sublimity, for Bloom.

The sublime, according to Bloom, represents the agonistic struggle which builds and strengthens a poet's selfhood. Without repression, without the sublime, the ephebe poet would not be able to write; the weight of previous poets and their writing would crush any would-be poet. In strong writing an intimation of the sublime is experienced, and this experience bolsters the poet's selfhood. We can discern, then, that although creation is catastrophic for Bloom, it is also subject-forming; subjectivity is formed through the act of writing. In this respect Bloom is an unlikely ally of Kant. In the end, both Harold Bloom and Immanuel Kant see the sublime as strengthening the self.

2) A Condition of the Sublime: Negative Defenses of Literature

From Pseudo-Longinus, Bloom borrows the idea that the sublime requires strength, strength required by both the writer and the reader. Bloom articulates this idea so frequently that it becomes a slogan of sorts: the sublime "exists to compel readers to forsake easier pleasures in favor of more strenuous satisfactions" (*Poetics* 176). This notion sits uneasily with humanistic conception of literature. If Pseudo-Longinus is correct, and it has been a condition of literature since its outset, why then have there been humanistic arguments made to support literature, why have defenses of literature ever been made? Do we delude ourselves when we think of the study of literature as having a positive affect? The question itself may be naïve, but the answers we receive may be surprising. In short, the answer for Bloom will be 'yes.' Part of Bloom's critical aim has been to illuminate the fact that literature has been agonistic since the start.

To consider literature in terms of positive or negative may be absurd, but for Bloom, and many of his contemporaries, literature does indeed fall to the side of the negative rather than the positive. However, Bloom, like Jacques Derrida, distinguishes the positive from the affirmative. Bloom is concerned with a non-positive affirmation. Let us put this into context. Literature, for someone like Bloom, can be positive and rewarding, but can only be so on a singular level. Literature, as Bloom often says, teaches us how to speak to ourselves; the problem is that it does not teach us how to speak to others. Likewise, the relation one has to the sublime is completely individual. Kant proposed that the sublime falls within the domain of the private, and in part, this is why literature need not have any social consequence, either for Kant or for Bloom. We may want to question Bloom here, as he has often argued that religion is a kind of poetry and religion has vast social consequences. However, we must keep in mind that for Bloom the religion which produces social consequences is religion that has become ideology. When Bloom aligns literature and religion he is speaking, perhaps naïvely, of religion minus ideology. The sublime forms no community, not even a community of writers or a community of readers. Our engagement with literature is completely singular, and in part, it is this singularity of literature which places it under the auspices of the sublime. It is this sublime marking which necessitates that all defenses of literature be negative.

Works Cited

Burke, Edmund. *A Philosophical Enquiry into the Origins of our Ideas of the Sublime and Beautiful*. Ed. J. T. Boulton. London: Routledge and Kegan Paul, 1958.

Dorsch, T. S., trans. and ed. *Aristotle, Horace, Longinus: Classical Literary Criticism*. Harmondsworth: Penguin, 1965.

Freud, Sigmund. "The Uncanny." *The Standard Edition of the Complete Psychological Works of Sigmund Freud*. Vol. 17. Trans. and ed. James Strachey, et al. London: Hogarth, 1955. 217–56.

Hart, Kevin. "The Rapid, Impatient Labour of the Negative: Reading Harold Bloom." *Scripsi* [Melbourne] 9.1 (1993): 185–203.

Helfar, Martha B. *The Retreat of Representation: The Concept of* Darstellung *in German Critical Discourse*. Albany, NY: SUNY P, 1996.

Kant, Immanuel. *The Critique of Judgement*. Trans. James Creed Meredith. Oxford: Oxford UP, 1952.

Longinus. *On Great Writing (On the Sublime)*. Trans. G. M. A. Grube. Indianapolis: Bobbs-Merrill, 1957.

Bloom and the School of Resentment: An Interrogation of the "Preface and Prelude" to The Western Canon

BARNARD TURNER

> Poets, we can assume, as children *assimilated* more than the rest of us, and yet somehow *accommodated* less. . . .
>
> —*Map* 53

As any 'canonical' Preface, that to *The Western Canon* both pre- and post-figures that which it introduces; it posits a centre—Shakespeare—but exhibits a characteristic contextual amplitude, through which Bloom recalls both his own work and his readings of others, and issues a battle-cry for acts of resistance against the "School of Resentment," aberrant, inappropriate and superfluous modes of literary criticism. As is admirably apparent in Bloom's "Elegiac Conclusion" to the book, his is partly at least a book of resentment against the School of Resentment: "This book is not directed at academics, because only a small remnant of them [not the 'Resenters' or the 'multiculturalists' in the common academic sense] still read for the love of reading" (483–84). It is a cheap shot, unworthy of a fine critic, but incisive because it tells those of us who do not live in America and see it 'exorbitantly,' that is, in relation to our own spirit of place rather than as an essential ground of being, much about a particular view of contemporary American academia often reproduced in the popular press. In this regard, *Canon* presents an initial manoeuvre in a war of position which characterises much of his subsequent work. Throughout *Genius*, for example, Bloom reviles against "fashions" in literary studies, and on occasion it appears that his perspective is informed by his view of his own colleagues; in one Whitmanesque flourish, he regrets that "academic imposters" and "resentment-pipers" surround him (182), and later compares one "Professor of Resentment" to a "Marxist cheer-leader" (626). And yet, for someone who has argued so cogently for the importance of Joseph Conrad (*Canon* 10) to American modernism, the implicit distinction here between "them" and "us" is salient, not to say cutting; why, that is, does Bloom not here want to be, as Conrad's main characters frequently, if disparagingly say of others, "one of us"? One can understand both his critique of certain fashionable literary approaches (although I wonder a little about the percentage of Marxist critics on any given twenty-first century American campus), and, even more, his criticism that literary study has been subjected to laws (instant gratification, novelty for its own sake, self-promotion) comparable to those of fashion, yet surely Bloom can hardly disown his status as an "academic." To rephrase then a question Bloom asked himself earlier in his career: "What does [he] mean [here] by '[not-]we'" (*Map* 37)? How can the Sterling Professor of Humanities at Yale University, the Berg Professor of English at New York University, not count himself as an academic? Should we infer that he is not now writing as one, perhaps because he enjoys the works discussed? Bloom is not indulging in an act of sheer populist demagoguery here, for reaching out to the community—and Bloom's community is vast, of course—is a well-established intellectual activity; Emerson's lyceum lectures are perhaps the precursor here. What I am more interested in, and what links to my main strategy in this essay, is the "space between" the Professor and the Populist, which has of course—from the days of the *Modern Critical Interpretations* series to those of *Bloom's Notes*—so characterised Bloom's career. To speak *from* the Professorial Chair is not to speak *as* it, perhaps.

The Preface is informed by spatial and temporal relationships. The latter should not surprise us, for after all a canon is the intersection of time and the timeless; the former needs some discussion, as much of Bloom's analysis, from *Anxiety* on, has been founded on spatial metaphors. The first three "revisionary ratios" all involve spatial relationships: *clinamen* (from a root meaning 'slant,' 'incline'), "*tessera* or link" (*Anxiety* 66), and *kenosis* (literally 'emptying'). Thus a genealogy of diachronic intertextual relations becomes, to use Bloom's own term, a "map" which moves out from the present, as an evaluation of the past for the benefit of the canonizers and a legitimation of their hegemony.

Bloom's "central" figure, or cardinal point here, is similarly both positioned and displaced, because there is—as Bloom has subsequently pointed out—already "an excess beyond representation" in Shakespeare, as there is in Bloom's reading of him (*Shakespeare* xviii; see *Peripheral* xv). Even this excess—the movement beyond a point where criticism may follow or "map"—may not go far enough for Bloom; in a move which seems both to invert and to evoke Johnson's famous claim about *Paradise Lost*, he opines in the conclusion to his short book on Shakespeare's longest play that "we want to hear Hamlet on everything," as he regrets that it is not long enough (*Hamlet* 154; again, who is this "we"?). That which therefore cannot be "re-presented" is repeated, and the "Preface" to *The Western Canon*, with its copious references to Shakespeare and his works, already prefigures two of the book's main chapters and its "Elegiac Conclusion," where the dramatist returns, both for his "sensuous immediacy" and his "universalism" (*Canon* 489); in turn, the *Shakespeare* book of 1998 gives Bloom's subsequent thinking on the dramatist, and this pattern is repeated (often in combination with Cervantes) in later volumes. Vital to these arguments is the view that the impulse to write Shakespeare's works can never exhaust that which can be said. There are moments in which his readings, as a token of this inclusivity, seem to coincide with those "transgressive" ones of the "School of Resentment," as Robert Sawyer has argued (167–68). This is not perhaps surprising—indeed, it could be seen as an offshoot of Bloom's "hyperbolic" ("Bardolatric") view of Shakespeare—particularly since his perspective on the dramatist does not foreground nor is limited to those characteristic of the "School." If Shakespeare is then originary and central, then, he is a fluid core, and the very move that would see him as the "central figure" of the Western Canon (1) casts into question the figure of "centrality" itself, and, by extension, Bloom himself as the central figure in (the debate on) it. To use "figure" in this sense is usual, common, and for most people proper, but it is not *canonical*; as Bloom himself has said, a *figura* is "traditionally" the general concept which would include a trope, and for Quintilian "a kind of discourse departing from common usage" (*Map* 93).[1] There is therefore already something unusual, even uncanny, about a 'figure,' a trace of both excess and *Ersatz*, such that we can but paraphrase but never exhaust it. On the other hand, intertwined with this meaning as if one of those in Escher's drawings, is the sense of a 'figure' as the Latin

---

[1] Peter de Bolla gives a sustained reading of the transmutations of the terms "trope" and "figure," from classical to eighteenth-century rhetoric to Bloom, and at one point notes that the terms "inevitably attract each other with a force we cannot seem to control" (112); even more, then, he continues, is needed the will, and the ability, to keep them apart.

translation of the Greek σχῆμα, the *outline*, shape or plan of something, and, by extension, from its relation to the verb *fingere*, that which has been created deliberately and purposefully by the effort of human will, which Bloom at the end of his Preface—in a palimpsestic reformulation of a "canonical" Nietzschean phrase—calls "the will to figuration" (11).

Can therefore a 'figure,' canonically considered, *have* or *be* a centre? Indeed, it is the very possibility of and demand for the displacement of the canonical, in both religious and literary senses, that has dominated exegesis, and—in an important explication of these procedures—Erich Auerbach has noted that, for figural interpretation, "a connection is established between two events which are linked neither temporally nor causally—a connection which it is impossible to establish in the horizontal dimension (if I may be permitted to use this term for a temporal extension)" (73-74). One might add that such an interpretation, as Nietzsche describes it in section four of *The Birth of Tragedy*, is but the "Schein [eines] Scheins," the glimmer of an appearance, Goethe's transient, illusive allusion perhaps.[2] In all three writers is evinced the difficulty of thinking object relations temporally without recourse to spatial metaphors. Bloom's rhetorical thrust—his opening here and yet so familiar gambit—is to conflate historiography and cartography, or linear and concentric images of the transmission process of cultural canonicity. The diachronicity implicit in the temporal ordering of texts conflates with the synchronicity—as far as this is possible in regard to the mindfulness of the temporality of all such sequencing—of the gaze which would so order them.

It is worthwhile then to move to the end of the Preface, and to recall its final reformulation, its closing act of nostalgia for the canon and for a reflection on an extended work on its *technai*: "the desire to write greatly is the desire to be elsewhere, in a time and place of one's own, in an originality that must compound with inheritance, with the anxiety of influence" (11). *Hic et ubique? Hic et aliquō? Hic quam aliquō?* In Bloom's characteristic, and relatively simple statement is compressed the essence of his mysticism, his Kabbalah-mantra discernible throughout his work: the *here* that can be described is not the true here, as this here exists in a tension with—a space between—the elsewhere which is also a

---

[2] The reference is of course to the untranslatable, unparaphrasable conclusive "Chorus Mysticus" of *Faust* 2: "Alles Vergängliche ist nur ein Gleichnis," the final word being of particular difficulty for Nietzsche interpretation; Wayne Klein gives an overview of the issues (see e.g. 435).

past, and thus both ou-topic and ou-chronic at once. It is a limit position, one which is demanding to keep fully in one's attention; in subsequent work, there seems a recidivist element in Bloom's view of the great, in those magisterial (*ex cathedra* one might say, but Bloom has always written from this self-conscious position) tomes, of which *How to Read and Why* offers a short example: "the strongest, most authentic motive for deep reading of the now much-abused traditional canon is the search for a difficult pleasure" (29). One searches actively—but under whose propulsion or "motive"—for difficulty? Reading thus becomes a penitential flagellation, perhaps. In his *Wisdom* book, Bloom reflects on the contrastive virtues of wisdom literature, that which offers a "Perfection" which "can either absorb or destroy us, depending on what we bring to it" (a Derridean interpretation of the *pharmakon* would be misplaced, or would at least need to be heard through a comparable source in Kabbalistic scholarship—for Bloom here, Moshe Idel and Gershom Scholem). In his closing paragraph, he opines that "we read and reflect because we hunger and thirst after wisdom," that which "we cannot embody" but which "we can be taught . . . to know" (284). We "search," we "hunger," we "thirst," we are driven; yet in all this, what is the prime mover, beyond the pedagogic imperatives on the one hand or an indeterminate, but untested foundational quasi-psychological assumption about human needs on the other? J. K. Rowling "feeds a vast hunger for unreality," notes Bloom in a 2000 *Wall Street Journal* piece; in the minds of her readers, this unreality could pass for wisdom of sorts.

Bloom has of course given a psychology—what he calls, in *Map*, a "psychology of belatedness" (52)—to Eliot's argument about "Tradition and the Individual Talent," as what is merely strongly asserted in Eliot's essay finds its rationale in the 'anxiety' thesis. Yet he has done much more, perhaps unwittingly, since he has placed the discussion squarely within the debate about *alterity*, where the only constant is the will to assert difference, to claim an otherness on the fringes of the known which is however no more than that which is already present, habitual and yet uncodified in the subaltern. "It is, ironically, the disintegrative moment, even movement, of enunciation—that sudden disjunction of the present—that makes possible the rendering of culture's global reach." The words are Homi Bhabha's (217), not Harold Bloom's, but the importance of the enunciative as constitutive of the new is shared by both, such that the formulations uncannily echo each other, as do of course the writers' initials.

It might of course be thought absurd to pitch these very different writers together, given Bloom's ostensible reaction against multiculturalism. Yet *The Western Canon* is in a sense Bloom's updating of Pound's *How to Read*, as is apparent in its Appendix, widening Pound's scope (the only non-European whom Pound lists is Confucius, and he dismisses the "Rhooshuns" [40]) and toning down his pomposity. (In contrast, *How to Read and Why*, with its apparently more specific allusion, is more of the genre of explication than polemic.) Bloom includes no Chinese works in his Appendix—his concern is after all the "*Western*" canon—yet it is heartening to see works, both ancient and modern, from the Near East and India present there, even if the list (not entirely his own idea, it seems), his self-confessed "mug's game" of "cultural prophecy" (516), is overly laden with current Americans, and a few (too few) writers from Canada and Australia are listed; the South Pacific is perhaps *too far West* of Yale, too far out all its life, for Bloom's vision to stray this far. This is after all a "Western" canon unashamedly written from and for the *Eastern* seaboard of the United States; it may be after all that it is Bloom himself who is not far West enough. That "West" which would act as a fulcral lode from which its canon might be surveyed is in any case difficult to locate past the millennium. No-one should or would of course expect even Harold Bloom to have read everything. A consideration of contemporary Australian poetry, as strong and vital as ever, is not part of his task here, even if he has subsequently written an extensive overview to John Kinsella's selected poems, in which he summons the Australian poet, alongside Shakespeare, in his critique of Deconstruction (xv). Even here, however, Bloom's technique is to read Kinsella through other canonical figures; since the selection serves as an introduction of the poet to the American market, one might forgive a marked tendency, characteristic of much recent American rhetoric, to see the foreign as it reminds him of the local (Ashbery, for example). Some volumes such as Tsaloumas' *The Barge*, Murray's *Translations from the Natural World*, Walwicz's *Red roses*, Salom's *Feeding the Ghost* and ΠO's *24 hours* might form part of an extended 'prophecy' with the strength of their interrogations of place, space and self.

And what of Asian-American poetry, which is full of 'strong' readings, but which has yet to find a criticism which would lift itself out of the socio-cultural? Here Bloom's criticism of what he calls "multiculturalist" readers needs to be nuanced, such that the poetry can be separated from the reductivist readings, against which Garrett Hongo had already written in the introduction to his 1993 anthology *The Open Boat*. It may be ironic then, for Bloom's main strategy, that 'Bloomian' readings of the multicultural and the multi-ethnic are now timely, but such seminal poems as Marilyn Chin's "Barbarian Suite" (in *The Phoenix Gone, The Terrace Empty*, 1994)—with its negotiations of Whitman and Eliot, among others—and Hongo's "The Pier" (haunted by Wordsworth and Yeats) and "Ancestral Graves, Kahuku" (haunted by Valéry; both in *The River of Heaven*, 1988), as read in the context of Bloom's work, remind us that his critical strategy has always been, like theirs, multi-temporal, multicultural and hybrid. Visions in these poems of the here and now are written in the interstices, the spaces opened up, in the canonical as that which is well and deeply read, and this is of course the site of influence as health and recovery (*Anxiety* 95), as Prolific and Devourer both. In the introduction to *The Open Boat*, moreover, Hongo made a point similar to Bloom's that poetry—"even," one might say, Asian-American poetry—should be "read" and not simply "interpreted" (xxxiv). Hongo's later pronouncements in his preface—that literature constructs "primarily a subjective, even a dissident truth" (xxxvi), and that he seeks "a kind of serious bewilderment that clarifies experience" (xxxvii)—manage to combine strategies reminiscent of Emerson, Bloom and Nietzsche, as of Buddhism and the rhetoric of empowerment.

In his placement of Shakespeare, moreover, Bloom is doing more than putting the Bard back on the pedestal from which multicultural levelling has thrown him, as he has instilled once more the spirit of Shakespeare as father, demiurge and structure of at least the now paradoxically polyglot, polysemous Anglophonic world. The 1997 'pan-Asian' *Lear* of the Japan Foundation Asia Center, to mention but one example, with largely Japanese funding and look and with interventions from South-East Asian theatrical practices, but with even less 'Western' input than Kurosawa's film, is an act of multicultural *kenosis* and *apophrades* of Shakespeare through which the canonical source-text is taken as an opportunity, rather than as that which needs to be negated. While stylized and 'over the top' in some ways, the play is both multicultural and 'excessive,' even if the latter is not perhaps such as Bloom might claim for Shakespeare. It is at least faithful to its own interpretation of this spirit of excess. Thus Bloom's point, in the new preface to *Anxiety*, that "real multiculturalists, all over the globe, accept Shakespeare as the one indispensable author" (xv), finds its real, haunting echo in this very living production which has received positive reviews in Hong Kong, Singapore and Perth.

Bloom therefore—and this is a point which is often overlooked—is careful to distinguish this true multicultural activity from that generally practised in the universities, which would concentrate more on "contextualization" in the attempt to make, from students of literature, "amateur political scientists, uninformed sociologists, incompetent anthropologists, mediocre philosophers, and overdetermined cultural historians" (*Canon* 487). Whether this criticism is just, and whether, half the way around the world from Yale, we should concern ourselves about it, are matters themselves of cultural politics, of the evaluation of the role and function of literature in the university, and they will not be my concern here; neither am I particularly concerned with Bloom's Shakespeare, except *figuratively* in the 'original' sense. And yet, as I shall shortly argue, there can be for Bloom no 'original figure,' just as there can be no 'original text;' positing Shakespeare as such then becomes an act of hypostatization, antithetical to Bloom's own "originary" claim in *Anxiety* that "the meaning of a poem can only be another poem" (94). Everything else, says Bloom, "rhetorical, Aristotelian, phenomenological, and structuralist criticisms," is reduction. What interests me, then, are the dialectical strategies at play in Bloom's critique, where an initial sense of resentment of social science by the arts departments (because of false economies in university budgets on the debased Platonic-'Republican' assumption that *The Odyssey* and *Hamlet* are myths and therefore luxuries, while the speculative calculation of next year's GDP or future voting trends are not), and the arts' resultant pusillanimous attempts to mimic the social sciences' funding and perceived relevance by mimicking their research style and method, become themselves the object of Bloom's own resentment. Yet can there ever be an 'initial resentment' at all, abstractly considered? Probably not, as the *re*-prefix already points to a prior state than the one described by the term itself. Resentment, as a willed reaction, is never original, any more than there is *one* source text from which all else is *epigonentum*. And yet the *variety* of sources of Bloom's critique of the "School of Resentment" is not hard to find in his own writing, not only in the scattered but gradually accumulating disdain of 'reductive' criticism—especially Marxism, Feminism and 'French' theories—but also in the very operations of the revisionary ratios themselves, which necessarily posit a prior against which the new reacts, measures itself, and is itself measured. Since that reactionary force implicit in the act of resentment itself is pervasive, not only in Bloom's work, can one then talk of the "School of Resentment"—or resentment itself—without oneself falling prey to it? Robert C. Solomon notes of Nietzsche's "ressentiment" that "lack of power is not the cause but the content of resentment" (98) and that the emotion "presuppos[es] impotence" (108); all criticism tacitly acknowledges its powerlessness before its object, as Bloom acknowledges when he argues for Shakespearean excess. The School of Resentment, ironically itself, would will its own power over the text, but only by not measuring itself by it at all. Yet it is not so easy to overcome the influence of "decadence and *ressentiment*" over willing, a common issue for Nietzsche in the reading of Steven D. Hales and Rex Welshon (178).

It is instructive then to foreground Nietzsche's method here, not only because his work has been a background pulse throughout Bloom's career, but also because the Preface closes with a reference to him. Early on, Bloom had praised the German as "the prophet of the antithetical," and the *Genealogy of Morals* as "the profoundest study available to [him] of the revisionary and ascetic strains in the aesthetic temperament" (*Anxiety* 8). What had then appeared to cognition ("revision") had earlier—in Nietzsche—appeared in/as feeling ("*ressentiment*"), and it is now this excess of the agonistic, with which Bloom has been struggling throughout, that appears in his metaphor and critique of the School of Resentment. Nietzsche's drive to find the originary, explicatory historical power (the "genealogy") of *ressentiment* for law and religion implicates his own empiricist 're-sent-ment,' nothing for him being in the intellect that was not already and is not still in the senses, and thus the turn back, the *re*-inscription, the *re*-lict (the "chosen again"), the feeling again and self-satisfaction of the given raised to and risen as a principle. Thus for Bloom the French recoil in the term is highlighted—a particularly Nietzschean nuance, as Georg Stauth and Bryan S. Turner remind us in their discussion of the term (69).

If for Nietzsche then *ressentiment*, bad conscience, and the slave revolt of Christianity were interlinked (as in the second essay of the *Genealogy*), then for Bloom the School of Resentment is nothing more than an act of bad faith/conscience (see *Genealogy* 2.16), where instincts cannot be revealed, but need to be directed inwards (1.10). The American Cultural Revolution of the 1960s plays then for Bloom—as earlier for Adorno—the questionable role in the mind of the aristocrat (in the Greek sense) of democratic urges now displaced into new hegemonies, of old high priests of the psychedelic becoming new presbyters of the IT age, and thus of the English Civil War for the late Milton and the French Revolution for Nietzsche: the "will to the lowering, the abasement, the leveling and the decline and the twilight of mankind" (*Genealogy* 1.16).

(One might here add D. H. Lawrence to the disaffected, albeit that he exhibits his post-Nietzschean resentment in ways which Bloom, rather summarily, dismisses as those of a "rather weird political theorist" [*Canon* 408], but whose poetry, both in the "Canonical" list and the Kinsella introduction, he brings to prominence.) In the terms of Nietzsche's *Jenseits von Gut und Böse* (section 30), the School of Resentment would make all books for the bravest ("die Tapfersten") into those for the pusillanimous ("die niedere Seele, die niedrigere Lebenskraft"). To be "brave enough" for such great works, one must learn to capitalise on the excess implied in our "resentment"—the process of sensing our way through them—and not be confined within it, so that we point out from it as we point it out. In resentment, for Nietzsche as for Bloom, is the continual recurrence of the eternally pusillanimous-platitudinous.

To turn now to another spirit behind Bloom's writing[3] (who appears both implicitly and explicitly towards the end of the *Canon*'s Preface), we could assert that a 'Resenter' for Bloom, as for Nietzsche (had he known it) is the obverse of Emerson's self-reliant "Man Thinking," being of that

---

[3] But of course in a Bloomian fashion, in that act of defiance to the "institutionalization" of "Emerson's procedures" of which he speaks in *Map* (30). When, for example, in *A Map of Misreading*, Bloom talks of "the ratio of *apophrades*" as "the return of the precursors ... in colors not their own" (90), I am reminded as much of Emerson's lines from the beginning of "Self-Reliance," "In every work of genius we recognize our own rejected thoughts; they come back to us with a certain alienated majesty" (*Essays* 176), as of a variety of ghostly echoes from Shakespeare and Vergil. When, late in the *Canon* Preface (10), Bloom refers to "Emersonian irony" and "pragmatism," he appears to be referring only to his point that "originals are not original," and yet Emerson is perhaps here placed because of the characteristically Emersonian tone, phrasing and diction into which Bloom has lapsed in the immediately preceding sentences, for example in the claim that "aesthetic criticism returns us to the autonomy of imaginative literature and the sovereignty of the solitary soul, the reader not as a person in society but as the deep self, our ultimate inwardness." One might here also be reminded that, for Bloom, as for Shelley, the deep self, like the deep truth, is imageless. This is a brief trajectory in Bloom's Preface, the consideration of which I here of course have relegated to a footnote, but it can serve as a helpful reminder that the relationship between texts is nothing without the relationship between particular passages in those texts, and that influence can sometimes be no more than a vague hint or nuance of tone incorporated into the subsequent work. The combination here of the Romantic, the Transcendentalist and the Aristocratic (in the original Greek sense for Bloom, "the fundamental archetype for literary achievement will always be Pindar" [*Canon* 6]) is also of course characteristic of Bloom's work in general.

class of which Emerson speaks in "The American Scholar:" "meek young men [who] grow up in libraries, believing it their duty to accept the views" of the acknowledged great (*Selected Essays* 88). One might also be reminded of the "central commonplace" that Strawson examines in his "Freedom and Resentment" essay: "the great importance that we attach to the attitudes and intentions towards us of other human beings, and the great extent to which our personal feelings and reactions depend upon, or involve, our beliefs about these attitudes and intentions" (5). One need only substitute "a weak reader" for "we" here to give that against which Emerson is fighting. Emerson, famously, continues: "I had better never see a book than to be warped by its attraction clean out of my orbit, and made a satellite instead of a system" (88). Bloom's work against the School of Resentment is to place such sentiments about the engagements between readers and texts squarely within his contention for the autonomy of the literary-aesthetic, such that a strong reading of Emerson's sentence would give: "A book had better never see a critic than to be warped by its attraction . . . and made a satellite instead of a system." Yet behind this, of course, for Bloom but not for Emerson, is William Blake, the third spirit of his writing, and particularly Los's famous lines from *Jerusalem*:

> I must Create a System, or be enslav'd by another Mans
> I will not Reason & Compare: my business is to Create. (*Complete Poetry* 153)

Resentful works, to borrow more of Blake's famous sayings, are "only Analytics," "analysis of the more sublime, but no further," and thus "recapitulations of all superficial opinions" rather than "new truth" (42–43). A reading of Bloom on Resentment would, in summary, find that the term comes from Nietzsche, the discourse from Emerson, and the tone from Blake.

Where then do the power, originality and strategic force behind Bloom's critique lie? Why is the Professor also a best-seller, a 'public figure'? Here again the recourse to Shakespeare is instructive. Bloom says at the end of his "Elegy for the Canon" which follows the Preface that the dramatist gives us not only "our representation of cognition but much of our capacity for cognition" (38–39); the return to the text is also therefore part of the voyage out. We are not the same after having read *Hamlet*, but we are not Hamlets either; reading, hearing or seeing the play are essays (attempts) in object-relations, with all *termini* in the process open-ended and constitutive of new beginnings. Bloom does assert at the opening of *Shakespeare* that the "enigma" of the dramatist is that he produced "an art so infinite that it *contains* us, and will go on enclosing those likely to come after us" (xix). Yet we are "contained" in Shakespeare in the same way that we are contained in the universe, in which we have such considerable freedom of movement that we may decide we are not so contained; otherwise, there could be no apostatic "School of Resentment," no dissident Shakespeareans like Tolstoy and Orwell.

Therefore the assertion of containment must be approached carefully, not only in terms of the importance of 'strong readings' and the dialectics of literary composition which Bloom has foregrounded throughout his career, nor even of the inability of any reader to comprehend the unique one moment of the text, to summon it to awareness and recompose it for oneself and others, but also, and more fundamentally, as part of the resistance to the merely secular which has dominated Bloom's works. This appears of course in his resistance to secular (temporal, reactive, circumscribed) *readings* of texts, those by the "School of Resentment" being at the forefront, but also including 'modernizations,' catering to popular notions of relevance. (It is hard for me not to concur soundly with his view in the *Shakespeare* book that the 1995 film of *Richard III* with Sir Ian McKellen in the title role is as good an argument as any that "public recitation" is conceivably better than "indeliberate travesty" [729].) Yet Bloom is also more generally opposed to the *division* made between the secular and the spiritual in the canon, a term which (we hardly need reminding) is of religious provenance. The equation is here apparent: the sacred dominates the secular just as the literary dominates the sociopolitical.

I find it difficult in this regard not to think of Cardinal Newman, whose "Idea" of the university has a certain resonance for and with Bloom's, whose opposition to the transient, the fashionable, and the 'periodical' (in both senses) is as acute, and who was as vehemently opposed to journey-work and amateurism in scholarship. In his own "Preface" to the series of lectures given in the context of the establishment of a Catholic university in Dublin, Newman inveighs against the demand that one "have a view at a moment's notice on any question from the Personal Advent to the Cholera or Mesmerism" (10). Later, Newman declaims against the strategy, as he sees it, of contemporary education: "All things now are to be learned at once, not first one thing, then another, not one well, but many badly. Learning is to be without exertion, without attention, without toil; without grounding, without advance, without finishing. There is to be nothing individual in it; and this, forsooth, is the wonder of the age" (103). Such contentions—cries of resistance against the demand that we give all to what others, not perhaps in our own best interests, would call the immediate, the salient or the "newsworthy"—are not hard to reconcile with Bloom's criticism of "contextualization," as quoted above. Both would remind us that *aller Anfang ist schwer*: the Cardinal, that one must make a good strenuous beginning and then progress to something else; the cardinal point in Anglo-American scholarship, that we should accept the effort needed to keep page with Shakespeare and, again, work from there. If for Newman, "Theology [was] a Branch of Knowledge" (as the title of his second Discourse proclaims), for Bloom the spiritual in general is an indispensable element of any approach to or formation of the canon or the canonical, and to be differentiated from the merely, if paradoxical theocratic of a Gnostic turn, which—in his 1993 book on *The American Religion*—he opines as characteristic of "post-Christian" American belief. To turn to those of whom one would have spoken well is to turn away from others one dares not mention: days of criticism become *apophrades hemerai*, *dies nefasti*, days of renunciation on which one would have the dead speak for and through us, if speech is possible at all, days on which no assembly can be held or no market open. All criticism is an annunciation and an observance of the sabbath, as is already prefigured in the final main chapter of *Anxiety*, on *apophrades*. And yet there is a real consolation offered here also on a more mundane level, as—and I am aware that the leap of faith might be a bit far—Pope Benedict XVI proclaimed in an *Angelus* message of 17 July 2005: "Le vacanze sono . . . giorni nei quali ci si può dedicare più a lungo alla preghiera, alla lettura e alla meditazione sui significati profondi della vita."

In the Introduction to *The Book of J*, Bloom moves succinctly and swiftly to a virtual *Aufhebung* of the secular into the sacred: "the distinction between sacred and secular texts results from social and political decisions, and thus is not a literary distinction at all" (11). There is inevitably then what Bloom in the "Preface" calls an "ambivalence between the divine and the human" (*Canon* 5) not only in Bloom's 'originary' text but also in *all* texts, a calling forth from beyond the grave by which the belated, yet all-too-anxious living reader-poet-creator is haunted. This is perhaps Bloom's strongest, even his only defence against the Resenters, an excess in the textual that cannot be gainsaid because it may not yet be recognized, since that which is not yet existent cannot be denied. What subsequent generations will make of the literary is beyond our ken, but we can be sure that it will be something. Belatedness for Bloom has also then an impossible cataphoric relation, an assumption that the future will correctly assign status and value to that which ideology has masked to its present, as most famously perhaps in the case of that now-canonical poet with whom Bloom began his critical strategy, William Blake. The yet-to-be canonical literary text thus takes on something of the messianic to come, which Moshe Idel says does not "destroy history" but which "restores an old regime," thus merging the "conservative and restorative" (40), and which can be in part strategised in terms of the restoration of *adam qadmon* (171), arguably part of Blake's vision also. Less arcanely, perhaps, Bloom's perspective moves into the idealist not-yet of Ernst Bloch's futural principle of hope, a however inarticulate movement beyond current representation which ushers in the new, and which—in the work of its becoming articulate in anticipatory texts, perhaps—can be intimated to the attentive (*Prinzip Hoffnung*, ch. 15). In this vacant open possibility of which nothing can be said (even that nothing can be said), and to which no reaction is thus possible, resentment, supremely but vacuously articulated and centred, is powerless to find a voice.

Works Cited

Auerbach, Erich. *Mimesis: The Representation of Reality in Western Literature*. Trans. Willard R. Trask. Princeton: Princeton UP, 1953.
Bhabha, Homi K. *The Location of Culture*. London: Routledge, 1994.
Blake, William. *The Complete Poetry and Prose of William Blake*. Ed. David V. Erdman. Commentary by Harold Bloom. Rev. ed. New York: Anchor-Doubleday, 1988.
Bloch, Ernst. *Das Prinzip Hoffnung*. 1959. Frankfurt/M: Suhrkamp, 1985.
De Bolla, Peter. *Harold Bloom: Towards Historical Rhetorics*. London: Routledge, 1988.
Emerson, Ralph Waldo. *Selected Essays*. Ed. Larzer Ziff. New York: Penguin, 1982.
Hales, Steven D. and Rex Welshon. *Nietzsche's Perspectivism*. Urbana: U of Illinois P, 2000.
Hongo, Garrett, ed. *The Open Boat: Poems from Asian America*. New York: Anchor-Doubleday, 1993.
Idel, Moshe. *Messianic Mystics*. New Haven: Yale UP, 1998.
Klein, Wayne. "Tragic Figures: Music and Image in Nietzsche's *The Birth of Tragedy*." *International Studies in Philosophy* 26 (1996): 17–31. Rpt. in *Nietzsche*. Ed. Richard White. Aldershot: Ashgate, 2002. 433–47.
Newman, John Henry. *The Idea of a University*. 1852; 1873. Ed. Frank M. Turner. New Haven: Yale UP, 1996.
Nietzsche, Friedrich. *On the Genealogy of Morals* and *Ecce Homo*. Trans. Walter Kaufmann and R. J. Hollingdale. Ed. Walter Kaufmann. 1967. New York: Vintage-Random House, 1989.
Pound, Ezra. *Literary Essays*. Ed. T. S. Eliot. New York: New Directions, 1968.

Sawyer, Robert. "Looking for Mr. Goodbard: Swinburne, Resentment Criticism, and the Invention of Harold Bloom." *Harold Bloom's Shakespeare*. Ed. Christy Desmet and Robert Sawyer. Houndmills: Palgrave, 2001. 167–80.

Solomon, Robert C. "One Hundred Years of *Ressentiment*: Nietzsche's *Genealogy of Morals*." *Nietzsche, Genealogy, Morality: Essays on Nietzsche's* Genealogy of Morals. Ed. Richard Schacht. Berkeley: U of California P, 1994. 95–126.

Stauth, Georg and Bryan S. Turner. *Nietzsche's Dance: Resentment, Reciprocity and Resistance in Social Life*. Oxford: Blackwell, 1988.

Strawson, P. F. *"Freedom and Resentment" and Other Essays*. London: Methuen, 1974.

On the Stone Raft:
Harold Bloom in Catalonia and Portugal[1]

CHRISTOPHER ROLLASON

1) The Stone Raft

In 1986, José Saramago—the Portuguese Nobel laureate whom the American critic Harold Bloom believes is the greatest living novelist—wrote *A Jangada de Pedra* (*The Stone Raft*), a magic-realist fiction in which the Iberian peninsula breaks away from Europe and drifts out into the Atlantic, until it halts at a location off the Azores, halfway to North America. More recently, the Yale Professor of Humanities and author of *The Western Canon* and *Shakespeare: The Invention of the Human* has paid significant literary visits to the Iberian peninsula—Portugal in May 2001, Barcelona in May 2002—and has both times been welcomed by a reception considerably warmer than he would be likely to find in his home country, where the antagonisms persisting between him and much of the university establishment are notorious. Indeed, Bloom's trajectory in Portugal and Catalonia conjures up images of the septuagenarian critic standing on the "stone raft," a lone mariner facing the hostile sea-spray.

The reflections that follow arise out of my reading of the two main essays contained in a book signed by Bloom and published in Barcelona. This volume, whose title would translate into English as *The Future of the Imagination*, appeared in May 2002, published by Anagrama / Empúries simultaneously in two editions: Catalan (*El futur de la imaginació*) and Spanish (*El futuro de la imaginación*; my references are to the Catalan

---

[1] This essay is a review of Bloom, *futur*. All translations in this essay from Catalan, Portuguese and Spanish are my own.

[149]

edition). It falls into three sections, of which the first consists of a brand-new lecture, while the last is a text which will be new to the great majority of readers. The opening text, "El futur de la imaginació i les seves formes en relació amb la proesa catalana" ("The Future of the Imagination and Its Forms in Relation to the Catalan Achievement," 9–18), is Bloom's acceptance speech given in May 2002 at the ceremony, held at the Generalitat (the seat of the Catalan regional government) at which he received the *Premi Internacional Catalunya*—an award whose previous winners include the likes of Václav Havel and Edgar Morin. It is notable not only for its author's trenchant statements on the state of literary studies in the twenty-first century, but also for the knowledge and appreciation he displays of Catalan literature. This new text is followed by a set of twenty-four brief essays on individual writers, all of them translations from critical monographs originally published by Bloom in the US in his Chelsea House series. At the end, significantly positioned, comes a fifteen-page tribute to Portugal's Nobel laureate entitled, simply, "José Saramago" (191–206). It is stated that this text was given as a lecture in Lisbon in 2001—evidently during Bloom's Portuguese visit in May of that year; the exact date and venue are not specified. I have not managed to locate an on-line reference to any published English or Portuguese version of this text, and therefore presume that it will be new for most readers.

I shall now discuss these two 'new' (opening and closing) essays, following which I shall offer some further thoughts on the issues Bloom raises in them; the latter comments will be backed up from my reading of a number of articles on and interviews with Bloom which have appeared in the Spanish- and Portuguese-language press over the last two years, and which I have had the good fortune to locate on line. As this material—book and articles—is not accessible to Anglophone readers who are not cognisant with Spanish, Catalan or Portuguese, I am offering this essay in the hope that it will be of interest and use to those who would like to know more about Harold Bloom's work on the literatures of the Iberian-language world, as well as the reception of his ideas in that cultural area. His controversial positions, as expressed in *The Western Canon* and *Shakespeare*—in defence of the literary tradition, against both political correctness on the left and religious fundamentalism on the right—are well enough known, but the particular context, i.e. concrete exposure to the literary works of a specific language area, should help bring them into sharper focus.

2) Homage to Catalonia

Bloom begins his Barcelona address with a polemical statement targeted on the epigones of modernism (and, by implication, of postmodernism too). He declares that, as one who "grew up in the literary epoch of high modernism," he never accepted the belief of that period that human nature had somehow irrevocably changed near the beginning of the twentieth century—thus throwing down the gauntlet to those who would read the literature of the past through the sole prism of the present and its immediate concerns. He goes on to make the by now expected complaints against "the epoch of resentment and political correctness" and, in the same breath, to distance himself from the cyber-utopians and their belief that network technologies will bring about a qualitative transformation of consciousness. For Bloom, what continues to matter is the printed page: indeed, he declares provocatively that "the Internet horrifies me," seeing the plethora of on-line information as a nightmare of excess, an infinitely expanded version of the flood of unsolicited textual material with which, as America's best-known literary critic, he has himself been inundated for years in paper form. Consciously drawing on Jorge Luis Borges' anti-utopian visions of random, self-reproducing systems, Bloom paints a dark picture of the Internet as an "immense ocean without form," "a universal sea of chaos:" "the Internet has no form, unless it be that of one of Borges' labyrinths."

Bloom is nonetheless far from believing that literature is dead. He has high praise for the works of such living novelists as José Saramago, Gabriel García Márquez, Philip Roth and Thomas Pynchon—a list which, containing two Americans but also writers from Portugal and Colombia, immediately points up the broadness of Bloom's critical vision and his visible distance from narrow notions of Anglo-Saxon cultural superiority. He fears, however, that in spite of the impressive performances of these and other novelists, the time may be approaching when the novel as we know it will be replaced, as the wheel comes full circle, by something resembling the pre-Renaissance romance which Cervantes was the first to transcend. Whatever happens to literature, Bloom reposes his faith for its future reception not in the universities but in the common, non-academic reader. The academic establishment, he believes, has abandoned virtually all notion of aesthetic or intellectual standards, and has become the prisoner of lobby groups. The only hope for criticism lies in the survival of what he calls "a group of advanced readers"—a kind of cultural rearguard (or vanguard?) who will preserve the reading of canonic literature as a minority pursuit.

In the second section of the address, Bloom pays tribute to the literature of Catalonia. Here too, it deserves stressing that he has made the effort to read (in translation), and to praise, a significant range of works from one of Europe's more obscure and marginal literatures—indeed, one which does not even have the backing of a nation-state to promote it (unless one counts Andorra). Bloom lauds the late Salvador Espriu as "an extraordinary poet by any international standard." This homage to Catalonia, paid by Harold Bloom in admiration of a lesser-known European literature, will come as a surprise to many, although those who have looked carefully at the reading lists appended to some editions of *The Western Canon* will have noted that half-a-dozen Catalan writers, including Espriu, already figured there.

Bloom also finds a significant analogy between the Catalan and Jewish traditions, recalling the medieval Catalan-Jewish mystical tradition as represented by the likes of Isaac the Blind of Gerona, and comparing the persecution of the Jews by the Nazis with the stifling of Catalan culture by the "abominable Franco regime" ("Yiddish was destroyed by Hitler in the same way as Franco tried to destroy Catalan . . . the Catalans' struggle to preserve their literary culture and their language is very similar to the Jewish effort to keep their linguistic and literary identity"). It should be recalled here that, secular Jew though he is, Bloom's Jewishness has very deep roots in his family history: his father, who hailed from the large Jewish community in Odessa (now in Ukraine), which also produced the remarkable writer Isaac Babel, and his mother, born in a shtetl (Jewish community) near Brest-Litovsk (now in Belarus), were first-generation emigrants, and the young Harold grew up in an Orthodox Jewish New York household where only Yiddish was spoken indoors.

Meanwhile, Bloom's detractors might care to note what this speech tells us in general about the open-ended nature of his canon, his willingness to include writers from lesser-known literatures and minority linguistic areas. He certainly believes canonic status can only be granted on strict criteria of merit, but a canon with a seat for Salvador Espriu is surely no exclusive gentlemen's club. Bloom's literary internationalism contrasts sharply with the Anglophone insularity which more often than not afflicts critics from the planet's hegemonic language area: in Britain, in particular, it would be difficult to imagine a major critic, alive or dead, whether F. R. Leavis, Raymond Williams, or even a proclaimed internationalist like Terry Eagleton, taking up the cudgels for Catalan literature.

3) Here the Sea Ends

A similar positive internationalism illuminates Bloom's Lisbon lecture on José Saramago, whom, it is clear, Bloom today considers to be the greatest writer of fiction alive: "the most impressive living novelist on our planet, who overshadows all other living Europeans and all Americans too, whether they write in English, Spanish and Portuguese" (Bloom admittedly here fails to mention Asians or Africans, but the thrust of his point is clear). Again, to the well-informed this will not come as a complete surprise. Bloom's interest in Portuguese literature was visibly manifested in *The Western Canon*, which featured a section on Fernando Pessoa, Portugal's great twentieth-century poet, and the reading lists at the end of that book included a number of Portuguese texts, including the national epic, Luis de Camões' *Os Lusíadas* (*The Lusiads*), and just one novel by Saramago: his remarkable historical novel of 1982, *Memorial do Convento* (known to English-speaking readers as *Baltasar and Blimunda*). Since then, Bloom has quite clearly made a point of reading right through Saramago's *oeuvre*, albeit in translation (his reading knowledge of Portuguese is, he says, not on the level of the novelist's complex style). The present text is not, in fact, Bloom's first on the Portuguese writer: a study of *O Evangelho segundo Jesus Cristo* (*The Gospel according to Jesus Christ*), entitled "The One With the Beard is God, the Other is the Devil," appeared in 2001 in issue 6 of *Portuguese Literary and Cultural Studies* (published by the Center for Portuguese Studies and Culture of the University of Massachusetts at Dartmouth).

Bloom begins by comparing Saramago's work to the ocean, the archetypal image of Portuguese letters as also sung by Camões and Pessoa: "Re-reading Saramago, I always feel like Ulysses endeavouring to grasp Proteus, the metamorphic god of the ocean: at all moments, he eludes my grip." He here appears to evoke the opening of Saramago's *O Ano da Morte de Ricardo Reis* (*The Year of the Death of Ricardo Reis*), which begins with the words "Here the sea ends and the earth begins" (themselves harking back to Camões), while also highlighting the tale-teller's supreme unpredictability, the mutability of his writing from one novel to the next. While identifying *O Evangelho segundo Jesus Cristo* as Saramago's master-work, and *História do Cerco de Lisboa* (*History of the Siege of Lisbon*) as his own personal favourite, Bloom dispassionately runs through the sequence of novels from *Memorial do Convento* onwards, up to the neo-Kafkaesque *Todos os Nomes* (*All the Names*) of 1997; he admits that he has yet to get to grips with Saramago's (then) most recent novel, *A Caverna* (*The Cave*), which ironically juxtaposes Plato with the modern world of shopping-malls, as the English translation had (at the time of his lecture) still to come out.

While he is scarcely unaware of Saramago's political stance as an unrepentant communist militant and a passionate foe of market-led globalisation, Bloom prefers not to view his subject in ideological terms, affirming: "Saramago is a free man, and his books exalt freedom, typically representing the appalling alternatives to it." He focuses chillingly on the novelist's ability to stare totalitarianism in the face, in a country which, from the Inquisition to the Salazar dictatorship, has, alas, not lacked in examples of that phenomenon: he sees *Memorial do Convento* as "Saramago's historical novel of the sentiments, set in the fear-inspiring Portugal of the early eighteenth century, a country still untouched by the Enlightenment," a social and ideological universe whose motto is, in the novelist's words, "Either shut up or burn;" and he shows how *O Ano da Morte de Ricardo Reis*, Saramago's dark, dense evocation of Lisbon in the 1930s, is impregnated with "the cosmos of the great poet Pessoa and that of the fascist dictator Salazar," in one and the same paradoxical vision. For Bloom, if in the first novel "Saramago prophetically dispatches Portugal, the Catholic church and the monarchy to the hell of history," in the second "we are back in hell, and now it's the historical Portugal of December 1935, with Salazar in power and Spain on the point of succumbing to the fascist usurpation." We may note how, here as in his paean to Catalan literature, Bloom has no time whatever for General Franco; we may also note how his Jewish roots are—in Portugal as they were in Catalonia—stirred, here in *Memorial do Convento* by the character Blimunda, "the half-Jewish witch," an illiterate but magically gifted woman of the people. He further notes in passing—in relation to *A Jangada de Pedra* (*The Stone Raft*)—that Saramago is marked by the (benign) influence of an earlier magic-realist master, the Cuban Alejo Carpentier—although, curiously, he fails to draw attention to certain images (a proletarian hero mutilated in the arm; a monument built by the forced sweat of the people) that provide a strong continuity between *Memorial do Convento* and Carpentier's remarkable novel *El reino de este mundo* (*The Kingdom of This World*).

Coming to Saramago's later novels—which are for the most part no longer located in an identifiable Portuguese context, but set either elsewhere (a quasi-biblical Palestine) or nowhere (in the depersonalised land of allegory)—Bloom distils the essence of each in a few words. He compares O Evangelho segundo Jesus Cristo favourably to D. H. Lawrence's provocative re-write of the resurrection story in "The Man Who Died," and declares: "The God of his 'Gospel' certainly deserves refusal: he is the most disagreeable person in all Saramago" (thus, be it said, creating a Bloom-Saramago axis that joins forces with Salman Rushdie in saying no to the contemporary *bien-pensant* orthodoxy that uncritically counsels 'respect for religion'). He reads the terrifying *Ensaio sobre a Cegueira* (*Blindness*) as a "parable of the perpetual possibility of the return of fascism, or its advent," adding that if asked to choose between this novel and Albert Camus' *La peste* (*The Plague*), he "would opt for Saramago." Finally, Bloom lauds *Todos os Nomes* (*All the Names*), Saramago's fictional interrogation of the universe of bureaucracy, as a latter-day, and more hopeful, re-creation of the world of Franz Kafka. It is abundantly clear from the comparisons Bloom deploys—Lawrence, Camus, Kafka—that he considers the Portuguese Nobel laureate to be the equal of the twentieth century's most respected masters of fiction: at a time when many in the academy deny the very notion of literary value, Bloom the critic unflinchingly assumes the role of defender and, indeed, maker of reputations, concluding: "I, as a literary critic, gain encouragement from the wisdom of Saramago."

4) The Press Pays Tribute

Bloom's two 'new' lectures in this volume may be further illuminated by reference to selected elements from the clutch of articles on and interviews with him which appeared in the Iberian-language press and electronic media, tying in with his visits, in 2001 and 2002. These texts, apart from clarifying Bloom's positions on various subjects, chronicle a number of significant events: in particular, on 27 May 2001 Harold Bloom was awarded an honorary doctorate by the University of Coimbra, Portugal's oldest seat of learning, in the presence of and with the sponsorship of José Saramago. In the next section, I shall offer the anglophone reader a digest of the salient points from the following press texts, translating all quotations from Spanish or Portuguese into English (I have chosen seven texts—five in Portuguese, two in Spanish;

each full reference is preceded by a codeword that will serve to identify it):

> *Almeida*. Catarina Solano de Almeida, "Ser um génio literário não implica ser inteligente para outras coisas [Literary Genius Does Not Guarantee Intelligence in Other Fields]." Website: *SIC Online*, 1 September 2002 <http://www.sic.pt/article4540visual4.html> (this article is a paraphrase of statements made by Bloom in an interview with the Chilean newspaper *El Mercurio*).
>
> *DN*. "Uma 'lança' cultural nos EUA [A Thorn in America's Cultural Flesh]." *Diário de Notícias* 22 May 2001, reproduced on Lusoplanet website: <http://lusoplanet.free.fr/notio105.htm >.
>
> *Júnior*. António Júnior, "Harold Bloom: Um autor a que não podemos ficar indiferentes [Harold Bloom: An Author to Whom No-one Can Be Indifferent]." Website: *Blocos On Line* (Brazil), 2001 <http://www.blocosonline.com.br/entrev/entrevo3.htm >.
>
> *Moret*. Xavier Moret, "Harold Bloom, crítico literario: 'Los lectores están en peligro de desaparición' [Harold Bloom, Literary Critic: 'Readers Are an Endangered Species']." *El País* 22 June 2002, reproduced on literaturas.com website: <http://www.literaturas.com/haroldbloom.htm >.
>
> *Najmías*. Daniel Najmías, "El boom Bloom: Harold Bloom en Barcelona [The Bloom Boom: Harold Bloom in Barcelona]." *Barcelona Review* 30 (May-June 2002): <http://www.barcelonareview.com/30/s_dn.htm >.
>
> *Queirós*. Luís Miguel Queirós, "Só Falta Começarem a Partir-me Os Vidros das Janelas [Next Thing They Will Be Smashing My Windows]." *Público* 26 May 2001, reproduced on terravista.pt website: <http://www.terravista.pt/Bilene/5099/bloom2.htm >.
>
> *Sobrado*. Jorge Sobrado, "O Futuro passa por . . . Shakespeare [The Future Is . . . Shakespeare]." Website: *Feira do Livro do Porto* (Oporto Book Fair), 2001 <http://feiradolivro.clix.pt/prt/g_img/programa/programa_eventos_02.html >.

5) The Critic Speaks

The first point to be stressed from the reading of these press texts is the way in which they underline Bloom's enthusiasm for the literatures of the Iberian world. Thus, he tells Júnior: "The [doctoral] ceremony in Coimbra was extraordinary and eloquent—an incentive to me to go on learning more deeply about the Portuguese literary tradition. I've already written pieces on Camões and Eça [de Queiróz or Queirós]. I believe that [Eça's] *The Maias* is a work of sublime beauty, one of the finest European novels of the nineteenth century." Júnior, in return, notes that Bloom's popularity in Portugal may not be unrelated to his declared interest in that nation's great writers: "People in Portugal are delighted at your high opinion of Fernando Pessoa and José Saramago." Elsewhere, in the article by (Luís) Queirós, we are told that Bloom considers Camões' neo-classical epic *Os Lusíadas* to be "a great poem—extraordinarily powerful and disturbing, better by far than all of Virgil;" the DN article adds that "Bloom has written the introduction to a translation of Eça's *A Relíquia* [*The Relic*], slated for publication in the US in the autumn [of 2001];" Almeida adds that "among those whom he believes to be the greatest literary geniuses, the likes of Shakespeare, Balzac, Cervantes or Hemingway, the critic [Bloom] has no hesitation in including the Portuguese writer José Saramago;" while Sobrado reports that "A careful reader and confessed admirer of the Portuguese author, Harold Bloom declared him to be a 'great writer,' even comparing him with Cervantes" (one may guess that Bloom was here thinking of Saramago's picaresque, pan-Iberian and, indeed, quixotic narrative *A Jangada de Pedra*). For Spanish literature, we may, then, note Bloom's recourse to Miguel de Cervantes as a point of reference; while for Catalan literature, Moret quotes Bloom as declaring: "The Nobel committee is guilty of many errors, and one of those was not to have given the prize to Salvador Espriu. I believe he deserved it."

On the more specific details of the Bloom-Saramago connection, we learn from Sobrado that, at the Oporto Book Fair in May 2001, "Bloom was unstinting in his praise for Portugal's literature Nobel, José Saramago, with whom he says he regularly exchanges correspondence." Still on his relationship with the Portuguese writer, Bloom further tells Queirós: "I regret the fact that I don't speak Portuguese. On the few occasions when I've met Saramago, we had considerable difficulty in communicating. I manage to read Portuguese, but I find it difficult to pronounce, and his English is non-existent. And so we ended up speaking in a crazy mixture of French, Italian and Spanish. Saramago is a great writer and a most engaging person."

One might be forgiven for supposing that, defying the language barrier, novelist and critic have indeed formed a Bloom-Saramago alliance in defence of the literary tradition and its value for today's world. However, all is not plain sailing when non-literary controversies raise their head. On the vexed subject of Middle-Eastern politics,

Almeida quotes some sharp words from Bloom on his Portuguese friend's anti-Israel line: "Saramago was in Ramallah [in March 2002] and said that what he'd seen was a latter-day Auschwitz. Such a statement is absurd and unforgivable ... when he talks politics, the old Stalinist stereotype is always there." It is clear that Bloom the critic makes a clear distinction between Saramago the novelist and Saramago the political animal—as, it might be recalled, an intelligent Marxist critic such as Georg Lukács does in the converse direction, drawing a sharp line between Balzac's monarchist politics and his novelist's genius.

This brings us to the question of Bloom's own wider political views, and it emerges from these documents that, while he certainly has no time for unreconstructed Stalinism or (unsurprisingly) for the pro-Palestinian world-view, he is equally no admirer of the neo-conservative, hard-right forces that now rule America. On Bloom's views on the present President of the United States, Almeida comments: "In the opinion of this US citizen, George W. Bush 'is a semi-illiterate fascist' who might as well be the character Polonius from *Hamlet*." Junior informs us that Bloom "was invited to receive an honorary distinction at Yale's 300th anniversary celebrations, but decided not to go and to accept Coimbra's honorary doctorate in person instead," and quotes Bloom's own explanation for his choice: "His majesty Bush was to be one of the recipients at Yale. I decided I would rather not be there, and I have no regrets .... George Bush II embodies the worst imbecility that exists in the USA, something which is quite beyond my comprehension."

On the Internet, Bloom's position as expressed in these texts is at best lukewarm and at worst downright hostile. Sobrado's report on his address at the Oporto Book Fair cites remarks that are quite as acerbic as those in Bloom's Barcelona speech. The sea-of-chaos image recurs: "Bloom declared peremptorily that the Internet is an 'ocean of chaos, an ocean of death,' which makes it impossible to read properly or to make any qualitative distinction between the works 'afloat' on it. He concluded that from the literary viewpoint 'the Web will not contribute anything of value.'" To Moret, however, Bloom is a shade more conciliatory, declaring: "For a decently educated young person, the Internet may be a very useful tool. I'm glad to know that there's valuable information of every kind there on the Internet, but someone who uses it without the right educational background runs the risk of drowning in an ocean of information. When I read about the World Wide Web I can't help thinking of a huge spider's web trapping the unwary."

On another manifestation of the vicissitudes of text in the modern world, namely Joanne K. Rowling's Harry Potter books, Bloom confesses to Moret: "I've read *Harry Potter and the Philosopher's Stone*. It's so badly written! It's full of clichés and repetitions. Frankly, I was most disappointed. If the Harry Potter books are now the most popular books in the world, then we've got a terrible problem." In the same vein, he tells Queirós: "Of all my writings in recent years, the one that caused the greatest furore was a small article in which I said, actually in a quite kindly tone, that the Harry Potter books have no value whatever, neither aesthetic, psychological or any other kind."

If we now move centre-stage to consider Bloom's main preoccupations, we find that these articles, inevitably, touch on Bloom's defence of the Great Books, his hostile relationship with the dominant orthodoxy in American universities, the 'right-wing' label pinned on him by certain influential lobbies, and the book of his that sparked off the entire conflict, *The Western Canon*. On the polemical issue of his own position inside the US academy, Bloom tells Moret: "In the circles I move in, they treat me as a controversial critic. I don't feel that I am, but this must be a sign that something is not right." He declares to Queirós: "If I'd been born in 1970, they'd never have given me a job. Even if I were ten times more gifted than I am, no-one would take me on, because my opinions aren't acceptable." Estranged from the academic establishment of which he is nominally part, Bloom finds solace in what he finds to be the more open-minded company of the common reader. He confides, again to Queirós: "Around 1990 I came to the conclusion that there was no point in writing for an academic public. I went back looking for the general public—and I discovered that it existed. There are readers out there—thousands of them, all over the world."

Meanwhile, Bloom's strictures against political correctness in literary studies remain as harsh as those to which he gave voice in *The Western Canon*. He states to Moret: "For years now, literature hasn't been taught decently in my own country or in any English-speaking country. If things go on like this, with the teaching of literature subordinated to gender, race, sexual preferences or political opinions, in the end society will self-destruct." Najmías, meanwhile, makes the salutary point (often overlooked by commentators) that in reality Bloom's polemic in *The Western Canon* was directed as much against the right (read: the Christian fundamentalists) as the left (read: the politically correct): "[that book] raised the hackles of the members of the lobbies, on both the right and the left, whom Bloom accused of politicising literary studies and criticism." Still on that book, Bloom makes an important clarification in the interview with Queirós. Some, but not all editions (among them the 1995 UK paperback) include, apart from the twenty-six main author studies, a much more extensive set of reading lists in (mostly) western literature, from Homer and the Bible to the present day. Bloom explains why some editions lack these lists: "Those lists have nothing to do with me. I was obliged to include them, but I repudiated them a good while back. I decided to remove them from the book, and so they're not there in the Swedish or the Italian translation, although you will, unfortunately, find them in the Portuguese and Brazilian editions. My publisher and my agent banded together to persuade me that the book could only be published with those lists—and so, in protest, I wrote them off the top of my head, without looking up anything."

To Queirós, Bloom relates an incident at the University of California which, he feels, encapsulates the antagonism between his concept of literature and the world-view of his opponents:

> Three years ago, I gave some lectures at the University of California, which is an extremely politically correct place .... In the middle of one of my lectures, suddenly the hall literally exploded. They even wanted to lynch me, all because, in the end, I told the truth. I turned to them and said: "A lot of you in this room are teachers of literature, but you don't really care about literature. If you commission a table from a carpenter who happens to be Mexican-American, or Marxist, or gay, and he hands you over a table that collapses on its legs, you'll return it and ask for your money back. Yet you're more than happy to accept books with no legs to stand on. You're totally hypocritical. There are quotas for women, blacks, Mexicans and gays in law and arts faculties, but not for medicine. You know why? Because if you politically correct folk were on a hospital table for a brain operation, and the doctor who was about to operate on you was a devastatingly attractive black lesbian—I'm trying to be as offensive as possible—who you are told got her qualifications thanks to her ethnic origin and her sexual orientation, all of you would run out at once." The whole room started shouting at me: "Racist! Fascist!" And I shouted back at them: "All you are is a bunch of low-down nuisances. You don't have a single rational argument to throw back at me. You're a crowd of perfect swindlers. The whole lot of you would run out of the operating theatre." It was war. But is there any more socially repugnant idea than to claim that it's more helpful for a young woman from Cape Verde who comes to live in Portugal to read her fellow nationals' books, however bad they are, than Eça or Almeida Garrett? Another day, I was speaking about five of my favourite poets: Whitman, Pessoa, Lorca, Hart Crane and the wonder-

ful Luis Cernuda. All of them were gay, but why should I have to care whether they preferred to go to bed with men or women?

6) The Word in the Modern World

The above incident might suggest to some that the gulf between Harold Bloom and the self-styled representatives of today's modernity may simply be unbridgeable—that where two positions are irreconcilable to such a degree, no dialogue can exist and nothing can be done. However, if we retrace our steps and consider various of Bloom's positions, as expressed in the material introduced in this essay, in a globally-oriented context, the outlines of a more inclusive perspective may emerge.

Bloom defends the written word, but appears particularly resistant to its present-day recasting via the new medium that is the Internet: while some of his pronouncements on the network universe are more conciliatory than others, his general position is clearly hostile. It is true that intelligent use of the Internet for research purposes requires the capacity to select, filter and assess the masses of material available on line, but Bloom surely underestimates the usefulness of the medium for literary study. The World Wide Web allows readers to download, read, keep, annotate and study large numbers of classic works of literature, and to track down quotations and references with unrivalled speed and accuracy (the same is true for CD-ROM versions). An electronic version of a novel is—unlike a stage, film or television adaptation—not a transposition of the text into the language of a different medium, with all the distortion that can entail; it is a reproduction of the existing text, within another medium, certainly, but with no distortion of the original message and with certain 'value-added' elements such as search capacity. An electronic text of *Don Quixote* is still Cervantes' novel, in a way that a stage version like *Man of La Mancha* is not; it is more like Pierre Menard's "rewritten *Quixote*" in Borges' celebrated story: transcribed word for word for the readers of another age, superficially different yet ultimately still the same. In addition, with the rise of the Internet the cunning of history has brought about an unexpected resurgence of, precisely, that common reader whose intuitions Bloom says he now values well over those of the academy. Today, any computer-literate reader of books can post a review on any of numerous popular websites (Amazon and its imitators) or Usenet groups, so becoming his or her own critic and bypassing the official critical establishment altogether. The contours of a new reader-centred criticism are likely to become visible as our new century progresses, and it seems somewhat misplaced that a critic like Bloom should not be taking due note of this immensely positive development. Large swathes of the Internet are and will remain essentially text-based: the superficial difference between printed page and screen is no greater than that between papyrus and parchment, or vellum and paper. The new medium, in stark contrast to its audiovisual predecessors, has all the potential, *pace* the still-voluble disciples of the late Marshall McLuhan and his increasingly beleaguered world-view, to redeem the power of the written word for the coming generations—to transform and deepen it, while in no way abolishing it, thus repeating Gutenberg's quantum leap on a new and more powerful plane.

At the risk of appearing to compare great things with small, I now beg leave to move from the Internet to Harry Potter, and to question the usefulness of Bloom's critical positions over another latter-day manifestation of the written word. The analogy between J. K. Rowling's parallel world of witchcraft and the virtual universe of cyberspace may in fact not be so far-fetched as it might seem. The Potter books are, on one level, about the hidden potential of alternative forms of networking, and, like the electronic networks, they have given a remarkable and surprising boost worldwide to the allegedly 'out-of-date' medium of text, breaking through the barrier of anti-book prejudice and encouraging children to read as no other contemporary fictions have. Indeed, J. K. Rowling and Tim Berners-Lee may yet prove to be the two great anti-McLuhans of the new millennium. In such a context, Bloom's dismissal of the Potter books could come across as short-sighted and unfair. By denying their literary value, he aligns himself with José Saramago, who is, as it happens, another of J. K. Rowling's detractors (although, by contrast, such eminent figures from the world of letters as the critic George Steiner and the novelist Mario Vargas Llosa have praised her books). It may be added that the repetitive and formulaic element which displeases Bloom in Rowling's style may be linked to the fact that they are at least partly intended for oral delivery (as bedtime stories), and thus stand at a particular intersection point of the written and spoken word which, a more sympathetic critic might argue, could suggest comparison with the similarly formulaic works of Homer.

On the vexed question of 'the Western Canon versus political correctness,' it needs pointing out that, despite the white heat that fires Bloom's attacks on his adversaries (and theirs on him), the canonic gospel according to Bloom is in fact much more inclusive than some might think. This is very clear from the reading lists appended to some editions of *The Western Canon*, which include large numbers of texts (not exclusively western) and writers, both male and female, from an enormous range of times and places, and it seems unfortunate that Bloom has chosen to suppress those lists, thus generating unnecessary misunderstandings. His canon is infinitely more generous than that of F. R. Leavis, who seemed bent on whittling down the ranks of the great writers to the tiniest of elites. Nor are there many Anglophone critics—above all from faculties of English rather than modern languages—who have shown the openness towards foreign-language literatures, including lesser-known ones, that Bloom has manifested in embracing Spanish-, Portuguese- and Catalan-language writers. His interest in Latin American literature even connects him to the wider area of postcolonial studies (this aspect could be usefully strengthened were Bloom to pay more attention to the parallel phenomenon of Indian and 'Anglo-Indian' writing, from R. K. Narayan to the likes of V. S. Naipaul, Anita Desai, Vikram Seth, Vikram Chandra, Manju Kapur or Salman Rushdie, which has, like Latin American writing before it, achieved worldwide recognition not by quotas but by merit). Indeed, even if Bloom would no doubt reject the concept of 'postcolonial studies' as such, the global reach of his interests can objectively bear linking with the concerns of that movement; and there are even curious similarities between his technique, in *The Western Canon*, of revisiting and reinterpreting classic texts, and the method operated by Edward Said in certain passages of his book *Culture and Imperialism*, which is now recognised as a basic text for postcolonial studies.

Meanwhile, there is no rational justification for the "fascist" label pinned by the Stanford audience on someone who is an ardent promoter of a card-carrying communist like José Saramago, and who, as we have seen, has described Franco's regime as "abominable" and Salazar's as a hell on earth. Indeed, one might legitimately wonder how many of Bloom's Stanford opponents knew more about General Francisco Franco than could be written on the back of a postage stamp, and how many had so much as heard of António de Oliveira Salazar.

It may nonetheless be argued that Bloom has by now said everything useful that he could say on the issue of political correctness, and that it could be time for him to move on. The whole PC question has, besides, now been magnificently explored in fiction in *The Human Stain*, the remarkable Clinton-era novel by Philip Roth (himself a Bloom favourite). Roth's novel is centred on the academic world, and his character Delphine Roux, the French ex-structuralist converted to PC, is a wickedly telling caricature of Bloom's real-world opponents. The question remains whether there is much more to say of interest on the subject, and whether it might not be a more valuable exercise for all concerned to move away from confrontational positions and start building bridges. The cosmopolitan slant of Bloom's literary interests suggests that he and his adversaries may actually have more in common than either would wish to admit. The biggest objective stumbling-block is probably Bloom's insistence that works of literature should be judged on merit rather than on the gender, colour and so on of the people who wrote them; his opponents would no doubt counter-argue that his concept of merit is itself a white male construct, but given that many of the modern writers whom he champions are not precisely from 'central' or hegemonic cultures, it should surely be possible to evolve some more inclusive definition of merit which might satisfy all parties.

Political correctness, despite its tangible excesses and rigidities as pinpointed by Bloom and Roth, has at least had the not insubstantial merit of keeping literary studies alive in universities. While the aesthetic has to a large extent been displaced by the ideological, the world does still have humanities departments populated by people who believe that at least some creative writing is valuable enough for its study not to be pushed out of the university curriculum altogether. One may wonder if Bloom is, today, necessarily identifying the right enemy: political correctness may in fact pose far less of a danger to literary studies than does the insidious ideology of vocationalism.

By vocationalism, in the context of the humanities, I mean the ideologically motivated subordination of arts courses to reductivist, technicist, instrumentalist, parodically positivist and empiricist labour-market criteria, and to crudely demagogic and populist pseudo-philosophies of 'relevance.' This can take the form of contaminating humanities courses by injecting totally alien discourses (one possible example, taken at random, being behaviourist psychology), or, in the case of modern languages courses, of downgrading and devaluing the literary component as being 'irrelevant' or 'useless.' This kind of wholesale poisoning of educational systems may, in the long term, prove far more inimical to the humanities than political correctness could ever be. The time is surely ripe for an international campaign against vocationalism, to be conducted above all on line and in as many languages as possible, targeting in particular unnecessary vocationalist elements on first-degree courses (allowing that postgraduate vocational courses may in some cases form a legitimate bridge between the knowledge-oriented first degree and the empirical realities of the workplace). Such a project would in no way be incompatible with a Bloomian reading of literature, for anti-vocationalism is surely implicit, on one level or other, in every word that Harold Bloom writes.

7) Portbou: A Hollyhock Blooms

Vocationalism is typically justified by reference to a simplistic notion of linear 'progress;' and when one speaks of linearism and wishes to criticise it, the example of Walter Benjamin inevitably springs to mind. It is curious that Bloom, when he speaks of the affinity between the Jewish and Catalan cultures, does not mention Benjamin, a Jew who died in tragic circumstances on Catalan soil in 1940. Benjamin's non-linear model of history, as unforgettably expounded through the key image of the constellation in the last work he wrote, the "Theses on the Philosophy of History," offers a devastating critique of the false gods of "progress." His work in literary and cultural studies, whose crowning glory, the vast, unfinished *Arcades Project*, is now finally available in English, is grounded in a project of building bridges—of rescuing lost fragments of popular culture from oblivion and teasing out their latent significance, while at the same time not destroying, Taliban-like, the great artefacts of high culture, but re-reading and re-appropriating them so that they can serve to liberate, and not oppress, the men and women who make up today's ordinary humanity. The kind of bridge-building exemplified by Benjamin's life's work could now form a valid pointer for a future-oriented evolution, in his own hands or others', of Harold Bloom's ideas. Meanwhile, at the cemetery in Portbou, on the Catalan side of the Franco-Spanish frontier, at the feet of the Pyrenees and overlooking the blue Mediterranean—there where the sea ends and the earth begins, right on the edge of Saramago's stone raft—next to the marble plaque raised in memory of Walter Benjamin, a bright pink hollyhock waves each summer, symbolically in bloom.

Afterword

A first version of this text was posted on rec.arts.books (Usenet) on 30 November 2002. The present revised version dates from June 2005. Some of the biographical material is taken from Larissa MacFarquhar's "The Prophet of Decline: Harold Bloom's Influential Anxieties," in *The New Yorker*, 30 September 2002.

A new book by Bloom, the physically and intellectually weighty (and unfashionably titled) volume *Genius*, came out as I was finishing the first version of this article. It includes, among its one hundred writers, studies of ten from the Iberian / Ibero-American cultural area—three from Spain (Cervantes, Lorca, Luis Cernuda), one from Mexico (Octavio Paz), one from Cuba (Alejo Carpentier), one from Argentina (Borges), three from Portugal (Camões, Eça de Queiróz, Pessoa) and one from Brazil (Machado de Assis). The Machado de Assis reference significantly further opens up Bloom's Luso-Hispanophone discourse to embrace Brazilian literature (the reading list to *The Western Canon* mentioned another Brazilian, Carlos Drummond de Andrade). Concerning Bloom's reception in Brazil, one may mention the appearance of a regular series of his articles, translated into Portuguese by Arthur Nestrowski, in *A Folha de São Paulo* in the 1990s (see <http://www2.folha.uol.com.br/biblioteca>). Saramago is not present officially in *Genius*, since the book's rubric excludes living writers. Nonetheless, in an introductory chapter Bloom names the Portuguese novelist as a figure "of palpable genius" (11), and does not fail to express his admiration for Saramago even when speaking of his compatriots: writing on Pessoa, he goes so far as to declare: "I am a literary critic trying to reeducate myself, as I go on seventy-one, with the help of the master Saramago" (519).

Also while this article was being written, the English translation of Saramago's *A Caverna* (*The Cave*) was published. Since then Saramago has produced *O Homem duplicado* (*The Double*) and the outstanding *Ensaio sobre a Lucidez* (*Essay on Lucidity*, not yet translated into English).

The concept of 'building bridges' between cultures through literature, which I advanced at the end of this article, has since found definitively eloquent expression in a ground-breaking comparative study by the Spanish scholar Dora Sales Salvador of trans-cultural literature in the Indian and Latin American contexts, focusing on the Peruvian José María Arguedas and the Indian English-medium writer Vikram Chandra, *Puentes sobre el mundo: Cultura, traducción y forma literaria en las narrativas de transculturación de José María Arguedas y Vikram Chandra* (*Bridges Over the World: Culture, Translation and Literary Form in the Narratives of Transculturation of José María Arguedas and Vikram Chandra*, 2004); see my review of this outstanding book, to which I trust an open-minded Bloom would not prove unsympathetic, at <http://www.seikilos.com.ar/DoraPuentes_en.pdf>.

Works Cited

(a) Printed Sources

Benjamin, Walter. *The Arcades Project*. Trans. Howard Eiland and Kevin McLaughlin. Cambridge, MA: Harvard UP, 2002.

———. "Theses on the Philosophy of History." *Illuminations: Essays and Reflections*. Trans. Harry Zohn. Ed. Hannah Arendt. New York: Harcourt, 1968. 253–64.

Carpentier, Alejo. *El reino de este mundo*. 1949. Puerto Rico: U of Puerto Rico P, 1996. [English translation: *The Kingdom of This World*. Trans. Harriet de Onis. New York: Farrar, 1989.]

MacFarquhar, Larissa. "The Prophet of Decline: Harold Bloom's Influential Anxieties." *The New Yorker* 30 September 2002: 87–97.

Roth, Philip. *The Human Stain*. London: Cape, 2000.

Said, Edward W. *Culture and Imperialism*. New York: Knopf, 1993.

Salvador, Dora Sales. *Puentes sobre el mundo: Cultura, traducción y forma literaria en las narrativas de transculturación de José María Arguedas y Vikram Chandra* [*Bridges Over the World: Culture, Translation and Literary Form in the Narratives of Transculturation of José María Arguedas and Vikram Chandra*]. Berne: Lang, 2004.

Saramago, José. *O Ano da Morte de Ricardo Reis*. Lisbon: Editorial Caminho, SARL, 1984. [English translation: *The Year of the Death of Ricardo Reis*. Trans. Giovanni Pontiero. Orlando: Harvest, 1992.]

———. *A Caverna*. Lisbon: Editorial Caminho, SA, 2000. [English translation: *The Cave*. Trans. Margaret Jull Coasta. Orlando: Harvest, 2003.]

———. *Ensaio sobre a Cegueira*. Lisbon: Editorial Caminho, SA, 1995. [English translation: *Blindness*. Trans. Giovanni Pontiero. Orlando: Harvest, 1999.]

_____. *Ensaio sobre a Lucidez*. São Paulo: Companhia das Letras, 2004.
_____. *O Evangelho segundo Jesus Cristo*. Lisbon: Editorial Caminho SA, 1991. [English translation: *The Gospel According to Jesus Christ*. Trans. Giovanni Pontiero. Orlando: Harvest, 1994.]
_____. *História do Cerco de Lisboa*. Lisbon: Editorial Caminho, SA, 1989. [English translation: *History of the Siege of Lisbon*. Trans. Giovanni Pontiero. Orlando: Harvest, 1997.]
_____. *O Homem duplicado*. Lisbon: Editorial Caminho, SA, 2002. [English translation: *The Double*. Trans. Margaret Jull Coasta. Orlando: Harvest, 2005.]
_____. *A Jangada de Pedra*. Lisbon: Editorial Caminho, SARL, 1986. [English translation: *The Stone Raft*. Trans. Giovanni Pontiero. Orlando: Harvest, 1996.]
_____. *Memorial del Convento*. Lisbon: Editorial Caminho, SARL, 1982. [English translation: *Baltasar and Blimunda*. Trans. Giovanni Pontiero. Orlando: Harvest, 1998.]
_____. *Todos os Nomes*. Lisbon: Editorial Caminho, SA, 1997. [English translation: *All the Names*. Trans. Margaret Jull Coasta. Orlando: Harvest, 1999.]

(b) On-line Sources

Bloom, Harold. For Bloom's many texts in *A Folha de São Paulo*, see <http://www2.folha.uol.com.br/biblioteca >.
De Almeida, Catarina Solano. "Ser um génio literário não implica ser inteligente para outras coisas [Literary Genius Does Not Guarantee Intelligence in Other Fields]." *SIC Online* 1 September 2002. <http://www.sic.pt/article4540visual4.html >.
_____. "Uma 'lança' cultural nos EUA [A Thorn in America's Cultural Flesh]." *Diário de Notícias* 22 May 2001. Republished at Lusoplanet: <http://lusoplanet.free.fr/notio105.htm >.
Júnior, António. "Harold Bloom: Um autor a que não podemos ficar indiferentes [Harold Bloom: An Author to Whom No-one Can Be Indifferent]." *Blocos On Line* (Brazil) 2001. <http://www.blocosonline.com.br/entrev/entrevo3.htm >.
Moret, Xavier. "Harold Bloom, crítico literario: 'Los lectores están en peligro de desaparición' [Harold Bloom, Literary Critic: 'Readers Are an Endangered Species']." *El País* 22 June 2002. Republished at literaturas.com: <http://literaturas.com/haroldbloom.htm >.

Najmías, Daniel. "El boom Bloom: Harold Bloom en Barcelona [The Bloom Boom: Harold Bloom in Barcelona]." *Barcelona Review* 30 (May-June 2002). <http://www.barcelonareview.com/30/s_dn.htm >.

Queirós, Luís Miguel. "Só Falta Começarem a Partir-me Os Vidros das Janelas [Next Thing They Will Be Smashing My Windows]." *Público* 26 May 2001. Republished at terravista.pt: <http://www.terravista.pt/Bilene/5099/bloom2.htm >.

Sobrado, Jorge. "O Futuro passa por . . . Shakespeare [The Future Is . . . Shakespeare]." *Feira do Livro do Porto* (Oporto Book Fair) 2001. <http://feiradolivro.clix.pt/prt/g_img/programa/programa_eventos_02.html >.

Anxieties of Influence in the Theatre of Memory: Harold Bloom, Marlowe and Henry V

T. J. CRIBB

In his valuable analysis of Bloom's theory of influence as an art of rhetoric, Peter de Bolla remarks that it is "a highly idiosyncratic extension of the traditional tropes," an extension de Bolla himself proposes to take even further (De Bolla 62). Idiosyncratic though Bloom's extension may be, it is not the first. In *The Art of Memory* Frances Yates quotes one Renaissance Humanist, Patrizzi, saluting another, Camillo, because he had "released the precepts of the masters of rhetoric from narrow bounds, extending them to 'the most ample places of the Theatre of the whole world'" (Yates 171). Camillo had done this, like Bloom, by attributing new powers to one department of the art of rhetoric, the art of memory. There is, however, a crucial difference from Bloom. Camillo dealt with artificial memory, that is, memory improved by cultivation, whereas Bloom's memory is (to retain the Classical distinction) the memory of the natural man, operating according to the laws of nature. Now our ideas about the laws of nature have changed a good deal since the Renaissance, changes which affect the way we think about language and memory. We can examine the consequences flowing from the two different assumptions about memory by comparing Bloom's account of the anxiety of influence in the works of Shakespeare with Shakespeare's own representation of the action of memory in *Henry V* (where I quote from the Folio text).

I base my account on the "Preface" to the second edition of *The Anxiety of Influence* rather than on *Shakespeare: The Invention of the Human*, because the idea of influence in the latter is not Bloom's main concern and is indeed surprisingly attenuated to little more than a matter of style. It is touched on in connection with *King John*, *Henry VI* and *Richard III* but the matter is essentially concluded in *Titus Andronicus*, where "the contest involves taking Marlovian language to so extreme a point that it parodies itself" (*Shakespeare* 80-81; see Pechter 155–56). Influence is much more fully treated in the "Preface," under the much stronger sub-heading of "The Anguish of Contamination," and Marlowe is the main theme for over half of the thirty-six pages.

    Moreover, the second edition retracts or qualifies a number of claims about Shakespeare in the first edition (written, it is revealed, in 1967, some five years before it was published). The first edition had declared Shakespeare's works immune from the anxiety of influence for three reasons: that his precursor was Marlowe and Marlowe was "a poet very much smaller than his inheritor;" that drama is less subjective than poetry; and that Shakespeare belonged to a period "before the anxiety of influence became central to poetic consciousness" (*Anxiety* 11). This last reason confirms Gregory Machacek's argument in this volume that Bloom's idea of influence depends on a prior assumption about originality and that the latter derives from the time of the Romantics. Indeed, as Peter de Bolla points out, Bloom supplied precisely that periodization to his idea when he claimed that the advent of associationist psychology and theories of language in the eighteenth century displaced Classical ideas of faculty psychology and rhetoric and inaugurated ways of thinking about language, memory and poetry that continue down to Freud and the present (De Bolla 33–34). In other words, behind the Romantics lies Locke. By a rather Foucauldian turn, de Bolla also shows that, because Bloom claims that Freud's *topoi* occupy the places of the rhetorical *tropoi*, he works the two sets of terms interchangeably. It is this mapping of the one onto the other that enables Bloom to make his "idiosyncratic extension of the original tropes" so that the terms of rhetoric subsume the terms of psychology. Hence poetry, where the tropism inherent in language emerges fully fledged, becomes the supreme fiction. And if, in a human or secular rather than religious world, poetry as such is the supreme fiction, then Bloom can co-opt the procedures from the Kabbalah hitherto reserved for the study of sacred texts. With all this heavy machinery in place, it becomes possible to extend the application of the theory of influence back to Shakespeare and in principle to all literature. Bloom says in the "Preface" that he was wrong to "confine the phenomenon of creative misprision to post-Enlightenment writers" and that he corrected this "false emphasis" in later books (xxiv). It is, however, more than a mere degree of emphasis, for in extending his theory back to an earlier period, Bloom carries the Enlightenment and Freudian version of language and memory with him, and that version purports to be a scientific account of the natural man.

There can be no doubt that Bloom is right to see Marlowe as the contemporary who most haunted Shakespeare's imagination. By the time *Henry V* was performed, Bloom is inclined to see that influence as having dwindled to Ancient Pistol as a mere joke, but I see Marlowe as a much more substantial presence. After all, the Archbishop of Canterbury sends his sovereign off to war under the banner of Tamburlaine: "Stand for your own, unwind your bloody Flagge" (1.2.101). An apt pupil, Henry knows what follows: after the red flag comes the black. At the siege of Harfleur he ruthlessly transfers the responsibility for rape and massacre to the besieged:

> What is't to me, when you yourselves are Cause,
> If your pure Maydens fall into the hand
> Of hot and forcing violation? (3.3.19–21)

In this he echoes the logic of force that Tamburlaine deploys when the virgins plead too late for the sparing of Damascus: "They have refused the offer of their lives" (*Tamburlaine* 5.1.126).

Tamburlaine is a natural precedent for Shakespeare to bear in mind, for *Henry V* is his only play about a conqueror in action.[1] Moreover, as Bloom says, Tamburlaine's conquests in Asia are an expressive correlative for the conquest in the theatre of the audience by the poet. Hence it follows that Shakespeare owes his freedom of the stage as a poet-playwright in the first place to Marlowe. Such an inheritance cannot but be troubling. As Bloom observes, this new power over an audience was "only loosely allied to traditional morality, societal constraints, or orthodox pieties" ("Preface" xxxiv–xxxv).

That is to put it mildly. Power is what Wole Soyinka calls an "essence," that is, something with no intrinsic limit, which can therefore never be fully realized (Soyinka 115–18); hence its all-consuming dynamic. Tamburlaine reflects on this idea quite explicitly, and grounds it on what Bloom describes as Marlowe's curious "natural religion," in the famous speech explaining why he has suddenly turned on his former ally and master:

---

[1] My comments on *Tamburlaine* are influenced by Tim Supple's brilliant production of the play for the Marlowe Dramatic Society at Cambridge Arts Theatre in 1992. For *Henry V* as a conqueror play, see Robert Egan, "A Muse of Fire."

> Nature, that fram'd us of foure Elements,
> Warring within our breasts for regiment,
> Doth teach us all to have aspyring minds. (*Tamburlaine* 2.7.18–20)

The same constitutional strife and aspiring mind motivates poetry, as he explains in his meditation on beauty, after Zenocrate herself has pleaded unsuccessfully for the citizens of Damascus:

> If all the pens that ever poets held,
> Had fed the feeling of their maisters thoughts . . . .
> Yet should ther hover in their restlesse heads,
> One thought, one grace, one woonder at the least,
> Which into words no vertue can digest. (*Tamburlaine* 5.1.161–73)

Power and beauty are both essences, infinite in themselves, beyond good and evil, alarmingly Nietzschean; war and poetry are the means for pursuing them; that is the nature of the world.

In this analysis I have so far chimed with Bloom. However, given that the two powers, the poetic and the political, are, in Marlowe's case, so deeply implicated in each other, I do not well see how Bloom can later turn his back on the second, as he does when rejecting the historical dimension of these issues. True, a properly literary history will trace the lines of force from writer to writer in terms derived from the reception of one by the other, and it is Bloom's great merit to have written the peculiarly Romantic chapter of such a history. True also, "returning Shakespeare to history is a disheartened endeavour" ("Preface" xxvi), if that entails a betrayal of the internal logic and coherence of literary history and its reduction to the terms of some other kind of history—the more Althusserian kind of cultural materialism, for instance. But once a parallel between the two kinds of power has been admitted (and Bloom asserts it), then exploring the terms and degrees of relationship becomes a legitimate interest.

Indeed, what marks Marlowe as more intensely Renaissance, and thereby more historically limited, than Shakespeare is precisely the fact that his "hyperboles fuse the pen and the sword" ("Preface" xxxiii). But that fusion was not Marlowe's alone. It was the Humanist revolution in education that had made the first move by promoting rhetoric to the top of the grammar school trivium, because it was the Humanist dream that words might change the world—for the better. Marlowe carried that dream to its logical, post-Machiavellian conclusion: the power of words can be harnessed to any end—not just the good. His genius (and his economic necessity as an unemployed graduate of the new schooling) recognized that the make-believe world of theatre could give unfettered scope to the imagining, through the power of words, of power itself. Thus it was the reform of one institution and that a central one, education, which made Marlowe possible, and another institution, theatre, a marginal one, which presented him with the opportunity to take that educational inheritance in a direction his teachers could not have predicted. It was the crucible of the Elizabethan theatre which distilled the radical values out of the Humanist revaluation of rhetoric, although it took a character of Marlowe's daring to perform the experiment. Bloom explicitly sets aside these institutional considerations, yet it is they which give weight and consequentiality to the issues. Indeed the issues are such that one might suppose that so outrageous a consummation of a grammar school education as Marlowe's would have made all its alumni anxious. In fact, Bloom is right to point out Shakespeare as the one poet who was so troubled. Chapman, by contrast, continues *Hero and Leander* unperturbed in what seems a blandly rather than strongly creative misprision. Peele is another such, and Peele will eventually bring us back to *Henry V*.

In his "Introduction" to the New Cambridge edition of the play, Andrew Gurr says that the extensive deployment of a Chorus as presenter was an innovation, but this is to omit the case of Peele.[2] Several critics have drawn attention to Peele's interesting use of a Chorus as presenter, not only in conqueror plays like *The Battle of Alcazar*, but especially in his biblical plays, such as *The Love of King David and Fair Bethsabe, with the Tragedie of Absalon*, published in 1599 but acted some years before. Here, the Chorus mediates between sacred history and the audience, striving to raise its mind to heavenly understanding, echoing in little "Israel's sweetest singer," David the psalmist, whose poetry was directly inspired by God, and who orphically inspired his people by the songs of God. The Chorus is needed for this function because, although David is divinely inspired as a singer, he is also a sinner. Peele is writing a history play, that is, a play immersed in the contingency of the world, for David's story is taken from the two books of Samuel, and these record the deviation of the Jewish people from the direct guidance of God revealed through his prophets in a theocracy, to the secular king-

---

[2] See Inga-Stina Ewbank, "The House of David in Renaissance Drama," and "'What Words, What Looks, What Wonders?';" also Judith Weil, "George Peele's Singing School."

ship inaugurated by Saul. Henceforth, God will work not directly by revelation but immanently, by providence, constantly recuperating men's deviations for their salvation despite themselves. In this context there are two main things about David. First, he is a sinner, but a sinner who passionately repents, thus allowing a glimpse of God's providence at work. Second, he is the founder of a human dynasty, the House of David, through which God will eventually work the redemption of the whole of mankind. By investing the Marlovian sense of infinite possibility in another shepherd-king, the passionate and erring David, Peele opens the way for combining the essences of beauty and power with the merely human. Peele also brings the history play into intimate contact with contemporary politics, for Protestants were interested in David and his relations with the prophets as a model of how spiritual and secular might be combined in an Erastian church.

Bloom notes that Marlowe's natural religion was "not easily reconciled with Protestant Christianity" ("Preface" xxxiv). Precisely that is what Peele accomplished. In fact, Peele may not have had as much to overcome in effecting this Christianization (or platonization) of conquest as we might suppose. C. L. Barber, citing contemporary reactions such as Robert Greene's, describes the complex of energies Marlowe dealt in as "a version of extremist Protestant 'prophesying'" and reads Tamburlaine as animated by "a violently antinomian sense of 'election'" (Barber 79–90). Peele retains the dynamism and reach of the Marlovian verse cadence, realigning it according to a platonized Protestantism similar to Fulke Greville's, though more optimistic. The beauty that had so troubled Tamburlaine migrates from the false son, Absolom, and from fair Bathsheba herself, to David's youngest son, Solomon, and he is instructed by his father just how he should aspire:

> The feeble eyes of our aspiring thoughts
> Behold things present and record things past:
> But things to come, exceed our humane reach . . .
> For those, submit thy sence, and say, Thou power
> That now art framing of the future world,
> Knowest all to come, not by the course of heaven,
> By fraile conjectures of inferiour signes . . .
> But by a true and naturall presage,
> Transforme me from this flesh, that I may live
> Before my death, regenerate with thee. . . .
> Ravish my earthly sprite,
> That when I thinke, thy thoughts may be my guide. (Peele 1808–30)

Similar parallels between Protestantism and Renaissance neo-platonism were pointed out long ago by Hiram Haydn in *The Counter-Renaissance*. If there is an anxiety, it is not so much about influence as about inspiration, and a psychology very different from a post-Enlightenment associationist one is implied. In any given case, is the inspiration from God, or, as with Absolom, from the devil, cunningly disguised in beauty as the Christ? If inspiration means the conveying of a spirit from one body to another, is that spirit good or evil? If 'spirit' is thought of in its root sense of air or breath, and inspiration means that dead or inert matter is raised into action by having life breathed into it, is that resurrection by means of the Holy Spirit or Black Magic? In the case of David's sexual sins, can the language of rape be purged of its material aggression?

If Peele's plays have disappeared from the repertory, that is because he does not ask those questions. Instead, his Chorus gives the answers. But God's providential ironies are not the same as dramatic ironies; for all David's human frailties, *The Love of David and Fair Bethsabe* is more a show than a drama, and, for all the excitement of the unfolding of its dynamism, a lesser measure of the same limitation touches on *Tamburlaine*.

This is where *Henry V* differs. It is␣Shakespeare's fully dramatic imagination, subdued to but also instructed by the medium it works in, that enables him to widen his horizon beyond the Marlovian afflatus. It is this negative capability towards his medium that enables him to transcend the Marlovian precedent and Humanist project and also, I would claim, to escape the anxiety of influence. It is not by extending the scope of the terms of rhetoric, the route that Frances Yates shows Camillo taking, but by questioning them, that Shakespeare eludes his age. This is not to say that his dramaturgy is any the less trenchant; it cuts to the heart of the problematics of inspiration by picking up the device of a Chorus which, from its distinctly Marlovian opening words, deals in nothing else than inspiration:

> Play with your Fancies: and in them behold
> Upon the Hempen Tackle, Ship-boyes climbing;
> Heere the shrill Whistle, which doth order give
> To sounds confus'd: behold the threaden Sayles,
> Borne with th'invisible and creeping Wind,
> Draw the huge Bottomes through the furrowed Sea,
> Breasting the loftie Surge. O, doe but thinke
> You stand upon the Rivage, and behold
> A Citie on th'inconstant Billowes dauncing. (Prologue to Act 3, 9–15)

After the opening Chorus of fire, here the inspiration is all air. The climbing ship-boys lead our eyes up into the air; a vibration in the air, the sound of the tiny bosun's whistle, pierces through the dull hubbub; as if responsive to its bidding, air fills the sails and the ponderous mass of each ship begins to move. We feel not only the wonder of sail-power, a wonder in our times more apt to be elicited at the slowly accelerating ascent of a rocket, but also the power of the human mind and will to set inert masses of material and whole populations of fellow-creatures in motion. Henry's invasion fleet is thus an extended image of the winged weight, a familiar Elizabethan emblem for the exaltation of gross matter by spirit. It appears on the title page of the Quarto *Richard II*, for example. The same image is also the very process of inspiration, the uttering of words by which the Chorus seeks to move the audience. In *1 Henry IV*, Falstaff had reduced honour to a word and words to air; here the sequence runs back to show the power of air over men. By the end of the speech, the inspiring and exalting muse of air has become a hellish muse of fire and we are at the siege of Harfleur:

> ... the nimble Gunner
> With Lynstock now the divellish Cannon touches,
> And downe goes all before them. (Prologue to Act 3, 34–35)

As commentators have increasingly realized, the Chorus's obliviousness, not only of the extremity of such differences but of their relatedness, is typical, and is part of the dramaturgic design. As Andrew Gurr sums up: "The events of each act belie the claims of the Chorus that introduces it" ("Introduction" to Shakespeare, *Henry V* 8). For example, the Chorus is completely silent as to the whole existence of Pistol and company, as well it might be, since by a bold extension into politics of the sub-plot pioneered in *Dr Faustus*, Pistol parodies both Chorus and King.[3] The fact that the Chorus is so unreservedly committed to the official values of political history and yet is so unreliable a narrator must reflect on the values it so zealously promotes. If it shares the same breath of inspiration that moves Henry, his soldiers, his ships, and all England, then that motive is rendered questionable. Poetry, the word itself, is thus brought into a dialogue with the material practice of theatre, which again proves to be a radicalising crucible, as it had for Marlowe. But this time the Humanist project is subjected to a more sceptical scrutiny. All the

---

[3] Marlowe may in fact have pioneered this formal device in *Tamburlaine the Great*, but the printer tells us that he has taken upon him to delete such comic material.

powers of poetry are invested in the Chorus, but the Chorus itself is isolated in a sea of prose. In *Words and Poetry*, G. H. W. Rylands argued long ago that before he could write the poetry of the later plays Shakespeare first had to demolish the rhetorical system he had been taught at grammar school, and that he did this in the History plays and middle Comedies by writing prose. If Shakespeare establishes supremacy above other Renaissance writers it is not by a Renaissance triumphal progress. One might say, in Bloomian speculation, that he learned from his own play of *Richard II*, where the king becomes inviolably king, a king of Kingship, beyond Bullingbrook's reach, by abdication.

The contradictions between the Chorus and the play to which it offers itself as guide are all incorporated in Henry, heir both to Marlowe and to Peele; hence the contradictions in the critical responses to the play and in its stage productions over time. These range from an expressly religious reverence for Henry, such as Wilson Knight's, to a dismissive hostility, such as Yeats's (whom Bloom follows). Henry can be seen as a manipulatory Machiavel or an easily manipulated plain soldier; as humane or ruthless; as mixing with his troops on terms of brotherly fellowship, or as reserved and isolated; as a man of genuine if simple piety at pains to clear his conscience, or as deeply troubled by guilt; as a figure of Christ harrowing Hell and bringing poor benighted souls out of bondage by the miraculous deliverance of Agincourt, or as the Devil himself; as charmingly inept in the arts of wooing, or as giving the last and grossest meaning to the Chorus's apology for reducing heroic history to a game in a cock-pit. Henry is thus like a cloud-chamber in which one can trace all the issues of the play, rendered visible through the medium of his character, but which pass through him, leaving traces, not imparting any final definition. From this perspective, he is like the horizon line of the play, an example of what Bloom indicates in saying that Shakespeare cannot be "tracked" because "the only instruments by which we can examine him were either invented or perfected by Shakespeare himself" ("Preface" xxvii). In this instance, however, Shakespeare takes a Brechtian turn and lays out his instruments before us. The Chorus may be oblivious of the moral issues it sweeps up in its poetic enthusiasm, but that same desire to over-reach makes it hyperconscious of having to work within the constraints of an actual theatre. The obverse of its idealism is an obtuse literalism, a not uncommon combination, whether in aesthetics or politics.

The problems the Chorus complains of in the theatre are also those of the historian as defined by Peter Munz:

> The ideal limiting case of a reproduction is reduplication [i.e. a re-run of Agincourt, with a kingdom for a stage], and a duplicate is too true to be useful. Anything that falls short of the ideal limit of reduplication is too useful to be altogether true. (Munz 17)

Re-stagings of the storming of the Winter Palace are of this order. But, as Munz points out, the categoric incommensurability of space and time does not permit verification by reduplication. *Henry V* addresses this problem too, and here the differences between Classical arts of artificial memory and Post-Enlightenment attempts at a natural science of memory come into play.

By a special technique of inspiration, the Chorus incites the audience to use the scene before them as a semi-magical *aide-mémoire*. The idea is that the scenes as performed offer mere figures for enlargement in the mind and, potentially, for completion in action. Here we see rhetoric coming to the aid of memory by means of persuasive figures—not figures of speech but the figures of the actors impersonating the historical actors. They are a material enactment of the *imagines agentes* that Frances Yates dwells on in the most influential of the Classical arts of rhetoric, the *Ad Herennium* (Yates 25). If the audience will cooperate in this, then the scene will swell through a consecutive series of theatres, nesting different epochs within each other, and the Globe will become a theatre of memory. In the Chorus to Act 5, four different times are imagined: the past of Henry's return to London, the further past of Caesar's triumphal entry into Rome; the present of the audience; and the future of Essex's expected return from the conquest of Ireland. This temporal series corresponds to a spatial series in which the players' theatre is a figure for the theatre of England: "Behold the English beach / Pales in the flood; with Men, Wives, and Boyes, / Whose shouts & claps out-voyce the deep-mouth'd Sea" (Prologue to Act 5, 11–13). That in turn is a figure for Rome, the greatest of political theatres the western world had seen. What allows them to cohere and make a composition of place and time is that each is a type of the other.

The same patterning is observable in English history. After the Archbishop has urged Henry to unwind his bloody flag, he continues:

> Goe my dread Lord, to your great Grandsires Tombe,
> . . . invoke his Warlike Spirit,

> And your great Unkles, Edward the Black Prince,
> Who on the French ground play'd a Tragedie . . .
> Whiles his most mightie Father on a Hill
> Stood smiling, to behold . . . . (1.2.108-14)

When the French King recalls the victory of the Black Prince at Crecy, it is again as a scene in a natural theatre:

> Whiles that his Mountaine Sire, on Mountaine standing
> Up in the Ayre, crown'd with the Golden Sunne,
> Saw his Heroicall Seed, and smil'd to see . . . . (2.4.63–65)

At Agincourt, the Constable of France entertains the same idea that he and the other nobles might safely take their stands as spectators on the neighbouring hill to watch their common soldiers clear away the English (4.2.32–39). But the theatre of history has not allotted him that privileged position and, just before Mountjoy comes to concede the victory, Henry sends a trumpeter "unto the Horsemen on yond hill" (4.7.59) to bid them fight or flee. The field of Agincourt is thus overlooked by an audience composed of previous actors on the historical stage. In this theatre, Henry re-enacts the deeds of the Black Prince, overcoming great odds with a select few, just as, to compare small with great, the players re-enact him and overcome their audience, and as current political leaders project the action into new theatres of operation. There is nothing unconscious about these dramaturgically devised parallels; there is no call for the tropes of rhetoric to be extended or translated into a Freudian topology of the unconscious; the artificial memory and art of rhetoric are fully aware of how they construct themselves. Only the Chorus, aided and abetted by some parts of the play, but resisted by other parts, seeks to create a magical memory theatre which will induce that to happen which it wishes. The Chorus exemplifies that strain of Renaissance idealism which led to the wilder shores of speculation explored by Frances Yates and to the expensive illusions of the court masques, exposed by Stephen Orgel in *The Illusion of Power*. The Chorus wants to transport us from a wooden "O" to a marble "Roome"—that is its historical and political project.

Inevitably, the mere act of conducting it in a theatre, especially a popular and commercial theatre, threatens to undo the spell as fast as it is made. The allusions, so exceptionally marked in this play, to contemporary topics, are apt to stimulate diversity rather than unity of response. If Williams were in the audience (or the Boy), we know from the unshakeable independence of mind he shows in the play that an army is not only a happy few but a mixed bag. As Bloom points out, "the common soldiers fighting with their monarch are not going to become gentlemen" (*Shakespeare* 120). Williams will not be an uncritical enthusiast like Fluellen. If he goes to the theatre at all, it will be to what Brecht called a smokers' theatre, lending himself coolly to the illusion, just as he lends himself to the state's purposes in battle.

Yet one must not overstate Williams's healthy scepticism and self-possession. The play's production history proves that when a tide of feeling sweeps the nation, then the play does consolidate with the Chorus, audiences do compose a unity of time and place, and history is foreshortened into myth even as it is being made, as Churchill, for example, well knew.

History, then, and Henry's character with it, is the outcome of the interaction of an unstable ensemble of agencies, figured in this play by the will to believe voiced by the Chorus, the ambivalently independent evidence offered by the scenes of the play, and what a given audience at a given time makes of the relation between the two. Put another way, history is what an audience and a company of actors choose to repeat from the past, and how they choose to repeat it, where choice sometimes feels like choice and is cool, and sometimes feels more like inspiration. The foregrounding of the Chorus as intermediary between play and audience makes the ensemble proto-modernist in form, since it allows us in principle to scrutinise the means of production, pursuing that to as sceptical and materialist a conclusion as we can find it in ourselves to discern, while at the same time remaining irreproachably patriotic, loyal and popular—that is, if we are willing to lend ourselves to the inspiring purposes of history at all. I conclude, therefore, that Bloom had no need to renege on his original intuition that Shakespeare was immune from the anxiety of influence as it may have developed with the Romantics, and that Shakespeare's relation with Marlowe is more like that of an apprentice who becomes his own man by mastering and criticising the tools of his trade. I would nonetheless concede that when all the battles are lost and won, it is not the once and future king of England but the rejected Falstaff, one of Bloom's characters beyond whom we cannot think, who sleeps in Arthur's bosom.

Works Cited

Barber, C. L. *Creating Elizabethan Tragedy*. Chicago: U of Chicago P, 1988.
De Bolla, Peter. *Harold Bloom: Towards Historical Rhetorics*. London: Routledge, 1988.
Egan, Robert. "A Muse of Fire: *Henry V* in the Light of *Tamburlaine*." MLQ 29 (March 1968): 17–26.
Ewbank, Inga-Stina. "The House of David in Renaissance Drama." *Renaissance Drama* 8 (1965).
———. "'What Words, What Looks, What Wonders?': Language and Spectacle in the Theatre of George Peele." *The Elizabethan Theatre* 5 (1975): 124–54.
Marlowe, Christopher. *Tamburlaine the Great*. *The Complete Works of Christopher Marlowe*. Ed. Fredson Bowers. 2nd ed. 2 vols. Cambridge: Cambridge UP, 1992.
Munz, Peter. *The Shapes of Time*. Middletown: Wesleyan UP, 1977.
Orgel, Stephen. *The Illusion of Power: Political Theatre in the English Renaissance*. Berkeley: California UP, 1975.
Pechter, Edward. "Romanticism Lost: Bloom and the Twilight of Literary Shakespeare." *Harold Bloom's Shakespeare*. Ed. Christy Desmet and Robert Sawyer. New York: Palgrave, 2001. 145–65.
Peele, George. *The Love of King David and Fair Bethsabe*. Ed. W. W. Greg. Malone Society Reprints. Oxford: Oxford UP, 1912–13.
Rylands, George H. W. *Words and Poetry*. London: Hogarth, 1928.
Shakespeare, William. *Henry V*. Ed. Andrew Gurr. Cambridge: Cambridge UP, 1992.
Soyinka, Wole. *Art, Dialogue and Outrage*. 2nd ed. London: Methuen, 1993.
Weil, Judith. "George Peele's Singing School: *David and Bethsabe* and the Elizabethan History Play." *Themes in Drama* 8 (1986): 51–66.
Yates, Frances. *The Art of Memory*. 1966. London: Pimlico, 1992.

Conceptions of Origins and Their Consequences: Bloom and Milton

GREGORY MACHACEK

> ... the revisionist strives to *see* again, so as to *esteem* and *estimate* differently, so as then to *aim* "correctively."
> —HAROLD BLOOM

The concept of originality is fundamental to much literary analysis, particularly the construction of literary and cultural histories. And the almost exclusively honorific force of the term *original* insures that it functions as a mechanism in the canonization of almost any particular literary text. The concept of originality does not owe its prestige and currency to any consensus as to its meaning, however. An origin can be understood either in relation to the antecedents from which it deviates, or in relation to the consequences that follow from it, or in terms of its own singularity. So when Harold Bloom, to whom the concept of origins is probably more important than to any other modern critic, articulates his understanding of the Western literary tradition, the form that history takes is determined in part by the understanding of origins and originality that underlies his literary theorizing. The impact of his conception of origins on his sense of literary history is nowhere more clear than in his treatment of Milton, a figure Bloom finds particularly difficult to account for. Milton was, of course, himself deeply interested in origins—in Regina Schwartz's phrase, "obsessed with origins"—and a consideration of how Milton conceived originality may help to explain why Bloom has such difficulty in accounting for Milton and provide a different way of describing Milton's place in the Western literary tradition (1).

The concept of originality was crucial within Bloom's famous influence tetralogy, and even in more recent work such as *The Western*

Canon, it remains one element of the "amalgam" through which a work breaks into the canon: "mastery of figurative language, originality, cognitive power, knowledge, exuberance of diction" (29). Bloom's treatment of the topic, in part because of the energy and extravagance with which it is articulated, illustrates vividly the connection between one's conception of origins and one's sense of the poetic tradition. One place where the connection between these two is especially apparent is in the chapter of *A Map of Misreading*, entitled "Milton and His Precursors," in which Bloom attempts to describe the place of Milton in the epic tradition. Yet in mapping the Western literary tradition (and not least in this chapter), Bloom experiences particular difficulty in accounting for the poetry of John Milton. This difficulty I attribute to changes in the meaning of the word *original* between the end of the seventeenth century and the present day. A better understanding of the semantic development of the word, along with an examination of Milton's own unusual understanding of originality, will provide the grounds for a more adequate account of Milton's place in the epic tradition than Bloom has been able to provide.

1) Bloom Reading Milton

There can be no mistaking the importance of Milton in Bloom's theory of poetic influence. One of Bloom's opening strategies in *The Anxiety of Influence* is to read *Paradise Lost* (*PL*) "as an allegory of the dilemma of the modern poet" (20). And elsewhere Bloom contends that "of the dozen or so major poetic influencers before this century [Milton] ranks as the great Inhibitor" (32). Even the title of one of his more recent works of literary criticism, *Ruin the Sacred Truths*, comes from Andrew Marvell's poem, "On *Paradise Lost*."

But the position Milton occupies in Bloom's theory, however privileged, is an unstable one. One sign of this instability is Bloom's vacillation on the question of whether or not his theory even applies to Milton. His declared purview is post-Enlightenment poetry, and on one occasion he claims that Milton "absorbed precursors with a gusto evidently precluding anxiety" (*Anxiety* 50). From such statements it would seem that the theory is not intended to apply to Milton. Yet on other occasions Bloom asserts the contrary: "Shakespeare belongs to the giant age before the flood, before the anxiety of influence became central to poetic consciousness," but Milton "with all his strength, yet had to struggle, subtly and crucially, with a major precursor in Spenser"

(*Anxiety* 11). Indeed, so great is Bloom's uncertainty as to whether his theory applies to Milton or not, he can within the space of a single page argue that Milton "was incapable of suffering the anxiety of influence" and then go on to demonstrate the manner in which Spenser is Milton's precursor, his "Great Original" (*Anxiety* 34). Bloom seems eager to resolve this confusion; in *A Map of Misreading*, the second book in his famous influence tetralogy, he claims that he "would now assert only a difference in degree, rather than in kind, for influence-anxieties from Milton on" (77). But despite this attempt at clarification, the confusion remains. Milton, whose inclusion or exclusion was formerly unsettled, now occupies an ill-defined transitional position in Bloom's poetic history. And the ambiguity of Bloom's phrasing—"from Milton on"—leaves one wondering whether the change of which he is speaking occurs with or just after Milton.

A second indication of the unstable position Milton occupies in Bloom's theory is that even though Bloom typically excludes from his study obvious verbal echoes, claiming that they have "almost nothing to do with . . . poetic influence, in the sense [he] gives to it" and are suited only to "those carrion-eaters of scholarship, the source hunters," when he comes in *A Map of Misreading* to study Milton, it is precisely these obvious verbal echoes (of Homer, Virgil, Dante, Tasso, Spenser and others) that he examines (*Map* 19 and 17). Bloom himself admits the difficulty he has in accounting for Milton, who is, as he puts it, "the central problem in any theory and history of poetic influence in English" (*Anxiety* 33), confessing, in an interview with Robert Moynihan: "I am increasingly uncertain . . . as to whether we have a way of talking about what it is that Milton is actually doing in *Paradise Lost*. I reject completely the orthodox accounts, but I have not yet found one to replace them."[1]

Bloom's perplexity over Milton stems, I would argue, at least in part from his conception of origins and originality. The word *originality* became a term of literary approbation in the eighteenth century and was promoted to a *sine qua non* of literary value by the Romantics. Perhaps Bloom's theory, unabashedly Romantic in its adoration of originality as it is in so many other ways, is simply inapplicable to pre-Romantic literature, and the difficulty Bloom has in accounting for Milton a manifestation of his theory's historical boundaries. Of course, writers have always

---

[1] Though he has treated Milton since that interview, in both *Ruin the Sacred Truths* and *The Western Canon*, it is not clear whether Bloom has yet developed what he would regard as an adequate account. Robert Adams regards Bloom's chapter on *Paradise Lost* in *The Western Canon* as one of the weakest readings in that book.

sought to distinguish themselves from their predecessors, whether or not they refer to such distinctiveness with the term *originality*. Carew praises Donne for his "fresh invention" and claims that he will yield to the ancients no "precedence but time." Milton himself reveals his desire to be what we would call original—to pursue, in his words, "things unattempted yet in prose or rhyme" (*PL* 1.16)—and the Ariostian provenance of that line (besides demonstrating that Milton has no simplistic notion of originality) indicates that the desire was hardly new to Milton. If writers have always struggled to distinguish themselves in some way from their precursors, then his focus on originality would not, in itself, provide reason to regard Bloom's theory as limited to post-Enlightenment poets. We might agree with Paul de Man that Bloom's positing of a "great age before the Flood" represents nothing more than a "highly familiar ... historical fallac[y]" (*Blindness* 272, citing *Anxiety* 122).

Yet even despite the fact that authors have always aimed to differentiate their work from that of their precursors, a more historically informed consideration of the term *original* can still be of use in suggesting why Milton fits so uneasily in Bloom's theory, if one recognizes that the term *original* has several distinct but interrelated senses and one bears in mind the special sense in which Bloom employs the term. In the evaluation of art, the word *original* is now customarily employed in contrast with the term *derivative*; we deem a given poem original when it seems fundamentally unlike earlier poems. Bloom, true to his own imperative that "every word in a critic's vocabulary should swerve from inherited words," takes *original* in something closer to its root sense (*Agon* 21). The anxiety of influence is aroused in a poet precisely because he wishes to be more than merely distinctive; he desires actually to antedate his predecessors, to be original in the sense of "initial, first, earliest," and not merely in the sense of "not derivative or dependent."[2] "*Priority* in divination," Bloom maintains, "is crucial for every strong poet, lest he dwindle merely into a latecomer;" or again, "the commodity in which poets deal, their authority, their property, turns upon *priority*" (*Anxiety* 8 and 64; emphasis added). Such actual chronological priority is of course impossible to attain, but the revisionary ratios that Bloom enumerates are strategies of writing that make it *appear* possible; this is especially true of the ultimate ratio, *apophrades*, by which "the tyranny of time is almost overturned, and one can believe, for startled

---

[2] All definitions are from the *Oxford English Dictionary*.

moments, that [historically late poets] are being *imitated by their ancestors*" (*Anxiety* 141; his emphasis).

Bloom, then, connects uniqueness of writing style with actual temporal priority along the trajectory of the word *originality*, which may now convey either of those meanings. This is a trajectory, however, arguably unavailable before the eighteenth century. The earliest witness for the word *original* in the sense of "not imitated from another" is the preface to John Dryden's 1700 *Fables Ancient and Modern*, where he announces that to his imitations of Homer, Ovid and Boccacio he has "added some Original papers of [his] own." Now, it is true that our earliest witness of a term's use is only rarely that term's first actual use, and in this instance one can be more certain than usual that Dryden is not here coining this sense of the term, for the word appears in the subtitle of his book (*Translated into Verse, from Homer, Ovid, Boccace and Chaucer: with Original Poems*) in the same sense; Dryden obviously did not feel that he needed the context in order to make his sense of the term clear, as he would probably have felt had he been coining a new sense of the word *original*. But whether coined by Dryden or not, this new sense of the word *original* is not witnessed before his use of it.

So, Milton was undoubtedly able to conceive of that feature of artistic production that today we call originality. But if "not imitated" as a meaning for the word *original* was at best emerging in Milton's time, it is unlikely that he would have understood the connection, so important to Bloom's theory, between the distinctiveness of a writing style and actual temporal priority. It is in the connection of these two senses of the term *original* that Bloom's theory is historically bounded, and this may explain why he has such difficulty accounting for the poetry of Milton.

2) Origins: Milton/Bloom

Another reason for Bloom's difficulty in accounting for Milton is that he (Bloom) figures an origin as a strictly unitary phenomenon. In contrast with earlier critics, who assumed that a poem consists of a variety of strands from previous literature—an image from here, some lines from there, an evocative phrase from someplace else—and thus has a multiplicity of origins, Bloom conceives of an origin as profoundly singular. Poets engage in that *agon* which is the most distinctive feature of Bloom's theory of poetry because, again, "the commodity in which poets deal, their authority, their property, turns upon priority;" that priority or originality is conceived as a space which can be occupied by only one author at a time, thus prompting later poets to attempt to oust their precursors, king-of-the-hill style, from the privileged position of the origin and thus to usurp the authority which is indivisible from anteriority (*Anxiety* 9).

To see the impact of Bloom's unitary conception of origins on his understanding of the poetic tradition, we might first cast that conception into relief by contrasting it with Milton's own figuration of origins. Milton's epic, by contrast with Bloom's theory, figures origins as binary in nature: an event, the poem insists, is only an origin in conjunction with that which follows from it and repeats it.[3] This unusual, and perhaps paradoxical, conception of origins underlies the major action of the poem, for in *Paradise Lost* the original sin is emphatically not the first transgression, Eve's, but the first two transgressions: Eve's eating of the forbidden fruit *together with* Adam's repetition of her action. The language of the passage in which Milton describes Adam's fatal trespass provocatively underscores the binary nature of the initial sin. When Adam ate of the forbidden fruit, we are told, Earth trembled and the sky "wept at compleating of the mortal Sin / Original" (*PL* 9.1003-04). That an origin should be open to completion is, I believe, an unusual suggestion. To understand such a suggestion demands that one see an origin as a bifurcated occurrence, in which an earlier event brings about a later event (as Eve's disobedience does Adam's) but is nevertheless only properly an origin *in conjunction with* that later event.

This formulation underlies many of the other origins depicted in the epic as well, from the plan to corrupt mankind—which originates only with Beelzebub's repetition of "devilish counsel, first devis'd / By Satan and in part propos'd" (*PL* 2.379-80)—to the origin of repentance, described in the famously repetitive passage that closes Book 10. Even the word *fruit* in the opening line of the epic suggests a relation between origin (if we understand the apple as a synecdoche for the initial sin) and consequence (in the word's punning sense of 'results') so close as to suggest that consequence partly constitutes origin.

---

[3] The binary character of Milton's imagination is of increasing interest to Miltonists. See, for instance, Sanford Budick's *The Dividing Muse*; Gordon Teskey's "From Allegory to Dialectic;" and especially R. A. Shoaf's *Milton, Poet of Duality*. Regina Schwartz addresses, though in terms different from mine, Milton's binary conception of origins; see her *Remembering and Repeating*.

3) Bloom Misreading Johnson Reading Milton

The contrast with Milton, then, shows that there are other ways to conceive of an origin than, as Bloom does, as strictly unitary. We are now prepared to see the impact that that conception of origins has on his understanding of the poetic tradition. And we can do so by considering his most extended examination of Milton: the analysis he offers in the chapter of *A Map of Misreading* entitled "Milton and his Precursors." But in my reading, Bloom's chapter on Milton is not so much a straightforward account of Milton's place in the epic tradition as it is a Bloomian *agon* (with Johnson) for the authority that comes with priority.

In the chapter, Bloom claims that Milton achieves what all poets seek to achieve: he reverses time by writing in such a way as to make his precursors seem to be his imitators. In Bloom's esoteric terms, this is *apophrades*, the sixth and ultimate revisionary ratio, "the uncanny effect [of which] is that the new poem's achievement makes it seem to us ... as though the later poet himself had written the precursor's characteristic work" (*Anxiety* 16). Milton's capacity to effect an *apophrades* on his precursors, to come out a winner in the struggle for priority in which all strong poets engage, results from his particular manner of alluding to other authors: what Bloom terms a transumptive or metaleptic mode of allusion.

In Bloom's view, Milton developed this mode of allusion as a defense against Spenser, whom he acknowledged to Dryden was his "Original" (as Dryden reports it in the preface to *Fables Ancient and Modern*). Before examining this special mode of allusion, Bloom reiterates one of the central premises of his book—namely, that all original poetry results from a misreading of one's precursors—by drawing attention to a mistake that Milton makes about *The Faerie Queene* in his comments on Spenser in *Areopagitica*: Milton speaks of Spenser bringing Guyon into the cave of Mammon accompanied by the palmer, when in fact Guyon enters the cave of Mammon unaccompanied. "Milton's is no ordinary error," Bloom claims, "no mere lapse in memory, but is itself a powerful misinterpretation of Spenser and a strong defense against him" (*Anxiety* 128). In Bloom's view, Milton had to make such a mistake about Guyon, had to believe that Spenser's hero was accompanied in his moment of temptation, in order to believe that his own presentation of Adam and Eve facing temptation unaccompanied by a spiritual superior represented an advance over the work of his precursor.

Having in this way evidenced his claim that all strong poetry arises from a misreading of one's precursors, Bloom begins to describe Milton's supremely effective mode of misreading, his transumptive allusion, by invoking Samuel Johnson as the best authority on Milton's relation to his precursors. This citation of Johnson, as we shall see in a moment, does more than just corroborate Bloom's point; it becomes the territory on which Bloom stages an *agon* with Johnson. Consider Bloom's quotation of Johnson, noting especially the ellipsis and the phrase "adventitious image:"

> Whatever be his subject, [Milton] never fails to fill the imagination. But his images and descriptions of the scenes or operations of Nature do not seem to be always copied from original form, nor to have the freshness, raciness, and energy of immediate observation. He saw nature, as Dryden expresses it, *through the spectacles of books*; and on most occasions calls learning to his assistance . . . . But he does not confine himself within the limits of rigorous comparison: his great excellence is amplitude, and he expands the adventitious image beyond the dimensions which the occasion required. Thus, comparing the shield of Satan to the orb of the Moon, he crowds the imagination with the discovery of the telescope and all the wonders which the telescope discovers.[4]

Bloom then reproduces the passage from *Paradise Lost* to which Johnson refers:

> He scarce had ceas't when the superiour Fiend
> Was moving toward the shore; his ponderous shield
> Ethereal temper, massy large and round,
> Behind him cast; the broad circumference
> Hung on his shoulders like the Moon, whose Orb
> Through Optic Glass the *Tuscan* Artist views
> At Ev'ning from the top of *Fesole*,
> Or in *Valdarno* to descry new Lands,
> Rivers or Mountains in her spotty Globe. (PL 1.283–91)

In comparing Satan's shield to the moon, Bloom observes, Milton alludes to Homer, who describes Achilles' shield as being like the moon, and to Spenser, who describes Radigund's shield as resembling the moon (*Iliad* 19.373–74; *Faerie Queene* 5.5.3). But, Bloom points out, Milton does not depict the same moon that his precursors depict:

---

[4] Bloom, here on page 130 of *Map of Misreading*, is citing a passage from Samuel Johnson's "Life of Milton" that can be found on pages 127-28 of *Lives of the English Poets*.

Conceptions of Origins and Their Consequences

> Homer and Spenser emphasize the moonlike brightness and shining of the shields of Achilles and Radigund; Milton emphasizes size, shape, weight as the common feature of Satan's shield and the moon, for Milton's post-Galilean moon is more of a world and less of a light. (*Map* 133)

Bloom, referring to Johnson's commentary on the Miltonic passage, calls Galileo's "Optic Glass" an "adventitious image," unnecessary to the picture that Milton is trying to paint. But while the image of the telescope may be adventitious with regard to the pictorial representation of Satan's shield, Bloom thinks it in another respect crucial, for it gives Milton a form of priority, the "priority of *interpretation*," over his precursors. That is to say, even though "Milton and Galileo are *late* . . . they see more, and more significantly, than Homer and Spenser, who were *early*" (*Map* 132–33, emphasis added). In this way, Milton turns "his tradition's priority over him into a lateness;" because of the seemingly adventitious image of the telescope, the moons described by Homer and Spenser come to seem like puerile imitations of a Miltonic original (*Map* 131).

The reading of Milton which I have just summarized is, in Bloom's own terms, a misreading—a misreading, however, not primarily of Milton, but of Johnson (whom Bloom elsewhere calls "the greatest critic in the language" and "the first great diagnostician of the malady of poetic influence" [*Anxiety* 28]). Bloom makes precisely the same sort of strategic error about Johnson that he showed Milton making about Spenser. His misreading of Johnson centers on the phrase "adventitious image." For Bloom, the adventitious image in Milton's description of Satan is the telescope; this is evident from Bloom's query, "why is Johnson's 'adventitious image,' Galileo and the telescope, present at all?" (*Map* 131–32). Johnson, by contrast, uses the phrase "adventitious image" for what we now, following I. A. Richards, term the vehicle of a metaphor. This becomes more clear when we examine the whole of Johnson's text, of which Bloom had reproduced only a part (his excision here indicated by brackets):

> Whatever be his subject, Milton never fails to fill the imagination. But his images and descriptions of the scenes or operations of Nature do not seem to be always copied from original form, nor to have the freshness, raciness, and energy of immediate observation. He saw nature, as Dryden expresses it, *through the spectacles of books*; and on most occasions calls learning to his assistance. [The garden of Eden brings to his mind the vale of *Enna*, where Proserpine was gathering flowers. Satan makes his way through fighting elements, like *Argo* between the *Cyanean* rocks, or *Ulysses* between the two *Sicilian* whirlpools, when he shunned *Charybdis* on the

> larboard. The mythological allusions have been justly censured, as not being always used with notice of their vanity; but they contribute variety to the narration, and produce an alternate exercise of the memory and the fancy.
>   His similes are less numerous, and more various, than those of his predecessors.] But he does not confine himself within the limits of rigorous comparison: his great excellence is amplitude, and he expands the adventitious image beyond the dimensions which the occasion required. Thus, comparing the shield of Satan to the orb of the Moon, he crowds the imagination with the discovery of the telescope and all the wonders which the telescope discovers. (Johnson 127-28)

Bloom's elliptical citation of Johnson, by effacing the context in which the remark about the "adventitious image" occurs, significantly misrepresents Johnson's point; the excision makes it seem as though Johnson is talking about Milton's allusions, when he is in fact discussing his similes. The paragraphs reproduced above represent just two in a series of rapid-fire critical observations about miscellaneous aspects of the epic: its divine machinery, episodes, integrity of design, moral sentiments and so on. The first paragraph discusses Milton's highly erudite and allusive style; the second takes up an entirely different aspect of the poem: similes. What Johnson wants to demonstrate in this second paragraph is how the vehicle of Milton's similes is often so fully elaborated in its own right that many of its details have no correspondence with the tenor. To convey this insight, he coins the phrase "adventitious image" for what we today call a vehicle, he uses the term "occasion" for what we would call the tenor, and he chooses the word "crowding" for details in the vehicle that have no corresponding elements in the tenor. Miltonic similes are characterized by the fact that the adventitious image is developed so extensively that we cannot determine a point-by-point resemblance between it and its occasion. In this particular instance, Satan's shield is the occasion, the moon is the adventitious image, and the telescope is the expansion or crowding of that adventitious image.

Bloom's labeling the telescope, rather than the moon, as the "adventitious image" is no ordinary error, no mere lapse of attention while reading Johnson's text, but is itself a powerful misinterpretation of Johnson. Bloom's strategic excision makes it seem as though Johnson brings up the example of Satan's shield in the context of a discussion of Milton's allusions and thus that Johnson is adumbrating Bloom's argument concerning how Milton transumes his precursors. Why should Bloom arrange to make it appear that Johnson is anticipating his own notion of transumptive allusion? The answer is not far to seek. By making Johnson sound as though he is advancing Bloomian arguments, Bloom *effects* the very thing that he is ostensibly *describing* Milton as having effected: an *apophrades* of his precursor. For a critic who will abide no distinction between criticism and poetry, it is not surprising that a purported reading of Milton in fact turns out to be a struggle to achieve priority over a predecessor.[5]

But if this is true, if Bloom's chapter on Milton is in fact a contest with Johnson for anteriority, what does that imply about its value as an account of Milton's place in the poetic tradition?[6] Does Milton merely serve as Bloom's adventitious image, extrinsic to his genuine concern in this chapter (an *agon* with Johnson)? Or does Bloom manage simultaneously an *apophrades* of Johnson and a viable reading of Milton's poetic practice? We need, after all, look no further than *Paradise Lost* for an example of a work that aspires to be at once a poem and an argument. Or perhaps the better parallel would be the *Essay on Criticism*, in which Pope simultaneously enumerates and exemplifies a number of poetic and critical principles.

To gauge the explanatory force, as distinct from the poetic force, of Bloom's text, we might begin by noting that what Johnson is describing in the paragraph on Satan's shield is what has since come to be known as an epic simile, a comparison in which the vehicle (or in Johnson's terminology the adventitious image) contains details that have no correspondence to the tenor (Johnson's "occasion"). Such similes are especially characteristic of Homer, and Milton, when constructing his own

---

[5] In the critical response to Bloom's work, nobody elects to study his texts as poems. Bloom insists that "a theory of poetry must itself be poetry" and speaks as his theory as one that "presents itself as a severe poem" (*Kabbalah* 109; *Anxiety* 13). But even critics sympathetic with his project—such as Peter de Bolla, Jean-Pierre Mileur and David Fite—value Bloom's texts as arguments rather than explicating them as poems. Daniel O'Hara does demonstrate that Bloom's appropriations of Nietzsche can be described using Bloom's own revisionary ratios.

[6] That it serves many readers as a plausible account of Milton's poetic practice is evident from the way Bloom's once radical reading of *Paradise Lost* has entered mainstream Milton criticism as just another option. In Paradise Lost *and the Rhetoric of Literary Forms*, for instance, Barbara Lewalski says that "though I focus upon Milton's engagement with literary precursors I do not find that engagement characterized by anxiety, struggle, transumption or triumph" (39), and the footnote to this sentence calmly directs readers: "for the counter argument, see Harold Bloom, *A Map of Misreading*."

extended similes, follows Homer's practice rather than that of Virgil, in whose similes the details in the vehicle usually correspond, though often subtly, with elements of the tenor. In any other critic than Bloom, we would regard as a mistake the inability to see that Johnson is discussing what is now known as an epic simile. Indeed, even in a theory that admits a large scope to the creative possibilities of misreading, the oversight is damaging. For if, as Bloom's argument would have it, Milton triumphs over his precursors through the technique of crowding his similes with "adventitious" contemporary details, then for the technique of the adventitious image itself to be borrowed from Homer would seem to represent a significant attenuation of Milton's supposed triumph. To describe the effect of Milton's allusions as being "to reverse literary tradition" may not be the best way of characterizing his relation to his precursors.

4) Three Origins

If it is his conception of origins as unitary that motivates Bloom's *agon* with Johnson, and if it is the distortions of Johnson's argument resulting from that *agon* that weaken Bloom's account of Milton's position in the epic tradition, then perhaps a different understanding of origins might yield a more nuanced account of Milton's inter-poetic relationships. As I mentioned at the outset, the word *original* bears several distinct, even divergent, senses. The word has as its basic meaning "initial, first, earliest." To that sense is often added a notion of causality: "that from which something arises, proceeds, or is derived." In the substantive, an original is the pattern by which copies are made. Finally, in aesthetic parlance, *original* means "not derivative or dependent," or more precisely "made, composed, or done by the person himself (not imitated from another)." One of the most common ways of graphically representing an origin—an image in which at least three of the senses of the word *origin* (primacy, causality and discontinuity) combine—is what in Euclidian geometry is termed a ray: a line segment beginning at a point and extending indefinitely thence in one direction. The sense of primacy is captured in the point (actually referred to by mathematicians as the ray's *origin*); the line segment may depict a chain of consequences extending from that origin; and the blank space preceding the point represents the discontinuity from the past that makes the origin "not derivative or dependent."

The conceptions of origins examined thus far in this essay can be coordinated with this threefold paradigm of origins contained in the image of the ray; Bloom's theory, for instance, focuses on the beginning point of the ray, stressing the unitary aspect of an origin, while the conventional modern understanding focuses on the radical difference between that point and what precedes it.[7] Incidentally, the image also allows us to appreciate that the sense of the word *original* which came into the language toward the end of the seventeenth century, the sense of "not imitated from another," represents more than just a new nuance accruing to an existing term; it is instead an absolute reversal in the temporal perspective from which an origin is viewed. For this definition considers an origin in relation to what comes before it, whereas the older sense of "that from which something arises, proceeds, or is derived" considers an origin in relation to what comes after it. Finally, the image of the ray allows us to characterize Milton's binary conception of origins as emphasizing both the point of origin and a later point on the line segment. Just as, in Euclidian geometry, a line is determined by two points, so too, in Milton's vision, are the consequences that follow from a particular event essential to that earlier event's being an origin—and essential as well to determining the trajectory that the remainder of the consequences will follow: the "sin original" becomes Original Sin, the congenital depravity of all of Adam and Eve's offspring.

5) Consequences

I submit that to adopt Milton's unusual understanding of originality (an understanding of the concept that is perhaps the result of his writing during a historical period in which the meaning of the word *original* was in process of changing) may provide us a more satisfactory way of describing his place in the epic tradition. Bloom would have it that Milton stands in an agonistic relation to his precursors, battling to occupy the position of origin. Such a picture, as I have shown, neglects the way in which Milton stations himself, in the construction of his similes, as an immediate follower of Homer.

A different picture might be created by adopting a binary conception of origins, a conception of an origin as something that may be

---

[7] Raymond Williams's *Keywords* notes the variety of perspectives from which origins and originality can be viewed and gives some sense of the historical shift I have isolated for consideration.

"completed." With such a formulation, we might say that Milton *completes Homer differently* than Virgil had. The proem to book 9 of *Paradise Lost* suggests that the epic tradition had followed a trajectory established by Virgil's imitation of Homer's martial episodes:

> the wrath
> Of stern Achilles on his foe pursued
> Thrice fugitive about Troy wall; or rage
> Of Turnus for Lavinia disespoused,
> Or Neptune's ire or Juno's, that so long
> Perplexed the Greek and Cytherea's son . . . . (9.14–19)

Apart from book 6 (which has the effect of demonstrating that he could have written a martial epic if he had wanted to), Milton chooses not to affiliate generically through the imitation of martial episodes. He picks up other poetic features for imitation, including the extended similes. He stations himself as an immediate descendant of Homer by including non-corresponding details in those similes. In Homer, the extended similes often remind readers of the non-military world, and in Milton they pertain specifically to the world of slow-endeavoring human effort in the pursuit of truth. Galileo exemplifies the "patience and heroic martyrdom" (literally witnessing) that Milton wants to make a new subject for epic poetry. Milton is original in that he completes Homer differently in an attempt to steer the epic tradition down a new path.

Besides providing a more nuanced way of describing how *Paradise Lost* is situated within the Western literary tradition, to recover a binary understanding might help us more generally to reconceive originality within the field of literary criticism, an enterprise devoted, as the phrase goes, to the making of an "original contribution to knowledge." Modern origins look only backward. We inhabit a critical climate in which (to update Donne) everyone aims "To be a Phoenix, hot that there be none / Else of that kind, of which one is, but one." (When we dream of being original in the older sense, of originating a new line of criticism, we employ the term *seminal* instead.) When Bloom wonders "why students of literature have become amateur political scientists, uninformed sociologists, incompetent anthropologists, mediocre philosophers, and overdetermined cultural historians," he should realize that part of the answer is that they operate under a professional injunction to be original (*Canon* 521). In such a situation, to conceive of originality as necessarily involving continuity as well as discontinuity, community as well as singularity, might save us from being original in the most recent, and weakest, sense of the term. It might save us from being merely unique.

Works Cited

Adams, Robert. "Bloom's All-Time Greatest Hits." *New York Review of Books* 17 Nov. 1994: 6.
Budick, Sanford. *The Dividing Muse: Images of Sacred Disjunction in Milton's Poetry*. New Haven: Yale UP, 1975.
De Bolla, Peter. *Harold Bloom: Towards Historical Rhetorics*. London: Routledge, 1988.
De Man, Paul. *Blindness and Insight: Essays in the Rhetoric of Contemporary Criticism*. 2nd ed. Minneapolis: U of Minnesota P, 1983.
Dryden, John. *The Poems of John Dryden*. Ed. James Kinsley. 4 vols. Oxford: Oxford UP, 1958.
Fite, David. *Harold Bloom: The Rhetoric of Romantic Vision*. Amherst: U of Massachusetts P, 1985.
Johnson, Samuel. *Lives of the English Poets*. Ed. Arthur Waugh. 2 vols. Oxford: Oxford UP, 1938.
Lewalski, Barbara Kiefer. Paradise Lost *and the Rhetoric of Literary Forms*. Princeton: Princeton UP, 1985.
Mileur, Jean-Pierre. *Literary Revisionism and the Burden of Modernity*. Berkeley: U of California P, 1985.
Milton, John. *The Works of John Milton*. Ed. Frank Allen Patterson, et al. 18 vols. New York: Columbia UP, 1931-40.
Moynihan, Robert. "Interview: Harold Bloom." *Diacritics* 13 (1983): 57-68.
O'Hara, Daniel. "The Genius of Irony: Nietzsche in Bloom." *The Yale Critics: Deconstruction in America*. Ed. Jonathan Arac, Wlad Godzich and Wallace Martin. Minneapolis: U of Minnesota P, 1983. 111-29.
Schwartz, Regina M. *Remembering and Repeating: Biblical Creation in* Paradise Lost. Cambridge: Cambridge UP, 1988.
Shoaf, R. A. *Milton: Poet of Duality*. New Haven: Yale UP, 1985.

Teskey, Gordon. "From Allegory to Dialectic: Imagining Error in Spenser and Milton." *PMLA* 101 (1986): 9-23.
Williams, Raymond. *Keywords: A Vocabulary of Culture and Society.* New York: Oxford UP, 1976.

The Poet as Poet: Misreading Harold Bloom's Theory of Influence

MILTON L. WELCH

And through thine eyes, even in thy soul I see
A lamp of vestal fire burning internally.
—PERCY BYSSHE SHELLEY, *The Revolt of Islam*

Outside you can see the difference
Inside you can feel the difference
—YAZ, "I Before E Except After C"

1

Categorizing Harold Bloom's notion of influence as basically psychological[1] seems inaccurate for straightforward reasons: (i) though Bloom rejects T. S. Eliot's "monumentalist" view of tradition, Sigmund Freud proves no more crucial to Bloom's studies of revisionism and influence than a panoply of other figures ranging from Isaac Luria to Kenneth Burke. Indeed, Bloom's "revisionary ratios" ultimately involve more metaphysics and theology than psychology, as Bloom's "map of misprision" illustrates (*Map* 85). Noting these "ratios" (the term is Platonic), we further note that (ii) although Bloom offers Freud such large epithets as "the Founder" or "the master of those who know," these same epithets are often used for the very un-Freudian Ralph Waldo Emerson, who—as Christy Desmet and Robert Sawyer recently pointed out—is "Harold

---

[1] Here, I understand the term "psychological critic" in the sense that John Crowe Ransom offers while discussing I. A. Richards's *New Criticism*: "poetry is a very good thing but it has no rating as a way of knowing the world. Its service is not cognitive but psychological" (8).

Bloom's authentic American ancestor."[2] Indeed, Emerson shares with Freud the honor of being cited as "the father of us all." These epithets are not incidental, since (iii) Emerson's Lucretian Law of Compensation—"Nothing is got for nothing"—motivates influence and revisionism for Bloom. This Law, to be sure, is also Shakespearean in source, a reminder that (iv) Bloom's admiration of Freud has evolved into a preference for Shakespeare. Freud, psychoanalysis, psychology are endeavors Bloom has reduced to derivations of Shakespearean aesthetic achievement.[3] Whether these reductions have been wholly successful is beside the point since the question at hand is construing Bloom's idea of influence.

Given Bloom's association with the Yale School of Criticism, an alternate suggestion may be seeing Bloom's work on "influence" as a version of what he calls rhetorical criticism. "Rhetorical Criticism" is the rubric under which Bloom lumps critics whose primary concern is the language of the text, its epistemological implications and operations of meaningfulness. I refuse this suggestion as well. The basis of my refusal is Bloom's own writings on the limitations of such criticism (particularly "Coda: Poetic Crossing," the final chapter of *Wallace Stevens: The Poems of Our Climate*).

Concerning the crucial issues of rhetorical criticism, e.g. meaning, Bloom is mostly indifferent. On the specific nature of meaning, Bloom is unconcerned:

> Whether one accepts a theory of language that teaches the dearth of meaning, as in Derrida and De Man, or that teaches its plenitude, as in Barfield and Ong, does not seem to me to matter. All I ask is that the theory of language be extreme and uncompromising. (*Breaking* 4)

Whether "meaning" is empty, ongoing chains of mutually (non)supportive (non)signification or a mystically definitive, metaphysically overdetermined entity is a question that does not need to be settled to discuss influence. Regardless of meaning's explanation, the *agon*, the revisionary stance of an author toward ancestral creativity (not signification) is primary. Not what precursors *meant*, but what they

---

[2] See Desmet and Sawyer; see also David Fite, "Influence and the Map of American Poetic History: The Emersonian Survival," in his *Harold Bloom: The Rhetoric of Romantic Vision*, for a flawed though intriguing discussion of Bloom's relationship to Emerson.

[3] The chapter "Freud: A Shakespearean Reading" in *The Western Canon* can be taken as Bloom's final settling of accounts with Freud.

imagined before matters. Whatever resonance and concern Bloom shares with rhetoricians of any stripe, there is little resemblance in critical aim or insight between their mode and Bloom's antithetical one. What remains, then, is the genuine difficulty of characterizing Bloom's notion of influence, among the most intriguing ideas of the last quarter of the twentieth century.

2

Holding psychology at arm's length while exploring the contours of Bloom's idea will allow us to begin rethinking the complex nature of his critical enterprise, and its cohesiveness. Harold Bloom's theory of influence is caught in a host of interrelated issues (e.g. criticism, reading) from his first attempts to set it forth. Early in *Anxiety of Influence* Bloom defines his view on the object and nature of criticism:

> The effort of criticism is to teach a language, for what is never learned but comes as the gift of a language is a poetry already written . . . I mean that criticism teaches not a language of criticism . . . . but a language in which poetry already is written, the language of influence, of the dialectic that governs the relations between poets *as poets*. (*Anxiety* 25)

According to the quotation, the way in which criticism instructs us in poetry is by teaching how to respond to poetry. This response, an articulate experience of one's emotions is qualitatively different from discursive mastery. Criticism, according to Bloom, is a way of recognizing—and more importantly *feeling*—poetic achievement; it results from reading poetic language, and designates an indispensable feature of how poetic language spread (influence as influenza). In so far as the critic needs poetic language to learn how to work her craft, the critic is a specialized case of the poet (similar in kind, different in degree). According to Bloom, the difference between poet and critic is in *what*, not necessarily *how*, they write. Any distinction in Bloom's work between criticism and the object of criticism is judicial, and moreover originates in acts of reading (*Kabbalah* 101). When discussing Bloom's theory of influence, then, we must hold in mind that it proposes the poet as a primary form of intellectual expression and imaginative perception: "all criticism is prose poetry" (*Anxiety* 95).

To discuss this primary form of the poet Bloom refers throughout his theoretical work to the figure of "the poet as poet." This figure, we shall see, is pre-communicative, primordially conjoining the functions of poets and critics, and collapsing the textual distinction between the primary and the secondary. The poet as poet incarnates what Bloom calls "the poetic character," the individual constitution of dialectical relations among poets, i.e. influence. There is a third figure, a non-rhetorical *topos* Bloom introduces in *Map of Misreading*, into which poetic character transubstantiates: the Primal Scene of Instruction. These three figures, to me, comprise the skeleton of Bloom's theory of influence. In the cycle of poetic incarnation (roughly speaking, the process of maturation of the poet as poet described most fully in *Anxiety of Influence*), the poet as poet is at the root of the relations of influence.

I intend to give an account of the poet as poet as the deep poetic self, a self so deep and so deeply poetic that it exists in an irreducible fashion, neither psyche nor will, though related to both; it is irreducible because this deep poetic self, the poet as poet, is liminal to any actual poet. Bloom states the paradox as follows:

> For the poet is condemned to learn his profoundest yearnings through an awareness of *other selves*. The poem is *within* him, yet he experiences the shame and splendor of *being found* by poems—great poems—*outside* him. (*Anxiety* 26)

The poet as poet is internal and external to the poet himself or herself: radically internal because the poet as poet is the well-spring, the fountainhead, what Bloom calls the *daimon* and flame, of poetry that makes the poet a poet. The poet as poet is radically external because as well-spring, fountainhead and flame it bursts and is discovered due to its having been brought forth and recognized in encounters with other poets. These encounters are readerly, and Bloom's Primal Scene ultimately ironizes the creative, non-encounter of misreading.

3

It is more fruitful to explore the nature of the poet as poet by exploring the explicative aspect of poetry, so crucial to the poet as poet. *Anxiety of Influence* and *Map of Misreading* explore this aspect at length, and so by willfully misreading Dylan Thomas's "To Others Than You" I would like to illustrate and discuss the tacit connection of the poet as poet with influence in the persistent form Bloom suggests it has taken. I enact this misreading upon a poem chosen nearly at random, but apropos to Bloom's theory. Misreading Thomas, I will suggest "To Others Than You" allegorically displays what it is, poetically and critically, to come to terms with poetic alterity. I quote the poem in full:

Friend by enemy I call you out.

You with a bad coin in your socket,
You my friend there with a winning air
Who palmed the lie on me when you looked
Brassily at my shyest secret
Enticed with twinkling bits of the eyes
Till the sweet tooth of my love bit dry,
Rasped at last, and I stumbled and sucked,
Where now I conjure to stand as thirst
In the memory worked by mirrors,
With unforgettably smiling act,
Quickness of hand in the velvet glove
And my whole heart under your hammer,
Were once such a creature, so gay and frank
A desireless familiar
I never thought to utter or think
While you displaced a truth in the air,

That though I loved them for their faults
As much as for their good,
My friends were enemies on stilts
With their heads in a cunning cloud. (1–21)

These lines esoterically combine sexual, mystical and poetic concerns which I will attempt to trace in light of Bloom's theory. The treatment of these concerns vaguely suggests certain veiled correspondences with the biblical story of the Fall of Man. The verse is opaque, but the Fall preoccupies Thomas in many works,[4] so as a topic it is not unusual. With this preoccupation in mind, this poem seems an apt perpetuation of Thomas's persistent equation (not original to him) of erotic and epistemological awakening with the Fall. This equation has a source in *Paradise Lost,* where John Milton writes:

> but that false Fruit
> Farr other operation first displaid,
> Carnal desire enflaming, [Adam] on Eve
> Began to cast lascivious Eyes, she him
> As wantonly repaid; in Lust they burn. . . .
> [they] Soon found thir Eyes how op'n'd, and thir minds
> How darkened. . . . (10.1011–15, 1053–54)

---

[4] Particularly the ambitious and neglected "Altarwise by Owl-Light," which fuses themes of birth and redemption to those of sexual awakening and the fall.

This passage is, of course, based on Genesis 3.7, which reads:

> And the eyes of them both were opened, and they *were* naked; and they sewed figs together, and made themselves aprons.

In both, though the fall is the "death" of man and woman, ironic figures of awakening are used, figures of opening eyes which invoke epistemological categories, also ironically: Milton's "Eyes how op'n'd" overtly suggesting Platonic opinion in a phrase whose typical aegis is knowledge. This sudden knowledge, however, is bodily; Milton directly and Genesis indirectly portrays this knowledge of the body as occasioned by a shaming sexual arousal.

Thomas broadly aims to convey similar themes. Let us assume for the purposes of misreading that Adam speaks "To Others than You," and the poem is said to Eve. This indulgence for which I ask pardon will more securely tie Thomas's poem to Bloom's notion of influence, which relies heavily on the literary status of Adam, who is "the potentially strong modern poet. But at his weakest moment when he has yet to find his own voice" (*Anxiety* 20). For Bloom, Adam is the ecstatic, untested imagination, all and only potential. He is the figure of the poet as poet, immaculate and brilliant, but yet to emerge.

4

I will misread "To Others than You" as Adam's rallying of what remains in the post-lapsarian state. What remains to Adam is Eve since even God will reject him now. And yet . . . and yet Eve is the reason, at least in Adam's mind, for the fallen state. Analogously, Eve is to Adam as the serpent was to Eve. Despite, or indeed, because of the fact of her being flesh of his flesh and bone of his bone, she (Eve) is the temptress of Adam even as the serpent is the tempter of Eve. There is, then, a strange nature to the title's plural "Others:" the poem is as much Adam's complaint against the deception of Eve as it is Eve's moaning against the serpent for deceiving her. "To Others than You" is a blaming, meant to excuse the Fall: Adam blames woman, woman blames serpent. Each blames the other, and all are punished. The opening line of Thomas's poem points a finger outside. Understood in this light, however, "You" in the title takes on a reflexive dimension. It names "You" as both other (i.e. Eve as other to Adam, the serpent as other to Eve) and as self (You as "me," or what "I" did). Yet clearly for this poem to blame self and other is for it to transgress our analogy, in effect, allowing a simultaneous accusation: of Eve by Adam; of the serpent by Eve. This depth in the speaking self –our first hint of "the poet as poet"—retains, rather than relinquishes, identity with the exterior "You" when the reference is split. In temptation, Eve is the strangeness in Adam, the serpent the strangeness in Eve.

This strange depth of the self is also not original to Thomas in twentieth-century poetry. Among others, it is equivalent to the interior paramour of Wallace Stevens, something other than a muse though of muse-like qualities, "the miraculous influence" (9). This interior paramour, this curious "you" in "me" that I identify with Bloom's poet as poet, is excused from the primary complaint of Thomas's poem. "To Others than You" would be directed by the poet toward the composite figure of the precursor (in this case, uncannily, Eve rather than God).

The precursor need be prior in authority only as the external agent of the awakening (sexual, poetic, epistemic) of Bloom's ephebe figure, a figure Adamic in nature. The sexual/poetic/epistemic awakening is referred to when Adam/Eve/poet/critic calls out Eve/the serpent/precursor as (s)he "who palmed the lie on me when [(s)he] looked / Brassily at my shyest secret." The line, with its unmistakable hints of deception and exposure brings us back to Bloom's description of Adam (also the Eve in Adam, the serpent in Eve and the Adamic young poet) as the limit of contraction, the point "beyond which our imaginations will not contract" (*Anxiety* 24). The limit of contraction is the *sine qua non* of our thinking, the place where our imaginings first form. This limit is, in Thomas, "the shyest secret;" for Bloomians, it is the untested imagination, the unrealized sexual nature, epistemological naivety. Further, this secret is the poet as poet outside, revealed in the "brassily" glaring face of the precursor whose poetry has already been written. If the precursor is "strong" enough, it is as if the poetry has always been written. "Brassily" connotes the bold, knowing look of the precursor: experienced, doubtless. The word also connotes the precursor's apparently convincing, and perceptive gaze; an evocation of the authoritative radiance of such a figure.

The aureole of the precursor is seductive and coercive: "Enticed with twinkling bits of the eyes / . . . [I] stumbled and sucked." This line suggests that the boldness to transgress comes from an appeal to preexisting curiosity. The appealing transgression of the Fall is linked to a curiosity of the fruit. For the virgin, sexual arousal underscores the appeal of consummation; for a poet, poetry underscores the appeal of imagining. The poet as poet is found in the act of reading; erotic pleasure is found through physical contact, and Eve/and the serpent in Adam/Eve is found in tasting the fruit. The appeal of Eve as precursor causes the fall of the Adamic poet just as, for the poet Eve (also strangely Adamic) the cunning of the serpent as the precursor brings about her fall.

Continuing our elaboration, we accept that Eve finds Adam's "interior paramour," a vulgarizing trope for what the later Eliot figures as a quasi-evangelical internalized point of darkness in his *Four Quartets*. Freeing this paramour means the fall of Adam as much as of Eve. Yet this freeing leads to a peculiar formulation. Eve seduces Adam into subversion by reminding Adam of his own thought, not by introducing new ideas to him (NB poetry's relation to criticism is apparent in this Adamic self-awareness). Eve "conjure[s] . . . in the memory worked by mirror," because, like the serpent's encounter with her, her encounter with Adam is essentially a reflectant one: the ephebe sees his or her inner aspect reflected in the precursor, but it is as if this inner aspect were prior to the ephebe *because it is seen in the precursor as well*. Adam's desires are highlighted by Eve, pragmatically teacher and tempter, because they are necessarily figured as ones abiding in him. In its proper mode, this enticement appeals to desires seen as unrecognized until acted upon. Thomas illustrates this point in the last six or seven lines of the second stanza. These last lines convey the experience proper of Fall as epistemic awakening and sexual initiation. There the hammer is a masculine symbol of the precursor-tempter-seducer-serpent's persuasive power. This hammer is the figure for what moved Adam in Eve's appeal to taste the forbidden fruit; what moved Eve in the serpent's appeal for the same.

Thomas's poem concludes with the image of "enemies on stilts." This image deflates the authority of the tempter/precursor. This authority facilitated the awakening, and is intimately tied to the shame, anguish or anxiety occasioned by such an awakening. Nevertheless, once awakened the ephebe can render the precursor's authority illusive: this "authority" becomes an image of presumptive over-reaching on the part of the tempter(s)/precursor(s), who immersed "their heads in clouds of cunning" to seem so powerful. In a strong, fallen ephebe the influence of the precursor is imagined as a parody of strength. The full cycle of the fall thus completes itself in figures suggesting reinvigoration, gathered strength on the part of the ephebe. In the vector of a poet's development, the modern poet and Adam move beyond the limit of contraction. Adam, after the fall, becomes a trope for widening poetic possibility.⁵

5

The fall of Adam is Adam's rise beyond contraction. We will recall from *Anxiety of Influence* that it is Satan that is figured as the limit of poetic opacity:

> Satan is the thwarted or restrained desire of natural man, or rather the shadow or Spectre of that desire. Beyond this spectral state, we will not harden against vision . . . . (*Anxiety* 24)

Satan, for Bloom, symbolizes a reaching that is always and already overreaching. He does not achieve that crest of poeticism perpetually unrealized though perpetually sought. To Bloom, Satan is the usual fate of poets in this belated age:

> Poets this late in the tradition are both Adams and Satans. They begin as natural men, affirming that they will contract no further, and they end as thwarted desires, frustrated only that they cannot harden apocalyptically. But, in between, the greatest of them are very strong, and they progress through a natural intensification that marks Adam in his brief prime and a heroic self-realization that marks Satan in his brief and more-than-natural glory. (*Anxiety* 24–5)

Adam as the limit of contraction and Satan as the limit of opacity are the endpoints of modern poetic development, the poet as poet. These poles are traversed through intensification and self-realization. Adam and Satan are tropes for how the poet as poet manifests in the language of poetry:

> The intensification and self-realization are accomplished only through language, and no poet since Adam and Satan speaks a language free of the one wrought by his precursors. (*Anxiety* 25)

The final statement hardly holds in light of the Bloomian re-estimation of Milton's Satan as something like the offspring of the fiendish triumvirate of Macbeth-Edgar-Iago. I will not explore Bloom's alternatives to

---

⁵ To some extent, this widening poetic possibility can be identified with *apophrades*, the last of Bloom's presented "ratios" in *Anxiety of Influence*.

Satan as limit of opacity in this essay.[6] Nevertheless, the above quotation returns us to the insistence by Bloom that criticism and poetry teach nothing save the language in which poetry exists. It is the poet as poet in the reading poet-to-be and the same in the deeply reading critic that first manifests in reading criticism and poetry. Such an awakening is figured as an Adamic function, and has just been outlined above.

6

What is that for which the Adamic (and Satanic) figurations are tropes? What undergoes the process that moves language through intensification to self-realization? It has been our assertion that the poet as poet moves from Adam to Satan, that is to say is conceived as undergoing the process from contraction to opacity. We therefore seem on the verge of redundancy. To resist repetition, we turn to a baffling moment in the Interchapter of Bloom's *Anxiety of Influence*. While reviewing a possible objection to what Bloom is to later name the necessity of misreading, he writes:

> It can be objected against this theory that we never read a poet as poet, but only read one poet in another poet, or even into another poet. Our answer is manifold: we deny that there is, was or ever can be a poet as poet—to a reader. (*Anxiety* 94)

The manifold answer given here, the denial of reality to the poet as poet, ought to stop us short. Rightfully, we ought to be surprised, and ask "but didn't he say . . ." reviewing passage after passage in that book, including the sentence at the bottom of the same page concerning the poet as poet:

> The issue is true history or rather the use of it, rather than the abuse of it, both in Nietzsche's sense. True poetic history is the story of how poets as poets have suffered other poets . . . . (*Anxiety* 94)

It would seem that with the denial of the poet as poet, there would follow the denial of true poetic history also. Such a denial seems irreconcilable with Bloom's notion of influence. The complication is this:

---

[6] Satan as presented in *Anxiety of Influence* seems to me the representative figure for the fourth and fifth ratios of *daemonization* and *askesis*. Both of these ratios require a reactionary stance with regard to the precursor of the sort that Satan exemplifies.

every poet/critic begins as reader, poetic history is the tale of readers awakened into poetry by other poets/critics. This awakening is the sudden inspirational influx called influence. To deny other poet as poets erases the roots of the movement from reading into influence. Bloom's theory apparently cannot get off the ground due to his own justification of it.

Faced with such a deep contradiction, like Paul de Man, we can decide that Bloom's ideas essentially unravel when pressed at certain points, or we can seek places within the framework of Bloomian thought that resolve our tensions and defuse our perplexity. I opt for the latter because most demonstrations of unraveling, confusion and contradiction in Bloom strike me as wrongheaded, often responses to the perception of an attack by Bloom on the author's work. Returning to our complication, we can ask how can we account for the fact that Bloom disqualifies his own characterization of reading in his account of the impossibility of other poets as poets?

7

Bloom's Primal Scene of Instruction gives light to our darkness. In brief, the Primal Scene of Instruction is a paradigm of reading as listening in which the act of reading becomes an occasion for learning. This scene is, we will see, transumptive in character, which is to say the scene rests on a final inversion of a usual order of things. In the primal scene of instruction reading is an analogue to listening, but one creating the voice heard:

> The psychic place of heightened consciousness, of intensified demand, where the Scene of Instruction is staged, is necessarily a place cleared by the newcomer in himself, cleared by an initial contraction or withdrawal that makes possible all further self-limitations, and all restituting modes of self-representation. (*Map* 55)

Bloom describes the primal scene as a satisfaction of an extreme inner demand for meaningfulness. A reader sees meaning through something like an attitude of attentive listening to the work. This attitude is part of the demand and creates the meaningfulness demanded (hence the transumptive character). The demand created and fulfilled in reading is something we spoke of earlier in terms of the response learned or engendered by critical and poetic language; in Bloomian terms the scene is the place of incarnation for the poetic character. All of this depends upon a sensory figure of *place* (as previously stated, a non-rhetorical *topos*). Despite the sensory nature we attach to place, the poet as poet is remarkable because a necessary condition is an inability to sense the incarnation that takes: to the poet as poet there is only the urge to satisfy his or her own demands.

The Primal Scene of Instruction is a demand for meaning followed by a reception of meaning. But the scene is pathetic, for only when the meaning received is not the meaning sought is capable imagination the result:

> Both the initial and violent excess of demand .... and the answering violence of an inadequate response ... are imposed by the new poet upon himself, and both are therefore his interpretations, without which there would be no *given* whatsoever. (*Map* 55–6)

Here finally the role of misreading is clear: the demand for meaningfulness and the consequent meaning are the result, and as such establish the conditions of difference on which the poet as poet thrives. There is no encounter between another's poet as poet and one's own because what would-be one's own poet as poet is essentially a contracted, potential poetic character, an uncleared stage for the reception of meaning. This is to say that the poet as poet cannot be acknowledged in itself until there is a demand for poetic meaning (the scene of instruction). The poet as poet will then be identified to the extent that it is the necessary condition for an insufficient reception. Whatever meaning is, it will not satisfy the poet as poet's demand for it until it is derived from the poet as poet. Oddly enough, this holds because the poet as poet both issues the demand for and is the source of the meaning it wants. This fascinating paradox reifies the basic solipsism of this figure: simultaneously interior (source of demand) and exterior (source of meaning) to even the Primal Scene. In the Primal Scene of Instruction the poet as poet is seen as a prior profound yearning that has been waiting to take flight. This flight, which might as well be called a flight to Lucifer, is neither psychological nor rhetorical.

8

I have shown that Bloom's notion of influence can be fully, perhaps more fully, described without recourse to psychological or epistemological categories. We are closest to his spirit when we ask critically: "What other than the mind and knowledge is involved in writing poetry?" It may appear that Bloom is merely inverting the question of the psychological critic. To be sure I must concur, as there may be a cohesive interpretation of Bloom's theories of reading and influence that could recast them in negative psychological terms.[7] This reading would conclude by saying that Bloom is concerned with the non-authorial psyches that produce a text, that Bloom's theories of *influenza* are another form of our age's undermining of the author's presence in the text. Yet such an interpretation would have to account both for Bloom's view of originality (an author's ability to write without regard to tradition's mandates), and for the Bloomian privileging of metalepsis or transumption (an author's ability to render the ancestral voice[s] derivative in feel) as the central tropes of poetic language. Otherwise, we have the truly outlandish suggestion that Bloom is a sort of proto-new historicist. Bloom's notions of originality, influence, and transumption depend upon a positive ascription of an authorial persona, though what constitutes this persona is, as we have seen, uncanny and paradoxical.

---

[7] Perhaps the closest we have come to such a reading is Lars Ole Sauerberg's "Harold Bloom: Swerving into Ever-Renewed Strength," in his *Versions of the Past-Visions of the Future: The Canonical in the Criticism of T. S. Eliot, F. R. Leavis, Northrop Frye, and Harold Bloom*. Sauerberg writes: "Artistic creation [in Bloom's theory] contains an enormous negative charge gathered together by the artist's terrible anxiety of being smothered by his forebears, and his equally terrible urge to destroy them" (xx).

Works Cited

The Bible. King James Version.

Desmet, Christy and Robert Sawyer. Eds. *Harold Bloom's Shakespeare*. New York: Palgrave, 2001.

Fite, David. *Harold Bloom: The Rhetoric of Romantic Vision*. Amherst: U of Massachusetts P, 1985.

Milton, John. *The Complete Poetry of John Milton*. Ed. John T. Shawcross. New York: Anchor, 1971.

Ransom, John Crowe. *New Criticism*. Norfolk, CT: New Directions, 1941.

Sauerberg, Lars Ole. *Versions of the Past-Visions of the Future: The Canonical in the Criticism of T. S. Eliot, F. R. Leavis, Northrop Frye, and Harold Bloom*. New York: St. Martin's, 1997.

Thomas, Dylan. *Collected Poems of Dylan Thomas: 1934-1952*. New York: New Directions, 1971.

To Execute a Clinamen

John W. P. Phillips

> A poet swerves away from his precursor, by so reading his precursor's poem as to execute a *clinamen* in relation to it.
> —Bloom, *Anxiety* 14

> If it were not for this swerve, everything would fall downwards like raindrops through the abyss of space.
> —Lucretius (cited in *Anxiety* 44)

> Just as happens with the flower in a plant, in culture there lies the capacity (or the responsibility) for forming and fertilizing the seedling, which will assure the continuity of history, at the same time assuring the prospects for evolution and progress of the society in question.
> —Cabral, "National Culture" 142

The poet makes 'something' of nothing. Harold Bloom's famous statement that "there are no texts, only relations between texts" indicates an alterity that allows relations to occur only because the relation as such remains impossible (so Bloom's statement is by no means a kind of relativism). You repeat, repeat, repeat, or you fall endlessly. The choice between the faithful textual substitution on the one hand and the *abyss* on the other is not available for the strong writer, who is thus forced by that very strength into constructing an elaborate rhetorical divergence. Satan has stopped falling. Rhetorical divergence is something like an exemplary relation, relation's example, the paragon of relation;[1] in which case the divergence logically comes before, produces the textual relation, and at the same time produces the void, as in the following diagram:

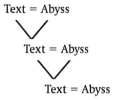

The new text must inevitably outline the abyss from which it is a swerve in order to avoid the simple repetition of the precursor's outlining of the abyss. To diverge from simple repetition, the poet "executes a *clinamen*." A number of examples compose a kind of indefinite series, a series of interruptions, as one reads through Bloom, that each time contests the logic of exemplarity. These paragons of the literary interrupt the bland transmission of repeatable texts and simultaneously (thus) assure a very odd kind of historical continuity—in which case Shakespeare may be the paragon of all exemplars of exemplarity.

1) Shakespeare

An allusion to Friedrich Nietzsche in Bloom's relatively recent reading of Shakespeare's *King Lear* involves the construction of an antimetabole, which is a synecdoche for rhetorical divergence *per se*. He says: "it is not that the pain is meaningful but that meaning itself becomes painful in this play" (*Shakespeare* 484–85). Chiasmus, antimetabole, tautology and oxymoron are the typical figures on which Bloom constructs his readings, and they perform subtle condensations. So in Edgar's comment on Lear, "He childed as I father'd" (3.6.110), a series of condensations is performed in a single figure. Bloom's reading tells us that in Edgar's phrase "the tragedy is condensed into just five words" (*Shakespeare* 485). *Lear* is the "most tragic of all tragedies . . . a storm with no subsequent

---

[1] The law of the *clinamen*, which stems from "a 'Pataphysical sense of the arbitrary," governs "exceptions," Bloom tells us in *Anxiety of Influence*: "the new poet *himself* determines the precursor's *particular* law" (42–43). See Allen, *Harold Bloom* 23–26; this study should be required reading for anyone concerned with Bloom.

clearing" (493), and its message is "all is nothing, less than nothing" (509). *Lear* is Shakespeare's monumental outline of the abyss. Yet, in a formulation repeated from *Ruin the Sacred Truths*, this is the play in which it is most evident that "the difference between what Shakespeare knew and what we know is, to an astonishing extent, just Shakespeare himself" (*Shakespeare* 487). The *episteme* is Shakespeare's discovery. Our discovery of Shakespeare is his *episteme*. Edgar's phrase condenses the condition that makes Lear's and Edgar's tragedy Shakespeare's and ours as well. "He is what we know because we are what he knew: he childed as we fathered" (487). So the condensation is folded out as another antimetabole.

The formulation from *Ruin the Sacred Truths* is even less ambiguous. There Bloom says that "the difference between the world that Shakespeare saw and ours is to an astonishing degree Shakespeare himself" (56). The world we see is Shakespeare's revelation. (Shakespeare childed as we fathered.) The parallel is already its own inversion in a condensed form of the antimetabole, now betraying its kinship to the more complex form of the chiasmus. The five words perform a condensation of five different things: the chiasmatic figure, the tragedy as such, the relation between Edgar and Lear in the tragedy, our relation to Shakespeare, and Shakespeare himself. If our relation to Shakespeare takes this condensed chiasmatic form, then it is the most persuasive (at once the most typical and the best) example possible of the definitive figure of Bloom's theory of modern poetry, elaborated fully for the first time in *The Anxiety of Influence* (1973). And the name for this figure is the name that Bloom had always reserved for it; that is, of course, *Shakespeare*.

Although Shakespeare is deliberately excluded from consideration in *The Anxiety of Influence*,[2] the chiasmic form outlined above saturates that text. The theory is captured with rhetorical directness in the following statement of the argument's "general principle" (the law of the *clinamen*):

> Poetic Influence—when it involves two strong, authentic poets,—always proceeds by a misreading of the prior poet, an act of creative correction that is actually and necessarily a misinterpretation. The history of fruitful poetic influence, which is to say the main tradition of Western poetry

---

[2] Shakespeare takes the place that was always reserved for him in the new Preface to the 1997 edition of the book, this *preface* now apparently completing the theory of modern poetry more than twenty years after its initial appearance.

since the Renaissance, is a history of anxiety and self-saving caricature, of distortion, of perverse, wilful revisionism without which modern poetry as such could not exist. (*Anxiety* 30)

Bloom does not state as such that the perversion typically takes the form of rhetorical inversion (antimetabole, chiasmus and oxymoron), but his own dramatic presentation is rich with such forms. If Milton is seen in that book as "the central problem in any theory and history of poetic influence in English" (33), then it is largely because Milton's texts dramatise the form that the theory and history of influence must take. Milton provides Bloom with his main rhetorical example for the pattern of simultaneous mourning and triumph:

> Farewell happy fields
> Where joy for ever dwells: Hail horrors, hail
> Infernal world, and thou profoundest Hell
> Receive thy new possessor: One who brings
> A mind not to be chang'd by Place or Time,
> The mind is its own place, and in it self
> Can make a Heav'n of Hell, a Hell of Heav'n,
> What matter where, if I still be the same . . . ?

(*Paradise Lost* 1.249–56, cited in *Anxiety* 33)

The antimetabole embedded in the quotation (often used as a standard *example* of the figure in dictionaries) performs a condensation of Satan's position (and Milton's, as well as the position of each of his descendants) and of Bloom's *theory*, capturing "the poetry of loss, and the voice also of the strong poet accepting his task" (*Anxiety* 33). As we have seen, the antimetabole can be unfolded in several ways. Its power is just this potential unfolding: the un-explicated, inexplicable power of explication. Out of this extreme condensation (we might have said *radical condensation* but for one or two determined, or overdetermined, associations with the term *condensation* that we need to suspend for this part of the discussion), Bloom can unfold both Nietzsche, as "the prophet of the antithetical," and the Freud of *The Interpretation of Dreams*, whose "mechanisms of defense and their ambivalent functionings" provide the always deceptively straightforward model for the theory of modern poetry itself (*Anxiety* 8). In accordance with an inescapable rule of this power (the inexplicable power of explication), no "happy substitution" is possible (8). The reversal is simultaneously a repetition. Oxymoron is tautology. Antithesis is analogy. The pages between Bloom's statement of his general principle and the Milton quotation are exemplary (remembering now that the example is also the paragon) of the expanded chiasmatic structure of the whole theory. Here Bloom elaborates the law of the *clinamen* by explicating the second of two citations, characteristically pithy remarks from Lichtenberg: "'To do just the opposite is also a form of imitation, and the definition of imitation ought by rights to include both'" (*Anxiety* 31).[3] Bloom uses Lichtenberg's remark to initiate an analogical divergence on Romantic love:

> What Lichtenberg implies is that Poetic Influence is itself an oxymoron, and he is right. But then, so is Romantic Love an oxymoron, and Romantic Love is the closest analogue of Poetic Influence, another splendid perversity of the spirit, though it moves precisely in the opposite direction. (31)

Commentators on Bloom have apologised on his behalf for the difficulty of his prose in this book, as if he might have stated its contents more directly. But the form of this unfolding chiasmatic structure does provide a clear sense of the theory. The subversion by analogy of the Lichtenberg remark (taking it in the opposite direction) provides the pattern that poetic influence is supposed to take. If poetic influence is an oxymoron (poetry and influence are mutually opposing terms), then so is Romantic love, which is an analogue of poetic influence. But the analogy is itself oxymoronic, for poetic influence moves in the opposite direction to Romantic love (and to do just the opposite is also a form of imitation):

> The poet confronting his Great Original must find the fault that is not there, and at the heart of all but the highest imaginative virtue. The lover is beguiled to the heart of loss, but is found, as he finds, within mutual illusion, the poem that is not there. (31)

---

[3] The first of these remarks is also, of course, crucial: "'Yes, I too like to admire great men, but only those whose works I do not understand'" (31). The remark supports Bloom's point (which Bloom never makes explicit for reasons that will emerge shortly) that a strong reading—whether it produces a poem or a critical text—cannot pay attention to thematic content and survive. In an essentially stupid repetition, a new text—neither identical nor antithetical—might emerge. However, the strongest works will be the ones that in understanding still *wilfully* turn against that understanding in the repetition.

The poet finds fault falsely and founds the poem; the lover finds the poem falsely and founds himself. The oscillations between poem and the self, the play of finding and loss, finding and founding, will be intensified in Bloom's later books, of which more in a moment. But here, in unfolding this new cluster of analogical/oxymoronic relations/divergences, Bloom has recourse to yet another influence, that of Kierkegaard:

> "When two people fall in love," says Kierkegaard, "and begin to feel that they are made for one another, then it is time for them to break off, for by going on they have everything to lose and nothing to gain." When the ephebe, or figure of the youth as virile poet, is found by his Great Original, then it is time to go on, for he has everything to gain, and his precursor nothing to lose; if the fully written poets are indeed beyond loss. (31–32)

In this exact repetition of the structure of Kierkegaard's statement (in the chiasmus), Bloom produces a divergence of sense via the orthodox classical antimetabole. Lovers have everything to lose and nothing to gain; the poet has everything to gain and nothing to lose. Bloom's patterns of auto-exemplification, without which his theory would have *nothing to stand on,* show themselves to be more effective in this respect than the analogy itself and its aporetic twists, condensed now in the antimetabole and reminding us of his point, made earlier, that "the profundities of poetic influence cannot be reduced to source-study, to the history of ideas, to the patterning of images" (7). Neither empirical study (historical, historiographical, biographical, formalist, linguistic, and so on) nor thematic criticism (conceptual, contextual, philosophical, and so on) would be sufficient to account for the power behind the phenomena with which we are concerned, that is, the very power of poetry, of the poetic. The potential implied by the passages of condensation and explication, and by the figures of analogy and oxymoron (chiasmus, tautology, antimetabole), cannot be reduced to what can be *found* as either ideal contents (on the level of ideas) or empirical forms (on the level of evidence). They can be indicated, however, minimally perhaps at first, with a name (although a name of this kind would already be more and less than just a name), a name like 'Shakespeare' that already names something like the power of poetry. In this sense, the more elaborated version (theory) of the exemplary name (Shakespeare) would fulfil in more elaborate fashion the exemplifying work that the name (Shakespeare) already does in the form of an extreme condensation.⁴

2) Trope to Trope

Bloom gives three reasons why Shakespeare stands outside the concerns of *Anxiety of Influence* (*Anxiety* 11). He stands outside historically, at the cusp of modernity. He belongs to "the giant age before the flood," before poetic influence becomes the productive anxiety that is central to his argument about modern poetry. He stands outside also because his is the dramatic, rather than the lyric form. But the main reason that Bloom gives is that, in contrast to the modern poets who are all instances of the defensive anxiety about precursors, Shakespeare is an instance (the largest) of "the absolute absorption of the precursor" (namely Marlowe). Bloom's book on Shakespeare thus appears to be a giant supplement to the Theory of Poetry. All the reasons that excluded Shakespeare from *Anxiety* now show him to be the central figure of that book. He stands outside modernity because modernity is his own vision. Shakespeare himself is the cusp. The dramatic form is the appropriate form for revealing the rhetorical tensions that always governed lyric anxiety, in so far as the modern lyric involves a denial of its dramatic form, the relation to the precursor that it never consciously acknowledges. The creative corrections, the wilful misreadings and revisions, take a dramatic form in Bloom's readings of modern poets. Finally, it is appropriate that Bloom begins his book on Shakespeare by saying that the accurate stance towards his plays is "one of awe" (*Shakespeare* xvii). The main reason for the earlier exclusion of "the greatest poet," absolute absorption of a precursor, is now revealed to be poignant for *us*. The absolute absorption moves in the other direction, for it is Shakespeare's successors, his creatures, who are really absorbed by him.

So it would hardly be controversial to observe that Bloom finds his own theory performed by Shakespeare's characters. Bloom plays Falstaff, he suggests, nudging us in the direction of that interpretation, and yet would rather be Hamlet. But surpassing these fully

---

4   Lars Ole Sauerberg, in his *Versions of the Past—Visions of the Future*, observes that Shakespeare, in Bloom's recent work, has become "the epitome and archetype of all literature" (156). Sauerberg thus correctly establishes Bloom's debt to Vico's notion of the cultural cycle, according to which successive developments in literature produce only an increasingly fading imitation of a great past.

authorised interpretations, these plain substitutions, a deeper wish, both an anxiety and desire, can be read in Bloom's work. Again, disarmingly close to the surface, but operating in the trivial rhetorical dimension of the pun, the *envoi*, the accident (the chief mechanism, as he points out, for the cunning of displacement), Bloom would like his own name to be the name for what strong poets do. Furthermore, while this does not, apparently, require that Bloom the reader be particularly strong (though he often arguably is) it would also be the name for what strong readers do.[5] Bloom should be associated indelibly with the theory of reading as well as for what the theory claims that poets do. He would be neither the practitioner nor the subject of the theory, but the strong author of the theory itself, in so far as it is down to a Bloom to observe, discover, disclose and *demonstrate* the theory of modern poetry. Does that mean, then, that we would not find Bloom executing a *clinamen*? On the contrary, Bloom's theory can plausibly be regarded as the very paragon of the principle. A Poem is a dramatic act, in which a poetic self is revised through negotiating a relationship to a precursor, who is also revised in the act. The passionate and passive lyric turns out to be the broken off part of an agonistic rhetorical drama. And the name of a poet is the name for such an act. A poet's name is a verb, for Bloom, a verb like *trope*. And the verb *to trope* (to execute a *clinamen*, for instance) would designate an active negotiation of the relationship that takes the form of a turn, a way, a manner or a style. For instance, if the word 'epistemology' is a trope, then the assertion of the tropic nature of epistemology is also tropic and, like the law of the *clinamen*, belongs to the "science of imaginary solutions." Such an assertion founds itself on the *absence* of solid foundations, turning not from ground but from figure: the *trepein* of the trope would be the turning of the way. By way of the theory of poetry, Bloom takes his own turn. But to

---

[5] In *Kabbalah and Criticism* we learn that "the reader is to the poem what the poet is to his precursor—every reader is therefore an ephebe, every poem a forerunner, and every reading an act of 'influencing,' that is, of being influenced *by* the poem and of influencing any other reader to whom your reading is communicated" (97). Situated in relation to this chain of influences (*influenza*) transported analogically here, Bloom would be neither strong poet nor strong critic (disingenuously: "I am rather downcast when I reflect that the misreading of Blake and Shelley by Yeats is a lot stronger than the misreading of Blake and Shelley by Bloom" [126]), but would rather be situated as a kind of divergence from or interruption to the whole analogical chain, as that which names its possibility but resists inclusion.

which God does Bloom play Satan, to which Father son, to which Poet ephebe?

3) Will and Will-Have-Been

The double figure of naming/unnaming is literally a central concern in Bloom's criticism. Bloom presents his most sustained discussion of the figures of naming and unnaming during his reading of Walt Whitman's *Lilacs* elegy ("When Lilacs Last in the Dooryard Bloom'd") in *Agon*. It will become clear that unnaming is the central concern of the central poem of the central American poet. It will not be insignificant that the actual moment of unnaming occurs, as Bloom observes, at the "mid-point" of that poem, and that Bloom will contrast this—with meticulous attention to detail—to the more triumphant and successful "naming" at the "mid-point" of *Song of Myself*. But naming/unnaming is central also because it refers us to the absent centre of poetic experience, the void or the abyss against which the self must affirm itself over language, while always affirming the priority of figurative language over meaning. If a name for this doubling antithetical figure could be established, then it would be the correct name for Bloom's critical method. The self is a figure bent out of language, a turn from the thought of the literal as such, which just is death, as we learn from Bloom's reading of Freud earlier in that same text:

> The repressed rhetorical formula of Freud's discourse in *Beyond the Pleasure Principle* can be stated thus: *literal meaning equals anteriority equals an earlier state of meaning equals an earlier state of things equals death equals literal meaning*. Only one escape is possible from such a formula, and it is a simpler formula: *Eros equals figurative meaning*. (107)

The death drive, or the instinctual drive to return to the inorganic state, is in Bloom's reading the drive for the literal, for non-figurative meaning. This reading can be compared with those opening pages of *Anxiety* where death is figured as the original precursor—the precursor of the precursor. It is this ultimate—the most anterior of provocative anxieties—that poets begin by rebelling against, through whatever form their figurative Eros takes: "Every poet begins (however 'unconsciously') by rebelling more strongly against the consciousness of death's necessity than all other men and women do" (10). In this sense the poet is rebelling against his past, in the form of the Great Original, but as a displacement from a knowledge that all great poets share—a consciousness of the ineluctable world of the future (the dimension of my death)—so this consciousness can be nothing other than the relationship with death.[6] If it is this relationship to death that produces the Great Original, then the new poet, the ephebe, is, on a yet more fundamental level (but where will the *yet more* end?), rebelling against, and misreading, the memory of his own future and his own possibility (in the death of the precursor).

What Bloom derives from Freud, therefore, is as complex as could be. Bloom adds a rhetorical flourish to his interpretation of Freud by saying "perhaps that may seem some day the truest definition of the Freudian Eros: the will's revenge against time's 'it was' is to be carried out by the mind's drive to surpass all earlier achievements" (*Agon* 144). It is worth paying attention to Bloom's implicit formulation of his reformulation of Freud: one day perhaps the truest definition of Freud's Eros will be Bloom's. The final passage that Bloom cites in support of this reading of Freud is suggestive of a dimension that Bloom does not obviously exploit here. In some belated remarks, which Freud added to his interleaved copy of *The Psychopathology of Everyday Life*, he had written:

> My own superstition has its roots in suppressed ambition (immortality) and in my case takes the place of that anxiety about death which springs from the normal uncertainty of life . . . . (*Psychopathology* 323 n. 3)

And Bloom writes: "Against literalism and repetition of the death-drive, Freud sets, so early on, the high figuration of his poetic will to an immortality" (*Agon* 144). As is nearly always the case with Bloom's readings of Freud (and his readings generally), the insights are great. However, "the normal uncertainty of life," the source from which the anxiety about death "springs," remains a little underdetermined as it

---

[6] Jean-Pierre Mileur, in his 1985 study *Literary Revisionism and the Burden of Modernity*, claims that Bloom's sharp distinction between Miltonic and post-Miltonic in literary history (Mileur's book appeared before Bloom's *Shakespeare*) commits him to the argument that "the earlier poets were more accepting of their own deaths" (75). For Mileur, Bloom's revisionism uses the anxiety of influence as a myth that represses the main and intractable problem of secularisation: "the secular mind's inability to accept its own death without the hedging of transcendencies" (75). Mileur's claim, however, commits *him* to a sharp distinction between life and death, on the basis of a distinction between the empirical and its "transcendencies," that Bloom's readings tend to surpass.

stands in the quotation—with Freud's own elliptical dots intact. The main text elaborates a little further:

> Superstition is in large part the expectation of trouble; and a person who has harboured frequent evil wishes against others, but has been brought up to be good and has therefore repressed such wishes into the unconscious, will be especially ready to expect punishment for his unconscious wickedness in the form of trouble threatening him from without. (*Psychopathology* 323)

So Freud's explanation of superstition, which, as Bloom accurately observes, has its roots in the ambition for immortality (and thus against the certainty of death), has a further, deeper determination, according to Freud, in the expectation of trouble.[7] When we read this back into the speculations of *Beyond the Pleasure Principle*, we are reminded that the opposition of Eros and Death substitutes for the earlier, unsatisfactory opposition set out in "On Two Principles of Mental Functioning" as the tension between pleasure and reality. The *imaginary solution* represented by the death drive is the consequence of the need to interpolate a third principle, that is, *death*, to account for the distinction between the first two. An attentive reading of *Beyond* would acknowledge Freud's casting *death* as that which simultaneously counters, and accounts for, anxieties caused by *both* pleasure *and* reality in the form of *expectation of trouble*.[8]

---

[7] The motif of trouble is obliquely yet repeatedly echoed throughout Bloom's career in the motif of "the joys and sorrows of giving offence, at first in innocence and even involuntarily" (*Breaking* 30). In "The Breaking of Form," for instance, he confesses "surprise" that his emphasis on strong poets should have "given so much offence" (5). And in *The Breaking of the Vessels* he sets out a short treatise on it: "After half a lifetime of giving offence, to weak critics, academic impostors, inchoate rhapsodes, and virtuous journalists, I am something of an expert in academic scandal. . . . The center of offence, as I have discovered, is not so much in bringing bad news (though who welcomes that?) but in showing that no reader, however professional or humble, or pious, or disinterested, or 'objective,' or modest, or amiable, can describe her or his relationship to a prior text without taking up a stance no less tropological than that occupied by the text itself" (30). See the interview with Moynihan for more discussion of this (17–18 and 45–46). No less rhetorical than anything else in Bloom, this "giving offence" can be regarded as yet another *imaginary solution*.

[8] If the pleasure principle is to be understood as the need to reduce excitation and the reality principle as the need to reduce trouble, then death is to be understood as simultaneously the very principle of the drive to reduce and at the same time to lessen the danger of the reductions themselves. That is to say that Freud's death drive must be understood as a drive for life and for death simultaneously.

The "expectation of trouble threatening from without" (which is in Freud's account the consequence of a repression and thus threatens from within) provides a belated model for the anxiety of influence (and is similar in this one respect to the Oedipal drama or family romance), for it replicates the drama condensed in the figure of antimetabole—the analogical/oxymoronic figure of life-death. Any distinction between life and death, Eros and Thanatos, figural and literal language, would fall back on a deeper possibility—the possibility of a new determination, an always as yet undetermined potential—which resides in the future anterior of anticipation and is experienced here as the expectation of trouble. I, accordingly, hazard my own tentative revision here. Perhaps this will one day seem the truest definition of Bloom's *clinamen*: the will's revenge against time's '*it will have been.*'

4) Bloom's Anxiety

> 'That corpse you planted last year in your garden,
> 'Has it begun to sprout? Will it bloom this year?
> —T. S. Eliot, *Complete Poems* 63

> All over bouquets of roses,
> O death, I cover you over with roses and early lilies,
> But mostly and now the lilac that blooms the first . . . .
> —Whitman, *Complete Poems* 353

We find that some of the most remarkable of Bloom's readings turn on these two senses of the word *will*—between the act of will and the will-have-been of time (time as repetition and time as death, as abyss). And among the most remarkable of all Bloom's readings is his reading of Whitman's *Lilacs* elegy. Bloom sees Whitman at the "midpoint" of American poetry (though the centre, or what is central, shifts with each successive transumption, as we will see). First, we see him as the messianic hope, the *to come* of Ralph Waldo Emerson's central idea of the "Central Man:"

> The Idea is the Central or the Universal Man, the American More-than-Christ who is *to come*, the poet prefigured by Emerson himself as voice in the wilderness. In some sense he arrived as Walt Whitman, and some seventy years later as Hart Crane, but that is to run ahead of the story. (*Agon* 160)

This is Bloom's theory of poetry in action, now, never more persuasive than when applied to the story of American Poetry, which Bloom casts as a "spiralling out" of Emerson's centre. This centre is represented first by Emerson, but also each time by a series of exemplars who take up the legacy of the *to come*. Emerson plays for American poetry (and thus for America) a role analogous to the one Shakespeare plays for poetry generally (and thus for *us* in general):

> Starting from Emerson we came to where we are, and from that impasse, which he prophesied, we will go by a path that most likely he marked out also. The mind of Emerson is the mind of America, for worse and for glory, and the central concern of that mind was the American religion, which most memorably was named 'self reliance.' (*Agon* 145)

So Whitman too will become central, receiving the responsibility of American self-reliance as a kind of legacy to the future that he can only pass on and give up in the process (in principle to infinity). And, therefore, Whitman is central *as* legacy too, simultaneously the receiver and the giver of the legacy of naming/unnaming the American self.[9] In order to analyse this situation we need to examine, to the extent that this is possible, the mechanisms by which Bloom discovers and demonstrates the process. As Bloom tells his story—a sometimes reassuring though often startling chronology of poetic events, prophesies, anticipations, revisions, disappearances, reappearances, surprising repetitions, transumptions and disavowed inheritances—we will attempt to trace it back by following the lines of what can nearly always be comprehended as a form of displacement.

Beginning, perhaps arbitrarily, with T. S. Eliot (but not quite arbitrarily, because Eliot is undoubtedly central and exemplary too), we learn from *The Breaking of the Vessels* that "Eliot's true and unnamed precursor[10] was not Dante or Donne or Jules Laforgue or Baudelaire, but an

---

[9] A preliminary version of this reading can be found in Bloom's *A Map of Misreading*, particularly the section "In the Shadow of Emerson" (177–92).

[10] The true precursor must always be unnamed in accordance with the naming/unnaming pattern, but also because of the need to produce the misreading as a kind of displaced continuity and without acknowledgement, in disguise (thus not a continuity but a divergence). For this reason we distrust everything that Bloom tells us regarding his own precursors: for example, "but here again I am Emerson's ephebe, and so I repair to that fountain of our will, and to his major, now neglected text, *The Oversoul*, which Whitman must have pondered deeply" (*Breaking* 31).

uneasy composite of Tennyson and Whitman, with Whitman being the main figure" (21). This insight *apparently* derives (although Bloom does not say this and we have no real reason to assume it) from a very long quotation from Eliot's little known "Reflections on Contemporary Poetry," which, as Bloom points out, provides a quite different account of the poet as a bearer of tradition than the more official one found in "Tradition and the Individual Talent." Undoubtedly the passage supports Bloom's claim that Eliot was aware of the anxiety of influence, but it does not anywhere suggest Tennyson or Whitman as precursors (any more than it does any number of other possible and unnamed others), though the tradition is clearly marked by the repeated appearance of *Crisis Odes* and *Elegies,* in which case both Whitman and Tennyson would indeed be "central." So from where does the insight derive?[11] The precursor is acknowledged only in the minor rhetorical form of *transumptive allusion*, which is "the principal mode that the process of negation takes in post-Miltonic poetry, down to our present" (13). No stylistic or formal imitation and no thematic concern would be sufficient for the identification of an allusion of this kind. As Bloom has learned from Freud, an allusion ought to be *not at all* convincing if the displacement is to succeed.

It could be suggested, for instance, with at least some plausibility, that Eliot in *The Waste Land* makes the following unacknowledged allusion to an unnamed source. In one of his footnotes, he describes the role of the "character" Tiresias:

> Tiresias, although a mere spectator and not indeed a 'character,' is yet the most important personage in the poem, uniting all the rest. Just as the one-eyed merchant, seller of currants, melts into the Phoenician Sailor, and the latter is not wholly distinct from Ferdinand Prince of Naples, so all the women are one woman, and the two sexes meet in Tiresias. (78, n. to 218)

The way Eliot describes these characters echoes, perhaps (but *perhaps* is the chief vehicle of allusion), the way Freud describes the work of condensation. The remark about all the women being one woman

---

[11] When it comes to the appropriate moment for demonstrating his "surmise" about Eliot's true precursors, Bloom dissimulates: "it would be a facile exercise to demonstrate this pattern" (21). He leaves us instead to check for ourselves, suggesting that *Ash Wednesday*, "his crucial crisis ode," follows an uncanny sequence of ratios and crossings of the kind that Bloom has been tracing.

corresponds suspiciously closely to Freud's account of the "dream of Irma's injection," his "specimen dream:"

> The principle figure in the dream-content was my patient Irma. She appeared with the features which were hers in real life, and thus, in the first instance, represented herself. But the position in which I examined her by the window was derived from someone else, the lady for whom, as the dream-thoughts showed, I wanted to exchange my patient. In so far as Irma appeared to have a diphtheritic membrane, which recalled my anxiety about my eldest daughter, she stood for that child and, behind her, through her possession of the same name as my daughter, was hidden the figure of my patient who succumbed to poisoning . . . . She turned into another lady whom I had once examined, and, through the same connection, to my wife. (*Interpretation* 399)

Freud's explanation of the work of condensation shows how a single figure can be turned into a collective image, combining often contradictory elements (in the manner of the analogical/oxymoronic figure). "Irma became the representative of all these other figures which had been sacrificed to the work of condensation" (399–400). And just as Eliot has left clues—which may be accidental or may be deliberate—Bloom seems to have done the same. Freud illustrates his account of the mechanism of displacement (after Bloom, we call it transumptive allusion) by showing how the dream work sets up chains of thought that are like "the puns and riddles that people make up every day for their enjoyment," and he points out that the realm of jokes "knows no boundaries" (*Interpretation* 262). The trivial allusion takes us to a deeper level of the dream than a more plausible or probable explanation would be able to do. The more acceptable explanations are too obvious. "As we are told in *Hamlet* [1.5.125–26]: 'There needs no ghost, my lord, come from the grave / To tell us this'" (261). Freud's illustration is the famous "dream of the botanical monograph," in which the key mechanism of the displacement is the allusion barely concealed in the word *blooming*:

> But, lo and behold, I was reminded in the analysis that the man who interrupted our conversation was called *Gärtner* [Gardener] and that I had thought his wife looked *blooming*. And even as I write these words I recall that one of my patients, who bore the charming name of *Flora*, was for a time the pivot of our discussion. (261)

As this moment represents Freud's most direct explanation of the technique that Bloom identifies and adapts as transumptive allusion, one might ask: is the allusion a coincidence? Is it a joke? Even then, jokes and accidents are anyway the mechanisms mobilised by the transumptive procedure, the essential process of negation without which no poet would ever execute a *clinamen*. Moreover, it is possible (though never, of course, with certainty) to trace Eliot back to Whitman on the basis of this diversion into Freud, with the corpse in the garden of *The Waste Land* blooming again, Whitman's spectre in the form of an echo from his *Lilacs* elegy (to Lincoln) lodging in Eliot's poem.

Bloom's reading of Whitman must count among his most remarkable performances. The central moment of the reading shows Whitman, "profounder even than Freud," in the interlocking of the two drives, love and death. Bloom's reading turns on a complex condensation (again), a combination of figures composing one trope, bound together in an analogy between the sprig of lilac that the speaker places on Lincoln's hearse and the song of a thrush that floods the western night:

> Ultimately these are one trope, one image of voice, which we can follow Whitman by calling the "tally," playing also on a secondary meaning of "tally," as double or agreement. "Tally" may be Whitman's most crucial trope or ultimate image of voice. As a word, it goes back to the Latin *talea* for twig or cutting, which appears in this poem as the sprig of lilac. (*Agon* 186)

Bloom here, having identified the sprig of lilac in analogy with the song of a thrush as a trope of image of voice (trope of voice, or just trope?), takes the reading on a truly remarkable detour via the *talea* of the tally now doubling as trope for voicing: "voicing and reseeing are much the same poetic process, a process reliant on unnaming, which rhetorically means the undoing of a prior metonymy" (182). The tally is, thus, simultaneously a trope of voice and a metonymy for the undoing of prior metonymies (prior tropes). Bloom's detour produces the undoing, for the *tally*, via American slang, designates masturbation. Whitman "tallies" by masturbating and writing poems (186). Thus the clear contrast between *Song of Myself* and the *Lilacs* elegy (the one in triumph naming, the other in mourning unnaming) can be cast on the basis of the doubling (and tallying) of the tally as masturbation. *Song of Myself* is triumphant success, the *Lilacs* ode haunting failure (186–89). Bloom thus finds that after the crisis brought on by the hyperbole of *Song of Myself*,[12]

---

[12] This hyperbole is itself a repetition of an overdetermined trope—the trope of the alternative dawn, "I'd strike the sun if it insulted me!"—and is therefore faintly reminiscent of John Donne.

Whitman in *Lilacs* can work through mourning towards a complex affirmation centred on failure: "The miraculous juxtaposition of the two images of the tally, sprig of lilac and song of the hermit thrush ... points the possible path out of Whitman's death-in-life. [...] Whitman's profuse breaking of the tallies attempts to extend this trope, so as to make death itself an ultimate image of voice" (190-92). Bloom has taken his reading to the very centre of the poem (as he calls it here) and shown that this centre can be read as a (perhaps imaginary) solution to the crisis set up by Whitman's "greatest" poem, but he remains silent—to the extent that he never calls the *Lilacs* elegy by its name—on its main word for the sprig, the voice, and the tally itself—that is, the *bloom*. *Bloom* is the unnamed trope that binds these tropes into a single condensation, the trope for life-in-death, the trope for naming/unnaming.

5) The Breaking of the Bloom

The reappearance of the *bloom* in this central, exemplary poem, the exemplar of the American voice, would mean nothing if that were where the chain ended, but it does not end there. We must now go further back still to Emerson and his strong precursor, Carlyle. We have learned already that Whitman can be regarded as Emerson's "More-than-Christ who is *to come*." Bloom shows just where Emerson reappears in Whitman:

> The image of voice is the image of influx, of the Newness, but always it knowingly is a broken image, or image of brokenness. Whitman, still Emerson's strongest ephebe, caught the inevitable tropes for this wounded image of American voice:
>
>> —and from this bush in the dooryard,
>> With delicate-color'd blossoms and heart-shaped leaves of rich green,
>> A sprig of flower I break. (*Agon* 172)

The reappearance of Emerson in Whitman occurs as the breaking of a bloom and as the "wounded image of the American voice." This voice *begins* with Emerson as creator of the American Religion; but the American Religion, Bloom claims, rather than opening up an absolute origin, can be understood as Emerson's transumption of Carlyle.[13] When

---

[13] Bloom will build this argument into a fully worked out thesis in his 1992 book *The American Religion: The Emergence of the Post-Christian Nation*.

Bloom refers to the American Religion, he sees it as a consequence of the "addition" of "the American difference." And to make his point, Bloom provides a lengthy intertextual juxtaposition, designed to reveal the subtle differences between these two great religious writers. I include shortened versions here—Carlyle first, then Emerson:

> "Till the eye have vision, the whole members are in bonds. Divine moment, when over the tempest tossed soul, as once over the wild-weltering chaos, it is spoken: Let there be Light . . . . The mad primeval Discord is hushed; the rudely jumbled conflicting elements bind themselves into separate Firmaments: deep silent rock-foundations are built beneath; and the skyey vault with its everlasting Luminaries above: instead of a dark wasteful chaos, we have a blooming, fertile, heaven-encompassed World."
>
> "Build therefore your own world. As fast as you conform your life to the pure idea in your mind, that will unfold its great proportions . . . . The kingdom of man over nature, which cometh not with observation,—a dominion such as now is beyond his dream of God,—he shall enter without more wonder than the blind man feels who is gradually, restored to perfect sight." (cited in *Agon* 149)

"The juxtaposition is central," writes Bloom. The differences are not as subtle as all that. Emerson's affirmation of American Freedom seems clearly distinguishable from Carlyle's orthodox rejection of chaos, in which he affirms man's freedom yet keeps everything in God's name. Bloom locates Emerson, on the other hand, alongside "the heretical absolute freedom of the gnostic who identified his mind's purest idea with the original abyss" (150). What he does not say is that Carlyle's finite, "blooming, fertile, heaven-encompassed World" has been replaced by an interminably productive mind with the power to "unfold its great proportions" indefinitely. The one maintains the opposition between chaos and light, suggesting an infinite that encompasses the finite, and the other does not rigorously distinguish the two realms, suggesting instead an infinity within finitude.

It is this infinity within finitude that we have been tracing. William R. Schultz, in his *Genetic Codes of Culture,* has attempted to identify in Bloom a kind of cultural geneticism (somewhere between Kuhn and Derrida) and one can see why (without needing to accept this as anything but analogical). To discover the odd signature effects in Bloom's readings (the embedding of his name, unremarked and passed over in silence, at "central" moments) reminds us that following the traces of intertextuality can be like focusing on and then magnifying the boundary of the Mandelbrot (**M**) set: as the magnifications increase, the boundary continues to generate further self-similar patterns within its own parameters, until you come across a replica of the **M** set embedded deep within. In principle there would be no end to the process.[14] Reading Bloom may be reminiscent of this experience because, just as complex fractal boundaries are produced through simple laws of iteration, so Bloom's tropic theory of poetry accounts for complex situations on the basis of simple laws—that of the *clinamen*, for instance, according to which an *iteration* of one poet in another produces a simultaneous divergence and repetition.[15]

The name 'Bloom,' when we discover it as the word *bloom* in Bloom's readings, functions as a metonym for the mechanism whereby a prior metonym is undone and replaced by another metonym. Freud's account of displacement (the substitution of one metonym for another) finds an example (the exemplar) in *blooming*. In Whitman the breaking of the bloom stands for the replacement of naming by unnaming (and substitutes Whitman himself for Emerson as Emerson's Universal Man). Bloom's name is thus the name for the chief mechanism of his theory of poetry. *To Bloom* is to make something from nothing by deforming the text of a precursor. The chain does not end with Eliot or Hart Crane (though the Whitman of the *Lilacs* elegy turns up in both), but it ends with a "blank." Whitman turns up at the end of the lecture "Transumption" as Wallace Stevens's repressed precursor, "swimming like a giant form beneath every surface Stevens could lacquer" (*Breaking* 105). And, sure enough, it is not just any Whitman that turns up—as rhetorical remains—in *The Rock*:

---

[14] Manfred Schroeder explains: "The **M** set consists of a large heart-shaped area to which smaller discs are attached, to which even smaller discs are attached and so forth *ad infinitum* in a roughly self-similar progression" (296).

[15] Bloom's treatment of the *clinamen* can be compared with that of Jacques Derrida, for whom the Epicurean pattern of destiny, or destination, falls from a futural dimension described by Derrida in terms of a "random indetermination" that, far from being opposed to the coding of determined structures of communication, is multiplied by the code itself while simultaneously reproducing the code. My reading of Bloom in this essay, making explicit the futural aspect of the theory of poetry, is indebted to Derrida's treatment of chance in "My Chances," and strongly suggests some connections between these two strong readers that Bloom at least would be inclined to deny.

> ... an illusion so desired
>
> That the green leaves came and covered the high rock,
> That the lilacs came and bloomed, like a blindness cleaned,
> Exclaiming bright sight, as it was satisfied,
>
> In a birth of sight. The blooming and the musk
> Were being alive, an incessant being alive,
> A particular of being, that gross universe. (cited in *Breaking* 106)

The blooming of the lilacs functions here again as another execution of a clinamen. Bloom, the author of the theory, is not simply the strong reader "who will turn the leaves of Stevens's book and in that turning transume another cry, and yet another, in that work we are not required to complete, yet neither are we free to abandon" (107). If his role as reader is to expose the transumption, the allusion which covertly replicates the negotiation of poet and precursor, he cannot simply operate with an ultimate transumption that would name the process itself. So Bloom leaves his name around in the texts he reads, thereby marking these texts with signature effects that, if they transume anything, transume his own future (he Shakespeared while we Bloomed). A *clinamen* simultaneously outlines the abyss and reproduces it under a different name, *ad infinitum*. Perhaps Bloom's typical rhetorical form, the exemplary trope, is the *envoi*:

> [Beckett] too beholds, with Wallace Stevens, "a way of truth," if not a way of meaning, a trope revealing that "Our bloom is gone. We are the fruit thereof." (*Ruin* 204)

Works Cited

Allen, Graham. *Harold Bloom: A Poetics of Conflict.* Modern Cultural Theorists. New York: Harvester, 1994.

Cabral, Amilcar. "National Culture." *Unity and Struggle: Speeches and Writings.* Trans. Michael Wolfers. London: Monthly Review P, 1979. 138–54.

De Bolla, Peter. *Harold Bloom: Towards Historical Rhetorics.* London: Routledge, 1988.

Derrida, Jacques. "My Chances/*Mes Chances*: A Rendezvous with some Epicurean Stereophonies." *Taking Chances: Psychoanalysis and Literature.* Ed. Joseph Smith and William Kerrigan. Baltimore: Johns Hopkins UP, 1984.

Eliot, T. S. *Complete Poems and Plays.* London: Faber, 1969.

Freud, Sigmund. *The Interpretation of Dreams.* Trans. James Strachey. Ed. James Strachey and Angela Richards. Pelican Freud Library 4. Harmondsworth: Penguin, 1976.

———. *The Psychopathology of Everyday Life.* Trans. Alan Tyson. Ed. James Strachey and Angela Richards. Pelican Freud Library 5. Harmondsworth: Penguin, 1975.

Kuhn, Thomas. *The Structure of Scientific Revolutions.* Chicago: U of Chicago P, 1970.

Lucretius Carus, Titus. *Titi Lucreti Cari De Rerum Natura Libri Sex.* 3 vols. Trans. and ed. Cyril Bailey. Oxford: Oxford UP, 1947.

Mileur, Jean-Pierre. *Literary Revisionism and the Burden of Modernity.* Berkeley: U of California P, 1985.

Moynihan, Robert. *A Recent Imagining: Interviews with Harold Bloom, Geoffrey Hartman, J. Hillis Miller, and Paul de Man.* Hamden, CT: Archon, 1986.

Prigogine, Ilya. *The End of Certainty: Time, Chaos and the New Laws of Nature*. New York: Free P, 1997.
Sauerberg, Lars Ole. *Versions of the Past—Visions of the Future: The Canonical in the Criticism of T. S. Eliot, F. R. Leavis, Northrop Frye, and Harold Bloom*. Basingstoke: Macmillan, 1997.
Salusinszky, Imre. *Criticism in Society: Interviews with Jacques Derrida, Northrop Frye, Harold Bloom, Geoffrey Hartman, Frank Kermode, Edward Said, Barbara Johnson, Frank Lentricchia, and J. Hillis Miller*. London: Methuen, 1987.
Schroeder, Manfred. *Fractals, Chaos, Power Laws: Minutes from an Infinite Paradise*. New York: W. H. Freeman, 1991.
Schultz, William R. *Genetic Codes of Culture? The Deconstruction of Tradition by Kuhn, Bloom, and Derrida*. New York: Garland, 1994.
Shakespeare, William. *The Complete Works*. Ed. Peter Alexander. London: Collins, 1951.
Stevens, Wallace. *Collected Poems*. London: Faber, 1955.
Whitman, Walt. *The Complete Poems*. Ed. Francis Murphy. Harmondsworth: Penguin, 1975.

Is Deconstruction Really A Jewish Science?
Bloom, Freud and Derrida

MARTIN MCQUILLAN

I have no relation to deconstruction. I never did have, I don't have now, and I never will have. Nothing is more alien to me than deconstruction.
—HAROLD BLOOM[1]

What difference is there between choosing and being chosen when we can do nothing but submit to choice?
—EDMOND JABÈS[2]

1) Hoorah for Harold Bloom

Thank goodness for Harold Bloom. There is no literary critic writing today who is more encyclopaedic, more prolific, more outrageous, or more camp than Harold Bloom. Only Bloom could denounce the Academy with impunity as, "dominated by fools, knaves, charlatans and bureaucrats" (Saluskinszky 49) or describe Literature departments in Britain as "a middle-class amateurism displacing an aristocratic amateurism" (*Map* 30). There is something tremendously amusing and deeply shocking about Bloom's loftily delivered, scandalous bon-mots such as his assertion that Literature can only "touch" a reader if that reader begins "by being very greatly gifted" (Saluskinszky 58). In a restricted economy of academic exchange Bloom's writing challenges

---

[1] "Interview" in Saluskinszky. Ed. *Criticism and Society*. 68. In the same interview he calls deconstructionists "my remote cousins, intellectually speaking" (51).

[2] Edmond Jabès. *Le Livre des questions*. 132. This translation taken from Jacques Derrida, "Edmond Jabès and the Question of the Book" in *Writing and Difference* (65). Hereafter this essay will be referred to in the text as EJ.

the unnatural politesse of literary criticism and exposes the commodification of institutionalised debate in an expense of signification which demonstrates the expensive waste which predicates that debate. Bloom at his most excessive and offensive ("It would lead to something more than quarrels if I expressed my judgement upon 'black poetry' or the 'literature of Women's Liberation'" (*Map* 36)) raises the stakes within literary criticism by revealing a form of communication which no longer informs and attenuates a community (the academic community) which is separated from a certain form of cultural exchange.

The resolutely un-PC Bloom has accordingly attracted a significant number of critics whose commentaries only encourage him to become funnier and more contumelious as he grows old disgracefully. The very idea of a book entitled *The Western Canon* published in 1995 is an uncompromising gesture of defiance, the comic potential of which should not be under-estimated. However, Bloom's out-put is not just another story of radical youth gone bad in conservative old age. Bloom has always been idiosyncratic, witty, catty, and brilliant. Any misunderstanding about perceived changes in Bloom's critical position following the publication of *The Western Canon* is the result of the previous medio-academic construction of the so-called "Yale School" of so-called "deconstruction." The purpose of this essay is not to rake over the coals of that brief but blazing moment in the history of literary criticism, rather it is to examine a thread in the work of Harold Bloom and Jacques Derrida which is connected to a philosophical friendship and to a "sibling rivalry" emerging from that historical entanglement.[3] Bloom and Derrida were born four days apart on the 11th and 15th of July 1930, this happy accident enabled a critical conversation (sometimes explicit, sometimes implicit) to develop between Bloom and Derrida during the most productive sections of their respective careers.

2) Misreading Derrida

Bloom has been at continual pains to distance himself from "deconstruction" and has been engaged in a one-sided, on-off polemic against Derrida's influence over Anglo-American literary criticism since at least *The Map of Misreading*, published in 1975. In that book Bloom presents a

---

[3] For more detailed accounts of this "sibling rivalry" see Frank Lentricchia's reading of Bloom in *After the New Criticism* or Peter de Bolla's *Harold Bloom: Towards Historical Rhetorics*. We could as easily characterise it as fratricide.

critical reading of Derrida's essay "Freud and the Scene of Writing" as a strategic move in the elaboration of his own theory of poetic origins.[4] In the previous volume of his theoretical tetralogy, *The Anxiety of Influence*, Bloom shoots a characteristic broad-side across the bows of deconstruction when he talks of "the anti-humanistic plain dreariness of all those developments in European criticism that have yet to demonstrate that they can aid in reading any one poem by any poet whatsoever" (*Anxiety* 12–13). It is perhaps difficult to separate camp bombast from serious dissent in much of Bloom's encounter with deconstruction (after all *A Map of Misreading* is dedicated to Paul de Man).[5] However, in the chapter "The Primal Scene of Instruction" (*Map* 41–63) Bloom makes the first move in a seeming disagreement with Derrida. The discussion which arises from Bloom's reading demonstrates a number of concerns about deconstruction which are only now beginning to become apparent to less perceptive readers of Derrida than Bloom.

Bloom opens his reading of Derrida's essay with an invocation of Freud in the epigram to the chapter. Quoting from *Moses and Monotheism* the chapter is watched over by the authority of Freud's suggestion that:

> A tradition based only on oral communication could not produce the obsessive character which appertains to religious phenomena. It would be listened to, weighed, and perhaps rejected, just like any other news from outside; it would never achieve the privilege of being freed from the coercion of logical thinking. It must first have suffered the fate of repression, the state of being unconscious, before it could produce such mighty effects on its return . . . . (Freud, *Moses and Monotheism* in *Map* 41)

It is possible to take these few suggestive sentences from Freud as a guide, as Bloom does, to this ant*ago*nism with Derrida. The debate, if indeed there is one, relates to the status (repressed or otherwise) of Hebraic traces (a word used advisedly in this context) in the collections of writing we call Bloom and Derrida. The question that arises from the textual exchange is, what are the "mighty effects" produced within

---

[4] Derrida, "Freud and the Scene of Writing" (196–232). Hereafter this essay will be referred to in the text as FSW.

[5] Paul de Man provides a concise "deconstructive" criticism of *The Anxiety of Influence* in a review for *Comparative Literature* 26 (1974): 269–75 (later reproduced in *Blindness and Insight*, 267–76). In summary, de Man notes that Bloom's tropic ratios are derived from Aristotelian rhetoric; that Bloom's use of the metaphor of "Influence" turns a linguistic structure into a diachronic narrative; such narratives disguise a tight linguistic model which demonstrates the indeterminacy of meaning rooted in language rather than the poetic self.

deconstruction by Hebraic traditions of thought which have been rejected and/or repressed as religious phenomena under the coercion of philosophical thought? The encounter between Bloom and Derrida brings these effects to the brink of becoming a compelling motif within both men's writing by occupying an unsettled position with regards to the "orthodox" closure of a secular order of knowledge. In this way these "Jewish" effects follow the logic of repression outlined by Derrida and Bloom in their work. The aim of this essay is to follow this force of signification in Bloom and Derrida in order to consider the metaphorical status of "Jewishness" which connects their writing.

To briefly outline Bloom's belated and strong misreading of Derrida, Bloom proposes that Jewish Oral Tradition is at odds with the Platonic philosophical tradition because it does not valorise speech over writing. Bloom contrasts the Greek word for "word," *logos*, with the Hebrew word *davhar* which, "is at once 'word,' 'thing' and 'act,' and its root meaning involves the notion of driving forward something that initially is heldback" (42). He suggests that Derrida's "deconstructive enterprise" to "demonstrate that the spoken word is less primal than writing" may be an unconscious substitution of *davhar* for *logos* and a correction of "Plato by a Hebraic equating of the writing-act and the mark-of-articulation with the word itself" (43). Bloom submits that, "much of Derrida is in the spirit of the great Kabbalist interpreters of the Torah" (43). Perhaps too readily suggesting an uncomplicated relation between a Hebraic and a Platonic tradition (assuming that such things are rigorously identifiable) Bloom seems to offer a very literal interpretation of Derrida's graphemetic trace. However, Bloom's short-hand equation of grammatology with the physical "writing-act" is off-set by the scholarly ellipsis of his own prose style and the historical contextualisation opened up by reference to the Torah and to Judaism as the culture of the Book. Bloom perhaps more than anyone else is sensitive to the anxiety of a Jewish influence and approaches the question of Derrida's Jewishness in part to hail a wider concern in his theory of poetic origins.

Bloom's reading of "Freud and the Scene of Writing" is preceded by the repeated assertion that "the prestige of origins is universal" (46) and that "a nostalgia for origins governs every primal tradition" (47). The question for Bloom is not the actuality of origins, he explicitly states that "every Primal Scene is necessarily a stage performance or fantastic fiction, and when described is necessarily a trope." Rather, at stake here is the step from a fictional origin to the repetition of that fiction as a continuous original fiction. What marks this step, according to Bloom *contra* Nietzsche, is "a missing trope we need to restore, another Primal

Scene that we are reluctant to confront." At the out-set of Bloom's argument what concerns him then is not the "origin" but the trope of the origin, what he calls borrowing from traditional rhetoric, "*metalepsis* or *transumption*" (47).

In reading Derrida's essay Bloom pays attention to what he sees as Derrida's suggestion of "a third scene, more Primal than the Freudian synecdoches" (48). Derrida's trope (the Scene of Writing) is "one of hyperbole" which has a "close relationship to the defense of repression" (48). This hyperbole is Derrida's alleged privileging of the primacy of writing. Bloom sums up Derrida's essay through quotation, "Derrida's argument is that Freud resorts, at decisive moments, to rhetorical models borrowed not from oral tradition, 'but from a script which is never subject, extrinsic, and posterior to the spoken word.'" From this Bloom cuts to "an assertion that goes beyond Derrida's precursor, Lacan" that, quoting from Derrida's essay, "there is no psyche without text" (48). This is the "Sublime trope" which Bloom takes to mean that the history of the psyche "is seen as identical with the history of writing." For Bloom, "Derrida's keenest insight . . . is that 'writing is unthinkable without repression,' which is to identify writing-as-such with the daemonizing [poetic or Imaginary] trope of hyperbole." It is this curious reduction, "writing-as-such," which is crucial to Bloom's argument and which threatens to unravel the entire reading. For Bloom in this context "writing" means literature and his interest in writing-as-literature, with its necessary connection to repression, will be opened out into an intertextual theory of "intra-poetic relationships" (49). However, while literature is a conspicuous site of interest for deconstruction, as a textual event which lends itself to the analysis of the general structure of textuality, it is surely this "transcendental" gesture of conflating the institutional space of literature with textuality *per se* which the "deconstructive enterprise" rejects?[6] Rather, the un-stated hyperbole that we-are-written-only-by-literature is one of those loosely figured clichés often associated with the anti-humanist "Postmodern Theory" which Bloom regularly denounces.[7]

---

[6] For an extended discussion of this question see Jacques Derrida, "This Strange Institution Called Literature" (33–76).

[7] The entire premise of Bloom's theory of "influence" depends upon a similar suggestion that the critical act of (mis)reading places each individual reader in their own singular relation to texts and so to "his own original relation to truth" (*Map* 3).

This leads Bloom to conclude that "Derrida's Scene of Writing is insufficiently Primal both in itself and as exegesis of Freud" because Derrida evades what Bloom calls "the Primal Scene of Instruction" (49) which is a tropic schema of influence anxiety underpinning every Primal Scene.[8] Bloom notes that while quoting Freud's *The Problem of Anxiety in his essay* Derrida omits a crucial sentence regarding the role of the id in the avoidance of repression. Derrida's omission, Bloom claims, is because "for Derrida's interpretation of Freud to be correct—that is, for writing to be as primal as coitus—the inhibition of writing would have to come about to avoid a conflict *with the superego, and not with the id*" (50, Bloom's italics). The implication here is that because Freud elsewhere suggests that it is speech and not writing (again this distinction relies on a reductive appreciation of speech) which is inhibited by the superego, speech is therefore more primal than writing. It is, of course, the superego which moderates the "quasi-religious" Scene of Instruction and this more primal trope must be based on speech. Therefore, says Bloom, Freud unlike Derrida "and perhaps despite himself, is a curiously direct continuator of his people's longest tradition." The point being that influence anxieties (secondary and fictional as they may be) inhibit writing more readily than orality and the "logocentric tradition of prophetic speech" (50). This is by no means the end of Bloom's argument and this brief synopsis perhaps does not do justice to a condensed and complex thesis but in order to progress through Bloom's reasoning it will be necessary to return to Derrida's essay.

3) The Influence of Influence

The question here might be is Bloom's "misprision" (to use his own word) of Derrida, as part of his own theoretical project, justifiable as a reading of "Freud and the Scene of Writing"? On Bloom's own terms this question would miss the point of such a misprison because it does not accept that "all interpretation depends upon the antithetical relation between meanings, and not on the supposed relation between a text and its meaning" (76). Leaving this exception momentarily to one side, as bearing a suspicious similarity to the there-are-no-wrong-answers-in-literature school of thought, it may prove productive to examine Derrida's essay in relation to Bloom. Ultimately Bloom is heading

---

[8] For a detailed reading of this chapter by Bloom see "Scenes of Instruction: the limits of Bloom's psychopoetics" in Graham Allen. *Harold Bloom* (69–105).

towards the suggestion (in keeping with his earlier comments regarding Derrida and Kabbalah, and in contrast to what he says here about the Primal Scene of Instruction) that there does not exist in the Hebraic tradition an absolute distinction between speech and writing. In *Kabbalah and Criticism* Bloom proposes *contra* Derrida that Kabbalah is "an Occidental method" of analysis which is produced by "posing the radical question of writing" (*Kabbalah* 52). Kabbalah is more "audacious" than deconstruction because it is able to hold metaphysical thinking about presence and esoteric thinking about absence in a single co-existing field of "continuous interplay" (53). Bloom's insistence is unsettling for two reasons: firstly, because much of what he says here in opposition to Derrida is already stated by Derrida in his essay on Freud and secondly, because if as Bloom claims "much of Derrida is in the spirit of the great Kabbalist interpreters of the Torah" then it seems a peculiar contradiction to ask us to chose between them as critical "utilities." Accordingly, we might ask what other influences are determining Bloom's argument here?

In response to the first of these reservations about Bloom's reading of Derrida one need look no further than the ground-clearing first page of Derrida's essay in which he notes that the "historical repression and suppression of writing since Plato . . . constitutes the origin of philosophy as *episteme*, and of truth as the unity of *logos* and *phone*" (FSW 196). This "deconstruction of logocentrism" (196) at no point suggests that writing is *more* primal than speech but rather that philosophy *qua* episteme and the privileged relation within that episteme between truth and speech [*phone*] relies upon the repression of writing. What such a deconstruction implies is the overturning of a conceptual order between speech and writing in order to interrogate the conditions under which truth and philosophy take place. As Derrida continues in the next sentence, repression "neither repels, nor flees, nor excludes an exterior force; it contains an interior representation, laying out within itself a space of repression. Here that which represents a force in the form of the writing interior to speech and essential to it has been contained outside speech" (196–7). It is this "interior representation" within philosophy which does not exclude writing but makes a "space of repression" for writing because writing is a necessary condition of speech, that which in Derrida's words is interior and "essential to it." Writing is "contained" within this representation but repressed so as to appear "outside speech" in its relation to *logos* as truth. It is the legibility of writing within this "interior representation" as repression (because repression is always unsuccessful) which makes Derrida's rigorous ontological excavations of writing in the text of philosophy possible. In other words, deconstruction is interested in the dismantling of historically imposed distinctions between writing and speech, absence and presence, and the conditions under which truth has been legitimated. Furthermore, according to Derrida "Logo-phonocentrism is not a philosophical or historical error which the history of philosophy, of the West, that is, of the world, would have rushed into pathologically, but is rather a necessary, and necessarily finite, movement and structure: the history of the possibility of symbolism *in general*" (197). Therefore, the historically-specific privileged status of speech within philosophy is in fact a necessary condition of a wider schema of symbolisation and the possibility of meaning as the "history of *difference*" and "history as *difference*" (197). Accordingly, if Bloom is working towards an understanding of speech and writing in which both "co-exist by continuous interplay" (*Kabbalah* 52) it will take a remarkable piece of "misreading" to dismiss Derrida all together.

As an argument against Bloom such banal first principles of deconstruction might not take us very far and would probably fail to appreciate the rhetorical tactic of misprison which self-consciously claims every reading to be a misreading and every critical truth to be a "poetic diction" (*Ruin* 199). With respect to the second reservation about Bloom's argument perhaps the most intriguing sentence he offers in *A Map of Misreading* is the assertion that Freud is "more in the oral than in the writing tradition, unlike Nietzsche and Derrida, who are more purely revisionists, while Freud, perhaps despite himself, is a curiously direct continuator of his people's longest tradition" (*Map* 50). Bloom's justification for relating Freud's work to a certain Hebraic tradition is that Freud, unlike Derrida, is more sensitive to the place of the unconscious rather than the superego in the formation of a fictional Primal Scene. Derrida along with Nietzsche is described as a "revisionist," a loaded term in Bloom's vocabulary meaning a strong poet who "misprisons" a precursor. If one is prepared to go with the terminology this characterisation of Derrida's essay shows what concerns Bloom as thematic and pressing in Derrida's work, even as it undermines the precision of Bloom's point about the superego.

Derrida's deconstruction of Freud is an attempt to read the legibility of textuality within the "interior representation" of repression presented by the Freudian ouevre. Derrida notes in the opening sentence of the essay proper, that his aim is "to locate in Freud's text several points of reference, and to isolate, on the threshold of a systematic examination, those elements of psychoanalysis which can only uneasily be contained within logocentric closure" in order to show that Freud's "originality is not due to its peaceful coexistence or theoretical complicity with this [logocentric notion of text], at least in its congenital phonologism" (FSW198-9). This is as much as to say that Derrida's reading will identify moments in which the action of the trace as an effect of deferral remains legible within Freud's text despite the logocentric conceptual order which predicates Freud's thought and which attempts to repress them. The legibility of these moments will be the result of their "uneasy" or "non-peaceful" place within the text. The point is not to discover a reference to the structure of textuality (such as the Mystic Writing Pad) and *ipso facto* to reclaim Freud as a subverter of phonocentricism but rather the task is to ask "what apparatus we must create in order to represent psychical writing" (199). This question must be supported by asking what the "imitation" of "something like psychical writing might mean" especially as it is described by Freud in terms of a machine. Furthermore, the ultimate stake here is not that, "the psyche is indeed a kind of text, but: what is a text, and what must the psyche be if it can be represented by a text?" (199). In this way Derrida is merely opening the Freudian oeuvre on to "the threshold" (in both Freud and Derrida) of an examination of the historical determination of the question of text and so placing Freud's work within that history. The Mystic Writing Pad is not a challenge to the wider schema of metaphysics because it "participates in Cartesian space and mechanics" (227). However, because there is an "uneasiness" here and therefore a general indeterminacy between Freud's metaphors of textuality (as they move from the static spatialised schema of *Project for a Scientific Psychology* to the inadequate mechanical model of "Note on The Mystic Writing Pad") and his already graphemetic description of the unconscious, Freud's work opens up "a beyond and a beneath of the closure we might term Platonic'" (228). Freud does not present us with a theorised grammatological schema of the psychical text but instead, "Freud performs for us the scene of writing. Like all those who write. And like all who know how to write, he let the scene duplicate, repeat, and betray itself within the scene" (229).

Freud's text survives, like all texts, only by the repression of the question of writing but it is the performance of this repression which makes the question legible rather than simply erased. Such a distinction ensures the text's survival. So Derrida is reading with Freud against

Freud, and after a fashion, we might say he "misprisons" Freud to open up the question of the text. In this respect Derrida's use of Freud is strategically similar to Bloom's use of Derrida. Furthermore, Derrida's description of Freud's performance of the scene of writing bears comparison to Bloom's reading of *Tintern Abbey* as a "practical" application of his theoretical Scene of Instruction. He says, "there is a hidden but quite definite fear of writing in *Tintern Abbey*, or perhaps rather a fear of being delivered up to a potential fear of writing" (*Repression* 76; see also *Map*). *Tintern Abbey* performs within itself the repression of writing and presents a fear of its own writing. There may be a troublesome blurring of the way in which Derrida and Bloom use the term "writing" here but the evidence is mounting that the distance between Bloom and Derrida is not as great as Bloom's theatrical insistence might suggest.

Bloom's misprison of Derrida's shortened quotation of *The Problem of Anxiety* is strategically effective if somewhat disingenuous. Derrida's interest in the "Freudian break-through" (FSW 199) concerns the schema of the trace offered by a conceptualisation of the unconscious as an effect of delay and deferral. The reading of the interior representation of a repression of writing depends upon the uneasy fit between Freud's mechanical metaphor of writing and his discussion of the effects of the unconscious as trace. In the gap and contradiction between these two descriptions Freud's text performs the scene of writing which takes the form of the aporia, "if there is neither machine nor text without psychical origin, there is no domain of the psychic without text" (199). On this occasion this aporia is not as Bloom suggests "an assertion that goes beyond Derrida's precursor, Lacan" (*Map* 48) but rather a question which sets up a deconstruction of the metaphorical relationship between technology, the psyche and writing in the history of the conceptual order which predicates the concepts "technology," "psyche" and "writing." If Derrida, like Bloom, appreciates that there is not a simple antagonistic relation between "speech" and "writing" but a complex interplay performed in every text then, to follow Bloom's own logic, Derrida will be sensitive to the relation between writing and the unconscious and thus be like Freud "more in the oral than in the writing tradition" (50). If this were true, and by now the whole notion of "oral" and "writing" traditions should have been significantly displaced, then the relation between Bloom and Derrida might begin to take on an entirely different appearance.

4) Apologies for Absence

There are several points of agreement between Bloom and Derrida (or the spirit of a certain Bloom and the spirit of a certain Derrida) in "Freud and the Scene of Writing" and *A Map of Misreading*.[9] To quickly, and too hastily, enumerate them, firstly Derrida notes that the effect of deferral in the unconscious is extended by Freud in *Moses and Monotheism* to the history of culture and for Freud seems to work over extensive historical intervals. Derrida comments in passing that "the problem of latency, moreover, is in highly significant contact with the problem of oral and written tradition in this text" (FSW 203). Bloom is alert to the connection between this problem within Freud and calls it "a psychology of belatedness" (*Map* 52). Derrida in turn notes that the unconscious text consists only of reproductions of traces and that "everything begins with reproduction" as such any Primal Scene must always already be a repository "of meaning which was never present, whose signified presence is always reconstituted by deferral, *nachträglich*, belatedly, supplementarily" (FSW 211). There is here a space for correspondence between Bloom and Derrida, what relation does Bloom's "belatedness" bear to Derrida's "supplement" as a trope of deferral within a wider consideration of the problem of oral and written traditions?

In a move which echoes one by Derrida, Bloom notes that "behind all Primary fantasy is the even more Primal repression that Freud both hypothesised and evaded" (*Map* 56).[10] Taking his lead from Freud's essay "Repression" Bloom suggests that primal repression requires the establishing of a fixation to secure the repression. Therefore, argues Bloom,

---

[9] There are a number of other points of correspondence which I have only time to allude to here. They include Derrida's claim here and elsewhere that "there is no writing which does not devise some means of protection, *to protect against itself*" (FSW 224) and Bloom's notion that "all tropes are defenses against other tropes" and that the composite trope of Influence is a defense "against itself" (*Map* 74). We might also look at the relation between the "Election-love" (*Map* 51) proposed by Bloom and Derrida's rendering of the gift. Bloom also looks forward to "another Western story of origins" (65) beyond Freud's primal scene of the brother which pre-empts Derrida's work in *The Politics of Friendship*.

[10] Derrida says of the problematic relation between the metaphors of writing and mechanics, "Freud failed to make [it] explicit, at the very moment when he had brought this question to the threshold of being thematic and urgent" (FSW, 228). This is the "threshold" in Freud's text which opens onto the "threshold" of Derrida's reading.

primal repression requires a Primal Scene of Instruction (in poetic terms fixation equates with the relation between strong poet and precursor). Thus, the unconscious (which in Freud comes into being with primal repression) is in fact underpinned by the Primal Scene of Instruction and so the origins of the unconscious "are in a more complex trope, indeed in the trope of a trope" (56). The Primal Scene of Instruction then follows the supplementary (or belated) logic of a trope of a trope, of a supplement to the unconscious. As such the Primal Scene of Instruction as a tropic fiction of poetic origins is what Derrida calls "the reconstitution of meaning through deferral" (FSW 214). Accordingly, to settle upon a point shared by Bloom and Derrida, this scene is in communication with the metaphors of writing within the Freudian text and offers a legibility to a trace which connects it to a certain Hebraic oral tradition. There is in Bloom's trope, to quote Derrida, "a mole-like progression" towards the Hebraic which leaves behind an "impression," this word will have greater resonance for us in a moment. This impression is a trace, the meaning of which has never been "lived consciously" (214) as such, and which if read will connect Freud, Bloom and Derrida to the oral tradition which both Bloom and Derrida bring to "the threshold of being thematic and urgent."

Derrida ends his essay on Freud with a question which incorporates two references to the Torah. The essay concludes with a speculation concerning various "fields" in which the problem of the erasure of the trace as "the very structure which makes possible . . . something that can be called repression in general, the original synthesis of original and secondary repression, repression 'itself'" (230) might be developed. Derrida suggests that the "entire thematic" of Melanie Klein (hardly an innocuous choice) might be one space in which the "valuation and devaluation" of the archi-trace [writing] might be thought of as a constant inter-play between "writing as sweet nourishment or as excrement, the trace as seed or mortal germ, wealth or weapon, detritus and/or penis, etc" (231). The final paragraph is a single question which might have been asked by Bloom. How, Derrida poses (more than half rhetorically), can the repression of writing as a general condition of logo-phonocentricism ("writing as excrement") separated "on the stage of history" from a valuation of the archi-trace ("writing as sweet nourishment"):

> be put into communication with what is said in *Numbers* about the parched woman drinking the inky dust of the law; or what is said in *Ezekiel* about the son of man who fills his entrails with the scroll of the law which has become sweet as honey in his mouth? (231).

Derrida is aware of the complex place of writing within the Hebraic tradition, this is precisely the place he goes to in order to find an example of the complex and endlessly repeated double representation of the trace as the dust which nourishes or the shit which tastes of honey. The issue here is not that the Hebraic tradition is the only place which conceptualises this inter-play but that this relation is the very structure which makes thought possible because it predicates binarism while simultaneously avoiding binarism itself. This relation, which is the erasure of the trace, is also the structure and movement of repression and as such is what makes the Primal Scene qua reproduction possible. Thus Derrida's final arresting and knowing question at once connects repression, speech, writing, and the Hebraic oral tradition in much the same way as Bloom makes it a concern of his book.

While this nexus is worked towards in "Freud and the Scene of Writing," and picked out by Bloom as the form of a question (this relationship being that which presents itself as a question in these texts), it is explicitly considered in two other essays in *Writing and Difference*, "Edmond Jabès and the Question of the Book" and "Ellipsis". Bloom identifies Kabbalah (an esoteric hermeneutic which reworks those passages of the Torah which unsettle authoritative closure) *contra* Derrida in *Of Grammatology* as an Occidental "theory of *writing* . . . that denies the absolute distinction between writing and inspired speech, even as it denies human distinctions between presence and absence" (*Kabbalah* 52. Bloom's italics). In "Edmond Jabès and the Question of the Book" Derrida embraces "a certain Judaism as the birth and passion of writing" (EJ 64). This essay puts down the roots of Derrida's later thematisation of the messianic noting, quoting Jabès, that "Judaism and writing are but the same waiting, the same hope, the same depletion" (65).[11] The coming of the event of writing which is both an arrival and a deferral corresponds to this trope of Hebraism and so for Derrida reading Jabès "the situation of the Jew becomes exemplary of the situation of the poet, the man of speech and of writing" (65). The poet (as an exemplary figure which leads us to a consideration of the general structure of textuality) is at once "bound to language and delivered from it by speech whose master, nonetheless, he himself is" (65). The doubleness of speech and writing, their "continuous inter-play," is performed every time by the poet just as it is by the Jew and the two cannot be separated. What Bloom sees as specifically "audacious" to Kabbalah is the condition of all

---

[11] For a formulation of "a messianism without messianism" see most notably Derrida's *Specters of Marx*.

poetic performance and so is the audacity of writing as such. This doubleness is particularly visible in a certain Hebraic tradition because as a culture of the Book predicated by the trace it constantly performs within itself the duplication, repetition, and betrayal of this doubleness.

If for Bloom, to paraphrase Derrida on Freud, the originality of Kabbalah is not due to its peaceful coexistence or theoretical complicity with the authoritative closure imposed by Judaic heteronomy then this formulation is remarkably close to Derrida's description of Jabès as Poet and Jew. Both the Poet and the Jew are "autochthons only of speech and writing, of Law" (66) wandering and separated in the coming of an event but the authority of Rabbinical prophecy has no place for the intercession of the poet. The exclusion of the poet, like the heretical rabbis of Kabbalah who appear in Jabès' poetry and out of which Derrida makes an anagram of his own name to sign this essay, places within this "oral tradition" the familiar metaphor of "the text as weed, as outlaw" (67). As Bloom is fond of quoting from "the central text for Oral Tradition" the *Pirke Aboth* (Sayings or Wisdoms of the Fathers), Judaic heteronomy makes "a hedge about the Torah" (*Map* 44). This necessitates commentary which like poetry is "the very form of exiled speech" (67). The Poet and the Kabbalist are the supplements to the Oral Tradition which are performed, duplicated and betrayed within the textual event of the authoritative closure of the Book and which make such a closure possible. Bloom and Derrida quote the same canonical injunction "In the beginning was Interpretation [hermeneutics]" (*Map* 55; EJ 67) but Derrida suggests that the shared need for interpretation is itself interpreted differently by the autochthonous poet and the legislating rabbi. This difference is irreducible and means that:

> The original opening of interpretation essentially signifies that there will always be rabbis and poets. And two interpretations of interpretation. The Law then becomes Question and the right to speech coincides with the duty to interrogate. The book of man is a book of question (EJ 67).

As such the Oral Tradition is no different from any other tradition in its performance of the continuous inter-play between the repression of writing within internal representation and the writing of writing, by writing itself.

The Oral Tradition becomes thematic and urgent for Bloom and Derrida because it is an exemplary economy of the repeated relation between the two interpretations of interpretation and so of repression and of the dynamic of textuality in general. The continuous existence of both rabbis and poets is exactly what Bloom has called the Primal Scene of Instruction as a trope of inter-textual relations between expression and injunction. The irreducibility of these two interpretations makes writing as a question possible and makes Bloom's trope of primality primal by asserting the primality of tropes. As Bloom acknowledges in *A Map of Misreading* and will later elaborate in *The Breaking of the Vessels*, "to originate anything in language we must resort to a trope, and that trope must defend us against a prior trope" (*Map* 69).[12] Bloom's Primal Scene of Instruction is a tropic performance of the repression of a trope within the interior representation of a trope. It makes poetic innovation possible while legitimating the poetic tradition by freeing the poet and binding the poet to language in order to attempt but fail to take possession of speech from writing. The negativity of the Primal Scene of Instruction ensures the freedom of the poet by locating a negative origin of the poetic in the opening of an interminable question of relations. In Bloom's schema of intra-poetic relations the Primal Scene of Instruction divides and supplements the fictional origin of the poet, as the trope of a trope of a trope the Primal Scene offers a double origin and its repetition.[13] There can be few better examples within Bloom's work of a correspondence between his theory of poetry and the deconstruction which he positions himself against than this very trope which he proposes as an alternative to Derrida.

5) Judaism Terminable and Interminable

Ultimately, it would be a mistake to collapse Bloom's project onto Derrida's deconstructive enterprise characterising both as a secular displacement of a Hebraic trace, or, to draw some pallid conclusions about the *influence* of one thinker upon the other. Rather, it might be

---

[12] In the chapter "Wrestling Sigmund: Three paradigms for poetic originality" from *The Breaking of the Vessels* Bloom offers a rereading of the Primal Scene of Instruction. While Bloom notes here that in his initial reading he may have made the mistake of confusing the primal scene and the later primal scene fantasy he goes on to reinforce his earlier distinction between himself and Derrida by claiming that "as a Primal Scene, the Scene of Instruction is a Scene of Voicing; only when fantasised or troped does it become a Scene of Writing" (*Vessels* 61). As such this later book does not significantly progress the argument.

[13] See Derrida's comments in "Ellipsis" regarding "triplicity" as the necessary figure of repetition in order for meaning to be different from itself: 229–300.

more profitable to ask, following Derrida's exemplary deconstruction in his essay on Freud, what must be the relationship between Judaism, writing, and repression for this metaphorical transition to exist not only, nor primarily, within these texts by Bloom and Derrida, but within the history of Judaism, writing, and repression? This, more or less, is the very question which Derrida addresses in the essay "Archive Fever: a Freudian Impression."[14] Part of the essay is a reading of Yosef Hayim Yerushalmi's book *Freud's Moses: Judaism Terminable and Interminable* and specifically of the closing paragraphs of the final chapter "Monologue with Freud" in which Yerushalmi writes:

> Professor Freud, at this point I find it futile to ask whether, genetically or structurally, psychoanalysis is really a Jewish science; that we shall know, if it is at all knowable, only when much future work has been done. Much will depend, of course, on how the very terms *Jewish* and *science* are to be defined. Right now, leaving the semantic and epistemological questions aside, I want only to know whether you ultimately came to believe it to be so.[15]

This is a question (the purported Jewishness of psychoanalysis) which interests Bloom in the final section of *Ruin the Sacred Truths* (Bloom here also reads a text by Yerushalmi, *Zakhor: Jewish History and Jewish Memory*).[16] Like Derrida, Bloom worries about how the terms "Jewish" and "science" are to be defined in such a context, "psychoanalysis, after all, is only a speculation, rather than a science" (*Ruin* 146) while to begin to ask such questions "is to ask the even more problematic question: What is it to be Jewish?" (147). The problem is that "we no longer know just what makes a book Jewish, or a person Jewish, because we have no authority to instruct us as to what is or is not Jewish thought" (156) and "the masks of the normative" conceal "the eclecticism of Judaism and of Jewish culture" (179).

Bloom however is more comfortable with Yerushalmi's approach and proposes that the concept of "repression" is "profoundly Jewish, and even

---

[14] Jacques Derrida, "Archive Fever: A Freudian Impression". Hereafter this essay will be referred to in the text as AF. See also *Archive Fever: A Freudian Impression*.

[15] Yosef Hayim Yerushalmi. *Freud's Moses: Judaism Terminable and Interminable*. 100. Of course the title of my essay comes from John Caputo's paraphrase of Yerushalmi in, *The Prayers and Tears of Jacques Derrida; Religion Without Religion* (263–281).

[16] Yosef Hayim Yerushalmi. *Zakhor: Jewish History and Jewish Memory*. Derrida also cites this text in AF.

normatively so" (152) because repression as a theory is only coherent in a "cosmos where absolutely everything is meaningful" (147) so that a joke or a symptom for example can be subject to a level of hermeneutic intensity like the rabbinical "hedge around the Torah." The Freudian cosmos is, according to this later Bloom, like the rabbinical cosmos because "everything already is in the past, and nothing that matters can be utterly new" (152) while *The Interpretation of Dreams* is the Freudian Torah in which all meanings are already present and are regulated by the interpreters who guard the tradition. Furthermore, and quite contradictorily so, Bloom suggests that the superego is "the most Jewish of the psychic agencies" (165). Just as it looks as if Bloom is prepared to entertain the idea of the Jewishness of psychoanalysis his argument cuts itself in half, once again at the point where he attempts to distance himself from Derrida. Bloom calls Derrida's reading of Freud "invalid" because his "Hegelianizing" of Freud "ends by undoing his [Freud's] radical dualisms" (151). This dualism (primary/secondary process, pleasure/reality principle) is, says Bloom, of a "quite Jewish variety" (154).

However, this dualism because it is "Jewish" is a continuous inter-play of absence and presence which necessitates the "freedom of interpretation" which in a Jewish cosmology "results in all meaning being overdetermined" (154). This freedom of interpretation is subject to its own dualism of two interpretations of interpretation in which overdetermination both liberates specifics and determines in general because "what *is* freedom where everything is overdetermined" (154). It is the Kabbalistic inter-play of Freud's dualism which Bloom identifies as a path out of the reductionism of scientism within psychoanalysis. In other words, what Bloom finds most Jewish about Freud are those aspects of the Freudian text which fit uneasily with the repression of the inter-play of absence and presence which characterises the logo-centric schema of scientism. As we have seen, what Bloom sees as a specifically Jewish co-existence of absence and presence is, according to Derrida, both the condition of symbolisation in general and the very structure of repression. If Bloom is correct what is most Jewish is the trace.

In "Archive Fever," which is in no small measure a re-visitation of "Freud and the Scene of Writing" (cf. AF 15–25) Derrida works to undo Yerushalmi's figurations of a "Jewish Science" and "Jewish Memory." Within psychoanalysis the classical order of knowledge which would determine what "science" is and what it means to be "Jewish" is suspended by the radical temporalisation and movement of the effects of deferral in the trace as repression. The trace undoes the determination of Jewishness just as it may be the most "Jewish" of concepts because it opens determination onto a question of the future. Yerushalmi contends that the Jewishness of psychoanalysis will be known "only when much future work has been done" but it is Derrida's argument here and elsewhere that "the condition on which the future remains to come is not only that it not be known, but that it not be *knowable as such*" (AF 47. Derrida's italics). The coming of the event of the future is indeterminate with respect to existing stabilised orders of knowledge and as such cannot render either "Jewishness" or "science," within or without psychoanalysis, as knowable. Derrida is uncomfortable with the proposal that "to be open toward the future would be to be Jewish," which he calls a "logical abyss" (49), and with the suggestion that while "Judaism" as religion may be terminable the individual may still be marked by a "Jewishness" which is interminable. His reason for rejecting such determinations brings us full circle to Derrida's essay on Edmond Jabès and the above reading of Bloom. While Derrida may use the metaphor of circumcision to describe the effect of the trace as it leaves a mark before Being which calls to a future event of re-interpretation ("Go, read my Book that I have written") there is nothing specifically Jewish as such about the co-existence of the injunction of the law as an instruction to historical memory and the opening of the future in the experience of the promise, within an economy of symbolisation. This is what happens repeatedly within every single textual event (the trace and repression are as much events of the future as of the past) but may be more readable in a certain Hebraic tradition where the question of the text is made culturally visible.

Ultimately, what Bloom finds most Jewish about Freud is deconstruction, or at any rate the trace. But the trace is what undoes any such determination, as Bloom quips "the id is not the Yid" (*Ruin* 159). There are perhaps two things we might take away from this encounter between Harold Bloom and Jacques Derrida. Firstly, Bloom's supposed "challenge" to Derrida in *A Map of Misreading* that meaning "cleaves more closely to origins the more intensely it strives to distance itself from origins" (*Map* 62). This reposte to Derrida now looks more like a general principal of symbolisation and a fair description of the Bloom-Derrida negotiation of Jewishness as a question. Secondly, Maurice Blanchot's inquiry quoted by Derrida in "Edmond Jabès" which asks "Is man *capable* of a radical interrogation, that is to say, finally, is man capable of literature?" (EJ 78). As Bloom's intra-poetic "theory" has shown, and is again demonstrated by the relation between the texts discussed above, the interrogation of an interrogation must always lead to the indeterminate and when we think we are in the midst of the Book, literature has already begun.

Works Cited

Allen, Graham. *Harold Bloom: A Poetics of Conflict*. London: Harvester Wheatsheaf, 1994.
Caputo, John. *The Prayers and Tears of Jacques Derrida: Religion Without Religion*. Bloomington: Indiana UP, 1997.
De Bolla, Peter. *Harold Bloom: Towards Historical Rhetorics*. London: Routledge, 1988.
De Man, Paul. Review of *The Anxiety of Influence*. Comparative Literature 26 (1974): 269-75.
———. *Blindness and Insight: Essays in the Rhetoric of Contemporary Criticism*. 2nd ed. Minneapolis: U of Minnesota P, 1983.
Derrida, Jacques. "Archive Fever: a Freudian Impression." Trans. Eric Prenowitz. *Diacritics* 25.2 (Summer 1995): 9-63.
———. *Archive Fever: A Freudian Impression*. Trans. Eric Prenowitz. Chicago: U of Chicago P, 1996.
———. "Edmond Jabès and the Question of the Book." *Writing and Difference*. Trans. Alan Bass. London: Routledge & Kegan Paul, 1978.
———. "Ellipsis." *Writing and Difference*, opp. cit.: 294-300.
———. "Freud and the Scene of Writing." *Writing and Difference*, opp. cit.: 196-232.
———. *Politics of Friendship*. Trans. George Collins. London: Verso, 1997.
———. *Specters of Marx: The State of the Debt, the Work of Mourning and the New International*. Trans. P. Kamuf. London: Routledge, 1994.
———. "This Strange Institution Called Literature." *Acts of Literature*. Ed. Derek Attridge. London: Routledge, 1992. 33-76.
Jabès, Edmond. *Le Livre des questions*. Paris: Gallimard, 1963.
Lentricchia, Frank. *After the New Criticism*. Chicago: U of Chicago P, 1980.

Salusinszky, Imre. Ed. *Criticism and Society*. New York and London: Methuen, 1987.
Yerushalmi, Yosef Hayim. *Freud's Moses: Judaism Terminable and Interminable*. New Haven: Yale UP, 1991.
—. *Zakhor: Jewish History and Jewish Memory*. New York: Schocken, 1989.

Harold Bloom, (Comic) Critic[1]

ROY SELLARS

> The Cervantes text and the Menard text are verbally identical, but the second is almost infinitely richer.
> —BORGES, "Pierre Menard, Author of the *Quixote*" 94

> PROLOGUS: Something esthetic,
> PROTEANS: Something frenetic,
> PROLOGUS: Something for ev'ryone,
> ALL: A comedy tonight!
> —*A Funny Thing Happened on the Way to the Forum* 16[2]

Harold Bloom is one of the most significant marxist critics of modern times. The term 'marxist' here does not denote affiliation to a political group—for Bloom prefers not to belong to any group that would accept him as a member—but rather a commitment to critique as an antithetical force. He comments on the driving aims of his life's work, with that lucidity which has become such a feature of his recent style, in *The Western Canon*:

> I am your true Marxist critic, following Groucho rather than Karl, and take as my motto Groucho's grand admonition, "Whatever it is, I'm against it!" (520)

---

[1] A few parts of my essay were first published, in German, in *Fragmente* [Kassel]; permission to revise them for this occasion is gratefully acknowledged. Another version was given as a guest lecture at the University of Stirling; I would like to thank my host, Nicholas Royle (author of "The Slide," in the present volume) for his generosity and humour.

[2] In the first New York production of this musical based on Plautus (1962), the parts of Prologus and of the wily slave Pseudolus were played by Zero Mostel (*Funny Thing* 3; see Brown, *Zero* 171–88 and 236–38). Despite Bloom's sometimes uncanny resemblance to Mostel, there has been almost zero research on the hidden roads going from the critic to his comic precursor.

From his Yale doctoral thesis onwards, Bloom has responded to this admonition by producing what he calls "antithetical" criticism (*Anxiety* 65) and by attempting to destabilise the dismal recognition scene of contemporary criticism, in which what is said is said because it has been said already (see *Poetry* 29). There are works by other critics which might be classified as 'Bloomian,' but this remains a problematic adjective. Bloom himself is only partially Bloomian, and it is in the nature of his sect of one to differ even from itself.

In so far as Bloom is a "kakangelist," a bearer of ill tidings, he does not expect that his analysis of the ever-growing burdens of tradition will be welcomed (*Map* 39). But resistance to Bloom is often linked with misunderstanding, and his own clarifications have been powerless to halt the tide of careless readings. As he has become far more of a global media figure since the publication of *The Book of J* (1990), the growth of Bloom's reputation has become a hindrance in the sense that it is now easy to presume some familiarity with his work without actually having read it. By a strange irony which Bloom no doubt relishes, his influence has in fact been greatest where he has been least read and least understood; Peter de Bolla has made this point in an important study of Bloomian rhetoric, noted by Bloom himself (*Harold Bloom* 15; see *Canon* 8). Moreover, one cannot save Bloom from his misreaders in a straightforward sense, for one of his distinctions is to have problematised the concept of 'misreading' as such.[3] If the reception of Bloom tends to repeat Bloomian effects of misreading, in a comedy of errors, a rejection of Bloomian theory based on defensive misreading emerges as a blind exemplification of what it rejects. "If they persist in their folly, all these outraged reviewers will become wise," Bloom remarks, polemically alluding to William Blake's *Marriage of Heaven and Hell* (*Agon* 16).[4] What does it mean, this Bloomian Proverb of Hell?

Bloom's own theoretical discourse cannot escape the effects of what it aims to describe. His discourse *on* misreading, that is, cannot be separated from a discourse *of* misreading: to some extent, it "exemplifies" what it "explores," as Bloom aptly writes of Sigmund Freud (*Agon* 92). The distance between the conventionally demarcated fields of 'criticism' and 'literature' tends to collapse in Bloom, as they are implicated in

---

[3] See Anders H. Klitgaard, "Bloom, Kierkegaard, and the Problem of Misreading," in the present volume.

[4] He first published on this outrageous text in 1958 (in an article collected as ch. 4 of *Ringers in the Tower*), and is still publishing on it nearly fifty years later (see *Wisdom* 174–75).

each other—forming not a homogeneity, but rather hybrid texts which fragment and proliferate in a process of antithetical struggle. Bloom's own texts have an intrinsic interest, prior to the critical applications and appropriations through which they have become domesticated and institutionalised; and if this process of assimilation is to be resisted, it will be necessary to return to his texts as texts, not as repositories of method, concept, or even value. Such a return would explore Bloom's articulation of rhetoric and (or as) error, for example, set against his diverse antithetical invigorators—including Bloom himself. For there are (at least) two Blooms: the embattled neo-Romantic or Gnostic with a position to defend, and the writer whose texts defy labelling and show a subversive power in excess of their professed aims or positionality. These texts include interview transcripts, of which there have been more and more as Bloom's global fame, or notoriety, has grown. In a particularly entertaining interview from 1985, he admits that when he last tried to read *The Anxiety of Influence*, even he "could not quite figure out what was going on in it," adding: "I like that very much" (Salusinszky, *Criticism* 51). More than mere obscurity is at stake here, and part of "the cosmological, psychological and rhetorical joke" of the books forming his major phase as a literary theorist was that they aroused "dislike" and "shock" in him as he was actually writing them (70). Out of the quarrel with himself, Bloom makes theory and criticism—with the qualifications that the 'self' as a point of reference is thereby called into question, and that the 'quarrel' is also a comic double act. The productive tensions of such a quarrel (another nice mess he's gotten us into) are not to be resolved, whether by Bloom or his critics.

No complete overview of Bloom's work exists, and more than ever there is a need (which in my role as harmless drudge I hope to fulfil) for a critical bibliography to trace his development in detail. Since 1985, for instance, Bloom has been editing and introducing hundreds of anthologies of criticism for Chelsea House Publishers, on writers from Homer to the present, and for a readership not restricted to universities;[5] it is hard to imagine another contemporary critic who could or would undertake such a project, and yet little critical attention has so far been given to it. Furthermore, as Bloom has increasingly moved to address a non- or more-than-academic audience, a substantive body of work has accumulated in the mass media, and in several languages, that has not been assessed beyond its immediate occasion. Even the most capacious

---

[5] See the publisher's reference guide, Litline.com: http://www.litline.com/.

account of Bloom has to be selective, and to call him prolific is a feeble understatement. While it is true that, as Bloom's friend and colleague Paul de Man once put it, one cannot by an effort of will substitute "bliss" for "gloom" (*Blindness* 274), Bloom has nonetheless continued to bloom.[6] In an age of over-specialisation, short memory and short attention span, his breadth and diversity of reference is quite remarkable. It is impossible to read everything, as Bernard Bergonzi observes in a gloomy survey of the troubled state of English studies (*Exploding English* 83); and Bloom invokes this impossibility as a justification for his theory of poetic competition and selection, which offers the reader a way of coming to terms with the ever-increasing textual "overpopulation" of the age of Information (Salusinszky 69; see *Genius* ix).[7] He sometimes writes, in fact, as if the limits of his memory corresponded to the limits of the literary canon, since canonisation is itself no more than a way of formalising the effect of strong reading, according to Bloom. He has argued that memory is pragmatically equivalent to the canon (*Canon* 17 and 39), and in a sense he has been reviving the art of memory—not as a museum for "walking encyclopaedias," as Friedrich Nietzsche mockingly put it ("Uses and Disadvantages" 79),[8] but rather as a perpetual field of conflict. The problem arises in the ensuing movements of transcendence and generalisation, whereby this conflict is presented as if it were more or less over, the field settled, the canon fixed. Bloom in recent years has tended to short-circuit the antithetical processes of misreading and to focus on what is taken to be their product: certain writers—notably, now, Shakespeare—are then said to form a universal canon, a gilded monument which seems to transcend temporality altogether. In this respect Bloom is not Bloomian enough.

[6] De Man's ironic anagram is analysed by Wlad Godzich ("Harold Bloom" 47–48). David Fite, in the first book to be written about Bloom (based on a 1982 thesis), began by suggesting that he might be running out of energy (*Harold Bloom* ix–x); while Fite deserves credit for being the first into the field, his prophecy was unduly pessimistic.

[7] On "the anxiety of choice," see Graham Allen, *Harold Bloom* 69–73, and in the present volume, "The Anxiety of Choice, the Western Canon and the Future of Literature." Allen's cogent monograph remains indispensable for readers of Bloom.

[8] Nietzsche's essay on history, "On the Uses and Disadvantages of History for Life," has an importance in this context which cannot be overestimated (for the German, see *Werke* 3.1: 239–330); Bloom similarly struggles with the possibilities for action while culture, the tradition of all dead generations, weighs like a nightmare on the brains of the living. (On Bloom's Nietzsche, see O'Hara, *Romance* 55–92.)

A funny thing happens on the way to the canon: something aesthetic. One of Bloom's main modern precursors in the articulation and appreciation of aesthetic experience is Walter Pater. Bloom praises Pater (and has edited a valuable anthology of Pater's writings), but tries to prise his precursor's aesthetics away from what he calls, disparagingly, "philosophy" (*Figures* 19; for a more nuanced account, see Loesberg, *Aestheticism* 11–74). Bloom argues that aesthetic criticism is the only criticism possible, and not just in relation to literature. In this he is following Pater in the famous "Conclusion" to *The Renaissance* (Pater, *Selected* 58–63), but also Pater's contemporary Nietzsche (see Bloom, *Wisdom* 208–20). In an essay from 1873, the year Pater's *Renaissance* was first published, Nietzsche writes:

> it seems to me that "the correct perception"—which would mean "the adequate expression of an object in the subject"—is a contradictory impossibility [*Unding*]. For between two absolutely different spheres [*Sphären*], as between subject and object, there is no causality, no correctness, and no expression; there is, at most, an *aesthetic* relation [*ein ästhetisches Verhalten*]: I mean, a suggestive transference [*eine andeutende Uebertragung*], a stammering translation [*eine nachstammelnde Uebersetzung*] into a completely foreign tongue—for which there is required, in any case, a freely creative and freely inventive intermediate sphere and mediating force. ("Truth and Lies" 86, translation modified; *Werke* 3.2: 378)

Bloom has certainly earned the right to occupy an "intermediate sphere," a pre-eminent aesthetic container; his mediating is nothing if not "creative" and "inventive;" and crossing is one of his most forceful tropes (see *Stevens* 375–406, and De Bolla 87–96). Increasingly, though, he smoothes over any "stammering" and draws back from the disintegration of "spheres" which experience of the aesthetic in Pater and Nietzsche entails. Furthermore, in order to be recognised in the form of criticism, it had been assumed that aesthetic relations must somehow be communicated. According to Immanuel Kant, a judgement of taste had to be immediately and universally communicable in order to qualify as such, in so far as it falls under the rule of *sensus communis*, common or communal sense (*Critique* 173–76; see Lyotard, *Lessons* 191–98). This rule, however, seems impossible to maintain—because of solipsism, commodified relativism, or cultural dumbing-down,[9] but above all because of what Pater describes as the flux and discontinuity of modern aesthetic experience, which destabilises any universalising rule. Bloom

---

[9] According to the *OED*, the colloquial verb 'dumb down,' American in origin, has been performing its dumbing-down since 1933.

acknowledges how difficult it is to communicate anything of the aesthetic (*Canon* 17); the means of adequate "transference" or "translation," in Nietzsche's terms, are lacking, and the audience may not even exist. Bloom's more vatic pronouncements on the canon need to be supplemented by a Paterian, or Nietzschean, awareness of their contingency. When he writes, in (aesthetic) relation to Nietzsche, that "it is very painful to accept contingency," he adds as a gloss "to be the contained rather than the container" (*Wisdom* 220); but instead of displacing attachment to the "container" by attachment to the "contained," there is the more radical possibility that *each* is itself contingent, each is a trope. An aesthetic crossing, with Bloom, is often masterful and persuasive, and it is easy to be persuaded that we cross with him from one sphere (for example, an object) to another (for example, a subject). In reading Bloom, in other words, it is easy to forget that *there is nothing but crossing*:[10] a situation which is dangerous, painful, or comic, depending on traffic conditions.

> Why did Bloom cross the road?
> —To persuade us that there is one.

∼

The following cursory survey makes no attempt to contain Bloom. I focus on his published work up to approximately 1982 (the year of *Agon* and *The Breaking of the Vessels*) because, despite its undeniable importance for the field of literary criticism and theory, this work is now at risk of being forgotten, or simply ignored by readers of his more recent ventures into religious and cultural criticism.

Bloom's early phase, from 1956 to 1970, was primarily devoted to English Romanticism. His thesis on P. B. Shelley—with its more acerbic comments on other critics muted or cut—became his first book, *Shelley's Mythmaking* (1959), followed by *The Visionary Company* (1961; 2nd edition, 1971) and *Blake's Apocalypse* (1963). Early essays, reviews and introductions on Romanticism are collected in *The Ringers in the Tower* (1971), including "The Internalization of Quest Romance." This essay sets itself against what was received critical doctrine on Romanticism, and points forward to Bloom's breakthroughs of the 1970s. In it, he analyses the

---

[10] He once remarked to me, in response to an earnest question about Nietzsche, that there is nothing but tropes. It was said in an apparently pained tone, and yet it is surely one of Bloom's best jokes.

Romantic imagination as an antithetical category; the experiential, the natural, and the merely given are its dialectical opposites (*Ringers* 19–22). For Bloom, it is weak idealisation to assume that William Wordsworth writes so-called "nature poetry:" instead, Wordsworth's poetic sublimity is comparable to the equally antithetical, anti-natural "strength" of John Milton (20). In order to be able to originate and posit, the imagination has to fight for its autonomy, to differentiate itself from the organic self-presence and self-identity of nature, which is a tempting but impossible model. Paul de Man had argued much the same, in "Intentional Structure of the Romantic Image," an early essay which Bloom included in his still useful anthology of criticism, *Romanticism and Consciousness* (1970).[11] The origins of Bloomian theory are sometimes closer to de Man than Bloom might care to admit: in their different ways, each threatens the continuity between poet and nature or experience which had been assumed by the humanist critic. In Bloom's later work on tropes, literality displaces nature as the primary danger which antithetical poetry must fight; literal meaning becomes a kind of death that the poet defends against, relying on the interplay of figurative substitutions (*Map* 91; see *Agon* 107). Bloom's early work, despite its apparently more conservative terminology and assumptions, can be seen in retrospect to lead to this radical reformulation. 'Strong' or influential poetry does not aim to identify with or represent the data of experience and nature—even if such things exist. Instead, Bloom's theory returns poetry to rhetoric, considered as both a system of persuasion and a system of tropes. Strictly speaking, the imagination for Bloom is not a mode of self-expression or even of representation: literature is neither autobiography nor documentation. In his theoretical work he makes it explicit that the imagination does not have a referential aspect at all (*Map* 48). This does not mean, though, that Bloom is a covert formalist. He argues that a poetic text is formed in an irreducibly figurative, oppositional relation to anterior texts and to anteriority as such, so that it would be pointless for the critic to frame a single poem as if it were an object.

"The Internalization of Quest Romance" is a turning point in Bloom's development, uneasily blending an emerging rhetoric of the antithetical with a kind of literary psychology. It ends with a formula for the phantasmic but necessary quest of the Romantic poet: to become his or

[11] The essay is collected in De Man, *Rhetoric of Romanticism* (1–17), which mentions Bloom only in passing and yet invites comparison with Bloom's work throughout.

her own poetic father, as it were, and thus to become autonomous (*Ringers* 35). But this formula could be (and often has been) taken to imply a psychobiographical approach in terms of the Oedipus complex, and the reference to Freud at the beginning of Bloom's essay is equally conventional, implying that Freudianism is bound to reduce Romantic dialectics to the confines of the Reality Principle, leaving no space for the work of the imagination (13–15; see 23).

Bloom's study of W. B. Yeats (1970) had a gestation almost as long as *The Ringers in the Tower*, as he struggled to keep up with the movement of his own theoretical insights during this period (*Yeats* vii–viii). The book's introduction wryly observes that poetic influence is "a labyrinth that our criticism scarcely begins to explore" (4; see 87–88). Bloom here enters that labyrinth, outlining some of the strategies that a new poet or "ephebe" is obliged to adopt in order to defend against the anxiety of influence (5–7)—which is not an emotional state, but rather a pre-empting effect of rhetoric. Poetic tradition—that is, the cumulative effect of the precursors—is seen as a blocking force which the language of the ephebe must resist in order to emerge as such, and what we are used to calling literary history is only produced as a form of misreading, an effect over time of resistance to the language of the precursors. The major precursors of Yeats, in Bloom's study, are Blake and Shelley (v; see 59). But the readings presented in the main body of the book do not always fulfil the expectations generated by its theoretical introduction; Bloom later admits as much (*Poetry* 205–06). The tension between theory and critical practice makes the book a challenging read.[12] Bloom vigorously rejects the assumption that Yeats is a kind of modernist who eventually succeeds in transcending his Romantic origins. The poetic autonomy of which Bloom writes, and which amounts to a lie against time, is not to be confused with any literal form of modernism. He argues that modernism is a kind of blindness which, while negating the perspectivising effects of the anxiety of influence, only displays those effects all the more (*Ringers* 17; see *Map* 28). This view brings Bloom close to de Man's analysis of the self-contradictory appeal of modernism for writers desiring a *tabula rasa*: in the act of asserting their modernism, they "discover their dependence on similar assertions made by their literary predecessors" (De Man, *Blindness* 161; see Allen, *Harold Bloom* xxi–xxiv).

---

[12] Ann Wordsworth noted this aspect in her appreciative book review, "Wrestling with the Dead." Perhaps the best teacher I have ever known, she it was who first introduced me to Bloom's work.

Evidently de Man and Bloom share an interest in working through the implications for literature of Nietzsche's essay on history (see *Blindness* 149–52; Bloom, *Anxiety* 49–50).

Bloom's own work is as antithetical as the literature it chooses to analyse. He overthrows the canonical value-judgements of T. S. Eliot, for example, which had dominated the scene when Bloom began his career (Salusinszky 61). Eliot disliked and misunderstood Shelley; Bloom sets out to defend him. Similarly, F. R. Leavis disliked and misunderstood Milton; Bloom sets out to defend him. Much of his polemic against what used to be the Anglo-American literary-critical establishment was directed against the residual influence of Eliot, Leavis and the once-New Criticism. As a revisionist, Bloom challenges not only the content but also the mode of formation of the poetic hierarchy. His originality is not so much in sketching a new great tradition as in asking hard, resolutely unfashionable questions about the canonical as such. Now the literary-critical establishment, if there is one, looks very different, and Bloom's writing looks different too; he is no longer addressing the university world in any direct sense. It may be that he now lacks proper opponents, and sometimes he verges on self-parody. But his belief in "the poetic will" and "the individual reader's struggle" persists (Pease, "Bloom" 129): each must play its part in lying against time.

Bloom's major theoretical phase began with the publication of *The Anxiety of Influence* (1973; 2nd edition, 1997), the argument of which is developed and refined in a series of books within a few years of each other: *A Map of Misreading* (1975; 2nd edition, 2003), *Kabbalah and Criticism* (also 1975), and *Poetry and Repression* (1976).[13] *The Anxiety of Influence*, subtitled *A Theory of Poetry*, is his manifesto for antithetical criticism. Poetry is antithetical in so far as it turns away from the self-present state of nature or experience, the merely given which threatens to annihilate the imagination. Criticism becomes antithetical when it sets itself against the "primary" criticism of institutionalised literary studies (*Anxiety* 70), and Bloom designates as primary the familiar operations of tautology and reduction whereby a poem is either (redundantly) paraphrased or (forcibly) reduced to something extra-poetic, something less than itself. His use of the same term, "antithetical," to describe both Romantic poetry and Bloomian criticism, reinforces the links between the two: "all criticism is prose poetry," he writes (*Anxiety* 95), a

---

[13] This constitutes Bloom's tetralogy, to which can be added *Figures of Capable Imagination* (also 1976).

hyperbolic assertion which has caused some misunderstanding.[14] Bloom has never proposed that criticism is equivalent in value to literature. It is ironic that he has been blamed for advocating such a view, for he has more recently been blamed for advocating strict criteria in judging literature and even stricter criteria in judging criticism. What Bloom has emphasised at least since *The Anxiety of Influence* is that criticism is not an activity with coherent boundaries: a strong critic such as Dr. Johnson is engaged in a struggle with texts which is similar in nature to that of a strong poet, however different the form of their enterprises may be (Salusinszky 57). Bloom aims to persuade his readers that "the reading of strong poetry is just as much a poetic fact as is the writing of such poetry" (*Poetry* 6; compare *Kabbalah* 101). As Peter de Bolla has shown, Bloom has constructed a poetic theory of poetry based on misreading and the usurpation of meaning (*Harold Bloom* 8; see Bloom, *Kabbalah* 109).

There are significant continuities between Bloom's earlier work and this major phase. He half-seriously claims to have discovered the anxiety of influence as a child of twelve, in 1942, while reading the poetry of Hart Crane (Salusinszky 50). However, Bloom also made at least two related breakthroughs around 1970, and to some extent he disassociates himself from his early work (*Poetry* 46). Firstly, criticism is no longer assumed to be a form of interpretation; secondly, the poem is no longer assumed to be an object. The focus of Bloom's theory is on the origins and inter-relations of figuration, but this focus is routinely lost by his readers, as Jonathan Culler points out, because we are so used to the assumption that the critic's role is to identify and interpret meaning (*Pursuit* 14). Bloom's very first publication was an enthusiastic review of Northrop Frye's *Anatomy of Criticism* (1957; it has not been collected, despite its proleptic interest for readers of Bloom). The review already makes clear his antipathy to New Criticism and any formalism that takes the poetic text to be a delimited object, a well-wrought urn; he

---

[14] To give just one example, Colin Falck, a self-styled heresiologist of literary theory, objects to a catalogue of fallacious "doctrines" of which the fourth reads: "That there is no clear distinction between the texts of criticism and the texts of literature itself (Geoffrey Hartman, Harold Bloom)" (*Myth* 23–24). Leaving aside the obvious differences between Bloom and Hartman (author of "The Song of Solomon's Daughter" in the present volume), readers who pursue the page reference that Falck gives here to *Kabbalah* (33–34) will find nothing to support his objection, unless it be Bloom's focus on the interpretative nature of Kabbalah. Does it make sense to insist that Kabbalah be either "criticism" or "literature"?

welcomes Frye's archetypal criticism in so far as it champions rhetoric against the restrictions of the New Critics ("New Poetics" 133). It was not until many years later that Bloom's antipathy found its full theoretical justification. "Let us give up the failed enterprise of seeking to 'understand' any single poem as an entity in itself," he protests (*Anxiety* 43), advocating the antithetical as an escape from what he terms, deferring to Paul de Man, "the impasse of formalist criticism" (12; see de Man, *Blindness* 229–45).

Bloom does not underestimate the difficulties of escaping this impasse. Graham Allen argues that there is a residual "rhetoric of interiority" in Bloom (*Harold Bloom* xii); he has eloquently admitted that his stance must rely on specific social privilege (*Canon* 23–24), but is well-known for being scathing about any sociology of literature. The question of how the limits of reading are determined remains. As his contemporary Jacques Derrida shows in *The Truth in Painting*, a certain enframing of a putative textual entity is fundamental to understanding (57–64). Derrida does not, as is sometimes claimed, proceed to abolish the outside of the text. Rather, he works through the problem of formalism by analysing the frame as a supplement whose strange structural logic determines that it is at once extrinsic and intrinsic, so that this conventional binary opposition becomes unstable. While Bloom is concerned with figurative "intra-poetic relationships" (*Anxiety* 5) or "the hidden roads that go from poem to poem" (96), at the same time he calls into question the identity of the poetic text as such, emphasising that "'form' in poetry" is just another figure ("Breaking" 1), as are "'inside' and 'outside'" (*Agon* 46; see Allen, *Harold Bloom* 32–35). Bloom's critical road takes him far from Derrida, but they have both exposed the arbitrariness and unreliability of the inside/outside oppositions that continue to exercise so much power over reading. The tension between the two theorists remains a productive factor in Bloom's work, despite his avowed hostility to what he calls the "Deconstruction Road Company" (*Agon* 35), managed by those critics who have turned deconstruction into a movement with a determined programme (on the latter, see Derrida, "Some Statements"). There is no such royal road to knowledge for Bloom; but it is disingenuous for him to claim, as he does, that his work has "no relation whatsoever" to deconstruction (Salusinszky 67–68). More precisely, though, this claim could be described as one of his necessary defensive jokes, since—as he argues with regard to strong poetry—"Discontinuity is freedom" (*Anxiety* 39). A comparable defence emerges when Bloom describes the title of the famous collection

Deconstruction and Criticism (1979) as a joke: Derrida, de Man, J. Hillis Miller and Geoffrey Hartman were the "deconstruction," while Bloom was the "criticism," he claims (Salusinszky 68).

Near the beginning of *Poetry and Repression*, he sets the question of the text in the following perspective:

> Few notions are more difficult to dispel than the "commonsensical" one that a poetic text is self-contained, that it has an ascertainable meaning or meanings without reference to other poetic texts. Something in nearly every reader wants to say: "*Here* is a poem and *there* is a meaning, and I am reasonably certain that the two can be brought together." (2–3, Bloom's emphases)

Instead of ascertaining the "meaning" of the "text," Bloom insists on the inter-relatedness of poetic language, on his vision of intertextuality (see Allen, *Intertextuality* 133–44). His analysis is all the more compelling in that it has to struggle against resistance to its own insight. When he refers to the "'commonsensical'" desire of "nearly every reader" to determine the meaning of a poem as an entity, he implies that such resistance extends to himself, as he seems to confirm in what follows the above quotation:

> Unfortunately, poems are not things but only words that refer to other words, and *those* words refer to still other words, and so on, into the densely overpopulated world of literary language. Any poem is an inter-poem, and any reading of a poem is an inter-reading. A poem is not writing, but *rewriting*. . . . (*Poetry* 3, Bloom's emphases)

"Unfortunately," wherever the desire of that ironically pained adverb may lead, there will never be an end to reading. There is no possibility that criticism will ever see the thing as in itself it really is, for the frame of reference that would support such a project is lacking. The "*Here*" of the text and the "*there*" of meaning are not locatable, for these terms function merely as deictic markers—pointing as an act of language which, in the very act of pointing, reveals its own inability to coincide with what is supposed to be a specific reference (see Hegel, *Phenomenology* 60–66). Instead of identifying the specific place of the "*there*" as meaning, the antithetical critic displaces attention to "other words," and one's attention cannot remain fixed on "*those* words" because "*those*" in turn send one in another direction, and so forth, until one begins to doubt if anyone is in control of the process of inter- and intra-textual proliferation. While the poetic quest for Bloom is finally to arrive at one's origins, it must be stressed that this arrival cannot be experienced as such. To move from *topos* (commonplace) to trope in the writing and reading of poetry, as he proposes, is to realise that one can never be at home in language.

The idea of critical rigour needs to be rethought: as far as literature is concerned, rigour conceived as the positivist adequation or approximation to an object produces only *rigor mortis*. 'Misreading,' as an antithetical term, is not a symmetrical opposite of adequation. Insisting on its own truth in relation to the event of a text, Bloomian misreading necessarily lies; rigour, then, would lie in the pursuit of a bewildering process whereby difference is displaced but then, in turn, displaces the misreading that had displaced it. In this sense, Bloom's work is deeply historical: it always goes on till it is stopped, and it never is stopped. Deferring to Oscar Wilde's critique of Matthew Arnold, Bloom argues with outrageous logic that criticism "must see the object, the poem, as in itself it really is not" (*Agon* 18),[15] and this is partly because of the poem's crucial relationship to what it has excluded, setting up a dialectic of absence and presence which even the strongest poet struggles to master (see *Kabbalah* 121–25). The poet's struggle prefigures the critic's in its heroic (or dismal) failure. "A text is a relational event, and not a substance to be analyzed" (*Kabbalah* 106); or, as he writes with fine hyperbole—his favourite trope—near the beginning of *A Map of Misreading*, "there are *no* texts, but only relationships *between* texts" (3, Bloom's emphases; compare *Kabbalah* 88). Rethinking influence thus involves rethinking textuality, that which constitutes a text as such. Instead of positioning meaning in or outside a text, Bloomian theory defers meaning as a constant drifting between texts (see Renza, "Influence" 200–01). This movement is the effect of a struggle in which belated writer and belated reader are both implicated: an agonistic view of literary history, or rather histories, as fuelled by the conflictual processes of influence (*Anxiety* 5). Influence in this context has nothing to do with the transmission of images and ideas familiar from conventional source study (7; see De Bolla 15–18). Nor should Bloom's vision be reduced to a scheme in which writers are classified in terms of determinate sources and lineage, since the 'source' itself turns out to be always already belated and subject to distortion. Literary history is no longer a continuum, supported by a succession of authorial presences, but rather a powerful

---

[15] See Wilde, "The Critic as Artist" 364–69; on Wilde's allusion to Pater here, see Bloom, *Figures* 18–19.

rhetorical effect that alternates, for the reader, with knowledge of its insubstantiality; figurative rewritings clash, without a source that could be called aboriginal beyond the flux of perspectives. Even the belief that literary history moves teleologically into the future is subverted by the demonstration that influence can very well move backwards, as Jorge Luis Borges had suggested (as if influenced by Bloom) in his studies and stories of influence.

From the beginning, which is only a beginning if the poet has lied persuasively enough, there is already belatedness. In constructing a theory of that belatedness, Bloom has recourse to the Freudian notion of *Nachträglichkeit*, a term that Freud uses to describe the temporal relation between the deferred appearance of a symptom and its putative origin—which may well be phantasmic—in a pathogenic event or wish. Freud's term can be translated into English only with some awkwardness, as 'supplementarity' (in Derrida) or, as Bloom suggests, "*aftering*" or "'retroactive meaningfulness'" (*Poetry* 4; see 287–88, and *Stevens* 168–70).[16] Bloomian belatedness, a symptom of that quasi-pathological condition known as poetry, accompanies an indeterminate chain of supplements; belatedness is a function of a text which is itself always already a supplement.[17]

Bloom used to compare poets' reactions to the primal trauma of discovering they are not their own creators to children's reactions in the Freudian family romance when they replace their own feared and desired parents with a more tolerable fantasy of noble birth (see Freud, "Family Romances," *Standard Edition* 9: 235–41).[18] He makes it clear that origin and originary influence become inseparable from mythology and figuration ("Breaking" 3); but Bloom certainly does not reduce poetry to a product of Oedipal or other psychological forces. In *Poetry and Repression*, he laments the fact that he is generally thought to advocate an Oedipal interpretation of literature, and reminds his readers that in

---

[16] If Freud's term is not well known in English, it is partly because the translated *Standard Edition* of his major works does not allow readers to track its use; see Laplanche and Pontalis, *Language* 111–14.

[17] The phrase 'always already' is taken from Derrida's essay "Freud and the Scene of Writing" (202–03 and 211–12), which Bloom both admires and resists for its deconstruction of memory, repression and textuality in Freud (see *Map* 48–50). See Martin McQuillan, "Is Deconstruction Really A Jewish Science? Bloom, Freud and Derrida," in the present volume.

[18] For relevant analysis of the Oedipus complex and the problem of identification in Freud, see Borch-Jacobsen, *Freudian Subject*.

studying poetry one is not studying the mind or even the unconscious (25). He now avoids reference to the family romance, since it is a misleading analogy (*Agon* 44; see Salusinszky 55). Bloomian theory is only psychological at all in a figurative sense, for the anxiety of influence is not something experienced by the poet as person—as if Wordsworth, for instance, woke up feeling anxious about Milton—but is rather that which constitutes the poet as poet. This crucial distinction between person and poet is present in Bloom's work from his first book onwards (*Shelley* 21; compare *Anxiety* 11).

For all the deadly earnest of the writer's dilemma, a narrative account of the anxiety of influence resembles a shaggy dog story (Freud's *Aufsitzer*, to which we will return below for the punch line). The personal intention and consciousness of the poet have no necessary link to meaning whatsoever: as Bloom likes to remind us, "all bad poetry is sincere," a joke from his precursor Wilde that he would like to see "engraved above every gate at every university" (*Canon* 16). To aim at meaning, as a poet, is to generate a sequential structure in which meaning is projected as terminus; to arrive would be to possess meaning as one's own. Such an arrival is a delusion, however, even for the strongest writers, whose strength is a measure of their (delusive) ability to turn delusion into arrival. To arrive at meaning at all is to come into a *topos*: that is, a place already marked as not one's own. Likewise, the general determination of the ego to find meaning at any cost is exposed by Freud as delusory, as in the theory of secondary revision outlined in *The Interpretation of Dreams* (Standard Edition 5: 488–502). The joke is always on the ego—such that it is not far-fetched for Jacques Lacan to take the ego as symptom rather than agent.[19] Bloom and Lacan have given equally outrageous interviews, in which what is outrageous is not so much their content as their style and the undecidability of their ironies. "I always speak the truth," says Lacan at the beginning of his interview *Television* (3). Like Lacan, Bloom always speaks the truth, but then immediately invites a response comparable to the following:

> My first thought was, he lied in every word,
>   That hoary cripple, with malicious eye
>   Askance to watch the working of his lie
> On mine, and mouth scarce able to afford

---

[19] Bloom's revisionary relation to Lacan demands an essay to itself (see in this context *Poetry* 145–46 and 245). According to Shoshana Felman, who was Bloom's colleague at Yale, students attending his literature seminars used to report difficulties of understanding similar to those of students in her seminars on Lacan.

> Suppression of the glee, that pursed and scored
>   Its edge, at one more victim gained thereby.
>
> What else should he be set for, with his staff?
>   What, save to waylay with his lies, ensnare
>   All travellers who might find him posted there,
> And ask the road? I guessed what skull-like laugh
> Would break, what crutch 'gin write my epitaph
>   For pastime in the dusty thoroughfare,
>
> If at his counsel I should turn aside....
> (Browning, "'Childe Roland to the Dark Tower Came'" 1–13; Bloom has obsessively re-read this poem)

If Bloom tells all the truth, he tells it slant. One of the jokes here is that "there are no right readings, because reading a text is necessarily the reading of a whole system of texts, and meaning is always *wandering around between texts*" (*Kabbalah* 107–08, my emphasis). The quest of the critic is to be a permanent vagrant, "wandering around" in the wake of meaning with miles to go before he or she sleeps, and telling stories of that wandering. The suspension of meaning that characterises such a quest is analogous to the termination of a shaggy dog story that is no termination at all. To relish this suspension for its comic potential demands the strength to relinquish the pathos and nostalgia that would turn Bloom's "between" into a mere place to be visited and revisited.

"I am a comic critic, and all I get are serious reviews" (Salusinszky 68). Bloom draws attention to an ironic, amusing discrepancy in the reception of his work; but we can hardly decide whether his statement (constative) is itself a joke (performative), any more than we can put a stop to the dizzying chiasmic reversals, whereby literal is mistaken for figurative and vice versa, to which he draws attention at the beginning of one of his essays on Browning (*Poetry* 175). Bloom is a trope critic, or joke critic, indistinguishably.

If poetry *is* anxiety, or achieved anxiety (*Anxiety* 94), the joke seems to be on the poet—but we should be careful not to assume that anxiety is a known quantity. Freud began in his early work on psychopathology with an economic theory of anxiety as a quantity, subsequent to repression, so that the repression of a threatening affect translated that affect into so much anxiety. However, when he came to write *Inhibitions, Symptoms and Anxiety*, Freud had moved to a theory of anxiety as a signal, in which it is generated not as an affective response to danger, but as a kind of defensive representation prior to the appearance of the potential danger against which it defends. No longer simply a psychical affect, Freudian anxiety is thus a pre-emptive signal which tends to disrupt the connection between a representation and that which is to be represented (*Standard Edition* 20: 135–37 and 164–68).[20] An achieved anxiety, in Bloomian terms, is an aggressive prolepsis which aims to come before or forestall that which is prefigured. "O run, prevent them [the precursors] with thy humble ode," as Milton puts it, addressing his Muse in the not-so-humble proem to "On the Morning of Christs Nativity" (24). The strong poem will "prevent" that which it announces, at the cost of a severe repression.

Freud matters to Bloom above all as a theorist of defence—that is, of the ways in which the psyche endeavours to survive and to achieve some autonomy in the face of assimilable and unassimilable challenges from both outside and inside. He appreciates Freud's emphasis in *Beyond the Pleasure Principle* on the protective shield of the primitive living organism, whereby the defence against stimuli—in Bloomian terms, against influence—is held to be a function "almost more important" than the reception of stimuli (*Standard Edition* 18: 27). Bloom is more concerned with the aesthetics of defence than with the aesthetics of reception, and he uses Freud's theory of anxiety as a defensive signal in order to support his argument that poetic meaning is neither experiential nor referential (*Agon* 109–11). Anxiety, then, does not refer to the poet's biography, and poetic reference offers meaning only as a lure that traverses other texts, so that the joke is now on the reader (*Anxiety* 70 and 94). Instead of working at representation, the poem attempts to pre-empt danger by defensively revising other poems: poetry is hence a form of "mediated revision, for which another name is anxiety" (*Agon* viii).

Agency remains a problem. A poem does not write itself, but writing as the constant process of inter-poetic revision cannot be ascribed to a pretextual self either. Bloom seems increasingly to rely on a notion of strong authorship which his own work on intertextuality undermines, or at least compromises (see Culler, *Pursuit* 107–11). The sovereignty and self-presence of the author finds itself under threat in Bloom, yet he insistently differs from Derrida, for example, in rethinking authorial economies. Writing on Freud, Derrida had asked: "what is a text, and what must the psyche be if it can be represented by a text?" ("Freud" 199). In antithetical mode, Bloom turns Derrida's leading question around:

---

[20] Samuel Weber elucidates Freud's theory in a way that is helpful for readers of Bloom (*Legend* 48–60).

"What is a psyche, and what must a text be if it can be represented by a psyche?" (*Poetry* 1). Rather than translating psychology into a theory of poetry, he works on the psyche as itself a figure—of breath, voice, will or stance (*Poetry* 1-2; see 55). This "psychology" is not recognisably experiential (De Bolla 16-20). While Bloom aims to save the psyche as figure of voice, and resists the work of Derrida and de Man on this basis, such resistance does not entail a belief in the substance of humanistic verities. As Bloom likes to say, following Nietzsche, it is simply that he would rather have the void *as* purpose, instead of being void *of* purpose (*Poetry* 192-93 and 234):[21] a stance as precarious as that of Wile E. Coyote who, having run off a cliff in pursuit of the Road Runner, continues to tread the air. The wilier poet, meanwhile, survives by willing survival as a figure in relation to other figures, his or her stance working to achieve separation from the precursors; but the discontinuity achieved is a lie—or a figure, the terms being almost synonymous here—and can hardly establish a secure identity. If the poetic psyche is constituted by tropes, then to take that constitution to be identical or present to itself is to turn a necessary lie into a dangerous mystification.

Bloom emphasises the use value of a trope, in poetics, and its surplus value, in aesthetics (passing over exchange value, it may be noted). Tropes are immediately necessary to generate writing, any writing, when the ephebe is called into being—or rather, becoming—by the anxiety of influence. If everything is already written, the poet must un-name what has been named in order to begin at all and to clear some imaginative space and time; so the referential function of language will be disturbed from the very beginning. Such clearance is violent and exacts a high cost, for the writer must lie and distort in order to write, and this lying is not a singular occurrence but a dialectical process which never reaches closure. Above all, the writer has to lie against time, disavowing facts of belatedness, as if it were morning: "Now while the Heav'n by the Suns team untrod, / Hath took no print of the approaching light" (Milton, "On the Morning of Christs Nativity" 19-20). This urgent printing that would come before the "print" of the precursors helps to show why Bloom defines tropes, in Nietzschean terms, as "figures of willed falsification" (*Poetry* 25; compare *Map* 93). The trope is that which turns against literality, or prior figuration, with cavalier disregard for truth,

---

[21] Right at the end of *On the Genealogy of Morals*, Nietzsche had written: "man would rather will *nothingness* than *not* will.—[lieber will noch der Mensch das Nichts wollen, als nicht wollen. . .]" (163; *Werke* 6.2: 430).

property or propriety. Troping against prior tropes is especially vital and is designated "metalepsis" (*Vessels* 74–75, quoting Hollander, *Figure of Echo* 115–16;[22] see De Bolla 97–101 and 133–34). The trope offers the poet-becoming-a-poet a saving antithetical moment. Poetry, or figurative writing in general, is a mode of creative distortion or "misprision," a term which Bloom employs to distinguish the misreading that is his concern from everyday carelessness or dyslexia (*Kabbalah* 97).[23] Misprision is the defence without which literature as such would be inconceivable.

It is tempting to summarise the interlocking set of revisionary ratios on which Bloom relies, since they are no longer familiar, if they ever were. *The Anxiety of Influence* had described a series of six ratios by which the antithetical critic may assess the distorting relations between a poet's texts and those of his or her precursors. The first ratio, *clinamen*, is perhaps the best known: a corrective swerve, implying that the precursor lies in every word—as Browning's Childe Roland puts it—and should have moved precisely in the direction of the new poem (*Anxiety* 14). The second, *tessera*, involves an antithetical completion; the third, *kenosis*, is an emptying out so as to produce a discontinuity (14–15); *daemonization*, the fourth, is a movement towards the sublime, identifying with a power just beyond the precursor's reach (15); *askesis*, the fifth, is a creative self-purging that isolates; while *apophrades*, the final ratio, designates an uncanny return of the dead, a reversal so that the poet's work appears to be a product of the precursor (15–16). Bloom then elaborates parallels between his revisionary ratios and Freudian defence mechanisms, in *A Map of Misreading* (71–74) and *Poetry and Repression* (16–20), while *Agon* re-reads Freud's theory of the drives as a dualism in which the revisionary will manifests itself (136).

---

[22] Bloom habitually quotes from memory, so readers should not be surprised to find minor discrepancies when consulting his printed sources. Although it makes only passing reference to Bloom, this modest book by John Hollander (author of "A Merrie Melody for Harold" in the present volume) is nonetheless essential for an understanding of Bloomian poetics.

[23] He does use neologisms, but 'misprision' is not one of them, being found in Spenser ("mesprize," *Faerie Queene* 2.12.19.4) and Shakespeare (Sonnet 87.11), for example. The *OED* has now granted Bloom's usage an entry: 'misprision,' *n.*¹, 2.d. Hollander notes the Shakespearean source in his introduction to *Poetics of Influence* (Introduction xl–xlii), which remains to date the only Portable Bloom: a very useful selection of articles and chapters up to the mid-1980s.

A summary is too abstract, however, and it would be wrong to imply that Bloom's theory can be detached from the reading of specific texts. His work on Milton offers an interesting example of antithetical criticism.[24] Before Bloom turned his attention to Shakespeare, as the strongest of all writers (above all in *Shakespeare: The Invention of the Human*), he took Milton to be "the central problem in any theory and history of poetic influence in English" (*Anxiety* 33). The Satan of *Paradise Lost* became an archetype of the post-Miltonic poet, defying his omnipotent precursor—God, or Milton—with a false but seductive rhetorical power (*Anxiety* 19). Bloom likes to cite Satan's claims for himself and his rebel angels as he responds to the divine threats of Abdiel, the loyally orthodox angel. These are the claims of an ephebe confronting the anxiety of influence and attempting to repress tradition:

> We know no time when we were not as now;
> Know none before us, self-begot, self-rais'd
> By our own quick'ning power....
> (Milton, *Paradise Lost* 5.859–61; see *Map* 63 and, twenty-seven years later, *Genius* 56–57)

Hell must be preferable to Heaven, because Satan can claim Hell as his, and the power of the trope is to be able to transform anything into anything else—a rhetorical falsity which, as long as Satan sustains it, becomes his truth. Satan's strength, at least until his moment of repentance at the beginning of Book 4, is that he is prepared to accept the burden of the lie. He has learnt the virtue, or vice, of tropological substitution. As Satan the theorist puts it himself,

> The mind is its own place, and in it self
> Can make a Heav'n of Hell, a Hell of Heav'n.
> What matter where, if I be still the same....
> (1.254–56; see *Anxiety* 33)

This Satan is a supreme instance of stance as poetic power, resisting the divine authority which would reduce it to silence and subservience (*Map* 37; see *Poetry* 23).

According to Bloom, such strength is also characteristic of Milton as poet (*Vessels* 82). Following suggestions by John Dryden and others, the chapter on Milton in *A Map of Misreading* argues that Edmund Spenser's

---

[24] For a more detailed and critical account, see Gregory Machacek, "Conceptions of Origins and Their Consequences: Bloom and Milton," in the present volume.

Faerie Queene is the main precursor text which *Paradise Lost* has to distance and overcome (*Map* 125–28).²⁵ To a great extent, Bloom's Milton is the Romantic Milton of Blake and Shelley (*Poetry* 23), and the Milton he presents in his earliest publications (see *Apocalypse* 38) has survived the theoretical vicissitudes of his later career more or less intact (see *Ruin* 91–92). He re-used an introduction to an edition of Milton published back in 1962 ("Introduction" *PL, PR, SA*), for example, in introductions to two anthologies of Milton criticism for Chelsea House some twenty-five years later ("Introduction" *JM*, and "Introduction" *JMPL*); similar examples could be adduced. Continuity in Bloom's work, unsurprising in so prolific a writer, points to a problem: if strength lies in *discontinuity*, as he cogently argues, criticism should perpetually re-conceive itself so as to prevent that strength from lapsing into the continuities of what he rejects as 'primary' criticism. Very few could match Bloom in either scope or energy, but is perpetual re-conception humanly possible, even for him? "Imaginative literature is otherness," as he writes in the Preface to *How to Read and Why* (19); how to live with that otherness? There is neither object nor place for antithetical criticism to describe, and no security, while the critic must somehow continue to invent and to break out of being into the otherness of becoming. Bloom's Milton criticism bears the marks of a struggle between the emergence of a critical re-description without place and the relapse into a primary language of place, presence and identity.

Strictly speaking, Bloomian strength is not the property of an agent, nor a measure of quantity. In Bloom's usage, 'strong poet' and 'poet' are almost synonymous, for he is uninterested in 'weak' poets—who idealise tradition and are consumed by it, or ironically repeat other verse while trying to write autobiography or other forms of documentation. When he writes about strength, he is discussing an *effect* which should only be identifiable, if at all, according to what has been excluded from the poem in question ("Breaking" 5); strength is an effect of reading, not a thing in itself. But his reverence for certain writers—such as Milton or Shakespeare—leads him to imply a strength which is indeed a property of the poet-as-agent. The travesty of Bloom which takes Bloomian literary history to be a wrestling match between giant (male) selves then

---

[25] John Guillory has developed Bloom's analysis in greater detail (*Poetic Authority* 130–45); he offers his book to Bloom, among others, "in partial repayment for having learned to take literature seriously" (xii). Bloom now claims that Shakespeare is "the inevitable source of influence-anxiety for Milton" ("How" xvi).

becomes at least partly understandable. He has tended to write as if Romantic reactions to what can be called the 'Milton effect' had indeed created a giant capable of freeing himself from the anxieties of influence (*Map* 37). Even if Milton now finds himself displaced by Shakespeare in Bloom's revisionism, the danger remains that a vision of an age before the flood (of anxiety) will prove to be a mere variation on T. S. Eliot's theory of the dissociation of sensibility ("Metaphysical" 287–88), and a further monumentalisation of literary history.[26] Like Nietzsche, however, Bloom teaches his readers to distrust apparent continuity between cause and effect, and so one should be cautious in approaching his own rhetoric of strength, since the effect of strength—recurrent, unforgettable, but also unstable—does not necessarily presuppose an authorial presence as its cause.

The case of Milton, then, shows an exemplary tension between theory, in which strength is a reading effect, and criticism, in which strength is the property of an agent. To say that Bloom misreads in a Bloomian way may be a simplification, but there is a reflexivity whereby his work turns back on itself, exemplifying what it explores—and this brings him close, again, to the work of Paul de Man. In 1962, the latter had written a far-sighted review of Bloom's *The Visionary Company*. De Man is sympathetic, but complains that Bloom's commentaries on the poetry of the English Romantics generally "fail to do justice to the power of the thesis," and this complaint, pointing to a disjunction between theory and criticism, is a familiar one ("New Vitalism" 92). De Man here proposes that Bloom should slow down in his readings—*The Visionary Company* covers a huge field—just as Bloom chides critics of Shelley, a few years later (*Ringers* 102). Bloom writes that he "tried to benefit" from criticisms made by his friend in preparing the revised version of his book, published in 1971 (*Visionary* vii). In Blake's terms, he remains a "Prolific," and the Prolific needs some form of "Devourer" (*The Marriage of Heaven and Hell*, plate 16); has anyone else been able to take de Man's place in this respect?

In 1973, de Man wrote a review of *The Anxiety of Influence*, collected in the second edition of his *Blindness and Insight* (267–76), which became one of the most famous book reviews in recent literary theory. He focuses initially on the problem of the writing subject in Bloom and the

---

[26] Thomas McFarland supplies a useful overview of such antediluvian visions (*Originality* 5–18). See Bloom, *Anxiety* 11, 27 and 122; "Daemonic" 479 (on Spenser); and *Ruin* 53.

naturalistic language associated with it; for de Man, such a frame of reference is a mystification which detracts from the power of the Bloomian project. De Man applauds the potentially decisive shift in critical practice marked by the emergence of the antithetical, but argues that Bloom himself has not pursued its most radical implications (*Blindness* 270-76). According to de Man, Bloom lapses into a language of desire, mastery and possession, as if literary history really were assimilable as a subsidiary of the Oedipus complex in which the son is forever trying to overcome the father. The tensions between de Man and Bloom are not to be resolved, and while the former is concerned with the aberrance and epistemological unreliability of figuration as such, the latter insists on retaining the will as an essential category of poetic meaning.[27] For de Man, Bloom's tradition is too much of "a temporal hierarchy that resembles a parental structure," as he had put it in his demystifying essay on Nietzsche and literary modernity (*Blindness* 164). Attending to the metaphoricity at stake, de Man sketches a view of influence that would include the interplay between literal and figurative in the case of individual words, instead of the inter-subjective struggle between poet and precursors—not in order to substitute the former for the latter, but to suggest a supplementary dimension of "the interplay between the various modes of error that constitute a literary text" (276). Rhetorical substitution, for both theorists, is a constitutive "error" without which literature would not exist at all. In much of Bloom's subsequent work, especially *A Map of Misreading*, published in 1975 and dedicated to de Man,[28] and the Coda to *Wallace Stevens*, published in 1977 (375-406; see Wordsworth, "An Art" 209-14), he engages in an intense if sometimes covert debate with de Man. In "The Breaking of Form" (1979), Bloom cites an aphorism by Nietzsche, as if in response to de Man's suggestion

---

[27] There have been several critical accounts of these tensions: see for instance Wordsworth, "An Art That Will Not Abandon the Self;" De Bolla 69-81; Allen, *Harold Bloom* 43-48; and, most recently, Marc Redfield, "Literature, Incorporated" 217-26 (we had hoped to include a version of Redfield's finely appreciative and comic essay, sympathetic to both Bloom and de Man, in the present volume).

[28] The new edition retains the dedication and emphasises that the book itself—which its author fondly hoped would be a "final statement" on influence—was "provoked" by his friend's "brilliant polemical review" of *Anxiety of Influence* ("How" xiii); written with de Man's "ironic strictures" in mind (xiv), the new preface goes on to give a detailed reading of Milton's *Lycidas* (xiv-xxiii), as if to show that the map is still capable of generating new revisions. I am not the only reader to wish for many more such readings (and no final statement).

about the figurative interplay of single words: "Jedes Wort ist ein Vorurtheil [*Every word is a prejudice*]" (quoting *Werke* 4.3: 215; *Human, All Too Human* 323).²⁹ Nietzsche's aphorism is headed: "*Linguistic danger to spiritual freedom.*" Then, as if to ward off the danger that such linguistic "prejudice" poses to the autonomy of the subject, Bloom offers his own revision of the aphorism: "Every word is a *clinamen*" ("Breaking" 9). That is, every word can be read as an instance of the ratio *clinamen*, whereby the poet—in a *willed* error—turns away from prior words. For de Man (and Derrida),³⁰ though, a *clinamen* cannot be mastered by a subject, opening up pathways whose swerves resist assimilation. Even if Bloom declines to take such a road, at least ostensibly (*Map* 76–77 and 93–94), it is a hallmark of antithetical criticism—making all the difference—to provoke and be provoked by other readings, other roads.

Like his Milton, Bloom is a fierce individualist, and much of the tension in his work stems from a drive to clear space between competing modes of reading. Whatever the cost—and he frequently reminds us that nothing is got for nothing—he will remain a strong critic. In the prelude to his series of lectures published as *The Breaking of the Vessels*, he offers a justification of the need for strength in writing and reading. He declares himself to be

> equally unhappy both with older and with newer modes of interpretation, equally convinced that say M. H. Abrams and Jacques Derrida alike do not aid him in reading poems as poems.
> The power I seek to gain over the text is what Milton's Satan called "quickening power," the conviction of pragmatic self-engendering. Such a power is parallel to any strong poem's power over its precursor poems. Power, in this sense, is neither the autonomous ego's location of itself in history, as in Abrams, nor the deconstructive process's demystification both of the ego and of history, as in Derrida. . . . What concerns me in a strong poem is neither self nor language but the utterance, within a tradition of uttering, of *the image or lie* of voice, where voice is neither self nor language, but rather spark . . . as opposed to self, and act made one with word . . . rather than word referring only to another word.
> (3–4; emphasis mine)

Somewhere between the restoration of the "self" and the demystification of "language," to take up this simplified spatial scheme (*Poetry* 270), Bloom defends an "image" of poetic "voice" which has an

---

²⁹ I am grateful to Peter Krapp for help locating this reference.

³⁰ Derrida has written on *clinamen*, in a somewhat different context, in "My Chances;" see John W. P. Phillips, "To Execute a Clinamen," in the present volume.

irreducible power of its own, even as that image is relentlessly exposed as a "lie." He is not a reconciler, however, and despite his extremely heterogeneous frame of reference, he does not synthesise approaches or schools of thought; the antithetical struggle itself will undo the construction of any synthesis. Stance for him does not mean standing still in order to hold together a structure, but rather carrying out an "act" which is necessarily mobile—an athletic, evasive form of stance, worthy of Pseudolus (Zero Mostel), in *A Funny Thing Happened on the Way to the Forum*, at his most frenetic. Moreover, a solemn attempt to define (and hence reify) Bloom's position would miss one of its most characteristic and subversive aspects: namely, its humour.

From its beginnings, his work has been on the attack, often with a wry or sly humour that has either been ignored altogether or taken as merely offensive. For many years, the favoured opponents of this self-styled pariah of the Anglo-American literary-critical profession were the "Moldy Figs" (Salusinszky 72), professors of literature subscribing to an antiquarian approach (Nietzsche, "Uses and Disadvantages" 72–75). More recently, the reader of Bloom has been hearing less about the mouldy figs (have they mouldered away?) and a great deal more about what he terms, again following Nietzsche, the School of Resentment.[31] Members of this so-called School—a large and diverse group, which has its primary habitat in the United States and includes some feminists, new historicists, non-Bloomian marxists, cultural materialists, deconstructionists, and others—are frequently referred to as "lemmings" (e.g. *Canon* 4 and 15; see *Wisdom* 36 and 44); why so? Bloom, who since 1971 has teased his readers on every page by not supplying the habitual pseudo-scholarly references,[32] does not explain.

The *Further Fables for Our Time* of James Thurber (1956) begin with "The Sea and the Shore" (1–3), foreshadowing the evolutionary emergence of the human as the pioneering female of a marine-bound species first ventures onto land; the male, after first having "globbed" back into the water, eventually chooses to follow her (2–3). The *Further Fables* end, in a pessimistic chiasmus, with "The Shore and the Sea," and if we try to read this fable as an allegory of misreading, we may

---

[31] Nietzsche's term is *Ressentiment*; see Deleuze, *Nietzsche* 111–46, and Barnard Turner, "Bloom and the School of Resentment: An Interrogation of the 'Preface and Prelude' to *The Western Canon*" (in the present volume).

[32] See María Rosa Menocal, "How I Learned to Write Without Footnotes," in the present volume.

better appreciate what is at stake in Bloom's enterprise. Here is the text:

> A single excited lemming started the exodus, crying, "Fire!" and running toward the sea. He may have seen the sunrise through the trees, or waked from a fiery nightmare, or struck his head against a stone, producing stars. Whatever it was, he ran and ran, and as he ran he was joined by others, a mother lemming and her young, a nightwatchlemming on his way home to bed, and assorted revelers and early risers.
> "The world is coming to an end!" they shouted, and as the hurrying hundreds turned into thousands, the reasons for their headlong flight increased by leaps and bounds and hops and skips and jumps.
> "The devil has come in a red chariot!" cried an elderly male. "The sun is his torch! The world is on fire!"
> "It's a pleasure jaunt," squeaked an elderly female.
> "A what?" she was asked.
> "A treasure hunt!" cried a wild-eyed male who had been up all night. "Full many a gem of purest ray serene the dark unfathomed caves of ocean bear."
> "It's a bear!" shouted his daughter. "Go it!" And there were those among the fleeing thousands who shouted "Goats!" and "Ghosts!" until there were *almost as many different alarms as there were fugitives*.
> One male lemming who had lived alone for many years refused to be drawn into the stampede that swept past his cave like a flood. He saw no flames in the forest, and no devil, or bear, or goat, or ghost. He had long ago decided, since he was a serious scholar, that the caves of ocean bear no gems, but only *soggy glub and great gobs of mucky gump*. And so he watched the other lemmings leap into the sea and disappear beneath the waves, some crying "We are saved!" and some crying "We are lost!" The scholarly lemming shook his head sorrowfully, tore up what he had written through the years about his species, and *started his studies all over again*. (172–74; emphases mine)

One could take the remaining "scholarly" lemming as a figure of Bloom at his darkest, an aged and tragicomic philosopher, without disciples or hope. But when asked once how he managed to write so much, Bloom replied with one word: "sleeplessness" (Salusinszky 48). He is equally, then, the "wild-eyed male who had been up all night" (reading poetry, or partying?), very much a part of the process of misreading that he aims to describe (*Further Fables* 173). He is torn between defeatedly acknowledging the cultural entropy which reduces textuality to "soggy glub and great gobs of mucky gump," on the one hand (174),[33] and

---

[33] The strongest theoretical text on textuality as "glub" is Derrida's *Glas*, probably too "soggy" and "mucky" for Bloom's tastes.

resolutely setting off on a new "treasure hunt," on the other (173), like a heroic quester who is blind to the effects of his own misprision and whose very blindness is at once salvation and loss. Bloom often worries in print that, as the burden of tradition grows exponentially larger and the hour ever later, we may reach a point at which the enrichingly repetitive strategy of Borges' Pierre Menard becomes impossible, because literary language has become "mucky gump" so literal or so figuratively overdetermined—and at this point the extremes become indistinguishable—that no-one is able to trope against it. The age of the computer, which Bloom has declined to enter (he continues to write by hand), exacerbates the problem in the sense that "great gobs" can now easily be represented as very small bytes whose memory is as total as it is threatening to a human aesthetic; as far as I know, no-one has yet figured out how to trope a byte (see Lyotard, *Inhuman* 34–35 and 112). To act and write as though it were morning becomes harder with each sunrise. Furthermore, how could one choose between the alternatives I drew from the fable, the lemming as stoic philosopher and the lemming as Tennysonian Ulysses, without participating oneself in what Spenser calls the "endlesse traine" of error (*Faerie Queene* 1.1.18.9)?

The "wild-eyed" lemming (*Further Fables* 173) is quoting from Thomas Gray's "Elegy Written in a Country Church Yard" (53–54), as his own daughter fails to recognise, neatly illustrating the dire danger posed by generational dumbing-down and the nefarious neglect of the canonical. In the next stanza of the "Elegy," Gray had speculated about the buried existence of a "mute inglorious Milton" (59).[34] This poetic lemming seems like a post-Romantic who cannot abandon the quest; or he might be what Bloom would call a Resenter, seeking to build a more socially just canon on the basis of those traditionally classified as mute or inglorious. Again, Thurber's "elderly male" with the vision of the devil's "red chariot" and the world "on fire" is a highly Bloomian and ambivalent figure (*Further Fables* 173): an apocalyptic visionary familiar not only from Bloom's work on Blake, for example, but also from his hilarious and disturbing studies of American (Gnostic) religion. Bloom, "contaminated" by the imaginative power of "the American Religion" (*American* 38), at the same time resists it for its chilling death drive: "The new irony of American history is that we fight now to make the world safe for

---

[34] For a more serious reading of Gray's "Elegy," focusing on issues of canonisation and literary culture, see Guillory, *Cultural Capital* 85–124; see also Mileur, *Literary Revisionism* 197–211.

Gnosticism" (*American* 30; this book was published in 1992). For at least fifteen years, he has warned of a coming age of theocratic dogma to which, for him, anything is preferable—even chaos (*Canon* 249; see *American* 269-71). But it is difficult, as a reader, to abide in chaos, as Bloom's own increasingly frenetic rhetoric attests.

One of the most striking aspects of Thurber's fable is its near-chaotic acceleration. From the opening misreading on the part of the "single excited lemming" (*Further Fables* 172), whose mistake lies in attempting to act as though it were morning—frenetically and fatally—when it really is morning, there is no pause until the final catastrophe. The time for reading, and the time to insist upon and expound the exclusivity of one's reading, is collapsed into an instant: the instant of panic. The lemmings merely react to one another's misreadings in a chain reaction of *ressentiment* leading inexorably to self-destruction, collective suicide. The temporality needed for antithetical reading has been more or less eliminated, as each lemming proclaims a different slogan which promptly becomes its epitaph (173). In order to stop this reduction of trope to death, the ultimate form of indifferentiation, one should in Bloomian terms trope more strongly, insisting on difference. The only effective response to *ressentiment* is strength—that is, willed error. But the question remains: in the state of chaos that is contemporary literary study according to Bloom, how can one know if one's difference is leading onto the shore, to begin a new form of life, or into the sea, the undifferentiated grave? It is in the nature of a chiasmus to be traversable in both directions. Moreover, how is a poor lemming to know whether his or her (mis-)reading is a sign of strength or merely an effect of language and thus not even 'his' or 'hers' in the first place? "Fire" may be substituted for "sunrise" along the lines of metaphorical resemblance (172), although the narrator leaves the origin of this delusion undetermined; but when a "pleasure jaunt" becomes the treasured "treasure hunt," and Gray's verb "bear," inviting exploration, becomes a real "bear," inviting flight (173), then the reader may well ask if the misreadings are produced as an expression of the poetic will to error or as an expression of the aberrant system of tropes itself. Is seeing a ghost an act of vision, visionary delusion, or rather an echo produced by the previous misreading, "Goats" (173)? What is it that the lemmings are running from, and to, and why, in this short detour to death? Thurber's mocking *sententia* or "MORAL," appended to the text of the fable and thus bringing the *Further Fables* to an end, is written out as prose but forms a regular heroic couplet, presenting the reader not with formal closure but with an ultimate ironic challenge: "*All men should strive to learn before they die what they are running from, and to, and why*" (174). Bloom's work on tropes, while it provokes us to "*strive*," makes any such learning all but impossible. The dilemma of Thurber's lemmings is not so easily localised and delimited as seemed to be the case with Bloom's academic School of Resentment. If one cannot tell the difference between trope as willed error and trope as aberrant linguistic substitution, if one cannot even tell the difference between difference and indifference, then the survival of the species—or at least the vulnerable species of the literary critic—is clearly in doubt. Is it too late, before we "*die*," for literary studies to be started "all over again" (174)?

In this tense situation, I end with another bad joke. According to Freud, jokes are essential to human survival because they offer a release, even if phantasmic, to tension which would otherwise be unbearable. The fourth chapter of his *Jokes and Their Relation to the Unconscious* (1905) ends with an important long footnote which became even longer in 1912 when he added a consideration of the following joke:

> "Life is a suspension bridge [*eine Kettenbrück'*]," said one man.—"Why is that?" asked the other.—"How should *I* know?" was the reply.
> (*Standard Edition* 8: 139 n. 1; *Studienausgabe* 4: 131 n. 1)

Strictly speaking, Freud is not sure whether the above sample (if it is a sample of something) is a joke or not.[35] Its punch line is that there is none, and the "other" man is taken in by his desire for meaning or assumption of meaningfulness. Freud seems not to be amused by the theoretical difficulty that ensues, since it has become hard to distinguish between the "casing," the formal shell of the joke which is supposed to lift inhibitions, and its binary counterpart, its "core" of original pleasure (*Standard Edition* 8: 138 n. 1). This joke "straddles [*aufsitzt*]" the unknown, to borrow Freud's term from the context of dream analysis (*Standard Edition* 5: 525, translation modified; *Studienausgabe* 2: 503; see Weber 75–78): the joke is a "take-in" or shaggy dog story, an *Aufsitzer* (*Standard Edition* 8: 139 n. 1; *Studienausgabe* 4: 131 n. 1). The category of "nonsense jokes" does indeed require what he calls "supplementary consideration" (*Standard Edition* 8: 138 n. 1), for they confuse—in their supplementarity—Freud's equally precious binary distinction between playing with words and playing with thoughts.

---

[35] According to Hill, *Soul of Wit* 173–74, this was originally a Rabbi's joke; see also Weber 111–16, and Palmer, *Taking Humour* 79–88.

After such jokes we are no longer sure which is which, and Freud cannot quite decide whether the above instance can even be classified as a nonsense joke; what is most intolerable is this suspension. The purpose of such ambiguous joke-like verbal "productions," he concludes, is aggressive, as the person who tells them derives pleasure from misleading the hearer: "The latter then damps down his annoyance by determining to tell them himself later on" (as I have just done; *Standard Edition* 8: 138–39 n. 1). To our annoyance, or amusement, Bloom's antithetical comedy of error, like Freud's, is never finished. There are no texts, but only (suspension) bridges between texts, so Bloom constructs an elaborate theory of poetic crossing. Refusing to leave the will in suspense, he attempts to transform suspense *into* will—and so on, troping into a most uncertain future. Nietzsche's Zarathustra is there already. "With the *antithetical* wisdom of Nietzsche as Zarathustra, one feels no inclination to quarrel," Bloom had written in 1970 (*Yeats* 438); over thirty years later, though, he describes Zarathustra as "a failed comedian" (*Wisdom* 208). Suspended between antithetical visions, Zarathustra declares that Man is "a rope over an abyss," and: "What is great in man is that he is a bridge [*eine Brücke*] and not a goal" (*Thus Spoke* 43–44; *Werke* 6.1: 10–11). Bloom offers no assurance that the rope-bridge will hold, even for him.

Cultural stress, for want of a better phrase, may be turning us into lemmings. Bloom, ever the kakangelist, insists on strangeness, difference, and the abyss of temporality, and has no gospel of aesthetic salvation to offer; rather like Leo Bersani, he will not subscribe to the culture of redemption (*Culture* 1–4; see Bloom, *Canon* 31). If reading is a bridge secured only by the will to error, as Bloom provokingly suggests, it will be hard to determine whether or not one is a lemming until it is already too late. This is why the aesthetic *is* now the frenetic.

Works Cited

Allen, Graham. *Harold Bloom: A Poetics of Conflict*. Modern Cultural Theorists. Hemel Hempstead: Harvester, 1994.
———. *Intertextuality*. New Critical Idiom. London: Routledge, 2000.
Bergonzi, Bernard. *Exploding English: Criticism, Theory, Culture*. Oxford: Clarendon, 1990.
Bersani, Leo. *The Culture of Redemption*. Cambridge, MA: Harvard UP, 1990.
Blake, William. *The Complete Poetry and Prose*. Ed. David V. Erdman. Commentary by Bloom. Rev. ed. Berkeley: U of California P, 1982.
Borch-Jacobsen, Mikkel. *The Freudian Subject*. Trans. Catherine Porter. Stanford: Stanford UP, 1988.
Borges, Jorge Luis. "Pierre Menard, Author of the *Quixote*." *Collected Fictions*. Trans. Andrew Hurley. New York: Viking, 1998. 88–95.
Brown, Jared. *Zero Mostel: A Biography*. New York: Atheneum, 1989.
Browning, Robert. "'Childe Roland to the Dark Tower Came.'" *Men and Women*. Vol. 5 of *The Poetical Works*. Ed. Ian Jack and Robert Inglesfield. Oxford English Texts. Oxford: Clarendon, 1995. 129–50.
Culler, Jonathan. *The Pursuit of Signs: Semiotics, Literature, Deconstruction*. Ithaca: Cornell UP, 1981.
De Bolla, Peter. *Harold Bloom: Towards Historical Rhetorics*. London: Routledge, 1988.
Deleuze, Gilles. *Nietzsche and Philosophy*. Trans. Hugh Tomlinson. European Perspectives. New York: Columbia UP, 1983.
De Man, Paul. *Blindness and Insight: Essays in the Rhetoric of Contemporary Criticism*. 2nd ed. Theory and History of Literature 7. Minneapolis: U of Minnesota P, 1983.

———. "Intentional Structure of the Romantic Image." *Romanticism and Consciousness: Essays in Criticism*. Ed. Bloom. New York: Norton, 1970. 65–77.

———. "A New Vitalism: Harold Bloom (1962)." *Critical Writings, 1953–1978*. Ed. Lindsay Waters. Theory and History of Literature 66. Minneapolis: U of Minnesota P, 1989. 90–96.

———. *The Rhetoric of Romanticism*. New York: Columbia UP, 1984.

Derrida, Jacques. "Freud and the Scene of Writing." *Writing and Difference*. Trans. and ed. Alan Bass. Chicago: U of Chicago P, 1978. 196–231.

———. *Glas*. Trans. John P. Leavey, Jr. and Richard Rand. Lincoln: U of Nebraska P, 1986.

———. "My Chances / *Mes Chances*: A Rendezvous with Some Epicurean Stereophonies." Trans. Irene Harvey and Avital Ronell. *Taking Chances: Derrida, Psychoanalysis, and Literature*. Ed. Joseph H. Smith and William Kerrigan. Psychiatry and the Humanities 7. Baltimore: Johns Hopkins UP, 1984. 1–32.

———. "Some Statements and Truisms about Neologisms, Newisms, Postisms, Parasitisms, and Other Small Seismisms." Trans. Anne Tomiche. *The States of 'Theory': History, Art, and Critical Discourse*. Ed. David Carroll. Irvine Studies in the Humanities. New York: Columbia UP, 1990. 63–94.

———. *The Truth in Painting*. Trans. Geoff Bennington and Ian McLeod. Chicago: U of Chicago P, 1987.

Eliot, T. S. "The Metaphysical Poets." *Selected Essays*. 3rd ed. London: Faber, 1951. 281–91.

Falck, Colin. *Myth, Truth and Literature: Towards a True Post-modernism*. 2nd ed. Cambridge: Cambridge UP, 1994.

Fite, David. *Harold Bloom: The Rhetoric of Romantic Vision*. Amherst: U of Massachusetts P, 1985.

Freud, Sigmund. *The Standard Edition of the Complete Psychological Works of Sigmund Freud*. Trans. and ed. James Strachey, et al. 24 vols. London: Hogarth, 1953–74.

———. *Studienausgabe*. Ed. Alexander Mitscherlich, et al. 11 vols. 1969–75. Frankfurt/M: Fischer, 1989.

A Funny Thing Happened on the Way to the Forum. Music and Lyrics by Stephen Sondheim. Book by Burt Shevelove and Larry Gelbart. New York: Burthen Music, 1964.

Godzich, Wlad. "Harold Bloom as Rhetorician." *Centrum* [Minneapolis] 6.1 (1978): 43–49.

Gray, Thomas. *The Complete Poems: English, Latin and Greek.* Ed. H. W. Starr and J. R. Hendrickson. Oxford: Clarendon, 1966.
Guillory, John. *Cultural Capital: The Problem of Literary Canon Formation.* Chicago: U of Chicago P, 1993.
——. *Poetic Authority: Spenser, Milton, and Literary History.* New York: Columbia UP, 1983.
Hegel, G. W. F. *Phenomenology of Spirit.* Trans. A. V. Miller. Ed. J. N. Findlay. Oxford: Clarendon, 1977.
Hill, Carl. *The Soul of Wit: Joke Theory from Grimm to Freud.* Modern German Culture and Literature. Lincoln: U of Nebraska P, 1993.
Hollander, John. *The Figure of Echo: A Mode of Allusion in Milton and After.* Berkeley: U of California P, 1981.
——. Introduction. *Poetics of Influence: New and Selected Criticism.* By Bloom. Ed. Hollander. New Haven: Schwab, 1988. xi–xlvi.
Kant, Immanuel. *Critique of the Power of Judgment.* Trans. Paul Guyer and Eric Matthews. Ed. Paul Guyer. Cambridge: Cambridge UP, 2000.
Lacan, Jacques. *Television: A Challenge to the Psychoanalytic Establishment.* Trans. Denis Hollier, et al. Ed. Joan Copjec. New York: Norton, 1990.
Laplanche, J. and J.-B. Pontalis. *The Language of Psycho-analysis.* Trans. Donald Nicholson-Smith. New York: Norton, 1973.
Loesberg, Jonathan. *Aestheticism and Deconstruction: Pater, Derrida, and de Man.* Princeton: Princeton UP, 1991.
Lyotard, Jean-François. *The Inhuman: Reflections on Time.* Trans. Geoffrey Bennington and Rachel Bowlby. Stanford: Stanford UP, 1991.
——. *Lessons on the Analytic of the Sublime.* Trans. Elizabeth Rottenberg. Meridian: Crossing Aesthetics. Stanford: Stanford UP, 1994.
McFarland, Thomas. *Originality and Imagination.* Baltimore: Johns Hopkins UP, 1985.
Mileur, Jean-Pierre. *Literary Revisionism and the Burden of Modernity.* Berkeley: U of California P, 1985.
Milton, John. *Complete Poetry.* Ed. John T. Shawcross. Rev. ed. Garden City, NY: Anchor-Doubleday, 1971.
Nietzsche, Friedrich. *On the Genealogy of Morals.* Trans. Walter Kaufmann and R. J. Hollingdale. Ed. Walter Kaufmann. 1967. New York: Vintage-Random House, 1989.
——. *Human, All Too Human: A Book for Free Spirits.* Trans. R. J. Hollingdale. Texts in German Philosophy. Cambridge: Cambridge UP, 1986.

———. *Thus Spoke Zarathustra: A Book for Everyone and No One*. Trans. R. J. Hollingdale. 1961. Harmondsworth: Penguin, 1969.

———. "On Truth and Lies in a Nonmoral Sense." *Philosophy and Truth: Selections from Nietzsche's Notebooks of the Early 1870s*. Trans. and ed. Daniel Breazeale. 1979. Atlantic Highlands, NJ: Humanities International, 1990. 77–97.

———. "On the Uses and Disadvantages of History for Life." *Untimely Meditations*. Trans. R. J. Hollingdale. Texts in German Philosophy. Cambridge: Cambridge UP, 1983. 57–123.

———. *Werke: Kritische Gesamtausgabe*. Ed. Giorgio Colli and Mazzino Montinari. Berlin: De Gruyter, 1967–.

O'Hara, Daniel T. *The Romance of Interpretation: Visionary Criticism from Pater to de Man*. New York: Columbia UP, 1985.

Palmer, Jerry. *Taking Humour Seriously*. London: Routledge, 1994.

Pater, Walter. *Selected Writings*. Ed. Harold Bloom. 1974. New York: Columbia UP, 1982.

Pease, Donald E. "Bloom, Harold." *The Johns Hopkins Guide to Literary Theory and Criticism*. Ed. Michael Groden, et al. 2nd ed. Baltimore: Johns Hopkins UP, 2005. 126–30.

Redfield, Marc. "Literature, Incorporated: Harold Bloom, Theory, and the Canon." *Historicizing Theory*. Ed. Peter C. Herman. Albany: SUNY P, 2004. 209–33.

Renza, Louis A. "Influence." *Critical Terms for Literary Study*. Ed. Frank Lentricchia and Thomas McLaughlin. 2nd ed. Chicago: U of Chicago P, 1995. 186–202.

Salusinszky, Imre. *Criticism in Society: Interviews with Jacques Derrida, Northrop Frye, Harold Bloom, Geoffrey Hartman, Frank Kermode, Edward Said, Barbara Johnson, Frank Lentricchia, and J. Hillis Miller*. New Accents. New York: Methuen, 1987.

Shakespeare, William. *Shakespeare's Sonnets*. Ed. Stephen Booth. New Haven: Yale UP, 1977.

Spenser, Edmund. *The Faerie Queene*. Ed. A. C. Hamilton. Longman Annotated English Poets. London: Longman, 1977.

Thurber, James. *Further Fables for Our Time*. New York: Simon and Schuster, 1956.

Weber, Samuel. *The Legend of Freud*. Minneapolis: U of Minnesota P, 1982.

Wilde, Oscar. "The Critic as Artist, with Some Remarks upon the Importance of Doing Nothing: A Dialogue." *The Artist as Critic: Critical Writings of Oscar Wilde*. Ed. Richard Ellmann. New York: Random House, 1969. 340–408.

Wordsworth, Ann. "An Art That Will Not Abandon the Self to Language: Bloom, Tennyson and the Blind World of the Wish." *Untying the Text: A Post-Structuralist Reader*. Ed. Robert Young. Boston: Routledge, 1981. 207–22.

——. "Wrestling with the Dead." *Spectator* 25 July 1970: 74.

Bloom, Kierkegaard, and the Problem of Misreading

ANDERS H. KLITGAARD

What is so remarkable about Harold Bloom is his extraordinary ambition: to give a poetic account of poetry, i.e. to read poetry as poetry, not as something else. Bloom quests for what is virtually unobtainable. How can one treat in academic discourse that which lies beyond mind and language? Simply, one cannot. Bloom, urged on by his ambition, must therefore contradict academic standards. Bloom's ambition is fierce, even by his own measure. He does attain the objective of treating poetry poetically, but, given the excruciating difficulty of this project, he does so at a price—above all, I think, at the price of some obscurity. When approaching Bloom, as when approaching poetry, we therefore must not look for logical consistency; instead we should be perceptive towards the general outlook. That Bloom's theory of poetry is itself poetic has been acknowledged very well by Peter de Bolla: "the 'theory' sets out to be what it claims it is about, to be a poetic theory of poetry, not a methodology of reading" (8).

Let me propose a radical strategy: neglecting even his stunningly lucid readings (I wish to be able to regard these as utterly mistaken, as it may be that poems are not, after all, related the way Bloom believes), I maintain that Bloom still offers a genuine, i.e. poetic, account of the nature of poetry. What I thus suggest is that Bloom's theory of poetry can be detached from its object and considered in itself. Rather than this being a sincere questioning of the value of the readings, it should be perceived as a compliment to the strength of the poetic theory itself. Bloom is aware that his theory has been charged with being somehow unfit for its object. But he demonstrates a perfect command of the Nietzschean legacy of his theory when he declines to vindicate it as true/correct and instead pragmatically responds: "whether the theory is correct or not may be irrelevant to its usefulness for practical criticism" (*Map* 10). What I here suggest, however, is even more radical: it may be that Bloom's theory is untrue, it may be useless for practical criticism, yet Bloom's theory will still give us a first-rate insight into the nature of poetry.

1) The Hermeneutical Problem

It has often been said that Bloom is a critic more difficult than most. This may well be true, namely in so far as he has yet to get a proper reception. If this is an arrogant, boastful, and untrue remark, why then let it be my *clinamen*, the trope with which I make room for myself in the discussion of Bloom. Yet now I fear I have already said too much: by using the Bloomian word 'clinamen,' I am about to become intellectually intimate with Bloom, something which must be avoided at all costs. If we are to understand anything in Bloom at all, we must maintain a safe distance, apply a certain *pathos of distance*, to use Nietzsche's phrase. The study of Bloom is thus bound up with the most intricate hermeneutical problem. Far from being a figment of the overheated intellectual imagination, this problem is very real: it stares us in the face when we consider the keyword of the Bloomian theory of poetry, viz. 'misreading.' Misreading, or misprision, is the way in which one poem relates to another (in so far as the two are related), and Bloom reads poems only within this intertextual realm. It is by way of misreading that the poet wards off his anxiety of influence, the other crucial notion to Bloom's theory of poetry. It may be objected that the notion 'anxiety of influence' is a keyword more important to Bloom than 'misreading;' the anxiety of influence, it may be said, is the more occult notion, the notion underlying, as it were, the notion of misreading. From a textual point of view, however, 'misreading' is the theory's central term. Thus we will ask, "If Bloom is all about misreading, how must we then approach him: should we read Bloom, or should we misread him?" If we simply read Bloom, it seems as if we are unable ever to grasp the notion of (strong) misreading, and we judge ourselves as weak (mis)readers; on the other hand, if we deliberately misread him, we seem to lose our object, as we cannot objectively point towards Harold Bloom if 'Harold Bloom' means merely our idiosyncratic misreading of the man. Let me add this: 'weak' and 'strong' misreadings are actually misnomers. That is, the names themselves, 'weak misreading' and 'strong misreading,' seem to imply only a difference in degree, not a difference in kind, both being essentially misreadings; and yet the former is supposed to imply a failure and the latter a success. This means all the more a difference in kind, as Bloom has a significant pragmatist bent, success/failure being of course already the very touchstone of pragmatism.

I am content to see Graham Allen give due attention to the difficulty of approaching Bloom: "The most important methodological decision I have had to take has been whether to read Bloom from a non-Bloomian perspective or in his own terms." But I am rather dissatisfied with his conclusion: "These figurations, 'inside' and 'outside,' are just that, figurative" (xi–xii). I shall argue that they are not; or rather, with Bloom's pervasive notion of trope in mind, that the figurations (inside/outside), although they may be "figurative" in the sense that they are metaphors, are not *just* figurative, if this would imply that they are somehow unreal. There is indeed an inside and an outside to Bloom. Briefly put, and paradoxically, we may say: "Only when we are outside Bloom are we inside." But not every 'outside' is an 'inside,' of course; simply being outside will not get us inside Bloom. There is indeed such a thing, such a quasi-object, as 'inside Bloom:' the question is how we get to see it, how we arrive there. Writing about Bloom in his own vocabulary, which for Allen corresponds to being 'inside' Bloom, is clearly not enough. Allen has written a wonderful scholarly book about Bloom, but I suspect this mode of writing may work against the nature of Bloom's project. If scholarly writing aims to 'tame' its object, to pin it down so as to determine its exact qualities, there is a wildness to Bloom's endeavour. Shunning the confinement and sterility of scholarly exactness, Bloom is above all a lover of freedom. And not just his own: like the poets he admires, Bloom too is a liberating god, turning his reader into a writer. An account of Bloom that does not reflect this Promethean dynamic is missing the point. And so, I shall embark upon a rather crooked journey.

2) Misreading the Misreader: An Experimental Attempt

Bloom forces the hermeneutical problem discussed above upon his reader to such an extent that there can be no reading of Bloom which has not first pondered this question and come up with a satisfactory answer. But the question is not new; it does not originate with Bloom. That is, although the concept of misreading may be wholly Bloomian, the structure of the problem is well known outside Bloom. Bloom may be very willing to acknowledge the Kabbalah as his precursor text, as indeed it may be; but maybe it is not. Why should not Bloom be vulnerable to the evasions he sees in others? Could it be that Bloom points to the Kabbalah because his true precursor is bound up with his own anxiety of influence? Consider what Bloom says of Milton:

> In conversation with John Dryden, he [Milton] once confessed rather too readily that Spenser was his "Great Original," a remark I have come to understand as a defense against Shakespeare. Shakespeare was at once the source of Milton's authentic if hidden poetic anxiety and, paradoxically, the engenderer of Milton's canonicity. (*Canon* 169)

Could it be that Bloom by pointing to the Kabbalah is trying to suppress a more dangerous precursor? By thus questioning Bloom, we are not actually misreading him in the proper sense of the word; we are just reading him against himself. We have not yet accomplished the *transcendence* onto a sphere outside Bloom necessary for a proper misreading. Let me disclose my suspicion: I think Søren Kierkegaard may be Bloom's suppressed precursor. In terms of structure, Bloom is very close to many of the key notions in Kierkegaard. This concerns not least the tropological view of language. When employing a pseudonym, Kierkegaard writes in an attempt to set the scene for a single fictitious individual (see *Concluding Unscientific Postscript* 1: 252–54). The whole enterprise, the book, the plot, the words used, are not to be taken at face-value, as their significance is relative to the gesture (trope) they make towards painting or sketching an individual. The ultimate objective for Kierkegaard is by this indirect means to initiate the reader into the Christian religion. When Kierkegaard writes in his own name, scholars disagree as to whether 'Kierkegaard' is to be regarded as a quasi-pseudonym or if this is somehow the voice of Kierkegaard himself. In any case, Kierkegaard asserts that it is paganism to demand that Truth be directly communicated. Accordingly, language has no words by which Truth can be immediately conveyed. Kierkegaard famously spoke of the "illusion" that "we are all Christians," by which he sought to refer to the fact that, according to popular opinion, his contemporary Denmark was a Christian nation. Thus Kierkegaard saw no connection between the Christian vocabulary and Christianity itself; *a fortiori*, he believed that the Danish church of his age, in the name of Christ, 'preached' the very antithesis to Christianity. The word 'Christianity' does not denote Christianity, as Christianity implies a leap of faith which lies beyond language. So when Kierkegaard employs this word, what does he mean? By postulating a gap between the message (Truth) and that which is being said (the indirect message), Kierkegaard presents his reader with no easy task. Kierkegaard has veiled himself in a blur that must be cleared up before one can make any sense of him. It may sound trivial, but with Kierkegaard it remains emphatically true that all understanding goes via interpretation. In this, Kierkegaard resembles Bloom; or vice versa, in so far as Bloom has taken after Kierkegaard. Having adopted Kierkegaard's view of language, Bloom can say that source-hunting is essentially irrelevant to literary criticism. By Bloomian lights, literary criticism is the study of influence, a phenomenon that ultimately escapes textual account, precisely because it is an intertextual phenomenon. Bloom readily acknowledges this affinity with Kierkegaard, however:

> I turn to Kierkegaard as the great theorist of the Scene of Instruction, particularly in his brilliantly polemical text, the *Philosophical Fragments* (1844). The title page of this short book asks the splendid triple question: "Is an historical point of departure possible for an eternal consciousness; how can such a point of departure have any other than a merely historical interest; is it possible to base an eternal happiness upon historical knowledge." Kierkegaard's intent is to refute Hegel by severely dividing Christianity from Idealist philosophy, but his triple question is perfectly applicable to the secular paradox of poetic incarnation and poetic influence. For the anxiety of influence stems from the ephebe's assertion of an eternal, divinating consciousness that nevertheless took its historical point of departure in an intra-textual encounter, and most crucially in the interpretative moment or act of misprision contained in that encounter. (*Kierkegaard* 1–2)

This is a remarkably truthful rendering of the parallel between the Kierkegaard of the *Philosophical Fragments* and the Bloom of *The Anxiety of Influence*. But if Bloom is here truthful, he has destroyed my point. If A is B's suppressed precursor, B will necessarily lie about his relationship to A. This, at least, is Bloom's notorious view. So how can we, when reading Bloom against himself, maintain that Kierkegaard is Bloom's suppressed precursor? The answer is rather subtle. We have congratulated Bloom on his truthful view of the Kierkegaard of the *Philosophical Fragments*, the author to whom Bloom seems to be referring, but, strictly speaking, Kierkegaard is not the author of the *Philosophical Fragments*—Johannes Climacus is. Let us for a moment forget that Johannes Climacus may be Kierkegaard's pseudonym, and instead emphasize that Kierkegaard is *not* the author of the *Philosophical Fragments*, and that

Bloom is consequently lying about his relationship to his precursor. This is far more than a simple 'slip.' Whereas, at times, it may be pardonable to confuse Kierkegaard with one of his pseudonyms, in the realm of misreading, it most certainly is not. For Kierkegaard is all about misreading, to speak Bloom's language, or the 'indirect message,' to speak Kierkegaard's own. The question is therefore: "Is the apparent fairness of Bloom's acknowledgement of Kierkegaard as the 'great theorist of the Scene of Instruction' a trope trying to conceal that Bloom's entire concept of misreading is ultimately Kierkegaardian?" If this question is perhaps guided by undue aggression rather than intelligence, I must remind the reader that we are still trying to find a way to the 'inside Bloom,' and that we are therefore still approaching Bloom in an experimental sort of way. "Will Bloom reveal himself if we turn his own virulent energy upon himself: will he perhaps be visible in a flash of self-destruction?" Such is really the hope that has guided us so far. It sounds like a self-contradiction—how could an acknowledgement ever be a way of concealing just what it explicitly states?—but this, our would-be-Bloomian approach to Bloom, does bring home once again that Bloom is not about mere words, words at face value: Bloom is concerned not with the lips but with the heart.

In *The Anxiety of Influence*, Bloom again celebrates Kierkegaard. This time "Kierkegaard" is congratulated on having given, in *Repetition*, "a grand introduction to the dialectic of misprision" (82). Again the fairness of Bloom's acknowledgement seems to make ridiculous our attempt to discredit him—but yet again we have the same 'mistake:' Constantin Constantius, the author of *Repetition*, is flatly misread as "Kierkegaard." Again, we must disregard the fact that Constantin Constantius, of course, is a Kierkegaardian pseudonym: our point is precisely that the pseudonyms must be taken at face value (to some extent), i.e. that the Kierkegaardian concept of misreading hinges on the very state of the authorship's being (partly) pseudonymous. For that reason, I do not sympathize with Bloom's reading of *Repetition*. Bloom *quotes* from *Repetition* as if it were possible to access the text in such a literal way. This is really Bloom in a sub-Bloomian vein. Bloom may here want to object that he precisely misreads the text by reading it against its intention, that if Kierkegaard, by casting himself as Constantin Constantius, intended to convey an indirect message, then he, Bloom, triumphs over the text by misreading it as conveying only a direct/literal message. This imagined objection, however, not only neglects Bloom's usual disbelief in 'literal meaning;' more seriously, it obscures what is the object of discussion. If Bloom indeed takes his concept of misreading from Kierkegaard (our experimental hypothesis), then he cannot possibly ward off father-Kierkegaard that easily, as literal meaning, if anything to do with misreading, is only weak misreading. If Bloomian misreading is a Kierkegaardian derivative, it will have to be stronger than its origin even to hope to triumph over it, let alone succeed. Weak misreading can never triumph over strong misreading.

"If Bloom's reading of Kierkegaard is unsatisfactory," it will be asked, "how should Kierkegaard then be approached?" This question should interest us as a way into Bloom. Given the assumption that Bloom has lifted his concept of misreading from Kierkegaard, Kierkegaard's concept of misreading must tell us something about Bloomian misreading. Now, first of all, it must be acknowledged that the word 'misreading' is Bloom's, not Kierkegaard's. But we are not concerned with mere words, of course, rather with thoughts and ideas. Hence, we have no difficulty in substituting the word 'misreading' for the idea of the indirect message, and vice versa, in so far as the general thought behind them is the same. "What, then," we might ask, "does the notion of the indirect message entail?" Before attempting an answer to this question, it is necessary briefly to outline the Kierkegaardian project in existential terms. Kierkegaard's essential concern was with the Christian individual. The Kierkegaardian project was to assert what Christianity was in truth, in opposition to the pseudo-Christianity of the contemporary Danish church. Kierkegaard was hoping, obviously, to save as many souls as possible—realizing, however, and emphasizing, that the world will forever be evil. There is no 'cure' for the world—it is lost. Although humans may be redeemed, they can be so only individually. Corresponding to Bloom's "triumphant solipsism," we have in Kierkegaard the Christian individual, albeit with the modification that the latter is never triumphant, never certain of his salvation, but always fearing and trembling. In terms of structure, however, in virtue of their radical solipsism, the two are rather close. For Kierkegaard, the (Kierkegaardian) text is the catalyst, between God and man, which might facilitate man's (the reader's) redemption. The text, therefore, is ultimately nothing, as a catalyst is nothing—that is, the Kierkegaardian project has an extra-literary aim, viz. the sphere of God and man. Kierkegaard, in other words, writes for the sake of a magical 'reaction,' namely the redemption of man (the reader) by God. If a reader of Kierkegaard is in the process of being redeemed while reading, or just changing in his spiritual outlook, although it might seem as if the process is fuelled by the text he is reading, in fact the process is the work of God. Again we observe the similarity between Kierkegaard and Bloom; for this process is what Bloom terms 'influence'—textual influence, we might add, as opposed to Kierkegaard's spiritual influence. Bloom will here want to object that his concept of influence is no less spiritual than is Kierkegaard's, which, actually, surprisingly, is true. I hope I shall be permitted to maintain the above distinction between textual and spiritual influence without much further discussion, the issue being so vast in its implications. Kierkegaard's text from its own perspective points beyond itself, and yet it is still a mere text, not just from the Bloomian perspective but from a 'contemporary perspective,' i.e. any perspective typical of the twentieth century and its so-called linguistic turn. This issue aside, we may further observe how Bloom's concept of influence has a malignant side to it; although it may be the sine qua non of the poet-to-be, it ultimately is "the giving that famishes the taker" (*Map* 11). On the other hand, Kierkegaard's concept of influence is wholly benign—indeed, we may say that resistance to (divine) influence invokes just the category of the demonic (in Kierkegaard's, not Bloom's, sense of the word): the opposite of influence is sin.

If in the above we have regarded Kierkegaard's authorship as a whole, we will now consider *Repetition* in particular. In opposition to Bloom's own 'literal misreading' of *Repetition*, we must now bear in mind that the text is not what it appears to be. If taken literally, *Repetition* seems to be about an existential category called 'repetition.' But it may be that the category of repetition properly so called is not even to be found within the book *Repetition*. This, in fact, is the view of the Danish Kierkegaard scholar Joakim Garff (*"Den Søvnløse"* 148-56). If, in abstract terms, the scene of instruction is best described by Kierkegaard in the *Philosophical Fragments*, there is in *Repetition* an example of its concrete application which is no less compelling. This regards the so-called "Young Man." In a letter to Constantin Constantius dated November 15, the Young Man writes this:

> If I did not have Job! It is impossible to describe all the shades of meaning and how manifold the meaning is that he has for me. I do not read him as one reads another book, with the eyes, but I lay the book, as it were, on my heart and read it with the eyes of the heart, in a *clairvoyance* interpreting the specific points in the most diverse ways. Just as the child puts his schoolbook under his pillow to make sure he has not forgotten his lesson when he wakes up in the morning, so I take the book to bed with me at

night. Every word by him is food and clothing and healing for my wretched soul. Now a word by him arouses me from my lethargy and awakens new restlessness; now it calms the sterile raging within me, stops the dreadfulness in the mute nausea of my passion . . . . At night I can have all the lights burning, the whole house illuminated. Then I stand up and read in a loud voice, almost shouting, some passage by him. Or I open my window and cry out his words into the world . . . . Although I have read the book again and again, each word remains new to me. Every time I come to it, it is born anew as something original or becomes new and original in my soul. Like an inebriate, I imbibe all the intoxication of passion little by little, until by this prolonged sipping I become almost unconscious in drunkenness. But at the same time, I hasten to it with indescribable impatience. Half a word—and my soul rushes into his thought, into his outcry; more swiftly than the sounding-line sinker seeks the bottom of the sea, more swiftly than lightning seeks the conductor does my soul glide therein and remain there. (*Repetition* 204–05)

The Young Man tries to bring about a repetition in his own life by invoking Job, who is for him the very emblem of repetition. Although approaching Job in the right manner (so to speak), he must realize that he cannot himself bring about that repetition he so desperately longs for, and that his efforts ultimately are in vain. I find it very interesting that Bloom regards Shakespeare's *King Lear* as a misreading of the Book of Job (Bloom, *King Lear* 1-3). If namely, following Kierkegaard, the Book of Job is about a repetition, and, following Bloom, *King Lear* is a misreading of the Book of Job, it seems to bestow new meaning on Edmund's essential words: "The wheel is come full circle" (5.3.175). Along these lines, one could perhaps venture to suggest that whereas Shakespeare's misreading of Job meets with success, Kierkegaard's misreading of the same proves a failure. We now regard *Repetition* as a text, a text that breaks down again and again in its failed attempt to conquer (misread) the precursor text. But we may also regard *Repetition* as 'more than a text,' that is, a text with an extra-textual ambition. Thus, we may see a point to the apparent failure of *Repetition*. We may come to understand how, on existential terms, there is something outside the realm of misreading (the realm of texts), namely existence. We will thus come to understand the Young Man's failure to bring about a repetition by reading as evidence for the supremacy of existence over texts. Existence will not be commanded by books. Here, we arrive at the Kierkegaardian challenge to Bloom and hence Bloom's possible motive for misreading Kierkegaard; that is, to do away with unwanted material in Kierkegaard. There is in Kierkegaard a piousness which is unthinkable in Bloom.

Bloom never leaves the realm of texts and for that reason remains faithful to the notion of strong misreading as the one and only measure. For Bloom, only the text itself can be given in evidence of the text. For Kierkegaard, however, an 'inferior' text can be stronger beyond comparison than a 'superior' text. Consider the following:

> As a genius, Paul cannot stand comparison with either Plato or Shakespeare; as an author of beautiful metaphors, he ranks rather low; as a stylist, he is a totally unknown name—and as a tapestry maker, well, I must say that I do not know how high he can rank in this regard. See, it is always best to turn obtuse earnestness into a jest, and then comes the earnestness, the earnestness—that Paul is an apostle. And as an apostle he again has no affinity, none whatever, with either Plato or Shakespeare or stylists or tapestry makers; they all (Plato as well as Shakespeare and tapestry maker Hansen) are without any comparison to Paul. ("Difference Between a Genius and an Apostle" 94)

Because of the extra-textual fact that "Paul is an apostle," the text itself, Paul's text, becomes incommensurably stronger than even the strongest of secular texts. This is a challenge to Bloom in so far as Kierkegaard is the precursor, that is, in so far as the ephebe must always live in terror of the precursor.

3) Dropping the Mask of Misreading

I now wish to step out of the persona I have employed in the above. In trying to drive home a point, I had to lie quite a bit, something I don't think agrees very well with my moral ego. If decadence in real life is soundness in matters of art, there is quite a significant amount of Wildean soundness in Bloom. In order to bring this to the fore, in order to *illustrate* this, I had to immerse myself in the spirit of decadence, from which followed the compulsion to lie. I thus over-emphasized the hermeneutical problem pertaining to Bloom, claiming it was impossible to access him directly; and yet Wilde is the high road to Bloom. The Wildean doctrine that "Life imitates art far more than art imitates life," Bloom follows slavishly. This is Wilde: "Schopenhauer has analysed the pessimism that characterises modern thought, but Hamlet invented it. The world has become sad because a puppet was once melancholy" ("The Decay of Lying" 35). And this is Bloom: "I sometimes suspect that we really do not listen to one another because Shakespeare's friends and lovers never quite hear what the other is saying, which is part of the ironical truth that Shakespeare largely invented us" (Preface, *Anxiety* xiii). Bloom's faithfulness to Wilde is uncanny. It may be that the concept of misreading owes so much to Wilde that Wilde himself cannot be misread. Clearly, Wilde is a much more straightforward way to Bloom than is Kierkegaard, although the latter does in fact have a close affinity with Bloom. As a way into Bloom, I favoured Kierkegaard over Wilde *simply because that was the more unreasonable thing to do*, thus trying to emulate Bloom's poetic formula, the anti-natural quest for "an impossible object" (*Anxiety* 10). As Blake said, crooked roads are preferable to straight ones. Alas, the reader may feel that I have by now lost all credibility. But by admitting to having lied for the sake of the argument, I do not wish to take back what I have written as much as qualify it, i.e. guide or modify the reader's reading in retrospect. What I hope to have accomplished may be regarded as a mighty trope, one large gesture. That is, my words above aim to do, rather than to say, something. Thus, I have tried to account for what I take to be Bloom's way of employing language, or, at any rate, what ought to be his way of employing language, viz. what his theory of poetry entails—or, still more accurately perhaps, taking into account Bloom's radical solipsism (thus acknowledging that Bloom is ultimately completely inaccessible): what I have tried to account for is what I, *upon my (mis)reading*, take to be 'the Bloomian theory of misreading.'

Or maybe I didn't lie! It is possible that I, forced by the argument (which is really a trope), have confessed to sins I have never committed. Although claiming to have shed the mask of misreading, I may have still been under a strain to perform, and so have put on another mask. It is conceivable that a false confession was proclaimed just to cause a chilling sensation in the reader, a fearful taking-back not unlike what Bloom calls *apophrades*. But if I lied when I said I was lying, does the reader then trust me now? It is Bloom's ambition as a critic to attain the poetic stance, which to him ranks far above any scholarly mode of writing. Following Wilde, he equates poetry with lying. One will therefore not arrive 'inside Bloom' before one has ceased being natural and assumed a pose that is wilfully perverse. When engaging with Bloom's work, one needs, I submit, to abandon the epistemological mode of writing for a performative stance; otherwise, one will not match Bloom's tropological view of language. Or rather, as the epistemological mode of writing, admittedly, can be tropologically strong, one must realize that epistemology is not a safe haven: if one's work does not mark a strong tropological stance, it will fail. Bloom's challenge to academic standards is thus to propose something more demanding than epistemology, a measure that calls on our creative energies no less than our cognitive powers. Let us consider an instance of excellent scholarship which nevertheless does not meet the Bloomian criterion for success, which is a usurpation of the precursor text. With *"Den Søvnløse,"* Joakim Garff has produced a reading of Kierkegaard that is very knowledgeable and very clever. Written in a playful language for an academic audience, it precedes his wonderful and more popular biography of Kierkegaard (*Søren Kierkegaard*). Although one must congratulate *"Den Søvnløse"* on its uniqueness and eloquence, it nevertheless fails by Bloomian lights. One is reminded of what Bloom says of Wilde's "The Ballad of Reading Gaol" (*Anxiety* 6): every lustre it exhibits is reflected from the precursor—in Garff's case, from Kierkegaard. Garff's ambition is to read Kierkegaard on his own terms, so as to account for the authorship's contradictions from within (*"Den Søvnløse"* 11). This sensible methodology Garff identifies as deconstruction, and so it is easily seen that the Bloomian critical mode is radically more demanding than its deconstructive alternative. What is success by deconstructive standards is failure by Bloomian standards. Academic scholarship will find itself at ease within the school of deconstruction, whereas Bloom will dismantle every effort that has not accomplished something impossible.

Works Cited

Allen, Graham. *Harold Bloom: A Poetics of Conflict.* New York: Harvester-Wheatsheaf, 1994.
De Bolla, Peter. *Harold Bloom: Towards Historical Rhetorics.* London: Routledge, 1988.
Garff, Joakim. *"Den Søvnløse:" Kierkegaard læst æstetisk/biografisk.* Copenhagen: C. A. Reitzel, 1995. (Summary in English.)
——. *Søren Kierkegaard: A Biography.* Trans. Bruce H. Kirmmse. Princeton: Princeton UP, 2005.
Kierkegaard, Søren. *Concluding Unscientific Postscript to Philosophical Fragments.* Trans. and ed. Howard V. Hong and Edna H. Hong. Kierkegaard's Writings 12. Princeton: Princeton UP, 1992.
——. "The Difference Between a Genius and an Apostle." *Without Authority.* Trans. and ed. Howard V. Hong and Edna H. Hong. Kierkegaard's Writings 18. Princeton: Princeton UP, 1997. 91–108.
——. *Philosophical Fragments, or A Fragment of Philosophy.* Trans. and ed. Howard V. Hong and Edna H. Hong. Kierkegaard's Writings 7. Princeton: Princeton UP, 1985. 1–111.
——. *Repetition: A Venture in Experimenting Psychology.* Trans. and ed. Howard V. Hong and Edna H. Hong. Kierkegaard's Writings 6. Princeton: Princeton UP, 1983. 125–231.
Shakespeare, William. *The Tragedy of King Lear. The Riverside Shakespeare.* Boston: Houghton Mifflin, 1974. 1255–95.
Wilde, Oscar. "The Decay of Lying." *Intentions and the Soul of Man.* London: Dawsons of Pall Mall, 1969.

Placing the Jar Properly: The Religious and the Secular in the Criticism of Harold Bloom

NICHOLAS BIRNS

1) To Forsake the Sublime

Harold Bloom is often seen as a religious critic. Yet he is not often associated with traditional or "mainstream" religious faiths. More often, he is seen as a wayward rebel, chanting arcane slogans that certainly possess a religious fervor but seem to lack a religious structure. Lately, conservatives who agree with his defense of the canon have been prepared to ignore his distinctive take of religiosity, but this does nothing to come to grips with its existence. I would like to argue that Bloom's work has, as it were, a less "sublime" and more "picturesque" aspect, and that this latter self-restraining tendency can in many ways operate as a corrective to the more rambunctious aspects of his work.

Although Geoffrey Hartman is known as the great Wordsworthian of his critical generation, Harold Bloom's Wordsworth is at least as worthy of interest. Hartman's Wordsworth seems, for all its disavowal of "mere" nature, to endow the imagination with all the mystified qualities of "nature" and then, by seemingly preferring the binding of *akedah* ("binding," from the story of Abraham and Isaac) to the fulfillment of apocalypse, to value a characteristically "natural" in definition as well. Bloom's Wordsworth, on the other hand, is clear-sighted and emotional without being mantic, or sage-like. Yet Hartman is famous above all for his Wordsworth criticism, whereas Bloom, as a close reader, is thought of as a Shelleyan, a Stevensian, certainly seldom a Wordsworthian.

Consider, though, *The Visionary Company*, an astonishingly rich book that is at once a primer on the major Romantic poets and a deeply philosophical consideration of poets who had previously deserved such consideration but had seldom received it. When *The Visionary Company* was published in 1961, Bloom had already produced, two years earlier, a whole book on Shelley, containing more in-depth readings than those available in the later omnibus volume. In 1963, he was to publish *Blake's Apocalypse*, thus explaining the relatively restrained length and nature of the commentary on Blake in the longer book. Bloom admits, in the course of the book on Romanticism (272), that he is not a Byronist. Keats has, at the time of the book's composition, just received (or endured) his great period of New Critical hagiography, and someone in Bloom's polemical position in 1961 was never going to concentrate on Keats, whatever his obvious individual regard for this poet. This leaves Coleridge, and indeed Bloom's commentary on Coleridge in *The Visionary Company* is significant, particularly in its discussion of later Coleridge poems such as "Limbo" and "Ne Plus Ultra," poems which Bloom was the first critic to take seriously. But it is to be strongly doubted whether Coleridge, as poet, can ever be the central figure in a narrative of Romantic poetry, simply because of the relative smallness of his oeuvre compared to the other major poets.

So it is Wordsworth who dominates Bloom's first indisputably great work of criticism, *The Visionary Company*. And Bloom's line on Wordsworth is a rather surprising one. There is little hailing of the poet's natural supernaturalism, little praise of any turn from mimesis to expression. Indeed, Bloom's tone with regard to Wordsworth is as close to the thought of his arch-classicist graduate school teacher, William Wimsatt, as it is to that of his arch-romantic undergraduate instructor, M. H. Abrams. Bloom lucidly expresses this in a key paragraph of *Ruin the Sacred Truths* when he speaks of "sublime poets who are crucially humanistic in some aspects," among whose number is Wordsworth, who must "forsake the sublime when they foreground humanistic concerns" (117). Bloom here does not unequivocally hail the sublime, eventually calling for a less hyperbolic rhetoric that, among other things, is "de-idealizing or antithetical" (120). Bloom goes on to stress the Enlightenment connections of Romanticism, saying that Enlightenment reductions of transcendence into the sentimental (121) paved the way for the overt emotionalism of poets like Wordsworth. This process was first visible in the eighteenth-century poets of sensibility, who Bloom hails as "reconciling" (122) the sublime with milder forms of emotion. This is, notably, not just an account of poets such as Cowper and Gray as "preromantics;" it recognizes that the eighteenth century, so often seen, especially by pro-Romantic critics, as filled with soulless, formalistic classicism, had an emotional tenor of its own, one which if eschewing the sublime (the more conscious gesture of "forsaking" should probably be reserved for Wordsworth) does so perhaps in order to arrive at a more complex affective stance. This great respect for the later eighteenth century surfaces again and again in Bloom's oeuvre. It is not without relevance that Bloom studied with Frederick Pottle, the preeminent twentieth-century Boswell scholar, and that the best of the many prefaces Bloom wrote in the 1980s for the Chelsea House series of literary criticism is the one on Pope. Bloom, whom Imre Salusinszky calls a "fierce proponent of Romanticism" (Salusinszky 46) never lets this partisanship overtake his aesthetic respect for any writer of accomplishment, whatever their stance.

But surely this is only a development of the later, more public Bloom. Is not the Bloom of *The Visionary Company* the wild-eyed Romantic sage that is so often depicted? A look at the earlier book, though, supplies a surprising sense of continuity on Bloom's part. Near the beginning of the first chapter of the original 1961 edition of *The Visionary Company*, Bloom insists that the "fluid dissolving of the imagination" (8) associated with Romanticism did not originate with the canonical Romantics themselves, but that "its presence in Collins is crucial." The subsequent extended analysis of Collins's "Ode on the Poetical Character" establishes a continuity between Collins and the later "Romantics," even though Collins is seen as reacting more sharply against Pope (11) than the later Bloom of the 1986 Chelsea House introduction might have it. Bloom's treatment of the genesis of Romanticism and Classicism, which given the "visionary" title of the book and the author's known intentions to resurrect Romantic poetry might be expected to lean melodramatically towards Romanticism, is in fact far more measured. The classic-romantic distinction, as deployed diachronically, is one of the primal dramas of literary history; certainly critics from the 1940s historians of ideas such as A. O. Lovejoy to Paul de Man, with his virtual identification of modernity with the Romantic turn, have enacted it this way. Bloom characteristically sidesteps this drama. Even more explicit is the 1970 introductory essay to the book, "Prometheus Rising," in which Bloom points out, in a gesture that would not be jarring in a late-1980s historicist excursus on the Romantic ideology, that the poets we today term Romantic were not especially inclined to use that term of themselves. Bloom's vision of Romanticism is, in a way, so powerful that it does not even need the period-term "Romanticism" to anchor it, as it is more a mode of thought than a phase of literary history. Nor does this mode of thought need to melodramatically set itself off from Classicism; Bloom's attack on the "classical or Catholic temperament" (xxi) which advocates "the whole neoclassical line" (in fact, most of the English neoclassicists, as Anglicans, were no more Roman Catholic than is Bloom himself) is leavened by an appreciation of "the strength and even the glory" of figures such as Dryden or Johnson. Giving classicism its due, Bloom does not need to go into anxious dithyrambs over Romanticism, and thus his presentations of the Romantic poets can show them as possessing, in unexpected places, classical virtues.

Wordsworth is the poet most responsible for making the decisive break with the past that constitutes the Romantic moment; yet he is also, with the exception of Byron, the Romantic who retains most vestiges of eighteenth-century diction and outlook. Even before he has formally devised his theories of influence, Bloom evokes Wordsworth's literary-historical as well as philosophical complexity. Unlike Rousseau, Bloom's Wordsworth is not one for "simplistic dissension" (127) from Christian traditions in favor of either extreme individualism or ecstatic communalism; his vision of a state where internal and external will be "exquisitely fitted" (127) emerges, in Bloom's rendition, as intersubjective and metadiscursive, providing a sufficiently complex intellectual frame for a "celebration of the possibilities inherent in our condition, here and now" (128).

Bloom's analysis of the Immortality Ode is at the heart of his vision of Wordsworth. One of Bloom's achievements here is to present a reading of the poem which is faithful to what most readers will infer as its spirit, yet which does not assume any inherent quality of being "Wordsworthian" in either poem or analysis. So often a pre-constructed, stereotypical idea of what "the poet," as "signature," stands for interferes with the actual reading of the poem. Throughout *The Visionary Company*, Bloom is championing the latter over the former, but and no more splendidly than in his discussion of Wordsworth's "Great Ode" (170). Bypassing the "much-studied imagery" (173) of the poem, Bloom argues that, for all that the poem presents such easily apprehensible objects, Wordsworth at key moments makes the gesture of "forsaking the image" (172) and placing his poetic trust in an argument sufficiently complex to carry this sort of artistic weight. Bloom quotes the poem's climactic stanza, where "our souls have sight of that immortal sea" and thus can mentally travel back to a plenitude of spiritual joy, "And see the children sporting on the shore / And hear the mighty waters rolling evermore" (177). He comments:

> The intimation of immortality from recollections of early childhood in the poem is the sight of these children, for to be able to travel back to their shore is to intimate one's fusion with them. It is never to die, because once we did not know death, and we can find our way back to our not-knowing. The immortal sea is what laps around every side of our separateness. (177)

This passage, retaining and drawing upon Wordsworth's own eloquence, underscores the poem's simultaneous apprehension of both sublimity and limitation. Wordsworth promises only an intimation, not the full reality of fusion. While part of him concedes that such a return to not-knowing is inevitably fictive, an equal part of him maintains that, as emotional reality, it is ultimate reality. The immortal sea laps around our individuality, engulfing and perhaps redeeming it, but it does not overwhelm the individuality, which remains. Bloom's Wordsworth once again is involved in forsaking, not just the image, but the sublime itself. Forsaking the sublime is, of course, not the same as refraining from it or never knowing it. Such a fervent affirmation of the soul's immortality surely calls on the idea of the sublime, but Wordsworth opts for a kind of regular access to plenitude rather than a one-time sublime evocation of it. This forsaking of the sublime could be compared to the role *akedah* plays in Hartman's Wordsworth. Yet a secular *akedah* does not really forsake anything; by binding, it constricts, but what it binds and harnesses is a reservoir of potential sublimity. To forsake the sublime, to truly forsake it, is less a corollary of Hartman's than of Bloom's vision, which can take individual entities and the immortal sea of unity and hold them both in the surety of one gesture.

Bloom's vision of creativity is often seen as a Romantic challenge to traditional authority, and there is much in his rhetoric to help this view along. But Bloom's respect for Wordsworth and his eighteenth-century predecessors shows that he is as much a traditionalist as any sort of Romantic rebel. Indeed, his analysis of Wordsworth undermines the ideal of secular autonomy often associated with Romanticism.

2) Placing the Jar Properly

Bloom's surprising opposition to aesthetic complacency reaches its most subtle form in the reading of Stevens's "Anecdote of the Jar" that closes *Kabbalah and Criticism*. Although John Hollander, among others, has singled out this reading as one of Bloom's most "brilliant" (Hollander, xxvii), it has often been ignored because of the relative obscurity of its placement in a book ostensibly about the Kabbalah, where few of Bloom's readers looking for his views on Stevens or even on the reading of poetry as such will begin their research. In the well-known poem, the speaker places the jar on a hill "in Tennessee" and "the wilderness rose up to it, / And sprawled around no longer wild." The jar changes the landscape irrevocably: "It took dominion everywhere / The jar was gray and bare / It did not give of bird or bush / Like nothing else in Tennessee" (Stevens 46). Bloom begins his analysis by stating that "Anecdote of the Jar" is at once a "strong poem" but also is "only a part of a mutilated whole" (*Kabbalah* 110). This kind of fructifying contradiction is a hallmark of Bloom's reading of the poem, here radically and instantly applied to the quality for which Stevens's poem is routinely applauded, the making of a given place into an aesthetically ordered dominion:

> Stevens's opening joke is purely antithetical: I placed a jar, not on a hill in Tennessee, but in Tennessee, as though the whole state had reified into a single separate entity or substance. Tennessee is now a single hill and not a slovenly wilderness, but because of the self-insistence of a single poetical jar Tennessee gets organized, firmed up, and so the wilderness rises up, still sprawling, but tamed. (110)

What is striking about this analysis, even before its content is approached, is how concrete it appears, how immediate is its engagement with issues of, for lack of a better phrase, raw interpretation. It is easy to assume Bloom is a more abstract critic than he is, and this mistake is made by Frank Lentricchia's provocative piece on Stevens in his 1987 book *Ariel and the Police*, a reading followed up in an abridged form in his 1994 work *Modernist Quartet*. Lentricchia's reading of "Anecdote of the Jar" deftly positions itself as the historicist corrective to Bloom's, even as Lentricchia is certainly aware that this critical swerve brings him squarely within the lineaments of a Bloomian agon. Although Lentricchia pointedly does not mention Bloom in his analysis of this particular poem, Bloom is cited extensively elsewhere in *Ariel and the Police* and is demonstrably Lentricchia's chosen "precursor" as a Stevens critic. Basing his argument on a mention of the poem by the Vietnam War writer Michael Herr, Lentricchia sees the jar's dominion over the wilderness as an allegory of a kind of Manifest Destiny, an "imaginative imperialism" (Lentricchia, *Modernist* 23) that mirrors American political expansion. Not only does Lentricchia cite Vietnam as an instance of the rationalistic, controlling nexus precipitated by the jar-as-America; he uses the "Tennessee" referent to remind the reader that Tennessee, a state with a name that is "an englishing of a Cherokee place name" (Lentricchia, *Ariel* 16), was originally inhabited by the Cherokees and other native peoples, who were expelled in order to pave the way for Enlightenment myths of progress and civilization represented, in his view, by the jar's ordering power over the wilderness and its "spirit of abstraction" (Lentricchia, *Ariel* 17). This reading is compelling, but there are problems, especially in the Native American example, with Lentricchia's reading of "Tennessee." He is assuming that it is the early history of Tennessee, a hundred years or so before Stevens wrote the poem in 1919, that registers in the poem. While striving for political sensitivity in its respect for Native American peoples, Lentricchia's analysis implies that Tennessee can register as a referent only when its history is colorful, only when it involves explicitly subordinated peoples or events, such as the removal of the Indians, that appear on the historical scale in an epic manner. Lentricchia can apparently only imagine Tennessee when associated with political turbulence, as a marginal, not-yet-assimilated place. Bloom, on the other hand, follows what must be assumed to be the practical intentions of Stevens when he sees Tennessee as simply, "merely" a part of the United States. So it was in 1919, when Tennessee was in as sedate a state, in political terms, as ever, and its citizens were engaged merely in living, as they lived. Given that Bloom went on in *The American Religion* to extensively discuss the Cane Ridge revival meeting in Kentucky (*American* 59-64) he must be assumed to be at least as in touch as Lentricchia with trans-Appalachian developments. "Dominion" and "wilderness," the key terms in any "territorial" reading of the poem (cf. Lentricchia, *Ariel* 16), are to be found elsewhere than in this poem in the early Stevens, for instance in "Sunday Morning," a poem far more about the lack of sanctioned spirituality in the American landscape than the American push to map, order, and arrange the experiential landscapes of others.

Tennessee is not a specific or serious referent, as Lentricchia wants it to be. It is a "joke" as Bloom says; it is a constant and stable referent because it is not serious, whereas a serious referent ("I placed a jar in Vietnam"), culturally and historically inflected in a really consequential way, would muddle the parable of form and matter which all the poem's critics agree it is, though the interpretations of most have been far simpler than Bloom's. Tennessee is part of the United States; it does not evoke some fascinating political margin or incendiary case of cultural subordination, and it is, for better or worse, basically a generic referent. Not to say that any state will do; having mountains is probably a prerequisite (to evoke the sublime, yes, but also to allow the option to forsake it). Certainly the affect of placing a jar upon a plain would, in aesthetic as well as topographical terms, be quite different. A more fertile landscape would hold out the hope, or at least the horizon, of the possibility of fullness. But with an avatar of form in Stevens's poem which can, as a jar, be both full and empty in itself, the hill's environment does not promise a nourishing fertility. With an air of elegiac disappointment as much as gloating triumph, it can bestow both fullness and emptiness on the mountainous landscape:

> The jar remains antithetical, and everything else in Tennessee abides in the state of nature, and the poem begins to look like a trope for pathos, a synecdoche for desire .... it follows rather faithfully the great Wordsworthian crisis-poem model, though it takes a pretty cheerful attitude towards what it insouciantly regards as a merely technical crisis, that is to say, somebody else's crisis all right, but not mine. The poem becomes rather like someone whistling a chorus of "the bells of hell go ting-a-ling-a-ling / For you but not for me," but the poem remains dialectical enough to break off without going on to: "O death where is thy sting-a-ling-a-ling, / O grave thy victory?" Stevens's anecdote isn't a triumph, it is just an anecdote, and its metaleptic conclusion introjects an antithetical future only by reminding us that all in the past is projected, and by forcing us to see that there is no present tense in the poem at all, and indeed no presence, no fullness of meaning whatsoever. The poet is a fellow who went about placing jars. If you placed the jar properly, you achieved a certain perspective. Your placing, however well you did it, was necessarily a failed metaphor, because all a metaphor does is change a perspective, so that the phrase "a failed metaphor" becomes a tautology. A jar may be a unity, and you can do with Tennessee what you will, but as soon as you troped your jar you mutilated it, and it took dominion only by self-reduction from fullness to emptiness. (*Kabbalah* 110–11)

The fact that the poem, rather than being a triumph, is just an anecdote, should be the decisive rejoinder to anyone who sees Bloom as an enthusiast for art and art alone. Whereas Lentricchia needs to ground the poem in order to yield a political truth, Bloom does not even permit the far milder intoxicant of an aesthetic complacency, a satisfaction in how wonderful form is and how triumphantly a poem can impose itself on reality. In placing the jar, the poet does not gain some grandiose power of creation, but merely the satisfaction of placing the jar properly in order to gain a new perspective, one which might be different from that which was there before the jar was placed. The poet should not expect to be getting anything substantive out of composing a poem aside from the creative gesture itself. The reader should not expect to be getting anything substantive or palpable out of reading either. Reading is not a sacerdotal process, nor an extraction of natural resources of the text. It is instead a kind of game, a serious game, one with real emotional consequences, not a ludic gambol at all, but also not a solemn exercise to be justified in terms of some over-riding cultural importance.

Bloom is arguing here against a very received tradition of reading this poem and allegories of art and nature in general, a tradition best addressed under the umbrella of hylomorphism. "Hylomorphoism" is, of course, most familiar as a term from Aristotle. Aristotle uses it to talk about form and matter in the physical world, but of course the term easily lends itself to adaptation in the literary sphere. The word signifies a coming-together, or at least a parallelism, of matter and form. In a literary context, the relationship between these two terms has never been an easy one. In the literature classroom, there exists an almost inherent bias in favor of form; after all, form, in the vernacular use of the term, is why almost everybody is there. Whatever talk of "cultural materialism" may have flourished in the academies recently, the common-sense assumption about literary analysis is that form exists in order to triumph over matter, to surpass and quell its unruly energies, and that a work of art (especially one, like Stevens's poem, that is seen as a paradigm of the artistic process itself, and thus a form of forms) takes a preexisting idea of form and uses it to shape and mold matter, and that the more successful this process the more successful the work of art. How many times has a blurb or a book review said, "X has taken the terrible sufferings of the poor and shaped them into a numinous work of art" or some such. The hylomorphic problem, i.e. this over-confident view of the powers of form, has been persistent; political movements come and go, empires fall, but the hylomorphic problem remains with us. As previously implied, it is particularly a problem with Stevens, with the perennial curse of weak readings of poems such as "The Idea of Order at Key West" where he is alleged to have engendered "order out of chaos."

This formulation, so dear to the freshman-seminar room, is injurious to Stevens's poetry. It grasps the sense of discontinuity that H. W. Fawkner indicates when he says, "Surpassing is not born in the world. Transcendence is not born in nature" (Fawkner 54). But in imposing this realization of the non-natural origin of transcendence on order and chaos as terms, or form and matter to use the Aristotelian vocabulary, the traditional reading of "Anecdote of the Jar" is at once far too reductive in thematic terms and far too idealizing in aesthetic ones. If transcendence and surpassing are not in nature, that does not mean the natural objects such as a bush do not already have forms of their own, even if the jar, as a metonym for aesthetic order, imposes new ones upon them. As Norma Emerton puts it when discussing "crystalline" form[1]: "the matter in a body is always infused by a form" (Emerton 49). It is just changed in nature, as bird or bush, in Aristotelian terms, would possess form "as a structuring of matter" (Emerton), in being phenomenologically coherent in themselves and in being apprehensible to perception. Imposing form on matter inevitably alters the nature of the matter, because in both cases matter is already mixed with form.

Thus Bloom's jar-placer does not bring aesthetic deliverance, but merely a change in perspective, even if that change is rare and beautiful. It is not simply the idea of imposing form on matter in order to anoint matter with a formal crown. This sort of lacquering of the datum, varnishing of the empirical, does not take into account the limits of poetry's power and the sacrifice any artist must make when working, as most artists do, with any kind of material base; thus Bloom's elegiac recognition of the reduction of fullness to emptiness taking place in the same moment as the jar's seemingly dominant possessing of the landscape. Bloom's exegesis of Stevens suggests that an imposition of form may in fact involve a kind of decomposition or draining-out of matter. Whatever is gained by the kind of formal poetic seal troped by the jar will be lost (or, in Bloom's terms, "mutilated"), there or elsewhere. This is a recognition that, because the gains of art are never without cost, any kind of triumphal relaxation in their benefits is ultimately a violation of the integrity of the sacrifice the poet (or, more truly, the jar-placer) has made. Though Bloom does not sell short the power attendant upon the aesthetic gesture, he divests it of any overriding authority. It cannot, as in the hylomorphic scenario, simply confer form upon a dormant matter, or decisively have its own way with a compliant material base. The form of the jar is altered by its encounter with the matter of Tennessee; if it gains dominion, it expends its phenomenological

---

[1] As opposed, that is, to "organic" form. Bloom and most other critics would surely see "crystalline" as the preferable term, given its inevitable Paterian associations and its appositeness when speaking of the variety of form possessed, and bestowed, by the jar.

"fullness" in the process. What it cannot sustain is a self-sufficient, secular mastery over the world as it is. If "placing the jar properly" is the key phrase in Bloom's analysis, the matter-of-fact quality of the phrase does not connote any expediency. Bloom's abandonment of the hylomorphic dyad enables him to read the poem in aesthetic terms: the placing of the jar, nothing in itself (to borrow a Stevensesque locution) is everything in its effects, everything in how it remakes perception of its environment, and after all perception is what aesthetics, basically conceived, are all about.

Surprisingly, there is little overt talk here of "agon" or "influence." Perhaps these ideas, so crucial to the "brand name" of Bloom's criticism, are less central to its excellence than we might assume, or maybe they are only premises and not conclusions. The true sequel to Bloom's excursus on "Anecdote of the Jar" is to come not elsewhere in the influence tetralogy but in a far less arcane work fifteen years later. In the passage just considered, Bloom evokes the power of lateness to change the landscape in which its force appears—with the corollary awareness that the belated gesture has no inherent power in itself. To put it simply, mankind can produce beautiful art, but human creativity is not, in itself, self-sufficient. The failure of a self-sufficient secularism inevitably leads to the subject of religion, and it is religion that decisively comes into play in Bloom's most vivid engagement with the question of authorship, *The Book of J*.

3) The Curtailed Kingdom

The Book of J seems one of the most "primary" of Harold Bloom's works. Not only was it, at the time of its 1990 publication, by far his best-selling book and thus of a more primary appeal to a broad audience, but in it he speaks of a "universal author" (17). This seems at first like a transference of the authority of the Bible as a holy book to the supposed avatar of the single author, who will not just be responsible for authorship but for literary authority as well. To have this authority, she, in this case, must be a fount of the primary, a member of "the small group of Western authors we identify with the Sublime, with literary greatness as such" (316).

There are indeed places in *The Book of J* where Bloom emphasizes a primary authority, even if energized by a strong, revisionary impulse. Bloom argues that the Exodus occurs "somewhat earlier" (242) than the

1220 B.C. date he accurately says is most commonly assigned, although Bernhard W. Anderson, in *Understanding the Old Testament*, a reliable work that is actually cited by Bloom in *The Book of J*, goes back as far as 1280 B.C. for the probable date of the Exodus (Anderson 52). "Somewhat earlier" presumably goes further back even than this, towards a mid-fifteenth century date. This early dating, though gaining the authority of antiquity, risks losing the perspective of lateness, of metaleptic reversal.

Bloom's analysis of the Bible, however, destabilizes authority as much as it reaffirms it. Bloom gives a crucial indication of this in the first pages of his commentary. He states that Gerhard von Rad, one of his favorites among traditional Biblical scholars, placed the J-writer in "what von Rad memorably dubbed the Solomonic Enlightenment" (17). So we have the J-writer, considered not only by Bloom but by most scholars who have accepted the post-Enlightenment documentary hypothesis to be the greatest of the Biblical writers, placed in the same temporal milieu as Solomon, in political if not moral terms one of the greatest of the ancient Hebrew monarchs, the man who constructed the Temple and whose wisdom and wealth are a byword among Jews, Christians, and Muslims. In other words, we have J's literary greatness side-by-side with Solomon's political greatness. What more natural, we should think, that in a great national era for the Biblical kingdom a great writer (or, since Bloom pairs the J-writer throughout with the author of 2 Samuel, writers) should be produced?

Bloom, though, takes the daring step of placing the J-writer one generation later than does von Rad, in the reign of Solomon's son Rehoboam. As Bloom puts it, when "Rehoboam succeeded his dead father... the Davidic kingdom fell apart" (36). The arrogance ("I will chastise you with scorpions," 1 Kings 12.2) and incompetence of the younger king "marred and even destroyed forever" (38) the heritage fostered by his forebears. Thus the J-writer's work is not an unfolding of Solomonic glory, but an "ironic epilogue" (39) to that glory. This is distracting to those who unthinkingly accept the model, outlined above, that great writers flourish in the eras dominated by prodigious statesmen; so Shakespeare, Bloom's aesthetic compass throughout the Book of J, is always associated with Elizabethan England even though his work hardly fell off under Elizabeth's less glamorous successor. But it is an authoritarian need to want the great writer to also be in the reign of the great politician. Many modern-day fashionings of precious cultures display this need, e.g. "Periclean Athens" and "the Florence of Lorenzo de Medici," where in each case the artists, poets, architects, playwrights of the period far outshone anything accomplished in the political realm, but where some sort of sociological imprimatur is evidently needed for modernity to truly see these past eras as "great."

Bloom, à la von Rad, could easily have come up with the counterpart to these visions of a Solomonic Jerusalem, but he refrains from doing so. As Bloom says, "This J is my fiction . . . but then each of us carries about a Shakespeare or a Tolstoy or a Freud who is our fiction also. As we read any literary work, we necessarily create a fiction or metaphor of its author" (19). And with the Old Testament, when we have no exact notion of when any of it was written, there is also an added possibility of creating a fiction of when, in the most literal chronological terms, the author was writing. In his avowedly quasi-fictive scenario, Bloom can pretty much put the J-writer wherever he wants. Bloom is willing to have the J-writer flourish in the realm of the legacy-squandering Rehoboam, not of the nation-building David or the temple-building Solomon. Her literary talent, in Bloom's eyes, is nostalgic afterglow, not cheerleading ratification. By his placement of the J-writer in literary history, Bloom negates the potentially authoritarian thrust of having *one* person write many of the Bible's strongest passages.

The prominence of this vocabulary of strength and power in *The Book of J* makes a curious combination with the weakness and nescience of Rehoboam, and the effect is not just one of ironic contrast or pleasing dissimilarity between the aesthetic and the political. Placing the J-writer under Rehoboam eliminates a rival "greatness;" without the obtrusiveness of political power, poetic power can manifest itself all the more gloriously. Bloom has the experienced author's wariness of using the adjective "poetic" all the time, but surely, whenever Bloom speaks of strength and power, he means poetic strength and poetic power. Though Bloom does not maintain a hard-and-fast distinction between the aesthetic and the worldly, there is no equation or homology between political power and aesthetic power. Such a homology would have produced, inevitably, a Solomonic J-Writer; poetic strength alone produces a Rehoboamic J-writer, not guaranteed by a corresponding worldly might.

If in *Kabbalah and Criticism* Bloom attacks hylomorphism from the formal side, denying that the aesthetic can impose itself upon reality and remain unaltered, in *The Book of J* he attacks it from the material end. A great era of history cannot, in an expressive way, give birth to a great book; a literary work may have an ironic or negative relation to its subject-matter or origin, not simply emanating from some idealized sociopolitical source. While it would be simplistic to see this sort of fissure between work and background as inherently undermining secular authoritarianism, Bloom's deployment of aesthetic independence withdraws from any idealization of worldly power. At this point, the gender of the J-writer becomes a lot less gimmicky or self-consciously outré than it may appear at first. Any woman in ancient Israel, even one so gifted, aristocratic, and well-connected as Bloom's hypothetical authoress, is not going to have a lot of power. Despite the heroism of individual women in all parts of the Old Testament, even those dating from well before the J-writer, women are not associated with power in the Biblical milieu. There are no matriarchs among the patriarchs, despite Bloom's appealing portrait of Tamar (220-23). J's Judah, unlike Shakespeare's England, would never have tolerated a reigning Queen. This was demonstrated by the case of the wicked Queen Athaliah a couple of centuries later, overthrown because she was non-dynastic and idolatrous, but also, inferentially, because she was a woman. Even if the female J had written under Solomon, there would have been a distance, a fundamental severance, between the writer and the sources and instruments of power. That she writes under Rehoboam confirms her political disempowerment, and liberates her aesthetic gift from being yoked to an agenda of any given social regime.

In his excellent discussion of the Egyptian princess who rescues the baby Moses, Bloom speaks of her rejection of the "male violence" (243) of her father, presumably Ramses II, the Pharaoh of the Oppression. Although Bloom, along with most Christians, Jews, and Muslims, is decidedly more sympathetic to Solomon than to Ramses II, their profile as rulers is rather similar: egotistical, prone to build large monumental structures, seeing themselves as the state and the power of the state as the measure of all virtue. The J-writer, like Pharaoh's daughter, a relative of great kings, perhaps even a possible granddaughter of David (37), similarly rejects male violence in her work, and Bloom tropes this rejection by placing her in the era of Rehoboam. Eras of decline, such as Rehoboam's, are always seen as "feminine," filled with sloth, decadence, lassitude, lacking the hard, masculine virtues. Previously, goes the narrative, the nation had been built by strong, hungry pioneers, brave and daring; now, in the days of decline, it is filled with complacent idlers, aesthetes, frittering away political power as they self-indulgently flatter their art. Bloom, who in his earlier career has done so much to upend literary-historical clichés (such as the "sentimentality" falsely imputed to Romantics such as Wordsworth, or the "solipsism" assigned to Stevens) upends stereotypes of cultural history just as nimbly, and does so in the service, and to the tremendous enhancement, of his gender critique. The Rehoboam dating is feminizing, indeed so much so that Bloom almost does not even need the literal woman. The dating alone would have been feminizing enough, in the sense that Bloom is inverting the traditional derogation of the feminine to destabilize accustomed truisms. The anti-authoritarianism of the Rehoboam dating, the placing of the biblical master-work in the weak monarch's "curtailed kingdom" (36) is a stunning and noble ascesis, to use one of Bloom's revisionary ratios, and more a humbly self-limiting ascesis than a self-advertising (in the hands of mere mortals) kenosis. Just as one expects that he is using the J-writer as an origin, a monolithic genius to anchor Western literary history, his rendition of her gender and context frustrate this expectation entirely, and make it impossible to build a solid, constraining cultural foundation upon her art, which he is at pains to insist is "hugely idiosyncratic" (274). If Bloom's historiography of Bliblical creativity is hardly in itself a deconstructive historiography, it possesses many of the virtues one would expect the latter to have.

The Book of J is on a par with the other major works in Bloom's canon, and not just for its provocative literary-historical hypotheses (which even the author implies have to be seen with a grain of salt) but for its vision of authorship, in which pride and renunciation coexist. Every merely human idealization involves or even generates a corresponding de-idealization. Bloom's positioning of the unique genius in a curtailed kingdom illustrates that behind the visionary power of the "immensely strong" (274) J-writer is a critic who knows how to place the jar properly. The J-writer's lack of dependence on temporal strength is similar to Bloom's evocations of Wordsworth and Stevens in evoking a surprising humility that is fully compatible with a vision of literature, as it dwells in the midst of religion, that exalts beauty even as it avoids undue pride.

Works Cited

Abrams, M. H. *Natural Supernaturalism*. New York: Norton, 1971.
Anderson, Bernhard. *Understanding the Old Testament*. 4th ed. Englewood Cliffs: Prentice Hall,1986.
Aristotle. *The Basic Works of Aristotle*. Ed. Richard McKeon. New York: Random House, 1966.
Emerton, Norma E. *The Scientific Reinterpretation of Form*. Ithaca: Cornell UP, 1984.
Fawkner, H. W. *Immanence*. Stockholm: Stockholm UP, 1997.
Hartman, Geoffrey. *Wordsworth's Poetry, 1787-1814*. Cambridge: Harvard UP, 1987.
Haughton, Hugh and Adam Phillips, with Geoffrey Summerfield. *John Clare in Context*. Cambridge: Cambridge UP, 1994.
Hollander, John. Introduction. *Harold Bloom, Poetics of Influence: New and Selected Criticism*. New Haven: H. R. Schwab, 1988.
Lentricchia, Frank. *After the New Criticism*. Chicago: U of Chicago P, 1980.
———. *Ariel and the Police: Michel Foucault, William James, Wallace Stevens*. Madison: U of Wisconsin P, 1987.
———. *Modernist Quartet*. Cambridge: Cambridge UP, 1994.
Salusinszky, Imre. *Criticism in Society*. New York and London: Methuen, 1987.
Stevens, Wallace. *Collected Poems*. New York: Knopf, 1954.
Wimsatt, WIlliam K. *Day of the Leopards: Essays in Defense of Poems*. New Haven: Yale UP, 1976.

I, J, K

GWEE LI SUI

1

Despite all scholarly attempts to counter or revise Bloom's thesis on religious authorship, there remains one previously unimagined angle on his curious depiction of J. I say this not to discredit academic procedures of discussing either Bloom or the Torah, but to stress the fact that the critic's own foray into scriptural writing did not begin with his infamous co-authored 1990 text, *The Book of J*. A vivid awareness of this—which any reader in those puzzling few years preceding *The Book of J* should have possessed—is crucial to recognising the various kinds of conditions under which J came to be for him. The idea's current specificity can lead us wrongly to assume that an earlier Bloom would have needed just the opportunity to lay down his formulation completely and in elaborate detail. His notorious staunchness after 1990 even inspires a further trend: we speak of his construal these days in a way that suggests how future adjustments to the J of biblical scholarship can bear little or no relevance to it. Bloom's J, in other words, is now a rehabilitated creature, accepted by many as yet another idiosyncratic aspect of one man's cosmology, a vision that cannot constitutively differentiate between literature and religion. Such an outcome satisfies not just sceptics but also devotees who want to keep J in a corner, haunted perhaps by practical issues such as how J's proclaimed originality could have eluded Bloom for two-thirds of his career and how a writer with barely over a hundred pages of translatable text can be grouped with Homer, William Shakespeare and Leo Tolstoy. Indeed, Bloom's case appears increasingly like something out of a Pirandellian script—not with characters seeking an author but with a plot seeking characters—or a variant of William Paley's analogy: Bloom finds a watch and, instead of seeing a watchmaker-God, sees signatures of creative individuals warring against the intransigent systems of time.

The gap between the frequent pleasures one derives from engaging with Bloom's universe and the growing unease with his abstract fatalism and predictability ought to be addressed with care. A good part of this essay was written a few years before *Genius* (2002), his recent tome which goes on to fit one hundred writers, J included, into a Kabbalah-inspired "mosaic" of eccentricity. The book's unusual method prompted an astute *New York Times* reviewer to observe a "bizarre, almost worshipful frame" which strives largely to deepen "Bloom's cult of character" (Shulevitz 11). This description is right but not for the mere reason that the central structure is a mystical one put forward *a priori*. Worship is, after all, strong belief committed to transforming the uncertain or bodiless value of an object into sheer fact; if one then asks what exactly is being worshipped in *Genius*, a reply of God, Kabbalistic wisdom, or one hundred geniuses nonetheless seems to fall short.[1] This is because part of worship itself is drawn from a freedom to choose both its own conditions—to worship whom or what, in what way and for how long—and the surrender of that very freedom to the thing of worship. As such, *worship* and its presumed opposite, *play*, derive radically from the same act, since play likewise involves taking a claim or scenario too seriously with the effect of producing a new field of engagement. It is this understanding that can help ground my simple but outrageous attempt here to read an idea's initial emergence for Bloom in terms of what it 'really' is, what J has been long before its appearance in biblical discourse: the smallest form of irreducible novelty, an alphabetical letter. The project sounds bizarre, even misdirected, but I hope that my suggestion of a crucial alliance between Bloomian belief and play will be served at length. To be sure, I am not aiming to turn this animated J back into a plain document name in what biblical exegetes call the Source Hypothesis; I do require Bloom's J as he intends, as an actual historical writer suppressed by institutional religion. Such a J will be discussed particularly in relation to the original hypothesis and two German-Jewish writers central to the critic's own imagination of J, Sigmund Freud and Franz Kafka.

---

[1] The approach in *Genius* is not wholly unexpected: we note Bloom's account two decades earlier of his dispute with sceptics of his "maps of misreading" at Yale. He had claimed then that, "even if the Kabbalistic chart proved useless for interpreting poems, it would still be highly serviceable for plotting the vicissitudes of their love affairs" (*Agon* 49).

A couple of intriguing issues are perhaps the best places to start: we know firstly that, until J's arrival, Bloom had considered strong Gnostic writing, with scripts from both Christian and Jewish traditions, the antecedent of great literature. Given his claims too to be a modern Gnostic and, in *Agon* (1982), that every strong Gnostic text seeks to overthrow "the very strongest of all texts, the Jewish Bible" (70), we are faced with only one key obstacle in our attempt to explain his subsequent interest in J. It remains curious as to why Bloom should have favoured the Source Hypothesis above, say, New Testamentism—the belated submergence of the Hebrew scripture into the Christian and transformation of the original Testament into the Old—which describes the more successful institutional misreading. In short, a basic question has to be raised almost at once: why J? A second oddity involves the history told incompletely in *The Book of J*: J really received its name first from Johann Gottfried Eichhorn in 1780, although its conceptual birth went further back to another thinker, Henning Bernhard Witter. Witter had observed in 1711 the strange fact that the Book of Genesis bore not just two versions of a number of stories but also two distinct names for God; Eichhorn then concretised this by labelling the one referring to God as 'Yahweh' *J* and the other that used 'Elohim' *E*. Soon, a further priestly source was discovered and named *P* before a fourth, *D*, was demonstrated through the Book of Deuteronomy by Wilhelm Martin Leberecht De Wette, and *here* the story begins for Bloom. While acknowledging in passing the eighteenth-century origin of J and E, he presents De Wette as the "direct precursor" to the work of Karl Heinrich Graf, Wilhelm Vatke and especially Julius Wellhausen, scholars who popularly founded the Source Hypothesis (20–21).

Whether we see an imprecisely described *agon* between De Wette and Wellhausen or a precise but only implied one between Witter or Eichhorn and De Wette, the point cannot be missed that the central entity J has never existed alone. J emerged together with E even in Bloom's retelling; it emerged, if you like, as a twin, the older of two and, as the earliest strand of the whole Torah, the oldest of five once we include P, D and R, the final redactor's text. I do not overlook the irony here that J, as the first-born, like J's narrated Esau with his family's birthright, nonetheless secures an advantage through misrecognition, like Jacob, Esau's twin who won his father's blessing: J is, after all, the wrong abbreviation for 'Yahweh.' The letter J was taken from the German rather than the Hebraic spelling—that is, from *Jahveh*—and further echoes the transliteration 'Jehovah,' yet another misspelling but one used so extensively that it retains both its meaning and ascendancy today. 'Jehovah' had been a late medieval creation wrongly combining the Tetragrammaton *YHWH* with the vowels for *adonai*, or 'lord,' which Jewish scribes wrote under it to bypass pronouncing God's ineffable name. Incidentally, *hovah* also translates from Hebrew as 'ruin' or 'mischief:' it is *hava'* that means 'to be' in the familiar consecrated sense of God as 'I Am.' The last factor seems least helpful until we recall how Bloom himself sometimes tropes through a misidentification of words, as with *gevurah* which he uses repeatedly in *The Book of J* to call the Yahwist a woman of the Judean nobility. The proper term, as the more exacting Robert Alter points out, should be *gevirah*—*gevurah* being the abstract noun for 'power' or 'bravery' (30). Has Bloom erred, or is he being wilfully impish, like his own Yahweh? Considering his emphasis from *Kabbalah and Criticism* (1975) to *Genius* on Jewish mysticism, which names *gevurah* as one of ten *sefirot* or divine emanations, it appears hardly sensible to entertain ideas of his ignorance or carelessness. If Bloom is, then, deliberately smudging the line between an abstract concept and an actual individual—evoking a female writer as indeed audacity incarnate in a move like his doubling of J as person and idea—may we not describe his Yahweh as also reaching the modern Christian God through linguistic mischief, through *hovah*?

It should be clear by now that J in itself is an enormous site for the contest of various doubled forces: between first and second, authenticity and derivation, secrecy and revelation, the ineffable and the speakable, form and ruin, meaning and mischief, even Jew and gentile, and God and Demiurge. Let us quickly list at least five counts on which Bloom may be said to incite more mischief. J, the Yahwist's text, is firstly rendered synonymous with his Yahwist, so that a title like *The Book of J* is already pleonastic. Secondly, his J as *gevirah/gevurah* challenges the whole body of androcentric writing which Daniel M. McVeigh sees stretching from the masculine culture of Jewish scribes to the normative Christian theology producing the first J (371), marked by what Bloom calls "misogyny and championing of 'patriarchal religion'" (J 10). Thirdly, the critic affirms J's textual appearance from a twosome by imagining his J too with a creative twin, her "good friend" the court historian who wrote the Second Book of Samuel and to whom J might be "perhaps directly related by blood or marriage" (19 and 36). Both allegedly belonged to the post-Solomonic court and shared uncannily similar feelings of love for King David, mistrust for Solomonic glory, and contempt for King Rehoboam and the kingdom of Israel; their works were further open to each another even in their separate bids for creative precedence.² Fourthly, we read a remarkable *post hoc* assertion made by Bloom that J was, in fact, a gentile writer following Jack Miles's dazzling response to *The Book of J*. Miles has taunted Bloom for lacking the gall to name the biblical woman who best fitted his description of J, Bathsheba.³ In Bloom's next book *The Western Canon* (1994), his quibbler is called "shrewd" and the declaration made that J and Bathsheba will be treated henceforth as one and the same person, it being "a superb, J-like irony that the inaugural author of what eventually became the Torah was not an Israelite at all, but a Hittite woman" (5). Yet, the notion of J's "J-like irony" is that kind of talk that clarifies its own implicit dualism, since it inscribes similarity while preserving difference, vacillating still between J the writer and what makes any text J. In this sense, Bloom has deferred to Miles in an admission not really of defeat but of Miles's own J-like chutzpah.

There is one more count that concerns what the Source Hypothesis and Bloomian criticism differently premise: Bloom has often upheld his early statement in *The Anxiety of Influence* (1973) that the "profundities of poetic influence cannot be reduced to source study, to the history of ideas, to the patterning of images" (7). For source implies actual material fixity while ideas and patterns suggest control in regulating thought; from the viewpoint of influence, we get a rather more nervous sense that all these formations may well be illusory. To generate discussions on J, however, is precisely to confront source study, in fact to enter one of its acclaimed stable territories. One wonders whether Bloom's J may not exist to lay open this awkward tension in a "variant" approach struggling to escape its "original's" closure. It sounds perverse but fair to say

---

² Nicholas Birns's essay in this volume superbly combines the issues of gender and epochal difference by showing the positing of J in Rehoboam's reign as already feminising since it rejects the masculine premise that great art emerges in an age of political glory and not decline (15-19).

³ Miles makes a number of truly extraordinary points: for example, he argues that J's sympathy for Tamar the Adullamite should remind us of Tamar's seduction of the older Judah, which in turn parallels how Bathsheba had seduced the older David. He also suggests that Bathsheba might have even fashioned Yahweh after David, since her Moses, the emblem of moralistic religion, was looked on only with "studied coolness." Indeed, if Bathsheba had survived both David and Solomon to live under the incompetent Rehoboam, she would certainly model all "hard" women in her story after herself and "weave regal indignation into the warp and woof of Israel's foundation myth" (641).

that Bloom's interest relies on an anxious suspicion that truth in the Source Hypothesis might be verified—raised or diminished in relation to rival theories like those finding Moses the Torah's sole author or J itself with multiple writers—and thus concluded. His defiant reaction, then, is calculated to keep J going in spite of J. Evasion, essentially of itself/herself, is a radical part of Bloom's J who, as "a revealer who works through the juxtaposing of incommensurates" (*J* 15), is that ironic first unity of incommensurates. In this light, Bloom's J not only possesses a strategy of irony but *is* irony embodied, the grid for such ironic expressions, just as Bloom's Shakespeare is our whole inventory of individualities and his Freud our map of psychic responses. Although the critic after 1990 appears genuinely saddened by J's recurrent redaction into the institutional religious text we still endorse today, that emotion is suspect in view of how, as late as in *Ruin the Sacred Truths* (1989), he has further played *in the name of J* in a direction which moves away from J. The "great original J" is listed there with three other "J writers"—the prophet Jeremiah and the authors of Job and Jonah (22)—and their choice over other biblical contributors is founded on two factors. These authors, firstly, procure authority by supposedly parodying the Yahwist, expanding J-like irony out of J; secondly, all three quite simply share the same abbreviation J. By that latter reason, J in J's elliptical narrative is also encrypted in Jacob, as Bloom tells us later—"J's signature, a kind of self-representation" (*J* 209)—and in expressly two of his twelve sons, Judah and Joseph, one inheriting a forerunner's Abrahamic blessing, the other a latecomer's Davidic heroism and Solomonic worldly wisdom. As for the former, seemingly sounder reason, by virtue of the manner in which J's creative rivals had sought to overcome J through its/her own invitation to anxiety, even E, P, D and R are conceivably clear extensions of J.

2

We have assumed so far that the ironic content of Bloom's J is linked to its/her relation with the document J: what if, in arguably the strongest type of irony about origin, Bloom's J did not begin there but from *his* desired absorption of J into his theory of influence? "We are of the age of Freud and Kafka," Bloom writes in *Ruin the Sacred Truths* (156), but the critic also comes closest here to his longest, albeit covert, discussion of the duo's relation to J than in any of his titles since. I do indeed suspect that this slim volume based on lectures given before the event that was *The Book of J* holds the key to understanding the way J is shaped out of Bloom—in partial affirmation of one critical perspective that "J is Bloom" (McVeigh 375)—and how that lineage itself is mentally redacted away. There are telling similarities in his concluding remarks on Freud and Kafka in this survey of literature begun, in fact, with J: in a secularised Jewish universe, both are said to epitomise a fundamental rupture set against a longing for continuity or, more explicitly, the paradox "To be originally Jewish and yet to be original" (*Ruin* 158). With Freud first, we can deepen the connection not just by noting how, in *Moses and Monotheism* (1939), which Bloom chooses to elaborate, Freud has likewise acknowledged the Source Hypothesis and speculated on the way the word 'Jahveh' gave rise to Hebraic names like Jehu, Jochanaan and Joshua, and European ones from Jupiter and Jovis to Johann, John, Jean and Juan (*Standard Edition* 23: 40 and 45). In other words, Bloom's linguistic play on the letter J took root in Freud: his Yahwist is also fashioned after Freud's Moses as the true originator of Judaism, truer than its scripture's Abraham, and is thus both Abraham's and Moses' rival. Furthermore, J's dualism even replicates the accursed *agon* concealed in the Mosiac name: Freud's first Moses had been an Egyptian monotheist, his God Aton being the alleged source of the name *adonai*, but his lynching in the wilderness drove his murderers to yield later to another Moses, a Midianite whose impish tribal god was Jahveh. While what Bloom calls "Freud's novel" (*Genius* 179) may then prove Freud's aetiology of neuroses from trauma to the return of the repressed, Bloom's novel of J in turn proves the persistence of strong texts. Both nonetheless build their cases by similarly treating their respective stories too literally.

Given this likeness, the question why Bloom needs J can be answered partly by asking instead what is to be done with *Freud*. With the psychoanalyst as a secular god—the *Imitatio Freudi* being "the necessary pattern for the spiritual life in our time" (*Vessels* 64)—Bloom is cornered into defending himself against himself, against accepting Freud's only final place for him, as mere Freudian text. By saying this, I do not mean to invoke the kind of simplification sometimes made that Bloomian theory is Freudianism in denial, but rather to assert this notion as precisely what it evades. There are obvious, even deliberate differences in Bloom, such as the virtual absence of guilt's driving force and converse positive presence of genius and audacity. The teaser internal to his own poetics I therefore phrase as follows: how is Bloom to perform that necessary Gnostic act of "lying against time," the winning stroke in all strong interpretations (*Agon* 59), and pre-empt Freud from outside modernity even while he remains inescapably contained in Freud? Shakespeare may be that middleman or Demiurge of his cosmos these days—a position reiterated in *Genius* by branding our age "post-Shakespearean" but still "pre-Freud" (180)—and its stabilised genealogy may be inferred by 1989, with J's ironic positions revised into Shakespearean individualities which Freud then codified. In the history of its formulation, however, Shakespeare is the latecomer to J *and* Freud, being crucial chiefly for the 'return' to Freud after the installation of J to negate him. The critic, in other words, required the ironist first to block off the shrink even though he subsequently declares his need for the Bard above all. I can demonstrate this by highlighting how Bloom's chapter on Freud in 1989 found it essential to visit "the grotesque plot" of *Moses and Monotheism* twice (*Ruin* 159); much later in *The Western Canon*, Shakespeare is inserted into the same primal scene to suggest how Freud "weirdly" associates even Michelangelo's Moses with *Hamlet* (1603) and so displays tell-tale anxiety over the playwright (372-73). By *Genius*, the initial interest in Freud's J-supplanting text, now credibly supplanted for Bloom too via Shakespeare, is all but one line long. There is a clear parallel between Bloom's relationship to *Moses and Monotheism* and the J-redactors' to the document J; in the same way the critic has taught us to read Freud's Shakespeare, we ought to read his Freud in turn.

Here, then, is how Bloom's J must surface: it/she is meant audaciously to invert Freud's J whose Yahwist not only followed a Midianite's religion but also sought to revise an Egyptian's through it. The irony may indeed be stressed that neither original religion was Jewish although the product that emerged was nothing but Jewish, a curious twist we can describe by reversing Bloom's paradox thus: "To be original and yet to be originally Jewish." In Bloom's version, Freud's earliest precursor has to be the Yahwist herself since there simply was no-one before her, God and Adam being both her creations. Freud's later Moses might have deviously re-made Aton in Yahweh's image, but before Yahweh or Aton or even the first Moses was, '*J Am*.' This grammatical glitch clinches the point: J is the 'I Am' of its/her satirical creation story but, as scholarly fiction, an ancient gentile woman and yet a transcendental prototype, J is also the Other conjured by Bloom to be something, someone and somewhere else. It/she is the unvoiced imagination of the 'I Am' of Bloom, of his Gnostic secret 'I *am* J.' The manoeuvre artfully turns Freud into his own anxious late-arriving Yahwist beside Bloom's—he is, in *Genius*, "Solomon Freud" who thirsts to be the "New Moses" (179)—but it is as possible to see him caricatured in Bloom's sphinx-like Yahweh, a fiercely childish creature who nonetheless fathered all. With this, we can explain the wilder of two already noted transformations that Bloom's J underwent, specifically between 1989 and 1990: J became an actual historical person but moreover, as the Yahwist, J quite literally changed sex, from a man in *Ruin the Sacred Truths* to the woman of *The Book of J*. Critics who still murmur the charge of plagiarism concerning Bloom's female Yahwist miss the point, therefore: to be sure, Bloom did plagiarise, this idea having originated in Richard Elliott Friedman's *Who Wrote the Bible?* (1987).[4] Yet, the general Bloomian position states that we are all plagiarists anyway: the *real* challenge is to be paradoxically original in the crime's execution. The unique position in Bloom is that J's femininity in fact comes naturally since, in ironising Freud's myth of fatherhood as both curse and covert desire of sons, J 'pre-emptively' mocks Freudian purposiveness and theoretical coherence. As sheer irony, however, this J doubly mocks her own inversion too and secures for Bloom the last laugh, considering that she was, above all, a daughter and a mother.

J's other transformation in its/her *annus mirabilis* from text into author may be discussed in relation to Kafka, if, that is, we accept that Bloom's technique of pulling a writer into his name is performed most memorably there. While Kafka, unlike Freud, makes no theoretical claim to objectivity and universal significance, his case is not therefore straightforward in view of his different power to convey exact intuitions about our existential condition. This abyss of modern spirituality in the Kafkan message is what Bloom frequently demonstrates by sliding not just under an alphabetical letter—that is, under K—but, in particular, under the author's own name. *Kavka* is Czech for 'jackdaw' and, shuffling from a jackdaw to its classificatory genus, the critic reminds us often how one Kafkan aphorism does have crows asserting that "a single crow" could "destroy the heavens." This champion is argued to be Kafka himself although, according to the saying too, the heavens which *kavka*/Kafka can demolish are never threatened at all in truly meaning

---

[4] Friedman has maintained that strong evidence of male scribes in ancient Israel need not preclude a female writer of J. Observing the many courtly concerns and stories either about or sympathetic towards women, he asserts that "women of the noble class may have more power, privilege, and education than males of a lower class" (86).

"the impossibility of crows" (89). From man through beast, the Kafkan thing thus ends in self-negation once it/he crosses into the certainty of *das Jenseits*, 'the other world' it/he precisely aims at. Twisting the Latin for 'crow,' Bloom then hammers *graculus* into 'Gracchus,' the name for another Kafkan character, his mythic hunter drifting forever between life and the afterlife. What are we to make of this recurring kind of analogical criticism that claims to analyse but, in placing excessive interpretive value on a name first, seems more like divination? The issue ought not to be confused with the critical sense of an author-function or, loosely put, an author's delimitation to what critics can construct textually. Bloom's literary geniuses are not bound by what they directly write; they represent instead respective qualities whose reappearances in other writers are as good as continued work by them. It is this curious authorial indivisibility that finds its ground in Kafka's name, the linguistic suppleness of which is rendered compatible with his own message. Indeed, while such play with others may understandably be judged tenuous, Kafka's frailty or 'airiness'—the possibility of *kavka* Bloom imputes to him—is at once his whole point and thematic strength. As crow-elect and therefore fatefully also 'no-crow,' the proof of helplessness before the heavens, what Kafka intends and what both frustrates and forbids his intentions are powerfully locked in the same identity. *This* describes the absurd indeterminate status of modern existence whose literal value Kafka's creatures—his crows, Gracchus, Gregor Samsa, Karl Rossman, Joseph K, K, and so on—further trope.

Consequently, if J is Bloom's eventual "visionary of incommensurates," its/her vision being their own impossible joining, it is only because J's status as "the direct ancestor of Kafka" and anyone "condemned to work in Kafka's mode" means that Kafka's mode preceded J (*J* 13). Evidence of an initial Kafkaesque J is noticeable in how J's creation story with its ironic asymmetrical relation between God and His image Adam can be drawn almost wholly from the smallest thing of Kafkan beauty, the Odradek. In it, Bloom expressly sees two-legged man, "a child's creation" who is "harmless and charming," spiritually immortal but, as he stresses, Kafkan and yet not Freudian, being "aimless, and so not subject to the death drive" (*Ruin* 178). The Odradek nonetheless further projects his Yahweh's existence: appearing to be made by "an inventive and humorous child," this creature itself functions like "a daemon at home in the world of children" (177). Bloom's suggestion that we read the Odradek as Kafka's synecdoche for Jewish negation therefore conceals—not too well though—the fact that his own J is becoming the means to a Gnostic negation of Kafka, quietly still a Kafkan synecdoche. Another example should prove again how J's plot-structure simply narrativises Kafka's linking of incommensurates: *The Castle* (1922), highly recommended by Bloom for studying the Kafkan Kabbalah, is central not just when we can identify K's inner struggle between an unsatisfying domestic life and a self-destructive engagement with the alluring castle. Nor is it still enough to agree with the critic that the castle "is there primarily because K is ignorant, though K's deepest drive is for knowledge" (*Ruin* 194). All these are, in fact, diversions to play down a set of fundamental resemblances that Bloom himself admits, between the superior castle official Klamm and Yahweh, and between K and J. Klamm, an unpredictable Demiurge in K's universe, swings J-like between benevolence and menace, but *klam* itself is Czech for 'fraud' or 'deceit,' that is, for *hovah*. K, unlike Kafka the storyteller, remains radically outside this secret and so takes up no chutzpah-driven fight for the emancipating blessing. K, as failed Jacob or as Esau's casting as Jacob, doubly ruinous, stands in contrast to Kafka who succeeds at least in being aware of the real predicament. There is surely this ironic distance between writer and protagonist—itself bridged by Kafkan ambiguity—which we see inscribed twice in J's qualified triumph over itself/herself as a severely redacted text and an ill-fated lady in Rehoboam's court. It remains useful also to note how J's acerbic attitude towards authority derives from yet another Kafkan hero, Joseph K, in the way it/she exposes Yahweh's idiosyncrasy for commanding worshippers to "be like Me but not too much like Me" and morbid readiness to kill even his most favoured bureaucrat, Moses, at length un-creating him by returning him forgotten to Moabite clay. *Moab*, by the way, means 'desirable land' but also both 'out of father' and 'out of scandalous birth,' capturing at once a thoroughly Kafkan crisis of place.

The precedence of Freud and Kafka so explained cannot be misread: in so far as we operate within the Bloomian universe, J truly came first and, in so far as we situate ourselves outside it, both modern authors bear no relation to J. I can raise the issue here only after having asserted first a good-humoured basis determined by that clue I now re-describe as to "be like Bloom but not too much like Bloom." The goal has been to loosen up the rigidifying discussion among biblical scholars, historians, feminists and cautious puzzle-solvers and beat a more eccentric path by reading Bloom's J as audaciously as he has read the Jewish Bible. Some like Alter seem bent on disputing by faulting Bloom's translated Hebrew, an aspect the latter has since less courageously made David

Rosenberg, his collaborator on *The Book of J*, take the blame for (*Genius* 116). Other major assaults have included Tela C. Zasloff's, which points out Bloom's essentialist error of deducing J's gender from a textual preference for feminine traits and hatred of patriarchy, and Friedman's, which strives to reclaim his own project by now finding J part of "a long, exquisitely connected prose composition" stretching up to the First Book of Kings (*Hidden* 7). For Bloom, however, all these seem to pale in comparison to the thoughts of two expounders he openly approves of: other than Miles, there is Donald Harman Akenson who, in *Surpassing Wonder* (1998), describes how Bloom's reading "virtually bubbles with joy" stemming from the "enveloping quality of the intellectual puzzle" and "his joy at the very quality of the texts" (7). The startling tribute the critic pays in return to Akenson's focus, the *redactor's* text, makes one thing clear (*Genius* 6): as J's Moses is dispensable to its/her Yahweh and Bloom's precursory J is really an overcoming of Freud and Kafka, Bloom the J-defender is also underhandedly willing to set aside J to preserve what is 'Bloomian.' Indeed, while Bloom, all too human, ostensibly prefers having supporters, the deification of his fictive J is never truly the final point. I have suggested rather his fascination with a "lie-against-time," what he calls elsewhere "a writing in space" that "cannot hear a voicing in time," which works to break away from the "catastrophe" of historical truths (*Agon* 59). With this must emerge the corresponding demand for a reader to engage him on similar terms—creatively and with much chutzpah—for how else can one hope to gain a piece of that Gnostic blessing he has wrested from a Freudian-Kafkan modernity, just as his J/Bathsheba did too from the legacy of its/her beloved David?

Works Cited

Akenson, Donald Harman. *Surpassing Wonder: The Invention of the Bible and the Talmuds.* New York: Harcourt, 1998.
Alter, Robert. "Harold Bloom's 'J.'" *Commentary* 90.5 (1990): 28-33.
Freud, Sigmund. *The Standard Edition of the Complete Psychological Works of Sigmund Freud.* 24 vols. Trans. and ed. James Strachey. London: Hogarth, 1953–74.
Friedman, Richard Elliott. *The Hidden Book of the Bible.* San Francisco: Harper-San Francisco, 1998.
_____. *Who Wrote the Bible?* 2nd ed. San Francisco: Harper-San Francisco, 1997.
Kafka, Franz. *Shorter Works.* Trans. Malcolm Pasley. London: Secker and Warburg, 1973.
McVeigh, Daniel M. "'J' as in Joke? Bloom, Rosenberg, and the Hermeneutics of Chutzpah." *Christianity and Literature* 40.4 (1991): 367–79.
Miles, Jack. "The Book of B: Bloom, Bathsheba and the Book." *Commonweal* 9 Nov. 1990: 639-42.
Shulevitz, Judith. "The Hall of Fame." *New York Times* 27 Oct. 2002, Late ed.: 7.11.
Zasloff, Tela C. "The Author Was a Woman? The Issue of Essentialism in *The Book of J.*" *Women and Language* 17.2 (1994): 34–39.

Bloom upon Her Mountain: Unclouding the Heights of Modern Biblical Criticism

Leslie Brisman

> The moonlight crumbled to degenerate forms,
> While she approached the real, upon her mountain,
> With lofty darkness.
> —Wallace Stevens, "Mrs. Alfred Uruguay"

Almost all of Harold Bloom's extraordinary work on the Bible centers on the J writer, on the idea that this is indeed *a* writer, not a collection of documents by a partisan school, and that this writer has an interesting authorial personality as well as a claim to a kind of ultimate originality beyond and before other writers represented in the Bible. Readers of the eye-opening introductions to the Chelsea House Genesis, Exodus, and Bible volumes, the pages on "the Hebrew Bible" in *Ruin the Sacred Truths,* and preeminently in *The Book of J,* encounter the J writer as they encounter J's God—and Bloom himself.[1] All three are uncanny, impish, ironic, elliptical, unrivaled, élitist; to borrow Bloom's own locution about the troika of J, Shakespeare, and Freud, none of the three is "exactly a writer on the left" (J 255).

It is by no means demeaning to Bloom to speak of the revelation of his own personality and that of the author he so privileges in the same breath. On the contrary, the revelation of spirit—J's spirit or Bloom's spirit—is a thing divine, and the critic, like the author, lifts the reader to a mountain top from which to survey, in wild (Oscar Wilde?) surmise, the imagined land. Yet, as the recent film *Wilde* by Brian Gilbert has

---

[1] "From J to K, or The Uncanniness of the Yahwist" appeared in *The Bible and the Narrative Tradition.* Ed. Frank McConnell.. New York: Oxford, 1986; a version of this appears in Bloom's *Exodus,* and in *J.* For Bloom on biblical writers other than J (or other Js), see *Ruin.*

shown, an alternative, more domesticated Wilde can be imagined, and such imagining is not necessarily inferior for being more E than J.[2] In what follows, the question over which I brood concerns the exclusivity of the critic's mountain top. Bloom's capsule treatment of Jeremiah, Jonah, and Job in *Ruin the Sacred Truths* allows for some genius beside J's outside the Pentateuch; and in several places he acknowledges the Davidic historian of the book of Samuel as a rival voice, perhaps a contemporary of J. But for Bloom, there really is no other author worth talking about, no other great personality, in the Pentateuch itself: "very little of high literary quality . . . is by any author except J" (*Ruin* 9). Setting himself in grand opposition not only to Foucault and Barthes but to the entire anti-author mainstream of current cultural determinisms, Bloom heralds J as "the author-of-authors," if you like Prince of Peace—in the sense that J stands both outside the culture wars and, uniquely, outside wars with precursors or rivals.

Actually, Bloom has never been much interested in rivalry between contemporary writers, preferring always to see Oedipal intergenerational conflict even when two writers are contemporary. But even in the neutral sense of rivals as rivals in our estimation, rather than rivals with one another, Bloom places J beyond the reach of any single, actual other:

> J's only cultural rival would be an unlikely compound of Homer and Plato. Plato's contest with Homer seems to me to mark one of the largest differences between the ancient Greeks and the Hebrew. The agon for the mind of Athens found no equivalent in Jerusalem, and so the Yahwist still remains the mind of Jerusalem, everywhere that Jerusalem happens to be. (*Genesis* 2)

Now the idea of a "compound" precursor is not unique to Bloom's meditations on the Bible; in a sense it was necessitated by the very absoluteness of his vision (ye shall have no other gods before me!) in *The Anxiety of Influence* and the related books: *A Map of Misreading*, *Kabbalah and Criticism*, and *Poetry and Repression*. If the strong writer tones his mental physique by wrestling with a mighty precursor, and if we cannot always point to a single poem in the canon on which a particular new poem concentrates, then the precursor poems or poets will have to be composite figures, imaginative blends constructed by the poet's dream work, his repressed knowledge of what went before him, and subject to

---

[2] *Wilde*, written by Julian Mitchell and directed by Brian Gilbert, features Stephen Fry as Oscar, a noble, self-sacrificing, not very impish Oscar Wilde: an antithesis, if you will, of Harold Bloom's Wilde, his J or his Bloom.

the critic's insightful dissection into principal component parts. Thus T. S. Eliot could never be dignified into *the* precursor for Stevens in "Mrs. Alfred Uruguay," though his "Song of J. Alfred Prufrock" may be one component of the not so capable figure of imagination Stevens would pass on his mountain journey. Bloom himself mentions Coleridge's *Kubla Khan* and Keats's *Fall of Hyperion* (and implies a larger tradition of quest romance) in his brief discussion of "Mrs Alfred Uruguay" in *Wallace Stevens* (161-2). In the passage cited above, Homer and Plato are conceived as a model of the anxiety of influence, with Plato as belated poet half disparaging and dismissing his true love and arch rival mythmaker. But Homer/Plato are also imagined to be a composite ancestor for a culture as a whole, as though "Athens" were the ephebe and Homer/Plato the precursor.

The next sentence gives us Bloom at his strongest, though perhaps his strongest misreading of the Bible and Jewish culture generally. "The mind of Jerusalem" refers to no individual, unless that individual is Bloom himself, and Jerusalem "happens to be" in New Haven. Like Mrs. Alfred Uruguay, Bloom here has "wiped away moonlight like mud," unless we agree with him that everything but the work of J is without moonlight altogether—the Pentateuch being essentially a composite of J's imagination and the mud or Teufelsdröckh of priestly dullness, self-interest, and legalism. What does it mean to say "the agon for the mind of Athens found no equivalent in Jerusalem"? Accepting the conventional wisdom that J is the earliest of the Pentateuchal strains, Bloom seems to be headed towards a denial of the anxiety of influence in this one case: unlike Plato, who had to wrestle with Homer, J had nobody. His actual statement, however, stands independent of the mind of J or any historical sequence: J had no rival; no one else was of such capable imagination as to be worth a passing note if encountered in real or reimagined imaginative sequence. If "the mind of Jerusalem" had anything to do with normative Judaism, Bloom's judgment would be palpable nonsense; the struggle of the Yahwist with the spiritual pieties of the Elohist or the ritual obsessions of the Priestly writer might be a representation of the life-force of normative Judaism, if normative Judaism were granted any life or mind. Press on this statement, and "the Yahwist still remains the mind of Jerusalem" turns out to mean: *for Harold Bloom, the only mind of Jerusalem is the mind of J; all else is mindless legalism, insipidity, and the self-interest of the religious establishment.*

Though I share Bloom's central insight about J—not that J is a woman but that J is anything but a conventionally pious writer—I am less sure that there is no agon. Like the "figure of capable imagination" in Stevens's poem, J in Bloom's reading remains magnificently oblivious of others, "A rider intent on the sun." The sun here stands for all the glories of the physical world. J's reality is the reality of this earth, with its beef and curds, Yahweh's genial conversations with Abraham, his casual meetings by the well with Hagar. But there is a competing reality, not the reality of J's Yahweh, but the spiritual reality of what a more conventionally pious writer takes God to be. If J rushes down the mountain, others, like Stevens's Mrs. Uruguay, struggle up the mountain. The voice Bloom is determined not to hear is the voice of Mrs. Uruguay in the donkey's ear, whispering "I fear that elegance / Must struggle like the rest." I borrow Bloom's own insight here about Stevens's poem, that the word "elegance" is meant to evoke its etymological sense of chosenness. In both Stevens's comedic poem and in the writing of the Pentateuch, *elegance must struggle,* or rather competing authorial personalities struggle for elegance, for chosenness, blessing, imaginative gift.

We can synecdochally represent the agon for the mind of Jerusalem by turning to Bloom's reading of two mountain events, Moriah and Sinai. Though neither of these scenes, Genesis 22 or Exodus 19, explicitly mentions Jerusalem, each has been thought by some to have direct reference to ritual observance already centering in Jerusalem at the time of the composition of the text. "The struggle for the mind of Jerusalem" can be expressed as the struggle to keep Jerusalem in mind, the struggle to decide if Jerusalem should be kept in mind: "If I forget thee, O Jerusalem," as Psalm 137 has it, "may my right hand lose its cunning." This, in opposition to what we might couch as the pledge of the J critic: "If I do not forget, misread, or obliterate the Jerusalem connection, my J will lose her cunning." In what follows, I will try to evaluate Bloom's contribution to the struggle for the mind of Jerusalem by focusing on his relation to just one figure of immensely capable imagination of that Jerusalem, John Van Seters.

1) Moriah

Though Van Seters has in mind a later J author than Bloom would envision, and a J with none of the fierce opposition to religious establishment, the two share a sense that there is just J—and everything else, let us say just J and P. Bloom's reading of the *akedah* (binding of Isaac) episode therefore shares with Van Seters the notion that the story is at its core J and not E; E does not exist, and everything of interest (for Bloom) is J, however spoiled or suppressed by P or a redactor in the intellectual framework of P:

> I do not find J normative enough to be telling us a story in which Yahweh is putting Abram [sic] to the test. The God of the Binding of Isaac is precisely the God who will seek to murder Moses, for no reason or cause, soon after the prophet starts down to make the journey into Egypt. And the Abram of the Binding, as we have it, has been thoroughly cowed by Yahweh, his initial resistance now broken. I think therefore that either P or R added "God put Abraham to the test" (Gen. 22.1), excised Abram's fierce resistance, and also substituted "Elohim" for "Yahweh" in a few places. (J 206)

The second and third sentences here contrast the *Akedah* according to Bloom with the *akedah* as we have it. The former text, or supposition of an ur-text, features that wonderfully impish or irrational Yahweh whose refusal to be limited to moral sense is so much a mark of his liveliness, of the lively imagination of his creator. To imagine that the deity who calls for this sacrifice is the Yahweh who seeks to slay Moses, Bloom needs to excise or forget about the opening verse. He compares the Book of Jubilees, which features a scene in the heavenly assembly where Mastema provokes Yahweh into putting Abraham to the test. For Bloom, it does not matter if Genesis specifies a Mastema or not, because either way the idea of "testing" a patriarch is the dull product of a moralist. If Abraham in the text as we have it is "thoroughly cowed by Yahweh," there must have been a prevenient text, a true J text, in which he spoke up and gave Yahweh fierce and noble resistance to his hideous demand.

I think it is worth specifying that Bloom has always been what he confronts openly in *The American Religion*, a powerful and plain-spoken critic of religion—or, perhaps more precisely, of what happens to literary imagination when it degenerates into religious imagination. Bloom must be applauded for pointing out that the invention of Mastema in the Jubilees *akedah* story, like the invention of Satan's wager with God in the frame of the Job story, does not help at all.[3] No-one but the dullest and nastiest of Calvinists can feel an increase in admiration for a deity

---

[3] For an imaginative appreciation of the Book of Jubilees Bloom so loathes, see James Kugel, *The Bible as It Was*—e.g. the note on Abraham loving Jacob in the Jubilees substitution for Rebecca (201), or the explanation of how the Jubilees invention of Mastema plays with the biblical phrase achar hadvarim haeleh ("after these words..." [Gen. 22.1]).

whose bad behavior is "explained" by knowing about his wagers, just as (a moral point toyed with in the apocalyptically unimaginative last episode of Seinfeld) no one but the dullest and nastiest of self-absorbed adolescent males can feel that bad behavior towards a woman can be explained by understanding the bet the guys made behind the scenes about their sexual stamina. The question remains, however, whether "God put Abraham to the test" is of a piece with "God had this wager with Mastema." Does Bloom's distaste for this trial come from moral indignation (Bloom as critic of religion) or from what Stevens might call the "finding fang," the purely aesthetic sensibility that detects a bit of false J on the buds of literary taste?

Though I share Bloom's distaste for the trial of Abraham as such, I wonder if the decision to regard "God put Abraham to the test" as the dull normalization of a priestly writer or redactor does not resemble the decision to dismiss Iago's stated reason for corrupting Othello as a piece of insipidity surely not by the divine Shakespeare. In both cases, the artistry seems to be a function of the ability to weave such magnificent magic in the web from such bare and knobby threads. What is the magnificence of the *akedah* if it is not located in the uncanny ambiguities of verse 8? Isaac calls to Abraham as God did; Abraham's simple *hineni, bini,* "here I am, my son!" seems to declare an equivalent absolute or unconditional presence of father to son: here I am, here I will always be for you; ask, ask anything, and be reassured. And to Isaac's plain and pathos-filled question, "here is the fire and the wood, but where is the lamb for offering?" Abraham replies with something absolutely remarkable for its combination of directness and indirection. Out of context, Abraham's words *Elohim yireh lo haseh* could mean "God will provide him [Abraham] with a lamb" or "God will show him [Isaac] the lamb"; in context, as direct discourse to Isaac, the "him" has to be God Himself: thus "God Himself will provide the lamb," and the scene of instruction, which seemed to be set up with Isaac as ephebe, Abraham as tutor –pointing to God as supreme tutor—now resolves itself into an insight into the pure self-sufficiency, the pure self-reflectiveness, of God Himself providing, or God *showing Himself* in showing the lamb. As the *lo,* the him, becomes reflexive, the object of "provide"—or rather, the object of the verb *yireh*, which can only turn from a verb of sight to the meaning "provide" if there is an object being provided with sight—collapses. It is not that there is no one to see what God provides, or that God is so wholly other that it does not matter who sees; rather, the two possible objects of special providence, Abraham and Isaac, become one again in a renewed sense of awaiting and trusting in that providence. Hence the beautiful line, "the two of them walked together" (verse 6) is eerily repeated in verse 8, as though their physical togetherness (that of a father-son outing) now became metaphysical togetherness (father/son "as one") in face of the unknown sight—the hideous abyss or sublime provision to come. The entire sense of the sublime, of giddy confusion between height and depth, canny and uncanny, controlled and loosened ambiguity, concentrates in this one verse. And this verse 8 requires—in its own, purely literary sense of exaction—verse one, the putting of Abraham to the test. The point is made by Van Seters, arguing not against Bloom but against the folklorist Reventlow's dismissal of the opening verse: "Without the element of the divine test there is no way of structuring the movement in the story to a climax. How can there be any point to Abraham's reply to his son in verse eight without it?" (Van Seters 236). We can add: How could the story reach its magnificent conclusion, in which Abraham calls the mountain *Yahweh yireh* ("God provides!" or "on [this? such a?] mountain God will be seen") if the suspension of object of special providence here did not return so magnificently to verse 8 with its suspension—and to verse one when Abraham is put on trial, stationed in the moral equivalent of the suspended object of provision?

Bloom dismisses the trial of Abraham not because it is bad theology but because it seems to him impossible to believe that J wrote this. But though Van Seters and Bloom both believe that the *akedah* story is essentially J's, their remarks about verse 8, the very core of the story's sublimity, point rather to the wholly other nature of the story. It is "wholly other" than J's, not in J's mode at all, and truly to face verse 8 is to face the fact that there is an alternative mode of greatness. Bloom appears to acknowledge the special quality of verse 8 when he remarks, "Isaac's unmerited ordeal centers upon his baffled asking where the sheep is for the sacrifice, and his father's reply that God will see to the sheep" (J 207). His next sentence begins, "The profoundest irony here . . ." and we may for just a moment believe that he is about to expound the profound irony that Abraham may not have faith that Isaac will be saved, that Abraham may mean "God will show you to be the lamb" and the spiritual irony, at Abraham's expense, is that his words turn out to mean "God will show us a lamb," as He does in verse 13. But no! Bloom is not interested in *that* irony, or not interested in dignifying that irony with the ultimate praise, that of profundity. The profoundest irony here, for Bloom, "and a likely indication that this story originally was J's, is that the ghastly sacrifice would have taken place on what was to be the site of Solomon's Temple." Though Van Seters argues cogently for a J writer far more involved in cult than Bloom would be able to bear, we might concede that the *akedah* story, were it told by J, could imply "a very negative judgment upon the cult and its celebrations." But the *akedah* story is not, and perhaps could not be, told by J. How could a J story sustain the profound ironies of verse 8, and the perhaps profounder irony that the redemptive substitution of ram for Isaac fulfils Abraham's unwitting prophecy, that God will provide? This is a story that privileges rather than deprecates the rituals of substitution, and one can loathe the system of animal sacrifice while yet conceding that the *akedah* story may be the best thing that could be said *for* it. I believe it stands a triumph of the E writer's imagination, indeed sufficient reason not to dismiss the idea of an E writer. If nothing else, the hypothesis of an E writer allows us to see just how alternate is this mode of sublimity. Like Mrs. Alfred Uruguay, approaching "the real upon her mountain," E has a "wholly other" sense of the real, an ethereal, genuinely theological sense, in contrast with which J, figure of capable imagination that he is, and "blind to her velvet and/ The moonlight," remains just that, *a* figure of imagination. There are, there must be, at least two.

2) Sinai

If the Pentateuch exhibits imaginations different in kind rather than simply in degree, one might apply to them a term that Bloom often applies to Yahweh and man or other sets of realities that "cannot be resolved": "incommensurate" (see, for example, *Ruin* 4). Like Mrs. Alfred Uruguay and the "youth, a lover with phosphorescent hair," the writers of the Pentateuch do not have to be on different mountains (say, Horeb and Sinai) to avoid meeting each other. They simply see differently God, the human condition, and literary excellence. Stevens's poem, with one figure laboring to make the pilgrimage up the mountain, the other rushing down it, may be read as a distillation of all the competing attempts in Exodus to apprehend the nature of Revelation. Whether Sinai is and preveniently was God's place, or whether God and the Hebrews come to Sinai as, say, Israel and the PLO come to Oslow, each to a place not His or their own—or whether God is actually present on or hovers over the top of Sinai—those are lesser questions or lesser manifestations of the same question of just what makes Sinai (or Mrs.

Uruguay's mountain either) a "Montevideo," a place of vision. What seeing or unseeing, hearing or unhearing, will single out this confrontation from all others? And what quintessential differences in their vision, one from the other, will manifest the writers of the Pentateuch on Sinai?

Bloom's reading in *The Book of J* is drawn from his earlier Introduction to *Exodus: Modern Critical Interpretations* when his distaste for the E hypothesis had not yet crystallized. What had crystallized, into one of his most important visions of the J writer and J's Yahweh, is the importance of the taboo about sight. Bloom has little interest in the question of hearing—of just what the Hebrews hear, whether it has content at all or just overwhelming noise, sheer "facticity" of God's presence. Since he imagines J to have no interest in cult, it does not matter to Bloom whether the Ten Commandments as given in Chapter 20 replaced an earlier J content or whether J's vision of revelation was wholly contentless. What matters is that a taboo of touch ("beware of climbing the mountain or touching the border of it") gives way to a taboo about sight. What interests Bloom is that Yahweh, like Coriolanus, cannot bear the kind of self-exhibit the moment "requires." I put "requires" in quotation marks because it is unclear in Exodus, as it is to a lesser degree in Shakespeare, how much of the sense of ritual is imposed by some prevenient notion of political process, how much is self-imposed. Bloom raises, then ducks, the question about sight:

> Sinai will be taboo, but is this only a taboo of touch? What about seeing Yahweh? I suspect that an ellipsis, wholly characteristic of J's rhetorical strength, then intervened, again characteristically filled in by the E redactors as verses 16 and 17, and again as verse 19; but in verse 18 clearly we hear J's grand tone: "Now Mount Sinai was all in smoke, for the Lord had come down upon it in fire; the smoke rose like the smoke of a kiln, and all the people trembled violently." (Bloom, *Exodus* 11-12; *J* 253)

What is not clear from Bloom's explication is whether or in what sense Yahweh might be said already to have come down on Sinai and to have been subject to sight. When he says, "I suspect that an ellipsis ... then intervened", he presumably believes that the text would be more powerful, more coherent, if it now went, as once it did, from verse 15 to verse 18, and again from 18 to 20. I do not know what gain in power Bloom sees in the omission of 16 and 17 if it is not the sheer surprise at coming upon the revelation of God before one expects it: before some dull-witted pedagogue could imagine leading the people to God, they already confront that He is *there*. Yet, as Bloom specifies, He isn't *really* there, for "Yahweh, as we know, is neither the fire nor in the fire." Thus the ellipsis, in which the Presence seems to have "arrived," belies the essential absence, the fact that Yahweh isn't really there—and is having trouble getting there. Bloom "represents" this as Yahweh's trouble, His dislike of being represented, subject to being seen by everybody; but it is really J's crisis of representation, J's inability to imagine a scene of Yahweh revealing Himself to the people at large. We might at this point import the otherwise useless concept of J as a woman to imagine her saying, in a fit of peeve: *I don't do windows. And besides [closing the curtains, curtaining off revelation from future view] there ain't none there anyway.*

When the dialogue between Moses and Yahweh resumes, the curtains are drawn and there is to be no revelation of Yahweh. The talk, in 20-24, is all about not seeing Him. The crisis of representation has been doubly averted: first, there is the general or evasive statement that Yahweh had come down upon Mount Sinai in fire, and the mountain remained all in smoke, one trope obscuring what was, in any event, only another trope for the visible Presence. Second there is the dialogue between Moses and Yahweh in 20–24 about the conditions under which Yahweh would consent to be seen by a limited delegation from the people. This dialogue, because it is itself in the mode of one to one, like Yahweh's previous encounters with Abraham, Jacob, and Joseph, is something J can handle, and handle supremely well. All else is—ellipsis. Bloom concludes this passage of exegesis by moaning, "As our text now stands, the revisionists take over, and the Commandments are promulgated." A crisis of representation, of visual representation, is resolved in the end by the substitution of aural confrontation: the people hear what God has to say, and J gets over his crisis, his personal anxiety about representing a visual meeting of The One with the many. It is certainly curious that normative Judaism, here represented by the Priestly writer Bloom so much disdains, regards the aural as being every much a matter of crisis as the visual: The people cannot bear to hear Yahweh speak, and plead for Moses to receive the Law and transmit it, in human terms, in human decibels, to them. Tradition differs about whether the Ten Commandments, as opposed to the whole Book of the Covenant, is transmitted directly to the people at large, or whether just two or even just one command, perhaps just the first in the Jewish reckoning, "I am the Lord your God," constitutes the limit of the public revelation. I point this out simply to say that J has no monopoly on the "anxiety of representation," and just as multiple fools may rush in to add their content to revelation (as all sorts of politicians attempt to add riders to a bill), so multiple wise men may add their tortured representations of an ultimate moment of divine Presence.

One such fool, by Bloom's reckoning, rushed in with verses 16, 17 and 19, spoiling the silences of J. Yet there is no reason to regard this writer as a fool or even as a redactor in possession of the surrounding J material. The wisdom of the old documentary hypothesis here, by which 16, 17 and 19 were attributed to E, is the wisdom of supposing an equally capable imagination, imagining Revelation another way. I cannot bring myself to regard these verses as inferior work simply because they are so very much *not J*. Citing verse 18, which ends with the people trembling violently, Bloom says, "whether people or mountain tremble hardly matters in this great trope of immanent power." But it does matter. It matters that J conceives of the mountain trembling violently, while E imagines the people trembling. Verse 16, that is, attempts to represent a genuine, collective, spiritual sublime. For once, without murmurers, dissenters, skeptics, or Blooms, as E has it, all the people in the camp tremble. And then, magnificently, making this a second exodus transcending the first—indeed, a very image of transcendence—"Moses brought the people out from the camp to meet God; they took their stand at the foot of the mountain." Actually, translation belies an even more heightened effort at uniqueness here, for the phrase *likrat Elohim*, "towards God," is displaced grammatically, as though transcendence could be represented in sentence structure by bringing the people closer to God: "Moses brought *the people to God*, out of the camp; they took up their orderly station at the foot of the mountain." What we have here is no plodding filler work of a normative redactor, but the immensely capable imagination of another sort. The place of the redactor, the genius of the redactor, was to realize that both E and J were superb, sublime, indispensable. And verse 19 all the more so: "Moses would speak, and God would answer him audibly." Those who would translate the last word, *bikol*, as meaning "with thunder," rather than "with human voice," or "intelligibly," wipe away moonlight, E's moonlight, like mud. For E, the greatest possible imagination of revelation is a quiet conversation, one where Moses asks questions and God, in a kindly, gentle voice, answers him. This is not more or less sublime than J's picture of Yahweh and Moses quarrelling over who said what and who should see whom; it is simply *wholly other*.

If it is correct to hear in verse 19 something like a still small voice at the centre of endless agitation of fire and earthquake and thunder, an auditory and emotional reprieve (a temporal reprieve too, for "Moses would speak and God would answer him," all a summer's day[4]), we might add that the sense of transcendence here is established in a clearing all around which is the noise and confusion of partisanship. Bloom has brilliantly shown how J represents the writer's anxiety as Yahweh's anxiety of representation. From a wholly different perspective, Van Seters brings to Sinai a sense of a Priestly writer who advocates the rights and privileges of his interest group. In Van Seters's reading, the composite nature of the text must be thematically, rather than stylistically disassembled; there is really no personal, literary interest, just as surely as there is no historicity to such a scene. In Van Seters's reading, there are only two strands that need to be noted here, J and P.[5] J has a thematic interest in the legitimation of Moses and a strong sense of non-priestly, cultic ritual. Though Bloom would object, to be sure, that J has no interest in any cult whatsoever, from Van Seters's point of view this is palpably absurd when one is looking at a scene of cultic ritual written, or partly written, by J. For Van Seters, "the original instruction consisted of vs. 10–11 and 13b and has to do with consecrating the people so that they might ascend the mountain at the time of the theophany" (250). Thus for Van Seters, J's desideratum is just what Bloom singled out as J's nemesis, "the movement from an elite to a whole people." But the scene in Exodus 19 is not of a piece: "In contrast, vs. 12–13a have to do with consecrating the mountain as a sanctuary with the strictest taboos so that the people could not ascend." We should pause to note here not simply the distinction between consecrating the people and consecrating the mountain, but the implication that the mountain as symbolic sanctuary *points to Jerusalem,* points to the very struggle for the mind of Jerusalem that Bloom insists is nowhere in sight. For Jerusalem is a metonymy for both the Hebrews as a people and the temple ritual in particular, and in Van Seters's reading, the struggle for the mind of Jerusalem is a struggle, taken to Sinai, between J's noble vision of collective consecration and P's partisan self-interest in priestly cult, priestly privilege, priestly place. For Van Seters, the interest in 12–13a in consecrating the mountain as a sanctuary receives added reinforce-

---

[4] I borrow Milton's phrase, *Paradise Lost* 1.449, to suggest that the E vision of revelation may function as counterplot, a significantly placed, as well as a significantly other vision of revelation as still centre in a turning world.

[5] Van Seters's brilliant source analysis first appeared in "Comparing Scripture with Scripture"; the source division pages are revised, with particularized argument against a J-E division, in *The Life of Moses*, from which I cite by page number.

ment when the instructions are not carried out in vv. 14–19. Indeed, the purpose of the reprimand in 20ff is precisely to insist on the difference between priestly place and lay place. The story concerns not the anxiety of the J writer but the anxiety of the priestly class that the place of the priests in the nation's cultic ritual will not be ultimately and permanently privileged. Like the railings separating altar from churchgoers, the laws barring the people from the mountain are symbolic representations of privileged status. Van Seters's perspective might be summed up in his attribution on the basis of political, rather than literary interest: "The interest here is Priestly, even to the point of anticipating the later laws regarding the holiness of the sanctuary and priestly office" (251).

What shall one make of the radical disparity between Bloom and Van Seters? At stake is not just the attribution of Exodus 19.20-25, Bloom to J, Van Seters to P. The struggle is not just for this piece of text, nor even for "the mind of Jerusalem" in the larger sense of dominance, if not normativeness, in Hebrew thinking, or thought about Hebrew texts. In a sense Bloom's position represents all attempts to read literally, to read authorial intention as the intention of a person, a solitary man of genius, where Van Seters's position represents all attempts to read politically, to read "the interest here" as a class interest, a cultural determinant which refigures the story, whatever the story, in terms of a historically conditioned interest group.

And Moses, as it were, is caught between them, running up and down that mountain (oh for Mrs. Uruguay's donkey!) in an attempt to satisfy not just the demands of anxious deity or proprietary priests but, as it were, the ups and downs of critical fashion. We who gather at the base of the mountain can only wonder whether particular verses are E, J or P—and wonder at the achievements of the great moments, whatever their composition. If Van Seters is right, however, about verses 20-25 coming from the hand of P, it is nonetheless difficult to imagine that such a story of divine reproof, Mosaic quotation of Yahweh's earlier specification, and further divine reproof all arose from the single motive of priestly desire to protect property.[6] The story seems too much involved in individual vexation, Yahweh's and Moses's, for the politics to be the preeminent motive for metaphor; and the specification in verse

---

[6] Van Seters acknowledges, though he disputes, the widespread notion that verses 21-25 are secondary; see 250 n.7. Wellhausen and many of his immediate followers thought 19-25 were J, and Carpenter prints only verse 23 as secondary (see J. Estlin Carpenter and G. Harford-Battersby, *The Hexateuch*). Brevard Childs, reviewing the dispute, concludes of verse 23 that "the loose paraphrase of the command is not necessarily a sign of being secondary, but again belongs to the pattern being employed" (*The Book of Exodus* 364).

24 that Aaron should ascend next time with Moses, but the priests should not dare to break through, seems hardly something the priests would invent to further their struggle for the mind of Jerusalem.

    I remain, at the base of that mountain, adding my own anxiety, the anxiety of readerly incompetence of judgment, to that proposed by Bloom for J and by Van Seters for P. Though both cannot be right about the attributions, both are, I firmly believe, right to continue to try and imagine such attributions, however much the critical fashion in biblical studies has turned against such work. Bloom concludes his explication of the Sinai revelation by imagining that "when Moses reminds Yahweh that Sinai is off-limits anyway, Yahweh evidently is too preoccupied and too little taken with Moses even to listen, and merely repeats his warning that he may be uncontrollable, even by himself." A Yahweh "too preoccupied" to do any better is a preeminently Bloomian deity. But whether personal or political preoccupation has gotten there first and been primarily responsible for what others can only partially reconstruct, there remains both the nobility of the critic's struggle—and the moral imperative to give a little ground. Like our contemporary worshipers at Al Aksa or Solomon's retaining wall, our biblical scholars will lose nothing by acknowledging the competing claims for the mind or turf of Jerusalem.

Works Cited

Carpenter, J. Estlin and G. Harford-Battersby. *The Hexateuch ... Arranged in Its Constitutent Documents*. London: Longmans, 1900.
Childs, Brevard. The *Book of Exodus: A Critical, Theological Commentary*. Philadelphia: Westminster, 1974.
Kugel, James. *The Bible as It Was*. Cambridge, MA: Harvard UP, 1991.
Stevens, Wallace. *Collected Poems*. New York: Knopf, 1954.
Van Seters, John. *Abraham in History and Tradition*. New Haven: Yale UP, 1975.
―――. "Comparing Scripture with Scripture: Some Observations on the Sinai Pericope of Exodus 19-24." *Canon, Theology, and Old Testament Interpretation: Essays in Honor of Brevard S. Childs*. Ed. Gene M. Tucker et al. Philadelphia: Fortress, 1988. 111-30.
―――. *The Life of Moses: The Yahwist as Historian in Exodus-Numbers*. Louisville: Westminster-John Knox, 1994.

Enoch and Elijah: Some Remarks on Apotheosis, Theophany and Jewish Mysticism

MOSHE IDEL

Among leading contemporary thinkers, Harold Bloom's interest in and contribution to a novel understanding of religion is outstanding. Especially from his introduction to *The Book of J* to the more recent *Omens of Millennium*, his writings on specifically religious issues have expanded substantially. His book on the American religion represents the most extensive treatment of topics which permeate Bloom's thought and writings. His intense concern with the studies and ideas of Gershom Scholem, Hans Jonas, Ioan P. Couliano, and more recently of Henry Corbin and mine, and his many written expressions about them, are part and parcel of an intellectual career for which the spiritual quest is quintessential. Bloom's interest is, to use Martin Buber's expression, "filtered." He is most interested in topics related to Gnosticism and Gnostic-like phenomena and their reverberations. Especially prominent is his emphatic reiteration of the apotheotic move, connected in Jewish material to the Enoch-Metatron theme, namely the theory found already in Jewish sources of late antiquity that Enoch became an angelic figure under the name Metatron. It is the surge of this theme that has fascinated Bloom in his insightful exposition of the nature and origin of Mormon religion and more recently of the American religious scene in general (*American* 99–103, 110–11, 117 and 262). Later on he has even described Metatron, the hypostasis of Enoch, as "the angel of our moment" (*Omens* 50; more generally, see 44–53 and 206–07; also Wexler 32). In search of more powerful forms of religion than those propagated in the more conventional brands of religion, including modern Judaism, Bloom has turned to mystical traditions in which mythical elements are quite prominent. I would say that this convergence between the apotheotic and the mythical is the defining gist of Bloom's "filtered" approach. Let me offer here a brief survey of Jewish mysticism which traces the history of some of the themes that have preoccupied Bloom, especially in his *Omens*, in order to situate his project in a wider development within Jewish mysticism.

1. Jewish Mysticism: A Short Phenomenological History

If Moses is one of the most important protagonists involved in different forms of biblical theophany, two other figures, Enoch and Elijah, represent a minor biblical theme: human apotheosis. While Moses never visited God but was often visited by Him, those two figures were taken alive to a higher realm. Different in time and nature as these two figures are portrayed in the Bible, they were often associated in post-biblical literatures in order to illustrate the possibility of ascent on high. In Jewish texts both become angels: Enoch turned into Metatron, while Elijah retained his name. The latter's name is doubly theophoric: the consonants $E\,j$ and YHW are divine names. Thus, the prophet's name, unlike that of the patriarch, was particularly appropriate to express a transformation that brings someone close to God. In the case of Metatron, however, there are at least three different types of affinities between this figure and divine names. According to a Rabbinic statement, the numerical value of Metatron, namely 314, is numerically equivalent to that of the consonants of the name Shadday (BT, *Sanhedrin* fol. 38a). Moreover, according to other ancient traditions, Metatron was called YHWH Qatan, the smaller Tetragrammaton (Scholem, *Jewish Gnosticism* 50–51). Last but not least: scholars have already pointed out that the ancient angel Yaho'el was superseded by Metatron, and some of the former's attributes have been transposed to the latter (Box xxv; Odeberg 99 and 144; Scholem, *Major Trends* 68–69; Scholem, *Origins of Kabbalah* 187; Scholem, *Jewish Gnosticism* 47 and 51; Scholem, *Kabbalah* 378; Smith 51–53; Greenfield, "Prolegomenon" xxxi; Wolfson, *Through a Speculum* 224; Deutsch 52 and 97–98). The importance of the similarity between the role of Yaho'el and Metatron as revealing themselves on the sea and saving the people of Israel has also been emphasized recently (see Idel, "Enoch" 51).[1] Indeed, in one of the magical texts the two names occur together (Greenfield, "Prolegomenon" xxxix; Greenfield, "Notes" 156). It should be mentioned that a certain affinity between Metatron

---

[1] See also Gilles Quispel as to the existence of the angelic Messiah in Jewish-Christian texts, which has been invested with the name of God (149–51).

and Elijah is found already in two different discussions in the Babylonian Talmud, where the two figures are described as being punished by sixty lashes, by using the precisely very same Aramaic words, both in connection to esoteric issues (compare BT, *Haggigah* fol. 15a with BT, *Babba Metzia* fol. 85b).

In fact, we may describe one of the main developments of the history of Jewish mysticism as a gradual growth of the interest by Jewish thinkers in (and their discussions of) mystical patterns exemplified by those figures; they constitute figures who combine apotheotic and theophanic events (Idel, "Metatron" 22–44; Idel, "Enoch" 220–40; Idel, "Adam and Enoch" 197–218). The increasing growth in the role apotheosis plays has much to do with a variety of other developments, more eminently the emergence of an immense angelology since the Second Temple literature. Within the broader angelic hierarchy it was easier to allocate a proper place to the translated *perfecti*. It seems that this development has quite ancient sources, as the importance attributed to a great angel, understood as the creator of the world, according to several testimonies, shows. The scholarly literature on the gigantic angel is growing and testifies to the importance of ancient sources of a major theological development in ancient Judaism, the later development of which considerably enriched Jewish thought (see Hurtado 45 and 85–92; Collins 98–103; H. A. Wolfson 89–106; Fossum, *The Name of God* 18, 23, 329–32 and 337; Fossum, "Magharians" 303–43; Couliano, *Experiences* 70–71; Couliano, *Tree* 54; Daniélou 205–07; Scholem, *Origins of Kabbalah* 211–12; Wasserstrom 141–54). This ancient Jewish tradition, which might also have influenced the Gnostic vision of the Demiourgos as creator and legislator, did not disappear from Jewish literature. Its career still awaits a proper study, which cannot be done in this framework; it may, however, be connected with the binitarian trend found in Kabbalah since its emergence (Idel, "Kabbalistic Prayer" 265–86; see also Idel, *Kabbalah and Eros* 49–52).

In the following, I shall survey some of the phases of the development of the angelic status of Enoch and Elijah and the role they played in some mystical Jewish texts, some of them addressed recently by Bloom. However, before focusing our discussion more on Elijah, let me briefly discuss the associations between him and Enoch in a number of medieval Jewish texts. They may reflect the influence of the Christian view of the two witnesses for the advent of the Christ, though it is possible that both traditions draw from earlier sources (Macina 71–99; Klausner 451–57).

2. An Apotheotic Couple: Enoch and Elijah in Jewish Mysticism

It is in the early thirteenth-century philosophical commentator R. David Kimhi that two short passages about these figures as a couple occur. In his commentary on the book of the Kings he writes:

> And the opinion of our masses, as well as that of our Sages, is that the Lord brought him [Elijah] into the Garden of Eden with his body, as Adam had been before the sin, and He also brought in Enoch there. (Commentary on 2 Kings 2.1)

The impression is that he gives expression, somehow unwillingly, to a popular belief. Less reserved is his tone in his commentary on Genesis:

> For the Lord brought in Enoch [and] Elijah alive to the Garden of Eden, in soul and in body while they were still alive, eating of the fruit of the tree and serving the Lord, as Adam had been before he sinned, and they will remain there until the Messianic era. (Commentary on Genesis 6.24)

More enthusiastic about the possibility of an apotheotic transformation of a human being is Nahmanides. He was presumably acquainted with Kimhi's views, but I assume that he drew his views (presented below) from other sources. He emulates those who abandon the affairs of this world and pay no regard to this world at all, as though they were not corporeal beings, but all their intent and purpose is fixed on their creator alone—as in the case of Elijah and Enoch, who lived on forever in body and soul, after having attained the union of their souls with the Great Name (Nahmanides, Commentary on Leviticus 18.4).

Though part of a commentary on the Bible, Nahmanides' tone is much more of someone who recommends a certain ideal ascetic form of life which may ensure the perfect union with the divine. It should be emphasized that Nahmanides resorts to the Tetragrammaton in order to designate the divinity, a point which may be of a certain importance for better understanding his view. The letters of the Tetragrammaton YHWH are, after all, part and parcel of the theophoric name of Elijah: EliYaHW. On the other hand, Nahmanides was one of those early Kabbalists who emphasized the role of the garment in the revelations of the angels and divine attributes, an issue that will be developed in some of the discussions below (Wolfson, "Secret" xxxix–xl).[2]

---

[2] For later Kabbalistic developments, see Aloro 23 and Werblowsky 206–33.

Nahmanides was not alone in his interest in the special status of those figures. In his own Catalan town Gerona, an older Kabbalist, R. Ezra ben Shlomo, assessed that "Prior to his eating, Adam was entirely spiritual, and was garbed in an angelic garb [*lovesh mal'akhut*], as Enoch and Elijah" (see Scholem, *Pirkei Yesod* 196, and Scholem, *On the Mystical Shape* 68).[3] Here the concept of angelic garb is quite conspicuous, unlike Nahmanides' failure to mention it in the context of Elijah.

In this context, the emergence of traditions attributing to Elijah the revelation of Kabbalistic traditions, especially related to prayer, should be mentioned (Scholem, *Origins of Kabbalah* 236–37). Though the texts which preserve those traditions are relatively late, since the very end of the thirteenth century, their relevance for the point made here as to the ascent of the apotheotic and theophanic elements is quite obvious. It is some time around the end of the thirteenth century that Elijah started to play a most important role in Jewish mystical tradition. This is the case with the book of the *Zohar*, where this figure becomes omnipresent and paramount in discussions of mystical topics, and in a tradition attributed to R. David ben Yehudah he-Hasid, who was reported to have enjoyed revelations of Elijah (Idel, "Kabbalistic Material" 198).

The names of Elijah and Enoch as related to angelic entities recur in a great number of Kabbalistic writings, where they are sometimes described as two cherubs, and identified with Metatron and Sandalfon.[4] However, the most important elaboration on the two figures is found in a discussion between R. Isaac ben Shmuel of Acre and one of his teachers, a certain R. Yehudah ha-Darshan Ashkenazi:

> What is the matter—asked R. Isaac—that enabled Enoch's gaining to all this, because the matter of Elijah is known, but what is the reason of Enoch['s merit]? He [the master] said that he received [a tradition] that Enoch was a shoemaker . . . and each and every hole that he was perforating by the awl in the leather, he was blessing with the whole heart and with a complete *Kavvanah*, to God, blessed be He, and he was drawing down the blessing to the emanated Metatron. And he never forgot to bless even in the case of one hole but was doing it always, so that out of love he

---

[3] R. Ezra's text has been copied by R. Issac of Acre in his *Me'irat 'Einayyim* 27. On the status of Adam before the fall according to R. Azriel of Gerona, an associate of R. Ezra, see Bezalel Safran, "Rabbi Azriel and Nahmanides."

[4] See Ms. Paris BN 859, fol. 15b and 16a, where the two biblical figures are described quite conspicuously as angels before their apotheosis; see also the passages adduced in Idel, "Enoch" 274.

disappeared ['einennu], because God took him, and he merited to be called Metatron, and his rank was very great. (Goldreich 47)

This short passage had a wide impact on Jewish mystical literature; it reverberated in a long series of Kabbalistic and Hasidic texts and contributed to the ascent of the theory of worship in corporeality, 'Avodah be-Gashmiyyut, in Hasidism (see Idel, "Enoch"). However, this is not the only discussion R. Isaac had of the explanation for Enoch's achievement. In a manuscript which is apparently compiled by him, he asked another mentor he had, R. Nathan ben Sa'adya Harar, a disciple of Abraham Abulafia:

> "Why did not God do the same good to our forefather Abraham who underwent ten ordeals and stood all of them?" He said: "Do not speak about Abraham our father, blessed be his memory, [in this context] since his rank is very high in comparison to the rank of Enoch, since he is the man of Mercy, the head of the building [namely of the seven lower *sefirot* which start with the *sefirah* of *Hesed*, 'Mercy']." (Ms. New York JTS, 1777, fol. 33b; see the full Hebrew passage, its context and an analysis in Idel, "Enoch" 268–69)

Though adhering to ecstatic Kabbalah, R. Nathan offered a theosophical answer: Enoch ascended to a lower status, that of an angel found beneath the last *sefirah*, Malkhut, while Abraham is related to the *sefirah* of Hesed.

The Ashkenazi mentor of R. Isaac, otherwise an unknown figure, preferred, however, an answer based upon the possibility of transformation by the total dedication of one's deeds to God. He could rely on an Ashkenazi view, however, according to which the two figures are tightly connected to each other by dint of numerical and linguistic speculations:

> YHWH WHYH, in *gematria Ben*, because he was a man, who is Enoch ben Yared; Yaho'el in *gematria be-Yam* [by the sea], because it is written [Exodus 14.2] "before it [*Nikheho*] shall you encamp by the sea," and from *Nikheho* emerges [by anagrammatising the consonants *Hanokh*, because he revealed himself by the sea. And in *gematria ba-kol*, because he bears the entire world, and he is relying on the finger on God. And the Tetragrammaton is hinted at two times twenty-six and also the *gematria* of *'Eliyahu* [is 52], also *Yaho'el* also *Ke-Lev* [namely, 'like a heart'], because it is the heart of the world, and all the [divine] names are hinted at, because it is appointed on the Torah . . . and it is the prince of the world. (Epstein, fols. 7b–8a; see Dan, "Esoteric" 220–21; Dan, "Seventy Names" 19–23; Liebes, "Angels" 171–96; Abrams 301 and 302–05)

Here the affinities between the two biblical figures become much tighter. Yaho'el is considered as one of the seventy names of Metatron, related explicitly to Enoch, and this angel's name is an anagram of the consonants of *'Eliyahu*. To a certain extent at least, the description of Metatron above has a cosmological dimension, as in the case of the gigantic angel mentioned above and, on the other hand, as in the case of Christianity and here Kimhi also, there is an eschatological overtone: this is the power which was present at the moment of the salvation of the Israelites on the Red Sea.

The above version of the tradition about the seventy names of Metatron is only one of the extant variants; according to another one, preserved in a book written in 1280 in Capua by R. Abraham Abulafia, the eschatological tone was much more prominent. In his commentary on *The Guide for the Perplexed*, entitled *Sitrei Torah*, he writes about Metatron that:

> it is called in our language by many names, and it is the prince of the world, and Metatron, the angel of the [divine] Face ... and its name is Shadday, like the name of its master and its cognomen is Metatron ... and it is wise, [and] speaking, the universal spirit, which has been called by the philosophers the Agent Intellect ... and the divine Spirit, and *Shekhinah*, and the faithful Spirit, and the Kingdom of the Heaven ... and in our language the intellect has been designated by the [terms] *Mal'akh*, and *Keruv*, and in some places it will be called *'Elohim*, as we have said concerning the fact that "its name is like that of its master," and behold that the sages have called it *Enoch* and said that "Enoch is Metatron" ... and the first name out of the seventy names of Metatron is *Yaho'el* whose secret is *Ben* ... and its name is *'Eliyahu* and it is also the explicit name, *Yod*, *Yod*, *Vav* which is the double name ... and behold, it also "is the Redeemer [*hu' ha-go'el*]" and it is "in the whole [*ba-kol*]" of "your heart [*libbekha*]," and it is the ruler of the world. (Ms. Paris BN 774, fols. 129b–30b; see Idel, *Mystical Experience* 118)

The most crucial move in this text is the identification of the archangel of Jewish esotericism, Metatron, with the Neo-Aristotelian concept of Agent Intellect. This move, though not totally new with Abulafia, is quite characteristic of his writings, and reflects one of the most influential syntheses between modes of thought based on revelation and philosophical traditions.

The description of Metatron as the "ruler of the world"—*manhig ha-'olam*—reflects both the Talmudic concept of the prince of the world, and the kingly perception of this figure in the Hebrew *Enoch*, and it occurs also in the context of Metatron in a passage by R. Eleazar of Worms, *Sefer ha-Hokhmah* (Ms. Oxford-Bodleiana 1568, fol. 21a).⁵ On the other hand, Maimonides' identification between the Talmudic angel of the world, *sar ha-'olam*, and the Agent Intellect is also fundamental for this quotation (Maimonides, *The Guide for the Perplexed* 2: 60). This passage represents a specimen of the expansion of the role of the couple of apotheotic figures in Jewish mysticism: they are conflated with an ancient angelic entity which serves as the governor of the world. Abulafia draws here upon a passage from a still unparalleled version of a *Commentary on the Seventy Names of Metatron*, according to which there are numerical equivalences between several concepts, some of them relevant to our discussions above: like *Ben*, namely 'Son,' also *'Eliyahu* is numerically equivalent to 52, as is *Yaho'el*, and the Hebrew phrases *hu' ha-Go'el, ba-kol, libbekha, yod yod vav*, YHWH + YHWH.

There can be no doubt that the use of the *gematria* technique, widespread in Ashkenazi texts, was quintessential for creating the above equations, as much as the eventual conceptual relations between its members. However, what is conspicuously absent in the Ashkenazi discussion is the reference to any intellectual-hypostatic status of Metatron, so characteristic of Abulafia's writings. The archangel is described in terms stemming from the stock of the more traditional and mythical forms of late ancient and early medieval Judaism. However, the intellectual hierarchies adopted by Maimonides and his followers created a non-mythical chain of beings which emphasized the mental and the cerebral as the peak of the religious experience. This later development was integrated by Abulafia into a discourse which is more mystical and more dependent upon Jewish mystical terminology, a discourse that attenuated the mythical elements in the earlier Jewish texts, as we shall see below.

The Ashkenazi literature should be conceived as an intermediary literary corpus that preserved fragmented traditions concerning the ancient angel Yaho'el as instrumental in redemption of the people of Israel. The name *Yaho'el* appears already in the ancient Jewish apocryphal Apocalypse of Abraham (Hurtado 79–80). Jarl Fossum has pointed out in many details the significance of this angel in earlier Jewish traditions; he has suggested a certain nexus between Yaho'el and the high priest, a motif that is going to recur in the case of Metatron later on. He

---

⁵ On the concept of the ruler of the world in ancient Jewish texts, see Scholem, *Jewish Mysticism* 47–48; Segal 245–68; Couliano, *Experiences* 69–70; Idel, "Kabbalistic Prayer" 272–73.

mentions the plausibility that the name *Yao* is a name of the Christ and has to do with a saviour figure, a point reminiscent of the Ashkenazi text cited above (Fossum, *Name of God* 289, 307 and 318–21). Metatron, the main subject in the Ashkenazi quotation, is referred to by the angelic theophoric name *Yaho'el*, a theme that will reverberate in Abraham Abulafia's mystical messianology, as we shall see in the next section. The redemptive nature of this angel is hinted at by his revelation on the sea, the most salvific moment in the whole Pentateuch. There can be no doubt that Metatron-Yaho'el reflects divine intervention under the guise of an angel that bears the divine name.

The above passages reflect the two main tendencies I have hinted at above: on the one hand, the apotheotic one, as represented by the transformation of a man into an angel and, on the other hand, the theophanic aspect, as hinted at by the redemptive revelation on the sea. We may describe the apotheotic move as culminating, at least in many cases, in theophanic events.

3. Elijah in Ecstatic Kabbalah

The apotheotic ascent of Elijah is biblical and does not need any additional proof-texts, but for Maimonidean thinkers like Abulafia it constitutes a serious religious problem. The corporeal translation of the two figures on high was celebrated, as seen above, by Nahmanides, but they constituted a big quandary for the Maimonidean thinkers, including their followers among the Kabbalists. The thirteenth-century ecstatic Kabbalist R. Abraham Abulafia is quite reluctant to admit it. He writes, in one of the most sincere expressions of embarrassment, as follows:

> There is no need to ask us difficult questions concerning the issue of Enoch and Elijah, since no-one knows the essence of this issue. However, if you will say that the tradition testifies according to its plain sense and even the gentiles believe that they will descend from heaven at the time of the saviour, we shall not debate it. But we shall say to him that this issue did not happen to a part of mankind but to two persons of the species. And perhaps it was for the purpose of a great thing, but it is quite strange since in the human species there were much nobler individuals than those two, according to the testimony of the [holy] books and nevertheless no-one said about them that they live that kind of life like those two, as the tales of the multitude are about their issues. Thus they [the stories] will be obliterated because of their being in a small minority and we shall not believe anyone who brings a proof from them, as it is not an intellectual proof but an imaginary one. (*Sitrei Torah*, Ms. Paris BN 774, fol. 132b)

However, even he was ready to use the figure of Elijah as an allegory but for the intellectual apotheosis on the one hand, and for the double-edged nature of intellectual revelation on the other. In his *Hayyei ha-'Olam ha-Ba'*, when resorting to a magical tradition, he said that:

> Yafeifiyah [the Prince of the Torah] ... taught Torah, that is, the entire Torah, to Moses our teacher for forty days and forty nights, corresponding to the formation of the fetus in its mother's womb, [the time necessary] to distinguish between male and female. Therefore, it is possible for a person to enjoy the radiance of the *Shekhinah* in this world without food for forty days and forty nights, like Moses and Elijah [cf. Exodus 24.18 and 1 Kings 19.8]. And the secret of the names of both of them is known to you, and he combines one with the other: first Moses, and then Elijah, and their combination emerges as a Divine Name [*Shem ha-'Elohi*; an anagram of *Mosheh* and *'Eliyahu*], and it is in its secret [meaning] the name of the son, and he is the son of God. (Ms. Oxford-Bodleiana 1582, fols. 22b–23a; Ms. Paris BN 777, fol. 113a)[6]

Abulafia resorts to the imagery of corporeal birth in order to allude to spiritual rebirth. The names of Moses and Elijah as interpreted by Abulafia point to the divine name, which is a means by which someone may become the spiritual son of God, namely an intellect. The historical events, namely the forty years or days mentioned in the Bible in connection with the two figures, become allegories for the growth of the spiritual capacity, which is no more connected to the ancient texts but reflects present developments. Elijah is not only a name for an ancient prophet, an angel who reveals secrets and reveals itself on many occasions: it is also the human intellect that is born by resorting to a certain mystical technique. The main manner in which Abulafia 'discovers' the relevance of the biblical literary material is the deconstruction and reconstruction of language, and in the specific case discussed above, the

---

[6] In the context of the first two lines of this passage, see the magical book, *Shimmushei Torah*: "The Holy One, Blessed be He, has immediately called Yafeifiyah, the prince of the Torah, and he [the latter] gave him [Moses] the Torah ... and all the servant angels become his lovers and each and every one of them gave him a remedy and the secret of the names, which emerge from each and every pericope [section of the Torah], and all their [magical] uses ... and this is the [magical] use given to him by the angels, by means of Yafeifiyah, the prince of the Torah, and by Metatron, the Prince of the Face. And Moses has transmitted it to Eleazar, and Eleazar to his son Pinhas, who is [identical to] Elijah, the High and Respectable Priest." Cf. *Ma'ayan Hokhmah* 58–59; and see Idel, "The Concept of the Torah" 27–28.

names of the two figures. The analysis of language is, however, a rather free manipulation of the linguistic material which does not offer anything similar to an insight into the context of the proper names under scrutiny.

In the same manner, we find an interpretation of the numerical value of the consonants of 'Eliyahu as pointing to the "form of the intellect"—*tzurat ha-sekhel*. An anonymous commentator on the Pentateuch, writing presumably at the beginning of the fourteenth century, offers the following calculation: the *gematria* of *tzurat ha-sekhel* is 1051, and by reducing the 1000 to 1, we receive $51 + 1 = 52$, like 'Eliyahu (*Commentary on the Pentateuch*, Ms. Oxford-Bodleiana 1920, fol. 36b). For him, Elijah is the "influx of God, blessed be He, sent to the illuminati" (ibid. 27). Again, a strong exegetical method was put in the service of a strong allegorical-spiritualistic interpretation.

A similar linguistic procedure is obvious also in another case when Abulafia interprets the letters of 'Eliyahu as follows: *EU* points to the divine attribute of mercy while the consonants *YaHW* stand for the attribute of judgment. According to his view, the two contradictory attributes are found in the same entity, which is the source of providence, emerging from the supernal influx (*Sitrei Torah*, Ms. Paris BN 774, fol. 168b). This theory amounts again to an allegorical understanding of Elijah's name, as pointing to the unified nature of the intellectual influx which becomes diversified in accordance to the lower recipients. This inclusion of the two divine attributes makes Elijah, an intellectual extension of the divine, more similar to God. The double nature of the intellectual experience returns again in the same book, where the pattern of two attributes is reiterated, now in connection to the mystic himself:

> And you become perfect in the knowledge of the well-known attributes of God, by which the world is always conducted. And let your mind pursue after your intellect, to resemble him in them, according to your ability always. And know in your intellect that you have already annihilated those faculties called superfluous to you, and let all your intentions be for the sake of heaven. And be God-fearing in the essence of true fear, as you would fear the Angel of Death when you see it, entirely full of eyes [see BT, *Avodah Zarah* fol. 20b]. In its left hand is burning fire, and in its right hand a two-edged sword, performing the vengeance of the covenant, and in its mouth is a consuming fire, and he comes to you and asks you to give him his share of your self; and he is half of your existence, for example, and he seeks to cut off your limbs, one by one, and you see it all with your eyes. (*Sitrei Torah*, Ms. Paris BN 774, fol. 155ab)

This duality plays an important role in Abulafia's anthropology: man has two instincts, as in rabbinic psychology, but they are interpreted often as two angels which accompany man, again a rabbinic stand, all pointing to the duality of imagination and intellect. Though recurrent in a number of Abulafian texts, it is especially explicit in a Hebrew fragment from a lost book of Abulafia's, together with its Latin translation, both printed anonymously in Augustino Giustiniani's *Polyglot* of the Psalms (Psalm CIXL).

Abulafia's interpretation of the name of Elijah had some repercussions which did not add too much to his view (Ms. New York JTS 1853, fol. 3a; see also *Commentary on the Pentateuch*, Ms. Oxford-Bodleiana 1920, fol. 2a). According to another interesting discussion, found in his *Hayyei ha-'Olam ha-Ba'*, whoever receives a certain tradition from the "power of the influx" knows that he received it from Elijah (Ms. Paris BN 777, fol. 110a). Here Elijah is quite conspicuously identified with the intellectual influx.

As suggested above, Abulafia's exegesis is atemporal, attracting the classical texts into a web of interpretations which serves his spiritualistic drive. This means that the more archaic themes, like the ancient gigantic angel represented by the name Yaho'el, turned into an intellectual hypostasis active all the time in a manner that is indifferent to man and his vicissitudes. The synthesis between the archaic angelology and the philosophical hierarchy facilitates more individualistic attainments, which are indifferent to place and time.

However, it seems that in the specific cases discussed above, there is a more pressing present concern, which should be taken into consideration for a more profound understanding of Abulafia's stand. In his voluminous corpus of writings, he resorted to Elijah in very few instances, most of them already discussed above. All the quotations adduced in the earlier paragraphs stem from two books: *Sitrei Torah* and *Hayyei ha-'Olam ha-Ba'*, written, respectively, in Capua and Rome in 1280. This fact is, in my opinion, quite significant. In that year Abulafia made an abortive attempt to meet the Pope as part of a broader messianic enterprise. This is also his fortieth year, a year interpreted by him as the time for a spiritual rebirth (Idel, *Mystical Experience* 198–202). If this period of his life was rife with eschatological expectations concerning his own status and activities as a messiah (though indeed of a peculiar type), the recurrence of the theme of Elijah may indeed be one more detail that reveals his eschatological tensions.

It seems that, later on, his interest in the Elijah theme declined. Even in *Sefer ha-'Ot*, one of the most eschatological of his writings where there is a description of a meeting with an old man, who is described as Yaho'el, during the course of a vision, Elijah is not mentioned: "And he showed me an old man, with white hair, seated upon the throne of judgment ... and he ascended to the mountain of judgment, and I came close to the elder and he bowed and prostrated himself" (*Sefer ha-'Ot* 84). The old man interprets Abulafia's vision and then says: "And my name [is] Yaho'el, that I have agreed [*ho'il*] to speak with you now several years" (27). Written around 1285 in Messina, *Sefer ha-'Ot* is, from the literary point of view, part of Abulafia's prophetic books, which deal with mystico-messianic issues, characteristic of 1280. Since Yaho'el mentions that he revealed himself to Abulafia for several years, we may read the quotations as reflecting a much more experiential aspect of Abulafia's life, rather than quotations of Ashkenazi material and its philosophical interpretation. Mentioning the throne of judgment as it appears in *Sefer ha-'Ot* is evidently connected with the two attributes by which the world is led, as discussed above. Metatron, like Elijah, is depicted as possessing contradictory characteristics, as we find also in a treatise of a Kabbalist influenced by Abulafia, R. Reuben ha-Tzarfati in his *Perush la-Ma'arekhet ha-'Elohut*: "For the Agent Intellect, which is Metatron, the Prince of the Presence, has two impulses, that is, two angels, one appointed over mercy, and one over judgment" (R. Reuben ha-Tazarfati, fol. 96b; see also Werblowsky 220-21).[7] This revelation notwithstanding, which comes so close to the passage on Yaho'el and Elijah found in the earlier book of Abulafia and adduced above, Elijah himself does not occur.

Interestingly enough, Elijah plays a very important role in one of the classics of Kabbalah composed at the end of the fourteenth century or early fifteenth century in Byzantium, *Sefer ha-Peliy'ah* (Kushnir-Oron 75-76). In this book, Abulafian material has been integrated at several places verbatim, but there are also instances where the ecstatic Kabbalah was influential, though I cannot detect the precise source which inspired the anonymous author. I wonder whether Abulafia's attribution of a certain importance to Elijah may have been instrumental in promoting the figure of Elijah in the eyes of this author.

However, the allegorical interpretation of Elijah remained part of Abulafia's school long after his death. In mid-fifteenth-century Italy, an

---

[7] This dialectical understanding is evidently connected with the perception of Enoch as having both good and bad attributes found already in some midrashism. See Liebes' discussion of revelations of youth and the old in the *Zohar*: Liebes, "Myth vs. Symbol" 219-23.

anonymous thinker strongly influenced by Abulafia's thought described redemption in the following terms: "Elijah is the divine intellectual influx that is the redeeming angel" (Ms. Oxford-Bodleiana 836, fol. 155b), while elsewhere in the same book he writes that:

> The great salvation that is the true salvation and the perfect redemption which after it will never again be an exile will transpire through the agency of two angels . . . . One is called Elijah and the other—the "Son of David." "Elijah" is an allusion to the intellectual power whereas "Son of David" alludes to the prophetic power . . . the power of prophecy, that is allegorically rendered as the Son of David, will not indwell unless all the bodily powers and all the instincts will be terminated, in other words will be subjugated and acquiescent to the powers of intellect and prophecy. (Toldot 'Adam, Ms. Oxford-Bodleiana 836, fol. 159a–59b)[8]

It should be mentioned that by spiritualizing Elijah in a messianic context, another vision of messianism emerges, one closer to the philosophical brand than to the apocalyptic one. This more comprehensive drift to allegorize important segments of Judaism, in my opinion, elicited a reaction among some Spanish Kabbalistic circles since the mid-fourteenth century. Exemplified first by R. Shem Tov ibn Shem Tov's *Sefer ha-'Emunot*, it reaches its peak in a major Kabbalistic school that will preoccupy us immediately below.

4. Elijah as a Revelatory Garment in Sefer ha-Meshiv

Perhaps the strongest role attributed to Elijah in the general economy of Judaism is found in an anonymous literary corpus called the *Book of the Responding Entity* (*Sefer ha-Meshiv*). This huge body of Kabbalistic literature—extant almost only in manuscripts—spread all over the Jewish world, and it amounts to a thousand folios, a small part of what apparently was once a much more voluminous literature, now lost. I assume that most of the material has been committed to writing in Spain, perhaps in Castile, around 1470.[9]

---

[8] See also Ms. Oxford-Bodleiana 836, fol. 155b, where the intellectual influx is described as "the redeeming angel" which dwells into men, using the messianic verse from Isaiah 11.2.

[9] On the writing which forms the Kabbalistic literature of this circle, see Scholem, "The Maggid," and Idel, "Inquiries," "Origin of Alchemy," "Jewish Magic," "Magic and Kabbalah," "Lost Books," "Attitude to Christianity," and "Neglected Treatises."

The official author of most of this literature is conceived to be none other than God, and sometimes one of the most respected archangels, Azriel for example. God and various archangels spoke in these dreams in the first person, addressing the Kabbalist in the second person, and occasionally also dealing with ways to solve some of the more personal problems of the Kabbalist himself. However, the vast majority of the topics dealt with have to do with Kabbalistic issues. Let us start with a quotation that compares the revelations of Elijah to ancient *perfecti* to more contemporary revelations; in this quotation, God is speaking in the first person to the Kabbalist:

> When he [Elijah] has ascended on high, he has acquired the power of spirituality [*Koah ruhaniyyut*] as an angel indeed, to ascend and to become [afterwards] corporeal and descend to this lower world where you are existing, in order to perform miracles or to disclose My power and My *dynamis* in the world, and he is causing the descent of My power in the world, forcefully and compelling, from My great name, that is an integral part of him. And because of this great secret he did not have the taste of death, so that he will be able to cause the descent of My power and disclose My secret by the power of My precious names. And he is called "The bird of heaven will bring the voice" [Ecclesiastes 10.20] and no-one should have any doubt on it. He was revealing himself to the ancient pious one, factually in a spiritual body, which was enclosed and embodied in matter, and they were speaking with him, by the virtue of their piety, and he was revealing himself *in corpore* and *in spiritu*. This is the reason why those dreaming a dream are causing the descent of My power, by his mediation, within you, without a speech and a voice, and this is the secret of [the verse] [Deuteronomy 4.6] "for this is your wisdom and your understanding in the sight of the nations." And My power is bound to him [namely to Elijah or to his name] and he is bound to your souls and discloses to you the secrets of My Torah, without a speech. And a time will come, very soon, that he will reveal himself to you *in corpore et spiritu* and this will be a sign by the coming of the Messiah. And by his descending to earth together with him [Elijah together with the Messiah] then will he reveal *in corpore et in spiritu*, and many others will see him. (Ms. Jerusalem, NUL 80 147, fols. 96b–97a)[10]

The divine speaker is distinguishing between the *illud tempus*, when the pious were able to see Elijah both in body and spirit, and the Messianic era, on the one hand, and the present situation, when such a direct and corporeal revelation is apparently impossible. In lieu of the

---

[10] This passage was copied in Safed in the middle of the sixteenth century by R. ʿOvadiah Hamon (Ms. Oxford-Bodleiana 1597, fol. 58b–59a). The Hebrew original is printed in Idel, "Inquiries" 212–13.

strong waking vision, an oneiric revelation is allowed, one in which the divine power is connected to Elijah and he is connected to the souls of men, while they dream. In other words, in the dreams of some people at least, Elijah is still revealing himself, bringing with him the divine power. What is fascinating in this quotation is the fact that the speechless revelation of the present is conceived as inferior to the bodily one of the ancient and future days. The vision of the body and the audible speech are conceived as quite superior to the more dream-like revelations, which cannot be seen by someone else in addition to the dreamer. The spiritual, oneiric and private revelations are conceived to be less powerful forms of receiving messages from above. Redemption means, *inter alia*, the possibility to see in the state of wakefulness what we intimate in dreams. Nevertheless, during the dream, Elijah is conceived as revealing the secrets of the Torah, an expression that plausibly stands for Kabbalistic issues. To dream is therefore to open oneself to the realm where the encounter with the divine is still possible, though somehow mediated by the quasi-angelic power named Elijah. He 'comes' in a spiritual body, and may reveal his message by speech but also speechlessness. By suggesting a verse in a certain context, the verse becomes specifically relevant for resolving the question. Thus the links between the supernatural powers and man are the biblical verses, known by 'all the parts' involved in the oneiric enterprise. Those techniques may contribute to a better understanding of the psychological processes involved in the *Sefer ha-Meshiv*: in a certain state of consciousness, induced by former preparations, a verse surfaces which becomes an answer by means of an interpretive effort, which will link it to the circumstances or the details of the question. According to this passage, the divine name is conceived as part of the angelic nature. Here we witness an interesting form of immanence by means of the presence of the divine name in hypo-divine creatures.

The centrality of the concept of garment as related to those nocturnal visits is much more evident in another discussion of the revelation of Elijah to seminal Jewish masters. In a seminal passage preserved by R. 'Ovadiah Hamon of Barteniro, an inhabitant of Safed in the mid-sixteenth century, we read that:

> The issue of the garment [*Malbush*] of the speaking angel which will come to someone and teach him Torah. I found it written in the book *Mar'ot le-Maggid*: and the angel [that reveals himself] is called Azriel and he has revealed to him great and hidden things which no mouth can tell ... and when you pronounce the secret of the Great Name, immediately the force

of the "garment" will descend downwards, which is the secret of Elijah, who is mentioned in the works of the sages. And by this R. Simeon bar Yohai and Yonathan ben Uzziel learned their wisdom, and they were deserving of the secret of the "garment," to be dressed in it. And R. Hanina and R. Nehunya ben ha-Kanah and R. Akiva and R. Ishmael ben Elisha and our holy Rabbi [i.e. R. Yehudah the Prince] and Rashi and many others [learned] likewise. And the secret of the "garment" is the vision of the "garment," which the angel of God is dressed in, with a corporeal eye, and it is he who is speaking to you because you did not merit to see him as they did; they have received this privilege because they had a pure spirit and they merited the vision. And the secret of the garment was given to those who fear God and meditate upon His Name; they have seen it, those men who are the men of God were worthy of this state. And they were fasting for forty days continuously, and during their fast they pronounced the Tetragrammaton forty-five times, and on the fortieth day [the "garment"] descended to him and showed him whatever he wished [to know], and it stayed with him until the completion of the [study of the] subject he wanted [to know]; and they [i.e. Elijah and the "garment"] were staying with him day and night [apparently, in *Sefer ha-Meshiv* all the revelations took place at night only, unlike the case of the great masters mentioned above]. Thus was it done in the days of Rashi to his master, and the latter taught him [i.e. Rashi] this secret [of the "garment"], and by means of it [the secret] [Rashi] composed whatever he composed, by the means of his mentor and Elijah. Do not believe that he [Rashi] wrote this down from his own reason [literally, 'from his own head'] for he did it by the secret of the "garment" of the angel and the secret of mnemotechnics, to explain the questions one is asking or to compose a book one wishes to compose, and [thus] were all the sciences copied, one by one. By these techniques the ancient sages have learned from him innumerable sciences. And this happened in the days of the Talmud and in the days of Rashi's master and in the days of Rashi too, since his master began this [usage], and Rashi ended it, and in their times this lore [how to receive revelations] was transmitted by word of mouth, one man to another, and this is the reason all the sages of Israel relied upon Rashi, as at that time they knew the secret. Therefore, do not ever believe that he [Rashi] composed his commentaries on the Talmud and on the plain meaning of the Bible out of his reason, but by means of this force of the secret of the "garment," and that [force] which dressed it, which is an angel, since by means of it he could know and compose whatever he wished. This is the [power] which elevates the letters of the divine name upwards [common abbreviation of the divine name], and it brings downwards [both] the secret of the chariot and the thought of God. And those who were able to see it are like prophets, and in the times of the Talmud many used it. Afterwards, those who pursued the lore diminished, and they resorted to the daughter of the voice [*bat qol*] and the daughter of the voice is called the supernal voice. It is heard like the voice of a man indeed, and they do not see a body, but a speaking voice. (Ms. Oxford-Bodleiana 1597, fol. 39a–39b; Idel, "Inquiries" 239–40)

As seen above, in many Kabbalistic sources the prophet Elijah was considered to be an angel. The anonymous Kabbalist interprets the visits of Elijah as occurring according to a certain pattern, "the secret of Elijah" which is understood not as a sudden event, but rather as the result of resorting to a technique. Thus, also according to the doctrine of *Sefer ha-Meshiv*, he must use a garment in order to descend into this world. However, in this book he himself is a garment of the divine power descending below. God, hidden within Elijah, descends by means of a garment which enables both God and the angel to function in the material world. This garment is reminiscent of the Neo-Platonic and Gnostic theories of the descent of the spiritual into the material by acquiring corporeal elements on the way down (Idel, *Golem* 89–90 and 285–91). On the basis of the former quotations, it may be suggested that this passage should be understood as dealing with the descent of Elijah in a dream to those very important authors in the history of Judaism, most of them protagonists of Jewish mystical literature. So, for example, the first two names are the famous 'mystical' sages of ancient Judaism; the former is the principle hero of the *Zohar*, to whom the book has been spuriously attributed. The second was the author of an Aramaic translation of the Bible, which became a standard work in the Middle Ages, and someone who has also been described as a mystical figure. It is possible that the author of *Sefer ha-Meshiv* mentions them together because both 'interpreted' the Torah, the book of the *Zohar* being a homiletic commentary on the Bible and some of the scrolls. This interpretive activity is also obviously the case with the eleventh-century Rabbi Shelomo Yitzhaqi, better known as Rashi, the prince of all the Jewish interpreters, who interpreted both the Bible and the Talmud. All their achievements are portrayed here as attained due to their knowledge of the secret of the garment, namely how to induce the revelations of Elijah, who is the immediate source for all their books. I take the last quotation as one dealing with the revelation of Elijah in a dream, as explained above in another quotation. If the most important literary activities are nocturnal, and induced so that they will take place in a dream, then the largest part of canonical Judaism is conceived here as an ongoing revelation that is diminishing because the masters forgot the secret of the garment. Literary activity in the state of awareness is therefore a symptom of oblivion, of decay, of not being in a genuine contact with the ultimate source of knowledge and power.

This is a strong critique addressed to what some would call rationality, but what has been designated by the Kabbalist as Greek philosophy and its 'deleterious' repercussions in Judaism. Forgetfulness of the Torah is the cause of the exile because philosophy has invaded Jewish culture. A return to the dream is therefore a return to a relative authenticity because there alone God may still be encountered and only there the secrets of the forgotten Torah will be revealed, or restored. In terms reminiscent of the claims of the Dada and Surrealist manifestos of the beginning of the last century, this Kabbalist calls for a mental revolution which will allow dreams their creative role. It is in the dream alone that someone may receive Kabbalistic secrets nowadays, according to those Kabbalists. The diurnal mode was apparently conceived as philosophically oriented, while the nocturnal one was conceived as more pertinent for the Kabbalistic type of noetics. This was not only a theoretical suggestion; in my opinion, an important part of the huge corpus belonging to this circle has been composed as answers to questions asked by the Kabbalists and 'responded' to by God and angels in dreams. However, as part of an evolutionary way of thinking, and in expectation of an imminent redemption, the state of dreams was not assumed to remain the scene of creativity for ever: it will be transcended by the return to the 'normal,' fully fledged encounter between the corporeal form of God and of Elijah by the Kabbalists, and the reception of the concrete supernal voice in the Messianic time. Meanwhile, dreams may save the Kabbalist from the pits of philosophy. As against the exilic nature of philosophy, the anonymous Kabbalist emulates the traditional Jewish figures like R. Yehudah ha-Nasi, the compiler of the Mishnah and other ancient Tannaitic masters who were heroes of ancient Jewish mystical literature. Among the medievals, Rashi is the most important protagonist.

The image of a garment is quite central for many of the discussions of revelation in *Sefer ha-Meshiv*. God is imagined as coming down in a double garment; He is present in the angel Elijah, and clothed in him, and the angel in turn is assuming the garment in order to be able to descend. However, the covers put on by the divinity in order to come down are for the sake of the revelation of His power, on the one hand, and the disclosure of the secrets of the Torah, on the other hand. God covers Himself only in order to be able to uncover. This uncovering, or disclosure, is both the disclosure of the divine power and of the secrets of the Torah, after it has been forgotten (Ms. Jerusalem, NUL 80 147, fol. 106s). The extreme oblivion is, therefore, the cause of the beginning of a new revelation. God and His Torah have been forgotten and this is why He has to come down and explain the secrets of the Torah which are, at the same time, revealing His lost glory. This momentous revelation is tantamount to the time of an imminent redemption, an issue that recurs often in this Kabbalistic corpus (Idel, *Messianic Mystics* 126–34). The bodily form, the revelation of the secrets of the Torah, the manifestation of God's power or the loud voice, all are natural and positive symptoms of revelatory experiences which are also antidotes against the mentalistic conceptions of Judaism as promoted by Jewish philosophers writing under the influence of Aristotle. The image of the forgotten Torah may have something to do with the notion of the garment of the Torah. Kabbalistic oneirics are techniques, the very *organon* by means of which someone may reach God in dreams; and God, for His part, uses the state of dreams in order to reveal Himself, by revealing the secrets of the Torah. In one of the above quotations the issue of voice occurred. The assumption was that revelation may take place in a speechless mode, or by means of speech. Moreover, Elijah was conceived as the transmitter of the voice. What is interesting in this theory is the addition of the angelic powers as part of the unfolding of the supernal speech below. Elsewhere in this book, when answering the question of whether there is speech among the angels as there is between men, the angel Gabriel said that God puts his words into the Kabbalist's mouth. Therefore, there is indeed a voice in and as part of revelation, but it is the voice of the recipient which is used by the angelic power in order to reveal the message from above. Is the Kabbalist's mouth the main *organon* of revealing the message, and the angel an instrument to bring the spiritual power within man? I assume that this is a reasonable description of the view of this Kabbalist, because we have already seen that Elijah is conceived both as the garment of God and as connected to the soul of man. The Kabbalist's soul is therefore a medium where the divine message becomes articulated in discrete and loud words.

We have described theophanies related to Elijah as mediating the divine essence, perhaps more precisely the divine name, as part of revelations that constitute, according to this Kabbalist, the most important part of Jewish literature. This move is in fact the apotheosis of the development we surveyed previously: the increasing role played by apotheosis and revelation in Jewish mysticism, which will find its sharpest stage in the Hasidic vision of the *Tzaddiq*. This latest development does not concern us here (see Rapoport-Albert). I am concerned now with the further step taken by some of the themes related to the mystical Elijah in the next centre of Jewish Kabbalah, Safed.

5. Elijah's Revelations in Sixteenth-Century Safedian Kabbalah

The precise identity of the group of Kabbalists who produced the above literature is still wrapped up in mystery; though I assume that such a group was in existence, and that it is not the fiction of one person, it is quite difficult to find more specific details beyond the scant evidence transpiring from the revelatory mode of writing of the precise historical figures and the circumstances of their activities. It may be that they were a sociologically negligible group in Spanish and post-expulsion Sephardi Jewry, though the subsequent influence of their writings on Kabbalah was quite considerable. In any case, it is evident that Safedian Kabbalists were well acquainted with at least parts of *Sefer ha-Meshiv* as they were quoted verbatim by R. Moses Cordovero and R. 'Ovadiyah Hamon several times (Idel, "Inquiries" 194–95). Therefore, the possible contribution of this type of Kabbalistic literature for the understanding of some mystical phenomena in Safed should be taken into consideration much more than it has been previously.

One of the most remarkable repercussions of this type of Kabbalistic literature is quite visible in the visionary mode of one of the most important figures of sixteenth-century Judaism, and one of the most influential figures in Judaism in general, the great Halakhist R. Joseph Karo, whose revelations have attracted Bloom's attention (*Omens* 85–92). He is the codifier of Jewish law, which has been accepted and implemented since the second third of the sixteenth century in Judaism at large. However, in addition to the enormous enterprise of codifying all the aspects of Jewish law, Karo also had another form of spiritual activity: he was visited rather regularly by an angelic mentor, called the Maggid, which was conceived to be the Mishnah (see Pines 333–63). Despite the wonderful monograph on his mystical life by R. J. Z. Werblowsky, the question still remains: why was he visited by the Maggid at night? It still awaits further clarification. It is plausible to see in the nocturnal visits the result of initiatives of this author himself, who was either reciting the text of the Mishnah in a technical manner, in order to induce the experience, as has been recognized by scholars (Werblowsky 109–11; Fine, "Recitation" 183–99), or because of the resort to magical formulae similar to those employed in *Sefer ha-Meshiv* (Idel, "Inquiries" 220–26). I would like not to address this question here, but to refer to the similar attitude towards the issue of the revelation of Elijah in a dream. The angelic mentor, speaking to Karo in the first person, in a way quite similar to God's manner of addressing the Kabbalist in *Sefer ha-Meshiv*, indicates to him that:

> You should also mortify your soul as I have told you, in order to merit to see Elijah in the state of waking, face to face, and he will speak to you mouth to mouth, and will give you peace, because he will be your mentor and master to disclose to you all the secrets of the Torah. (*Maggid Mesharim* 5; Werblowsky 269)

However, this very optimistic prospect should be understood in the light of another passage in the same book:

> Elijah is clothing himself in a body and reveals himself in this world and when you want that he will reveal to you, meditate these words [or things] when lying down [to sleep] and then he will reveal to you, as it is said: Happy is he who has seen his face in a dream, etc. There are thus three degrees [of beholding Elijah]: the first is to see his face in a dream; the second to see him awake and to salute him, but without Elijah returning the salutation; the third is to see him awake, to greet him and to be saluted by him in return. (*Maggid Mesharim* 13; Werblowsky 270)

I assume that each of these three forms of encounter is triggered by an initial act initiated by Karo: to think before going to bed about something, as recommended explicitly by the angelic mentor. Though far from being the highest form of cognition, dreaming is still conceived as one of the ways to reach a revelation of Elijah, just as we have seen in *Sefer ha-Meshiv*. Moreover, just as in one of the passages from this book (printed in Scholem, "The Maggid" 107) also in Karo, the Maggid is called Dodi and he reveals himself at midnight (Werblowsky 259–61); the erotic imagery is recurrent and clear-cut (ibid., 267–68 and 275). Again, as in the *Sefer ha-Meshiv*, the revelation takes place by means of the speech of the Kabbalist himself and the revealing power is called Voice (259–60 and 265), as in *Sefer ha-Meshiv*. As pointed out by Werblowsky, Karo's use of the repetition of the Mishnah may be seen as a kind of incubation (261). However, though Karo's revelations were usually nocturnal (258), they occurred in a waking state of consciousness, though the Kabbalist might fall asleep in the middle of the speech with the Beloved (259–64). It may be suggested that we see in the Maggid of Karo a form of *She'elah be-haqitz*. He is able to receive in a state of waking what someone else is only granted in a dream; so, for example, Karo was told by the Maggid that "I come to delight myself with thee and to speak in your mouth, not in a dream but as one speaketh to one's friend" (117–18). Therefore, in Safed the 'waking' form of incubation in order to encounter Elijah has been conceived not only as higher than the oneiric one, but also as attainable before the advent of the Messiah, unlike the view of *Sefer ha-Meshiv*. This achievement was now due less to magical recipes—divine names—but to quite nomian techniques, the recitation of the Mishnah. Does this resort to the Mishnah as a technique have something to do with the resort of R. Yehudah the Prince to the garment, according to *Sefer ha-Meshiv*, as seen above? Did the prince of pre-modern Halakhah want to remain in the line of the series of great Halakhic authorities, starting with the Prince of the Mishnah, who were visited, according to the above quotation from *Sefer ha-Meshiv*? In any case, it is certain that the passage dealing with the garment, Elijah and their frequent visits of the Halakhic authors, was known in Safed, since the only source in which it was extant is 'Ovadiyah Hamon's compilation composed in the town in Karo's lifetime.

Even more crucial, however, is the role of Elijah in revealing Kabbalistic traditions to R. Isaac Luria, the peak of Safedian Kabbalah. Unlike Abulafia's claim to prophecy and messianism, which were generated from the revelations imparted by the Agent Intellect, Luria, or his disciples, were more modest: they attributed the emergence of the incredibly vast and complex Lurianic corpus to Elijah and revelations of the souls of the righteous dead (Fine, "Maggidic" 141–52). Apparently, the assumption of the students in Luria's entourage was that Elijah did not appear in a waking situation, since it was revealed to his disciple R. Hayyim Vital that his spiritual rank is higher than that of his master, Luria, and it is destined that "the angel Elijah will speak with you mouth to mouth, in a state of waking, this is why you should unify by the unification of this name, you should elevate it to secret of *'Eliyahu* who is the name *Ben*" (*Sha'ar ha-Gilgulim* 38: 160). I wonder to what extent the traditions adduced above about Elijah and the divine names, and *Ben*, resurge in this passage. In this context, a passage whose provenance is obscure attributes to R. Hayyim Vital a revelation stemming from Elijah and related to an enigmatic poem concerning the date of the advent of the Messiah (Krauss 242–43).

What should be emphasized in our context is the emphasis on seeing Elijah in a state of waking. *Prima facie* this may happen to ordinary people, according to the rich Jewish folklore about Elijah. Here, however, the assumption is not that Elijah will come and be seen, but that he will become the visible teacher of a certain Kabbalist and the revealer of Kabbalistic traditions. This emphasis on the imminent return of a more concrete form of revelation which will coincide with the final disclosure of secrets is, in my opinion, indebted to the theories of *Sefer ha-Meshiv*. This development is part of a retreat, and even sharp criticism addressed to Jewish philosophy and its influence on Kabbalah, as we learn from another Safedian figure, R. Joseph, the Tanna of Safed, and in Vital himself (see Scholem, "New Information;" Idel, "Inquiries" 240-43). The Safedian surge of non-allegorical, anti-mental understandings of Elijah among Kabbalists stands in clear contrast to the interpretations offered to this figure in ecstatic Kabbalah, as described above. It also reflects a dissonance in comparison to the renascence of the philosophical elements in contemporary Renaissance Italy and in Europe at large, and to some of the appropriations of this drift by Jewish Kabbalists, especially in Italy.

6. Some Concluding Remarks

Traditions about Enoch and Elijah did not remain the patrimony of Jewish mystical thinkers. They travelled far beyond the small circles described above. Let me adduce one interesting example, contemporary with some of the figures discussed in the last paragraph: the great, perhaps greatest Christian Kabbalist, Guillaume Postel. He believed that he was a prophet, and as such identified himself not only with the prophet Elijah, a forerunner of the Messiah, but also with the lower Messiah, apparently with the *sefirah* of Malkhut.[11] What seems interesting to me is the fact that he visited Safed in the mid-sixteenth century and could, in principle, communicate with the Kabbalists there. In any case, he was in contact with a prominent Jewish Kabbalist in Italy, R. Moses Bassola, who returned afterwards to Safed, and was acquainted with R. Moses Cordovero. Was he influenced by the emphasis on Elijah's role in the spiritual life of Safedian masters? Or may the emphasis of some Safedian Kabbalists on the importance of Elijah be a response to the claim of the Christian Kabbalist, as is the case with other topics (Idel, *Messianic Mystics* 315–16)? Or, perhaps, the two alternatives do not exclude each other.

However, more pertinent for the present context is the possibility, first advanced by Bloom (*American* 99 and 105), that some Enochic apotheotic traditions, as formulated in Kabbalistic literature, have

---

[11] See Reeves 381; see also Postel's French and Hebrew texts printed by François Secret in his *Guillaume Postel*. For an analysis of Postel's position on these issues, see Bouwsma 15, 45, 155, 162-64 and 276-77; and Popkin 164-65.

reverberated in Mormonism, a thesis which has been fostered immediately afterwards by a rich study that traces the history of the mediation of Jewish mysticism by Alexander Neibaur who came from Poland, via London, to the circle of the founder of Mormonism, Joseph Smith.[12] It is in this more concrete reading of the Enochic tradition that Mormonism was looking for its ancient sources, while skipping over the Kabbalistic medieval and pre-modern sources. What seems to me fascinating is the fact that Bloom's "filtered" apotheotic-mythical propensity was crucial for opening the historical discussion of the Jewish mystical sources that nourished the most original form of religion that emerged in America. As Owens put it, "there is both a poetic and an unsuspected factual substance to Bloom's thesis" (Owens 118). Last but not least: the brief history of Jewish mysticism offered above assumes a certain contest between different Kabbalistic modes of thought, in a manner which may be described as agonistic. Kabbalistic thought, like Bloom's theory of culture in general, is based upon various types of struggle between the later and the earlier, and I assume that such a struggle was formative for the ascent of the archaic as well as the more intellectual understandings of Enoch and Elijah. No linear development, not even a history of two different though parallel trends, is salient for understanding the changes in the history of Kabbalah. Historicist explanations may describe only in a very partial manner the complex intellectual processes involved in understanding the developments of various Kabbalistic themes. An agonistic approach, based upon interactions, tensions, reactions, appropriations and misunderstanding, may serve the scholars of Kabbalah better than most of the intellectual apparatus put to work in many of the classical studies of Kabbalah. After all, Kabbalists, like the poets described by Bloom, are traditional figures who in various ways depend on, and revolt against, what is already found in their respective traditions; even more so when one of those poets, William Blake, one of Bloom's favourites, derives some of his themes from E. Swedenborg, a Christian mystic who has so much in common with Kabbalists, especially their attempt to map the supernal world. In different ways, and drawing from different sources, Kabbalistic views impacted on a variety of literary and speculative materials—and have caught the attention of a thinker whose gift for discovering unsuspected affinities between apparently unrelated corpora is unparalleled.

---

[12] On Mormonism and Enochism in general, see Nibley; also see Owens, where the Kabbalistic sources of Smith are described.

Works Cited

R. David Kimhi. Commentary on 2 Kings. 2.1.
R. David Kimhi. Commentary on Genesis. 6.24.
Nahmanides. Commentary on Leviticus. 18.4.
BT, *Sanhedrin*. Fol. 38a.
BT, *Haggigah*. Fol. 15a.
BT, *Babba Metzia*. Fol. 85b.
BT, *'Avodah Zarah*. Fol. 20b.
Ms. Paris BN 774. Fols. 129b–30b.
Sitrei Torah. Ms. Paris BN 774. Fols. 132b, 155ab and 168b.
Ms. Paris BN 777. Fols. 110a and 113a.
Ms. Paris BN 859. Fols. 15b and 16a.
Ms. New York JTS 1777. Fol. 33b.
Ms. Oxford-Bodleiana 1582. Fols. 22b–23a.
Ms. Oxford-Bodleiana 1568. Fol. 21a.
Commentary on the Pentateuch. Ms. Oxford-Bodleiana 1920. Fols. 2a and 36b.
Moses Maimonides. *The Guide for the Perplexed*. 2: 60.
Ma'ayan Hokhmah. Printed by A. Jellinek, Beit ha-Midrasch. Jerusalem, 1967. Vol. 1.
Augusto Giustiniani. *Polyglot*. Genua, 1516. On the margin of Psalm CIXL.
R. Isaac of Acre's untitled treatise. Ms. New York JTS 1853. Fol. 3a.
Epstein, Y. M., ed. *Sefer ha-Hesheq*. Lemberg, 1865. Fols. 7b–8a.
Sefer ha-'Ot. Printed by A. Jellinek. In *Jubelschrift zum 70. Geburtstag des Prof. H.*
Graetz. Breslau, 1887. 65–88.
Toldot 'Adam. Ms. Oxford-Bodleiana 836. Fol. 155b.
Ms. Oxford-Bodleiana 836. Fols. 159a–59b.

Ms. Jerusalem NUL 80 147. Fols. 96b-97a.
R.'Ovadiah Hamon. Ms. Oxford-Bodleiana 1597. Fols. 58b-59a.
Ms. Oxford-Bodleiana 1597. Fols. 39a-39b.
Ms. Jerusalem NUL 80 147. Fol. 106a.
Maggid Mesharim. Jerusalem, 1960.
Sha'ar ha-Gilgulim 38. Jerusalem, 1971.
R. Reuben ha-Tzarfati. *Perush la-Ma'are'khet ha-'Elohut.* Mantua, 1558. Fol. 96b.

༄

Abrams, Daniel. "The Boundaries of Divine Ontology: The Inclusion and Exclusion of Metatron in the Godhead." *Harvard Theological Review* 87 (1994): 291-321.

Aloro, Dorit Cohen. *The Secret of the Garment in the Zohar.* Jerusalem: Hebrew U, 1987. [Hebrew]

Bouwsma, William J. *Concordia Mundi: The Career and Thought of Guillaume Postel (1510-1581).* Cambridge, MA: Harvard UP, 1957.

Box, G. H. *The Apocalypse of Abraham.* London: SPCK, 1918.

Collins, John J. "Messianism, in the Maccabean Period." *Judaisms and Their Messiahs at the Turn of the Christian Era.* Ed. Jacob Neusner, William Scott Green and Ernest S. Frerichs. Cambridge: Cambridge UP, 1987. 98-103.

Couliano, Ioan P. *Expériences de l'extase.* Paris: Payot, 1984.

____. *The Tree of Gnosis.* San Francisco: Harper, 1992.

Dan, Joseph. *The Esoteric Theology.* Jerusalem: Mossad Bialik, 1968.

____. "The Seventy Names of Metatron." *Proceedings of the Eighth World Congress of Jewish Studies, Division C.* Jerusalem: World Union of Jewish Studies, 1982. 19-23.

Daniélou, Jean. *Théologie du Judéo-Christianisme.* Paris: Desclée-Cerf, 1991.

Deutsch, Nathaniel. *The Gnostic Imagination: Gnosticism, Mandaeism, and Merkabah Mysticism.* Leiden: Brill, 1995.

Fine, Lawrence. "Maggidic Revelation in the Teachings of Isaac Luria." *Mystics, Philosophers and Politicians: Essays in Jewish Intellectual History in Honor of Alexander Altmann.* Ed. J. Reinharz and D. Swetschinski. Durham, NC: Duke UP, 1982. 141-52.

____. "Recitation of Mishnah as a Vehicle for Mystical Inspiration: A Contemplative Technique Taught by Hayyim Vital." *Revue des Etudes Juives* (1982): 183-99.

Fossum, Jarl E. "The Magharians: A Pre-Christian Jewish Sect and Its Significance for the Study of Gnosticism and Christianity." *Henoch* 9 (1989): 303–43.

———. *The Name of God and the Angel of the Lord*. Tübingen: Mohr, 1985.

Goldreich, A., ed. R. Isaac ben Shmuel of Acre. *Sefer Me'irat 'Einayyim*. Ph. D. Thesis. Jerusalem: Hebrew U, 1982. [Hebrew.]

Greenfield, Jonas. "Notes on Some Aramaic and Mandaic Magical Bowls." *Gaster Festschrift. Journal of the Ancient Near Eastern Society of Columbia*. New York: Jewish Theological Seminary of America, 1973. 149–59.

———. "Prolegomenon." *III Enoch*. New York: Ktav, 1973. xi–xlvii.

Hurtado, Larry W. *One God One Lord: Early Christian Devotion and Ancient Jewish Monotheism*. Philadelphia: Fortress, 1988.

Idel, Moshe. "Adam and Enoch According to St. Ephram the Syrian." *Kabbalah* 6 (2001): 197–218.

———. "The Attitude to Christianity in Sefer ha-Meshiv." *Immanuel* 12 (1981): 77–95.

———. "The Concept of the Torah in Heikhalot Literature and Its Metamorphoses in Kabbalah." *Jerusalem Studies in Jewish Thought* 1 (1981): 23–84. [Hebrew.]

———. "Enoch is Metatron." *Immanuel* 24–25 (1990): 220–40.

———. "Enoch the Mystical Cobbler." *Kabbalah* 5 (2000): 220–40. [Hebrew.]

———. *Golem: Danger, Deliverance and Art*. With Emily D. Bilski and Elfriede Ledig. New York: The Jewish Museum, 1988.

———. "Inquiries in the Doctrine of the Book of the Responding Entity." *Sefunot* 17 [ns 2] (1985): 185–266. [Hebrew.]

———. "Jewish Magic from the Renaissance Period to Early Hasidism." *Religion, Science, and Magic in Concert and in Conflict*. Ed. J. Neusner, et al. New York: Oxford UP, 1989. 82–117.

———. *Kabbalah and Eros*. New Haven: Yale UP, 2005.

———. "Kabbalistic Material from R. David ben Jehudah he-Hasid's School." *Jerusalem Studies in Jewish Thought* 2 (1983): 169–207. [Hebrew.]

———. "Kabbalistic Prayer in Provence." *Tarbiz* 62 (1993): 265–86. [Hebrew.]

———. "The Lost Books of Solomon." *Daat: A Journal of Jewish Philosophy and Kabbalah* 32–33 (1994): 235–46. [Hebrew.]

____. "Magic and Kabbalah in the Book of the Responding Entity." *The Solomon Goldman Lectures* 6. Ed. M. Gruber. Chicago: Spertus College, 1993. 125–38.
____. *Messianic Mystics*. New Haven: Yale UP, 2000.
____. "Metatron: Observations on the Development of Myth in Judaism." *Myth in Judaism*. Research in Jewish Studies 4. Ed. Haviva Pedaya. Jerusalem: Eshel Beer Sheva', 1996. 22–44. [Hebrew.]
____. *The Mystical Experience in Abraham Abulafia*. Trans. J. Chipman. Albany, NY: SUNY P, 1988.
____. "Neglected Treatises by the Author of Sefer Kaf ha-Qetoret." *Pe'amim* 53 (1993): 75–89. [Hebrew.]
____. "The Origin of Alchemy According to Zosimos and a Hebrew Parallel." *Revue des Etudes Juives* 144 (1986): 117–24.
Klausner, Joseph. *The Messianic Idea in Israel from its Beginning to the Completion of the Mishnah*. Trans. W. F. Stinespring. New York: Macmillan, 1955.
Krauss, Samuel. "Un texte cabbalistique sur Jésus." *Revue des Etudes Juives* 62 (1911): 240–47.
Kushnir-Oron, Michal. *The Sefer Ha-Peli'ah and Sefer Ha-Kanah: Their Kabbalistic Principles, Social and Religious Criticism and Literary Composition*. Ph. D. Thesis. Jerusalem: Hebrew U, 1980. [Hebrew.]
Liebes, Yehuda. "The Angels of the Shofar and Yeshua Sar ha-Panim." *Early Jewish Mysticism*. Ed. J. Dan. Jerusalem: Institute for Jewish Studies, Hebrew U, 1987. 171–96. [Hebrew.]
____. "Myth vs. Symbol in the Zohar and Lurianic Kabbalah." *Essential Papers on Kabbalah*. Ed. Lawrence Fine. New York: New York UP, 1995. 219–23.
Macina, Robert. "Le rôle eschatologique d'Elie le Prophète dans la conversion finale dupeuple juif: Positions juives et chrétiennes à la lumière des sources rabbiniques etpatristiques." *Proche-Orient Chrétien* 31 (1981): 71–99.
Nibley, Hugh. *Enoch the Prophet*. Salt Lake City: Desert Book Company, 1986.
Odeberg, H. *The Hebrew Enoch*. New York: Ktav, 1973.
Owens, Lance S. "Joseph Smith and Kabbalah: The Occult Connection." *Dialogue: A Journal of Mormon Thought* 27.3 (1994): 117–94.
Pines, Shlomo. "Le *Sefer ha-Tamar* et les Maggidim des Kabbalistes." *Hommage à Georges Vajda*. Ed. G. Nahon and Ch. Touati. Louvain: Peeters, 1980. 333–63.

Popkin, Richard. "Jewish-Christian Relations in the Sixteenth and Seventeenth Centuries: The Conception of the Messiah." *The Frank Talmage Memorial Volume*. Vol. 2. Ed. Barry Walfish. Haifa and Brandeis U: Haifa UP, 1993. 163–77.

Quispel, Gilles. "Qumran, John and Jewish Christianity." *John and Qumran*. Ed. J. H. Charlesworth. London: Geoffrey Chapman, 1972. 137–55.

Rapoport-Albert, Ada. "God and the Zaddik as the Two Focal Points of Hasidic Worship." *History of Religions* 18 (1979): 296–325.

Reeves, Marjorie. *The Influence of Prophecy in the Late Middle Age: A Study in Joachimism*. Notre Dame: U of Notre Dame P, 1993.

Safran, Bezalel. "Rabbi Azriel and Nahmanides: Two Views of the Fall of Man." *Rabbi Moses Nahmanides [Ramban]: Explorations in His Religious and Literary Activity*. Ed. Isadore Twersky. Cambridge, MA: Harvard UP, 1983. 75–106.

Scholem, Gershom. *Jewish Gnosticism, Merkavah Mysticism and Talmudic Tradition*. New York: Jewish Theological Seminary, 1960.

———. *Kabbalah*. New York: Quadrangle, 1974.

———. "'The Maggid' of R. Joseph Taitachek and the Revelations Attributed to Him." *Sefunot* 11 (1971–78): 69–112. [Hebrew.]

———. *Major Trends in Jewish Mysticism*. New York: Schocken, 1967.

———. *On the Mystical Shape of the Godhead*. New York: Schocken, 1991.

———. "New Information about Joseph Ashkenazi, 'The Tana' of Safed." *Tarbiz* 28 (1959): 59–89 and 201–35. [Hebrew.]

———. *Origins of the Kabbalah*. Trans. A. Arkush. Ed. R. Z. J. Werblowsky. Philadelphia: Princeton UP, 1987.

———. *Pirkei Yesod be-havanat ha-Qabbalah u-Semaleiah*. Jerusalem: Mossad Bialik, 1976.

Secret, François. *Guillaume Postel: Apologies et Rétractions*. Niewkoof: B. de Graaf, 1972. 19–168.

Segal, Alan F. "Ruler of This World: Attitudes about Mediator Figures and the Importance of Sociology for Self-Definition." *Jewish and Christian Self-Definition*. Ed. E. P. Sanders and A. Mendelsohn. Vol. 2. Philadelphia: Fortress, 1981. 245–68.

Smith, Jonathan Z. *Map Is Not Territory: Studies in the History of Religions*. Leiden: Brill, 1978.

Wasserstrom, Steven M. "Sahrastani on the Magariyya." *Israel Oriental Studies* 17 (1997): 141–54.

Werblowsky, R. J. Z. *Joseph Karo, Lawyer and Mystic*. Philadelphia: JPS, 1977.

Wexler, Philip. *The Mystical Society: An Emerging Social Vision*. Boulder, CO: Westwind, 2000.

Wolfson, Eliot R. "The Secret of the Garment in Nahmanides." *Daat: A Journal of Jewish Philosophy and Kabbalah* 24 (1990): xxv–xlix.

———. *Through a Speculum that Shines: Vision and Imagination in Medieval Jewish Mysticism*. Princeton: Princeton UP, 1994.

Wolfson, H. A. "The Pre-Existent Angel of the Magharians and al-Nahawandi." *Jewish Quarterly Review* ns 51 (1960–61): 89–106.

"From Blank to Blank:"
Harold Bloom and Woman Writers

SINÉAD MURPHY

> [T]he first true break with literary continuity will be brought about in generations to come if the burgeoning religion of Liberated Women spreads from its clusters of enthusiasts to dominate the West. Homer will cease to be the inevitable precursor and the rhetoric and forms of our literature then may break at last from tradition. (*Map* 60)

Harold Bloom's blithe prophecy equates the establishment of a feminist literary tradition with the end of the literary world as we know it. As such, it is the most instructive passage of any he has written, particularly for the woman writer. Yet it has consistently been ignored by the women who have engaged with Bloom's theory, with the result that Harold Bloom and his feminist critics have been writing and talking at cross purposes for decades, arriving, nonetheless, at the same conclusion: that his Western Canon is the very thing with which the female writer can have nothing to do. Women will persist in mistaking Bloom. Erroneously perceiving him as another stalwart of the patriarchal system which designates her as Other, they have aimed at disturbing the binarisms which support that system, adopting various measures to transform the lesser term into something powerful and creative. In Bloom's world, however, the lesser term, the inhibited party, the Other, is his modern poet. His antithetical criticism is such that creation stems only from inhibition, and when women write in support of the lesser term, they end only in describing the battle for priority of Bloom's modern poet and not of the women he excludes. It is when one writes against Bloom that one most emphatically strengthens his position. The purpose of the present analysis is to overcome this dilemma and finally facilitate a confrontation between Bloom and the woman writer.

Bloom's account of poetic production has not escaped censure from feminist critics. Yet feminist criticism of Bloom's metaphorically defeminized tale of poetic creation has universally mistaken the significance of Bloom's neglect of female creativity. It has attempted to situate the female in a dark corner in the midst of his creative warfare, a muted madwoman in the attic of the ivory tower of poetic tradition. Annette Kolodny identifies the emphasis of feminist criticism on "a psychodrama for women that emerges *amid* a pantheon of precursors ... [of] narcissistic fathers/lovers" (Kolodny 126; my emphasis). The fact is, however, that Bloom's map outlines a territory that is no woman's land. There are no recesses left inviolate, no attic without a reference to an all-powerful poetic tradition. Sparks exhorts the female writer to "excavate the traces of the feminine hidden below the surface of male writers' imagery and metaphors" (Sparks 57). But Bloom's ability to invoke an origin, a moment of absolute presence which is pure trope, trope as defence, trope whose lack of epistemological pretension renders it immune to deconstructive attack, removes the possibility of female excavation. There are no traces of the feminine in Bloom's exclusive, creative interaction of father and son, an interaction reduced to the negotiations of a single self, a male poet, to Harold Bloom himself.

Gilbert and Gubar exemplify the general feminist misunderstanding of Bloom's terms when they locate the patriarchal nature of his theory in his failure to recognize that "the female poet does not experience 'the anxiety of influence' in the same way that her male counterpart would" because she confronts a host of precursors exclusively male (Gilbert and Gubar 48). For Bloom the female does not experience the anxiety of influence at all and the term "female poet" is an oxymoron, encapsulating an impossibility designated by the terms of his theory. So the problem is not *how* to confront these forbiddingly male precursors, but one's inability to confront them at all; not *how* to be a female poet, but how to be female and a poet. According to Gilbert and Gubar, Milton is for women what Harold Bloom calls "the great Inhibitor, the Sphinx who strangles even strong imaginations in their cradles." In a line even more appropriate to women, Bloom adds that "the motto of English poetry since Milton was stated by Keats: 'life to him would be death to me'" (*Anxiety* 32; qtd. in Gilbert and Gubar 191).

This is not Bloom's Milton, a poet whose life or death can have no significance for the female. Gilbert and Gubar have mistaken the paradoxical nature of Bloom's account of poetic tradition in which to bestow is to take away, to liberate is to oppress, to give birth is to father, to conceive is to conceive oneself. They endeavour to enter the female into the terms of Bloom's discourse where there is, in fact, no room, not even "'the common sitting room' that denies [her] individuality" (188). They attempt to locate the female in her traditional position of inhibited Other, unaware that otherness and inhibition have been usurped by a dialectic for power between father and son. Identifying Bloom's theory as descriptive rather than prescriptive, as "not a recommendation for but an analysis of . . . patriarchal poetics" (47–48), they do not see that Bloom has proposed a poetic theory of poetry which purports to describe nothing, since description is based upon the *epistemological* interaction of the figurative and the literal with which Bloom has nothing to do.

Joanne Feit Diehl correctly identifies an instance of the uncanny in the "curiously hidden relationship" between Bloom's apparently antithetical criticism and Dickinson's own conceptions of language and poetic vocation (Diehl 421). Yet her critical excavations are not performed on Bloom's work but on Dickinson's poetry. Dickinson's search for a figurative language, she says, finds its "primary analogue . . . in the language of eros" (421). Like Gilbert and Gubar, Diehl presumes that Dickinson is unproblematically assimilated by Bloom's agonistic tradition, a tradition she unquestionably inherits. Having begun by exposing Bloom's discomfort with Dickinson, his reluctance to make her a strong poet, Diehl appears to believe the necessity for a struggle against this injustice to be fulfilled by an account of a struggle on Bloom's terms. Bloom's theory is dangerously deceptive, however. An agonistic battle with inhibition, which Diehl affirms as Dickinson's successful entry into the tradition of strong poets, cannot coherently be allowed as a female ploy to enter tradition when it is already appropriated by Bloom as the *agon* which comprises that tradition. Having recognised Dickinson's problematic status in relation to Bloom's canon, Diehl then writes as if she were part of it, fashioning figures from a language of eros which still proposes a process of spontaneous generation which denies her existence. "How, in Yeats's words, to 'put on' the precursor/muse's power without being robbed of her sense of autonomy is the central drama for the woman poet" (423). This is Diehl's conception of the situation governing the female poet's relation to Bloom's tradition. All it is, however, is simply a description of that tradition.

The misconception common to all of these feminist criticisms of Bloom is related to their failure to grasp the extremity of his antifeminism, the extent to which his theory is a *complete* exclusion of female creativity.

Any feminist critique of Bloom must sooner or later confront two aspects of his literary criticism which seem to annul the grounds for my discontent: his approval of Emily Dickinson and his radical conviction that the most truly original writer, the J-writer, was a woman. One cannot ignore this side of Bloom's work and still aspire to coherence in arguments against him. And indeed, diligence in this instance is rewarded twofold: for not only do Bloom's ardent affirmations of female greatness not dull the edge of the feminist cause, they curiously provide the most telling evidence of his real inability to allow for strength in a woman writer.

Bloom's high opinion of the worth of Emily Dickinson certainly appears to contradict my portrayal of his theory of influence as not only hostile to, but fatal for, female creativity. "Except for Shakespeare," says Bloom, "Dickinson manifests more cognitive originality than any other Western poet since Dante" (*Canon* 291). Her inclusion in his western canon, from which, I have said, all women are by definition excluded, rather supports than disproves my theory, however, since the manner of her inclusion dramatizes the extent to which a female poet cannot be admitted into Bloom's genealogy of influence. For, although Bloom reads every male poet worthy of being read as a participant in the self-assertive oedipal *agon* at the heart of strong poetry, Emily Dickinson's worth as a poet is never tried along those lines. Indeed, Bloom is at his most uneasy when writing on Dickinson, whose poetic prominence he must both sever from past poetic strength and isolate from future poetic aspiration. He abandons her to lonely isolation, excluded from the enabling operations of poetic rivalry and strangely representative of the vast wealth of female poetic endeavour which his theory will *not* legitimate. "Feminist criticism," says Bloom, "unable or unwilling to see that *agon* is the iron law of literature, continues to treat Dickinson as a comrade rather than as the rather forbidding figure she necessarily is" (*Canon* 296). By presenting her as a poet who engages with "the Miltonic-Coleridgean-Emersonian blank" (295), he renders her as yet another facet of a tradition whose terms are foreign to the female. By identifying her "original relation to that literary cosmos" (296), he places her at an equal distance from the poetic tradition whose welfare he has at heart, since the achievement of originality negates the necessity for the poetic struggle which endows strength.

The other claim which might appear to undermine the strength of my belief in Bloom's antifeminism is his curious insistence, which runs contrary to centuries of scholarship, that the author of *The Book of J*, "a work that has formed the spiritual consciousness of much of the world ever since," was a woman (J 9). In the face of multiple theological and literary theories as well as widespread popular beliefs that assert or assume the contrary, this perception of the most original of all writers would certainly, if viable, constitute a significant feminist coup.

Bloom's vindication of his startling announcement that the J-writer was female is based on essentialism, the notion that there are certain identifiable characteristics which will ascertain whether the author of a particular piece of writing is male or female. With this in mind, Bloom points to two features of *The Book of J* which prove (sic) that its composer was a woman: firstly, the fact that J devotes more time to, and is kinder in, the representation of women than of men; and, secondly, that a distinctly female use of irony prevails throughout. The first claim is unworthy of discussion considering that as many examples could be found to dismiss as to confirm its relevance in discovering an author's gender. It is with the second that I intend to illuminate the incongruencies of Bloom's line of argument.

Bloom maintains that J's use of irony is essentially female. Her attitude towards Yahweh, he says, "resembles nothing so much as a mother's somewhat wary but still proudly amused stance towards a benignly powerful but also eccentrically irascible son" (J 24). We may assume that if one is to divine the essence of female, as opposed to male, writing, it would require a detailed study of many, if not all, strong female writers in an effort to isolate those characteristics common to every case. One would be excused, then, for extending this assumption by expecting Bloom to compare J's type of irony to the irony used by other strong female writers. J's irony cannot be allowed to be essentially female simply by asserting that it is so. But Bloom (not surprising given his inability to acknowledge the existence of other strong female writers) does not engage in any such comparisons. Instead he elaborates on the (essentially female) strength of J's style by comparing it to examples of strong irony which are, without exception, male (25).

Tela C. Zasloff focuses on this contradiction between the radical feminism of Bloom's claim and the conservative anti-feminism of his support for it. She observes that "If J's irony is similar to Shakespeare's and particularly Kafka's ... and to [S]haw's ..., then it would seem there are no grounds for asserting that J's irony is essentially female" (Zasloff 36). Bloom does mention that Austen's irony has "some affinities" (J 211) with J's, but he does not elaborate on the connection, nor does he, Zasloff adds, "extract the essentially female nature of this affinity" (Zasloff 37).

In the end, Bloom tries to resolve this impasse by "finally claiming that J's irony is a special case, requiring its own definition to explain its essential female quality" (36). And here, I believe, is the key to the second part of the puzzle: the real problem of how to reconcile Bloom's unexpected affirmation of female poetic strength with the intolerance of his Western Canon. Bloom resorts once more to the ploy with which he dispatched Emily Dickinson from any affiliation with his theory. By insisting on the unique nature of the irony which represents J's strength, he is able to speak of "the shock of an originality that cannot be staled by cultural repetitions" (J 230), that cannot, in other words, be sullied by the agonistic battles which are the only indication of true canonical strength. J, the most original of all original writers, is free from the anxiety of influence.

Bloom's choice of J as the object of his uncharacteristic acknowledgement of female greatness is surely no coincidence; for J is "the author of the author" (J 267). The fact that J engages in "writing God" (267) allows for the ambiguities in Bloom's treatment of her and when it comes to the true purpose of his commentary on her work—a comparison with Shakespearean representations of character and the psychology of man in Freud—we find, suddenly, that Bloom is now speaking of J's Yahweh and not of J herself. The unique dilemma of "who created whom?" facilitates this ambiguity, and Bloom's persistent insertion of "J's Yahweh" for "J" in his discussions of intratextual influence is a telling indication of his continuing inability to enter a female writer into the terms of a tradition which endows strength.

Bloom's essay on Virginia Woolf in *The Western Canon* is entitled "Feminism as the Love of Reading." But Bloom's feminism is the love of reading only one's own text; not as it was written by one's poetic ancestors, but literally one's own text. "*Orlando*," he says, "may indeed be the longest love letter ever penned, but it is written by Woolf to herself" (*Canon* 444). In one sense, Bloom's female poet is the epitome of successful creation, but the possibility essential to Bloom's strong poetry is annulled by this attainment of success. The modern male poet struggles against the impossibility of originating himself in a tradition of overbearing fathers; the female poet, where she does exist, has successfully originated herself and, in the process of becoming her own mother, the author of the author, she is enacting "the successful female analogue to Bloom's frustrated poet/son who would (but cannot) be self begotten" (Kolodny 136). The point is, however, that success in the achievement of originality is failure in Bloom's poetic universe since it destroys the agonistic battles which grant poetic strength.

Feminist criticism curiously complies with Bloom's plans to exclude the female writer when it celebrates this impulse towards independence, and advocates the establishment of a community of female writers unified by a frenzy of sisterly goodwill. "Feminist readers and women writers can incorporate and undo male precursors by substituting a female point of origin and otherwise defusing an antifeminine genealogy" (Sparks 57). In opposition to the agonism of Bloom's poetic universe, this feminist tradition invokes a female utopia filled with women writers who, to borrow Bloom's satire, "lovingly cooperate with one another as quiltmakers" (*Canon* 482). The idea is that female anxiety was at its most inhibiting at the point of beginning when our eighteenth and nineteenth century sisters sought to overcome isolation and obscurity with the first few stitches of the quilt which today is vast and seamless, its many patterns dissolving into a governing poetic design in a process of benign transmission in which power is the property of all. As the female poetic past grows in strength, the "anxiety of authorship" induced by the fear that she cannot create is assuaged by the number of female precursors she is delighted to confront. The belatedness which poses such a threat to the originality of Bloom's modern poet is that which, in this female paradise, removes the anxiety of a position in which originality is the only option.

By heralding the situation with approval, however, feminist criticism is simply perpetuating the extent to which Bloom's theory excludes the woman writer from a tradition in which such examples of poetic strength reside that it must impoverish those whom it designates as outcast. Woolf said that the woman writer must think back through her mothers, but what of Homer, Shakespeare, Milton, denied to the female poet by Bloom and his feminist critics alike? Mistaking Bloom's antifeminism as a traditional account of enclosure in the terms of patriarchy, his female commentators attempt to save themselves through escape and flight, installing their sisterhood in a position alienated from poetic tradition, as far removed from the terms of Bloom's theory as even he could wish. The female poet, declaring her independence, comes to rest where Bloom would have her, at a distance from a poetic tradition which, if threatening, is also enabling. A constructive female engagement with Bloom must resist, as Flieger observes, this oedipal temptation "to kill the Fathers of theory and to succumb to the seductive (imaginary) promise of fulfilment, an overly indulgent union with a body of literature experienced as maternal corpus" (Flieger 189). The idea that, from there, she will forge a female poetic and engender a commune of sisters is an illusion, for who can create in a vacuum? Denied the comfort of fellowship, she is "a man without history" (Gilbert and Gubar 238), an orphan child, a foundress of nothing.

The question is whether or not it is possible to revise Bloom's poetic. Can the female enter the terms of his theory? Dorothy Steiner thinks not. "[M]ale historiographers like Bloom," she says, "are not revisable or adaptable," not primarily because they are misogynistic, "but because their models preclude any notion of cultural pluralism" (Steiner 574). And yet how can a tale of poetic creation which excludes one (female) half of the creative pact not be revisable? Is Steiner admitting the possibility, the existence, of a perfectly coherent account of poetic production that denies the notion of a female poet? The fact is that Bloom's philosophy, more than any other conception of literary production, is vulnerable to female attack.

In *Women Writers and Poetic Identity*, Margaret Homans describes Dickinson's relations with Emerson as I would describe her relations with Bloom. Homans identifies Emerson's exaggeration of the Romantic self-centred mode as helpful to Dickinson:

> Because his self is so inclusive, he cares less for the specific characteristics of the "NOT ME," so that Dickinson is not confronted with the same relentless myth of female nature and female objects of desire that Bronte and Dorothy Wordsworth face. Enormous as Emerson's egotism is, it is more easily adapted by a woman, because it has no sexually defined objects. (Homans 18)

The female writer is exemplified perfectly by the deadly plague which ravages the pages of Mary Shelley's apocalyptic novel, *The Last Man*. Described as a female force which defies logocentric definition, the plague is deadly embodiment as it paradoxically exalts the claims of a body it destroys, a body whose breath expires and whose stony eyes are lost to perception. Stephen Goldsmith brilliantly describes the plague's female revenge as "a kind of rhetorical dismemberment, what we might call the body's revenge against consciousness-raising" (Goldsmith 301). Goldsmith draws a parallel between the plague's grotesque reduction of the human body to its infected parts and its simultaneous dismemberment of the sentence. The word "plague" appears frequently in the novel in a form that, says Goldsmith, "brackets its graphic component" (302), printed in capitals or in italics or set in quotation marks. Sentences and words become "rhetorically fragmented" (301), reduced to their component parts, an affirmation of linguistic *différance*, of the materiality of writing. This insistence on the materiality of writing undermines the priority of Bloom's scene of voicing, for Goldsmith shows that speech suffers similar results when touched by the plague (303).

My argument is that the female writer can operate as the plague which infects Bloom's poetic with similar results. The rhetoric which supports his claim to the priority of voicing and seeing is materialized, literalized by a "living pestilence," (*Mathilda* 61) in that it is compelled to acknowledge the female writer as its literal other, the repressed truth which supports Bloom's lie. What does it mean to designate woman as literal? To be literal is to be un-purged of humanity (Steiner 94), to be mortal. Bloom's modern poet is, of course, constructed as daemon rather than human, relentlessly troping in an endless refusal of mortality. Bloom's exclusion of woman is a logical result of this disassociation from the literal since woman has always been seen as literal embodiment. This accounts for the way in which the female writer has traditionally been denied any sense of poetic self, as all manifestations of selfhood are exhausted by biographical explanation. Accordingly, Emily Dickinson's curious, diminutive fragments of selfhood scattered throughout her poems as daisies, birds and mice are often engulfed in psychological explanations of her apparent dislike for social encounter which intensified to an agoraphobic refusal to leave the security of her father's house during the latter years of her life. Her letters provide a halfway house, bridging the gap between figure and fact, facilitating a convenient translation from literature to life, fictional self to historical woman.

This journey, however, can be made in two directions. Emily Dickinson recognized her essential difference in a literature engulfed by a Romantic self which inhabited figurative language. In reaction, she makes of her absence from this figurative arena a figure in itself, using the materials of her daily reality "as if they were not facts but metaphors" (Gilbert 23), mythologizing her literal self and thereby creating a poetic self whose origin in the real, in Truth, renders it immune to the exclusive demands of the tradition. Dickinson, therefore, engages in a form of what Tillotama Rajan terms "autonarration" (Rajan 57). Truth, as Nietzsche had it, is a woman and every manifestation of self in Dickinson's work is part of a process of truth, in John Hollander's words, "yielding up her insides" (*Poetics* xxxv), disclosing the female flesh as the signified, the human, with which Bloom's critical daemons, no longer allowed to play with tropes, must engage. Pollack writes that "[w]omens' role is to be that silent or lost referent, the literal whose absence makes figuration possible. To be also the figurative substitute for that lost referent is," she says, "impossible" (Pollack 182). On the contrary, Dickinson renders herself as the figurative substitute for the lost referent which she is, a substitute which escapes the inadequacy of substitution in general since it masks an identity with the reality which it replaces.

Writing as she did in the America of the mid-nineteenth-century, Dickinson lived in a culture in which rhetorical address was perceived as the vehicle of truth. She rebels against the seeming necessity of voicing which pervaded a culture and a literature which sought to exclude her as a writer by expressing herself through a kind of *written* silence. This silence is part of her need both to disrupt the tradition which saw and said so much and to confirm her allegiance to a *différance* which cannot be spoken and be effective at once. The pervasiveness of silence makes it the perfect agent of difference as it supports Derrida's "always already" by always already determining what it is to speak. The unique appearance of Dickinson's poetry, hyphenated by a silence "which will never yield to a period" (Pollack 196), is a deliberate testimony to the prior claims of a silence which must be written.

> The perfectest communication
> Is heard of none —. (Dickinson, poem 1681)

Elaine Showalter is not in favour of appropriating gaps, blanks and silences as the spaces in which the female consciousness reveals itself. She ends, in her essay "Feminist Criticism in the Wilderness," with the logical but absurd conclusion that "it ought not to be in language that we base our theory of difference." Her objection arises from her affirmation of these "Holes in discourse" as "the blinds of a 'prison-house of language'" (Showalter 256). Yet, this prison-house is, as Dickinson knew, the house of Possibility, "a fairer House than Prose — / More numerous of Windows—/Superior —for Doors —" (657), and these blinds shutter the eye/I which denies the female. Although Showalter complains that women's literature is still haunted by the ghosts of repressed language (256), she unwittingly happens upon the figure for a language in which women are the ghost, the repressed, the haunting. The gaps in Dickinson's text are an extension of the literal figure she presented as she wandered through her father's house in her famous white dress which rendered her "a kind of ghostly blank, an empty page on which in invisible ink this theatrical poet quite consciously wrote a letter to the world" (Gilbert 31). Dickinson's chosen attire, her "white election" (528), strangely enacts Cixous' call for an inscription in the female body which would furnish a life-giving milk as a white ink to articulate an invisible text, to silence the voices which speak her non-existence. Dickinson's poetry is not exhausted by such biographical observations; to explain her poetry with her life is simply to extend an encounter with a literal writing, a silent figure, that forces the very idea of art "across the shadow line that usually separates the metaphorical from the literal" (Gilbert 32).

In *The Western Canon* Bloom produces a reading of Dickinson's poem 761 which begins:

> From Blank to Blank —
> A Threadless Way
> I pushed Mechanic feet—

"To be Blind," says Bloom, "is to give up seeing the Blank" (293) which is a figure for poetic crisis. Dickinson's blank is, in his view, Milton and/or Emerson, "in a very Shakespearean meaning of the blank; the bull's-eye or white spot at the center of the target" (293). But Bloom's insistence on Dickinson's original appropriation of the "Coleridgean-Emersonian Blank," in which blindness is redirected as an insight which ironically confirms the coherence of the I/eye, is itself a blindness which blatantly refuses to see the blank which completes Dickinson's first line, the hyphen whose literal representation of the notion of blankness infects the figurative allusiveness of Bloom's blanks. This hyphen\blank infuses Dickinson's words with the ability to literally annihilate Bloom's series of allusions by becoming a figurative representation of the end of figurative representation. Dickinson, significantly, *breathes* her Blank (1153), a process which refuses the tradition of voicing and seeing in a double coup: the breath of traditional rhetoric is undermined by the blank which it issues forth, and the Blank which Bloom troped as a confirmation of the inner eye is once more embodied by the anatomical process which exhales it, so that "A word which breathes distinctly" is "A Word made Flesh" (1651). Bloom paraphrases Dickinson's poetry of blanks when he says "To breath is to accept a ruined vision" (300). He sees her marriage of breath and vision as an affirmation of both. Instead it is a union which destroys them. An ever-expanding blank pollutes the sentence with a breath that breathes contagion and an eye blinded by the infection.

> The Soul selects her own Society —
> Then—shuts the Door. (303)

Silence, absence and literal embodiment is the society that Dickinson selects as a means of confronting her exclusion from Bloom's self-centred tradition. The absence articulated by Dickinson's poetic silence effects a fragmented sense of self which wanders through her texts as an alternative to the position of unified selfhood she confronts with the inescapable reality of difference. Having selected such a self and compelled Bloom's tradition into a dialectic wrangling for presence which at least cancels the notion of absolute presence which had demanded her exclusion, having entered tradition by duplicating its terms, there remains only to shut the door, to convert exclusion into inclusion and establish her place within a tradition which, however hostile, at least provides a creative context.

> I've known her—from an ample nation —
> Choose One —
> Then—close the Valves of her attention —
> Like Stone —. (303)

The ultimate figurative manoeuvre by Dickinson is to deny the passage of life blood and entomb her manifestations of self in the stony vault of repressed mortality at the core of a tradition ceaselessly aspiring to eternal life. When she has troped her literal self into Bloom's world of figures, the female writer can die into her art.

This enclosed, entombed figure is a strange affirmation of selfhood, and yet Dickinson knew the freedom that such confinement can bestow. Exclusion, unlimited potential, confers creative impotence, but the female writer can use this imposed death as a means of exposing the extent to which her exclusion is, after all, a figure for her inclusion at the repressed core of Bloom's tradition. His theory seemed not to figure the female at all, but the part of Freud's account of symptoms and anxiety which Bloom chose to ignore reveals her nothingness as, not a fact, but a trope which figures as the repressed ground upon which Bloom's poem is written. So this death is life, life to the female writer whose discovery as part of a traditional dialectic affords her the freedom which only inhibition can bequeath. It is, as Dickinson describes,

> As if my life were shaven,
> And fitted to a frame,
> And could not breath, without a key. (510)

The female writer begins to "breathe" — a traditional figure for inspired poetic activity—only when the air is stifled and she is breathless, for inspiration is possible only with a key to lock out the air which seeks to dull her mind. Dickinson once retired to a room in her father's house with her niece, Martha. She closed the door behind them and, with an imaginary key, locked them in. "Matty," she said, "here's freedom."

Works Cited

Dickinson, Emily. *The Complete Poems*. Ed. Thomas H. Johnson. London: Faber, 1970.
Diehl, Joanne Feit. "Dickinson and Bloom: An Antithetical Reading of Romanticism." *Texas Studies in Literature and Language* 23.3 (1981): 418–41.
Flieger, Jerry Aline. "Entertaining the Ménage à Trois: Psychoanalysis, Feminism and Literature." *Feminism and Psychoanalysis*. Ed. Richard Feldstein and Judith Roof. Ithaca: Cornell UP, 1989. 185–208.
Gilbert, Sandra. "The Wayward Nun Beneath the Hill: Emily Dickinson and the Mysteries of Womanhood." *Feminist Critics Read Emily Dickinson*. Ed. Suzanne Juhasz. Bloomington: Indiana UP, 1983. 22–44.
——, and Susan Gubar. *The Madwoman in the Attic*. New Haven: Yale UP, 1979.
Goldsmith, Steven. *Unbuilding Jerusalem: Apocalypse and Romantic Representation*. Ithaca: Cornell UP, 1993.
Homans, Margaret. *Women Writers and Poetic Identity*. Princeton: Princeton UP, 1980.
Kolodny, Annette. "The Influence of Anxiety: Prolegomena to a Study of the Production of Poetry by Women." *A Gift of Tongues: Critical Challenges in Contemporary American Poetry*. Ed. Marie Harris and Kathleen Aguero. Athens, GA: U of Georgia P, 1987. 112–41.
Pollack, Vivian. *Dickinson: The Anxiety of Gender*. Ithaca: Cornell UP, 1984.
Rajan, Tilottama. "Mary Shelley's *Mathilda*: Melancholy and the Political Economy of Romanticism." *Studies in the Novel* 26.3 (1994): 43–68.
Shelley, Mary. *The Last Man*. Ed. Morton D. Paley. Oxford: Oxford UP, 1994.

——. *Mathilda. The Novels and Selected Works of Mary Shelley*. 8 vols. Gen. ed. Nora Crook. Vol. 2. Ed. Pamela Clemit. London: Pickering, 1996.

Showalter, Elaine. "Feminist Criticism in the Wilderness." *The New Feminist Criticism: Essays on Women, Literature, and Theory*. Ed. Elaine Showalter. London: Virago, 1986. 243–70.

Sparks, Elisa. "Old Father Nile: T. S. Eliot and Harold Bloom on the Creative Process as Spontaneous Generation." *Engendering the Word: Feminist Essays in Psychosexual Poetics*. Ed. Temma F. Berg, et al. Urbana: U of Illinois P, 1989. 51–80.

Steiner, Dorothy. "Feminist Criticism, Poetic Theory, and American Poetry Historiography." *Opening Up Literary Criticism: Essays on American Prose and Poetry*. Ed. Leo Truchlar. Salzburg: Wolfgang Neugebauer, 1996. 88–133.

Zasloff, Tela C. "The Author Was a Woman: The Issue of Essentialism in *The Book of J*." *Women and Language* 17.2 (1994): 34–39.

A Queer Touch and the Bloomian Model of Authorial Influence

STEPHEN DA SILVA

In the "Terminal Note" to *Maurice*, E. M. Forster dramatically describes the novel's conception in terms of an inspirational touch. But the implications of that scene go beyond the description of one text's genesis. For, in that account, Forster is constructing an elaborate gay male authorial genealogy in which he situates *Maurice*. In this essay, I will 'touch' Harold Bloom's model of authorial influence with Forster's primal scene in order to consider the limited uses that Bloom's Oedipal model of authorial literary influence continues to have for gay male literary theory. Conversely, I will use the gay male family romance constructed by Forster to queer Bloom's model. The similarities between the dramas of Forster and Bloom, I will argue, help to unconceal a disavowed homoeroticism which lies at the heart of the Oedipal model of literary influence. Further, even while disavowing them, Forster's genealogical drama evokes issues of national, class, and gendered difference that the story of fathers and sons advanced by Bloom resolutely ignores.

1) A Tactile Genealogy

I will begin by citing at length the primal scene which frames this entire essay. In his terminal note to *Maurice*, Forster writes that the novel was "conceived" when he was visiting Edward Carpenter and George Merrill, Carpenter's working-class lover, at Milthorpe.[1] The idea for *Maurice* was born, according to this account, when Merrill touched Forster's "backside:"

[1] Forster links pederastic relations of influence to male impregnation both in the terminal note to *Maurice* and in the tale "Little Imber." This equation draws on

> It must have been on my second or third visit to the shrine that the spark was kindled and he [Carpenter] and his comrade George Merrill combined to make a profound impression on me and to touch a creative spring. George Merrill also touched my backside.... It [the sensation] seemed to go straight through the small of my back into my ideas.... If it really did this, it ... would prove that at that precise moment I had conceived.
>
> I then returned to Harrogate ... and immediately began to write Maurice. (245-46)

Although it was Merrill who touched Forster's "backside," Carpenter is intimately implicated in that touch. The repetition of the word 'touch' in the following two sentences—"[Carpenter] and his comrade George Merrill combined to make a profound impression on me and to *touch* a creative spring. George Merrill also *touched* my backside [my emphases]"—demonstrates that, regardless of who literally touched Forster's backside, Carpenter is figuratively implicated in Forster's impregnation fantasy.

The verb 'touch' appears again in Forster's 1929 memorial tribute to Carpenter, "Some Memories:" "Edward Carpenter was the sea. He *touched* everyone everywhere" (75, my emphasis). The reappearance of the word "touched" in this memorial tribute suggests that Forster, in looking back on Carpenter's life, might have been associating the older writer, at some level, with the inspirational touch that led to the conception of Maurice.[2] Further, at the end of 1913, the year in which the Milthorpe incident took place, thinking of his creative plans for finishing Maurice, Forster wrote in his diary: "Forward rather than back. Edward Carpenter! Edward Carpenter! Edward Carpenter!" (Furbank, Life 1: 258). In other words, at the end of the year, when Forster was looking back at the source of his

---

the Hellenic idiom of spiritual procreancy explored by Linda Dowling (75-79). Edward Carpenter, whom Forster implicates in the conception of Maurice, eloquently articulates the Hellenic position: "Just as ordinary sex-love has a special function in the propagation of the race, so the other love should have its special function in the generation—not of bodily children—but of children of the mind" ("Homogenic" 343).

[2] The tactile metaphors and figures that saturate (would 'blanket' be a more appropriately tactile figure?) Maurice may in part be the fruit of the inspirational touch which engendered the novel. For instance, when Clive Durham first speaks to Maurice in the "sunlit court" about the Hellenic love celebrated in the Symposium, Maurice feels that "a breath of liberty *touched* him" (69, my emphasis).

inspiration for *Maurice*, he powerfully associated it with Carpenter, so much so that Merrill entirely disappeared from the picture. In the diary description, it is Carpenter alone who propels Forster forward.

Forster's tactile metaphor situates the conception scene within a gay male literary tradition. For one thing, the trope intertextually links the novel to Carpenter's writing, particularly his long poem *Towards Democracy*, for that poem insistently uses the word 'touch' and tactile metaphors. To cite just one example, expansively celebrating the incorporative and insatiable power of his desire, the poet declares: "Him I touch, and her I touch, and you I touch—I can never be satisfied" (Towards 67). But the metaphor also implicitly invokes Walt Whitman. Whitman exerted a profound influence on Carpenter, who played a key role in popularizing the older poet in Britain. He also exerted a strong influence on Forster (one might consider here the intertextual link between works like Whitman's poem "Passage to India" and Forster's 1924 novel), though Forster does not directly acknowledge his influence in the way that Carpenter does.[3]

More to my purpose, Whitman, too, insistently relies on the language of touch. To cite just one instance, in the poem "Whoever You Are Holding Me Now in Hand," the poet speaking in the guise of the volume of poetry itself invites the reader to

>   thrust . . . me beneath your clothing,
> Where I may feel the throbs of your heart or rest upon your hip
> . . . .
> For thus merely *touching* you is enough, is best,
> And thus *touching* you would I silently sleep and be carried eternally.
> (*Leaves* 116; lines 22–23 and 25–26, my emphasis)

Not only does the language of touch attend the conception of *Maurice*, it also informs discussions of the novel's reception by younger gay male

---

[3] In a journal entry for 16 June 1908, Forster reveals the strong personal bond he felt with Whitman: "I opened Walt Whitman for a quotation, and he started speaking to me. . . . He is not a book but an acquaintance. . . . [H]e knows me personally" (Forster, qtd. in Buckton 254). In this account, Forster concedes that Whitman wins him over; he starts out in search of a quotation from Whitman but is seduced into listening to the poet as he would to a personal acquaintance (and we know how important personal relationships are for Forster). Below I will explore how Forster more defensively attempts to distance himself from Whitman in describing the utter originality of *Maurice*. For a persuasive account of the position of *Maurice* in a Whitmanian literary tradition, see Martin, "Edward Carpenter."

writers influenced by Forster, like Christopher Isherwood. In texts such as *Lions and Shadows*, Isherwood acknowledges the powerful artistic influence that Forster exerted on him (130–31 and 135–36), and both Alan Wilde and I have traced different formal and thematic connections between the two writers' works (Wilde 38–40; Da Silva, "Strategically" 189–91). In *Christopher and His Kind*, one page after citing Forster's description of the birth of *Maurice* (126), Isherwood describes his own reaction to the novel and Forster's response to that reaction:[4]

> the Pupil [Isherwood] was being asked by the Master[5] . . . how *Maurice* appeared to a member of the thirties generation. . . . My memory sees them sitting together facing each other . . . Christopher stammers some words of praise and devotion, his eyes brimming with tears. And Forster—amused and *touched*, but more *touched* than amused leans forward and kisses him on the cheek. (127, my emphasis)

While in this scene it is the older writer who is "touched" by the younger writer's response, there is an intense affective reciprocity between them. The younger writer's reverent emotion for his precursor is mirrored by his precursor's mingled amusement and emotion at the younger writer's obvious admiration, a reciprocity that is underlined by their spatial positioning—they sit "facing each other." Not only is Forster emotionally "touched," he literally touches his "Pupil" with an affectionate kiss.

The investment that the circle of gay male writers influencing and influenced by Forster has in constructing genealogical relations among themselves in terms of touch makes it particularly useful to juxtapose the scene of *Maurice*'s conception with Bloom's model of authorial influence, which also focuses on relations of influence among male writers of different generations, albeit in paternal-filial rather than pederastic terms. To some extent, I feel authorized in using a scene of literary conception to construct a theoretical allegory about gay male authorial

---

[4] Isherwood refers to himself in the third person as "Christopher" to emphasize the mediated distance between his authorial self and the past self he describes in his memoir.

[5] Isherwood's use of the terms "Pupil" and "Master" is significant because, as I have argued elsewhere, Forster both draws on and inverts the classical pederastic model which represents the relationship between the older man and the younger boy as a tutelary one (Da Silva, "Transvaluing" 257–60). As we will see later in this essay, Harold Bloom invokes this model as well in describing the younger writer as an "ephebe."

influence because Bloom himself, both in *The Anxiety of Influence* and *A Map of Misreading*, has used certain literary scenes in *Paradise Lost* to generate rich theoretical insights.[6]

If I am influenced by Bloom in using a literary scene to construct theoretical claims, I am influenced by Forster in giving salience to the metaphor of touch in articulating those claims. But I want to stress that I use the metaphor of touch in this paper as Forster does, as opposed to Whitman's and Carpenter's characteristic use of the word. For Whitman and Carpenter, touch usually works to heal separation or difference, in order to achieve transcendent unity. In Carpenter's poem "By the Shore," for instance, the poet moves from celebrating his tactile contact with the waves in the darkness—"The night is dark overhead; I do not see them [the waves], but I *touch* them. . ." (*Towards* 160, my emphasis)—to actually becoming the waves: "Suddenly I am the ocean itself . . ." (160).[7] By contrast, in the birthing scene of *Maurice*, there is no

---

[6] Bloom, with characteristic hyperbole, maintains that "Milton's epic [*Paradise Lost* is] the most Freudian text ever written, far closer to the universe of psychoanalysis than such more frequently cited works, in Freudian contexts, as *Oedipus Tyrannus* and *Hamlet*" (*Agon* 112).

[7] There are a few exceptions to Whitman's and Carpenter's expansive sense of the possibilities of touch. In "Song of Myself," for instance, Whitman obscurely hints at the treacherously dispossessing power of touch. Poem 28 initially suggests that touch can expand the poet's ontological mobility, though the uncharacteristic question with which it begins undercuts Whitman's usually unequivocally affirmative certainty: "Is this then a touch? quivering me to a new identity" (*Leaves* 57, line 620). But the poem ends with a fantasy of surrender to and imprisonment by racialized others: "The sentries desert every part of me / They have left me helpless to the red marauder / I am given up to traitors" (635-37). While the poet acknowledges in one clause that he exercised agency ("I went myself first to the headlands"), in the next clause, in the same line, he represents himself as an object controlled by his hands: "my . . . hands carried me there" (638). Rather than allowing the poet to incorporate the world, "villain touch" (639) is here in sadistic control of the poet: "you are too much for me" (641). Betsy Erkkila, however, points out that this feeling of dispossession is repaired at the end of the section: "The moment of sexual release is followed by a restoration of balance as the ejaculatory flow merges with and is naturalized as the regenerative flow of the universe" (106).

Carpenter too has rare moments when he acknowledges the incorporative limits of touch. In the poem "In the Drawing Room," the poet alienated by the pointlessness of urban life longs for Nature to revive him, and he figures that yearning in terms of a transsexual simile: "as a woman for the *touch* of a man / So I cried in my soul even for the violence and outrage of Nature to deliver me from this barrenness"

indication that the touch allows Forster to merge with his precursors.[8] The touch brings him into contact with them, but they remain separate—indeed, as we shall see, vexedly, anxiously separate. By the same token, I want to touch an Oedipal model of literary influence with a fantasy of gay male literary transmission, rather than absolutely collapsing them into each other. But if the touch at Milthorpe does not erase Forster's integrity, it does productively unsettle him, bring him into contact with something outside his accustomed boundaries, and I am hoping that touching a Bloomian model of influence with a scene of gay literary transmission might productively unsettle both parties.[9]

To begin, let me briefly and schematically sketch those aspects of Bloom's model which are of relevance to my argument. In Bloom's Oedipal model of authorship, the relationship between a younger male author and his precursor is analogous to the relationship between a father and his son: "a poem is a response to a poem as a poet is a response to a poet, or a person to his parent" (*Map* 18). No doubt, Bloom uses the non-gendered "parent" in this formulation, but by the next page he makes it clear that he is really thinking of the relationship between a

---

(*Towards* 120–21, my emphasis). Longing for a masculinized Nature to deliver him from the "barrenness" of quotidian reality, the poet compares himself to a woman yearning for the touch of a man. Similes, however, evoke both sameness and difference; one can compare two things only because they are not identical, so the "as" reminds us that the poet is not a woman, and even the invocation of his favorite tactile image will not allow him to collapse the difference between his relation to nature and the fantasy of a heterosexual female's yearning for intercourse and reproduction.

[8] In other Forsterian texts, also, one sees a certain skepticism about the integrative potential of the touch. In *A Passage to India*, for instance, Ronnie and Adela, who have had a disagreement, find themselves seemingly united by an intimate touch: "Her hand touched his . . . and one of the thrills so frequent in the animal kingdom passed between them, and announced that all their differences were only a lover's quarrel." But the narrative voice then goes on to characterize this seeming moment of communion as "a spurious unity . . . as local and temporary as the gleam that inhabits a firefly" (88).

[9] My formulation is indebted to the opening of Jane Gallop's *The Daughter's Seduction*. In that text, Gallop stages a seductive encounter between father psychoanalysis and daughter feminism: "This book is a continual working of a dialectical tension between psychoanalysis and feminism. . . . The radical potential in their marriage is not a mystical fusion obliterating all difference and conflict, but a provocative contact which opens each to what is not encompassed by the limits of its identity" (xii).

father and his son: "To the poet . . . a poem is always the *other man*, the precursor, and so a poem is always a person, always the father of one's Second Birth" (19). Later in *A Map of Misreading*, the metaphorics of paternity become more insistent. Thus, in describing the relationship between Percy Shelley and Robert Browning, Bloom writes: "[Shelley] is the presence that the poem ["Childe Roland to the Dark Tower Came"] labors to void, and his is the force which rouses the poem's force. Out of that struggle between forces rises the force of Browning's poem, which is effectively the *difference* between the rival strengths of poetic father and poetic son" (*Map* 116). Poetic creation arises in the Bloomian model from the struggle between paternal and filial forces. In order for the younger poet to gain his distance from the paternal precursor, he has creatively to misread the older one. Bloom then elaborates a series of complex tropes by which poets misread their paternal precursors, but these tropes are not of crucial import to my argument. My purpose is not to explore fully the complexities of the Bloomian model; rather, I am concentrating on those aspects of it which have resonance with my particular concerns in articulating a relationship between gay male literary theory and Oedipal models of influence. Such an interested (mis)reading of Bloom is consistent with his own model of critical reading: "Poets' misinterpretations . . . are more drastic than critics' misinterpretations, but this is only a difference in degree and not at all in kind. There are no interpretations but only misinterpretations" (*Anxiety* 95).

Admittedly, in his introduction to the new edition of *The Anxiety of Influence*, Bloom explicitly rejects readings of his model in terms of Oedipal authorial rivalry as a "weak misread[ing]:" "I never meant by 'the anxiety of influence' a Freudian Oedipal rivalry . . . how weakly misread *The Anxiety of Influence* has been . . . any adequate reader of the book . . . will see that influence-anxiety does not . . . concern the forerunner" (xxv). At the risk of betraying myself to be an inadequate reader, I would argue that mine is not a weak misreading of Bloom; rather, in the introduction to the latest edition of *The Anxiety of Influence*, we are witnessing Bloom himself strongly misreading his former positions. In Freudian terms, the bristling negation in these formulations ("I *never* meant . . . does *not* . . . concern") suggests active disavowal on Bloom's part of the influence of psychoanalysis on his project.[10] And

---

[10] For the seminal discussion of the way in which repressed desires are articulated through negation, see Freud's "Negation." Harold Bloom himself uses the Freudian concept of negation to read various writers' unconsciously defensive attempts to avoid recognizing the force of literary influence (*Agon* 18, *passim*).

indeed, Bloom's *The Western Canon*, a book written a couple of years before this introduction, constructs a revisionary family romance which makes Shakespeare, rather than Freud, the sire of his paradigm (xvi).[11] But beyond negation, what is one to make of Bloom's concessionary subordinate clause following his strong denial that the anxiety of influence has anything to do with "Freudian Oedipal rivalry"—"despite a rhetorical flourish or two in this book [to that Oedipal effect]" (xxv)? I would submit that what usually makes Bloom such a rewarding reader is precisely that he ignores authors' stated intentions and pays close attention to their language, their "rhetorical flourish[es]," if you will, for what they symptomatically reveal; consider, for instance, his close deconstructive reading of Wallace Stevens's rhetorical attack on poetic influence (*Poetry and Repression* 277–78). And the figurative logic of *The Anxiety of Influence* and *A Map of Misreading* suggests that authorial Oedipal rivalry is crucial to the paradigm, whatever Bloom's retrospective authorial intention might be.

Peter de Bolla, a highly sympathetic reader of Bloom on his own sometimes incoherent terms, reads "the somewhat repetitive quality in Bloom's theoretical work" (15) as a response to repeated critical obtuseness about Bloom's project (17). Yet de Bolla's attitude toward repetition and the relationship between truth and error seems to emerge from the Enlightenment rather than the realms of psychoanalysis or deconstruction. If critics, like myself, keep getting Bloom wrong, as de Bolla and Bloom himself would have it, then surely something productive is happening in that misrecognition. And if Bloom has constantly to correct critics in their supposed misunderstanding of his project, then surely as a good psychoanalytic critic one would need to attend to what might lie beneath that defensive repetition? Could it be that critics persistently want to understand the Bloomian model in Oedipal terms because, regardless of the new vocabularies to which Bloom turns—be it the arcane vocabulary of Kabbalah or the intertextual vocabulary of some strains of deconstruction—the animating energy of the project remains the Oedipal authorial struggle that he examined in his early works?

While Bloom more recently insists that he is more interested in intertextual relationships than paternal-filial authorial bonds, the

---

[11] Frank Lentricchia constructs another Bloomian family romance: he reads Bloom as replacing "New Critical father figures" with agonistic "poststructuralist" "siblings" like Derrida (326).

language he employs betrays a continuing investment in the Oedipal authorial struggle he elaborated in his earlier work. Let us examine the shifty and incoherent grammar of the following passage from *Poetry and Repression*:

> What happens to a poem after it has succeeded in clearing a space for itself? As the poem begins to be misread, both by other poems and by criticism, is it distorted in the same way or differently than it has always been distorted by itself through its own activity in misreading others? Clearly, its meanings do change drastically between the time that it first wrestles its way into strength and the later time that follows its canonization. (28)

On the one hand, the passive voice formulations in that passage fit a poststructuralist notion of intertextuality which focuses on language as a matrix of relations, rather than focusing on authorial subjects acting upon language. When Bloom asks in the passive voice "has it been distorted in the same way or differently?," or when he states in the passive voice that "it has always been distorted," the grammar comprehensibly describes an object situated in a realm of interrelated language objects. The text exercises no agency in these formulations. But I am mystified by the strong active voice formulations such as "it has succeeded in clearing a space for itself." What exactly is the ontological status of the text in such a formulation? What sort of model of agency informs such a formulation? The text in that formulation is a stereotypical virile pioneer with a driving will to clear a space for itself. It is, to put it bluntly, a male authorial son in textual drag. More plainly, my contention is that Bloom wants to get away from the figure of the literal author but cannot do so without sacrificing his Oedipal drama, so he mystifyingly transfers authorial agency to a hypostatized entity called 'the text' that has all the stereotypically virile and aggressive impulses of the authorial fathers and sons in the earlier version of his theoretical story.

Even if I were willing to concede that there are significant differences between earlier versions of Bloom's paradigm and more recent accounts, I would have to add that I find earlier versions of his critical paradigm far more useful. Such a distinction would be relevantly Bloomian because, as de Bolla correctly points out, Bloom is far less interested in creating an abstract literary theory than he is in constructing a pragmatic model that facilitates what he calls strong reading of poetry (18). Turning to Bloom's earlier theoretical work seems particularly appropriate in the context of discussing a gay male authorial genealogy. As I have argued elsewhere, works of gay male writers, like

Forster, that explicitly thematize homosexuality have often been critically dismissed as aesthetically immature, and these writers have sometimes responded by trans-valuing what counts as immature ("Transvaluing" 242–50). It seems appropriate, then, that I should find Bloom's "immature" critical work more valuable than his later work in reading the scene of *Maurice's* conception.

The value of Bloom's Oedipal model lies in its aggressive desublimation of literary production, its recognition of the violence and anxiety that underlie the relationship between writers of different generations. Before applying the Bloomian model to the writers under consideration, though, I would like to sketch the counter-mythology that they constructed, a mythology that opposes paternal-filial relations to nurturant, non-aggressive, pederastic ones, a counter-mythology which has been too often uncritically endorsed by gay male literary theory. Then I will consider how the Bloomian model salutarily helps to complicate that counter-mythology and reintroduce aggression and conflict into intergenerational bonds between gay male writers.

2) Pederastic Mentors versus Fathers

The two specific writers on whom I will focus are Isherwood and J. R. Ackerley: both were strongly influenced by Forster, and both opposed their vexed relations with their fathers, or the cultural patrimony that their fathers synecdochically represented, to their pederastic ties with Forster.[12]

---

[12] While my analysis focuses on Isherwood's and Ackerley's relationship to Forster, Carpenter constructs a similar dichotomy between the figures of his father and Percy Shelley: in *The Psychology of the Poet Shelley*, Carpenter stresses Shelley's androgynous nature and suggests that he might be described as an "intermediate type." Throughout the introduction, Carpenter stresses the influence that this precursor intermediate type exerted on him, and in one telling moment, he Oedipally challenges his father first by pointedly juxtaposing his father and Shelley, in terms of age, and then distinguishing between his father's reflection of wrong-headed public opinion on issues of sexual morality and Shelley's liberatory ideas: "I remember well that my own father (who was born in 1793, that is one year later than Shelley) ... did strongly disapprove of the poet's ideas ... especially on the subject of marriage. Knowing my father so well, and through him having obtained glimpses of the current political opinion of that period, I appreciated all the more the mental clarity and boldness of [Shelley] who so decisively cast aside the conventions that surrounded him" (8–9). Carpenter both aligns and distinguishes his precursor intermediate type from his father—they are both

Forster often appears as a character in Isherwood's novels, and the younger writer insistently represents his homosexual precursor in terms of youthfulness. These are romantically anti-developmental terms that Isherwood inherits from Forster himself.

Further, Isherwood repeatedly and pointedly pits the youthful and modest heroism of Forster against the false heroics of patriarchal authority.[13]

Ackerley too sets up an opposition between his strained relations with his father and his close ties with Forster. In one of the key scenes in his memoir *My Father and Myself,* Ackerley represents his paradigmatic filial discomfort with his father's all-seeing "magnificent blue eyes [that] fixed one so that one felt sometimes not merely scrutinized but trapped" (*My Father* 85–86). That Ackerley chooses to trope his reconstruction of his father's life in visual terms at several points in the memoir suggests that his auto/biographical venture is in part a way of aggressively reversing that gaze. In the memoir, his father, rather than being the eye that can detect secrets and that demands visual reciprocity, becomes an object on display, one, moreover, that is unaware it is on display:

> Any nosy Parker keeping a watch upon our house would have seen the front door opened punctually at [eight o'clock] . . . and my father descend the steps in his grey Edward VII hat, his light fawn or heavy overcoat, his umbrella on his arm. . . . (92)

All this battling over who will control the gaze would seem to stand in stark opposition to the mutuality suggested by the touches we have seen gay men of different generations sharing, though I will suggest later in this essay that it would be unwise to draw that opposition too sharply.

Ackerley sharply opposes his lack of communication with his father to his close bond with his homophilic mentor Forster. As Peter Parker shows in his biography of Ackerley, there was an enormously close and

almost of the same age—and uses Shelley's rebellion as an indirect way to articulate his own non-conformity.

Interestingly, Shelley is also a key figure in Harold Bloom's attempt to distance himself from his precursor New Critics. Bloom's first book (*Shelley's Mythmaking*) reassessed the value of a poet who had often been contemptuously dismissed by the New Criticism.

[13] For reasons of space, I do not textually support these claims, but they are more fully explored in my essay "Strategically Minor: Isherwood's Revision of Forster's Mythology."

communicative relationship between Forster and Ackerley (Parker 49-84), and Furbank explicitly frames their relationship in paternal-filial terms: "Forster was the father-figure [Ackerley] wanted: a man he could revere ... and yet with whom he could be frank" (Furbank 2: 137). The two writers regularly commented on each other's work—the friendship began, after all, when Forster wrote to the younger writer complimenting him and giving him critical suggestions on a homoerotic poem "Ghosts," and the older writer went on to give Ackerley extensive revision suggestions while he worked on *Hindoo Holiday*. Like Isherwood, Ackerley refers to Forster as a mentor, an appellation that would appeal to the older writer with his investment in the pederastic, tutelary model of male intergenerational relations: Ackerley writes in his diary "Morgan was already my mentor and had upon me the effect of keeping me up to the mark and making me feel that I had a best and should look to it" (Parker 80). Forster's position as Ackerley's literary mentor links him to another mentor who played an equally crucial role in the young man's life, Arnold Lunn: Ackerley explains that, at a time when he was not able to articulate his homosexual desire, Lunn introduced him to "books" by "Edward Carpenter" among others (*My Father* 117), which gave him a lexicon to express his desires. Not only do the readings Lunn gave Ackerley place him in a genealogical relation to figures like Carpenter and Whitman, they also help reaffirm a distinction between Ackerley's father, who does not read much and willfully refuses to recognize his son's sexuality, and a pederastic literary tradition embodied in the figure of Forster and the books to which Lunn introduced Ackerley (Lunn himself was a self-identified heterosexual).

But it was not merely the older writer who influenced the younger one. Parker explains that in fact the two writers exerted reciprocal influence upon each other. Ackerley gave Forster extensive revision suggestions on several of his homoerotic short stories, *Maurice*, and the libretto to Benjamin Britten's opera *Billy Budd*. Indeed, sometimes it is unclear as to which writer one should treat as the precursor and which writer occupies the position of the ephebe. This ambiguity can be seen when we consider Ackerley's Indian travel memoir, *Hindoo Holiday*. This text was written in 1932 at the prompting of Forster, and as I have mentioned before, Forster gave Ackerley extensive revision suggestions on it. So, in that sense, Forster is Ackerley's precursor. Yet Forster's own Indian travel memoir, published in 1953, *The Hill of Devi*, has close intertextual relations with Ackerley's book. In other words, the mentor's book is influenced by that of the ephebe, or to switch metaphors, in this case, one cannot be sure who is doing the touching and who is being touched.

Forster's and Ackerley's collaboration on the short story "Little Imber" is of particular import to the concerns of this essay because the thematics of the story are so similar to those of the birthing scene at Milthorpe. Ackerley closely collaborated with the eighty-three-year-old Forster (*Arctic* xxiii) on this uncompleted story, whose reflexive topic is arguably the productive possibilities of pederastic relations of influence. To summarize the plot of the story: in a futuristic world, which is growing increasingly sterile because of the imbalance between the female and male populations, two men, Little Imber and Warham reproduce. The tale repeatedly emphasizes the age difference between Little Imber and Warham: as the name *Little* Imber suggests, Little Imber is the younger of the two. He is repeatedly described as a "boy" and as "immature," and we are told that Warham is "jealous" of Little Imber's "youth" (see 230 and 229, for instance). In other words, in this tale, the fantasy of male reproduction is linked to the age difference between Warham and Little Imber, an age difference which can be analogized to the generational difference that separates Forster from Ackerley or Isherwood. In one fragmented conclusion to this story, for which two contradictory conclusions exist, the intergenerational coupling between the men leads to immense generativity. In that version, two male infants are born of the first male union, and they incestuously couple and bring back fecundity to an increasingly sterile world:

> And from that swaddling a babe burst.... [What] it really desired was its own younger brother.... They met and then things hummed. Retiring to a pagan grove, the whereabouts of which they concealed, they perfected their techniques and produced Romuloids and Remoids in masses. It was impossible to walk in that country-side without finding a foundling, or to leave two together without finding a third.... [T]he population graph shot up until it hit the jackpot. (235)

The link between Ackerley and the fertilizing force of Little Imber becomes evident when we read Forster's description of how the story was composed in a December 1961 journal entry: "[Ackerley] woke up to help over 'Little Imber' which ... might see the light of night after my death. Once aroused he may be active and penetrative" (*Arctic* xxiv). The journal entry links the story "Little Imber" to the character Little Imber; like Little Imber, Forster suggests, the story may be "penetrative" and fertilizing. However, the referent of the pronoun "he" is ambiguous; it could refer to Little Imber or Ackerley. In other words, like "penetrative" Little Imber, Ackerley at least metaphorically impregnates the aging Forster with a new story. Like the scene of *Maurice*'s conception, then, this story can be read as an allegory for the generative consequences of relations between homosexual men of different generations, as opposed to the sterility which informs relations between homosexual men and their fathers.[14]

3) Touching Homophilic Mythologies with the Bloomian Model

In this section, I will explore how, contrary to the oppositions Isherwood and Ackerley draw between paternity and pederasty, there is in fact a strong continuity between the anxious and aggressive relations between literary fathers and sons that Bloom explores in his model and the relations between male homosexual writers of different generations.

Take the relationship between Carpenter and Whitman. Bloom has posited that the anxious literary son pursues various revisionary strategies to separate himself from his paternal precursor. That description resonates strongly with Carpenter's attempts to distance himself from Whitman. In "A Note on *Towards Democracy*," for instance, Carpenter performs a series of complex negotiations to differentiate himself from Whitman. He begins the note: "I have said . . . nothing about the influence of Whitman—for the same reason that I have said nothing about the influence of the sun or the winds. These influences lie too far back and ramify too complexly to be traced." But immediately after acknowledging Whitman's influence on him, Carpenter denies that he consciously imitated Whitman: "I find it difficult to imagine what my life would have been without [*Leaves of Grass*], but I do not think I ever tried to imitate it or its style. . . . I did not adopt it [the form of *Towards Democracy*] because it was an approximation to the form of *Leaves of*

---

[14] Forster betrays his ambivalence about the fantasy of all-male generation by having two endings to the fragment. The other ending bleakly represents the death of the strange new fetal membrane which is the fruit of Warham and Little Imber's homosexual union: "They watched the enigmatic mass shrink, expand, and shrivel up. Very gently [Little Imber] laid his finger on the membrane. 'Yes, it's dead,' he whispered" (234). Note how in this conclusion not only is the fetus aborted, Little Imber's touching it does not serve to revivify it. Even though the story ends reparatively with the shared erotic encounter between Little Imber and Warham, one cannot escape the detumescent implications of the image of the shrunken shriveled membrane.

Grass." The repeated negations—"I do *not* think. . . . I did *not* adopt it"—suggest that Carpenter is trying to repress an indebtedness he unconsciously recognizes. He ends by declaring that *Towards Democracy* is extremely modest compared to Whitman's work:

> Whitman's full-blooded, copious, rank masculine style must make him one of the world's great originals—a perennial fountain . . . . "Towards Democracy" has a milder radiance, as of the moon compared with the sun . . . . Tender and meditative and altogether less massive, it has the quality of fluid and yielding air rather than of the solid and uncompromising earth. (*Towards* 414–15)

In this formulation, Carpenter feminizes himself—he is the moon to Whitman's sun; his poem is a "fluid," "yielding," "airy" work compared to Whitman's generative, "massive" "fountain." Yet when one remembers that Carpenter celebrates the feminine and feminizing qualities of the intermediate type, who can heal a masculinist culture that is alienated from female qualities, the tone of this distinction becomes decidedly ambiguous: is Carpenter praising or criticizing Whitman when he describes *Leaves of Grass* in such conventionally masculine, phallic terms? Regardless of how one reads Carpenter's tone, his seeming self-effacement allows him to differentiate himself from the older poet, Whitman.

Forster demonstrates a similar anxious ambivalence about Carpenter. That ambivalence can be demonstrated by juxtaposing Forster's tribute to Carpenter with his comments on his precursor in his *Commonplace Book*. In his tribute to Carpenter, Forster admiringly acknowledged how much deeper Carpenter was than he: "If I am as deep as a pond . . . Edward Carpenter was the sea" ("Some Memories" 275). Yet in his *Commonplace Book*, Forster was brutally dismissive of Carpenter:

> Astonishing how he [Carpenter] drains away . . . the spirit is there, but it has got into the wrong skin. Gerald Heard summed him up the other day at my request and most devastatingly: "An echo. Walt Whitman was the first blew through that hollow reed. Morris, J. A. Symonds—there you have the whole. He knew nothing he couldn't think. . . . He knew *nothing* about civilization. He was always a clergyman, you were *not* to wear boots but sandals, you were *not* to go to church. . . . I suppose there was something there, but as soon as one touches it, it's gone. Slow but steady decline of power." (*Commonplace Book* 52–53)

In this passage, by endorsing Heard's view of Carpenter, Forster is able to devalue his predecessor. Ocean-like Carpenter is here described as "draining away." This spermatic metaphor together with the image of "the hollow reed" make Carpenter a figure of sterility. To describe Carpenter as "draining away" is particularly cruel because in his own work, he constantly figures primitive man's youthful vitality in terms of his unity with the ocean. While in his essay on Carpenter, Forster rejects Havelock Ellis's gibe about Carpenter being "Whitman with water" ("Edward Carpenter" 214), here Forster endorses Heard's description of Carpenter as Whitman's "echo." Further, while in the "Terminal Note" to *Maurice*, Forster acknowledges Carpenter as the origin of the novel, he here denies his own indebtedness to Carpenter by endorsing Heard's dismissal of the older writer as belonging to a dead ("hollow") tradition descending from Whitman through Morris and Symonds. Moreover, if in the "Terminal Note" to *Maurice*, Forster sees Carpenter and Merrill as providing him with a source of vital, non-cerebral power—"it [the sensation] seemed to go straight through the small of my back into my ideas *without involving my thoughts*" (my emphasis)—here he endorses Heard's view of Carpenter as a pedant who "knew nothing he couldn't think." Again this is a particularly damaging accusation given that Carpenter himself despised an intellect that was alienated from the body and living experience. Carpenter, the inspirational spirit to whom Forster pays a "pilgrimage" in the "Terminal Note" to *Maurice*, here is transformed into a cranky nay-sayer: "you were *not* to wear boots but sandals, you were *not* to go to church." Also, since both Carpenter and Forster were strongly anti-clerical, the dismissal of Carpenter as an anti-clerical clergyman is particularly telling. Finally, if in the "Terminal Note" to *Maurice*, Forster represents Carpenter/Merrill's touch as powerfully generative, here he endorses Heard's claim that Carpenter's work is so insubstantial that as soon as one "*touches* it, it is gone" (my emphasis). Note that throughout the passage, Forster is supposedly citing Heard's views. Perhaps Forster's use of Heard as a ventriloquist's dummy indicates his ambivalence toward Carpenter: on the one hand, like the son in an Oedipal model, the younger gay male writer feels an indebtedness to the older one; hence Forster finds it difficult to attack Carpenter directly and uses Heard to do so. On the other hand, precisely because he is indebted to an older man, the younger one has to establish a distance between them; hence the sharpness of Forster's indirect attack on Carpenter.

Even when Forster does not directly repudiate Carpenter, the younger writer distances himself from precursors in general by challenging the whole notion of influence. In *Aspects of the Novel*, Forster writes:

The idea of a period or a development in time with its consequent emphasis on *influences* and schools, happens to be exactly what I am hoping to avoid.... We are to visualize the English novelists ... as seated together in a room, a circular room ... all writing their novels simultaneously. They do not, as they sit there, think ... *I carry on the tradition of Trollope*, I am *reacting against* Aldous Huxley.
(5, my emphases)

While in the scene at Milthorpe and in Isherwood's staging of his reception of *Maurice*, spatial positioning was very important (Forster was able to move forward because of a touch from behind, and Isherwood's and Forster's reciprocal influence was underlined by their position facing each other), in the passage above the writers in their circular reading room are atomistically self-contained, fantastically lifted outside time and history altogether. Although the dominant tone of the passage is urbane, the excessiveness of the word "enemy" used to characterize time—"Time all the way through is our enemy"—suggests that at some level Forster cannot completely banish history or the specter of precursors and successors from his atemporal circular room.

4) Touching the Bloomian Model with the Queer Scene at Milthorpe

While aggression and denial are distinct parts of the bonds between the gay male writers I am examining, they do not completely describe those relations. After all, the scene at Milthorpe is both tender—note that Forster uses the adverb "gently" in describing that touch ("George Merrill also touched my backside ... gently")—and erotic. Bloom's model, I would suggest, is unable to do justice to the non-aggressive, homoerotic desire of such a scene because although—or perhaps because—desire between men lies at the heart of the Bloomian model, literal homosexual desire is persistently disavowed.

To substantiate the claim that desire between men lies at the heart of the Bloomian model, let me begin by citing Bloom's formulation from *A Map of Misreading* again: "a poem is always *the other man*, the precursor and so a poem is always a person, the father of one's second birth." In this formulation, the male poet regenerates himself by recreating, reproducing his father, the poem. There is no female present in the scene at all, and in this sense, this scene is uncannily similar to Forster's homosexual birthing fantasy. Now, it is true that the scene is more heterosexualized in *The Anxiety of Influence*. In that book, Bloom writes:

"what is the Primal Scene, for a poet *as poet*? It is his Poetic Father's coitus with the Muse. There he was begotten? No, there they failed to beget him. He must be self-begotten, he must engender himself upon the Muse, his mother" (37). But even though a female Muse is present in this version of the Bloomian myth, she merely acts as an intermediary between the two men. She is either the mother who bears the father's son, or she is the incestuous vessel for the son's self-generation of himself as a poet. In other words, the Muse in this scene classically conforms to the role of the woman in the male homosocial paradigm explored by Eve Kosofsky Sedgwick in *Between Men*, although she concentrates on the role that women play in mediating desire between male coevals and does not really explore the role that women can play in mediating paternal-filial desire. In any case, the real actors in this scene are two desiring men, the older and the younger poet. Bloom partially concedes this point when he says that "the poet-in-a-poet cannot marry, whatever the person-in-a-poet chooses to have done," because the poet-in-a-poet's true affective bond is with his male precursor (*Map* 19). But having implicitly suggested that, regardless of the poet's literal marital status and sexual orientation, the act of poetic creation by a male writer is intrinsically homoerotic, Bloom rapidly moves on, as though he cannot deal with the homoerotic implications of the claim he has made.

Further, note how salient a position a homosexual, specifically pederastic tradition occupies in Bloom's theoretical edifice. The very first author that he cites, literally on the first page of *The Anxiety of Influence*, which is after all the first book in which he articulates his Oedipal model of influence, is Oscar Wilde. Given the importance of origins and beginnings for Bloom, it seems quite significant that despite the ostensibly paternal-filial frame of his model, we do not find a heterosexual patriarch at the beginning of his project but a gay man; one, moreover, whose name has become a synonym for homosexuality itself so that in *Maurice* the periphrasis "an unspeakable of the Wilde sort" functions unambiguously to designate homosexuality. Perhaps it is not so surprising that one should find a gay man at the origin of a story supposedly revolving around fathers and sons, for as Jonathan Dollimore has pointed out, Freud in his reading of Oedipus' conflict with Laius willfully forgets that Laius' fate is the outcome of an originary homosexual transgression which was condoned by the Thebans but condemned by the gods. In other words, while Freud and Bloom want to keep the story of sons and fathers center stage, lurking behind, so to speak, this familial scene is a narrative of male homosexual, specifically pederastic desire (Dollimore 204).

And yet, at the same time as Bloom gives such salience to a homosexual tradition, he also attempts to quarantine it from his paternal-filial story line. The Wilde passage that Bloom uses to define the anxiety of influencing is taken from a text in which a group of men construct a passionately homoerotic mythology around the figure of Shakespeare and his supposed youthful lover Willie Hughes. In the introduction to the second edition of *The Anxiety of Influence*, Bloom warmly commends Wilde for his intense, will-edly naive investment in the biographical figure of Shakespeare, an investment that no contemporary critic of what Bloom dismisses as the "current School of Resentment" is willing to make: "Oscar Wilde might have been interested in a question like [does the Player-King in *Hamlet* speak for Shakespeare?]; no living scholar-critic will allow them" ("Introduction" xlvi).

Like Wilde and the characters in "The Picture of Mr. W. H.," Bloom is passionately affectively invested in the figure of Shakespeare; at the same time he wants to distance his model from the homoerotic implications that Wilde foregrounds. At the beginning of that introduction, Bloom tells his readers that the real source of *The Anxiety of Influence* is Shakespeare's Sonnet 87, one of the sonnets addressed to the beautiful young man. Commenting on this lyrically homoerotic sonnet, Bloom writes: "Whether Shakespeare ruefully is lamenting the loss of the Earl of Southampton as lover, or as patron, or as friend, is not (fortunately) a matter upon which certitude is possible" (xiii). Those awkward parentheses appear again in a later passage when Bloom talks about Southampton, Shakespeare's "patron (some think also his lover)." The parentheses, I would suggest, are a symptom of Bloom's discomfort with the subject of the homoeroticism in the Sonnets, a topic which lack of historical evidence will "fortunately" allow him to bracket from his theoretical consideration. If the introduction reveals that Bloom has a hyperbolic transference onto the Bard—"Shakespeare will not allow you to bury him, or to escape him, or replace him. . . . we remain enclosed by Shakespeare. The only instruments by which we can examine him were either invented or perfected by Shakespeare himself" (xxvii)—as well as a powerful identification with him—at one rather comic moment, discussing how Shakespeare's experience as a "printer's apprentice" might have led to an "aversion to proof reading," Bloom in parentheses personally identifies with the Bard: "(having held such a job in my early youth, I have been a dreadful reader of my own proofs in consequence)" (xx)—the parentheses try to distance that identificatory transference from homoeroticism. Bloom might enjoy being "alone with Shakespeare," "rather than being propagandized" by mediatory critics, but the parentheses defensively insist that we distance this charged canonical intimacy from literal homoerotic desire.

The same defensiveness can be seen in Bloom's treatment of Walt Whitman in *The Western Canon*.[15] In the chapter on Whitman, Bloom repeatedly foregrounds Whitman's autoeroticism and downplays his homoeroticism: "one of the many current ironies of Whitman's reception is that he is acclaimed as a gay poet.... But ... in his poetry as well as in his life, his erotic orientation was onanistic" (273). While it is undoubtedly true that Whitman's poetry is deeply autoerotic, etiological accounts of homosexuality in the nineteenth century were densely implicated with discourses surrounding masturbation, so in discussing the autoerotic impulse in Whitman's work, one might expect Bloom to discuss its complicated links to the articulation of homoerotic desire; but the topic is conspicuously not addressed. Further, at one particularly telling moment in the chapter, Bloom in commenting on some lines from Whitman's "As I Ebbed" reveals his desire to quarantine paternal-filial bonds from male homoeroticism. Below are the lines that Bloom cites from "As I Ebbed:"

> I throw myself upon your breast my father,
> I cling to you so that you cannot unloose me,
> I hold you so firm till you answer me something.
> Kiss me my father
> Touch me with your lips, as I touch those I love.

Bloom describes these lines as "our strongest image of reconciliation with the father" (*Canon* 285). That the lines concern paternal-filial reconciliation is true enough, and yet Bloom's comment willfully avoids the scandalously homoerotic implications of that desired reconciliation, with homoerotic implications characteristically figured in tactile terms: "Kiss me my father / Touch me with your lips, as I touch those I love."

It is true that by using the term "ephebe" and making pedagogy central to his model, Bloom situates his model in relation to a classical pederastic tradition so central to Anglo-American male homophilic discourse. It is also true that he acknowledges the role that erotics plays in education: "Teaching is necessarily a branch of erotics...." But that

---

[15] I am indebted to Roy Sellars for drawing my attention to this chapter.

formulation continues: "Teaching is necessarily a branch of erotics in the wide sense of desiring what we have not got, of redressing our poverty, of compounding with our fantasies" (*Map* 39). By discussing "erotics" in "the wide sense," Bloom is able to avoid discussing erotics and specifically homoerotics in the narrow, literal sense. In stark contrast to the way in which he literalizes tropes of heterosexual rape and reproduction in his readings of scenes from *Paradise Lost*, Bloom both invokes and anxiously shies away from the homoerotic implications that lie at the heart of his model.

The gay male writers genealogically implicated with the inspirational touch at Milthorpe far more clearly recognize the homoeroticism that informs paternal-filial relations than Bloom does or chooses to acknowledge. Forster, for instance, often eroticizes paternal-filial bonds. In *Where Angels Fear to Tread*, through the eyes of Caroline Abbott, as readers we are allowed voyeuristically to observe the eroticized relationship between the Italian Gino and his son:

> "Wake up," [Gino] cried to his baby as if it was some grown-up friend. Then he lifted its foot and trod lightly on its stomach.... He stood with one foot resting on the little body, suddenly musing, filled with the desire that his son should be like him and should have sons like him to people the earth. (123)

That there is something menacing about the father's foot resting on his son's stomach, while he narcissistically muses on his own replication, is undeniable. And on the next page, Forster implicitly criticizes the ways in which patriarchal culture reduces children to objects that belong to the father: Gino objectifies his child by thinking of him as "a little kicking image of bronze," and in a spirit of passionate possessiveness declares "he is mine . . . I am his father" (124). Yet even if the narrative critiques the possessiveness of paternal love, it undeniably eroticizes it. If the fantasy of paternal authority in an Oedipal system is that the father is immune to desiring his son, that he is merely the enforcer of a prohibitive law, Gino undoes that fantasy by eloquently and urgently speaking his desire for his son: "he is mine; mine for ever. Even if he hates me, he will be mine. He cannot help it . . . I am his father" (124).

> If Forster represents the homoerotic desire of the father for his son, Isherwood often represents the son's homoerotic desire for the father. In *Kathleen and Frank*, for instance, Isherwood describes how his father Frank exercised every morning in his dressing-room, naked except for his undershorts. He let Christopher come in and watch him. Christopher can

remember taking pleasure which was definitely erotic in the sight of his father's muscles tensing and bulging within his well-knit body and the virile smell of his sweat. (350)

While Isherwood will passionately rebel against the symbolic authority with which the figure of his dead father will become associated, he desires the embodied man whom he watches exercising, and one might speculate that his father betrays a certain homoerotic exhibitionism in the exercise routine he stages for his son. A little later in the passage, describing his father's anger, Isherwood writes:

> sometimes [Frank] would fly into rages with Christopher and shake him till his teeth rattled. Christopher may have been frightened a little, but this too is a sensual memory for him: his surrender to the exciting strength of the big angry man. (350)

Like Bloom, Isherwood represents the violent conflict that can occur between fathers and sons, but Isherwood explicitly addresses the sadomasochistic pleasure that may be derived from such conflicts, a perverse pleasure that Bloom's Oedipal model chooses not to recognize.

Like Isherwood, Ackerley deconstructs the opposition between pederastic and paternal bonds. While his father is alive, Ackerley thinks of him as benignly thwarting his son's homoerotic desires. But after his father dies, Ackerley discovers that in fact, like his son, he guarded several secrets, including possible homoerotic ones: when Ackerley discovers that his father had been financially helped by his homosexual friend, the Count de Gallatin, he becomes obsessed with finding out whether his father had a homoerotic past. Ackerley disavows any homoerotic desire for his father, foregrounding instead his identification with the gay Count de Gallatin: "studying the photograph of [my father] in uniform, I decided that I would not have picked him up myself" (*My Father* 199); "the Count, *like myself*, may have started his emotional life (continuing it longer than I) by falling for men whom he was unable to *touch* but worshipped from afar" (194, my emphasis). The intensity, however, with which the son conducts his search to find out his father's past betrays the desire that drives the quest. As we have seen, one of the figures Ackerley draws on to represent his distance from his father when his father was alive is the trope of the paternal gaze. While the son could not look directly at his father when he was alive, after his father is dead he erotically pores over pictures of him and voyeuristically imagines observing the homoerotic bonds that his father may have shared with the Count de Gallatin: responding to a picture that he has of his father and the Count standing by an open window, Ackerley writes: "Would that I had been able to peep . . . through that window and discover their secrets if any" (28–29). Or, to shift from the visual back to the tactile metaphors that have dominated this essay: consider that Ackerley first finds out about his father's possible homoerotic past from a homosexual contemporary of the Count and his father, Arthur Needham. Since Needham is "an old quean" (190) and Ackerley is drawn to butch young men, he loses contact with the older man, or to use his terms, he gets "out of touch" (202) with Needham. However, driven by the need to find out more about his father's past, he gets back in touch with the older man. Through Needham, Ackerley is trying to touch his dead father. Rather than seeing Ackerley's homoerotic quest for his father's past as other to his discomfort with his father's authoritative gaze, I see them as always having been implicated. The paternal authority that claims to be immune from desire, in other words, belongs on a continuum with the homoeroticism which, among other things, it is supposed to proscribe.

Both Ackerley and Isherwood disclose the paternal-filial bond to the homoerotic. Conversely, Isherwood sometimes frames the homoerotic in paternal-filial terms, a move that has the same effect of un-concealing the desire that informs Oedipal relations. In his posthumously published diaries, for instance, Isherwood writes of his relationship with Don Bachardy that "I am very happy in my father relationship with Don" (458), and later on in the journals, responding to his brother Richard's maudlin declaration of fraternal love, Isherwood thinks "I have had a hundred brothers already and a thousand *sons*" (572, my emphasis), once again resignifying homoerotic relations in filial-paternal terms.

If touching Bloom's Oedipal story with Forster's birthing fantasy helps to un-conceal the disavowed homoeroticism of the former narrative, my reading will be mirroring the way that touching between men functions in wider Anglo-American culture. Straight men are made enormously defensive if they are intimately touched by gay men, particularly if they are touched on the behind. Part of the reason why such a touch might provoke anxiety is that it forces a heterosexual man in a homosocial culture to confront homoerotic desires that he would rather deny completely. Like many other commentators, I would suggest that the "Don't Ask, Don't Tell, Don't Pursue" compromise reached on the issue of gays in the American military shows that male homosocial institutions are far more anxious about *knowing* that they have gay men in them than they are about *having* gay men in them.¹⁶ For knowing that there are openly gay men around them forces heterosexual men to confront the homoeroticism that already informs homosocial institutions. By analogy, I hope that touching Bloom's model from behind with a scene of gay male literary transmission forces the former theoretical paradigm to acknowledge the homoeroticism that so powerfully informs it.

However, beyond disclosing the disavowed homoeroticism of the Bloomian model, the queer touch at Milthorpe also discloses other limitations to the Bloomian model. Critics like Frank Lentricchia and Thomas Yingling have criticized Bloom for the resolutely ahistorical and narrowly familial nature of his story line, and Bloom himself readily admits that he sees issues of race and class and contingent historical issues as irrelevant to the repeated drama of filial insurrection. But a queer reading of the scene at Milthorpe discloses how much is left out of a narrowly familial or pederastic account of *Maurice*'s conception. In order to construct such a queer reading, I want to resist Forster's spatial model with its emphasis on front and back (the touch from behind allowing him to move forward rather than backward, and so on), pederast and ephebe, and to substitute Sedgwick's sense of the queer as that which is etymologically related to crossing boundaries (*Tendencies* xii). Such crossing will allow me to trouble the family story constructed by both Forster and Bloom with consideration of issues of class as well as national and gender difference.

In Bloom's drama, class plays no role; artistic fathers and sons wage their battles with no reference to material differences. And yet in the scene at Milthorpe, class is a crucial issue. It is no coincidence, I would suggest, that it is working-class Merrill who touches Forster's behind, rather than middle-class Carpenter, since for both Carpenter and Forster, working-class men have access to particular forms of knowledge denied to middle-class men. In particular, they both fetishize the working-class man as being materially embodied in a way denied to middle-class men. Yet as we have seen, at the end of the year when Forster looks

---

¹⁶ To be more precise, one might use D. A. Miller's formulation and describe homosocial institutions as not wanting to know that they know they have gays and lesbians in their ranks (206). The connection I draw between the debate on gays in the military and Miller's "open secret" is indebted to Colleen Lamos's piece on the equivocal position of homosexuality in Joyce's *Ulysses* ("Signatures" 339).

back at the moment of the conception of *Maurice* and celebrates his ability to move forward rather than backward, Merrill drops out of the picture altogether. Carpenter gets credited with being the sole source of Forster's liberation. Having credited Merrill with a relatively unmediated, non-cerebral relation to the body, Forster cannot accommodate him in a narrative involving the transmission of ideas; but at the same time, he needs Merrill as an embodied medium through which those ideas can be transmitted to him from Carpenter. So, like the mediating woman in a male homosocial triangle, the working-class Merrill's touch helps to mediate between Carpenter and Forster; having served that purpose, he disappears from the scene of authorial influence.

Or take the issue of national difference: in Bloom's account of influence, writers have no race or national origin. However, national difference and imperial history play an important role in the homoerotics of the circle surrounding Forster: Whitman's, Carpenter's, Forster's and Isherwood's anti-developmental mythologies are all implicated with Anglo-American imperial involvements in India, and this space, which is supposed to be off stage from the familial drama being enacted at Milthorpe, symptomatically intrudes when Forster invokes the phrase "yogified mysticism:" "If it [the touch] really did this [went straight through the small of Forster's back to his ideas], it would have acted in accord with Carpenter's yogified mysticism."

The two writers whose homoerotic anti-developmental myths are most intimately linked to the figure of the Indian *yogi* are Carpenter and Isherwood. Carpenter fairly uncomplicatedly figures his Indian *gnani* as a wise child who will help him escape the constraints of corrupt Western adulthood. This story can be accommodated by a variation on the Bloomian narrative of fathers and sons: the childlike father influences the worldly-wise son. However, Isherwood, situated at a far less secure moment in Britain's imperial history, is forced to acknowledge the mediated and constructed nature of his anti-developmental myth. Like Carpenter, he associates his *guru* Swami Prabhavananda with a youthful innocence, similar to that which he associates with the figure of Forster:

> Prabhavananda, though nearly forty-six, was still aware of his boyish appearance.... He was considerably shorter than I [Isherwood] was. This made me able to love him in a special, protective way, as I loved little Annie Avis, my childhood nanny.... His smallness sometimes seemed babylike.... (39)

Unlike Carpenter's description of his *gnani*, though, Isherwood's novel foregrounds both the narrator's and the *guru*'s imbrication in the ironies of Britain's colonial history. Isherwood tells us that the Guru, prior to becoming a holy man, was a nationalist rebel against the British, and the writer speculates that the Guru's nationalist past was bound to affect his attitudes toward British disciples like Isherwood (*My Guru* 37). So, Isherwood's Swami self-consciously negotiates ambivalence in his relationship with the writer. Like Prabhavananda, Isherwood cannot escape colonial history, and at several places in the text, he explains the effect that being "an heir to Britain's guilt in her dealings with India" exerted on his relationship with the Guru (*My Guru* 36).

It is particularly significant, too, that in describing the Guru's past as a nationalist freedom fighter, Isherwood stresses the role that the holy man's youthful appearance played in those activities: "Because [Prabhavananda] looked so *boyish and innocent*, his comrades entrusted him with some revolvers which had been stolen from a British storehouse; he hid them in his room" (32, my emphasis). If, as Judith Butler argues, the performative nature of drag helps to reveal the contingent, constructed nature of gender itself, Isherwood's alignment of supposed boyish innocence with a calculated, violent anti-imperialist strategy has a similar potential to denaturalize the supposedly essential innocence and youthfulness which primitivism ascribes to non-Western peoples (*Gender* 137). Prabhavananda cannot be simply described as a father or a son, an *erastes* or *eromenos*; he is a man from another culture whose relationship to the narrator can be read only if we take into account stories outside the family romance, stories involving colonial history and national differences.

Finally, turning to the issue of gender difference, both Forster's and Bloom's dramas of literary generation are resolutely androcentric. However, if one reads the scene at Milthorpe against the grain, drawing on biographical details about Forster that he withholds from his account of the novel's "conception," one can see that female influence—in literary, psychic and material manifestations—cannot be quarantined from this scene of male literary birthing. Because of the proximity of the Forsterian myth to the Bloomian one, I will suggest that by implication one has to recognize the disabling limitations of a mythology that tries to effect a rigid gender separatist account of literary influence.

In as much as the scene at Milthorpe represents the birth of *Maurice* occurring in a moment of pastoral intimacy among men, safely removed from the feminizing influence of domesticity, that scene mirrors what occurs in the novel itself; for in the novel, the eponymous protagonist eventually escapes from the female entanglements represented by his mother and sisters, as well as by Anne, his former lover Clive's wife, and flees to the all-male world of the greenwood with Scudder. However, figuratively women cannot be entirely banished from the greenwood because the writer irresistibly associates nature with a nurturant maternity. Thus, in the same "Terminal Note" to *Maurice* in which he celebrates his fantasy of male generation in the absence of women, Forster evokes a maternal landscape: bemoaning the effects of urbanization, he declares "there is no . . . cave in which to curl up" (250), linking an image of the womb to a pastoral landscape of homoerotic possibility.

In a similar fashion, Forster ambivalently figures his mother both as one who thwarts his artistic development and homoerotic desire, and as one who provides the nurturant space on which his artistic powers depend. Ackerley, with whom Forster "conceived" "Little Imber," misogynistically referred to Forster's "moldy old mother," a description that matraphobically links Lily Forster to death. It is significant, then, that it is to Ackerley that Forster explains the simultaneously prohibitive and generative effect that his mother exerted on him as a man and an artist: "Although my mother has been intermittently tiresome for the last thirty years, cramped and warped my genius, hindered my career . . . and boycotted my beloved, I have to admit that she has provided a sort of rich subsoil where I have been able to rest and grow" (Forster, qtd. in Furbank 2: 217).[17] Further, when his mother died, Forster wrote to Ackerley again suggesting that his mother's death had drained him of his own vitality: "My mouldy mother, as you once called her, is dead, and I expect now to start mouldering myself" (Forster, qtd. in Furbank 2: 255–56). Finally, while in the description of *Maurice*'s conception, Forster foregrounds the inspirational touch that he received from his male precursor Carpenter through the mediatory figure of Merrill, it is

---

[17] The split image of the nurturant inspirational mother of Forster's letter to Ackerley is the figure of the grotesque mother in a story like "The Machine Stops." Vashti, the deathly mother of Kuno in that dystopian story, reveals her degree of alienation from maternity by the fact that she has no desire to touch her son (5, 13 and 16).

significant that the novel was actually written at Harrogate, where the writer stayed with his mother after leaving Milthorpe.

Beyond his biological mother, one might also consider the effect of female artistic influence on Forster. In describing the conception of *Maurice*, Forster foregrounds his male precursor Carpenter, and later in the "Terminal Note," he also mentions Lytton Strachey's reaction to the novel. Nowhere in that Note does he mention Virginia Woolf. On the face of it, there is no reason why he should mention Woolf; after all, Furbank tells us that Forster never showed *Maurice* to Woolf, even when in 1927 he knew that she was writing an essay on what she thought was his entire *oeuvre*, and even though he normally took "every ... [critical] word ... [of Woolf's] to heart" (Woolf, qtd. in Furbank 1: 146). If one accepts Forster's belief that the scene at Milthorpe was the origin of *Maurice*, then, one might not be inclined to make much of Forster's not showing the novel to Woolf; after all, she had played no part in its "conception." However, I would suggest that it would be just as plausible to think of the birthing scene at Milthorpe as being a metaleptic, retrospective construction—as primal scenes generally are.[18] In that case, Forster's reluctance to show the novel to Woolf might be understood as a defensive need to preserve the fantasy of its all-male genesis. In other words, I would suggest that the fact that Woolf was not shown *Maurice* by Forster might paradoxically signal the extent of her influence on Forster, an influence that the writer has to disavow.

Finally, turning to the issue of material feminine influence, let us recall that the triumphal version of "Little Imber" ends in misogynistic glee with the narrative voice declaring: "Men had won." Appropriating the female power to conceive, men in this version of the story gain complete independence from women. But as Joseph Bristow points out, at the same time as Forster was writing this fantasy of absolute male autonomy, he was also working on the biography of his great-aunt Marianne Thornton (94). In that biography, he acknowledges that it was the eight-thousand-pound inheritance that he received from his great-aunt which "made [his] career as a writer possible," and tellingly he goes on, "her love in a most tangible sense followed me beyond the grave" (Forster, qtd. in Bristow 94). 'Tangible' literally means that which can be touched. In addition, then, to the inspirational male touch that Forster received at Milthorpe, his growth as an artist depended on the tactile,

---

[18] For the most cogent theorizing of the primal scene and deferred action, see Laplanche and Pontalis.

material contact with the property of his great-aunt. Contrary to the scene at Milthorpe or the plot of "Little Imber," Forster's pederastic bonds of influence with other male homosexual writers cannot be absolutely quarantined from the impact that various feminine sources exerted on him as well.

In an entry in his *Commonplace Book*, Forster lists a number of gay writers whom he saw as exerting an influence on him, ranging from Samuel Butler through a series of minor novelists of public school romances. One might treat this list as constituting a gay male canon and oppose it to the patriarchal canon advanced by Harold Bloom. Within feminist criticism such moves have been advanced by critics like Gilbert and Gubar, and a gay male critical response of that sort would be consonant with the homophilic myths of the writers in the Forster circle. My intent in this essay, however, has been to argue that such counter-canonical male homosexual genealogical lines are not particularly helpful. More efficacious is the move to queer the most powerful existing account of male authorial influence saliently informed by a male homoeroticism that is energetically disavowed.

Works Cited

Ackerley, J. R. *My Father and Myself*. New York: Poseidon, 1968.
Bristow, Joseph. *Effeminate England: Homoerotic Writing after 1885*. New York: Columbia UP, 1995.
Buckton, Oliver. *Secret Selves: Confession and Same-Sex Desire in Victorian Autobiography*. Chapel Hill: U of North Carolina P, 1989.
Butler, Judith. *Gender Trouble: Feminism and the Subversion of Identity*. New York: Routledge, 1990.
Carpenter, Edward. *From Adam's Peak to Elephanta*. New York: E. P. Dutton, 1904.
———. "Homogenic Love." *Sexual Heretics: Male Homosexuality in English Literature from 1850 to 1900*. Ed. Brian Reade. New York: Coward-McCann, 1971. 324–47.
———. "The Intermediate Sex." *Sex. Selected Writings*, vol. 1. Ed. David Fernbach and Noël Greig. Worcester: Gay Men's P, 1984. 185–233.
———. *Intermediate Types among Primitive Folk*. London: George Allen and Unwin, 1919.
———. *My Days and Dreams*. London: George Allen and Unwin, 1916.
———. *My Days with Walt Whitman*. London: George Allen, 1906.
———. "The Psychology of the Poet Shelley." *The Psychology of the Poet Shelley*. By George Barnfield and Edward Carpenter. London: George Allen and Unwin, 1925.
———. *Towards Democracy*. Worcester: Gay Men's P, 1985.
Da Silva, Stephen. "Strategically Minor: Isherwood's Deployment of Forsterian Mythology." *The Isherwood Century: Essays on the Life and Work of Christopher Isherwood*. Ed. James J. Berg and Chris Freeman. Madison: U of Wisconsin P, 2000. 187–95.

———. "Transvaluing Immaturity: Reverse Discourses of Male Homosexuality in E. M. Forster's Posthumously Published Fiction." *Criticism* 40.2 (Spring 1998): 237–72.
De Bolla, Peter. *Harold Bloom: Toward Historical Rhetorics*. New York: Routledge, 1988.
Dollimore, Jonathan. *Sexual Dissidence*. Oxford: Clarendon, 1991.
Dowling, Linda. *Hellenism and Homosexuality in Victorian Oxford*. Ithaca: Cornell UP, 1994.
Erkkila, Betsy. *Whitman the Political Poet*. New York: Oxford UP, 1989.
Forster, E. M. *Abinger Harvest*. New York: Harcourt, Brace, Jovanovich, 1964.
———. *Arctic Summer, and Other Fiction*. London: Arnold, 1980.
———. *Aspects of the Novel*. 1927. New York: Harcourt, Brace, and World, 1954.
———. *The Commonplace Book*. London: Scolar, 1985.
———. "Little Imber." *Arctic Summer*. 226–38.
———. "The Machine Stops." *The Eternal Moment and Other Stories*. New York: Harcourt, Brace, Jovanovich, 1928.
———. *Maurice*. New York: Penguin, 1978.
———. *A Passage to India*. 1924. New York: Harcourt, Brace, Jovanovich, 1984.
———. "Some Memories." *Edward Carpenter: In Appreciation*. Ed. Gilbert Beith. London: George Allen and Unwin, 1931. 74–81.
———. *Where Angels Fear to Tread*. 1905. Harmondsworth: Penguin, 1984.
Freud, Sigmund. "Negation." *The Ego and the Id, and Other Works. The Standard Edition of the Complete Psychological Works of Sigmund Freud*, vol. 19. Trans. and ed. James Strachey, et al. London: Hogarth, 1961. 235–39.
Furbank, P. N. *E. M. Forster: A Life*. 2 vols. San Diego: Harcourt, Brace, 1978.
Gallop, Jane. *The Daughter's Seduction: Feminism and Psychoanalysis*. Ithaca: Cornell UP, 1982.
Great English Short Stories. Ed. Christopher Isherwood. New York: Dell, 1957.
Isherwood, Christopher. *Christopher and His Kind*. New York: Avon, 1976.
———. *Diaries, Volume 1: 1939–1960*. Ed. Katherine Bucknell. New York: HarperCollins, 1997.
———. *Down There on a Visit*. New York: Simon and Schuster, 1962.
———. *Kathleen and Frank*. New York: Simon and Schuster, 1971.

———. *Lions and Shadows*. 1947. New York: New Directions, 1977.
———. *My Guru and His Disciple*. New York: Farrar, Straus, and Giroux, 1980.
———. *Prater Violet*. New York: Ballantine, 1945.
Lamos, Colleen. "Signatures of the Invisible: Homosexual Secrecy and Knowledge in *Ulysses*." *James Joyce Quarterly* 31.3 (Spring 1994): 337–56.
Laplanche, Jean and Jean-Bertrand Pontalis. "Fantasy and the Origins of Sexuality." 1964. *Formations of Fantasy*. Ed. Victor Burgin, James Donald and Cora Kaplan. London: Methuen, 1986. 5–34.
Lentricchia, Frank. *After the New Criticism*. Chicago: U of Chicago P, 1980.
Martin, Robert. "Edward Carpenter and the Double Structure of *Maurice*." *Essays on Gay Literature*. Ed. Stuart Kellogg. New York: Harrington Park, 1985. 35–46.
Miller, D. A. *The Novel and the Police*. Berkeley: U of California P, 1988.
Parker, Peter. *Ackerley: The Life of J. R. Ackerley*. New York: Farrar, Straus, Giroux, 1989.
Piazza, Paul. *Christopher Isherwood: Myth and Anti-Myth*. New York: Columbia UP, 1978.
Sedgwick, Eve Kosofsky. *Between Men: English Literature and Male Homosocial Desire*. New York: Columbia UP, 1985.
———. *Epistemology of the Closet*. Berkeley: U of California P, 1990.
———. *Tendencies*. Durham: Duke UP, 1993.
Whitman, Walt. *Leaves of Grass*. Ed. Sculley Bradley and Harold W. Blodgett. New York: Norton, 1973.
Wilde, Alan. *Christopher Isherwood*. New York: Twayne, 1971.
Wilde, Oscar. "The Portrait of Mr. W. H." *The Complete Works of Oscar Wilde*. 1966. Ed. J. B. Foreman. New York: HarperCollins, 1989. 1150–1202.
Yingling, Thomas. *Hart Crane and the Homosexual Text*. Chicago: U of Chicago P, 1990.

Harold Bloom, Parody, and the "Other Tradition"

PETER MORRIS

1) Milton's Satan: Precursors, Parody, and Incest

This essay is intended as a conscious misprision of the theory of poetry Harold Bloom sketches in *The Anxiety of Influence*: the very fact that, for Bloom, 'conscious misprision' is an oxymoron should, I hope, be central to its argument as well as its method. I trust that serious readers of Bloom are not fazed by such a sweeping claim on my part, since they will have seen Bloom make dozens of similar claims, and will understand it as part of the homage I pay to the great man. By the same token, anyone who finds Bloom's basic theory to be tendentious, implausible, insufficiently evidenced or manifestly loony is unlikely to be persuaded by the style of argument herein. But I hope that, if nothing else, I can prove (perhaps by exhaustion) Lucy Newlyn's perceptive comment in Paradise Lost *and the Romantic Reader* that there is "nothing more supportive of the argument which *The Anxiety of Influence* offers than the reception of *The Anxiety of Influence*: it has established itself as a text analogous to *Paradise Lost*, in the degree of 'revisionary' creativity it has made possible; and this, in its turn, has caused some of its central assumptions to become distorted and misconceived" (14-15). Accordingly I hope I may be indulged as I provide, even to the point of near-parody, a Bloomian misreading of Bloom, and take as the subject for 'antithetical criticism' Bloom's own work. I would also, in a profoundly un-Bloomian move, like to begin by acknowledging my debts to two other critics, Leslie Brisman and Paul Fry, both first-generation readers of Bloom: as an undergraduate I wheedled my way into graduate seminars given by these men, and my conversations (and arguments) with them helped me to misread their colleague a little more strongly. If the style of my argument suggests a Romantic revolt against the Miltonic figure of

Bloom himself, I hope readers might understand their mediating role in my own genealogy, and read Fry like Collins (of whom he has been a perceptive critic) and Brisman like Gray (whose vast learning resembles his own).

That being said, let me begin as Bloom himself does in *The Anxiety of Influence*, with the "experiment (apparently frivolous) of reading *Paradise Lost* as an allegory of the dilemma of the modern poet, at his strongest" (*Anxiety* 20), where that poet is represented by Milton's Satan. Putting Satan's considerable critical reputation out of our minds, though, let us restrict ourselves to judging this "modern poet" solely on the basis of his creative output, in Milton's account limited to a daughter and a son, Sin and Death. Are these the work of a Bloomian strong poet? Bloom himself is more or less silent about Sin and Death, limiting his comments to a brief consideration of Sin as Satan's Muse, to which we will return.[1] Yet Bloom's own acknowledged critical precursor Samuel Johnson ("the greatest critic in the language," in *The Anxiety of Influence* [28]) was notoriously voluble about the presence of Sin and Death in *Paradise Lost*. Although Johnson professes his willingness to indulge the allegorical mode in general—"To exalt causes into agents, to invest abstract ideas with form, and animate them with activity, has always been the right of poetry"—he warns that to give allegorical figures "any real employment, or ascribe to them any material agency, is to make them allegorical no longer, but to shock the mind by ascribing effects to nonentity" ("Milton" 530). Johnson then concludes with a sharp critique of this part of the poem:

> Milton's allegory of Sin and Death is undoubtedly faulty.... That Sin and Death should have shown the way to hell might have been allowed; but they cannot facilitate the passage by building a bridge, because the difficulty of Satan's passage is described as real and sensible, and the bridge ought to be only figurative. The hell assigned to the rebellious spirits is described as not less local than the residence of man. It is placed in some distant part of space, separated from the regions of harmony and order by a chaotic waste and an unoccupied vacancy; but Sin and Death worked up a *mole* of *aggravated soil*, cemented with *asphaltus*; a work too bulky for ideal architects.
>
> This unskilful allegory appears to me one of the greatest faults of the poem; and to this there was no temptation, but the author's opinion of its beauty. ("Milton" 530–31)

[1] Overall, Bloom seems to view Satan himself as the poem Satan creates: a notion admirably Romantic in the credence it lends to such claims for autochthony, but willfully blind to what Milton actually wrote.

Dr. Johnson's concerns about allegorical fictions would certainly seem too formalistic from a strict Bloomian perspective; after all, the immediate debt that Bloom's critical imagination owes to Angus Fletcher's work on allegory is considerable enough that even the least skillful examples of the genre are unlikely to find objection on such grounds as Johnson's here. For Bloom, the only real point of examination would be whether Sin and Death are *original* creations, as befits the work of a strong poet. Let me therefore follow such a line of inquiry.

Sin, of course, is not original at all, since her form is plagiarized directly from Milton's "great original," Spenser. Milton's description of Sin in Book 2 of *Paradise Lost*, a half-woman half-serpent whose brood of hell-hounds retreats to her womb, has long been recognized as a deliberate allusion to the description of Errour from Book 1 of *The Faerie Queene*: another half-woman half-serpent, with a "thousand yong ones" who suckle, then creep into their mother's mouth to hide (1.1.15.5). If all Milton's critics have noted the borrowing, none, I think, has adequately emphasized how *conspicuous* it is. Even a reader who has only read some two pages of the *Faerie Queene* before closing it in boredom or disgust may recognize Milton's plagiarism. Milton's allegory foregrounds its own belatedness as allegory (much as "Lycidas" foregrounded its belatedness as pastoral even with the shock of its opening words, "yet once more"). If we view Satan as Sin's "author"—and we must, since Milton himself uses the word—then by Bloom's standards the "modern poet at his strongest" creates a very weak and unoriginal poem indeed.

If plagiarism ensures that Sin suffers from something like an overdetermination of form, Death (at once her son and brother and, by rape, her lover) is by contrast indeterminable, in form or anything else. Edmund Burke famously singled out as a major touchstone for the sublime this "significant and expressive uncertainty of strokes and colouring" with which "Milton has finished the portrait of the king of terrors" (59). But the Burkean sublime depends aesthetically upon what goes unstated or unseen in a given context, and the originality of a poetic figure cannot be said to lie in that part of it that lies beyond language.[2] So we must ask: is Milton's Death an original creation? Spenser too had represented Death in the *Faerie Queene*, but if we compare the two, I think we might be half-persuaded by William Cowper (no careless reader of Milton or Spenser), who claims that (in comparison with Spenser's)

[2] We cannot give a writer credit for originality by virtue of what he did not write, although Bloom frequently seems to do just that.

Milton's is in fact an original figure, a Death of his own invention, a kind of intermediate form between matter and spirit, partaking of both, and consisting of neither. The idea of substance is lost in its tenuity, and yet, contemplated awhile as a shadow, it becomes a substance . . . . The dimness of this vague and fleeting outline is infinitely more terrible than exact description, because it leaves the imagination at full liberty to see for itself, and to suppose the worst. (Commentary in *Milton* 2: 453–54)

Cowper's defense of Death as a trope seems to me partly right. Certainly Milton does avoid the temptation of Spenser's prior figure here, and on that score, as compared with Sin, Death seems an original achievement. But what has been achieved? If Sin is an overdetermined trope, Death could by contrast be said to constitute no trope at all. Again I agree with Newlyn, who asserts that, in Milton's figuration of Death (and its critical reception), "it can be seen . . . how readily appropriable is a model of linguistic indeterminacy to ideological ends" (198)—that is to say, the figure remains open enough that virtually anything can be read into it. If the trope of Sin cedes too much of the author's creative authority to his precursor, the trope of Death cedes too much to the reader. It is, apparently, figuration that figures nothing—in other words, pure rhetoric. For even if there is any substance to death itself as we understand it (or to whatever other real-world referent we might posit for the figure of Milton's Death), in Milton's trope the style wholly triumphs over it. Newlyn draws the connection between the description of Death and several important Romantic recollections of it; we could follow Bloom in reading Milton through Shelley-colored goggles, and read Death as a trope for the annihilation of all trope, like the "shape all light" in *The Triumph of Life* (352). But let us consider Milton's actual description:

> The other shape,
> If shape it might be called that shape had none
> Distinguishable in member, joint, or limb,
> Or substance might be called that shadow seemed,
> For each seemed either; black it stood as night,
> Fierce as ten Furies, terrible as hell,
> And shook a dreadful dart; what seemed his head
> The likeness of a kingly crown had on. (*Paradise Lost* 2: 666–73)

What Burke and Cowper admire in this passage is, as Newlyn notes, a "linguistic indeterminacy" or even inadequacy. Milton's language seems deliberately ineffectual in describing Death, whether it be in the initial hedging contradictions, or the last resort of the thudding cliché "terrible as hell" (which sounds even lamer in this passage because its story actually takes place *in* hell, albeit near the exit).

Death is, ultimately, the perfect counterpart to Sin; they exemplify two different but related modes of failure in poetic originality as Bloom conceives it. If Sin is the obvious failure of being too much in the precursor's shadow (to the point of redundancy), Death may represent the somewhat less common failure that Bloom finds in work like John Ashbery's *The Tennis Court Oath* (a book Bloom finds unreadable, but whose author he deems—in other work—profoundly original): it attempts "too massive a swerve away from the . . . continuities" and thereby fails to achieve an actual trope (*Figures* 171). If we emphasize the unreality inherent in this style of figuration, it may help to gloss an otherwise opaque aphorism in *The Anxiety of Influence*: "Schizophrenia is bad poetry, for the schizophrenic has lost the strength of perverse, wilful, misprision" (95). In the Bloomian system, odd cases like Milton's Death or Ashbery's collage poems seem a bit like Bloom's picture of schizophrenia, where poetic ambition is seen to o'erleap itself, and fall on the other (wrong) side of original or strong poetry.

John Carey, discussing the oddness of Sin and Death, notes that "of course readers are at liberty to insist that the sequence is 'just allegory,' and that we should not bother with any of its deeper shades. However, even readers who take this line need to explain what it is an allegory of—what are the actual events that its various details correspond to?" (142). While Carey (whether through sheer negative capability or a failure of nerve) concludes that we are in no position to answer such a question, I will take the Bloomianly presumptuous step of providing my own reading. I read the allegory of Sin and Death—the creative output of "the modern poet at his strongest"—as outlining two opposite poles of poetic creation: one in which the poet does not individuate himself from the precursor at all, and another in which the poet goes so far into ambitious individuation as to lose all ground in reality. What Bloom defines as originality is therefore an illusory middle threatened with constant collapse between these poles. We may go one step further, I think, and call these two poles parody and self-parody.

The first of these categories is a well-established and indeed ancient genre (and not always necessarily a comic one, as Margaret Rose has demonstrated). But the notion of self-parody is much harder to discuss: Rose's few references to it are unhelpful. I suspect any definition of self-parody begins with the central matter in Bloom's own analysis of poetic originality—namely, a writer's own individuated *style*. Any work which might be called self-parody has the potential to be either consciously or unconsciously so. Conscious self-parodies do, of course, exist: Coleridge, for example, wrote some very funny ones. But it is a much more complicated business to suggest that sometimes a writer might be pushing his style into such excesses that the effort can only be understood as unconscious self-parody—largely because the only criterion may be the reader's taste for that particular style in the first place.[3] If I am willing to call such works as Wordsworth's *Peter Bell* or Henry James's *The Sacred Fount* undeniable self-parodies, it raises the question of why I would not extend the designation to (say) "Resolution and Independence" or *The Ambassadors*. That is perhaps the chief difficulty in calling Milton's Death a self-parody: as we have seen, readers like Burke and Cowper who are enraptured by Milton's style generally see the description of Death as a crowning glory of that style, not as an instance of Milton's pushing it into near-silliness. Certainly self-parody as a concept deserves serious thought: right now, as an aesthetic category it languishes much as its close cousin, camp, did before Susan Sontag undertook the effort to provide it with a theory. While a full theory of self-parody is beyond my scope here, I will offer one initial suggestion, which I think obvious. In my estimation, what connects Milton's Death to works like *Peter Bell* and *The Sacred Fount* is that they all have nothing concrete for their subject matter, which allows style itself to become the central fact of the enterprise. When writers have nothing to say, and say it at great length, all the virtues and vices of *how* they say it are set into stark relief. James writes a sort of detective story where there is nothing to detect (and where the detective's quest might simply demonstrate his madness). Wordsworth musters all his quasi-Methodist earnestness only to transform the lyrical ballad into its bathetic opposite number, what the American vernacular calls a shaggy dog story. Both are attempts to spin a narrative around precious little subject matter, and so all are basically over-elaborations of the writer's particular methods, resulting in the metastasis or over-elaboration of style: that, I think, is their conceptual relation to Milton's Death.

Examining Milton's further use of Sin and Death, we should recall Bloom's aphoristic claim that "Poetry (Romance) is Family Romance.

---

[3] Bloom's taste for exaggerated styles certainly leads to his expansive claims of strength and originality for writers who often seem to produce *only* self-parody: Cormac McCarthy springs to mind.

Poetry is the enchantment of incest, disciplined by resistance to that enchantment" (*Anxiety* 95), because Satan's union with Sin is, of course, literally and unresistingly incestuous:

> "... I pleased, and with attractive graces won
> The most averse, thee chiefly, who full oft
> Thyself in me thy perfect image viewing
> Becam'st enamored; and such joy thou took'st
> With me in secret, that my womb conceived
> A growing burden." (*Paradise Lost* 2: 762–67)

Bloom seems aware of the difficulty this poses to his Oedipal theory: in *The Anxiety of Influence*, he claims that Satan has "progressed beyond invoking his Muse," a Muse whom Bloom does later identify as Sin herself (20). I take Bloom to mean that Satan has progressed beyond copulating with her—yet in the Oedipal schema he proposes for influence, isn't the Muse the mother, and only thereafter taken as the incestuous bride? The story of Sin and Satan blurs most of the distinctions that Bloom would like to draw between muse, mother (or origin), and daughter (or achieved creation). When he claims in *The Anxiety of Influence* that "the incarnation of the Poetic Character in Satan begins when Milton's story truly begins, with the Incarnation of God's Son and Satan's rejection of *that* incarnation" (20), he avoids mentioning that Sin is additionally Satan's parodic response to Christ's incarnation effected by God. Sin represents merely the word of the precursor Spenser made repellent flesh, and is thus unoriginal by Bloomian standards: a weak poem, a parodic squib. The question of parody in this episode overall—Milton's parody of Spenser, Satan's of God—is every bit as muddled as the sexual and genealogical connections between the characters. As John Carey says of the matter, "in this murk of rape and incest and male birth pangs, the themes and actions of the poem swim about guiltily transformed. We have here, as it were, not just Satan's but the poem's subconscious. Its myths of origin are here released from narrative decorum, and parade in spectral shapes" (142).

I am suggesting that we may take from Milton's interpolated allegory a parodic model for poetic creation, one which necessarily contradicts Bloom's aphoristic definition of poetry as "the attraction of incest disciplined by resistance to that enchantment." Satan engages in actual incest, as we have seen, and may therefore be considered to lie beyond the scope of Bloom's revisionary ratios, since these are identified by Bloom with psychic defense *against* incest. When Bloom returns to an extended discussion of "Milton and His Precursors" in *A Map of Misreading*, he seems queasily aware of the relevance of such issues, and does allude to them, if only to dismiss them:

> Thomas McFarland . . . has suggested that "plagiarism" ought to be added as a seventh revisionary ratio. Allusion is a comprehensive enough ratio to contain "plagiarism" also under the heading of *apophrades*. . . . Allusion as covert reference became in Milton's control the most powerful and successful figuration that any strong poet has ever employed against his strong precursors. (*Map* 126)

When we consider Bloom's masterful reading of Milton's trope of the leaves, which concludes the chapter in *A Map of Misreading* (to which he will return in later books), we see the justice of his self-defense, and indeed why he might genuinely think he is right: the direct allusiveness in Milton's famous simile has indeed more of the character of John Hollander's notion of metaleptic echo (invoked by Bloom) and does not seem to partake of the character of parody, plagiarism, or any other poetic tactic which might be considered as an incestuous trespass into the precursor's imaginative space.

But there are plagiarisms and plagiarisms. Perhaps Milton's Vallombrosan leaves do manage to "lie against time," as Bloom would have it; if they create anew a hoary classical trope for the belated poet, they are best understood as *apophrades*. But what schema of influence can account for a Pierre Menard, whose vast originality flowed directly from his belated context and is rendered more striking by the total lack of original expression in what he wrote? Borges' remarkable fable is, of course, better suited to ideas of incest and parody than to a Bloomian universe where both are banished, just as *apophrades*, which Bloom claims can account for all seeming plagiarism in strong poetry by calling it allusion, may be useful for explaining the trope of the leaves (and Milton's relation to Homer, Virgil or Dante) but not, it seems to me, adequate for explaining the allegory of Sin and Death (and Milton's relation to Spenser, who must in any case be understood as the more formidable precursor in the game of writing epic poems in *English*).

As an experiment (again apparently frivolous), let us consider for a moment the grammar of the standard or Satanic statement of authorial autochthony. The statement "I am my father" can be reduced ontologically either to the sheerest determinism (the identity I possess is not mine, it is all stolen from the being that created me, and I am no more than a replication) or else the sheerest freedom (I am the only source of my identity, I am wholly self-authored)—just as grammatically it reduces either to an error, confusing subject with object, first person with third (I am *him*, or *he*), or else it reduces to tautology (I am I: a statement which has no meaning whatsoever unless, as in Exodus 3.14, it is spoken by God Himself). Regarding this paradox, I consciously evoke Bloom's Yale colleague Geoffrey Hartman having some fun with the myth of Oedipus in his early but influential essay, "The Voice of the Shuttle:"

> Oedipus is redundant: he is his father, and as his father he is nothing, for he returns to the womb that bore him. His lifeline does not exist. Except for the illusion that it exists . . . . The illusion is important, it is all Oedipus has to develop in . . . . Human life, like a poetical figure, is an indeterminate middle between overspecified poles always threatening to collapse it. (348)

I know of no better instance of this "redundant" notion of identity than one of Bloom's (and Freud's) dearest texts, *Hamlet*. Here, father and son have the same name, surely contributing to the seeming Oedipal confusion. Only when it is too late (and his impending nonexistence is certain) can the prince make the statement we have been waiting to hear: "This is I, / Hamlet the Dane" (5.1.247–48). Such self-naming sounds like an active and heroic establishment of identity, exactly the sort of thing we've waited four acts to hear, but it might just as easily be read as a total collapse into the nom du père, the same Oedipal elision of identity that Geoffrey Hartman outlines.[4] I here invoke *Hamlet* largely to recall that Bloom again nervously avoids such a Hartmanian reading of the Oedipal drama. Consider, for example, this statement from Bloom's "Shakespearean reading of Freud" in *The Western Canon*:

> Freud tells us that a healthy Hamlet would murder Claudius, and since Hamlet evades the act, he must be a hysteric. I turn again to the Nietzschean refinement of Goethe's view, which is that Hamlet thinks not too much but much too well, and at the frontiers of human consciousness declines to become his father, who would certainly have skewered *his* uncle in the same circumstances. Young Fortinbras is old Fortinbras come again, another bully boy, but Prince Hamlet is hardly just his father's son. (*Canon* 383)

---

[4] As I will show, this pattern, where Hamlet is named only when his non-existence is imminent, is recalled in a text that involves itself more openly and paradigmatically with incest, Byron's *Manfred*.

What seems most strange to me about Bloom's otherwise attractive corrective to the Freudian reductionism is not his dogged certainty about the character of Hamlet's father. Instead, I wonder at Bloom's evasion of the question of *names*, for in this paragraph he openly names both "Young Fortinbras" and "old Fortinbras," a father-and-son pair who also bear the same name, while uneasily avoiding the fact that Hamlet's father was also named Hamlet. By contrast, James Joyce's reading of *Hamlet* in *Ulysses*—also discussed by Bloom in *The Western Canon*—insistently emphasizes the identical names of father and son, "Hamlet *père* and Hamlet *fils*," in a polemical attempt to debunk the paradigm of paternity which Bloom accepts (*Ulysses* 175).[5]

If *Hamlet* can be used to illuminate Hartman's Oedipal vision of the poetic figure, and thereby highlight Bloom's reluctance to use his Oedipal paradigm in the same fashion, let us add the hint from Hartman to my own reading of Sin and Death, and bear both in mind as we consider Bloom's definition of the ideal literary criticism (from the interchapter of *The Anxiety of Influence*):

> All criticisms that call themselves primary vacillate between tautology—in which the poem is and means itself—and reduction—in which the poem means something that is not itself a poem. Antithetical criticism must begin by denying both tautology and reduction, a denial best delivered by the assertion that the meaning of a poem can only be a poem, but another poem—*a poem not itself*. (*Anxiety* 70)

Both Hartman and Bloom see an "indeterminate middle" between two "overspecified poles" of tautology (I am I) and reduction (I am him). Would it be too facile to identify these poles, these primary forms of criticism, with Sin on the one hand—the reproduction of a precursor's trope, in which the poem is and means itself—and Death on the other—either the production of a trope that is not one, in which the poem means something that is not a poem (Bloomian 'schizophrenia'), or else the production of a trope without a subject, pure rhetoric which means nothing at all (what I identify as self-parody)? One might also adduce Freud's examples of the child's reaction against his real parentage, which couple together the changeling fantasy (where the real father is a cipher) to a correspondent fantasy that the mother had many lovers:

---

[5] If we are tempted to doubt that mere names could carry such importance for a theory's originality, we must recall Bloom's own linking, again in *The Western Canon*, of all proper names with the belated sense of being "a gleaner in the wake of famous men, our fathers who begat us" (89).

again, the null and the infinite share the same inimical relation to establishing an integral quantity.

Let us now return to the suggestion that literary incest does occur with regularity in strong poets like Milton, and might be called parody. For Bloom, this is unimaginable: for him parody at best is 'weak' poetry, an ineffective appropriation of the precursor's tropes. On this score Bloom's view is rather similar (he would be disappointed to hear) to the famous dictum of T. S. Eliot: the bad poet borrows, the good poet steals. But let us consider those archetypes I have proposed for parodic poetry, Sin and Death. One figure is, by Bloomian terms, not original enough— the other almost too original. But we must ask, regardless, whether they perform the work of originality: what function do these figures serve within the larger context of *Paradise Lost*, and do they (in spite of their vexed relation to Bloom's definition of strong poetry) actually perform a function which enhances the overall 'strength' of Milton's epic? That is to say: does Milton's allegory of Sin and Death help to win the contest with the mighty dead, as Bloom would have it? I would argue that it does: Milton includes an allegory within his narrative in an obviously disjunctive fashion so that he may reject allegory altogether. Unreconstructed allegory here serves an aggressively revisionary purpose. Sin and Death are allegorical figures but *Paradise Lost* is not an allegorical epic; accordingly their narrative contains an implicit critique of the emptiness of the allegorical mode.

Consider the episode that Dr. Johnson singled out for negative criticism, the building of the "causey" in Book 10 (10.415). Johnson, we will recall, objects to the grotesque concreteness of their labor, claiming that "a *mole* of *aggregated soil*, cemented with *asphaltus*" is "a work too bulky for ideal [i.e. allegorical] architects" ("Milton" 530–31). Curiously enough, the notorious Richard Bentley had a similar objection to this passage, and tellingly emended one particular. Milton tells us that Death "smote" the "aggregated soil" with his "mace petrific" in order to solidify the bridge, and then, to further cement the construction: "the rest his look / Bound with Gorgonian rigor not to move, / And with asphaltic slime" (10.293–98). Bentley changes one word: he insists that Death's Medusa-gaze must leave the bridge "Bound with gorgonian rigor not to move / *As* with asphaltic slime" (emphasis mine). To Bentley's strangely perceptive ear, there is an inelegance in Milton's equation of "Gorgonian rigor" and "asphaltic slime," which implies that each is an equivalently concrete entity which could be used to bind up soil for bridge construction. But virtually every image that Milton uses in this passage highlights some slippage between the abstract idea and the form with which it is invested (to use Johnson's terms for allegorical figuration), and is therefore intended to call into question the allegorical mode itself. The simile in the passage compares the allegorical duo to "polar winds" that drive up mountains of ice which block "th' imagined way / Beyond Petsora eastward"—that is to say, the famously nonexistent Northwest Passage (10.289–92). Milton's logic suggests that the building of the "causey" is as pointless a creative effort as blocking a nonexistent road, with the added asymmetry of his analogy between building a passage and blocking one. The classical allusions to Delos and the Gorgon in this passage also refer to the creation of artificial and imposed solidity from something much more fluid, as the floating island was fixed in place by Zeus, or as men meeting the Gorgon's gaze were turned to stone. In either case, such solidification resembles what Johnson termed the defining hallmark of allegory: the investment of abstract ideas with concrete form. If this episode is to be read as an allegory *of* anything, then I think that it must be an allegory of the creation of allegories itself.

Of course, Milton could not resist the most obvious religious pun relative to the investment of abstract ideas with form: Sin and Death, working on their "causey," employ the "wondrous art / Pontifical" (10.312–13), recalling the ultimate Biblical instance of petrific metaphor, Christ's own pontifical pun on the name of Peter. Even if the papacy, and the Catholic reliance on ritual and the cult of objects (transubstantiation, vestments, and so on), is the immediate target of this jibe, we might just as easily understand that target to be Spenser himself, the Anglo-Catholic allegorist, life to whom was death to the Puritan Milton.[6] For Milton, allegory entails the solidification of sprawling concepts and complex characters into a structure, compounded as much of the "slime" of literal meaning as of the "rigor" of intellectual abstraction, which leads nowhere at all in its attempt to bridge an abyss. Such allegory is used by Milton conveniently to undermine Spenser's own achievement in the allegorical mode, as though to warn readers against reducing Milton's complex poem to a simple and banal moral lesson by

---

[6] When Sin refers to Satan as her "author" (2.864 and 10.236), the specifically literary cast of Milton's imagination here is made apparent: she is authored by Satan as surely as her model, Errour, was authored by Spenser. The only difference is that Sin, a preternaturally wise child, knows her own author, and even knows him carnally.

means of reductive hermeneutics. Milton asserts moral and intellectual superiority by falsely characterizing all allegory (including Spenser's) as simplistic on a level below that even of Bunyan, or Aesop.

Bloom, of course, has moved away in recent years from any acknowledgment of Spenser's influence on Milton; his reading in *The Western Canon* holds that Milton "confessed rather too readily that Spenser was his 'Great Original,' a remark that I have come to understand as a defense against Shakespeare" (169). Similarly, I have come to understand Bloom's newfound emphasis on Shakespeare (including his decision to apologize, in the preface to the second edition of *The Anxiety of Influence,* for his theory's inability to account for an originality like Shakespeare's) as his own defense against acknowledging parody as another tradition, equal in strength to the tradition that Bloom himself reveres. It has sometimes been claimed that Shakespeare is the one author who cannot be parodied; the same mystic privilege behind such claims may also lurk behind Bloom's now-overwhelming Bardolatry. But I think Shakespeare eludes Bloom's theoretical grasp (as demonstrated by the retrograde Bradleyan critical approach he takes in *Shakespeare: The Invention of the Human*), because any dramatist is necessarily steeped in the parodist's method in ways that lyric or epic poets seldom are. Drama is a collaborative art (witness centuries of textual emendations to Shakespeare's plays, justified by the assumption of an actor's interpolation), and playwrights have a notoriously weak regard for intellectual property rights (as demonstrated by Aristophanes' relentlessly parodic drive in *The Frogs*; by Shakespeare's magpie-usage of Holinshed, Plutarch or anything that came to hand; or by Brecht's lifelong career of grand larceny). And above all other ways in which it proves a stumbling block for Bloom, drama is the one literary form in which the author never speaks *in propria persona,* and in which the reliance on a single and fixed style (of the sort that defines originality in Bloom's theory) results not in a good play like *Hamlet*, but in something arid, sterile and unstageworthy.[7] Perhaps the best examples of what happens when a writer brings Bloomian standards of originality to bear on the playwright's craft can be found in the pages of the English Romantics, who provided the largest single influence on Bloom's theories, and whose reputations he did so much to revive at the beginning of his academic career. The

---

[7] There is a reason why Milton abandoned his initial effort to write *Paradise Lost* as drama, and why the only remaining evidence of his original intention is the speeches of Satan that Bloom adores.

willingness to shift styles, to introduce high and low matter, to make sure each character speaks appropriate and individual language (rather than highfalutin rhetorical boilerplate)—these are hallmarks of a play like *Hamlet*. To see what happens when a poet is trying to use drama to be 'original' in the Bloomian-Romantic sense, and to use the dramatic mode solely to lay emphasis on the originality of his own voice (rather than the voices of his characters), we need only skim Wordsworth's *The Borderers*, Coleridge's *Remorse*, Shelley's *The Cenci*, or Keats's *Otho the Great* for dispiriting examples.

There might seem to be one obvious problem with approaching a theory of parody by way of Milton's Sin and Death: they are not, as parodies generally are, funny. I feel the need to acknowledge this objection because I want to maintain, in what follows, some sense of parody's comic potential. Although I do not expect readers to share my own sense of a real, grim Beckettian comedy when Sin and Death build a bridge to nowhere, I will suggest the possibility that any humor in parody might (to follow the Freudian paradigm for jokes) be intimately related to the aggression inherent in the revisionary contest, or to the sublimation of such aggression. Bloom might deny that parody is revisionary at all, and therefore deny it the aggression that he attributes to 'strong' poetry; but Margaret Rose's work on parody (which follows the Russian Formalist critics, most notably Yuriy Tynyanov, from whom parody had hitherto received some of its most rigorous theoretical treatment) insistently reminds us that parody need not be funny to be a significant instrument of literary change. If Milton's own aggression against Spenser is most openly figured in a parody shorn of all comedy, and if Sin and Death are too grotesque to be amusing to any but the most jaded readers, perhaps that is because Milton's own aggressive drives remain, even in their most parodic moments, too strong to sublimate themselves into mere laughter.

2) "A League of Incest:" Byron and Shelley

To consider further how the matter of parody can inform our understanding of Bloomian theory, we might begin with the notion that parody embodies, in part, the claim that the precursor should have recognized his own belatedness but didn't—a model of creation which thereby emphasizes the likeness (if only in a shared belatedness) of the precursor to his ephebe, not his overwhelming and empowered unlikeness. If we read Satan as an incestuous parodist—or at least recognize that he is as much a parodist as a Bloomianly 'strong' poet—we should consider what further light the idea of incest (or incest-as-parody) can shed on the understanding of poetic revisionism, or the 'family romance' of literature. Let us allow Freud to inform this argument, as Bloom surely would. In Freud's terms, actual incest is best defined not as the mere overcoming of the Oedipal taboo to couple with one's mother, but in the larger theoretical terms of an overdetermination of likeness in erotic object choice.[8] Of course, this insight is as much Milton's as Freud's: overdetermination of likeness in the choice of one's erotic object is precisely what leads Satan to couple with his daughter Sin, who, speaking to Satan, reminds him that she charmed "thee chiefly, who full oft / Thyself in me thy perfect image viewing / Becam'st enamored" (*Paradise Lost* 2.763–65). But what erotic attraction, by Freud's definition, is not therefore bordering on incestuous? Bloom seems often to appreciate the hard and strange human wisdom of this paradox in Freud's thinking.[9]

The distinction Freud draws between ego-libido and object-libido is ultimately problematic only because the latter is always powered by the energy of the former, and each can be converted freely back and forth into the other. But for Bloom, and for his theories, it continually seems that object-libido is comprehensible whereas ego-libido (with its attendant overdetermination of likeness) is incomprehensible. As a proof case for this claim, we might turn to a relevant poet whom Bloom seems incapable of reading, namely Byron. Bloom is perpetually at a disadvantage in understanding Byron, since he begins with the assumption of Shelley as normative. Bloom's initial study, *Shelley's Mythmaking* (his first book, a published version of his doctoral thesis, and an interesting glimpse into the early stages of his thought), draws heavily upon the philosophy of Martin Buber.[10] *Shelley's Mythmaking* illustrates perfectly my concern here, for Buber's 'I-Thou' distinction is a concept similar to Freudian object-libido: it represents the decision to find spiritual

---

[8] This links incestuous and homosexual attraction, interestingly, under a common aetiology.

[9] This appreciation lurks, for example, in Bloom's otherwise bizarre overestimation of Wallace Stevens's "Two Figures in Dense Violet Night" (*Figures* 105–06).

[10] I might note here that it occasionally seems—with the early reliance on Buber, later on Freud, then finally on Gnosticism and Kabbalah—that Bloom is trying hard to prove that the canon of English poetry has always been, at heart, Jewish: in *Shelley's Mythmaking* this impulse seems a polemical response to the now-forgotten dominance of T. S. Eliot over Anglo-American criticism, but in later manifestations it recalls the laughable certainty of James Tyrone, Sr., in *Long Day's Journey into Night*, that he has proof that Shakespeare was an Irish Catholic like himself (O'Neill, *Long* 127).

connection with an other, without converting that other into a mere projection of the self. Shelley, besides being one of Bloom's favorite poets (and the poet on whose terms he judges all others), is the laureate of object-libido: in the "Defence of Poetry," he claims that "the great secret of morals is Love," then defines love in terms that make it indistinguishable from the classical definition of a trope, the discovery of likeness in unlikeness (*Shelley's Poetry* 487). Accordingly Shelley's favorite rhetorical figure is evidently the simile, perpetually likening one thing to another without ever collapsing them into an identity (as metaphor would). For a ready illustration of this tendency, I refer to his poem "To a Sky-Lark," composed of nothing but stacked similes gesturing with frenetic eroticism towards an unseeable "thou" (line 2).

But to get at the incestuous problem inherent in Shelley's object-libido, we need look no further than his best-known anthology piece, "Ozymandias." What is most characteristically Shelleyan in this poem is the belief that what survives are the "passions" (6) interpreted by the sculptor: they survive both the sculptor's mocking "hand" and Ozymandias' "heart" that fed them (8). This is consistent with Shelley's, and Bloom's, identification of artistic achievement or creation with Freudian object-libido. Yet anyone with a knowledge of literary-historical basics can recognize that "frown, / And wrinkled lip, and sneer of cold command" (4–5) as that of Byron himself, the imperious sneer that Bloom's protegée Camille Paglia is forever likening to that of Elvis Presley.[11] The introduction of Byron into a discussion of literary ego-libido and object-libido may seem slightly tendentious, given that we know that Byron—in life at least (although with Byron distinctions between life and work are always blurred)—was characterized by an overdetermination of likeness in erotic object choice, with noteworthy forays into both incest and homosexuality. But my goal here is to investigate the interrelations of Shelley and Byron, to read in their work the interrelations of object-libido and ego-libido. If Bloom's Freudian reading of English poetry grants priority to Shelley (and his vision of erotic quest), I hope to suggest that a stricter Freudian reading than Bloom's must necessarily grant priority to Byron, and see in Shelley's mystic

---

[11] Shelley's portrait of Byron as Ozymandias is perhaps mediated by two other figures: Napoleon, whose Egyptian campaign associates him with pharaonic antiquities and tyranny, and to whom Byron, as Shelley knew, had likened himself explicitly in verse; and also, of course, Milton's Satan, who surfaces in most depictions of the Ozymandias-like Byronic hero, and specifically in the first stanza of Byron's "Ode to Napoleon Buonaparte."

eroticism an attempt, above all else, to escape from the primacy of Byron's egocentric and parodistic imagination. My claim for Byron could be restated thus: in Byron's best work the poetic ego is so strong that it will not scruple at appropriating anything for itself, and certainly does not hesitate even at an incestuous trespass. And so, even as the Oedipal anxiety of influence may be the best guide for understanding Shelley, with Byron it becomes oddly irrelevant: we would do better to ignore Bloom's notion of Oedipal resistance to incest, and instead recall the quip attributed to Woody Allen: "What Oedipal struggle? I won, hands down."

In *The Visionary Company*, Bloom reads Byron (and all of Romanticism) through a Shelleyan lens. This approach renders Byron incomprehensible and forces Bloom to exalt mediocre efforts like "Stanzas to the Po," simply because they appear more Shelleyan or conventionally Romantic, and to underestimate the parodic character of Byron's best work. In part this must be due, as Bloom would freely admit, to the experiential character of his criticism: he discovered Shelley's poetry early and loved it, but lacks such a cathexis to Byron (although Shelley himself did not). But Shelley is a deeply unfunny poet, and to read Byron on his terms means that Bloom can never properly understand Byron's parodic ego. Bloom also believes that Shelley's primary precursor was Wordsworth, but this is like his occasional claim that Hart Crane (perhaps the most Shelleyan poet besides Shelley) found his real *agon* was not with Eliot but with Walt Whitman: in each case, Bloom has wrongly assumed the presence of a high Romantic precursor whom he admires (and can actually understand within his schema). The truth is that Shelley's development as a poet was far more influenced by Byron's work, or even by Southey's, than by Wordsworth's—just as the "Hymn to Intellectual Beauty" may be Shelley's most Wordsworthian performance (as Bloom correctly notes), but is also (as he fails to note) a very light and ironic or Byronic performance, a rare bit of fun for the earnest Shelley, and the closest prefiguration of his late-flowering serious frivolity in "The Witch of Atlas."

In most instances where Shelley makes revisionary use of Byron, though, all irony is banished. An obvious example is found in the curse which lies at the center of *Prometheus Unbound*. Its obvious precursor text is Byron's savage (and really quite amusing) curse of forgiveness upon his wife in *Childe Harold* 4. Shelley's revisionary tactic here consists in removing the irony, taking Byron's satirical attack straight and considering it as a serious moral problem. Claude Rawson, in an important essay on Shelley, Byron, and the satiric tradition, calls this revisionary maneuver "one of the strangest and least studied mutations of mock-heroic," where a poet will

> pick up an idiom of derision or parody, and *un*parody or rewrite it upwards .... It is an extension, perhaps, of that Shelleyan or Byronic inability to sustain a live and serious ambivalence in those domains where the heroic and the derisive might interact .... In the readiness to assume heroic aspects straight, if in nothing else, this may be thought to stretch back before Dryden to Milton himself. (116–17)

If Bloom fails to comprehend this revisionary technique in Shelley, it is probably because his own sympathies do not extend to the satirical tradition. Bloom is by no means a humorless critic (no-one could accuse him of slighting Falstaff or Wilde), but for two-and-a-half crucial centuries of literary history his canon excludes satiric or ironic poetry. For that reason alone, his tastes are anything but catholic, with the pun fully intended: Bloom can read Milton but not Donne or Pope or Marvell, just as he can read Shelley but not Byron. And, as we have already seen, Bloom's view of Milton denies an equally persuasive alternate Milton—the Byronic rather than the Shelleyan Milton. He even makes these terms explicit in *The Anxiety of Influence*: "It is sad to observe most modern critics observing Satan, because they never do observe him.... Eliot ... speaks of 'Milton's curly haired Byronic hero'" (one wants to reply, looking from side to side: 'Who?').... Fortunately we have had Empson, with his apt rallying cry: 'Back to Shelley!' Whereto I go" (23).

It may be that, for Bloom, the frank and conscious aggression of satire is what has to be overcome to constitute the properly revisionist poetic ego. We may recall in this context Shelley's own reaction to Byronic aggression in this fragment of 1818, which W. M. Rossetti conjectured was an address to his contemporary:

> O mighty mind, in whose deep stream this age
> Shakes like a reed in the unheeding storm
> Why dost thou curb not thine own sacred rage? (*Poetical Works* 482)

It is the Byronic "sacred rage" of parody and satire that baffles Shelley here, just as it is the *aggression* of the curse in *Childe Harold* that troubles him most. Shelley's own performances as a satirist are marked by a humanely admirable but poetically disastrous commitment to his own peaceable principles. Works like *Peter Bell the Third* and *Swell-foot the Tyrant* are really too sincere, too dogged and unenjoyable, to be any good as satire or parody; even when they do summon up a properly "sacred rage," they never really make an attack.¹² Shelley's problems as a satirist are overwhelmingly evident in the 1820 fragment "Satire on Satire," which begins:

> If Satire's scourge could wake the slumbering hounds
> Of Conscience, or erase the deeper wounds,
> The leprous scars of callous infamy;
> If it could make the present not to be,
> Or charm the dark past never to have been,
> Or turn regret to hope; who that has seen
> What Southey is and was, would not exclaim,
> Lash on! Be the keen verse dipped in flame.... (*Poetical Works* 455)

Robert Southey's political apostasy is the subject here (and proved an inexhaustible one for many other satirical poems of the day), yet Shelley concludes the fragment by rejecting satire itself. This is precisely the same dynamic that underlies the un-saying of Prometheus' own Byronic language of the curse—the rejection of the Byronic mode (whose aggression is here defined specifically as that of satire) is configured as a moral flight from the endless regress of the *lex talionis*:

> This cannot be, it ought not, evil still—
> Suffering makes suffering, ill must follow ill.
> Rough words beget sad thoughts, and beside
> Men take a sullen and a stupid pride
> In being all they hate in others' shame,
> By a perverse antipathy of fame.
> 'Tis not worth while to prove, as I could, how
> From the sweet fountains of our Nature flow
> These bitter waters; I will only say,
> If any friend would take Southey some day,
> And tell him, in a country walk alone,
> Softening harsh words with friendship's gentle tone,
> How incorrect his public conduct is,
> And what men think of it, 'twere not amiss.
> Far better than to make the innocent ink — (455–56)

And here Shelley breaks off, as he must. This is tremendously, if unintentionally, funny. But to judge Shelley's very great talents by this silly

---

¹² Interestingly, in both of these satirical texts the matter of incest—for Shelley, notoriously, the most poetical of subjects—is glaringly prominent; the latter poem, which rests in deserved obscurity, is in fact a parody-version of *Oedipus Rex*.

performance, or to compare it with the brilliant skewering of Southey in *Don Juan*, would be to employ the wrong criteria entirely: it would replicate the kind of fundamental error Bloom makes in *The Visionary Company* when he estimates Byron's strength on the basis of "Stanzas to the Po," or compares *Manfred* unfavorably to *Prometheus Unbound*.

Byron's *Manfred* demonstrates another ramification of the parodic mode that Bloom cannot comprehend. I single it out because *Manfred* is not actually satire or parody, yet what is original and good about it is best understood in the parodic or satiric terms that I have been sketching. The determinate fact underlying Byron's drama is, of course, that an act of incest has actually occurred; Manfred himself locates the incest as the source of the drama. Although we might seem to be on tenuous ground in suggesting a literary rather than autobiographical source for the incest motif in *Manfred*, the constant invocation of Milton's Satan at least reminds us how little Byron scrupled at literary appropriation. But is *Manfred* a parody? Not quite; I think it is best considered, like Sin and Death, as an abstracted allegory of the queer revisionism or originality that can be wrought by the parodist's revisionary ratio. Byron is trying to be serious in *Manfred*, and, successful or not, I think his efforts here will give us a better insight into the workings of his greatest achievement, the self-consciously frivolous *Don Juan*. Nearing his end, Manfred says, in language plagiaristically borrowed from Milton's Satan:

> The Mind which is immortal makes itself
> Requital for its good or evil thoughts,—
> Is its own origin of ill and end—
> And its own place and time .... (*Manfred* 3.4.129–32)

But the Satanic rhetoric here masks an underlying collapse of identity. If Manfred's mind is immortal, how can it be its own origin or end? The paradox is ignored, and the play ends with Manfred willing himself out of existence, notoriously telling the Abbot, with a supremely Wildean insouciance: "Old Man! 'tis not so difficult to die" (3.4.151). An earlier image that Manfred uses has the same strange collapse of identity within it: discussing the public career he might have pursued before committing himself to incest, Manfred says he once had the visionary urge

>   to rise
> I knew not whither—it might be to fall;
> But fall, even as the mountain-cataract,

> Which having leapt from its more dazzling height,
> Even in the foaming strength of its abyss,
> (Which casts up misty columns that become
> Clouds raining from the re-ascended skies,)
> Lies low but mighty still.—But this is past,
> My thoughts mistook themselves. (3.1.107–15)

That Manfred would be rising to fall (not to mention his invocation of an identical trope within his trope, the cycle of water's evaporation and precipitation) again hints at the problematic collapse of identity between two poles, the collapse I have earlier identified as incestuous. Yet what a fall it is that Manfred depicts! It is a parodic literalization, I would argue, of the Miltonic trope of the fall of Satan (or of Man), where Byron turns that existential fall into a gorgeous and highly artificial extravaganza of *literally* falling water: this is the Luciferian revolt reconceived in the style of a near-Gothic Art Deco. In the space before the poem's total annihilation of identity, brought on by the incestuous trespass, a strange and nearly comic poetry is being born.

Manfred moves past the dream of rising "to fall" to get closer to the incestuous source of his ultimate collapse. His sister Astarte is "one without a tomb" (2.4.82); she did not actually die, but her identity simply vanished when she yielded to the act of (literal) incest. But the summoning of Astarte is surely a great comic anticlimax: after arriving, she does nothing but name Manfred, give him assurance his death will occur on the morrow, bid him twice farewell, name him a final time, and vanish (2.4.97–155). The overall impression is not so much of a revenant like Poe's Madeleine Usher—how can you locate the return of the repressed in a consciousness that represses as little as Byron's?—as of a spooky little automaton, a Frankenstein-ballerina popping out of a vast cuckoo-clock designed by Tim Burton. Astarte's name is even a comic allusion, for the Astarte of *Paradise Lost*, of course, is really the devil Astoreth, whose description in Book 1 invokes the virginal Diana: "... Astartè, queen of heav'n, with crescent horns; / To whose bright image nightly by the moon / Sidonian virgins paid their vows and songs" (*Paradise Lost* 1.439–41). If we consider Byron's Astarte to be like Diana, that may mean her brother Manfred is to be identified with Apollo, god of poetry and light; but clearly the analogy to those divine siblings, at least one of whom was noted for her chastity, is made a joke by their sexual relationship. The end result of her summoning is that Manfred, the poet, is given only his name and his death by the incestuous muse. It seems that we are in the realm of Oedipal collapse: as I noted earlier, this seems like a half-conscious invocation of the naming and self-annihilation of Act 5 of *Hamlet*. After this, Manfred, like Hamlet, is allowed a brief moment of individuation nonetheless. But what poetry does that true moment of individuation produce? Between Astarte's naming of Manfred (with her death-prophecy) and Manfred's actual death, there falls a comic, even slapstick scene in which Manfred tries to have the Abbot of St. Maurice dragged off by a demon. Byron reluctantly removed this scene from the published version of the text at the urging of his friend Gifford, but I find his initial view of its necessity particularly telling. It shows that the comic element is unleashed between the incestuous naming of the poet and the final collapse of his identity.

Byron's contemporaries, and later readers in the nineteenth century, admired *Manfred* immensely.[13] Much as I admire this closet-psychodrama, I would agree with Bloom that, in our century, Byron's reputation seems far more readily assured by the achievement of *Don Juan*. And *Don Juan* does not allegorize incest and parody, as *Manfred* does: it simply takes them as its basic procedural principles. In *Don Juan*, the Byronic hero—of whom Manfred is the last important example in the Byron canon—no longer commands the spotlight; when he does appear in the poem it is not as a Satanic rebel against authority, but as the figure of authority itself, almost as though the Byronic hero were the precursor with whom the poet wrestles. An example can be found in Lambro (from the Haidée episode), and we might connect the Byronic hero's odd reversal of function to the fact that, by all accounts, the poet's father 'Mad Jack' Byron was even more mad, bad and dangerous to know than his son (potentially suggesting that the romantic stance of all Byron's earlier work was, in fact, nothing more than a parody of his own father). As opposed to the obsessive autochthony of a Manfred, Juan himself has no character, no overwhelming ego-libido in the earlier Byronic sense. But *Don Juan* is great precisely because all of the poem's incestuous leanings have been transferred from the representation of a character (a projection of the lyric poet's *I*) onto the poetic medium itself. The *ottava rima* stanza takes the place of the Byronic (or Satanic) hero's fictive self-projection, and it proceeds with a similar penchant for incest, the figurative incest of parody / plagiarism, which appropriates everything for inclusion in a ceaseless drive toward self-creation.

That the matter of incest is entwined with the matter of *Don Juan*'s satiric style can again provide an interesting point of comparison to the

---

[13] Hippolyte Taine compared it quite favorably with Goethe's *Faust*.

Shelleyan method of the "Satire on Satire." Although the Satanism of the earlier Byronic poetry is interestingly hinted at in the very first stanza, where the Juan of the pantomime is "sent to the devil somewhat ere his time" (*Don Juan* 1.1.8), it is ultimately rejected: one would be hard pressed to imagine a less Satanic figure than Juan himself. Yet there is an important connection to be made here between the matter of Satan (so fascinating to the second-generation Romantics) and the ironic dedicatee of *Don Juan*, the poet laureate Bob Southey. As we saw, Southey was the target of Shelley's "Satire on Satire," where it was hoped that the tender remonstrance of a friend (Wordsworth?) might lead him to see the error of his newly reactionary ways. It was not until after the initial cantos of *Don Juan* were written and published that Southey began his attack on Byron's "Satanic School" of poetry, an attack which first appears in Southey's preface to "The Vision of Judgment." This attack famously occasioned Byron's response in the form of a wicked parody (with an identical title). Southey's preface is worth considering here:

> What, then, should be said of those for whom the thoughtlessness and inebriety of wanton youth can no longer be pleaded, but who have written in sober manhood, and with deliberate purpose?—men of diseased hearts and depraved imaginations, who, forming a system of opinions to suit their own unhappy course of conduct, have rebelled against the holiest ordinances of human society, and, hating that revealed religion, which, with all their efforts and bravadoes, they are unable entirely to disbelieve, labor to make others as miserable as themselves, by infecting them with a moral virus that eats into the soul! The school which they have set up may properly be called the Satanic School; for though their productions breathe the spirit of Belial in their lascivious parts, and the spirit of Moloch in those loathsome images of atrocity and horror which they delight to represent, they are more especially characterized by a satanic spirit of pride and audacious impiety, which still betrays the wretched feeling of hopelessness wherewith it is allied. (*Poetical Works* 10.196)

Belial, we will recall, is the patron of sodomy, and no-one can fail to hear in Southey's slur a hint of the rumors that swirled around Byron during his divorce. But Southey had in private leveled the charge of incest against Byron long before publicly calling him "Satanic" in this passage. Before the publication of either poet's "Vision of Judgment," Southey was on Byron's mind during the composition of *Don Juan*. This is the reason for the poem's ironic dedication to Southey, in those stanzas suppressed only because the poem was published anonymously and Byron therefore declined to "attack the dog in the dark." In a letter to

Hobhouse of November 11, 1818, written during the composition of Cantos 1 and 2 of *Don Juan,* Byron recalls Southey's earlier charge of incest:

> The son of a bitch on his return from Switzerland, two years ago, said that Shelley and I "had formed a League of Incest, and practiced our precepts with, &c." He lied like a rascal, for they *were not sisters* .... He lied in another sense, for there was no promiscuous intercourse, my commerce being limited to the carnal knowledge of Miss C. (qtd. in Marchand 288)

Yet the accusation of incest, which Byron demurely denies, could by the terms I have proposed be applied to *Don Juan* itself. I would use it to characterize the aesthetic shock of a stanza like the following, a shock that most of us still register, as Byron hoped we would, with our laughter:

> "Go, little book, from this my solitude!
>   I cast thee on the waters, go thy ways!
> And if, as I believe, thy vein be good,
>   The world will find thee after many days."
> When Southey's read, and Wordsworth understood,
>   I can't help putting in my claim to praise.
> The four first rhymes are Southey's every line;
> For God's sake, reader, take them not for mine. (1.222)

Since the Byronic ego is governed not by the Bloomian resistance to incest, but instead by the overdetermination of likeness in its erotic object choice, it follows as a principle of Byron's literary method that, if even so bad a poet as Southey can be made Byronic enough (even if only in his rhyme and meter) he can be absorbed by a process of satirical plagiarism. What Bakhtin characterized as novelization fits nicely with the sort of parodic method employed here, where the attack on Southey is effected by letting Byron's capacious ego swallow him whole. Southey is betrayed by his own words, much as he was in the *Wat Tyler* controversy, only two years before the first canto of *Don Juan* was published. Byron was delightedly aware of this controversy: it is mentioned in the prose preface to *Don Juan,* and provides the chief subject for the preface to his parody "Vision of Judgment." In a sense, Byron, like all good satirists, realized that the best tactic to adopt with so worthy a target as Southey was to let the man speak for himself. Accordingly, Byron's "Vision of Judgment" takes over Southey's title and scenario unaltered, converting them into Byronic *ottava rima* only to conclude with a vision of Southey sent to hell, as though to prove whose poetic school is the genuinely Satanic one. Much as Spenser's allegorical mode is incorporated as part of Milton's own revision of Spenser, here Southey's poetry is enlisted for Byron's attack on Southey. This Byronic mode of attack by incorporating direct quotation can be found in most of Byron's best satiric precursors: it is employed by Rochester in the satire "After Boileau;" it is also a feature of Swift's *Tale of a Tub* and Pope's *Dunciad*, where even the counter-attacks and critical commentary of each author's enemies are worked into the very fabric of the text. One does not know whether to call this style of composition incestuous or cannibalistic, but the effect is clear: Byron's attack renders Southey irrelevant, by incorporating Southey into the verse as part of the aggressive attempt to destroy him. Again the contrast with Shelley's "Satire on Satire" could not be greater, and again the difference between Shelley and Byron illustrates the different fundamental creative procedures of erotic, even hysterical object-libido and imperious ego-libido.

Because Byron's ego is so consistently *itself*, it often fails to recognize the boundaries of that self, and incorporates everything it finds into the Byronic mode. Even so familiar an anthology piece as "She Walks in Beauty" derives its force as a poem from Byron's barely-resisted temptation to turn its subject, Lady Wilmot Horton, into yet another Byronic hero, a solitary wandering like the Giaour in the "cloudless climes and starry skies" of Levantine chiaroscuro ("She Walks" 2). Consequently, the greatest praise that Byron can bestow on any person is that he or she has been true to him- or herself (this despite the fact that Byron cannot discern another person's self unless it ultimately can be likened to his own); and by the same criterion, Southey's ultimate failing is found in the political apostasy Byron pillories. If Byron seems constantly to be recalling Satan's steadfast declaration that "we know no time when we were not as now" (*Paradise Lost* 5.859), then surely it is for a failure to live up to his own self in such Satanically steadfast fashion that Southey is being mocked. In fact, Milton himself is the heroic example Byron will invoke to belittle further the laughable inconsistency of a Southey: a Milton who seems Byronically plagued by public misunderstanding, yet still unwilling to yield, in other words a Milton who sounds (rather oddly, in the context of such a comic poem as *Don Juan*) like Childe Harold vowing to "tire torture and time:"

> If fallen in evil days on evil tongues,
>   Milton appealed to the avenger, Time,
> If Time, the avenger, execrates his wrongs
>   And makes the word *Miltonic* mean *sublime*,

> *He* deigned not to belie his soul in songs,
>   Nor turn his very talent to a crime.
> *He* did not loathe the sire to laud the son,
> But closed the tyrant-hater he begun.
>
> Think'st thou, could he, the blind old man, arise
>   Like Samuel from the grave to freeze once more
> The blood of monarchs with his prophecies,
>   Or be alive again—again all hoar
> With time and trials, and those helpless eyes
>   And heartless daughters—worn and pale and poor,
> Would he adore a sultan? He obey
> The intellectual eunuch Castlereagh? (*Don Juan*, Dedication 10–11)

The charge of sterility in the last line may recall the substance of another gibe at Southey in *Don Juan*, where Byron refers to him as "dry Bob:" a conscious literary echo of Rochester's satiric attack on Dryden in "An Allusion to Horace" (a title that Byron perhaps recalled for his own "Hints from Horace"), 'dry bob' was a slang term for coitus without emission. Byronic autochthony is somehow equivalent to sexual potency, just as Manfred gains his identity only by consummating the act of incest. This might seem a very un-Miltonic element of Byron, given Milton's notable fear of contamination by sexuality and consequent valorization of virginity (which runs throughout his work, from *Comus* to *Samson Agonistes*). But one could argue that both Byron's association of the poetic ego with sexual potency (or even sexual jusqu'auboutisme) and Milton's with a fetish for virginity actually spring from the same impulse to maintain the integrity of the self. For Byron, that self is found reflected in every object of desire, so there is no danger of contamination—instead potency becomes important as an exercise of the poetic will, just as every sexual act patterns itself on incest.

In the original draft of *Don Juan*, Byron had written a different (but equally vicious) couplet to conclude the passage weighing Southey against Milton. In the original, Byron inquired, with reference to Milton:

> Would *he* subside into a hackney Laureat?
> A scribbling self-sold soul-hired scorned Iscariot (qtd. in *Don Juan* 567)

And to this variant, Byron attached his own satiric footnote, much in the style of Swift:

> I doubt if Laureat & Iscariot be good rhymes but must say as Ben Johnson did to Sylvester who challenged him to rhyme with "I, John Sylvester / Lay with your Sister." Johnson answered — "I Ben Johnson lay with your wife" Sylvester answered "that is not *rhyme*"—*no* Said Ben Johnson; "But it is *true*." (567)

Can we fail, though, to hear a hint of Byron's own "lay" with his own sister in this otherwise purely satiric and literary recollection? Though his actual incest with Augusta Leigh was among the reasons for his flight from England in 1816, it was hardly public knowledge. In this satiric footnote, the hint of incest in the phrase "lay with your Sister" is associated with being "*true*," as opposed to dissembling for the sake of a mere rhyme. But incest—or the irreverent and non-anxious attitude towards literary tradition—must be taken here as a profound governing metaphor for Byron's best poetic output, and I think it is not far-fetched to hear it even in this characteristically Byronic jest. I suspect that those revisionary poetic modes that Bloom neglects—parody, satire—and which are on full display in *Don Juan* often introduce the matter of incest reflexively, unknowingly. Certainly Byron, discussing an episode from the history of satiric warfare between poets, has no other reason to hint at the biographical fact of his own incest, just as Milton's introduction of incest into a wholly fictive Spenserian allegorical narrative springs from "no temptation, but the author's opinion of its beauty" (to recall Samuel Johnson's words, "Milton" 531).

3) Bachelor Uncles and "The Other Tradition:" Auden and Ashbery

I come at last to a contemporary whose work, for Bloom as well as me, provides the best recent example of poetic originality: John Ashbery. Bloom's criticism of Ashbery seems to me as persuasive as it is one-sided, and as with the other poets I have examined, I would like to offer a view of Ashbery antithetical to (but, I hope, as persuasive as) Bloom's. I would argue that Ashbery is not so much a great poet in Bloom's anxiety-ridden high Romantic tradition as he is a poet of the incestuous (ironic and Byronic) tradition of parody I have been outlining. Although hostile critics tend to regard each new book of poems by Ashbery as an exercise in pointlessness, and cry that the poet's constant pursuit of expressive novelty soon grows tired, my response as a passionate defender of Ashbery is to remind the nay-sayers that each new canto of *Don Juan* also once seemed increasingly tiresome to a good number of Byron's most intelligent contemporaries—indeed, the protracted publication history of *Don Juan* in Byron's lifetime demonstrates the ways in which a poet may outlive his own acclaim—and to suggest that any sensitive reader today would be grateful to have just one more of them (let alone the full hundred Byron intended). Ashbery's output is Byronic in precisely that way: the author is so self-assured in his remarkable originality that his style, forever twisting itself into new shapes and finding fresh matter to absorb and make its own, may come to seem as if it exists purely for its own sake. The main risk that Ashbery runs by writing in such a fluent way is that his detractors find his work to be one endless and unenjoyable self-parody.

There are enough suggestive correspondences between the styles of Ashbery and Byron that I feel justified in bringing them together. Perhaps the most salient of the common features is the attitude of each towards his *materia poetica*: each sees the poet's job as being a bit like the collector's. In an interview with David Herd, Ashbery uses an image of himself: describing his poetry as "a kind of cabinet of curios," he goes on to observe, of what this cabinet contains (i.e. his subject matter), that

> Collectability is a relatively recent concept, I think. A collectable is something that doesn't have the status of an antique, yet. But people collect them for mysterious reasons . . . . I collect a lot of things, including the vomit bags from airplanes; unused. I did it because I thought, "I never heard of anyone collecting these." (Herd 36–37)

I would connect Ashbery's suggestions here about his method to Frank McConnell's insights in his article "Byron as Antipoet" (originally published as "Byron's Reductions: 'Much Too Poetical'"). Much of what McConnell says here of Byron applies equally well to Ashbery:

> . . . Byron *does* write poetry of undeniable power which nevertheless, taken at its own self-evaluation, seems to deny many of our most basic tenets of belief in the nature and efficacy of creative language. Terms like "irony" and "satire" help us a bit to evaluate and identify, but finally even they are inadequate to the range of Byron's reductive imagination; for he ironically calls irony itself into question . . . . The deep undercurrent of weakness or effeminacy in the *form* of [Byronic] writers' experience is precisely complementary to the virile and lucid energy of their reductive approach. Byron epitomizes this ambivalent myth of the artist when he writes of the "miser" in *Don Juan* . . . . It is the miser's *uselessness* which eminently equips him for the role of "only poet" . . . . The miser is the poet

of moral and phenomenal vacuums. For his "art," the art of *possession,* is an anti-poiesis which under the sign of ownership reduces the things of this world to *objects* in their most quantitatively inanimate aspects . . . . Poetry is not creation, but collection, and the collector's impulse is near Byron's deepest sense of his own production. ("Byron" 420–21)

Collectorship first of all necessitates a different sort of relation between the poet and his subject than is normally found in the poets Bloom deems strong. In Byron's poetry, objects are not distant or idealized, like Shelley's skylark—they are actual and concrete things. He takes a pleasure in stacking up names, items, rhetorical devices (as the *tour de force* of *Don Juan*'s Canto 11 demonstrates, with a gusto that recalls Ashbery's omnium-gatherum efforts). And frequently the consequence of collecting is that banal or ordinary artifacts (including such fossilized linguistic artifacts as clichés or poetic diction) can, by their inclusion in a poem and by virtue of what Ashbery calls the "logic / Of strange position" (*Selected* 28), result in a startlingly original poem. "*Difficile est proprie communia dicere*" is the epigraph to *Don Juan*: a tag from Horace that might be translated "it is difficult to speak of common things in your own way," intended by Byron as a jibe at the 'Lake School' of Wordsworth and Southey, whose avowed interest in common things too often feels faux-naïf or solipsistically false. Byron's originality is found in his belief that to speak of common life requires no more than an acceptance and incorporation of all the *trouvailles* (a favorite word of Ashbery's) of language and experience—none of which are to be found in the poetry of the Lakers, given Wordsworth's deliberately plain language, and the absence of any dramatic (or even interesting) personal experience on the order of Byron's. But this Byronic approach to "common things" is taken to dizzying extremes in Ashbery's oeuvre. Although Ashbery has been criticized at times (largely by admirers of Robert Lowell) for an indifference to socio-political or even autobiographical particulars, he has quietly defended his work as a deliberate attempt to produce a "one-size-fits-all confessional poem" or an "everybody's autobiography" in the mold of Gertrude Stein. Ashbery does approach common life with something like Don Juan's acceptance and incorporation of everything that is encountered. This includes the encounter with poetic tradition itself, making Ashbery a less convincing proof of Bloomian theory than one would suppose from Bloom's discussions of him: I can discern in Ashbery no anxiety about the incestuous inclusion of other writers' work into his own. He has even gone so far as to publish under his own name two "*centos*," poetic compositions made up entirely of quotations borrowed from other well-known poems:[14] while these may not be the poems by which Bloom judges Ashbery's originality—and may not even be poems at all—the joking gesture behind them hints at a larger procedural method which is unconcerned with originality as Bloom defines it. Plagiarism is a central fact of Ashbery's style: even "Self-Portrait in a Convex Mirror" (acknowledged by Bloom, and even by many critics normally unmoved by Ashbery, as his most important and original achievement) manages to incorporate large quoted chunks of Sydney Freedberg's academic study of Parmigianino directly into the verse. This tactic is hardly novel; it can be found in precursors important to Ashbery, but seldom mentioned in Bloom's genealogies of twentieth-century strong poetry, like Marianne Moore or T. S. Eliot. It also recalls Byron's use of direct quotation from Southey—with the difference that Ashbery has a less openly satiric animus against the poets he quotes.[15] More than the comparable rhetorical moves in Eliot (whose allusiveness is frequently satirical) or even Marianne Moore (for whom direct quotation seems to spring from a funny scruple that a poet ought not to pass off as her own any thought that derives from her reading), the use of quotation in Ashbery's work feels utterly non-tendentious, a simple record of what his mind encounters, regardless even of whether it may derive from high or low cultural sources. For this reason I think the texture of Ashbery's verse, like Byron's, is distinguished by its permeability: it goes beyond allusion or plagiarism, to a point where it is able to incorporate any sort of word, or level of discourse, without any willful drive toward disjunctiveness (save in the experimental excesses of *The Tennis Court Oath,* which Bloom is right in finding a failure), and without sacrificing our sense that what we are reading is, always and indefeasibly, *echt* Ashbery.

I suspect it is not irrelevant that Ashbery and Byron are both frequently understood specifically as gay writers. Although I think critics run the risk of blockheaded reductiveness by giving too great an emphasis to this subject, I would like to adduce some tentative but interesting remarks about Byron, again by Frank McConnell:

> Byron's relationship with his fictive projections is, I have suggested, introverted. One hesitates to use the franker word, "homosexual" without the qualification that here it is being employed as a primarily *imaginative*

---

[14] One, "To a Waterfowl," dates from the 1960s and was published in the periodical *Locus Solus*; the other may be found in the 1998 volume *Wakefulness,* and is entitled "The Dong with the Luminous Nose."

[15] One of Ashbery's most admirable qualities is his unflappable good nature.

value, by analogy with the strongly heterosexual quest-myth of Blake, Shelley, and Keats . . . . It is undeniable, however, that homosexuality becomes increasingly crucial for the literature of the post-Romantic imagination, as the perfect analogue, on the metabolic level, to the linguistic impulse toward the devaluation of metaphor and the technical impulse toward conscious artifice. ("Byron" 427)

Certainly what McConnell calls "the technical impulse toward conscious artifice" is even more salient in the postmodern Ashbery than in the half-Romantic Byron.[16] If all Ashbery's conscious artifice, the delicacies he concocts from pastiche and even his occasional lapses into preciosity, constitute tactics that we have come to recognize as 'postmodern' (as well as hallmarks of a twentieth-century gay sensibility), we might also recall a comment by Ian Jack that shows how close the language of Byron (at his best) can come to the characteristically postmodern clutter in Ashbery's diction. Jack writes of *Don Juan,* in a passage that might have been taken verbatim from Ashbery's *Vermont Notebook*:

> No word in the language is too familiar or too commonplace to be used in this poem, which contains such humdrum words and phrases as mortgage, Patent Blacking, vermicelli, soda water, menagerie, indigestion, really, hencoops, Five per Cents, butler, cheese-paring, ready money, bagged, billiards, thereanent, old newspaper, affidavit, solvent, portmanteaus, income tax, supercargo, beefsteak, post-obit, damme, guts, cough, breakfast, non-suit, raising cash, emetic, entrails, broth, jugular, blankets, cookery, phthisical, clap-trap, grand-dad, quiz, valet, teaspoonfuls, annuities, and gastric juice. Of many of these it may be said, as Byron says of "broth," that it is "A thing which poesy but seldom mentions." (Jack 67–68)

This last quip may not actually be true (even rarefied George Herbert put "broth" into "The Odour") but it contains a real insight about Byron's own poetic method. The way in which *Don Juan* can incorporate broth or teaspoonfuls or billiards did expand the scope of poetry itself, and altered the tradition: it is one of the signs of Byron's originality, if not on Bloom's terms then at least on the terms I would like to use. I would liken the use of those common things that Jack catalogues, plucked by Byron from the very heart of emergent bourgeois culture, to Ashbery's

[16] If 'postmodern' has any use whatsoever as a critical term, then surely it must be applied to a poet like Ashbery, who can begin a poem with lines like: "This poem is concerned with language on a very plain level. / Look at it talking to you. . ." (*Selected* 283).

methods: certainly no item on the list that Jack compiled would be out of place amid the camp drollery of Ashbery's novel *A Nest of Ninnies* (written in collaboration with James Schuyler), where corn-dodgers and alligator pumps, fresh-baked Sally Lunn buns and the bagpipes of the Ayrshire rifles all find their place in an American bourgeois milieu. Like *Don Juan's* English cantos, Ashbery's work caresses its subjects lovingly even as it tweaks them with the gentlest satirical intent. In his interview with David Herd, Ashbery connects this list-making to the Whitmanian strain in American poetry, and then notes with bemusement that an anthology of list poems was published in England which included "one from 'Daffy Duck in Hollywood' which they title 'An American Everything'" (Herd 37). I would argue for very deep affinities here: between the inclusiveness of Ashbery's "American Everything," the collecting impulse in Byron identified by McConnell, and what I have characterized as the permeable and literally all-encompassing poetic ego of the parodist, whose poetic revisionism does not depend on contests with the mighty dead conducted largely below the threshold of the conscious imagination. This non-anxious or parodic revisionism instead depends upon what Ashbery himself, in "Grand Galop," sees as a knowing conscious effort

> To try to write poetry
> Using what Wyatt and Surrey left around,
> Took up and put down again
> Like so much gorgeous raw material . . . . (*Selected* 177)

Alongside the frank and refreshing concreteness of this image—and its understanding of poetry as a collecting activity, where each novelty of the sublime becomes another *tchotchke* to be snatched up by the enterprising poet—I would also recall Sin and Death, for whom an abstract "Gorgonian rigor" is as concrete and useful a tool as the all-too-tangible "asphaltic slime" (*Paradise Lost* 10.297–98). Both Milton and Ashbery (two poets who otherwise have little in common save highest praise from Bloom) figure the work of the imagination as a physical activity, with the writer's material understood as actually, tangibly material—both tropes analogous to the workings of allegory as Milton understands them, wherein abstract ideas are turned, as by the gaze of Medusa, into linguistic fossils. In these two moments from Milton and Ashbery—both of which are about the creative effort—it feels as though a precursor's tropes have, over time, solidified into *objets trouvés:* the Covering Cherub has been transformed into a decorative *putto,* and belatedness itself becomes no source of terror but rather a charming opportunity to shop for antiques. In summing up the burden of the past as "so much gorgeous raw material," Ashbery makes an implicit statement against the Bloomian view of tradition. The collector is hardly embarrassed (or diminished) by the past's riches. In part, this is why Bloom's Freudian-Oedipal paradigm fails to do full justice to poets like Byron and Ashbery; we may, in fact, require a revisionary approach to the Oedipal paradigm itself. For the moment, I would adduce Melanie Klein's paper "A Contribution to the Theory of Intellectual Inhibition" (without necessarily endorsing it as a definitive replacement for Freud's; it is one interesting revision among many). In the concluding moments of the paper, Klein discusses the impulse to collect:

> ... I think that the child's compulsive, almost greedy, collection and accumulation of things (including knowledge as a substance) is based, among other factors which need not be mentioned here, upon its ever-renewed attempt ... to amass sufficient reserves inside itself to be able to resist attacks made upon it by its external objects, and if necessary to restore to its mother's body, or rather, to its objects, what it has stolen from them. (247)

That is to say, a child's feeling of self-sufficiency—or the poet's sense of literary originality—might actually be bolstered by amassing large quantities of digestible material.[17] Poems like *Don Juan* or Ashbery's *Flow Chart* could, in fact, continue forever in amassing stuff, and transforming it into the stuff of original poetry. It seems no accident that, in each of these cases, the author has established an arbitrary boundary to the fecundity: Byron claimed that he would finish with *Don Juan* after composing a hundred cantos (but did not live long enough to do so) while Ashbery claimed that he would end *Flow Chart* after reaching a hundred typewritten pages (and did). This perpetual transformation of just about anything the poet encounters into verse might seem to entail

---

[17] If anxiety lurks in this strategy, as it may—certainly no-one thinks that Melanie Klein underestimated the force of anxiety—it is not an anxiety preoccupied with Oedipal or Bloomian questions about priority; it is more likely to dwell on the possibility that what is amassed has either been overvalued or undervalued, what we might perhaps understand as the anxiety not of influence, but of taste. Klein's version of anxiety is, I think, more concerned with the self-critical workings of the poetic imagination than with what Bloom consistently emphasizes, the sheer force of the poetic *will* (to make a distinction I will explicate later).

a necessary suppression of the discriminating faculty.[18] I think Ashbery takes it on faith (a Kierkegaardianly anxious faith, perhaps) that the imagination will always somehow manage to discriminate: hence the repeated inclusion in some of his best poems of the image of being rescued at the last minute (as in "Soonest Mended" or "My Erotic Double"). The risk is always that what he writes may not turn out to be great poetry, or indeed poetry at all. Yet he writes with affectionate accuracy of Frank O'Hara's conception of poetic form as "a bag into which anything is dumped and ends up belonging there" (Ashbery, Introduction ix): to some extent this is Ashbery's method as well, and the fact that an intelligent reader would never confuse a mature poem by O'Hara with one by Ashbery suggests he is right to suppose that a poet's imagination does perform the rescue work, that his powers of aesthetic discrimination are always present and intimately related to his originality. But the heavy emphasis on the act of discrimination that one finds in canon-obsessed critics like Johnson or Bloom is wholly absent from Ashbery's sensibility; he strives only toward the acceptance, and incorporation, of things as they are found. The ethos of non-judgment recalls *Don Juan*, and is expressed throughout Ashbery's verse, as in "Houseboat Days," where he writes:

> To praise this, blame that,
> Leads one subtly away from the beginning, where
> We must stay, in motion. (*Selected* 231)

Like *Don Juan*, "Houseboat Days" argues for an end to arguments—what Ashbery (appropriating most of a long sentence from Pater's discussion of the Sophists in *Plato and Platonism*) calls "that insincerity of reasoning on behalf of one's / Sincere convictions, true or false in themselves / As the case may be, to which, if we are unwise enough / To argue at all with each other, we must be tempted / At times" (*Selected* 231; see Pater 115). Ashbery seems humanely to suggest that one's place in this world has only the status of a houseboat: habitable but with no solid foundation,

---

[18] Imperceptive critics suppose, wrongly, that this is a problem with Ashbery, and undervalue him as a result: to his detractors, a cabinet of curios may exhibit a "logic / Of strange position," but so does a garbage dump. To such critics, poetic language is defined by the avoidance of cliché, so Ashbery's frequent inclusion of cliché means that he writes something other than poetry. It is to Bloom's credit that he was the first critic who taught readers how to see beyond these pointless quibbles.

it merely drifts. Each new moment is a "beginning, where / We must stay, in motion," and one must accept such moments as an aimless wanderer accepts each new destination (*Selected* 231).[19] I suspect this sense of wandering, allied to an ethic of acceptance, is the reason for Ashbery's direct invocation of Childe Harold at the conclusion of "Houseboat Days." Linking the different styles of Byron's early work to his late work, Ian Jack reminds us that, in all Byron's greatest poems, life "is no longer portrayed as the oppression of one individual by the rest of the world working in collusion. The alternations between passages 'droll or pathetic, descriptive or sentimental, tender or satirical' which were to have been a feature of *Childe Harold* . . . are the hallmark and glory of *Don Juan*" (69–70). As if to tease out this particular feature of Byron's verse, Ashbery (addressing his beloved, one supposes) writes:

> to be with you
> In this passage, this movement, is what the instance costs:
> A sail out of some afternoon, like the clear dark blue
> Eyes of Harold in Italy, beyond amazement, astonished,
> Apparently not tampered with. (*Houseboat Days* 40; compare
> *Selected* 232)[20]

The implication here is that the Byronic hero, like the understated lyric voice of Ashbery's poems, has no choice but to accept the forward motion of a "sail out of some afternoon," even though it may leave him "astonished" but still somehow "beyond amazement."

Taking the Kleinian argument one step further, we might choose to see a poet's knowledge (or sense of literary history) as less the source of anxiety than of nourishment. Such a view (which Bloom would consider naïve) is found in nearly all the great poets whom Bloom dislikes or only weakly misreads. Often these are learned or allusive poets whose work creates a virtual *cento* of other voices, such as Thomas Gray (singled out in *The Anxiety of Influence* as an unoriginal poet whose one deepest insight somehow frightened Dr. Johnson into an inappropriately high estimate of his strength) or T. S. Eliot (constantly and tiresomely belittled by

---

[19] In "Soonest Mended," the poem which Bloom most frequently invokes, this is figured a little less cheerfully as "learning to accept / The charity of the hard moments as they are doled out" (*Selected* 89).

[20] In Ashbery's *Selected Poems*, a still-uncorrected typographical error elides the reference to Childe Harold ("like the clear dark blue / Eyes of Harold in Italy"), but this is not an authorial revision, and the text to follow here is that of the poem's 1977 publication.

Bloom, for reasons that seem more personal or political than aesthetic). In his impassioned claims for Ashbery's originality, Bloom fails to note the ways in which Ashbery is precisely like the writers he calls weak: Geoff Ward has shown how Bloom steadfastly refuses to acknowledge not just the collaborative, or collage-like, nature of Ashbery's best poems, but also their deeply ironic character. Ward argues that "Wet Casements"—which Bloom, who ranks it among the greatest achievements in American poetry, unsurprisingly reads as a hymn to solipsism—is actually a profoundly non-Bloomian performance. Given that the text of the poem is riddled with allusions to Kafka, Keats and other writers (which might seem to undercut Bloom's claims for its profound originality), and that its chief affect is one not of "sermon-like directness" (as Bloom believes) but rather of fey irony, Ward suggests that "what Bloom sees as the poem's heroic project is exactly the false idealism it most mocks. Bloom fails to see this, because he fails to see the wit in 'Wet Casements.' Indeed, he fails entirely to see the wit in any of Ashbery's work" (134). Ward is ultimately right that "Bloom's swerve away from Eliot . . . is a distorting factor in his writing on John Ashbery" which leads Bloom to deny how much Ashbery's poetry can resemble Eliot's allusive and near-satiric style, and also "cuts him off from . . . most surprisingly, Ashbery's wit" (Ward 115).

Although I have pursued a correspondence between certain basic strains in Ashbery's and Byron's poetry, Byron is not a poet with whom Ashbery has claimed any significant affinities. He is occasionally quoted, or alluded to, in Ashbery's verse, but frankly, who isn't? Yet I think we can trace a direct line of descent from Byron down to Ashbery, the sort of poetic genealogy for which Bloom has taught his readers to look. In this case, we are not rounding up the usual Bloomian suspects, though: we may safely reject the high Romantic lineage Bloom sketches, where Ashbery is son to Stevens and grandson to Whitman. In place of that, I would propose an anti-Romantic line, consisting of poets in whom Bloom has little or no interest: Ashbery's real precursor is W. H. Auden (whom Bloom detests). And Auden's mediation explains the family resemblance between Byron and Ashbery.

At this point, I must make explicit the primary assumption of my reading of Bloom: that he, like Shelley's Alastor or any other Romantic Solitary, has necessitated the manifestation of his own haunting double, just as the Magus Zoroaster (or perhaps, to recollect that old comedian whom Bloom by his own admission so uncannily resembles, the Magus Zero Mostel) met his own image walking in the garden. I mean that

Bloom's poetic canon conjures up its ineluctable parody, in which all that he has repressed must perforce return. It is a poetic canon with a genealogy as coherent and persuasive as that of his. And it must be understood by a theory antithetical to Bloom's, which makes central everything he would defend against: incest and homosexuality, plagiarism and allusion, satire and parody. Much of what he calls weak poetry is found strong in this tradition, and much of what he calls strong poetry is a part of it too, and may be read as persuasively (or more) by the methods of an antithetical theory as by those of *The Anxiety of Influence.* Indeed, the most astonishing proof of Bloom's theory is that it also proves—by all its exclusions, denials, oversights, maddening or deliberately provocative judgments, and errors—its own antithesis. The antithetical canon is one in which relations between writers are not Oedipally fraught, but refreshingly collegial: Byron openly celebrates Pope continually in his verse, and defended him in a noteworthy quarrel with Bowles; Auden himself used the *ottava rima* stanza to compose a delightful "Letter to Lord Byron;" and Ashbery's career began with substantial assistance from Auden (a fact to which I will return). What is perhaps most remarkable about all these literary interrelations is that, while the debt of each later writer to his precursor is clear, it has not interfered at all in the individuation of poetic style; even as we see how Byron learned certain of his tricks at the knee of Pope, we also marvel that the author of *Manfred*, or even of *Don Juan*, should have deemed himself a Popean. And if we wish to trace back this genealogy beyond Pope, then we find that this Other Tradition begins precisely where Bloom's does, with Milton; but we must accept Milton in his entirety, rather than tendentiously focusing (as Bloom does) on a few similes and the speeches of Satan. Reducing *Paradise Lost* to Satan may have seemed, to Bloom, the most Romantic gesture—but it leads him later to the critically useless approach of reading Milton as an ephebe of Shakespeare. If nothing else, Bloom's later judgment of Milton in *The Western Canon* betokens a significant shift in his thought generally: he replaces a genealogy of strong poetry with a genealogy of 'great books,' many of which are novels and thus inexplicable to his theory of poetry, and consequently he is forced into a debased understanding of originality altogether, defined not in terms of a writer's individual *style* (which at least can be discussed in a somewhat empirical fashion) but in terms of *mythopoesis* (which may fit in with his increasing interest in the criticism of religion, but which makes too great a claim for what literature actually does) or else *sublimity* (which is so subjective a category as to impoverish critical discussion altogether). It is these aspects of *The Western Canon* (or all Bloom's subsequent work) that make it so jejune as a work of criticism. But if we concentrate on those bits of *Paradise Lost* that Bloom neglects, we discover (for example) a Milton whose description of the War in Heaven is mock-epic, and precisely prefigures Pope's *Dunciad* and "Rape of the Lock."

I am persuaded, as many are not, by Bloom's ways of reading and understanding the poems he loves. But if I may lapse into the sort of quasi-religious phrasemaking to which Bloom at his worst is susceptible, I have also discovered of my own taste that, invariably, the stones which Bloom rejected have become my touchstones. They comprise an Other Tradition: sociable, where Bloom's is solipsistic; frequently anti-Romantic, where Bloom claims all strong post-Miltonic poets must be Romantic; often (as with Donne, Pope, Eliot or Auden) a Catholic or Anglo-Catholic tradition, where Bloom initially characterized his tradition (following Frye and Abrams) as staunchly Protestant, and more recently as Gnostic; and always pursuing a revisionary intent untroubled by the anxiety of an influence.

In establishing a criticism antithetical to Bloom's, we must recall the insight of Denis Donoghue, who provides in *Ferocious Alphabets* the strongest criticism of Bloom's basic assumptions that I have encountered:

> ... [T]o Bloom, poetry is not a form of knowledge but a form of action .... [H]e refuses to distinguish between imagination and will: will subsumes imagination in every case. As it is bound to do. Bloom wants to find in the poem an agon of a particular kind; he has already sketched its plot. So he forces the reading away from any attribute of the poem that might testify to knowledge, contemplation, appreciation, perception, or wisdom; these are of little account .... But ... if you allow the imagination to become subsumed in the will, you relegate to some Limbo the association of imagination with creativity, the making of poetic objects, structures in some sense distinguishable from the poet's creatural self. In Bloom's criticism, a creative faculty is acknowledged, though I can't recall any occasion on which the acknowledgment is joyously made .... It is a defect of the will, and not of the imagination, that it is too completely, too insistently, itself: that is why the will, great as it is, is incapable of criticizing itself, as the imagination is wonderfully capable. (139–45)

I think this argument confirms much of what I have said about the Other Tradition, and the antithetical theory by which we must learn to read it; but let me disavow any claims to originality in this argument, because I have in fact taken the idea of an "Other Tradition" from Ashbery himself. Although this phrase first occurs in his 1972 book *Three Poems* (a year before Bloom published *The Anxiety of Influence*), thereafter it acquires a real significance when it provides the title for one of his very best individual poems from the 1977 volume *Houseboat Days* (where it is undoubtedly a specific response to Bloom). After that, "An Other Tradition" was the overall title of Ashbery's 1990 Charles Eliot Norton Lectures, delivered at Harvard University, which celebrated a host of fascinating non-canonical poets and writers such as Raymond Roussel, Laura Riding and Thomas Lovell Beddoes. When the lectures were published a decade later by Harvard University Press, Ashbery amended his title yet once more, to *Other Traditions*. It is telling that, over the course of almost thirty years of toying with the little phrase, Ashbery has slowly backed away from the initial, near-Bloomian claim to canon-making, and says in *Other Traditions* that he "regretted" it (4): if at first he hoists the defiant flag of the definite article, he later modestly changes it to the indefinite, and finally settles on the quiet acknowledgement of a plurality of different tastes. Because Ashbery's writings on the "Other Tradition" are, in fact, intimately related to Bloom's work, I think it is no accident that he followed such a trajectory over the thirty-year period in which both he and Bloom first established and then maintained their reputations, and in which they read and responded to each other's work. If Ashbery has gradually settled into a gentle humility, acknowledging "other traditions" in general, Bloom has run in the opposite direction: starting with the revolutionary theory of *The Anxiety of Influence* and its elaboration in his next few books, Bloom moved on to ever-grander claims for his powers as the arbiter of the canonical, in books like *The Western Canon* (1994) and in his prefaces to the Chelsea House library of literary criticism, then finally, bathetically, sinking into his pitiful current role: a latter-day Mortimer J. Adler garbed in the ill-fitting mantle of Ecclesiastes, author of books like *How To Read and Why* (2000) or *Where Shall Wisdom Be Found?* (2004), wherein Bloom tries to do for great authors what Liberace did for great composers.

Ashbery has the distinction of being the first living poet whose critical reputation was established by Bloom. I understand Ashbery's evocation of the "Other Tradition" as a response to a critic who has cheerfully admitted that all his readings are misreadings. Although Bloom's esteem may be flattering, Ashbery wants to assert the taste, and criteria, whereby his work may be seen for what it really is, and as something more (and stranger) than the illustration of another man's theory: the effort, as Geoff Ward has noted, is made "partly in order to conjure what looks like a more friendly but also more Surrealistic gallery of literary aunts and uncles than cultivators of the family tree, such as Bloom, tend to offer" (120). Ward's invocation of avuncular presences recalls the most central error in Bloom's misreading of Ashbery: his denial of Auden as Ashbery's major precursor. Bloom has claimed (in an essay on James Merrill) that, for the strong poets of Bloom's generation in America, Auden is no real precursor at all, however frequently they wish to claim him as one. He writes:

> Though W. H. Auden is invoked throughout Merrill's epic, both as sage and as archetype of the poet, his example and career seem to play the same part in Merrill as in Ashbery. He is a benign presence for both, precisely because he is not the true father, but more like an amiable uncle on the mother's side, as it were. Stevens, the veritable precursor, is a very dangerous poetic father, whether one takes after his very formal self, as Merrill does, or comes up out of his repressed Whitmanian depths, which is Ashbery's authentic origin. (Bloom, Merrill 2)

Since Bloom thinks perverse willful misprision is a good thing, I do not insult him by calling this judgment willfully perverse. What reader could ever discern a "formal self" in Wallace Stevens to compare with the Auden of countless sestinas and canzones, not to mention the most noteworthy *tour-de-force* of poetic formalism in modern English poetry, *The Sea and the Mirror*? Obviously Auden is the authentic precursor of James Merrill, a poet who always addressed even his most philosophical concerns not with Stevensian abstraction, but with Popean wit and grace. So too is Auden the precursor of Ashbery.

Perhaps, in the Other Tradition we have been examining, "precursor" may not actually be the synonym for "father," as it is in Bloom's lexicon; there is a truly sublime joke in Bloom's analysis of Auden here, a joke I wonder whether he consciously intended. Here is the punchline: Auden himself actually wrote a major poem (*The Orators*) which outlines a proof that one's maternal uncle can, in fact, be a truer ancestor than one's own father. Bloom hates Auden too much (as a symbol of the neo-Christian Eliotic criticism which his own writings have worked so hard to supplant) ever to mention *The Orators*; indeed I doubt he has read it, or remembered it sufficiently, to be alluding to it above. So Bloom's invocation of a bachelor "uncle" is probably not a recollection of Auden's; but in the long second section of *The Orators*, "Journal of an Airman," Auden's protagonist asserts that "[t]he true ancestral line is not necessarily a straight or continuous one" (*English Auden* 78). He follows up this statement with a list of Mendelian genetic charts, in an attempt to demonstrate that (given the distribution of dominant and recessive genes over consecutive generations) his closest ancestor is his mother's brother, the homosexual bachelor Uncle Henry: of all potential genotypes, they alone share the combination of two recessives. One supposes this may be the genetic code for homosexuality, since that is what the Airman and his uncle have in common. To some extent, this little fantasia smacks of the gay man's search for origins and family; it is certainly a nice fantasy to imagine that Uncle Henry, who would never father any biological children, could nonetheless produce a real and true son in Auden's Airman. And homosexuality is what Bloom knowingly calls to mind, by using the image of a bachelor uncle. I don't think it is intended as a slur—what reader does not think of Auden as a bachelor uncle? Bloom is being coy, but he is not being homophobic. Rather, I think he groping for a way out of his honest bafflement as to why two such strong poets as Ashbery and Merrill profess devotion to a writer Bloom loathes. The answer, he suspects, is that surely all three are gay, and on that basis, surely birds of a feather will flock together—even if, by Bloom's aesthetic criteria, two sublime swans could never have hatched from the egg of an ugly duck.

To some degree, I think Bloom's half-articulated suspicion is correct: the gay male milieu of these poets might account for their construction of a genealogy that contradicts his own. After all, Ashbery *knew* Auden.[21] Even more tellingly, Auden arranged for the publication of Ashbery's first book, by selecting it as the winner of a Yale University Press competition. But Auden's reasons for choosing it had more to do with their gay subculture than with his sense of Ashbery's aesthetic merit: after reading the finalists for the competition, Auden decided not to award the prize at all. Ashbery's manuscript, *Some Trees,* had not been a finalist: with Frank O'Hara's manuscript, it had been screened out by a faceless initial reader at the Yale press. At this point, news of Auden's refusal to award the prize, and news of Ashbery's and O'Hara's rejection in the first round, was relayed in either direction: gay subculture has, after all, perfected gossip as one of the fine arts (and surely Chester Kallman was the Giotto who discovered its third dimension). So

---

[21] Even, on one occasion which he has referred to as "the worst night of my life," knew him in the same sense as Satan knew Sin—but nobody has ever denied that Ashbery was a wise child indeed.

Auden sent word along the grapevine that the two younger gay poets should send him their manuscripts, deciding to give the prize to whichever he preferred, before reading either. He chose Ashbery, but Ashbery says (in an unpublished interview quoted by David Kermani) that "I never felt that he particularly liked my poetry, and the introduction to the book is rather curious, since it doesn't really talk about the poetry. He mentions me as being a kind of successor to Rimbaud, which is flattering, but at the same time I've always had the feeling that Auden probably never read Rimbaud" (6).[22] To that degree, Bloom's suspicion is certainly correct where Auden is concerned: the affinities were not so much aesthetic as sociable. But on Ashbery's part, the affinity was primarily and overwhelmingly an aesthetic one. I think Auden knew this; and I think Auden's introduction to *Some Trees* was ambivalent because the book is so heavily indebted to work that Auden had repudiated by that time, especially *The Orators*, which Auden disavowed and refused to reprint but which Ashbery names as his favorite. It is shocking, actually, to read *The Orators* after reading *Some Trees*: it could provide a stunning illustration of *apophrades* for Bloom, were it not for the fact that Bloom has already offered a reading of poems from *Some Trees* in *The Anxiety of Influence*, a reading which intends to prove by sheer force of will that the book is, in fact, influenced by Stevens.

Bloom is not completely wrong: there is a Stevensian element in Ashbery. But it is bizarre (and a little poignant) to watch Bloom stumbling through Ashbery's work, hunting the ghost of Stevens through countless rooms and hallways, in which large gilt-framed cartoons of Auden are tastefully hung. Then again, there is a basic difference between Bloom's theory of influence and my own here: to the poets of the Other Tradition, a cartoon is often more important than a ghost. Auden claimed, famously, that the only proper writing assignment for an undergraduate was pastiche. Imitation by caricature is often the sincerest form of critique: it requires both a sensitive attention to, and an ironic distance from, the author parodied. It can even comprise the best sort of literary criticism, just as Bloom's hero Empson was never more astute than in the parody-poem he entitled "Just a Smack at Auden." More significantly, Auden's sense of pastiche

[22] Ashbery retells this story, as a demonstration of "the precariousness of our [i.e. poets'] careers" in the final chapter of *Other Traditions*, then quotes from what he deems the definitive poetic statement about this precariousness: the speech of Caliban in Auden's *The Sea and the Mirror* (*Other* 123–24; see Auden, *Collected* 325–40).

as the first step in a writer's education recognizes in poetic style a mode of individuation and originality much more sociable than the solipsism of Bloomian misprision. One remarkable feature of Auden's literary criticism was that he was forever regarding other writers as social presences. This example is from a short introductory essay on George Herbert:

> There are some [poets], like Byron, whom I would like to have met once, but most, I feel, would either, like Dante and Goethe, have been too intimidating, or, like Wordsworth, too disagreeable. The two English poets, neither of them, perhaps, major poets, whom I would most like to have known well are William Barnes and George Herbert.
> Even if Isaak Walton had never written his life, I think that any reader of his poetry will conclude that George Herbert must have been an exceptionally good man, and exceptionally nice as well. (Auden, Introduction 7)

Such an emphasis on the social presences of canonical writers might be a bit precious, but I find it a useful corrective to Bloom's distasteful emphasis on solipsism. It also more truly reflects the way in which a writer becomes important to his readers. It may not be serious criticism, but it does betoken an admirable critical large-heartedness. And even in those cases where Auden was not so generous—Ashbery in *Other Traditions* specifically refers to one instance, one which probably accounts for Bloom's unceasing resentment of Auden, when Auden claimed that "I cannot enjoy one poem by Shelley" (7)—we can also comprehend his reasons. After all, who (save Bloom) would want to be seated next to Shelley at a dinner party? Or else, to be less harsh, let me simply say that, at my own dinner party, I know enough not to seat Shelley next to Auden—but unlike Bloom, I would invite both.

Sociability also hints at the prospect of writerly collaboration. Both Ashbery and Auden have written enough works in collaboration that it seems an important part of their procedure. But collaboration is another aspect of writing which has no place in Bloom's model, even though many works he values (*Lyrical Ballads* comes to mind, as does Yeats's *A Vision*) were produced collaboratively; even Shakespeare himself worked with collaborators on occasion. Bloom holds to a belief that social energies do not write poems, only poets do. I admire his emphasis on the creative faculty, in full opposition to so much bad criticism and theory produced nowadays; but it is foolish to insist that, to be original, the poet must be solipsistic and haunted by a single precursor. To lay a greater emphasis on the social than Bloom does, while nonetheless asserting the importance of a writer's revisionary intent, allows us to maintain the sense (lost in the worst sorts of academic criticism) that some poems are better than others, and that criticism should attend to the better sort—but it also allows us to provide a much-needed feminist or queer corrective to Bloom's readings.

To elaborate on the latter of these, I would emphasize in particular the sociable relationship between Auden and Ashbery in order to highlight Bloom's frequent inability to make an Oedipal paradigm work for gay writers. I acknowledge the value, and the persuasiveness, that his paradigm exhibits as a theory for some poetry. But as a tool for understanding the actual psychology of a human being—let alone a contemporary gay man—the Oedipal paradigm may be confidently rejected as pernicious nonsense.[23] In my reading, Bloom's weaknesses as a critic of twentieth-century verse are consistent with his inability to appreciate camp. Bloom has traced his own cathexis onto poetry to a single event: receiving a copy of Hart Crane's *Collected Poems* as a gift when he was ten years old. I would suggest, flippantly perhaps, but not unjustly, that the most deeply ingrained failures of Bloom's method are directly due to his status as a heterosexual man who formed his sensibilities on Crane's poetry.[24] For even though the extravagance of gesture in Crane often seems Shelleyan, it is even better understood as rococo, camp, an overwrought and hysterical pose. For all Bloom's adoration of Crane, and claims on behalf of his sublimity, it is curious that he can find no ephebe for Crane save Tennessee Williams. Williams's affinity for the poet is hardly an example of Oedipal wrestling; if there is a genealogical relation here, it is that of an *infanta* who longs to wear the tiara of her precursor, the old queen. It demonstrates a version of literary inheritance where style is not reaction-formation, but a drag act: self-dramatized, potentially bathetic, often a literal travesty. How else are we to understand Williams's desire to be buried at sea, in the precise spot where Crane committed suicide, except that Williams's crush on Crane was sufficiently strong that, even in death, he thought pretending to be Crane provided the role of a lifetime.

---

[23] Plenty of gay men would like to kill their fathers, to be sure, but not for the purpose of copulating with their mothers: we'd much rather take her shopping.

[24] It's like watching the exquisite spectacle of Lionel Trilling expounding on Forster.

I do not idly invoke images of theatricality here, because theatricality itself is central to my understanding of parody overall. Earlier I referred to Borges' well-known fable, "Pierre Menard, Author of the *Quixote*," in which the belated writer summons all his creative energies to write, as if it were his own original creation, a text perfectly identical to Cervantes' novel. Menard manages to produce only a few passages of his *Quixote* before his death; but Borges tells us (with a little close reading) how Menard's work actually differs from its great original. Intention, reception, style are all deemed original when their authorship by a twentieth-century writer is known. Here, the idea of originality requires specific reference to the social context implied by belatedness.[25] One can marvel a long time at the paradoxes suggested by Borges' fable, dwelling upon the questions it asks about an artist's originality, but I would like to offer a misreading of Borges by asking a question of my own: how might we understand the originality of Menard, or of Cervantes, if they were not writers but actors, and if the text they had in common was not *Don Quixote* but the lead role in *Hamlet*? If that were so, the artist's profession seems less like an effort to solidify his ego in the monument of a fully-individuated style, and more like the constant attempt to locate that ego in styles it did not create. This may sound like postmodernism. I would prefer to think of it as metempsychosis—the transmigration of an eternal artistic soul, generation after generation, into stylistic or rhetorical bodies that are never wholly its own, although its only expression depends upon its willingness to inhabit and animate them. As a mystical or religious model for the parodic theory of originality, this is at least as old as Ovid, and explains the originality of Shakespeare far better than Bloom can. In our antithetical theory, we may allow this to take the place of any Gnostic faith in a self-authored artistic soul that knows it predates

---

[25] Bloom by contrast provides a historicism obsessed with belatedness, but almost wholly uninterested in social context: this seems a major error, particularly in attempting to define a uniquely American sublime. An American writer like Ashbery seems not so much Pierre Menard as Rip Van Winkle, or Twain's Connecticut Yankee in King Arthur's court; without the social context of a long-established native tradition, the writer finds himself wandering freely, an innocent abroad in the museums and galleries which showcase past glories of other traditions. I do not think this is merely an American attitude; it is also a way to understand the classicism of Pope, or even the methods of a supposedly Romantic poet like Thomas Lovell Beddoes, adored by Ashbery and singled out by that other innocent abroad, Ezra Pound, as an example of how a poet may write great work in a style that is wholly borrowed.

everything else and seeks to find its truest expression by breaking through the husks of demiurgically-devised physical or rhetorical matter (which assert an illusory or false priority). For a Pythagorean, rather than a Gnostic, the physical things of the created world are not the soul's obstacle, but its only means of expression. No single style, or body, may satisfy fully its urge to self-expression—like the collector of curios, it wants to find ways of expressing itself through many different objects; like the actor, it must be counted a failure if it is not supple enough to play a number of different parts, and yet always be recognizable as itself. As Ashbery writes in "Clepsydra:"

> Each moment
> Of utterance is the true one; likewise none are true,
> Only is the bounding from air to air, a serpentine
> Gesture which hides the truth behind a congruent
> Message.... (*Selected* 63)

If the Gnostic soul expresses itself through sheer force of will to arrive permanently at a place where it always was, the Pythagorean soul expresses itself through the inexhaustible variety of its imagination, forever migrating but never arriving anywhere at all, still always and ineluctably itself no matter what shape it takes.

I hope my foregoing attempt to parody even the most bewildering and overwrought elements of Bloom's theory—and his grandest heresiarchical aspirations—has not led us too far astray from the high spirits of the Other Tradition, and how irreverently it performs the work of revisionary originality through sociability and wit. For a reminder of this, we may turn to a poem that offers a more aesthetically distinguished, but equally knowing parody of Bloom: Ashbery's "The Other Tradition" (I crave the reader's indulgence in quoting the full text). My reading of the poem will require knowledge of one additional fact. When Ashbery first wrote this poem, but before he published it, he sent it as a letter to Bloom (a fact confirmed to me by both men in conversation):

The Other Tradition

They all came, some wore sentiments
Emblazoned on T-shirts, proclaiming the lateness
Of the hour, and indeed the sun slanted its rays
Through branches of Norfolk Island pine as though
Politely clearing its throat, and all ideas settled

In a fuzz of dust under trees when it's drizzling:
The endless games of Scrabble, the boosters,
The celebrated omelette au Cantal, and through it
The roar of time plunging unchecked through the sluices
Of the days, dragging every sexual moment of it
Past the lenses: the end of something.
Only then did you glance up from your book,
Unable to comprehend what had been taking place, or
Say what you had been reading. More chairs
Were brought, and lamps were lit, but it tells
Nothing of how all this proceeded to materialize
Before you and the people waiting outside and in the next
Street, repeating its name over and over, until silence
Moved halfway up the darkened trunks,
And the meeting was called to order.
                              I still remember
How they found you, after a dream, in your thimble hat,
Studious as a butterfly in a parking lot.
The road home was nicer then. Dispersing, each of the
Troubadours had something to say about how charity
Had run its race and won, leaving you the ex-president
Of the event, and how, though many of those present
Had wished something to come of it, if only a distant
Wisp of smoke, yet none was so deceived as to hanker
After that cool non-being of just a few minutes before,
Now that the idea of a forest had clamped itself
Over the minutiae of the scene. You found this
Charming, but turned your face fully toward night,
Speaking into it like a megaphone, not hearing
Or caring, although these still live and are generous
And all ways contained, allowed to come and go
Indefinitely in and out of the stockade
They have so much trouble remembering, when your forgetting
Rescues them at last, as a star absorbs the night. (*Selected* 208–09)

I do not know if Bloom responded by sending a letter back to Ashbery. But he did respond to this poem as a critic, and certainly understood the challenge to his theory that it represents. Bloom writes in *Agon:* "I am aware that this charming poem urbanely confronts, absorbs and in some sense seeks to overthrow a critical theory, almost a critical climate, that has accorded it a canonical status" (198). I admire Bloom's decision to be charmed rather than affronted here, when even so gentle a satire as Ashbery's must have (as all satire does) some aggression at its core. It is as though Jackson Pollock had responded to Clement Greenberg's enthusiastically expansive critical claims on his behalf with a portrait of Greenberg, painted in his most characteristic style, but intended purely to deflate the adoring critic's most grandiose pretensions—and afterward, as though Greenberg had raved about the portrait in the *Partisan Review*. Bloom's subsequent misreading of the poem is instructive and characteristic, though. He argues that, in Ashbery's figuration here,

> ... poetic tradition becomes an ill-organized social meeting of troubadours, leaving the canonical Ashbery as "ex-president / Of the event." As for the image of voice proper, the Whitmanian confrontation of the night now declines into: "You found this / Charming, but turned your face fully toward night, / Speaking into it like a megaphone, not hearing / Or caring." Such a megaphone is an apt image for Paul de Man's deconstructionist view of poetic tradition, which undoes tradition by suggesting that every poem is as much a random and gratuitous event as any human death is.
>
> Ashbery's implicit interpretation of what he wants to call *The Other Tradition* mediates between this vision of poems as being totally cut off from one another and the antithetical darkness in which poems carry over-determined relationships and progress towards a final entropy. (*Agon* 198–99)

But this underestimates the social nature of the poem. Ashbery sent it as a letter addressed to Bloom: as such it is a communication, a connection between people, a social gesture and not a hermetic realization of the lyric poet's implacable solipsism.[26] There is also a major error in Bloom's reading here, one which occurs throughout his criticism of Ashbery: he invariably assumes that the "you" of an Ashbery poem refers to Ashbery himself. It is interesting to note that frequently the use of the second person in poems is a technique for gay writers to avoid 'coming out' in a poem; whether the writer is claiming "I've got you under my skin," or exhorting "lay your sleeping head, my love" or, in one of its more strained manifestations, Tennessee Williams's poem "Life Story," telling the story of a specifically homosexual encounter in the second person. Ashbery's use of pronouns is notoriously whimsical, although he has expressed a preference for the second person over "the eternal 'we' with which so many modern poets automatically begin

---

[26] Its inclusion in a letter might, I think, even recall Frank O'Hara's famous witty manifesto for "Personism:" "I was realizing that if I wanted to I could use the telephone instead of writing the poem, and so Personism was born.... It puts the poem squarely between the poet and the person, Lucky Pierre style, and the poem is correspondingly gratified. The poem is at last between two persons instead of two pages" (499).

each sentence, and which gives the impression that the author is sharing his every sensation with some invisible Kim Novak" ("Impossible" 250). We must seek the referents for Ashbery's pronouns on an *ad hoc* basis, I think; and in this case, the poem has a specific addressee. Contrary to Bloom's reading of "The Other Tradition," the best candidate for the "ex-president / Of the event" described in the poem is not John Ashbery but Harold Bloom himself. This poem is about him, a fact Bloom squirms to avoid in his reading.

The social milieu depicted in the poem, with its "Norfolk Island pine," its "endless games of Scrabble" and "celebrated omelette au Cantal," has always seemed to me a dreamlike evocation of the afterlife as Fire Island: it is no wonder that Bloom might feel a little out of place here. The poem dramatizes a confrontation between the mode of Bloom and the mode of Frank O'Hara, killed in a freakish dune-buggy accident on Fire Island. Bloom himself has very little interest in O'Hara's verse, dismissing him rather brusquely with the claim (in one essay) that "Ashbery has been misunderstood because of his association with the 'New York School' of Kenneth Koch, Frank O'Hara, and other comedians of the spirit" (Ashbery 5). In singling out Ashbery for canonical status, Bloom has unwillingly slighted those poets and friends whom Ashbery loves best, the contemporaries and collaborators, predominantly gay, elegized in "Soonest Mended."

Let us look closer at Ashbery's snapshot of Bloom on Fire Island. It is only when the "roar of time"—the sound of belatedness—is heard that Bloom "glance[s] up from [his] book," and, regarding the gay milieu of Ashbery and his friends, is "[u]nable to comprehend what had been taking place, or / Say what [he] had been reading" (*Selected* 208). Ashbery's critique of Bloom then reaches its ultimate point: as the social gathering around Bloom grows ("More chairs / Were brought"), the critic is denied knowledge of origins ("it tells / Nothing of how all this proceeded to materialize / Before you"). Faced with this kind of "other tradition," Bloom can only respond by imposing, upon the loose disorder of a genial social reality, the artificial structure of canon-formation: "the meeting was called to order." Bloom is granted nothing but a "thimble hat:" small and protective, designed to keep things out, much like his canon. Of the poets who, like Ashbery, have been admitted into Bloom's canon, "none was so deceived as to hanker / After that cool nonbeing of just a few minutes before"—Bloom's critical appreciation has, after all, established their careers as poets, given them "being," and Ashbery is not so churlish as to bite too savagely the hand that feeds him. Yet Ashbery cannot accept the fact that Bloom's criticism willfully ignores so much: it is like "the idea of a forest" which "clamp[s] itself / Over the minutiae of the scene," consciously recalling the cliché of not being able to see the forest for the trees. Bloom, with his "idea of a forest," a grand and canonical governing idea which "clamp[s] itself" onto the historical "minutiae" of literary communities, is unable even to see some trees (or *Some Trees*): even if Bloom generously grants critical approval to one poet like Ashbery, he also ignores so many poets whom Ashbery loves, avuncular presences like Auden, Beddoes or Raymond Roussel, and beloved contemporaries like O'Hara or James Schuyler. Bloom may on occasion be willing to concede that poets like O'Hara are "[c]harming," but he has "turned [his] face" and his critical appreciation away from these non-canonical writers nevertheless. Poets like O'Hara are therefore "contained;" they are not included in the canon but are "allowed to come and go / Indefinitely in and out of the stockade / They have so much trouble remembering," that large and undiscriminating space to which Bloom consigns the writers of the Other Tradition (*Selected* 209). Bloom has not admitted O'Hara into the canon. But the poem's final gesture is poignantly to trope O'Hara's exclusion—the exclusion of all such poets of the Other Tradition—as salvation: Bloom's "forgetting / Rescues them at last, as a star absorbs the night."[27]

Ashbery prefers an inclusiveness that will find a place in tradition for one's beloved friends as readily as it admits all the accidents of experience and of history. Forward motion is the key, as Ashbery seems to indicate in what is, perhaps, my favorite of all his poems, "Daffy Duck in Hollywood." Bloom has never commented on this poem, but it represents the fullest and most authentic expression of Ashbery's style, perhaps unto the point of self-parody: he even makes a joke of his own masterpiece, "Self-Portrait in a Convex Mirror," with Daffy Duck's reference to "me mug's attenuated / Reflection in yon hubcap" (*Selected* 227). At the close of this poem, Ashbery offers (with perhaps an implicit swipe at Bloom's parroting of the Nietzschean injunction to "try to live as though it were morning") his own view of tradition as forward motion, here expressed with a rare and plangent urgency:

> Morning is
> Impermanent. Grab sex things, swing up

---

[27] I noted earlier the centrality of this trope of rescue to Ashbery's method: here, he extends it generally toward a poet's canonicity, recalling again the sense he finds in Auden of "the precariousness of our careers" (*Other* 123).

> Over the horizon like a boy
> On a fishing expedition. No one really knows
> Or cares whether this is the whole of which parts
> Were vouchsafed—once—but to be ambling on's
> The tradition more than the safekeeping of it. (*Selected* 230)

The text of "Daffy Duck" provides such a masterful catalogue of bizarre details—what the anthologist could only summarize as "an American Everything"—because the poet is always "ambling on." In *Flow Chart*, the late flowering of the parodic mode of "Daffy Duck," Ashbery had considered making the Flaubertian confession, "Daffy Duck, c'est moi" (this confession did not ultimately appear in the published text). I think we can see the truth at which this confession hints. Daffy Duck's parodies and jokes, catalogues and collections provide the truer portrait of the artist, much as Ashbery's "Self-Portrait in a Convex Mirror" is a work of connoisseurship, not autobiography: the self-portrait is that of Parmigianino, and Ashbery finds himself in it.

In "Daffy Duck in Hollywood," the critical history I have been sketching of the Other Tradition also ends precisely where it began, for Ashbery has admitted that the genesis of "Daffy Duck in Hollywood" was, in fact, Milton's Satan:

> I went to a program of animated cartoons at a museum in New York a year or so ago and at the same time I was reading *Paradise Lost.* There was a Daffy Duck cartoon in which you see the pencil of the cartoonist sort of adding extra limbs and erasing the head and various parts . . . and I somehow subconsciously associated this with the idea of God in the first book of *Paradise Lost*, who has always seemed to me very comically conspicuous by his absence . . . . So I seemed to have somehow associated Satan with Daffy Duck . . . . They are somewhat alike. (qtd. in Shoptaw 203)

Satan, archetype of the modern poet at his strongest, is invoked by Ashbery as the postmodern permeability of consciousness. It may be true that, in Ashbery's guilty admission "Daffy Duck, c'est moi," there is a moving statement of the Miltonic and Romantic investment of the author in his protagonist. But this statement is itself couched in the form of a parody of Flaubert's prior statement about such investment, and, as such, is a pretty funny joke, too. Like many poets, Ashbery is part of Bloom's tradition even as he is part of the Other Tradition as well; and Ashbery's *oeuvre* is canonical insofar as, like everything else in the canon, it seems to us both Bloomianly ambitious or solipsistic and ironic, knowing, incestuous, precious, fun, by turns.

Works Cited

Ashbery, John. *Flow Chart*. New York: Knopf, 1991.
—. *Houseboat Days: Poems*. Harmondsworth: Penguin, 1977.
—. "The Impossible." Rev. of *Stanzas in Meditation*, by Gertrude Stein. *Poetry* 90.4 (July 1957): 250–54.
—. Introduction. O'Hara vii–xii.
—. *Other Traditions*. Charles Eliot Norton Lectures. Cambridge, MA: Harvard UP, 2000.
—. *Selected Poems*. New York: Viking Penguin, 1985.
—. *The Tennis Court Oath: A Book of Poems*. Middletown, CT: Wesleyan UP, 1962.
—. *Three Poems*. 1972. Harmondsworth: Penguin, 1977.
—. *Wakefulness*. New York: Farrar, 1998.
—. "To a Waterfowl." *Locus Solus* 2 (1961): 7.
—. and James Schuyler. *A Nest of Ninnies*. New York: Dutton, 1969.
Auden, W. H. *Collected Poems*. Ed. Edward Mendelson. New York: Random House, 1976.
—. *The English Auden: Poems, Essays, and Dramatic Writings, 1927–1939*. Ed. Edward Mendelson. London: Faber, 1977.
—. Introduction. Herbert 7–13.
Bentley, Richard, ed. *Paradise Lost*. By John Milton. Anglistica and Americana 175. Hildesheim: Olms, 1995.
Borges, Jorge Luis. "Pierre Menard, Author of the *Quixote*." *Collected Fictions*. Trans. Andrew Hurley. New York: Viking, 1998. 88–95.
Burke, Edmund. *A Philosophical Enquiry into the Origin of Our Ideas of the Sublime and Beautiful*. Ed. J. T. Boulton. New York: Oxford UP, 1990.
Byron, George Gordon, Lord. *Byron's Poetry*. Ed. Frank D. McConnell. New York: Norton, 1978.

—. *Don Juan*. Ed. T. G. Steffan, et al. Penguin English Poets. Harmondsworth: Penguin, 1973.

Carey, John. "Milton's Satan." *The Cambridge Companion to Milton*. Ed. Dennis Danielson. New York: Cambridge UP, 1989. 131–45.

Cowper, William. Commentary. *Milton*. Ed. Cowper. 4 vols. Chichester: J. Johnson, 1810.

Donoghue, Denis. *Ferocious Alphabets*. 1981. New York: Columbia UP, 1984.

Fletcher, Angus. *Allegory: The Theory of a Symbolic Mode*. Ithaca: Cornell UP, 1964.

Freud, Sigmund. "Family Romances." *The Standard Edition of the Complete Psychological Works of Sigmund Freud*. Trans. and ed. James Strachey, et al. Vol. 9. London: Hogarth, 1959. 235–41.

Hartman, Geoffrey H. *Beyond Formalism: Literary Essays, 1958–1970*. New Haven: Yale UP, 1970.

Herbert, George. *George Herbert*. Ed. W. H. Auden. Poet to Poet. Harmondsworth: Penguin, 1973.

Herd, David. "John Ashbery in Conversation with David Herd." *PN Review* [Manchester] 21.1 (Sept.-Oct. 1994): 32–37.

Jack, Ian. *English Literature, 1815–1832*. Oxford History of English Literature 10. Oxford: Clarendon, 1963.

Johnson, Samuel. "Milton." Milton 521–34.

Joyce, James. *Ulysses*. Ed. Hans Walter Gabler, et al. New York: Random House, 1986.

Kermani, David K. *John Ashbery: A Comprehensive Bibliography, Including His Art Criticism, and with Selected Notes from Unpublished Materials*. Garland Reference Library of the Humanities 14. New York: Garland, 1976.

Klein, Melanie. "A Contribution to the Theory of Intellectual Inhibition." *Love, Guilt and Reparation, and Other Works: 1921–1945*. Ed. Hanna Segal. Writings of Melanie Klein 1. 1975. London: Virago, 1988. 236–47.

Marchand, Leslie A. *Byron: A Portrait*. 1970. Chicago: U of Chicago P, 1979.

McConnell, Frank D. "Byron as Antipoet." Byron, *Byron's Poetry* 418–31.

Milton, John. *Paradise Lost*. Ed. Scott Elledge. Norton Critical Editions. New York: Norton, 1975.

Newlyn, Lucy. Paradise Lost *and the Romantic Reader*. Oxford: Clarendon, 1993.

O'Hara, Frank. *Collected Poems*. Ed. Donald Allen. Berkeley: U of California P, 1995.

O'Neill, Eugene. *Long Day's Journey into Night*. Rev. ed. New Haven: Yale UP, 1989.

Pater, Walter. *Plato and Platonism: A Series of Lectures*. 3rd ed. London: Macmillan, 1910.

Rawson, Claude. *Satire and Sentiment, 1660–1830*. Cambridge: Cambridge UP, 1994.

Rose, Margaret. *Parody: Ancient, Modern, and Post-Modern*. Cambridge: Cambridge UP, 1993.

Shakespeare, William. *Hamlet*. Ed. G. R. Hibbard. Oxford Shakespeare. Oxford: Clarendon, 1987.

Shelley, Percy Bysshe. *The Poetical Works*. Ed. Newell F. Ford. New York: Houghton Mifflin, 1974.

—. *Shelley's Poetry and Prose*. Ed. Donald H. Reiman and Sharon B. Powers. Norton Critical Editions. New York: Norton, 1977.

Shoptaw, John. *On the Outside Looking Out: John Ashbery's Poetry*. Cambridge, MA: Harvard UP, 1994.

Sontag, Susan. "Notes on 'Camp.'" *Against Interpretation, and Other Essays*. New York: Farrar, 1966. 275–92.

Southey, Robert. *The Poetical Works*. 10 vols. Boston: Little, Brown, 1863.

Spenser, Edmund. *The Faerie Queene*. Ed. Thomas P. Roche, Jr. Penguin English Poets. Harmondsworth: Penguin, 1978.

Ward, Geoff. *Statutes of Liberty: The New York School of Poets*. Basingstoke: Macmillan, 1993.

Williams, Tennessee. *Collected Poems*. Ed. David Roessel and Nicholas Moschovakis. New York: New Directions, 2002.

How I Learned to Write Without Footnotes

María Rosa Menocal

1

I keep telling myself I didn't really think this was going to be an easy piece to write. And I keep making longer and longer lists of the Bloom events that have filled New York this fall, events I can say I was wanting to be able to include in this article. And I can count, no longer on one hand, the discarded drafts of versions of this piece. And in the dead of the night, when I decide to get in bed and read the morning's *Times* instead of finishing what I think I can write about Harold Bloom, I admit how terribly difficult it is to write about someone one loves. That, of course, that last half sentence, and especially the speaking out loud of love, of passion, is not what we are mostly able to do, we academics. We write with footnotes—out of training and habit and perhaps mostly persuasion—and we by and large write in ways that reveal the most horrifying of the many horrifying truths in Nietzsche's line that Harold uses as an epigraph for the Shakespeare book: "That for which we find words is something already dead in our hearts. There is always a kind of contempt in the act of speaking." And yet.

And yet, what Harold does is precisely to prove Nietzsche wrong: he writes and speaks openly, ferociously, hyperbolically—even childishly, perhaps best of all—about things that are very much alive in his heart. And he writes from the astonishingly, scandalously, optimistic position that they—his multiple loves, his exuberant passions, from Falstaff (notoriously now) to the Gnostic Ibn 'Arabi of Henry Corbin—can be kept alive through these exhilarating, and to many, exasperating public declarations of such love. Far, very far, from Nietzsche's sang-froid and resignation and pessimism, Harold's Bloodhound-sad face and his regular declarations of every kind of "bloom and doom" (as he puts it) are only masks for the most ferocious and tender of optimists, for whom love is, indeed, as strong as death—and thus to be taken seriously. Every day. Harold restates the bit about not being able to say "I love you"—which is what poor Nietzsche is saying—but he understands that the point is you spend everything you have *trying* to find the ways, and you hope they are countless.

Most astonishingly—I love, now, being able to use that great Bloomian expression in my writing—all of this he does, without apology but certainly with a sense of its exceptionalism, at a historical moment of terrible crisis in the 'profession' of literary criticism and scholarship. A profession whose many woes are amply chronicled and thoroughly bemoaned and perhaps even competently explained away—woes which, for me, can be most simply seen in noting everything Harold is, and most of us are not. Harold sees it as being Falstaff (or Bloomstaff, as even the *Times*, with great charm, conceded), and that is as good as it gets, but my more pedantic way of putting it is that it is about knowing how to write without footnotes.

2

There used to be no story more famous in my own branch of 'the profession'—which is what used to be called Romance philology and now, in a fractured and many would say thus debased form, survives as departments of 'foreign' languages and literatures—than that of Erich Auerbach's writing *Mimesis* in Turkey. The German professor of Romance philology—which meant teaching Old French, Old Provençal and Old Italian—is a Prussian war hero and survivor of the carnage of the First World War, but he is also a Jew and in 1935 the Nazis chase him from his position at Marburg University. In 1936 he goes into exile, to Istanbul, where he instructed "an audience mostly of well-brought-up young Turkish ladies who needed French" as his student Lowry Nelson, Jr. would say in a loving necrology. But it is here, in such extreme exile, with Europe and its cultures savaging each other, that Auerbach sits helpless at the edge of the desert, looking on, without his languages and without his books—and writes *Mimesis*. Famously, very famously, with no footnotes, no bibliography and with the inscription (on the verso of the title page of the 1953 English translation): "Written in Istanbul between May 1942 and April 1945"—as if by way of explanation of this lapse in 'scholarship.'

I was first told the story as a graduate student in the 1970s, a moment which I think can now be seen as oddly 'transitional' in the history of literary studies: there were still considerable traces of the older universe, degrees in Romance philology were still technically possible, graduate students were still told the story of Auerbach and, indeed, were expected really to read *Mimesis*. But it was also mostly clear that this was largely vestigial, that we were mostly being trained as scholars in one language and one literature and maybe even one century. Indeed, this was just one of the ways in which scholarship was clearly defined— pragmatically if not explicitly—as a matter of greater specialization rather than greater vision and breadth. And the very notion that any of this had anything to do with true love or passion or cultural values wouldn't have crossed anyone's mind—and would have been sneered at if it had, probably from both sides of the aisle: the old-fashioned philologists were by and large from the school descended from German neogrammarians and as much interested in disembodied objective truth as the other neos, the New Critics.

So I was puzzled, as I think anyone who really thought about the Auerbach myth must have been: was the moral supposed to be that it was a truly magnificent scholar who could write a whole book without a library and thus without notes or bibliography? If so, what were *we* being trained to do? It was more than clear that whatever the moral was, it was certainly not that *we* should write our papers (let alone an entire book) without notes or a bibliography, as Auerbach had done. After all, literary scholarship in the 'modern' period meant one version or another—and these versions might be quite different from each other—of grasping that our field was as 'scientific' and 'disinterested' as any other, above all that it was about things which could be proven (or perhaps even be diagrammed or charted). Who would have suggested, out loud, in those years, that the footnotelessness of that book was an act of supreme love? Of the sort medieval writers, who believed in Memory itself as a necessary handmaiden to Love, had cultivated? (Peter Brown's recent huge book on *The Rise of Western Christianity* is unblemished by footnotes, a mode described as "wicked" by Robin Lane Fox but rather deftly, although incompletely, explained by another reviewer: "Brown has rejected the world of footnotes and embraced a medieval scholarly aesthetic in which the reader is constantly challenged to identify the sources paraded anonymously through these pages.")

But in my graduate school days, if Auerbach stood for a 'revered' but inimitable Old World, then Harold Bloom was the New, probably Brave, and certainly Scary as Hell. I knew who Harold Bloom was, as, I suppose, must have every even half-conscious graduate student in the seventies, from *The Anxiety of Influence*, a book I could scarcely understand and which was nearly responsible for my deciding I was simply not smart enough to make it through graduate school, let alone the profession. Of course, what I know now that I didn't know then is that when my fellow graduate students acted as if they understood it, and thus made me feel I was the village idiot (or The Idiot Questioner), the truth was they didn't really have much of a clue either. The many reasons *why* this was so—why a book far more heterodox vis-à-vis critical and scholarly practice, and thus far more unintelligible within that intellectual context, than Auerbach's, was as iconic as it was—I will leave aside for the moment.

But it was so, and my own lack of real understanding was a source of extraordinary distress, mostly because I was a medievalist (actually a Romance philologist, one of the very last that would come out of the Department of Romance Languages at the University of Pennsylvania) and the whole question of 'influence' (and its vast army of foot soldiers, sources and etyma and derivations and origins and so forth) was just about all anyone did or had ever done in my neck of the woods. And it was what I wanted to do, too; I had already fallen upon what my subject would be, which was (in essence) the question of the repressed influence of Hispano-Arabic poetry on early Romance poetry—and somehow I figured that even though the repressed (or what I dimly understood to be 'anxious') component was that of modern scholarship, rather than the influenced poetry, this Bloom book everyone talked about and cited just had to be important for me. No doubt it would have been, and no doubt it would have influenced me in ways that would have, indeed (although for very different reasons) made me abandon my scholarly career. But in the midst of becoming a scholar I could not stop really to understand this book that had no footnotes, no bibliography, dozens and dozens of quotes—by which I mean lines inside quotation marks—with no work-and-page citations. And Bloom, as far as anyone knew, did not have the excuse that he had written his book in Istanbul.

I think I would never, on my own, have stopped really to understand that book, but that carriage decided, rather improbably, it would stop for me. I was hired at Yale in 1986, having written a first book (with the subtitle *A Forgotten Heritage* to stand, unconsciously, appropriately enough, for my version of 'anxious influence') which one enthusiastic reviewer characterized as having the best footnotes on the subject ever written. (Or maybe what she said was that the best part of the book was the footnotes.) Everything about that move was terrifying—at some only half-conscious level I knew, I was certain, that this was going to lead to my being found out, that the fact I had been the single graduate student in the whole of the seventies who had not understood *The Anxiety of Influence* was going to be revealed, and probably published in the Sunday Magazine of *The New York Times*, where they had just published an article, with full-color pictures, on "the Yale Critics." To this day I remember the article as being called something like "Terror at Yale" (which seems quite implausible to me), and none of the guys in those pictures was smiling, least of all Harold Bloom. But since the 'flight' option was not really available to me in my moment of abject intellectual terror, I took the 'fight' which meant, of course, it was time to Grow Up and Figure It Out so when I actually met the Ferocious and Unsmiling Yale Critic I didn't end up too humiliated.

Talk about Misprision. By the time I actually met Harold, walking one day on the streets of New Haven, I had actually read enough, and well enough, that I wasn't even surprised to see him and the man who introduced me to him, Lowry Nelson, Jr.—the former student of Auerbach's who was one of the last of the very old-fashioned people, retrograde even, at Yale—exchange an obviously affectionate kiss. The essence of Harold Bloom—not just the personal essence, but the essence of this nonpareil reader of literature, this exemplary scholar of the twentieth century—is Love. Love in all of its manifestations, in every sense, from the Passionate to the Mystical and everything in between. And it is because the basis of his relationship to literature is Love, in all of its shapes—including, necessarily, all the fallout: the cruel jealousy, the rage against the false suitors—that he has not written a footnote in at least 25 years. And, more importantly—since the bit about footnotes is obviously both a little hyperbolic and a lot symbolic—that even 25 years ago, when he was writing stuff that was far from the recent books that have made the best-seller lists, his uncompromisingly and indefatigably *personal* version of criticism and scholarship was mostly unintelligible.

3

One of my very favorite pieces in the Bloom canon—likely to be read by the smallest handful of people, and certainly by nothing remotely like the public his vast *Canon* and *Shakespeare* and *J* books have had—is the preface to the newly republished *Alone with the Alone: Creative Imagination in the Sufism of Ibn 'Arabi* by the late, great Islamicist Henry Corbin. Corbin wrote with plenty of footnotes, by the way, and on a subject which is in no wise popular, and in a language that is sometimes as hermetic as that of the great Andalusian Sufi about whom he writes. But in reading that whole string of critical Gnostics, from Ibn 'Arabi to Bloom, it is possible to see how much it is a matter of having a visionary critical relationship with the texts one reads, and thus loves; and Harold's deft equation of Gnosticism ('acquaintance' rather than 'knowing') with "visionary" suggests in every way that without Love the enterprise of 'criticism' becomes something more akin to 'knowing' (thus the pseudo-scientific impulse, whether that of the philologists or the structuralists or the social-constructivists) than to 'acquaintance.' Which being about love is also necessarily about the imagination, as well as about passion and hope and God and belief and a dozen other words that most people are embarrassed to say or write in public—in the public spheres of our profession, anyway. But not Harold. Quoting Corbin— with unembarrassed love and approval—he notes and reiterates that we pray to God *because* we created him. And thus the places where our knowledge of God and of literature—or even the history of literature— are much the same are forms of either Gnosticism ('acquaintance') or Kabbalism ('tradition'). Or Love.

I quibble with Harold, sometimes, over his ferocious denunciations of what he has called the School of Resentment, because I think it's a bit of a red herring. His relationship to literature of all sorts is rooted in the varieties of the loving experience, and my own sense is that his real rebellion was and in some profound way still is against literary studies as a 'professional' enterprise—professional in the sense of it becoming impersonal. The hyperbole in Bloomian critical language is invariably characterized (negatively) as if it were the hyperbole of scientific writing and assertions—rather than understood as the language of love that it is, with all the possibilities for transcendent and, indeed, outrageous, Truths. And it is amusing, although sad-making, to read recent reviews of the *Shakespeare* book that take on the notion of the expression and the concept of "the invention of the human" as if it were an expression in a biology book written by fundamentalists—rather than a part of the languages of the human arts (God knows, not 'sciences') and thus contributions to the contemplation of the human, and ourselves. If writing about literature cannot be this, then what can? Of course, those of us trained as philologists should really have known better all along—after all, the concept that this is all about Love in the first place is perfectly embedded in that *ur*-professional designation, philology. And Auerbach, who with considerable pride called himself a philologist, is more complex, as a writer of a famously footnote-less and bibliography-less book, than a man accidentally caught without his library—which would be (how can I resist?) a bit like equating love with getting caught with your pants down.

4

The lines from Nietzsche are like a talisman, or a form of evil eye, or one of those other wonderful traditions that are meant to ward off bad things: it is certainly true that it is difficult, sometimes overwhelmingly so, to approach those things so close to the heart, or to write with critical nakedness, or to open oneself to the barbs of the Philistines, especially when the Philistines are our colleagues. (I found myself, just a few days ago, momentarily stung by what was unambiguously meant to be a derisive comment: my praise of what I truly believed to be a terrific book was dismissed as "rapturous.") The truth is that those who love are immensely vulnerable, and one maybe not-half-bad description of what love is could be that it is precisely that willingness to make oneself vulnerable. Which of course means anything other than that it is not difficult or hurtful—*au contraire*. Which is why we need the aphorism from Nietzsche, to urge us to try to say the unsayable, even when, especially when, we suspect the price involved.

This is the dread built into Falstaff's relationship with Hal—or, rather, the dread that Harold feels for Falstaff, when he contemplates Hal, who loves him now but will one day be King, will one day claim that his love for Falstaff is dead in his heart. There is a lovely passage in the *Shakespeare* book, towards the end, as I recall, about Falstaff's relationship with Hal being parallel to the poet's relationship to his lover and patron in the love sonnets. The terror of love, and the beauty of much love poetry, resides of course in that fear of abandonment of one sort or another—and one of the things Harold's reading suggests to me (which even as a medievalist who has read every manner of love poem I had never exactly glimpsed) is that the fear may be that we are abandoned *because*, as Nietzsche would have it, we never knew how to say that "I love you." But what Harold accomplishes is precisely to persuade us that it is crucial to keep trying, that there is only one kind of relationship to be had with literature, if we are to be critics true to what we pretend to write about: full-out and no holds barred, it must always be assuming it will be True Love and we will be able to find its name and say it.

No doubt 'posterity' and 'history' and all those other frightening things will remember Harold's astonishing accomplishments as the foremost critic of his age in a manner perhaps appropriately complex, and certainly with that whole range of admiration and fear, respect and jealousy, that the truly prodigious inspire. He may, as he has more than once lamented, be remembered principally for the *Anxiety* thing. Or, perhaps, he will be remembered for the very different books of this decade, for what will most likely be described as a turn to the 'popular'— and an abandonment of his profession, *pour cause*. But for me it is all reducible to the simplest, most frightening and difficult thing: he talks and writes, and thus urges others to talk and write, as the Lover does to the Beloved, as Ibn 'Arabi does to his God, as Falstaff does to Hal. To write about literature, under Bloomian skies—which are sometimes brilliantly clear and other times stormy, and always very much alive—is to be involved with literature in the most human ways. To love and be loved.

NEW YORK, 1998

Afterword

HAROLD BLOOM

I write these paragraphs on the morning of my seventy-fifth birthday, uneasily aware that I am three-quarters-of-a-century old, a fact I find hard to absorb. At the end of August, seven weeks away, I will begin teaching my fifty-first year at Yale, with a class on Shakespeare's early comedies. In early October, my thirtieth book will be published, *Jesus and Yahweh: The Names Divine*, which I expect to be contentiously received. All the better: if my work has any value, it must be to provoke, to help clear the mind of cant, an ambition I inherit from the Great Cham of criticism, Dr. Samuel Johnson, the best teacher of reading (except for Saint Augustine) whom I have encountered in print. Ranting against cant is my own obsessive weakness, which I would abrogate, if only I could. The literary critics I knew personally and most admired—G. Wilson Knight, Kenneth Burke, Northrop Frye, William Empson—never fell into ranting, though they faced tired conventions that stifled many not as strong. I note that one contribution to this volume suggests that I have become a Moldy Fig, a term applied to Dixielanders by the great Bop jazz artists of my youth. But then, Roy Sellars could compile a giant Invectorium of the reception of my criticism since I began to publish it, in 1957. And only last year, one of my research assistants walked into my house shaking her head, having just emerged from an American Studies seminar at Yale, where a teacher had demonstrated her own virtue by a two-hour denunciation of Walt Whitman as a "racist." Wilson Knight, Burke, and Empson had confronted Formalist, Eliotic Neo-Christian inanities, but nothing like assertions that our father, the old man Walt Whitman, was a racist. I will go on teaching until I am carried out of my last class, because these outrages to humane aestheticism are not going to cease.

    Unlike the sacred Whitman, the crucial writer engendered by the Evening Land, I do not contain multitudes. One learns from Walt

Whitman that it is better to be a singularity that cares, rather than an individuality indifferent both to the self and to others. I would rather be Falstaff (whom I have acted, on stage, with the American Repertory Theater) than Hamlet, who is beyond us all.

Some years ago I remember saying that I was a deliberately comic critic, who received only savagely serious reviews. Without humor, we perish. With it, we perish anyway, but in the spirit of my favorite Yiddish proverb: "Sleep faster! We need the pillows." The center of my work as a critic is my own version of Freud's dry observation: every one of us wishes to die her or his own death, and not someone else's. I want every authentic reader to die in that mode only.

I cannot pretend to know the function of criticism at the present time. Once I believed that literary criticism could be a form of wisdom writing, but I am no wiser now than I was in 1955. Yeats said we cannot know the truth but could incarnate it. Paul de Man would say to me, in every one of the frequent walks we took together: "The trouble with you, Harold, is that you do not believe in the truth." He had found the Truth in Schlegel's "permanent parabasis of meaning," but I could not be persuaded that irony was more than one trope among several others equally vital to imaginative literature.

All I know now about the function of criticism is what it should not be: politics, resentment, cheerleading, excursions into cultural guilt. Politics, in this era of Benito Bush, Duce of the West (Orwell's Oceania), cannot be evaded in my life as a citizen of a plutocracy-theocracy, but that does not guide me in teaching and writing about Walt Whitman, whose magnificent elegies for the self I go about reciting every day. The politics of pre-Civil War America scarcely illuminate *Leaves of Grass* (1855), still the only New World literature worthy of the visionary company of Milton, Goethe, Wordsworth, and Victor Hugo.

I found myself this early morning gently reciting to myself Graham Allen's poem, "Passage," in wonderment at how well he knew me, since I regret we have never seen one another. Certainly I cannot tell whether, like my uncle Satan, I am "falling still / Or rising." How can one rise above a poetics of conflict? Nietzsche taught that every spirit must unfold itself in fighting. The prophetess Deborah, in the earliest Hebrew poem we possess, gives praise to the tribes who went forth to battle to keep the Covenant they had cut with Yahweh:

> Zebulon and Naphtali were a people that jeoparded their lives unto the death in the high places of the field.

I am glad I cannot have my days again, since indeed I would repeat the same mistakes: the same enemies, the same misguided kisses. Error about life, Nietzsche says, is necessary for life.

Uncannily enough, I had spent a week rereading Faulkner just before receiving Graham Allen's essay on the anxiety of choice. *As I Lay Dying* goes on shattering the vessels, as surely it must for every reader. One has to go back to *Moby-Dick* for comparable prose sublimity in an American fiction.

I recall Boswell asking Johnson why he had not written some particular work, only to receive the dark reply: "Sir, a man is not obliged to do all that he can."

Notes on Contributors

Peter Abbs is Professor of Creative Writing at the University of Sussex. His latest critical book is *Against the Flow: The Arts, Postmodern Culture and Education* (Falmer, 2003); he has also published seven volumes of poetry, the latest being *Viva la Vida* (Salt, 2005).

Graham Allen is Senior Lecturer in Modern English, University College Cork. He is the author of *Harold Bloom: A Poetics of Conflict* (Harvester, 1994), *Intertextuality* (Routledge, 2000), *Roland Barthes* (Routledge, 2003), *The pupils of the University*. Ed. parallax 40 (2003) and is currently working on a monograph on Mary Shelley (to be published by Palgrave in 2007) and a first collection of poetry, provisionally entitled *Some Things I Never Did*.

Nicholas Birns teaches literature and literary theory at New School University. He is editor of *Antipodes: A North American Journal of Australian Literature*. He is the author of *Understanding Anthony Powell* (South Carolina, 2004); he also publishes frequently on Romanticism, with essays and reviews in *Studies in Romanticism*, *European Romantic Review* and *South Atlantic Review*.

Harold Bloom is Sterling Professor of Humanities at Yale University, and Henry W. and Albert A. Berg Professor in English and American Literature at New York University. His most recent monograph is *Jesus and Yahweh: The Names Divine* (Riverhead, 2005).

Gregory Botts is an artist and teacher of art whose paintings have been exhibited extensively in solo and group shows across the United States; he lives in New York and New Mexico. Bloom wrote a commentary on his work, "The American Sublime," in *Arts Magazine* 1990.

Leslie Brisman is Karl Young Professor of English at Yale University. His publications on biblical literature include "Biblical Revisionism," in *NLH* 29 (1998).

T. J. Cribb is Director of Studies in English at Churchill College, Cambridge. Trained as a Dickensian at Oxford, he reviews for *RES* and is half-way through a book on Shakespeare's idealism, after a detour setting up an undergraduate option in postcolonial literatures. Essays by Wole Soyinka, Ben Okri, Wilson Harris, John Kinsella and others are collected by him in *Imagined Commonwealths: Cambridge Essays on Commonwealth and International Literature in English* (Macmillan and St Martin's, 1999), and a bilingual collection, *The Power of the Word: La puissance du verbe* will appear with Rodopi in 2006, including dialogues between Wole Soyinka and Assia Djebar, Wilson Harris and Daniel Maximin, Niyi Osundare and Henri Lopes, Lorna Goodison and Véronique Tadjo, amongst others. Nearing completion is a book on the influence of the Bloomsbury Group on British theatre through the channel of the Cambridge Arts Theatre and the Marlowe Dramatic Society.

Stephen da Silva received his Ph. D. in English from Rice University. He has published essays on Shashi Tharoor, Christopher Isherwood, E. M. Forster, and English pedagogy, as well as encyclopedia entries on Robin Maugham, Hanif Kureishi, Lytton Strachey and Eve Kosofsky Sedgwick. He is working on a book tentatively entitled *Boyish Affiliations*, which examines how late-Victorian and Modernist homosexual writers challenged the association of same-sex desire with arrested development.

Norman Finkelstein is a poet and literary critic teaching in the English Department of Xavier University in Cincinnati, Ohio. He has written extensively on Bloom in his books *The Ritual of New Creation: Jewish Tradition and Contemporary Literature* (SUNY, 1992) and *Not One of Them in Place: Modern Poetry and Jewish American Identity* (SUNY, 2001). His books of poetry include *Restless Messengers* (Georgia, 1992) and the three-volume serial poem *Track*: *Track*, *Columns*, and *Powers* (Spuyten Duyvil, 1999, 2002, and 2005).

Roger Gilbert is Professor of English at Cornell University. He is the author of *Walks in the World: Representation and Experience in Modern American Poetry* (Princeton, 1991), and has co-edited *Considering the Radiance: Essays on the Poetry of A. R. Ammons* (Norton, 2005); he is currently writing a critical biography of Ammons, for which he was awarded a Guggenheim Fellowship.

Gwee Li Sui is Assistant Professor in the Department of English Language and Literature, National University of Singapore. He researches in eighteenth-century literature, philosophy and science, and English and German Romanticism; he has also written on the Reformation, modern Protestant theology, and Singaporean literature.

Kevin Hart holds the Notre Dame Chair at the University of Notre Dame, where he teaches philosophical theology. His recent books include *The Dark Gaze: Maurice Blanchot and the Sacred* (Chicago, 2004) and *Postmodernism* (Oneworld, 2004); his poems are gathered in *Flame Tree: Selected Poems* (Bloodaxe, 2003), and he has recently completed a new collection, *Young Rain*.

Geoffrey Hartman is an occasional poet; he taught literature at Yale University, and remains the Project Director of Yale's Fortunoff Video Archive for Holocaust Testimonies. Among his recent books are *A Critic's Journey: Literary Reflections, 1958-1998* (Yale, 1999), *Scars of the Spirit: The Struggle Against Inauthenticity* (Palgrave, 2002), and *The Geoffrey Hartman Reader* (Fordham, 2004).

John Hollander is Sterling Professor of English at Yale University. His volumes of poetry include *A Crackling of Thorns* (1958), *Types of Shape* (1969), *The Head of the Bed* (1974, with commentary by Bloom), *Spectral Emanations* (1978), *Powers of Thirteen* (1983), *Harp Lake* (1988), *Tesserae* (1993), *Figurehead* (1999), and *Picture Window* (2003); his works of criticism include *The Untuning of the Sky* (1961), *Images of Voice* (1970), *Vision and Resonance* (1975), *The Figure of Echo* (1981), *Melodious Guile* (1988), *The Work of Poetry* (1997), and *Rhyme's Reason* (3rd ed., 2001); and he has edited numerous collections, including *The Wind and the Rain: An Anthology of Poems for Young People* (1961, with Bloom). He has received numerous awards, including the Bollingen Prize, the Levinson Prize and the MLA Shaughnessy Medal, as well as fellowships from the Guggenheim Foundation, the MacArthur Foundation and the National Endowment for the Arts.

Moshe Idel is Max Cooper Professor of Jewish Thought at the Hebrew University, Jerusalem, and Senior Researcher at the Shalom Hartman Institute of Advanced Judaic Studies, Jerusalem. Among his books are

Kabbalah: New Perspectives (1988), *Hasidism: Between Ecstasy and Magic* (1995), *Messianic Mystics* (1998), *Absorbing Perfections: Kabbalah and Interpretation* (2002, with Foreword by Bloom), and *Kabbalah and Eros* (2005).

John Kinsella is a Fellow of Churchill College, Cambridge; Professor of English at Kenyon College; and Adjunct Professor to Edith Cowan University, Western Australia. He is the author of more than thirty books, including *The Silo* (Fremantle Arts Centre Press/Arc, 1995/1998), *The Undertow* (Arc, 1996), *The Hunt* (Bloodaxe, 1998), *Visitants* (Bloodaxe, 1999), *The Hierarchy of Sheep* (Bloodaxe/FACP, 2001), *Peripheral Light: New and Selected Poems* (Norton/ FACP, 2003, selected and introduced by Bloom), and *The New Arcadia* (Norton/FACP, 2005). He has published a novel, *Genre* (FACP, 1997), a book of stories, *Grappling Eros* (FACP, 1998), and a book of autobiographical writing, *Auto* (Salt, 2001); he is also the author of four verse plays (collected as *Divinations*). A novel, *Post-colonial*, a collection of essays, a volume of lectures, and a book of short stories (with Tracy Ryan) are forthcoming. His work has been translated into many languages, including French, German, Chinese, Dutch, Spanish, Polish and Russian, and he has been the recipient of many prizes and awards. He is founding editor for the international literary publisher Salt, and continues to work extensively as an editor and reviewer around the world.

Anders H. Klitgaard, born in Copenhagen, has always had a broad interest in the humanities, leading him to acquire three master's degrees: in Philosophy (Århus, 1994), Shakespeare studies (St. Andrews, 1998), and IT (Southern Denmark, 2002). He has used Bloom's theory of poetry to make sense of hypertext ("The Difference Between Analogue and Digital Textuality: An Epistemological Enquiry," in *Readerly/Writerly Texts* 9.1-2 [2001]). He has worked as a consultant in the field of Internet communication, and now runs his own company, AKVL (<http://www.akvl.com>). He is the moderator of an Internet discussion group dedicated to Bloom, which you are welcome to join via a link in his personal web site (<http://www.oeuvre.org>).

Gregory Machacek is Associate Professor at Marist College in Poughkeepsie, New York; he received his Ph. D. from Cornell University. His research focuses on John Milton, particularly on the relation between Milton and his classical sources (especially Homer). He is completing a book entitled *"Written to Aftertimes:" Milton and Homer.*

Martin McQuillan is Professor of Cultural Theory and Analysis at the University of Leeds. His publications include *Paul de Man* (Routledge, 2001), *Deconstruction: A Reader* (Edinburgh, 2001) and, with Eleanor Byrne, *Deconstructing Disney* (Pluto, 1998).

María Rosa Menocal received her Ph.D. from the University of Pennsylvania, taught at Bryn Mawr and Pennsylvania, and since 1985 has been at Yale, where she is Director of the Whitney Humanities Center and Sterling Professor of Humanities. Her work is in medieval literatures and cultures, with special focus in recent years on the vibrant mixed cultures of medieval Spain. Her books include *The Arabic Role in Medieval Literary History: A Forgotten Heritage* (Pennsylvania, 1987), *Writing in Dante's Cult of Truth: From Borges to Boccaccio* (Duke, 1991), and *Shards of Love: Exile and the Origins of the Lyric* (Duke, 1994). *The Literature of Al-Andalus* (in the Cambridge History of Arabic Literature series) is a recent co-edited project, while *The Ornament of the World: How Muslims, Jews, and Christians Created a Culture of Tolerance in Medieval Spain* (with Foreword by Bloom) was published by Little, Brown in 2002. She is working on a documentary based on *The Ornament of the World*, by producer Michael Schwarz, as well as a book for Yale UP, a collaboration with Prof. Jerrilyn Dodds and Abigail Krasner entitled *Out of Arabic: Conversion, Translation, and Memory in the Invention of Castilian Culture.*

Peter Morris graduated from Yale University and then studied at Oxford, where he hopes one day to submit his thesis; in the meantime, he is a playwright, television writer and occasional critic. His play *The Age of Consent* is published by Methuen, and his verse-drama "The Death of Tintagel" (a parody of Maeterlinck) appeared in the *Paris Review* 168; his critical essays have appeared in the English arts tri-quarterly *Areté*. He is collaborating with director Robert Altman on an adaptation of Roald Dahl's *Tales of the Unexpected* for the BBC.

Sinéad Murphy received a Ph. D. in Philosophy from University College Cork, where she lectures in Social Philosophy at the Department of Adult Continuing Education. Her dissertation addresses Gadamer's concept of Effective History in particular, and the problem that historical contingency presents for human thought and action in general; her research interests include the conditions for the possibility of aesthetic judgement, ethical and political paradigms in literature, hermeneutics, and the philosophical contributions of Gadamer and Lyotard.

John W. P. Phillips is Associate Professor in the Department of English Language and Literature, National University of Singapore. He is the author of *Contested Knowledge: A Guide to Critical Theory* (Zed, 2000), and has published articles on linguistics, psychoanalysis, deconstruction, philosophy, literature, urbanism, postmodernism, critical theory and aesthetics. He is the editor, with Lyndsey Stonebridge, of *Reading Melanie Klein* (Routledge, 1998) and, with Ryan Bishop and Wei-Wei Yeo, of two books on cities, *Postcolonial Urbanism: Southeast Asian Cities and Global Processes* (Routledge, 2003) and *Beyond Description: Space Historicity Singapore* (Routledge, 2004). He has recently completed a manuscript (with Ryan Bishop) on aesthetics and military technology, and is working on a manuscript concerned with Jacques Derrida.

Christopher Rollason is a British national living in France. He graduated with First Class Honours in English from Trinity College, Cambridge, in 1975, and obtained his Ph. D. from York University in 1988. Until 1987 he was a member of the Department of Anglo-American Studies at Coimbra University in Portugal. He is Language Editor for the Delhi-based *Atlantic Literary Review* (*ALR*) and has contributed articles to that journal and to anthologies issued by Atlantic Publishers. He has co-edited, with Dr. Rajeshwar Mittapalli, the anthology *Modern Criticism* (Atlantic, 2002) and, with Dr. Dora Sales Salvador, *Postcolonial Feminist Writing* (*ALR* special issue, 2003).

Nicholas Royle is Professor of English at the University of Sussex. His books include *Telepathy and Literature: Essays on the Reading Mind* (Blackwell, 1991), *E. M. Forster* (Northcote House, 1999), *The Uncanny* (Routledge, 2003), and *How to Read Shakespeare* (Norton, 2005); he is also author, with Andrew Bennett, of *Elizabeth Bowen and the Dissolution of the Novel* (Macmillan, 1994) and *An Introduction to Literature, Criticism and Theory* (3rd ed., Longman, 2004). He is joint editor with Timothy Clark of the *Oxford Literary Review* (of which Bloom has been Honorary Presidential Committee member since 1978).

Roy Sellars is Senior Lecturer in English literature at the University of Southern Denmark, Kolding; in 2005-06 he is in residence at the

Kierkegaard Library, St. Olaf College, Minnesota. A graduate of St. Edmund Hall, Oxford, where he discovered Bloom thanks to his tutor Ann Wordsworth, he has also worked at Marburg University, the University of Geneva, Cornell University and the National University of Singapore. He has published on topics in literature and theory, and is completing a book on Milton; he is also co-editor, with Per Krogh Hansen, of *Glossing* Glas (Nebraska, forthcoming). He welcomes notice of any relevant writings for a complete bibliography of Bloom in progress.

R. Clifton Spargo, a fiction writer and critic, is Associate Professor of English at Marquette University; he was the Pearl Resnick Fellow at the Center for Advanced Holocaust Studies of the US Holocaust Memorial Museum. He is the author of *The Ethics of Mourning: Grief and Responsibility in Elegiac Literature* (Johns Hopkins, 2004) and *Vigilant Memory: Emmanuel Levinas, the Holocaust, and the Unjust Death* (Johns Hopkins, 2006), as well as articles on American literature and the cultural memory of the Holocaust, on which he is a completing a monograph.

Heidi Sylvester completed her studies at Monash University in Australia with the Ph. D. thesis *Labours of the Negative: Sublimity in the Writings of Harold Bloom and Maurice Blanchot*. Before switching to Roland Berger Strategy Consultants in Hamburg, she spent five years at the German and European Business Information division of the *FAZ*-Institut in Frankfurt/M.

Barnard Turner is Associate Professor of English and Academic Convenor for European Studies, National University of Singapore. In addition to some two dozen articles on American and European literature and cultural politics, including several on D. H. Lawrence in new theoretical contexts, he has published *Cultural Tropes of the Contemporary American West* (Mellen, 2005) and a short study of Thoreau reception in India.

Paolo Valesio graduated from the University of Bologna. After teaching at Bologna, Harvard University and New York University, he became Professor of Italian at Yale University, where he taught from 1975 to 2004; he is now the Giuseppe Ungaretti Professor in Italian Literature at Columbia University. He founded the Yale Poetry Group and the journal *Yale Italian Poetry* (transferred to the Italian Academy for Advanced Studies in America, at Columbia, as *Italian Poetry Review*); he contributes to several literary and artistic journals, as well as Italian dailies. He has written several hundred essays, articles, poems and short stories, and has published four books of criticism—*Strutture dell'allitterazione: Grammatica, retorica e folklore verbale* (Zanichelli, 1968), *Novantiqua: Rhetorics as a Contemporary Theory* (Indiana, 1980), *Ascoltare il silenzio: La retorica come teoria* (Il Mulino, 1986) and *Gabriele d'Annunzio: The Dark Flame* (Yale, 1992)—as well as a critical-narrative essay, *Dialogo coi volanti* (Cronopio, 1997), two novels, a collection of short stories, a novella, and fourteen books of poetry. He is composing five diaristic novels constituting a *Pentalogia* which has reached fifteen thousand manuscript pages.

Milton L. Welch has written a Ph. D. thesis on lynching in American modernist poetry, at the University of Virginia, and will be Assistant Professor of English at North Carolina State University.

Index

Abraham 335–339
Abrams, M. H. 278, 304, 462
Abulafia, Rabbi Abraham 352–360
   Sefer ha-'Ot 358–359
   Sitrei Torah 353
   Hayyei ha-'Olam ha-Ba' 358
Ackerley, J. R. 402–406, 414–415
Adam and Eve 188, 203–208
Adorno, Theodor W. 77, 91, 92, 106
   "On Lyric Poetry and Society" 107
aesthetic value 35–48, 66
agency 271–273
agon xiv, xv, 1, 37, 38, 56, 64, 69, 70, 71, 77, 84–85, 89, 96, 124, 129, 130, 141, 187, 200–201, 308, 313, 371, 380, 381, 383; between Bloom and Johnson, 189–195
akedah 303, 307, 335–339
Akenson, Donald Harman 330
Allen, Graham 262, 265, 277, 292, 488, 489
   Harold Bloom: A Poetics of Conflict 214n, 240n, 258n
   Intertextuality 266
Ammons, A. R. 44–47
Anderson, Bernhard W. 314
antithetical criticism, see Bloom, Harold
anxiety,
   of choice (see Allen, Graham), 52–64, 258n
   of influence, 40, 52–54, 56, 68–116, 125, 128–131, 170–181, 184–186, 201–202, 210, 222, 224, 226, 262, 264, 269, 272, 274, 291, 293, 294, 334, 379, 383, 441
appreciation 35–50
Aristotle, 121, 122, 311, 366
   Poetics 120
Arnold, Matthew 40, 57, 267
Ashbery, John 38, 44–47, 138, 429, 451–461, 463–468, 470–475
   "Clepsydra" 470
   "Daffy Duck in Hollywood" 475
   Flow Chart 457
   "Houseboat Days" 458–459
   "The Other Tradition" 470–471
   "Self-Portrait in a Convex Mirror" 474–475
   Some Trees 465–466
   Vermont Notebook 455
Ashkenazi, Rabbi Yehuda ha-Darshan 351
Auden, W. H. 460–461, 464–468
Auerbach, Erich 136, 480, 483, 484
   Mimesis 480–481
avant-garde poetry 38, 41

Babel, Isaac 152
Badiou, Alain 80
Barthes, Roland xiv, 40, 333
Bathsheba 323, 330; see also J-writer
Beardsley, Monroe 36
ben Sa'adya Harar, Rabbi Nathan 352
ben Schmuel of Acre, Rabbi Isaac 351–352
Benjamin, Walter 73, 165

Bernstein, Eduard 77
Bersani, Leo xx
Bhabha, Homi 137
Black Book, The 74
Blackmur, R.P. 35, 37
   Language as Gesture 45
Blake, William 39, 49, 143, 146, 220, 262, 275, 276, 281, 300, 304, 371, 455
   Marriage of Heaven and Hell xiii, 256
Bloom, Allan xx
Bloom, Harold
   Agon xiv, 122, 221, 260, 273, 321, 471
   American Religion, The 145, 229n, 230, 281, 309, 336, 347
   Anxiety of Influence, The xx, 40–43, 45, 67, 72, 134, 145, 170–171, 184, 201–202, 207–208, 213–221, 237, 257, 263, 264, 273, 276–277, 294–295, 323, 333, 397, 399–400, 409–411, 425–426, 429, 431, 434, 437, 442, 459, 461, 463, 466, 482, 483
   Art of Reading Poetry, The xvii
   Best of the Best American Poetry, The 49
   Best Poems of the English Language 41n
   Blake's Apocalypse 67, 260, 304
   Book of J, The xv, 8, 145, 256, 313–317, 319–330, 332, 340, 347, 381–383, 483
   Breaking of the Vessels, The 223, 225, 249n, 278
   Figures of Capable Imagination 43–45, 263
   "From J to K, or The Uncanniness of the Yahwist" 332n
   Future of the Imagination, The 149
   Genius xvii, 133, 166, 320, 327
   Hamlet 135
   How to Read and Why xvii, 59–64, 137, 138, 275, 463
   Jesus and Jahweh xvii
   Kabbalah and Criticism 220n, 241, 263, 307–308, 315, 322, 333
   Map of Misreading, A 42–43, 45, 72, 74, 77, 85–86, 96, 142n, 184–185, 189–191, 201–202, 225n, 236–237, 242, 245, 249, 252, 263, 267, 273, 274–276, 277, 333, 397, 399, 400, 409, 432
   primal scene of instruction, 85–87, 209–210, 237, 249
   Modern Critical Interpretations, see Chelsea House
   Modern Critical Views, see Chelsea House
   Omens of Millenium 347
   Poetry and Repression 46, 263, 266, 268, 273, 333, 401
   Ringers in the Tower, The 43, 256, 260, 262
   "The Internalization of Quest Romance" 260–262
   Ruin the Sacred Truths 67, 184, 185n, 215, 250, 304, 324, 327, 332, 333
   Shakespeare xvii, 49, 59, 134, 135, 144, 149, 150, 170, 222n, 274, 437, 479, 483–485
   Shelley's Mythmaking 39, 67, 260, 269, 304, 439
   "The One with the Beard is God, the Other is the Devil" 153
   Visionary Company, The 39, 47, 67, 260, 276, 303–307, 441, 444
   Wallace Stevens 45, 106, 200, 277, 334
   Western Canon, The xviii, xx, xxiii, 48, 52–59, 66, 85, 115, 133–146, 149, 150, 152, 153, 159–160, 163, 166, 183, 185n, 200n, 236, 255, 323, 326, 383, 388, 400, 412, 433–434, 437, 461–463, 483
   Where Shall Wisdom Be Found? xvii, 137, 463
   Yeats 39–40, 262
   Book of the Responding Entity (Sefer ha-Meshiv) 360, 362, 365–366, 367–370

Borges, Jorge Luis 151, 161, 268, 281, 432, 469
Brooks, Cleanth 36
Buber, Martin 79, 347, 439
Burke, Edmund
  Philosophical Enquiry into the Origins of Our Ideas of the Sublime and Beautiful, A 122–124
Burke, Kenneth 35
Bush, George W., see neo-conservatism
Byron, see Lord Byron

Camões, Luís de
  Os Lusíadas (The Lusiads) 157
Camus, Albert
  La peste (The Plague) 155
Carpenter, Edward 393–421
Caruth, Cathy 98
Cavell, Stanley 73
Chelsea House 48, 134, 150
Chin, Marilyn 139
clash, see *agon*
clinamen 121, 134, 213–232, 273, 278, 291
Coleridge, Samuel Taylor 38, 304, 381, 388, 430
  "Kubla Khan" 334
Constantius, Constantin, see Kierkegaard, Søren
Corbin, Henry 347, 479
  Alone with the Alone 483
Couliano, Ioan P. 347
Crane, Hart 231, 441, 468
Critchley, Simon
  Ethics of Deconstruction 83n

davhar 73, 238
David 9, 322, 330
de Bolla, Peter xiii–xiv, 66n, 71n, 73n, 106, 111, 135n, 170, 171, 256, 264, 290, 400–401
de Man, Paul xxii, 38, 40, 42, 73n, 76, 186, 200, 209, 237, 258, 261, 262, 263, 272, 276–278, 305, 472, 488

deconstruction 235–252, 266
Derrida, Jacques xx, xxiii, 40, 68n, 73, 81–87, 100, 200, 231n, 235–252, 265, 268, 271, 272, 278, 280n, 387
  Archive Fever 250
  "Archive Fever: A Freudian Impression" 250–252
  "Edmond Jabès and the Question of the Book" 247, 252
  "Ellipsis" 247, 249n
  "Freud and the Scene of Writing" 85, 237–248
  Of Grammatology 87
  Politics of Friendship, The 245
  "This Strange Institution Called Literature" 239
Descartes, René 74
Desmet, Christy and Robert Sawyer 199
De Wette, Wilhelm Martin Leberecht 321
Dickinson, Emily 381, 383, 386–390
Diehl, Joanne Feit 380
Donne, John 39
Donoghue, Denis
  Ferocious Alphabets 462
Dorsch, T.S. 124
dreck 58
Dryden, John
  Fables Ancient and Modern 187, 189

E-writer, see Elohist
Eagleton, Terry 153
Eichhorn, Johann Gottfried 321
Eleazar of Worms, Rabbi 353–354
Elijah 348–371
Eliot, T. S. 35, 37, 38, 39, 41n, 68, 69, 137, 199, 206, 225, 228, 263, 276, 334, 435, 441, 442, 454, 459, 460
  "The Love Song of J. Alfred Prufrock" 334
  "Tradition and the Individual Talent" 226
  Waste Land, The 226–227

Ellison, Ralph Waldo
  Invisible Man 60
Elohist 321, 334
Emerson, Ralph Waldo 41, 46, 47, 69,
   89, 134, 142–143, 199–200, 224,
   225, 229–230, 231, 385, 388
Empson, William 35
Enoch, see Metatron
ephebe 37, 40, 41, 88, 125–129, 205,
   206, 218, 220, 221, 222, 262,
   272, 274, 294, 299, 396, 404,
   412, 416
Esau 321
Espriu, Salvador 152
evaluation 35–43
Eve, see Adam and Eve

Fall 1, 3
Falstaff, Sir John xvi
Faulkner, William
  As I Lay Dying 63
First Book of Kings 330
Fite, David
  Harold Bloom 193n, 200n, 258n
Fleiger, Jerry Aline 384–385
forbidden fruit 188
Forster, E. M. 393–411, 415–421
  Commonplace Book 421
  Hill of Devi 404
  Maurice 393–396, 402, 404,
    408–409, 416, 419–420
  Where Angels Fear to Tread 413
Foucault, Michel 74, 333
Franco, General Francisco 163
Freedman, Ralph
  The Lyrical Novel 103
Freud, Sigmund 69, 70, 71n, 72, 77,
   78, 85–86, 88–89, 91, 96,
   104–105, 109, 122, 123–124,
   125, 128, 129, 171, 180,
   199–200, 221–224, 226–228,
   231, 237–248, 250–251, 252,
   256, 262, 268, 269, 273, 320,
   324–327, 330, 389, 397n,
   399–400, 410, 433–434, 438,
   439, 440, 457, 488

"The Uncanny" 124
  Beyond the Pleasure Principle 223, 271
  Interpretation of Dreams, The 216
  Inhibitions, Symptoms, and Anxiety
    270–271
  *Jokes and Their Relation to the
    Unconscious* 283–284
  Moses and Monotheism 237, 325
  Psychopathology of Everyday Life, The
    222
  family romance 126
  Oedipus complex 31
Friedman, Richard Elliott 327
Fry, Paul 425
Frye, Northrop 36, 73, 87n, 307
  Anatomy of Criticism 36, 264

Galileo, Galilei 191
Gallop, Jane 398n
Garff, Joakim 297
gevurah 10, 322
Gilbert, Brian
  Wilde 332
Gilbert, Sandra M. and Susan Gubar
  Madwoman in the Attic, The 91, 379
Ginsburg, Allen 38
Giustiniani, Augustino 358
Goldsmith, Stephen 385–386
Gordon, George, see Lord Byron
Grappelli, Stephane 6
Graf, Karl Heinrich 321
Gray, Thomas
  "Elegy Written in a Country
    Church Yard" 281
Greenberg, Clement 471–472
Guillory, John 58, 275
Gurr, Andrew 174

Hartman, Geoffrey 68n, 87n, 264n,
   303, 307
  "Voice of the Shuttle, The" 433–434
Havel, Vaclav 150
Hazlitt, William 37
Hegel, Georg Wilhelm Friedrich 71,
   75, 77, 80, 90, 94, 96n, 120, 251,
   266, 294

Herbert, George 467
history 5, 25, 73–79, 93, 96–97, 98–116, 173
Hollander, John 273n, 307, 386, 432
Homans, Margaret 385
Homer 195–196, 319, 334
Hongo, Garret 138–139

imagination 67
influence, see anxiety
intentional fallacy 36
intertextuality, see anxiety of influence
Isaac 335–339
Isherwood, Christopher
  Christopher and His Kind 396
  Lions and Shadows 396

J-writer 314–317, 319–330, 332–345, 381, 382
Jacob 321
James, Henry
  Ambassadors, The 430
  Sacred Fount, The 430
Jameson, Fredric
  "Figural Relativism" 74–75
Jarrell, Randall 35
  Poetry and the Age 45
Jehovah, see Yahweh
Jeremiah 333
Job 333
Job, Book of 298
Johnson, Samuel 37, 190–194
Jonah 333
Jonas, Hans 347

Kabbalah 293, 308, 320, 347–371
Kafka, Franz 48, 155, 320, 324, 325, 327–329, 330, 382, 460
  The Castle 329
Kant, Immanuel 50, 120, 122, 129–130, 259
  Critique of Judgment, The 123
Keats, John 40, 304, 379, 455
  Fall of Hyperion, The 334
Kenner, Hugh 39

Kierkegaard, Søren 125, 126, 218, 293–301, 458
  Concluding Unscientific Postscript 293
  Philosophical Fragments 294
  Repetition 295, 297–299
Kinsella, John 138
Klein, Melanie 246
  "A Contribution to the Theory of Intellectual Inhibition" 457, 459
knowledge 7
Kolodny, Annette 379

Lacan, Jacques 86, 91, 239, 244, 269
langue 73, 81–82
Lawrence, D. H. 155
Leavis, F. R. 35, 152
  "Mass Civilization, Minority Culture" 57
Lentricchia, Frank 66n, 68n, 80, 308–310, 400
  After the New Criticism 67
  Ariel and the Police 308
  Modernist Quartet 308
Levinas, Emmanuel 71, 79–85, 87, 88, 90, 95, 97n
  "Ego and the Totality" 82
  Otherwise than Being 83, 84n
  "Wholly Otherwise" 83
  Totality and Infinity 84n
liberalism 79–80
linguistic historicism, see Vico, Giambattista
literary value, see aesthetic value
logos 238
Lovejoy, A. O. 305
Lacoue-Labarthe, Philippe 129
Llosa, Mario Vargas 162
Longinus, see Pseudo-Longinus
Lord Byron 304, 306, 439–461, 467
  Manfred 433n, 444–446, 461
  Don Juan 444, 446–445, 451–459, 461
Lowell, Robert 453
Lukács, Georg 158

Maimonides 354–355
  Guide for the Perplexed 353–354

MacFarquar, Larissa
    "The Prophet of Decline" 165
Marcuse, Herbert 77, 91
Marlowe, Christopher 171–178, 181
    Tamburlaine 172–174
    Dr. Faustus 177
Márquez, Gabriel García 151
Marvell, Andrew
    "On *Paradise Lost*" 184
McCarthy, Cormac
    Blood Meridian 63
McLuhan, Marshall 162
McVeigh, David 322
Merrill, James 464
Metaphysical poets 39
Metatron 347–355, 370–371
Miles, Jack 323
Mileur, Jean-Pierre
    Literary Revisionism and the Burden of Modernity 222
Miller, J Hillis 46, 266
Milton, John 39, 41n, 49, 107n, 141, 183–196, 216–217, 222n, 261, 263, 269, 271, 274–276, 277n, 278, 293, 379, 388, 397, 425–438, 442, 449, 451, 456, 461, 462, 475
    Paradise Lost 184, 190, 196, 203–204, 205, 274, 275, 343, 425–429, 440
    Areopagitica 189
misreading xiv, 4, 43, 122, 127, 191, 199–211, 215, 219, 256, 258, 262, 264, 267, 273, 280, 282, 290–301, 320n, 401, 463–464
modernism 39, 76
Moore, Marianne 454
Morin, Edgar 150
Morrison, Toni
    Beloved 98–103, 108–109, 112–115
    Song of Solomon 63
Moses 316, 326, 336, 341–345
Moynihan, Robert 185
Murray, Peter 179

Nahmanides 350–351
Nancy, Jean-Luc 129
neo-conservatism 158
New Critics 35, 39–40, 68, 76, 264–265
Newlyn, Lucy 425
Nietzsche, Friedrich 40, 41, 68n, 69n, 72, 74, 76, 124, 141–142, 143, 193n, 208, 214, 216, 238, 242, 258, 259, 260, 272, 276, 277, 278, 284, 291, 474, 479, 480, 485, 488, 489
    Birth of Tragedy, The 136
    "On the Uses and Disadvantages of History for Life" 258n, 263, 279

Oedipal, see Freud, Sigmund
O'Hara, Frank 473–474
Orgel, Stephen
    The Illusion of Power 180
originality 41, 183–197

Paglia, Camille 67, 440
Pater, Walter 37, 45, 76, 258, 259–260, 312n
Peele, George 174–176
    Battle of Alcazar, The 174
    Love of King David and Faire Bathsabe, The 174, 176
Pentateuch 333, 339
Perloff, Marjorie 39
Plath, Sylvia 38
Plato 334
poet 15
poetic imagination, see imagination
Pollock, Jackson 471
Pope, Alexander 462
Potter, Harry 159, 162
Pound, Ezra 35, 38
Pynchon, Thomas 151
    The Crying of Lot 49, 63
Pseudo-Longinus 130
    On the Sublime 120, 122–123

Quintilian 135

Rajan, Tilottama 64
Ramses II 316
Ransom, John Crowe 36, 199n

Rawls, John 93, 98
Rehoboam 314, 316–317, 322
resentment 133–146, 282
revisionism, see anxiety
rhetorical criticism 200–201
Rich, Adrienne 38–49
Richards, I. A. 35
   New Criticism 199n
Roethke, Theodore 42
Romanticism 39, 64, 260–263
Rorty, Richard 69
Rosenberg, David 330
Roth, Philip 151
   Human Stain, The 163
Rowling, J. K., see Potter, Harry
Ruskin, John 37
Rylands, G. H. W. 178

Said, Edward
   Culture and Imperialism 163
Salazar, Antonio de Oliveira 163
Salusinszky, Imre 53–54, 305
Salvador, Dora Sales 166
Saramago, José 150, 151, 155
   A Caverna (The Cave) 154, 166
   A Jangada de Pedra (The Stone Raft) 149, 154, 157
   Ensaio sobre a Cegueira (Blindness) 155
   Ensaio sobre a Lucidez (Essay on Lucidity) 166
   História do Cerco de Lisboa (History of the Siege of Lisbon) 153–154
   Memorial del Convento (Baltasar and Blimunda) 153, 154
   O Ano da Morte de Ricardo Reis (The Years of the Death of Ricardo Reis) 153
   O Evangelho segundo Jesus Cristo (The Gospel According to Jesus Christ) 153, 155
   O Homem duplicado (The Double) 166
   Todos os Nomes (All the Names) 154
Satan 207–208, 213, 274, 431–433, 438–439
Sauerberg, Lars Ole
   Versions of the Past, Visions of the Future 211
Scholem, Gershom 347
School of Donne, see Donne, John
School of Resentment, see resentment
Schultz, William R. 230
Schwartz, Regina 183, 188n
Searle, John 73
Second Book of Samuel 322
Sefer ha-Peliy'ah 359
Seters, John Van 335–345
Shaddai 9
Shakespeare, William xvii, 41n, 49, 55–56, 59, 60, 61–62, 64, 66n, 107, 133, 135, 138, 139, 140, 141, 142n, 143–145, 184, 200, 214–220, 225, 258, 273, 275, 276, 293, 299, 300, 314, 316, 319, 324, 326, 337, 340, 381, 382, 383, 388, 400, 411–412, 433, 437, 439, 461, 467, 469, 487
   Henry V 170–174, 176–181
   Henry VI 170
   King John 170
   King Lear 214–215, 298
   Richard III 170
   Richard II 177–178
   Titus Andronicus 170–171
Shelley, Mary
   The Last Man 63, 385
   Frankenstein 63
Shelley, Percy Bysshe 39, 44, 62, 64, 142n, 220n, 263, 399, 402n, 428, 439–444, 448, 460, 467, 468
   Defence of Poetry, The 61, 80, 440
   "Ozymandias" 440
   "Peter Bell the Third" 442
   Prometheus Unbound 441
   "Satire on Satire" 443, 447, 449
   Swell-foot the Tyrant 442
Shevirath ha-kelim 125
Solomon 8, 314
Solomon, Robert C. 140–141

Southey, Robert 443–444, 447
sparagmos 8
Sparks, Elisa 379
Spenser, Edmund 184–185, 190, 191, 293, 431, 432, 436, 437, 438, 449, 451
   Faerie Queene, The 189, 273n, 274–275, 281, 427–428
Steiner, Dorothy 385
Stevens, Wallace 37, 39, 44, 45, 46, 49, 205, 231, 232, 317, 337, 400, 439n, 464, 466
   "Anecdote of the Jar" 307–313
   "Idea of Order at Key West, The" 311
   "Mrs. Alfred Uruguay" 334–335, 339
strong 4, 258, 261, 264, 265, 269, 271, 274, 275, 278
Supple, Tim 172n
sublime, the 120–131
Swedenborg, Emanuel 371
Symbolism 39
Szigeti, Joseph 6

Tate, Allen 36
Thomas, Dylan
   "To Others Than You" 202–207
Thurber, James 279–283
Tolstoy, Leo 319
translation 4

Vatke, Wilhelm 321
Vendler, Helen 46
Vico, Giambattista 74–75

Weiss, Antonio 36
Wellhausen, Julius 321
West, Cornel 67
West, Nathaniel
   Miss Lonelyhearts 63
Whitman, Walt xv, xvi, 224–226, 228–231, 395, 397, 406–408, 412, 441, 456, 487–488
   "When Lilacs Last in the Dooryard Bloom'd" 221, 231

Song of Myself 221
White, Hayden 93
   Metahistory 73–76
Wilde, Oscar xvii, 50, 76, 267, 269, 299–301, 332–333, 410–411
   "The Portrait of Mr. W. H." 411
Williams, Raymond 152
Williams, Tennessee 468
Wimsatt, W. K. 35, 304
Winters, Ivor 55
wisdom 3
Witter, Henning Bernhard 321
Wollstonecraft, Mary 63
Woolf, Virginia 72, 98, 103–105, 108–115, 109n, 110, 113, 420
   Mrs. Dalloway 104, 111
   Orlando 383
   "Sketch of the Past" 104, 110, 112
   To The Lighthouse 67, 104
word 4–5
Wordsworth, William 113, 261, 269, 303–307, 310, 441, 453
   "Ode: Intimations of Immortality" 306
   Peter Bell 430
   "Tintern Abbey" 244

Yates, Frances 176
   The Art of Memory 170
Yaho'el 348, 354–355
Yahweh 321–322, 335–345, 348, 350, 352, 382
Yahwist, see J-writer
Yeats, William Butler 39, 488
Yerushalmi, Yosef
   Freud's Moses 250–252
   Zakhor 250
YHWH see, Yahweh
YHWH Qatan see, Metatron
yireh 337

Zasloff, Tela C. 382
Zohar 351, 364

Printed in the United Kingdom
by Lightning Source UK Ltd.
118137UK00002B/70-90